AS Accounting for AQA

the complete resource for the AS examination

David Cox

Michael Fardon

osborne
BOOKS

Published by Osborne Books Limited
Unit 1B Everoak Estate
Bromyard Road
Worcester WR2 5HP
Tel 01905 748071
Email books@osbornebooks.co.uk
Website www.osbornebooks.co.uk

Graphic design by Richard Holt

Printed and bound in Malta by Gutenberg Press Limited

British Library Cataloguing in Publication Data
A catalogue record for this book is available from the British Library

ISBN 978 1872962 733

Contents

Module 3
Financial Accounting: Determination of Income

Module 4
Introduction to Accounting for Management and Decision-making

Introduction

AS Accounting for AQA has been written to provide a study resource for students taking the Assessment and Qualifications Alliance's Advanced Subsidiary course in Accounting. The course is structured into four Modules. Candidates have to complete three Modules, either Modules 1, 3 and 4 or Modules 2, 3 and 4. The Modules are as follows:

either	**Module 1** **Financial Accounting: The Accounting Information System**	*or*	**Module 2** **Financial Accounting: Introduction to Published Accounts of Limited Companies**
plus	**Module 3** **Financial Accounting: Determination of Income**	*plus*	**Module 4** **Introduction to Accounting for Management and Decision-making**

AS Accounting for AQA has been designed to be user-friendly. It covers each of the Modules of the course in separate, 'stand alone' sections. Students will find all that they need to study for either Module 1 or Module 2 in the appropriate sections of the book, without the need for any cross-referring.

AQA recommends that those who wish to complete the full A Level should study Module 1. Module 2 has been designed specifically for those who do not wish to study the basic book-keeping techniques of Accounting which are contained in Module 1. It is particularly suitable for those who are studying A Level Business Studies or VCE Business.

The text of **AS Accounting for AQA** contains:

- clear explanations and numerous worked examples
- chapter summaries to help with revision
- a wide range of questions, many from past AQA examinations
- answers to selected questions, set out in full at the end of the book
- full coverage of the computer accounting content of Modules 1 and 2

For those questions where answers are not given in the book, a separate *Tutor Pack* provides the answers, which are set out in full, together with a range of photocopiable layouts and a web directory. Contact the Osborne Books Sales Office on 01905 748071 for details of how to obtain the Tutor Pack.

The Osborne Books website – www.osbornebooks.co.uk – is constantly developing its range of facilities for students and tutors. Popular features include the free downloadable resources and the on-line shop. Log on and try us!

David Cox, Michael Fardon

Summer 2004

Acknowledgments

The publisher wishes to thank Ruth Brown, Jean Cox, Mike Gilbert and Claire McCarthy for their help with the reading and production of this book. Particular thanks go to Roger Petheram of Worcester College of Technology for his excellent and patient editorial work.

The publisher is indebted to the Assessment and Qualifications Alliance (AQA) for its permission to reproduce past examination questions. Thanks are also due to Tesco PLC for permission to use extracts from their Annual Report and Accounts and to Microsoft UK and Sage PLC for their permission to use screen images from their software in the text.

Authors

David Cox is a Certified Accountant with more than twenty years experience teaching accountancy students over a wide range of levels. Formerly with the Management and Professional Studies Department at Worcester College of Technology, he now lectures on a freelance basis and carries out educational consultancy work in accountancy studies. He is author and joint author of a number of textbooks in the areas of accounting, finance and banking.

Michael Fardon has extensive teaching experience of a wide range of banking, business and accountancy courses at Worcester College of Technology. He now specialises in writing business and financial texts and is General Editor at Osborne Books. He is also an educational consultant and has worked extensively in the areas of vocational business curriculum development.

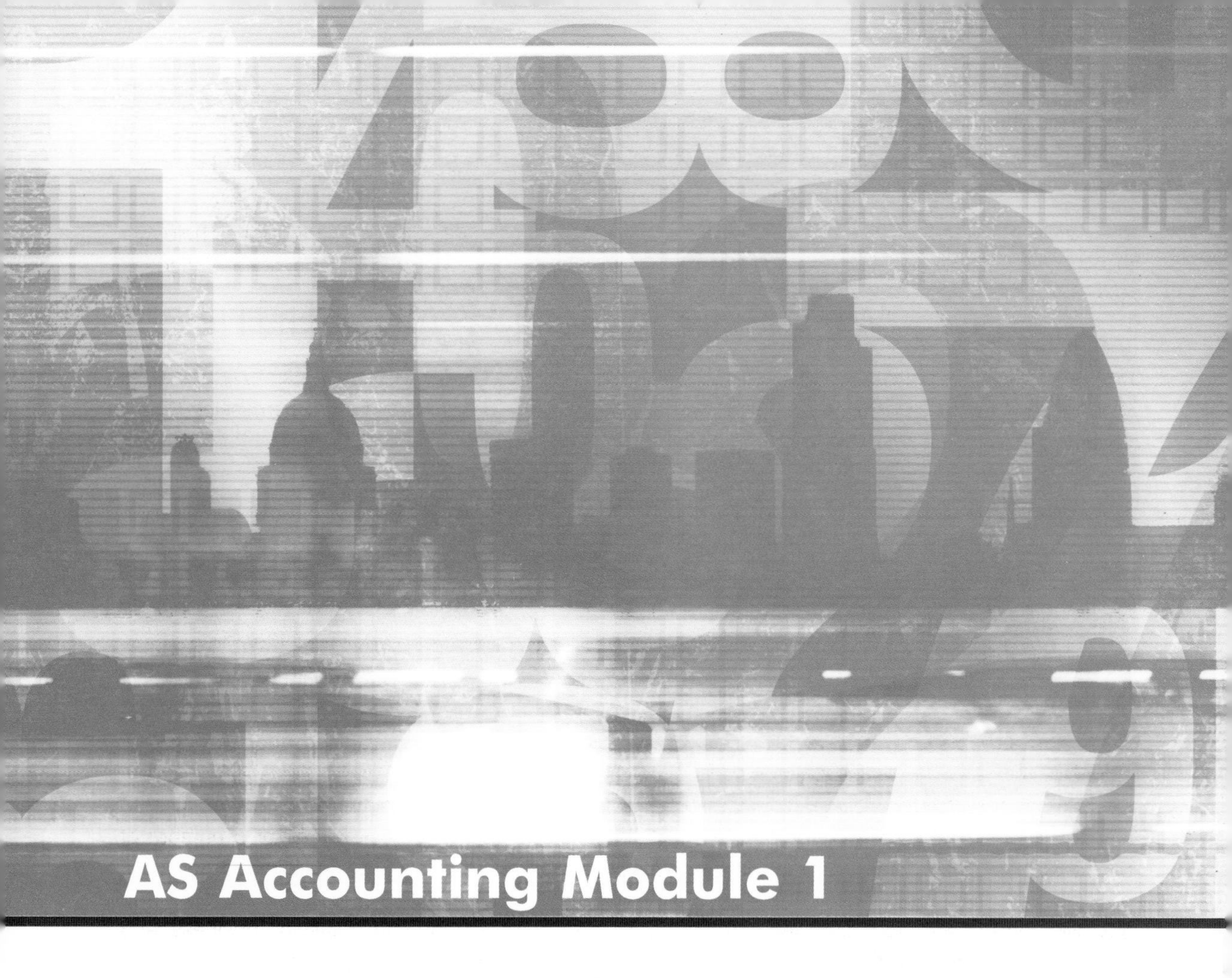

AS Accounting Module 1

Financial Accounting: the Accounting Information System

This Module for AQA AS Accounting is designed as a foundation for the course, with the emphasis on the accounting systems of sole traders. It covers:

- double-entry procedures, recording Value Added Tax, business documents
- verification of accounting records
- the trial balance, trading and profit and loss accounts, and balance sheets
- the use of computers in accounting

Note that, as an alternative to this Module, AQA offers Module 2 'Introduction to Published Accounts of Limited Companies'. This alternative module provides a foundation for the study of accounting, emphasising the accounts of limited companies. AQA recommends, however, that those wishing to complete the full A Level should study Module 1.

1 WHAT IS FINANCIAL ACCOUNTING?

Accounting – known as 'the language of business' – is essential to the recording and presentation of business activities in the form of accounting records and financial statements. Financial accounting involves:

- recording business transactions in financial terms
- reporting financial information to the owner of the business and other interested parties
- advising the owner – and other parties – how to use the financial reports to assess the past performance of the business, and to make decisions for the future

We will see how the three main elements of the definition – recording, reporting and advising – are often carried out by different types of accounting personnel. First, though, we will look at an outline of the financial accounting system.

THE FINANCIAL ACCOUNTING SYSTEM

Businesses need to record transactions in the financial accounting system for very practical reasons:

- they need to quantify items such as sales, expenses and profit
- they need to present these figures in a meaningful way to measure the success of the business

Business financial records can be very complex, and one of the problems that you face as a student is having difficulty in relating what you are learning to the financial accounting system of the business as a whole. In this chapter we will summarise how a typical business records and presents financial information in the form of accounts. The process follows a number of distinct stages which are illustrated in full in the diagram on the next page.

the financial accounting system

SOURCE DOCUMENTS

invoices – issued and received
credit notes – issued and received
debit notes – issued and received
bank paying-in slips
cheques issued
other banking documents

sources of accounting information

SUBSIDIARY BOOKS

day books
journal (or general journal)
cash books (also used in double-entry – see below)

gathering and summarising accounting information

DOUBLE-ENTRY BOOK-KEEPING

sales ledger – accounts of debtors

purchases ledger – accounts of creditors

general (nominal) ledger

- 'nominal' accounts for sales, purchases, expenses, capital, loans etc
- 'real' accounts for items, eg fixed assets

cash books

- cash book for bank and cash transactions
- petty cash book

recording the dual aspect of accounting transactions in the accounting system

TRIAL BALANCE

a summary of the balances of all the accounts at the end of the accounting period

arithmetic checking of double-entry book-keeping

FINAL ACCOUNTS

- manufacturing account
- trading and profit and loss account

and

- balance sheet

statement measuring profit (or loss) for an accounting period

statement of assets, liabilities and capital at the end of an accounting period

The financial accounting system can be summarised as follows:

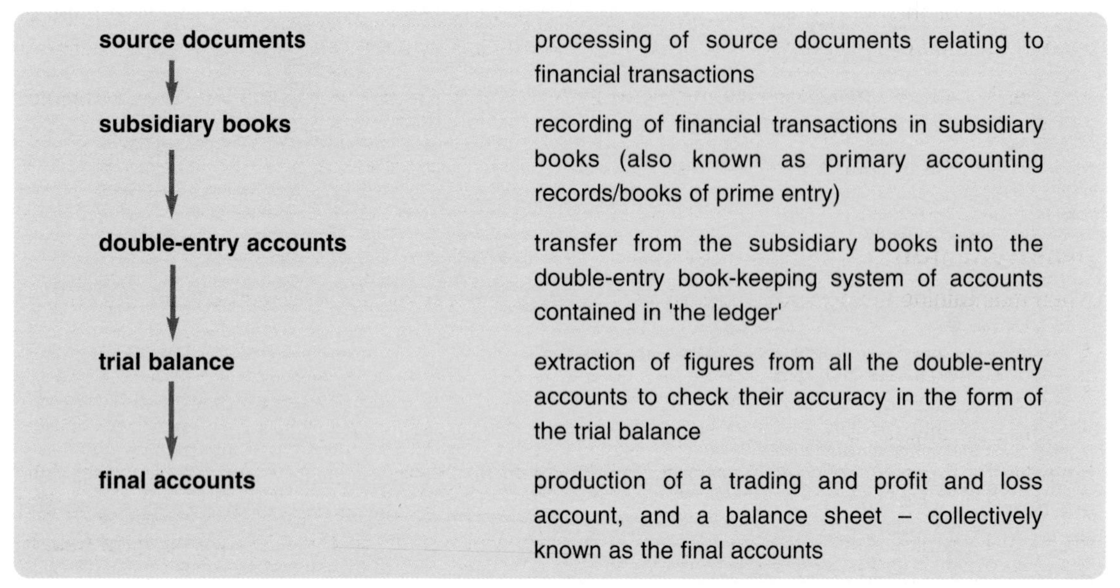

source documents	processing of source documents relating to financial transactions
subsidiary books	recording of financial transactions in subsidiary books (also known as primary accounting records/books of prime entry)
double-entry accounts	transfer from the subsidiary books into the double-entry book-keeping system of accounts contained in 'the ledger'
trial balance	extraction of figures from all the double-entry accounts to check their accuracy in the form of the trial balance
final accounts	production of a trading and profit and loss account, and a balance sheet – collectively known as the final accounts

Over the next few chapters we will look at these stages – the financial accounting system – in detail. If you should at any time lose sight of where your studies are taking you, refer back to this chapter, and it should help to place your work in context.

Before summarising each stage in the accounting system we will first examine what form accounting records can take.

ACCOUNTING RECORDS

Accounting records are usually kept in one of two forms: handwritten records or computer records.

written accounting records

This is the traditional form of keeping 'the books', particularly for the smaller business. The main record is the ledger which, at one time, would be a large leather-bound volume, neatly ruled, into which the book-keeper would enter each business transaction in immaculate copperplate handwriting into individual accounts. In modern times, the handwritten ledger is still used, and stationery shops sell ledgers and other accounting books, designed especially for the smaller business.

computer accounting records

Nowadays, computers are relatively cheap so that they can be afforded by all but the smallest business. With computer accounting, business transactions are input into the computer and stored on disk. The major advantage of computer accounting is that it is a very accurate method of recording business transactions; the disadvantage is that it may be expensive and time-consuming to set up, particularly for the smaller business. Interestingly, the word 'ledger' has survived into the computer age but, instead of being a bound volume, it is represented by data files held on a computer disk.

Whether business transactions are recorded by hand, or by using a computer, the basic principles remain the same. The first few chapters of this book concentrate on these basic principles; the use of computers in accounting is looked at in more detail in Chapter 11.

practical points

When maintaining financial accounts you should bear in mind that they should be kept:

- accurately
- up-to-date
- confidentially, ie not revealed to unauthorised people outside the business

Maintaining financial accounts is a discipline, and you should develop disciplined accounting skills as you study with this book. Your studies will involve you in working through many questions and practical examples. These will require you to apply logical thought to the skills you have learned. In particular, when attempting questions you should:

- be neat in the layout of your work
- use ink (in accounting, the use of pencil shows indecision)
- not use correcting fluid (errors should be crossed through neatly with a single line and the correct version written on the line below)

The reason for not using correcting fluid in handwritten accounts is because, in practice, the accounts will often be audited (checked by accountants): correcting fluid may hide errors, but it can also conceal fraudulent transactions.

SOURCE DOCUMENTS

Business transactions generate documents. In this section we will relate them to the type of transaction involved and also introduce other accounting terminology which is essential to your studies.

sale and purchase of goods and services – the invoice

When a business buys or sells goods or a service the seller prepares an invoice stating

- the amount owing
- when it should be paid
- details of the goods sold or service provided

An invoice is illustrated on page 47.

cash sales and credit sales – debtors and creditors

An invoice is prepared by the seller for

- **cash sales** – where payment is immediate, whether in cash, by cheque, by debit card or by credit card (Note that not all cash sales will require an invoice to be prepared by the seller – shops, for instance, normally issue a cash receipt for the amount paid.)
- **credit sales** – where payment is to be made at a later date (often 30 days later)

  A debtor is a person who owes you money when you sell on credit.

  A creditor is a person to whom you owe money when you buy on credit.

return of goods – the credit note and the debit note

If the buyer returns goods which are bought on credit (they may be faulty or incorrect) the seller will prepare a credit note (see page 49 for an example) which is sent to the buyer, reducing the amount of money owed. The credit note, like the invoice, states the money amount and the goods or services to which it relates.

A buyer who returns goods to a seller may use a debit note to request a reduction in the amount owed. The debit note is sent by the buyer to the seller and states the money amount and the goods and services to which it relates.

banking transactions – paying-in slips, cheques, BACS transfers

Businesses, like anyone else with a bank account, need to pay in money, and draw out cash and make payments. Paying-in slip counterfoils, cheque counterfoils and other banking documents are used frequently as sources for bank account transactions.

further reading

The subject of business documents is covered in detail in Chapter 4, while Chapters 8 and 10 deal with the use of information from bank statements.

RECORDING OF TRANSACTIONS – SUBSIDIARY BOOKS

Many businesses issue and receive large quantities of invoices, credit notes and banking documents, and it is useful for them to list these in summary form, during the course of the working day. These summaries are known as subsidiary books (primary accounting records/books of prime entry.).

These include:

- **sales day book** – a list of sales made, compiled from invoices issued
- **purchases day book** – a list of purchases made, compiled from invoices received
- **sales returns day book** – a list of 'returns in', ie goods returned by customers, compiled from credit notes issued

- **purchases returns day book** – a list of 'returns out', ie goods returned by the business to suppliers, compiled from credit notes received
- **cash book** – the business' record of the bank account and the amount of cash held, compiled from receipts, paying-in slip counterfoils, cheque counterfoils and other banking documents
- **petty cash book** – a record of cash (notes and coin) purchases for small items made by the business, compiled from petty cash vouchers
- **general journal** – a record of non-regular transactions, which are not recorded in any other subsidiary book

The subsidiary books are explained in detail in Chapter 6. The point you should bear in mind is that they provide the information for the double-entry book-keeping system.

DOUBLE-ENTRY ACCOUNTS: THE LEDGER

The basis of the accounting system is the double-entry book-keeping system which is embodied in a series of records known as the ledger. This is divided into a number of separate accounts.

double-entry book-keeping

Double-entry book-keeping involves making two entries in the accounts for each transaction: for instance, if you are paying wages by cheque you will make an entry in bank account and an entry in wages account. The reasoning behind this procedure and the rules involved are explained in detail in Chapters 2 and 3. If you are operating a manual accounting system you will make the two entries by hand, if you are operating a computer accounting system you will make one entry on the keyboard, but indicate to the machine where the other entry is to be made by means of a code.

accounts

The sources for the entries you make are the subsidiary books. The ledger into which you make the entries is normally a bound book (in a non-computerised system) divided into separate accounts, eg a separate account for sales, purchases, each type of business expense, each debtor, each creditor, and so on. Each account will be given a specific name, and a number for reference purposes (or input code, if you use a computer system).

division of the ledger

Because of the large number of accounts involved, the ledger has traditionally been divided into a number of sections. These same sections are used in computer accounting systems.

- **sales ledger** – personal accounts of debtors, ie customers to whom the business has sold on credit
- **purchases ledger** – personal accounts of creditors, ie suppliers to whom the business owes money

- **cash books** – a cash book comprising cash account and bank account, and a petty cash book for petty cash account (small purchases). Note: the cash books are also subsidiary books as well as being in the ledger
- **general (or nominal) ledger** – the remainder of the accounts: nominal accounts, eg sales, purchases, expenses, and real accounts for items owned by the business

trial balance

Double-entry book-keeping, because it involves making two entries for each transaction, is open to error. What if the book-keeper writes in £45 in one account and £54 in another? The trial balance – explained in full in Chapter 5 – effectively checks the entries made over a given period and will pick up most errors. It sets out the balances of all the double-entry accounts, ie the totals of the accounts for a certain period. It is, as well as being an arithmetic check, the source of valuable information which is used to help in the preparation of the final accounts of the business.

FINAL ACCOUNTS

The final accounts of a business comprise the profit statement and the balance sheet.

profit statement

income minus **expenses** equals **profit**

The profit statement of a business includes the trading and profit and loss account, and if the business manufactures goods, a manufacturing account. The object of these statements is to calculate the profit due to the owner(s) of the business after certain expenses have been deducted from income:

- manufacturing account shows the costs of producing a quantity of finished goods
- trading and profit and loss account shows the profit (or loss) after the deduction of cost of sales to give gross profit, and also after the deduction of all overheads (expenses) to give net profit

The figures for these calculations – sales, purchases, expenses of various kinds – are taken from the double-entry system. The layout of profit statements is explained in Chapter 12.

balance sheet

The double-entry system also contains figures for:

assets items the business owns, which can be

- fixed assets – items bought for use in the business, eg premises, vehicles, computers
- current assets – items used in the everyday running of the business, eg stock, debtors (money owed by customers), and money in the bank

liabilities items that the business owes, eg bank loans and overdrafts, and creditors (money owed to suppliers)

capital money or assets introduced by the owner(s) of the business; capital is in effect owed by the business to the owner

The balance sheet is so called because it balances in numerical (money) terms:

assets	minus	**liabilities**	equals	**capital**
what a business owns		*what a business owes*		*how the business has been financed*

The layout of balance sheets is explained in Chapter 12.

the accounting equation

The balance sheet illustrates a concept important to accounting theory, known as the accounting equation. This equation is illustrated in the diagram above, namely

Assets – Liabilities = Capital

Every business transaction will change the balance sheet and the equation, as each transaction has a dual effect on the accounts. However, the equation will always balance.

Consider the following transactions made through the business bank account:

	Transaction	**Effect on equation**
1.	Business pays creditor	decrease in asset (bank) decrease in liability (money owed to creditor)
2.	Business buys computer* (*VAT is ignored, for the moment)	increase in asset (computer) decrease in asset (bank)
3.	The owner introduces new capital by paying a cheque into the bank	increase in asset (bank) increase in capital (money owed by business to owner)

How is the equation affected by these particular transactions?

1. Assets and liabilities both decrease by the amount of the payment; capital remains unchanged.
2. Assets remain the same because the two transactions cancel each other out in the assets section: value is transferred from the asset of bank to the asset of computer.
3. Both sides of the equation increase by the amount of the capital introduced.

In short, the equation always balances, as will the balance sheet of a business.

In conclusion, every transaction has a dual aspect, as two entries are involved: this is the basis of the theory of double-entry book-keeping, and will be described in detail in Chapters 2 and 3.

Accounting Concepts

Accounting concepts are broad assumptions which underlie the preparation of all accounting reports. For the moment, we will consider two very important aspects:

- business entity
- money measurement

Business entity means that the accounts record and report on the financial transactions of a particular business: for example, the accounts of J Smith Limited record and report on that business only. The problem is that, when a business is run by a sole trader, the owner's personal financial transactions can be sometimes mixed in with the business' financial transactions: the two should be kept entirely separate.

Money measurement means that the accounting system uses money as the common denominator in recording and reporting all business transactions. Thus, it is not possible to record, for example, the loyalty of a firm's workforce or the quality of a product, because these cannot be reported in money terms.

Who Uses Financial Accounts?

Before answering the question of who uses the accounts, and why, it is important to draw a distinction between the two processes of book-keeping and accounting.

Book-keeping is the basic recording of business transactions in financial terms – literally 'keeping the books of account'. This task can be carried out by anyone – the owner, or by a full-time or part-time book-keeper. The book-keeper should be able to record transactions, and extract a trial balance (see Chapter 5).

Accounting involves taking the information recorded by the book-keeper and presenting it in the form of financial reports to the business owners or managers. Such reports are either retrospective:

- profit statement and balance sheet

or forward looking:

- forecast, or budgeted, accounts

In each case, these reports help the owners or managers to monitor the financial progress of the business, and to make decisions for the future.

information for the owner(s)

The accounting system will be able to give information on:

- purchases of goods (for resale) to date
- sales turnover to date

- overheads and expenses to date
- debtors – both the total amount owed to the business, and also the names of individual debtors and the amount owed by each
- creditors – both the total owed by the business, and the amount owed to each creditor
- assets owned by the business
- liabilities, eg bank loans, owed by the business
- profit made by the business during a particular time period

The owner will want to know how profitable the business is, and what it may be worth.

information for outsiders

Other people interested in the accounts of a business include:

- the bank manager, if the business wants to borrow from the bank
- HM Revenue & Customs – tax will have to be paid on the profits of the business
- the VAT office (operated through HM Revenue and Customs) – if a business is registered for Value Added Tax
- financial analysts who may be advising investors in the business
- official bodies, eg Companies House, who need to see the final accounts of limited companies
- creditors, who wish to assess the likelihood of receiving payment
- employees and trade unions, who wish to check on the financial prospects of the business
- general public, and interest groups seeking to influence company policy

ACCOUNTING PERSONNEL

If you are studying accounting you will encounter references to different types of professional accountant. It is important to have a general idea of who does what in the accounting world – see the diagram on page 12.

financial accountant

The function of the financial accountant is to take further the information prepared by the book-keeper. This will involve the preparation of final accounts, ie trading and profit and loss account, and balance sheet. The financial accountant may be also required to negotiate with the Inland Revenue on taxation matters.

Where the business is a limited company, the financial accountant will be also involved in preparing final accounts which comply with the requirements of the Companies Act 1985 (as amended by the Companies Act 1989). This Act requires the directors of a company to report annually to shareholders, with certain minimum financial accounting information being disclosed. The financial accountant of a limited company will usually report to the finance director.

accounting personnel in a medium-sized limited company

Shareholders

External auditors

Company Chief Executive

Finance director

Other directors

Internal auditors

Financial accountant

Management accountant

Book-keeper

Cost accountant

cost and management accountants

The cost accountant obtains information about the recent costs of the business, eg raw materials and labour, and estimates costs for the future. Often the cost accountant reports to the management accountant who prepares reports and makes recommendations to the owner(s) or managers of the business. The management accountant will usually report to the finance director.

The work of the cost and management accountant forms part of your studies for Module 4.

auditors

Auditors are accountants whose role is to check that accounting procedures have been followed correctly. There are two types of auditors:

- external auditors
- internal auditors

External auditors are independent of the firm whose accounts are being audited. The most common type of audit carried out by external auditors is the statutory audit for larger limited companies. In this, the auditors are reporting directly to the shareholders of the company, stating that the legal requirements laid down in the Companies Acts 1985 (as amended by the Companies Act 1989) have been complied with, and that the accounts represent a 'true and fair view' of the state of the business. External auditors are usually appointed by the shareholders at the Annual General Meeting of the company.

Internal auditors are employees of the business which they audit. They are concerned with the internal checking and control procedures of the business: for example, procedures for the control of cash, authorisation of purchases, and disposal of property. The nature of their work requires that they should have a degree of independence within the business and, in a limited company, they will usually report directly to the finance director.

ACCOUNTING TERMS

In the course of this chapter a number of specific accounting terms have been introduced. You should now study this section closely to ensure that you are clear about these definitions:

accounts financial records, where business transactions are entered

ledger the set of accounts of a business

assets items owned by a business

liabilities items owed by a business

capital the amount of the owner's (or owners') stake in the business

debtors individuals or businesses who owe money in respect of goods or services supplied by the business

creditors individuals or businesses to whom money is owed by the business

purchases goods bought, either on credit or for cash, which are intended to be resold later

credit purchases goods bought, with payment to be made at a later date

cash purchases goods bought and paid for immediately

sales the sale of goods, whether on credit or for cash, in which the business trades

credit sales goods sold, with payment to be received at an agreed date in the future

cash sales goods sold, with immediate payment received in cash, by cheque, by credit card, or by debit card

turnover the total of sales, both cash and credit, for a particular time period

CHAPTER SUMMARY

- Accounting is known as 'the language of business'.

- The accounting system comprises a number of specific stages of recording and presenting business transactions:
  - source documents
  - subsidiary books
  - double-entry system of ledgers
  - trial balance
  - final accounts

- Accounting records call for the development of skills of accuracy and neatness.

- The balance sheet uses the accounting equation:

  Assets – Liabilities = Capital

- Two basic accounting concepts which apply to all business accounts are:
  - business entity
  - money measurement

- Financial accounts are used both by the managers of the business and also by outside bodies.

- There are several different types of accounting personnel, including:
  - book-keeper
  - financial accountant
  - cost and management accountants
  - auditors, external and internal

- Accounting involves the use of very specific terminology which should be learned.

In the next chapter we will look at some transactions that are to be found in most financial accounts. By studying these we will begin to understand the principles of double-entry book-keeping.

QUESTIONS

NOTE: an asterisk (*) after the question number means that an answer to the question is given at the end of this book.

1.1* Fill in the missing words from the following sentences:

(a) The set of double-entry accounts of a business is called the ....

(b) A .... is a person who owes you money when you sell on credit.

(c) A .... is a person to whom you owe money when you buy on credit.

(d) The .... is a list of sales made, compiled from invoices issued.

(e) The business' record of bank account and amount of cash held is kept in the

....

(f) Accounts such as sales, purchases, expenses are kept in the ....

....

(g) The accounting equation is:

.... minus ....equals ....

(h) Accounts record and report on the financial transactions of a particular business: this

is the application of the .... concept.

(i) .... are accountants who check that accounting procedures have been followed correctly.

1.2 Describe the main stages in the financial accounting system. State five pieces of information that can be found from the accounting system that will be of interest to the owner of the business.

1.3 What types of accounting jobs are advertised in your local paper? Classify them in relation to accounting personnel described in this chapter. What tasks do the jobs involve?

1.4 Explain the accounting concepts of:

(a) business entity

(b) money measurement

1.5 Distinguish between:

- assets and liabilities
- debtors and creditors
- purchases and sales
- credit purchases and cash purchases

1.6 Show the dual aspect, as it affects the accounting equation (assets – liabilities = capital), of the following transactions for a particular business:

- owner starts in business with capital of £8,000 in the bank
- buys a computer for £4,000, paying by cheque
- obtains a loan of £3,000 by cheque from a friend
- buys a van for £6,000, paying by cheque

1.7* Fill in the missing figures:

Assets	Liabilities	Capital
£	£	£
20,000	0	....
15,000	5,000	....
16,400	....	8,850
....	3,850	10,250
25,380	....	6,950
....	7,910	13,250

1.8* The table below sets out account balances from the books of a business. The columns (a) to (f) show the account balances resulting from a series of transactions that have taken place over time.

You are to compare each set of adjacent columns, ie (a) with (b), (b) with (c), and so on and state, with figures, what accounting transactions have taken place in each case.

(Ignore VAT).

	(a)	(b)	(c)	(d)	(e)	(f)
	£	£	£	£	£	£
Assets						
Office equipment	–	2,000	2,000	2,000	2,000	2,000
Van	–	–	–	10,000	10,000	10,000
Bank	10,000	8,000	14,000	4,000	6,000	3,000
Liabilities						
Loan	–	–	6,000	6,000	6,000	3,000
Capital	10,000	10,000	10,000	10,000	12,000	12,000

2 DOUBLE-ENTRY BOOK-KEEPING: FIRST PRINCIPLES

As we have seen in Chapter 1, book-keeping is the basic recording of business transactions in financial terms. Before studying financial accounting in detail it is important to study the principles of double-entry book-keeping, as these form the basis of much that we shall be doing in the rest of the book.

In the previous chapter we looked briefly at the dual aspect of accounting – each time there is a business transaction there are two effects on the accounting equation. This chapter shows how the dual aspect is used in the principles of book-keeping. In particular, we shall be looking at accounts for:

- bank
- cash
- capital
- fixed assets
- expenses
- income
- drawings
- loans

LEDGER ACCOUNTS

Double-entry book-keeping, as its name suggests, recognises that each transaction has a dual aspect. Once the dual aspect of each transaction has been identified, the two book-keeping entries can be made in the ledger accounts of the accounting system. An account is kept in the ledger to record each different type of transaction. In a handwritten book-keeping system, the ledger will consist either of a bound book, or a series of separate sheets of paper – each account in the ledger will occupy a separate page; in a computerised system, the ledger will consist of a computer file, divided into separate accounts. Whether a handwritten or computerised system is being used, the principles remain the same.

A commonly-used layout for an account is set out on the next page. Entries in ledger accounts always include dates. Please note that dates used in this book, for the sake of simplicity, are often expressed as 20-1, 20-2, 20-3, etc, unlike in a real business where the actual year date is shown (ie 2001, 2002, 2003 etc). Occasionally in this book 20-9 is followed by 20-0, ie when the decade changes.

Debit		**Name of the account, eg Wages Account**					**Credit**
Date	**Details**	**Folio**	**£ p**	**Date**	**Details**	**Folio**	**£ p**
date of the trans-action	name of the other account	page or reference number of the other account	amount of the trans-action	date of the trans-action	name of the other account	page or reference number of the other account	amount of the trans-action

Note the following points about the layout of this account:

- the name of the account is written at the top
- the account is divided into two identical halves, separated by a central double vertical line
- the left-hand side is called the 'debit' side ('debit' is abbreviated to 'Dr' – short for DebtoR)
- the right-hand side is called the 'credit' (or 'Cr') side
- the date, details and amount of the transaction are entered in the account
- the 'folio' column is used as a cross-referencing system to the other entry of the double-entry book-keeping transaction
- in the 'details' column is entered the name of the other account involved in the book-keeping transaction

In practice, each account would occupy a whole page in a handwritten book-keeping system but, to save space when doing exercises, it is usual to put several accounts on a page. In future, in this book, the account layout will be simplified to give more clarity as follows:

Dr	**Wages Account**		Cr
20-1	£	20-1	£

This layout is often known in accounting jargon as a 'T' account; it will be used extensively in this book because it separates in a simple way the two sides – debit and credit – of the account. An alternative style of account has three money columns: debit, credit and balance. This type of account is commonly used for bank statements, building society passbooks and computer accounting statements. Because the balance of the account is calculated after every transaction, it is known as a running balance account (see page 26).

Debits and Credits

The principle of double-entry book-keeping is that for every business transaction:

- one account is debited, and
- one account is credited

Debit entries are on the left-hand side of the appropriate account, while credit entries are on the right. The rules for debits and credits are:

- **debit entry** – the account which gains value, or records an asset, or an expense
- **credit entry** – the account which gives value, or records a liability, or an income item

This is illustrated as follows:

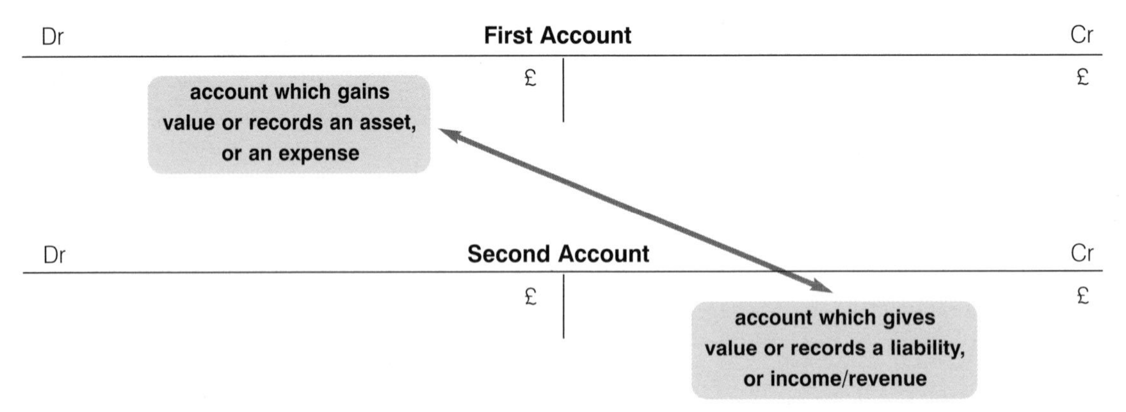

When one entry has been identified as a debit or credit, the other entry will be on the opposite side of the other account.

Example Transactions

In order to put the theory of double-entry book-keeping into practice, we will look at some financial transactions undertaken by a new business which has just been set up by Jayne Hampson in 20-1:

1 September	Started in business with capital of £5,000, a cheque paid into the bank
4 September	Bought office equipment £2,500, paying by cheque
7 September	Paid rent of office £500, by cheque
10 September	Received commission of £100, by cheque
12 September	Withdrew £250 from the bank for own use (drawings)
16 September	Received a loan of £1,000 from James Henderson by cheque

All of these transactions involve the bank, and the business will enter them in its bank account. The bank account records money in the form of bank receipts and payments, ie cheques, standing orders, direct debits, credit transfers, credit card transactions, and debit card transactions. (Most businesses also use a cash account to record transactions which involve money in the form of cash.)

With both bank account and cash account, the rules for debit and credit are:

- money in is recorded on the debit side
- money out is recorded on the credit side

Using these rules, the bank account of Jayne Hampson's business, after entering the transactions listed above, appears as:

Dr		Bank Account			Cr
20-1		£	20-1		£
1 Sep	Capital	5,000	4 Sep	Office equipment	2,500
10 Sep	Commission	100	7 Sep	Rent paid	500
16 Sep	J Henderson: loan	1,000	12 Sep	Drawings	250
		Money in		Money out	

Note: the bank account shows the firm's record of how much has been paid into, and drawn out of, the bank - it is not exactly the same as the record of receipts and payments kept by the bank (we will compare the two in Chapter 10).

To complete the double-entry book-keeping transactions we need to:

- identify on which side of the bank account the transaction is recorded – debit (money in), or credit (money out)
- record the other double-entry transaction on the opposite side of the appropriate account
- note that business transactions involving cash will be entered in the cash account

The other accounts involved can now be recorded, and we shall look at the principles involved for each transaction.

CAPITAL

Capital is the amount of money invested in the business by the owner (or owners). The amount is owed by the business back to the owner, although it is unlikely to be repaid immediately as the business would cease to exist. A capital account is used to record the amount(s) paid into the business; the book-keeping entries are:

- **capital introduced**
  - debit bank account, as in the case of Jayne Hampson, or cash account (or a fixed asset account where these form part of the capital)
  - credit capital account

Example transaction

1 Sep 20-1 Started in business with capital of £5,000, a cheque paid into the bank.

Dr		**Capital Account**		Cr
20-1	£	20-1		£
		1 Sep	Bank	5,000

Note: The dual aspect is that bank account has gained value and has been debited already (see account on page 21); capital account records a liability (to the owner) and is credited. Remember that the business is a separate entity (see Chapter 1, page 10), and this book-keeping entry looks at the transaction from the point of view of the business. The introduction of capital into a business is often the very first business transaction entered into the books of account.

Fixed Assets

Fixed assets are items purchased by a business for use on a long-term basis. Examples are premises, motor vehicles, machinery and office equipment. All of these are bought by a business with the intention that they will be used for some time in the business. Without fixed assets, it would be difficult to continue in business, eg without machinery it would prove difficult to run a factory; without delivery vans and lorries it would be difficult to transport the firm's products to its customers.

When a business buys fixed assets, the expenditure is referred to as **capital expenditure**. This means that items have been bought for use in the business for some years to come. By contrast, **revenue expenditure** is where the items bought will be used by the business quite quickly. For example, the purchase of a car is capital expenditure, while the cost of fuel for the car is revenue expenditure.

fixed assets and double-entry book-keeping

When fixed assets are bought, a separate account for each type of fixed asset is used, eg premises account, motor vehicles account, machinery account, etc. The book-keeping entries are:

- **purchase of a fixed asset**
  - debit fixed asset account (using the appropriate account)
  - credit bank account (or cash account)

Example transaction

4 Sep 20-1 Bought office equipment £2,500, paying by cheque.

Dr		Office Equipment Account			Cr
20-1		£	20-1		£
4 Sep	Bank	2,500			

The other part of the dual aspect of this transaction is a credit to bank account: this has been entered already (see account on page 21).

EXPENSES

Businesses pay various running expenses (overheads), such as rent paid, wages, electricity, telephone, vehicle running expenses, etc. These day-to-day expenses of running the business are termed **revenue expenditure**. A separate account is used in the accounting system for each main class of revenue expenditure, eg rent account, wages account, etc.

The book-keeping entries are:

- **payment of an expense**
  - debit expense account (using the appropriate account)
  - credit bank account (or cash account)

Example transaction

7 Sep 20-1 Paid rent of office £500, by cheque.

Dr		Rent Account			Cr
20-1		£	20-1		£
7 Sep	Bank	500			

Note: The accounting rules followed are that we have debited the account which has gained value (rent paid – the business has had the use of the office for a certain time). The account which has given value (bank) has already been credited (see page 21).

INCOME

From time-to-time a business may receive amounts of income, eg rent received, commission received, or fees received. These are recorded in separate accounts for each category of income, eg rent received account, commission received account. The book-keeping entries are:

- **receipt of income**
  - debit bank account (or cash account)
  - credit income account (using the appropriate account)

Example transaction

10 September 20-1 Received commission of £100, by cheque.

Dr **Commission Received Account** Cr

20-1		£	20-1		£
			10 Sep	Bank	100

Note: We have already debited the account which has gained value (bank – see page 21) and credited the account which has given value (commission received).

OWNER'S DRAWINGS

Drawings is the term used when the owner takes money, in cash or by cheque (or sometimes goods), from the business for personal use. A drawings account is used to record such amounts; the book-keeping entries for withdrawal of money are:

- **owner's drawings**
  - debit drawings account
  - credit bank account (or cash account)

Example transaction

12 Sep 20-1 Withdrew £250 from the bank for own use.

Dr **Drawings Account** Cr

20-1		£	20-1		£
12 Sep	Bank	250			

The other part of the dual aspect of this transaction is a credit to bank account: this has been entered already (see page 21).

LOANS

When a business receives a loan, eg from a relative or the bank, it is the cash account or bank account which gains value, while a loan account (in the name of the lender) records the liability.

- **loan received**
  - debit bank account (or cash account)
  - credit loan account (in name of the lender)

Example transaction

16 September 20-1 Received a loan of £1,000 from James Henderson by cheque

Dr			James Henderson: Loan Account		Cr
20-1		£	20-1		£
			16 Sep	Bank	1,000

The debit entry has already been made in bank account (see page 21).

FURTHER TRANSACTIONS

Using the accounts which we have seen already, here are some further transactions:

- **loan repayment**
  - debit loan account
  - credit bank account (or cash account)
- **sale of a fixed asset, or return of an unsuitable fixed asset**
  - debit bank account (or cash account)
  - credit fixed asset account

Note: sale of fixed assets is dealt with more fully in Chapter 24 under Module 3.

- **withdrawal of cash from the bank for use in the business**
  - debit cash account
  - credit bank account
- **payment of cash into the bank**
  - debit bank account
  - credit cash account

Running Balance Accounts

The layout of accounts that we have used has a debit side and a credit side. Whilst this layout is very useful when learning the principles of book-keeping, it is not always appropriate for practical business use. Most 'real-life' accounts have three money columns: debit transactions, credit transactions, and balance. A familiar example of this type of account is a bank statement. With a three-column account, the balance is calculated after each transaction has been entered – hence the name running balance accounts. For handwritten accounts, it would be rather tedious to calculate the balance after each transaction (and a potential source of errors) but, using computer accounting, the calculation is carried out automatically.

The following is the bank account used earlier in this chapter (page 21), set out in 'traditional' format:

Bank Account

Dr					Cr
20-1		£	20-1		£
1 Sep	Capital	5,000	4 Sep	Office equipment	2,500
10 Sep	Commission	100	7 Sep	Rent paid	500
16 Sep	J Henderson: loan	1,000	12 Sep	Drawings	250

The account does not show the balance, and would need to be balanced (see Chapter 5).

In 'running balance' layout, the account appears as:

Bank Account

20-1		Debit	Credit	Balance
		£	£	£
1 Sep	Capital	5,000		5,000 Dr
4 Sep	Office equipment		2,500	2,500 Dr
7 Sep	Rent paid		500	2,000 Dr
10 Sep	Commission	100		2,100 Dr
12 Sep	Drawings		250	1,850 Dr
16 Sep	J Henderson: loan	1,000		2,850 Dr

With a running balance account, it is necessary to state after each transaction whether the balance is debit (Dr) or credit (Cr). Note that the bank account in the books of this business has a debit balance, ie there is money in the bank – an asset.

In your studies you will normally use the traditional 'T' account format.

CHAPTER SUMMARY

- Every business transaction has a dual aspect.

- Business transactions are recorded in ledger accounts using double-entry book-keeping principles.

- Each double-entry book-keeping transaction involves a debit entry and a credit entry.

- Entries in the bank account and cash account are:
  - debit money in
  - credit money out

- Capital is the amount of money invested in the business by the owner. Capital introduced is recorded as:
  - debit bank account or cash account (or an asset account if an asset is introduced)
  - credit capital account

- Fixed assets are items purchased by a business for use on a long-term basis, eg premises, motor vehicles, machinery and office equipment. The purchase of such items is called capital expenditure.

- The purchase of fixed assets is recorded in the business accounts as:
  - debit fixed asset account
  - credit bank account (or cash account)

- Running expenses or overheads of a business, such as rent paid, wages, electricity, etc are called revenue expenditure.

- Expenses are recorded in the business accounts as:
  - debit expense account
  - credit bank account (or cash account)

- Receipt of income, eg rent received, commission received, fees received, is recorded as:
  - debit bank account (or cash account)
  - credit income account

- Drawings is where the owner takes money (or goods) from the business for personal use. The withdrawal of money is recorded as:
  - debit drawings account
  - credit bank account (or cash account)

- When a business receives a loan, it will be recorded as:
  - debit bank account (or cash account)
  - credit loan account in the name of the lender

In the next chapter we will continue with double-entry book-keeping and look at regular business transactions for purchases, sales and returns.

QUESTIONS

NOTE: an asterisk (*) after the question number means that an answer to the question is given at the end of this book.

2.1 James Anderson has kept his bank account up-to-date, but has not got around to the other double-entry book-keeping entries. Rule up the other accounts for him, and make the appropriate entries.

Dr **Bank Account** Cr

20-1		£	20-1		£
1 Feb	Capital	7,500	6 Feb	Computer	2,000
14 Feb	Bank loan	2,500	8 Feb	Rent paid	750
20 Feb	Commission received	145	12 Feb	Wages	425
			23 Feb	Drawings	200
			25 Feb	Wages	380
			28 Feb	Van	6,000

2.2* The following are the business transactions of Tony Long for the month of May 20-2:

20-2

1 May	Started a business with capital of £6,000 in the bank
4 May	Bought a machine for £3,500, paying by cheque
6 May	Bought office equipment for £2,000, paying by cheque
10 May	Paid rent £350, by cheque
12 May	Obtained a loan of £1,000 from a friend, Lucy Warner, and paid her cheque into the bank
15 May	Paid wages £250, by cheque
17 May	Commission received £150, by cheque
20 May	Drawings £85, by cheque
25 May	Paid wages £135, by cheque

You are to:

(a) Write up Tony Long's bank account

(b) Complete the double-entry book-keeping transactions

2.3 Enter the following transactions into the double-entry book-keeping accounts of Jean Lacey:

20-5

1 Aug	Started in business with capital of £5,000 in the bank
3 Aug	Bought a computer for £1,800, paying by cheque
7 Aug	Paid rent £100, by cheque
10 Aug	Received commission £200, in cash

12 Aug	Bought office fittings £2,000, paying by cheque
15 Aug	Received a loan, £1,000 by cheque, from a friend, Sally Orton
17 Aug	Drawings £100, in cash
20 Aug	Returned some of the office fittings (unsuitable) and received a refund cheque of £250
25 Aug	Received commission £150, by cheque
27 Aug	Made a loan repayment to Sally Orton of £150, by cheque

2.4* Tom Griffiths has recently set up in business. He has made some errors in writing up his bank account. You are to set out the bank account as it should appear, rule up the other accounts for him, and make the appropriate entries.

Dr		Bank Account			Cr
20-2		£	20-2		£
4 Mar	Office equipment	1,000	1 Mar	Capital	6,500
12 Mar	Drawings	175	5 Mar	Bank loan	2,500
			7 Mar	Wages	250
			8 Mar	Commission received	150
			10 Mar	Rent paid	200
			15 Mar	Van	6,000

2.5 Enter the following transactions into the double-entry book-keeping accounts of Caroline Yates:

20-7	
1 Nov	Started in business with capital of £75,000 in the bank
3 Nov	Bought a photocopier for £2,500, paying by cheque
7 Nov	Received a bank loan of £70,000
10 Nov	Bought office premises £130,000, paying by cheque
12 Nov	Paid rates of £3,000, by cheque
14 Nov	Bought office fittings £1,500, paying by cheque
15 Nov	Received commission of £300, in cash
18 Nov	Drawings in cash £125
20 Nov	Paid wages £250, by cheque
23 Nov	Paid £100 of cash into the bank
25 Nov	Returned some of the office fittings (unsuitable) and received a refund cheque for £200
28 Nov	Received commission £200, by cheque

2.6 Write up the bank account from Question 2.5 in the form of a 'running balance' account.

3 DOUBLE-ENTRY BOOK-KEEPING: FURTHER TRANSACTIONS

This chapter continues with the principles of double-entry book-keeping and builds on the skills established in the previous chapter. We shall be looking at the dual aspect and the book-keeping required for the business transactions of:

- cash purchases
- cash sales
- credit purchases
- credit sales
- returns
- carriage

PURCHASES AND SALES

Common business transactions are to buy and sell goods. These transactions are recorded in purchases account and sales account respectively. These two accounts are used to record the purchase and sale of the goods in which the business trades. For example, a shoe shop will buy shoes from the manufacturer and will record this in purchases account; as shoes are sold, the transactions will be recorded in sales account. Note that the book-keeping system does not use a 'goods account': instead, when buying goods, a purchases account is used; when selling goods, a sales account is used.

The normal entry on a purchases account is on the debit side – the account has gained value, ie the business has bought goods for resale. The normal entry on a sales account is on the credit side – the account has given value, ie the business has sold goods.

When a business buys an item for use in the business, eg a computer, this is debited to a separate account, because a fixed asset – see Chapter 2, page 22 – has been purchased. Likewise, when a fixed asset is sold, it is not entered in the sales account.

WORKED EXAMPLE: PURCHASES AND SALES

In order to put the theory of double-entry book-keeping for purchases and sales into practice, we will look at some financial transactions undertaken by Temeside Traders, a business which started trading on 1 October 20-1:

1 October	Started in business with capital of £7,000 paid into the bank
2 October	Bought goods for £5,000, paying by cheque
3 October	Sold some of the goods for £3,000, a cheque being received
5 October	Bought computer for £700, paying by cheque
10 October	Bought goods for £2,800, paying by cheque
12 October	Sold some of the goods for £5,000, a cheque being received
15 October	Paid rent £150, by cheque

These transactions are entered into the book-keeping system of Temeside Traders as follows:

Bank Account

Dr					Cr
20-1		£	20-1		£
1 Oct	Capital	7,000	2 Oct	Purchases	5,000
3 Oct	Sales	3,000	5 Oct	Computer	700
12 Oct	Sales	5,000	10 Oct	Purchases	2,800
			15 Oct	Rent paid	150

Capital Account

Dr					Cr
20-1		£	20-1		£
			1 Oct	Bank	7,000

Purchases Account

Dr					Cr
20-1		£	20-1		£
2 Oct	Bank	5,000			
10 Oct	Bank	2,800			

Sales Account

Dr					Cr
20-1		£	20-1		£
			3 Oct	Bank	3,000
			12 Oct	Bank	5,000

Computer Account

Dr					Cr
20-1		£	20-1		£
5 Oct	Bank	700			

Rent Paid Account

Dr					Cr
20-1		£	20-1		£
15 Oct	Bank	150			

notes to worked example

- Only one purchases account and one sales account is used to record the two different movements of the goods in which a business trades.
- The computer is a fixed asset, so its purchase is entered to a separate computer account.
- The purchases and sales made in the transactions above are called cash purchases and cash sales, because payment is immediate.

CREDIT TRANSACTIONS

In the previous section, we looked at the book-keeping for cash purchases and cash sales, ie where payment is made immediately. However, in business, many transactions for purchases and sales are made on credit, ie the goods are bought or sold now, with payment (for example, in cash, or by cheque) to be made at a later date. It is an important aspect of double-entry book-keeping to record the credit transaction as a purchase or a sale, and then record the second entry in an account in the name of the creditor or debtor, ie to record the amount owing by the firm to a creditor, or to the firm by a debtor.

Note that the term credit transactions does not refer to the side of an account. Instead, it means the type of transaction where money is not paid at the time of making the sale: payment will be made at a later date.

credit purchases

Credit purchases are goods obtained from a supplier, with payment to take place at a later date. From the buyer's viewpoint, the supplier is a creditor.

The book-keeping entries are:

- **credit purchase**
  - debit purchases account
  - credit creditor's (supplier's) account

When payment is made to the creditor the book-keeping entries are:

- **payment made to creditor**
  - debit creditor's account
  - credit bank account or cash account

credit sales

With credit sales, goods are sold to a customer who is allowed to settle the account at a later date. From the seller's viewpoint, the customer is a debtor.

The book-keeping entries are:

- **credit sale**
  - debit debtor's (customer's) account
  - credit sales account

When payment is received from the debtor the book-keeping entries are:

- **payment received from debtor**
  - debit bank account or cash account
  - credit debtor's account

WORKED EXAMPLE: CREDIT TRANSACTIONS

A local business, Wyvern Wholesalers, has the following transactions in the year 20-1:

18 Sep	Bought goods, £250, on credit from Malvern Manufacturing Co, with payment to be made in 30 days' time
20 Sep	Sold goods, £175, on credit to Strensham Stores, payment to be made in 30 days' time
18 Oct	Paid £250 by cheque to Malvern Manufacturing Co
20 Oct	Received a cheque for £175 from Strensham Stores

These transactions will be recorded in the book-keeping system of Wyvern Wholesalers (previous transactions on accounts, if any, not shown) as follows:

Dr **Purchases Account** Cr

20-1		£	20-1		£
18 Sep	Malvern Manufacturing Co	250			

Dr **Sales Account** Cr

20-1		£	20-1		£
			20 Sep	Strensham Stores	175

Dr **Malvern Manufacturing Co** Cr

20-1		£	20-1		£
18 Oct	Bank	250	18 Sep	Purchases	250

Dr		Strensham Stores			Cr
20-1		£	20-1		£
20 Sep	Sales	175	20 Oct	Bank	175

Dr		Bank Account			Cr
20-1		£	20-1		£
20 Oct	Strensham Stores	175	18 Oct	Malvern Manufacturing Co	250

Note: the name of the other account involved has been used in the details column as a description.

balancing off accounts

In the example above, after the transactions have been recorded in the books of Wyvern Wholesalers, the accounts of Malvern Manufacturing Co and Strensham Stores have the same amount entered on both debit and credit side. This means that nothing is owing to Wyvern Wholesalers, or is owed by it, ie the accounts have a 'nil' balance. In practice, as a business trades, there will be a number of entries on both sides of such accounts, and we shall see in Chapter 5 how accounts are 'balanced off' at regular intervals.

fixed assets bought on credit

Fixed assets are often purchased on credit terms. As with the purchase of goods for resale, an account is opened in the name of the creditor, as follows:

- **purchase of a fixed asset on credit**
  - debit fixed asset account, eg computer account
  - credit creditor's (supplier's) account

When payment is made to the creditor the book-keeping entries are:

- **payment made to a creditor**
  - debit creditor's account
  - credit bank account or cash account

PURCHASES RETURNS AND SALES RETURNS

From time-to-time goods bought or sold are returned, perhaps because the wrong items have been supplied (eg wrong type, size or colour), or because the goods are unsatisfactory. We will now see the book-keeping entries for returned goods.

- **Purchases returns** (or returns out) is where a business returns goods to a creditor (supplier).

  The book-keeping entries are:

  – debit creditor's (supplier's) account

  – credit purchases returns (or returns out) account

  Purchases returns are kept separate from purchases, ie they are entered in a separate purchases returns account rather than being credited to purchases account.

- **Sales returns** (or returns in) is where a debtor (customer) returns goods to the business.

  The book-keeping entries are:

  – debit sales returns (or returns in) account

  – credit debtor's (customer's) account

Sales returns are kept separate from sales, ie they are entered in a separate sales returns account rather than being debited to sales account.

WORKED EXAMPLE: PURCHASES RETURNS AND SALES RETURNS

Hightown Stores has the following transactions during the year 20-1:

7 October	Bought goods, £280, on credit from B Lewis Ltd
10 October	Returned unsatisfactory goods, £30, to B Lewis Ltd
11 October	Sold goods, £125, on credit to A Holmes
17 October	A Holmes returned goods, £25
26 October	Paid the amount owing to B Lewis Ltd by cheque
29 October	A Holmes paid the amount owing in cash

The transactions will be recorded in the book-keeping system of Hightown Stores (previous transactions on accounts, if any, not shown) as follows:

Purchases Account

Dr					Cr
20-1		£	20-1		£
7 Oct	B Lewis Ltd	280			

B Lewis Ltd

Dr					Cr
20-1		£	20-1		£
10 Oct	Purchases Returns	30	7 Oct	Purchases	280
26 Oct	Bank	250			

Purchases Returns Account

Dr			Cr		
20-1		£	20-1		£
			10 Oct	B Lewis Ltd	30

Sales Account

Dr			Cr		
20-1		£	20-1		£
			11 Oct	A Holmes	125

A Holmes

Dr			Cr		
20-1		£	20-1		£
11 Oct	Sales	125	17 Oct	Sales Returns	25
			29 Oct	Cash	100

Sales Returns Account

Dr			Cr		
20-1		£	20-1		£
17 Oct	A Holmes	25			

Bank Account

Dr			Cr		
20-1		£	20-1		£
			26 Oct	B Lewis Ltd	250

Cash Account

Dr			Cr		
20-1		£	20-1		£
29 Oct	A Holmes	100			

Carriage Inwards and Carriage Outwards

When goods are bought and sold, the cost of transporting the goods is referred to as 'carriage'.

Carriage inwards is where the buyer pays the carriage cost of purchases, eg an item is purchased by mail order, and the buyer has to pay the additional cost of delivery (and possibly packing also).

Carriage outwards is where the seller pays the carriage charge, eg an item is sold to the customer and described as 'delivery free'.

Both carriage inwards and carriage outwards are expenses and their cost should be debited to two separate accounts, carriage inwards account and carriage outwards account respectively.

General Principles of Debits and Credits

By now you should have a good idea of the principles of debits and credits. From the transactions we have considered in this and the previous chapter, the 'rules' can be summarised as follows:

Debits include

- purchases of goods for resale
- sales returns (or returns in) when goods previously sold are returned to the business
- purchase of fixed assets for use in the business
- expenses and overheads incurred by the business
- debtors where money is owed to the business
- money received through cash account or bank account
- drawings made by the owner of the business
- loan repayment, where a loan liability is reduced/repaid

Credits include

- sales of goods by the business
- purchases returns (or returns out) of goods previously bought by the business
- sale of fixed assets
- income received by the business
- creditors where money is owed by the business
- money paid out through cash account or bank account
- capital introduced into the business by the owner(s)
- loan received by the business

It is important to ensure, at an early stage, that you are clear about the principles of debits and credits. They are important for an understanding of book-keeping, and are essential for your later studies in financial accounting.

To summarise the double-entry book-keeping 'rules':

- **debit entry** – the account which gains value, or records an asset, or an expense
- **credit entry** – the account which gives value, or records a liability, or an income item

TYPES OF ACCOUNT

Within a book-keeping system there are different types of account: a distinction is made between personal and impersonal accounts. Personal accounts are in the names of people or businesses, eg the accounts for debtors and creditors. Impersonal accounts are the other accounts; these are usually divided between real accounts, which represent things such as cash, bank, computers, cars, machinery, etc, and nominal accounts, which record income and expenses such as sales, purchases, wages, etc.

These distinctions are shown in the diagram below.

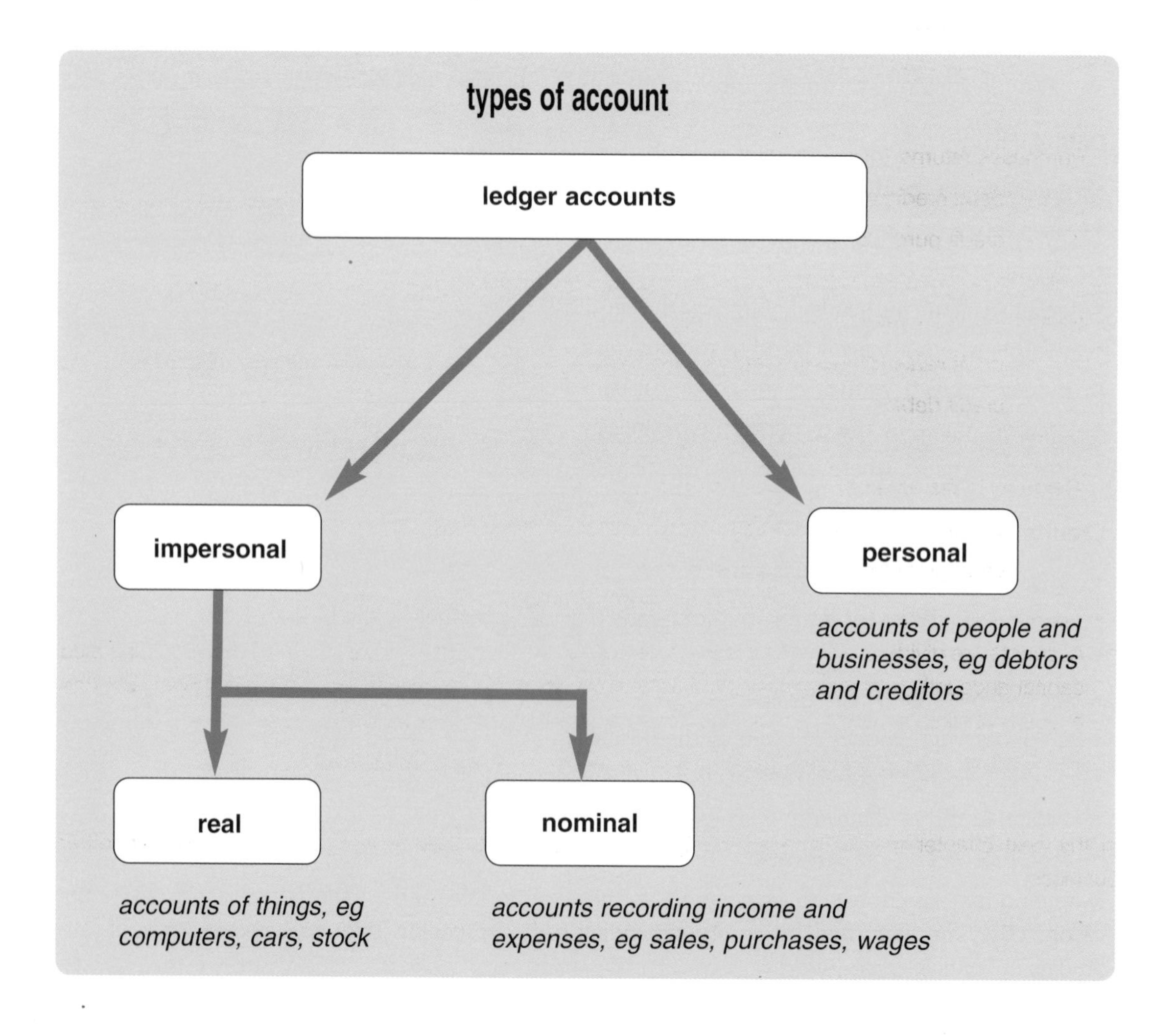

CHAPTER SUMMARY

- Purchases account is used to record the purchase of goods in which the business trades: the normal entry is on the debit side.

- Sales account is used to record the sale of goods in which the business trades: the normal entry is on the credit side.

- The purchase of goods is recorded as:
  - debit purchases account
  - credit bank/cash account or, if bought on credit, creditor's account

- The sale of goods is recorded as:
  - debit bank/cash account or, if sold on credit, debtor's account
  - credit sales account

- Purchases returns (or returns out) are recorded as:
  - debit creditor's account
  - credit purchases returns (or returns out) account

- Sales returns (or returns in) are recorded as:
  - debit sales returns (or returns in) account
  - credit debtor's account

- 'Carriage' is the expense of transporting goods:
  - carriage inwards is the cost of carriage paid on purchases
  - carriage outwards is the cost of carriage paid on sales

- Accounts are divided between personal (the accounts of people, firms, eg debtors and creditors; also capital account), and impersonal accounts; impersonal accounts are sub-divided between real (the accounts of things), and nominal (the accounts of income and expenses).

In the next chapter we will look at the business documents used when goods are sold to another business.

QUESTIONS

NOTE: an asterisk (*) after the question number means that an answer to the question is given at the end of this book.

3.1 The following are the business transactions of Evesham Enterprises for the month of October 20-2:

1 Oct	Started in business with capital of £2,500 in the bank
2 Oct	Bought goods, £200, paying by cheque
4 Oct	Sold goods, £150, a cheque being received
6 Oct	Bought goods, £90, paying by cheque
8 Oct	Sold goods, £125, a cheque being received
12 Oct	Received a loan of £2,000 from J Smithson by cheque
14 Oct	Bought goods, £250, paying by cheque
18 Oct	Sold goods, £155, a cheque being received
22 Oct	Bought a secondhand delivery van, £4,000, paying by cheque
25 Oct	Paid wages, £375, by bank giro credit
30 Oct	Sold goods, £110, a cheque being received

You are to:

(a) Write up the firm's bank account

(b) Complete the double-entry book-keeping transactions

3.2* The following are the business transactions of Oxford Trading Company for the month of February 20-1:

1 Feb	Started in business with capital of £3,000 in the bank
2 Feb	Sold goods, £250, a cheque being received
3 Feb	Bought goods, £100, paying by cheque
5 Feb	Paid wages, £150, by bank giro credit
7 Feb	Sold goods, £300, a cheque being received
12 Feb	Bought goods, £200, paying by cheque
15 Feb	Received a loan of £1,000 from James Walters by cheque
20 Feb	Bought a computer for £1,950, paying by cheque
25 Feb	Sold goods, £150, a cheque being received
27 Feb	Paid wages, £125, by bank giro credit

You are to:

(a) Write up the firm's bank account

(b) Complete the double-entry book-keeping transactions

3.3*

Write up the bank account from question 3.2 in the form of a 'running balance' account.

3.4*

The following are the business transactions of Pershore Packaging for the month of January 20-1:

4 Jan	Bought goods, £250, on credit from AB Supplies Ltd
5 Jan	Sold goods, £195, a cheque being received
7 Jan	Sold goods, £150, cash being received
10 Jan	Received a loan of £1,000 from J Johnson by cheque
15 Jan	Paid £250 to AB Supplies Ltd by cheque
17 Jan	Sold goods, £145, on credit to L Lewis
20 Jan	Bought goods, £225, paying by cheque
22 Jan	Paid wages, £125, in cash
26 Jan	Bought office equipment, £160, on credit from Mercia Office Supplies Ltd
29 Jan	Received a cheque for £145 from L Lewis
31 Jan	Paid the amount owing to Mercia Office Supplies Ltd by cheque

You are to record the transactions in the books of account.

3.5

The following are the business transactions for April 20-2 of William King, who runs a food wholesaling business:

2 Apr	Bought goods, £200, on credit from Wyvern Producers Ltd
4 Apr	Bought goods, £250, on credit from A Larsen
5 Apr	Sold goods, £150, on credit to Pershore Patisserie
7 Apr	Sold goods, £175, a cheque being received
9 Apr	Returned goods, £50, to Wyvern Producers Ltd
12 Apr	Sold goods, £110, a cheque being received
15 Apr	Pershore Patisserie returned goods, £25
17 Apr	Bought a weighing machine for use in the business £250, on credit from Amery Scales Limited
20 Apr	Paid Wyvern Producers Ltd £150, by cheque
22 Apr	Pershore Patisserie paid the amount owing by cheque
26 Apr	Returned goods, £45, to A Larsen
28 Apr	Sold goods, £100, cash received
29 Apr	Paid wages in cash, £90
30 Apr	Paid the amount owing to Amery Scales Ltd by cheque

You are to record the transactions in the books of account.

3.6 The following are the business transactions for June 20-3 of Helen Smith who trades as 'Fashion Frocks':

2 Jun	Bought goods, £350, on credit from Designs Ltd
4 Jun	Sold goods, £220, a cheque being received
5 Jun	Sold goods, £115, cash received
6 Jun	Returned goods, £100, to Designs Ltd
7 Jun	Bought goods, £400, on credit from Mercia Knitwear Ltd
10 Jun	Sold goods, £350, on credit to Wyvern Trade Supplies
12 Jun	Sold goods, £175, a cheque being received
15 Jun	Wyvern Trade Supplies returned goods, £50
17 Jun	Returned goods, £80, to Mercia Knitwear Ltd
18 Jun	Paid the amount owing to Designs Ltd by cheque
20 Jun	Sold goods, £180, cash received
23 Jun	Bought goods, £285, on credit from Designs Ltd
26 Jun	Paid rent in cash, £125
28 Jun	Received a cheque from Wyvern Trade Supplies for the amount owing

You are to record the transactions in the books of account.

3.7 For each transaction below, complete the table on the next page to show the names of the accounts which will be debited and credited:

(a) Bought goods, paying by cheque

(b) Cheque received for sales

(c) Bought goods on credit from Teme Traders

(d) Sold goods on credit to L Harris

(e) Returned unsatisfactory goods to Teme Traders

(f) L Harris returns unsatisfactory goods

(g) Received a loan from D Perkins, by cheque

(h) Withdrew cash from the bank for use in the business

Transaction	*Account debited*	*Account credited*
(a)	....	....
(b)	....	....
(c)	....	....
(d)	....	....
(e)	....	....
(f)	....	....
(g)	....	....
(h)	....	....

4 BUSINESS DOCUMENTS

Business documents are important because they are the source documents for the recording of business transactions. In this chapter we will look at the following:

- purchase order
- delivery note
- invoice
- credit note
- statement of account
- other source documents

We will also look at how cash discount – an allowance off the invoice price for quick settlement – is recorded in the book-keeping system.

DOCUMENTS FOR A CREDIT TRANSACTION

You will see that the documents to be explained involve credit transactions, ie selling or buying with payment to be made at a later date. The normal stages in a credit transaction are:

1 buyer prepares
- purchase order

2 seller prepares
- delivery note
- invoice
- statement of account

3 buyer sends payment by
- cheque, or
- bank transfer

If some or all of the goods are unsatisfactory and are returned, the seller prepares a credit note.

The flow of these documents is shown in the diagram on the next page.

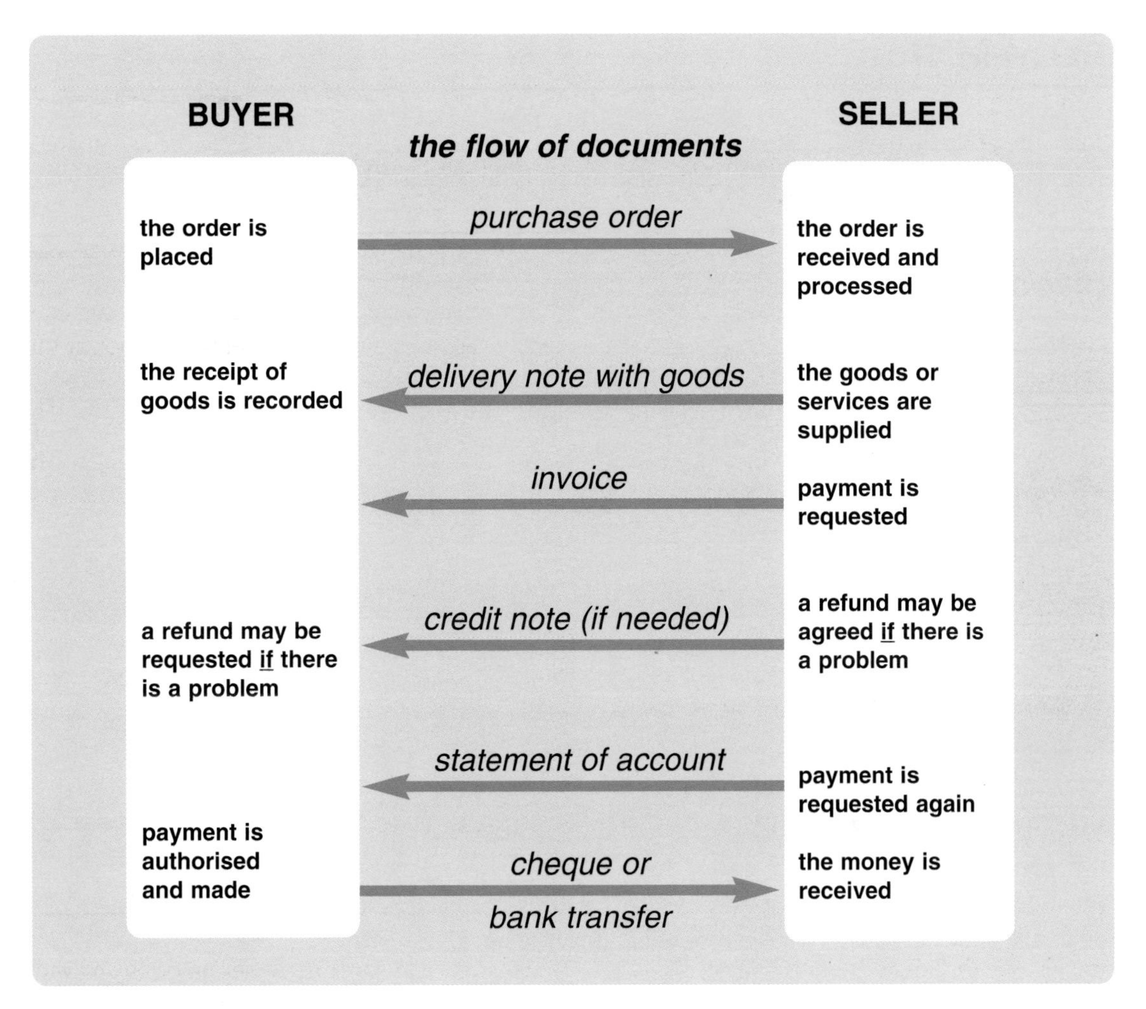

Purchase Order

A purchase order is prepared by the buyer, and is sent to the seller. Details found on a purchase order include:

- number of purchase order
- name and address of buyer
- name and address of seller
- full description of the goods, reference numbers, quantity required and unit price
- date of issue
- signature of person authorised to issue the order

In order to keep control over purchases many businesses authorise certain people as buyers. In this way, purchases are controlled so that duplicate or unauthorised goods are not ordered.

DELIVERY NOTE

When the business that is selling the goods despatches them to the buyer, a delivery note is prepared. This accompanies the goods and gives details of what is being delivered. When the goods are received by the buyer, a check can be made by the buyer to ensure that the correct goods have been delivered.

INVOICE

The invoice (see next page) is the most important document in a business transaction. It is prepared by the seller and is sent to the buyer. The invoice gives details of the goods supplied, and states the money amount to be paid by the buyer. The information to be found on an invoice includes:

- invoice number (serially numbered)
- name and address of seller
- name and address of buyer
- date of sale
- date that goods are supplied, including reference numbers, quantity supplied and unit price
- details of trade discount allowed (if any)
- total amount of money due
- terms of trade

value added tax

Where the seller is registered for Value Added Tax (VAT), tax must be charged at the appropriate rate on all sales subject to VAT. The invoice will normally state:

- the seller's VAT Registration Number
- the date for tax purposes (the tax-point) on which the sale is made
- amount of VAT charged
- total amount of money due including VAT.

If the buyer of the goods is VAT-registered, then the buyer can claim back the amount of VAT on the invoice from the VAT authorities (HM Revenue & Customs). The accounting implications of VAT are looked at in Chapter 7.

terms of trade

The terms of trade are stated on an invoice to indicate the date by which the invoice amount is to be paid. The term 'net' on an invoice means that the invoice total is the amount to be paid; 'net 30 days' means that the amount is payable within 30 days of the invoice date.

Other terms include 'carriage paid' and 'E & OE', which stands for 'errors and omissions excepted'. This means that if there is a error or something left off the invoice by mistake, resulting in an incorrect final price, the supplier has the right to correct the mistake and demand the correct amount.

INVOICE

TREND FASHION DESIGNS LIMITED

Unit 45 Elgar Estate, Broadfield, BR7 4ER
Tel 01908 765314 Fax 01908 765951
VAT REG GB 0745 4672 76

invoice to

Zing Fashions
4 Friar Street
Broadfield
BR1 3RF

deliver to

as above

invoice no	**787923**
account	**3993**
your reference	**47609**
date/tax point	**01 10 05**

product code	description	quantity	unit price	unit	total	trade discount %	net
45B	**Trend tops (black)**	**40**	**12.50**	**each**	**500.00**	**10**	**450.00**

terms
Net 30 days
Carriage paid
E & OE

GOODS TOTAL	**450.00**
VAT	**78.75**
TOTAL	**528.75**

trade discount

Trade discount is the amount sometimes allowed as a reduction when goods are supplied to other businesses, but not when the sale is made to the general public. VAT is calculated on the net amount of the invoice, ie after deducting any trade discount allowed. In the invoice shown above, trade discount of 10% is allowed on clothes supplied to Zing Fashions, a shop. Note that trade discount is never shown in the accounts – only the amount after deduction of trade discount is recorded.

cash discount

Cash discount is an allowance off the invoice amount for quick settlement, eg 2% cash discount for settlement within seven days. The buyer can choose whether to take up the cash discount by paying promptly, or whether to take longer to pay, perhaps thirty days from the invoice date, without cash discount. When cash discount is taken, it needs to be recorded in the accounts – see page 54.

It is important to note that where a cash discount is offered, VAT is calculated on the net amount of the invoice (ie value of goods supplied, less any trade discount allowed), less the amount of the cash discount, whether or not this discount is subsequently taken by the buyer. For example:

	net 30 days	2% cash discount for settlement within 7 days, otherwise net 30 days
	£	£
Net invoice amount	100.00	100.00
add VAT @ 17.5%	17.50	17.15
Invoice total	117.50	117.15

In the first example (net 30 days), the amount of £117.50 is due within 30 days of the invoice date.

In the case of the 2% cash discount, the VAT amount is:

(£100.00 - £2.00 cash discount) x 17.5% = £17.15.

In this example, £117.15 is due within 30 days of the invoice date if no cash discount is taken. If the buyer settles within seven days and takes the cash discount, the amount to be paid will be:

(£100.00 - £2.00 cash discount) + VAT £17.15 = £115.15.

format of invoices

Invoices (like other business documents) can be handwritten or typed on printed forms, or books of invoices can be bought in most stationers' shops. Invoicing is an ideal function for computerised accounting (see Chapter 11) and, for this purpose, pre-printed invoices are available in the form of continuous stationery. Also, increasingly nowadays, invoices are in electronic form (EDI – electronic data interchange) and the information needs to be 'captured' and put into the accounting system.

Credit Note

If a buyer returns goods for some reason (eg faulty goods supplied), or requires a reduction in the amount owed (the buyer may have been overcharged) the seller prepares a credit note (see next page) to record the amount of the allowance made to the buyer. Another document used with returned goods is the debit note. This is prepared by the buyer who sends it to the seller requesting a reduction in the amount owed.

CREDIT NOTE

TREND FASHION DESIGNS LIMITED

Unit 45 Elgar Estate, Broadfield, BR7 4ER
Tel 01908 765314 Fax 01908 765951
VAT REG GB 0745 4672 76

to

Zing Fashions
4 Friar Street
Broadfield
BR1 3RF

credit note no	**12157**
account	**3993**
your reference	**47609**
our invoice	**787923**
date/tax point	**10 10 05**

product code	description	quantity	unit price	unit	total	trade discount %	net
45B	**Trend tops (black)**	**2**	**12.50**	**each**	**25.00**	**10**	**22.50**

Reason for credit
2 tops received damaged
(Your returns note no. R/N 2384)

GOODS TOTAL	**22.50**
VAT	**3.93**
TOTAL	**26.43**

Statement of Account

At regular intervals, often at the end of each month, the seller sends a statement of account (see next page) to each debtor. This gives a summary of the transactions that have taken place since the previous statement and shows how much is currently owed. The details on a statement are:

- name and address of seller
- name and address of the debtor (buyer)
- date of the statement
- details of transactions, eg invoices, debit notes, credit notes, payments
- balance currently due

Most statements have three money columns: debit, credit and balance. The debit column is used to record the money amount of invoices and debit notes sent to the debtor; the credit column is for payments received and credit notes issued; the balance column shows the amount due, and is prepared on the 'running balance' (see page 26) basis, ie a new balance is shown after each transaction. The balance is usually a debit balance, which indicates that the buyer is a debtor in the seller's accounting records. Some statements of account also incorporate a remittance advice as a tear-off slip; this is returned to the seller together with the payment.

STATEMENT OF ACCOUNT

TREND FASHION DESIGNS LIMITED

Unit 45 Elgar Estate, Broadfield, BR7 4ER
Tel 01908 765314 Fax 01908 765951
VAT REG GB 0745 4672 76

TO

Zing Fashions
4 Friar Street
Broadfield
BR1 3RF

account **3993**

date **31 10 05**

date	details	debit £	credit £	balance £
01 10 02	**Invoice 787923**	**528.75**		**528.75**
10 10 02	**Credit note 12157**		**26.43**	**502.32**

AMOUNT NOW DUE **502.32**

PAYMENT

Before payment is made to the seller, the buyer must check that the goods have been received and are as ordered. The payment can then be authorised by an appointed employee and made by means of either a cheque (sent by post) or a bank credit transfer which passes the money from the buyer's bank account to the seller's account. Most bank credit transfers nowadays are made by BACS (Bankers Automated Clearing Services) computer transfer. If a cheque is posted to the seller, it is sent with a remittance advice, which shows the amount of the payment, and the transactions to which it relates. If a payment is sent through the bank a separate remittance advice will be mailed or faxed.

Other Source Documents

cash receipts

Often when payment is made to the seller, a receipt is given: this can take the form of a machine-produced receipt, such as is given in a shop, or a handwritten receipt. The copy of these receipts – in the form of a till roll/till summary and receipt book – form the source documents for the seller. The originals are the source documents for the buyer. Look at these examples:

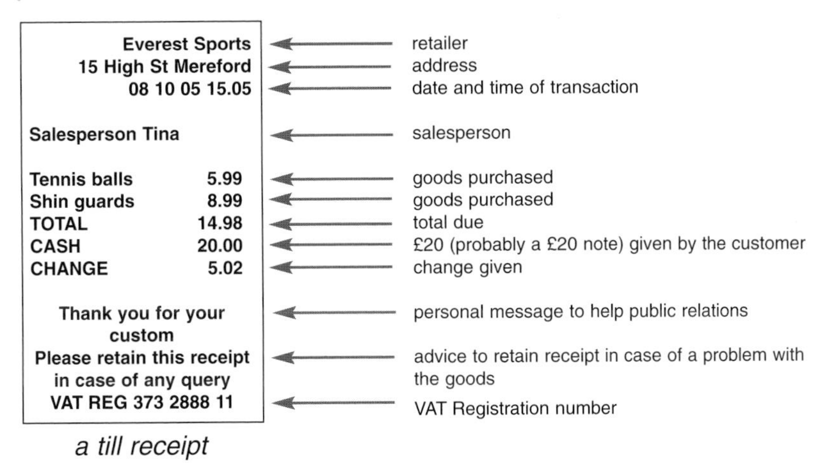

Everest Sports
15 High St Mereford
08 10 05 15.05

Salesperson Tina

Tennis balls	5.99
Shin guards	8.99
TOTAL	14.98
CASH	20.00
CHANGE	5.02

Thank you for your custom
Please retain this receipt in case of any query
VAT REG 373 2888 11

a till receipt

ENIGMA MUSIC LIMITED ***receipt*** **958**

13 High Street, Mereford MR1 2TF
VAT Reg 343 7645 23

Customer *R V Williams* date *3 Oct 2005*

'Golden Oldies' by J Moore	*£20.00*
	£20.00
VAT @ 17.5%	*£3.50*
Total	*£23.50*

a hand-written receipt

Note that, although the above are often described as 'cash receipts', they are issued whatever payment method is used – cash, cheque, credit card, debit card.

petty cash vouchers

Cash payments made for low-value purchases and expenses – such as small items of stationery and postages – are usually made from the firm's petty cash float. The source document for petty cash transactions is the petty cash voucher, an example of which is given below:

petty cash voucher — No. 807

date *12 May 2005*

description	amount (£)	
C5 Envelopes	*2*	*00*
5 Marker pens	*4*	*00*
	6	*00*
VAT	*1*	*05*
	7	*05*

signature *T Harris*

authorised *R Singh*

Note that the use of petty cash vouchers is covered fully in Chapter 9.

banking documents

Most businesses have a bank account into which they pay money using a paying-in slip, and make payments by issuing cheques. The paying-in slip counterfoils and cheque counterfoils form source documents for the accounting system. At regular intervals a bank sends a statement of account to its customers – the statement may show other receipts and payments – for example, standing orders, direct debits, credit transfers and bank charges.

We will be looking further at bank statements and banking transactions in Chapters 8 and 10 when we deal with the cash book and prepare bank reconciliation statements.

paying-in slip counterfoils

In a paying-in book, which is issued by the bank to business customers, the counterfoil is the part that is retained by the customer and stamped as a receipt by the bank cashier for the amount being paid in. A completed paying-in slip and counterfoil is illustrated on the next page.

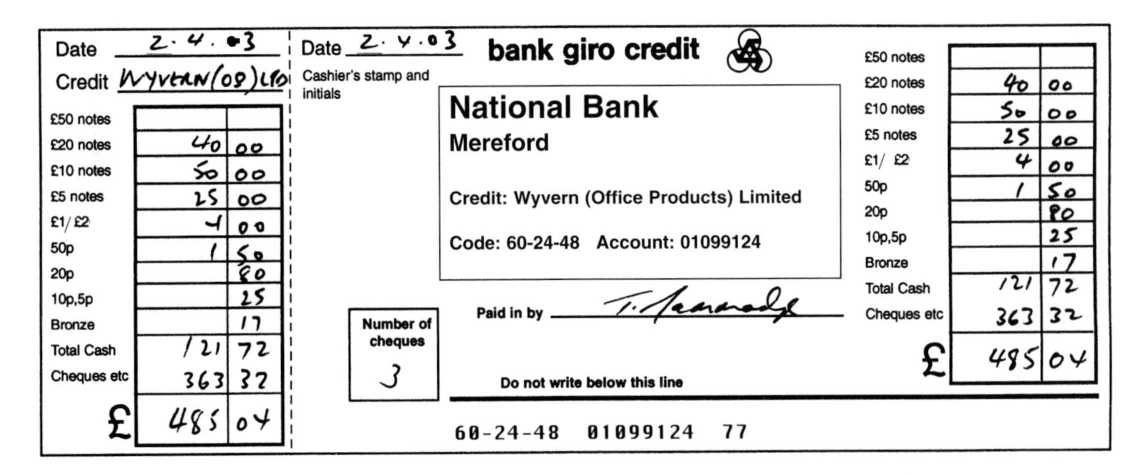

Date 2.4.03
Credit WYVERN (OP) LTD

£50 notes		
£20 notes	40	00
£10 notes	50	00
£5 notes	25	00
£1/ £2	4	00
50p	1	50
20p		80
10p,5p		25
Bronze		17
Total Cash	121	72
Cheques etc	363	32
£	485	04

Date 2.4.03
Cashier's stamp and initials

bank giro credit

National Bank
Mereford

Credit: Wyvern (Office Products) Limited

Code: 60-24-48 Account: 01099124

Number of cheques 3

Paid in by T. Kennedy

Do not write below this line

60-24-48 01099124 77

£50 notes		
£20 notes	40	00
£10 notes	50	00
£5 notes	25	00
£1/ £2	4	00
50p	1	50
20p		80
10p,5p		25
Bronze		17
Total Cash	121	72
Cheques etc	363	32
£	485	04

counterfoil *paying-in slip (front)*

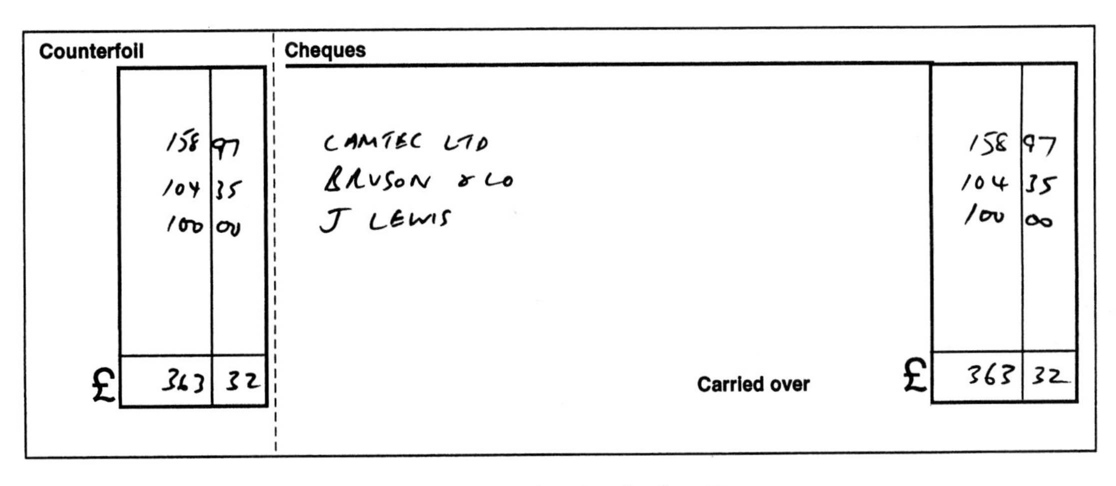

Counterfoil

158	97
104	35
100	00
£ 363	32

Cheques

CAMTEC LTD	158	97
BRYSON & CO	104	35
J LEWIS	100	00
Carried over £	363	32

counterfoil *paying-in slip (back)*

cheque counterfoils

In cheque books the counterfoil is the part retained by the payer when the cheque is sent off to the payee (the person who is being paid). The counterfoil gives information as to the date of the cheque, the payee, and the amount being paid; it also includes a note of the cheque number. A completed cheque and counterfoil is illustrated on the next page.

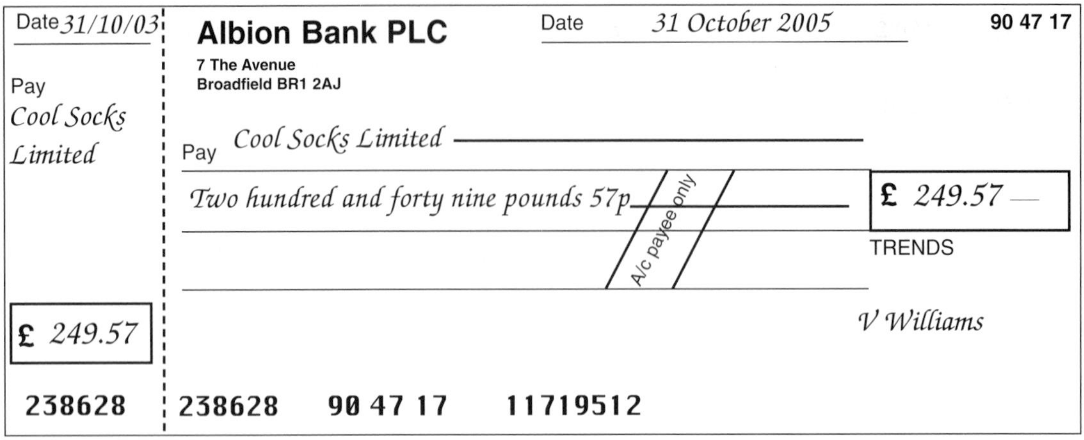

Date 31/10/03	Albion Bank PLC 7 The Avenue Broadfield BR1 2AJ	Date 31 October 2005	90 47 17
Pay Cool Socks Limited	Pay Cool Socks Limited		
	Two hundred and forty nine pounds 57p (A/c payee only)		£ 249.57 — TRENDS
£ 249.57			V Williams
238628	238628 90 47 17 11719512		

counterfoil — cheque

information from bank statements

The bank statement shows other receipts and payments:

- standing orders, for regular payments – eg hire purchase – made automatically by the bank on the instructions of the customer
- direct debits, for fixed or variable amounts – eg telephone bills – where the payment is requested by the receiver (beneficiary) of the payment through the banking system
- credit transfers, where money has been received through the banking system and credited to the account, eg where customers have paid the amount they owe
- bank charges, where the bank makes a charge for providing banking services; the charge may be calculated by reference to the number of transactions that have taken place on the bank account

These items are explained in more detail in Chapter 8, page 114.

Recording Cash Discount in the Book-keeping System

We saw earlier (page 48) that cash discount is an allowance off the invoice amount for quick settlement, eg 2% cash discount for settlement within seven days. A business can be involved with cash discount in two ways:

- discount allowed to debtors
- discount received from creditors

Note that, although the terms 'discount allowed' and 'discount received' do not use the word 'cash', they do refer to cash discount.

discount allowed

When cash discount is taken by a debtor it is entered into the accounts as shown by the following transactions:

10 October 20-2	Sold goods, £100 (no VAT), on credit to P Henry, allowing her a cash discount of 2% for settlement within seven days
15 October 20-2	P Henry pays £98 by cheque

Sales Account

Dr					Cr
20-2		£	20-2		£
			10 Oct	P Henry	100

P Henry

Dr					Cr
20-2		£	20-2		£
10 Oct	Sales	100	15 Oct	Bank	98
			15 Oct	Discount allowed	2
		100			100

Bank Account

Dr					Cr
20-2		£	20-2		£
15 Oct	P Henry	98			

Discount Allowed Account

Dr					Cr
20-2		£	20-2		£
15 Oct	P Henry	2			

Notes

- The amount of the payment received from the debtor is entered in the bank account.
- The amount of discount allowed is entered in both the debtor's account and discount allowed account:
  - debit discount allowed account
  - credit debtor's account
- Discount allowed is an expense of the business, because it represents the cost of collecting payments more speedily from the debtors.
- The account of P Henry has been totalled to show that both the debit and credit money columns are the same – thus her account now has a nil balance (the method of balancing accounts is looked at in the next chapter).

discount received

With cash discount received, a business is offered cash discount for quick settlement by its creditors. The following transactions give an example of this:

20 October 20-2	Bought goods, £200 (no VAT), on credit from B Lewis Ltd; 2.5% cash discount is offered for settlement by the end of October
30 October 20-2	Paid B Lewis Ltd £195 by cheque

Purchases Account

Dr					Cr
20-2		£	20-2		£
20 Oct	B Lewis Ltd	200			

B Lewis Ltd

Dr					Cr
20-2		£	20-2		£
30 Oct	Bank	195	20 Oct	Purchases	200
30 Oct	Discount received	5			
		200			200

Bank Account

Dr					Cr
20-2		£	20-2		£
			30 Oct	B Lewis Ltd	195

Discount Received Account

Dr					Cr
20-2		£	20-2		£
			30 Oct	B Lewis Ltd	5

Notes

- The business is receiving cash discount from its creditor, and the amount is entered as:
  - debit creditor's account
  - credit discount received account
- Discount received account is an income account.
- The money columns of the account of B Lewis Ltd have been totalled to show that the account now has a nil balance.

revision summary

- Cash discount – when taken – is recorded in the debtors' and creditors' accounts.
- Both discount allowed (an expenses account) and discount received (an income account) store up information until the end of the financial year, when it is used in the firm's profit and loss account – see Chapter 12.
- The cash book (see Chapter 8) is usually used for listing the amounts of discount received and allowed – transfers are then made at the end of each month to the respective discount accounts.
- Trade discount is never recorded in the double-entry accounts; only the net amount of an invoice is recorded after trade discount has been deducted.

CHAPTER SUMMARY

- Correct documentation is important for businesses to be able to record accurately buying and selling transactions.
- There are a number of documents involved – the two most important are the purchase order and the invoice.
- A purchase order is a document which states the requirements of the buyer, and is sent to the seller.
- The invoice is prepared by the seller and states the value of goods sold and, hence, the amount to be paid by the buyer.
- Trade discount is often deducted when goods are sold to other businesses.
- Cash discount is an allowance off the invoice amount for quick settlement.
- A credit note shows that the buyer is entitled to a reduction in the amount charged by the seller; it is used if:
  - some of the goods delivered were faulty, or incorrectly supplied
  - the price charged on the invoice was too high
- Statements of account are sent out regularly to each debtor of a business to show the amount currently due.
- Other source documents include cash receipts, till rolls, petty cash vouchers, cheque counterfoils, paying-in slip counterfoils.
- Information from bank statements gives details of standing orders, direct debits, credit transfers, bank charges.
- Cash discount allowed is entered in the accounts as:
  - debit discount allowed account
  - credit debtor's account

- Cash discount received is entered as:
  - debit creditor's account
  - credit discount received account

This chapter has looked at business documentation; the next chapter returns to double-entry book-keeping and looks at how accounts are balanced, and a trial balance is extracted.

QUESTIONS

NOTE: an asterisk (*) after the question number means that an answer to the question is given at the end of this book.

free download from website www.osbornebooks.co.uk
Blank financial documents for use in these questions are available for free download from the Resources section of the Osborne Books website.

4.1* Fill in the missing words from the following sentences:

(a) A .... is prepared by the buyer and sent to the seller and describes the goods to be supplied.

(b) The seller prepares the ...., which gives details of the goods supplied, and states the money amount to be paid by the buyer.

(c) .... is a deduction made in the price if the purchaser pays within a stated time.

(d) When the purchaser is in business, an amount of ....

.... is sometimes allowed as a reduction in the price.

(e) The term .... on an invoice means that the invoice total is the amount to be paid.

(f) A government tax added to an invoice is called ....

(g) If a buyer returns goods, the seller prepares a ....

(h) At regular intervals the seller sends a summary of transactions to the buyer in the

form of a ....

4.2 You work for Jane Smith, a wholesaler of fashionwear, who trades from Unit 21, Eastern Industrial Estate, Wyvern, Wyvernshire, WY1 3XJ. A customer, Excel Fashions of 49 Highland Street, Longtown, Mercia, LT3 2XL, orders the following:

5 dresses at £30 each

3 suits at £45.50 each

4 coats at £51.50 each

Value Added Tax is to be charged at 17.5 per cent on all the items.

A 2.5 per cent cash discount is offered for full settlement within 14 days.

You are to prepare invoice number 2451, under today's date, to be sent to the customer.

4.3 You work for Deansway Trading Company, a wholesaler of office stationery, which trades from The Model Office, Deansway, Rowcester, RW1 2EJ. A customer, The Card Shop of 126 The Cornbow, Teamington Spa, Wyvernshire, WY33 0EG, orders the following:

5 boxes of assorted rubbers at £5 per box

100 shorthand notebooks at £4 for 10

250 ring binders at 50p each

Value Added Tax is to be charged at 17.5 per cent on all the items.

A 2.5 per cent cash discount is offered for full settlement within 14 days.

You are to prepare invoice number 8234, under today's date, to be sent to the customer.

4.4 Enter the following transactions into the double-entry book-keeping accounts of Sonya Smith:

20-4	
2 Feb	Bought goods £200, on credit from G Lewis
4 Feb	Sold goods £150, on credit to L Jarvis
7 Feb	Sold goods £240, on credit to G Patel
10 Feb	Paid G Lewis the amount owing by cheque, after deducting a cash discount of 5%
12 Feb	L Jarvis pays the amount owing by cheque, after deducting a cash discount of 2%
16 Feb	Bought goods £160, on credit from G Lewis
20 Feb	G Patel pays the amount owing by cheque, after deducting a cash discount of 2.5%
24 Feb	Paid G Lewis the amount owing by cheque, after deducting a cash discount of 5%

Note: Ignore Value Added Tax

4.5 Trend Fashion Designs Limited has partially prepared the following invoice from the delivery note:

INVOICE

TREND FASHION DESIGNS LIMITED

Unit 45 Elgar Estate, Broadfield, BR7 4ER
Tel 01908 765314 Fax 01908 765951
VAT REG GB 0745 4672 76

invoice to

Fashion Shop
48 High Street
Wyvern
WV1 2AJ

invoice no	**7878106**
account	**2667**
your reference	**54208**
date/tax point	**10 11 05**

deliver to

as above

product code	description	quantity	price	unit	total	trade discount %	net
45B	**Trend tops (black)**	**30**	**12.50**	**each**		**10**	
35W	**Trend trousers (white)**	**20**	**25.00**	**each**		**10**	

terms
Cash discount of 5% for payment within 7 days

GOODS TOTAL	
VAT at 17.5%	
TOTAL	

REQUIRED

(a) Complete the invoice to show the total amount due.

(b) Explain the following terms:

- trade discount
- cash discount

4.6* Highfield Products is seeking to attract new customers and has decided to offer trade and cash discounts.

REQUIRED

(a) Explain the circumstances under which they would give each of these discounts.

(i) Trade discounts ....

....

....

....

(ii) Cash discounts ....

....

....

....

They supply goods to a customer on the following terms:

Selling price	£500
Trade discount	20%
Cash discount	5%
VAT	17.5%

(b) Calculate the total of the invoice for these goods.

Invoice total: £ ....

Workings ....

....

....

....

....

Assessment and Qualifications Alliance (AQA), 2003

5 BALANCING ACCOUNTS – THE TRIAL BALANCE

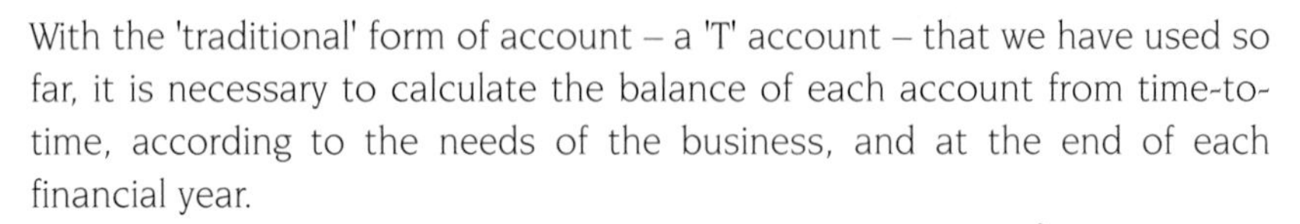

With the 'traditional' form of account – a 'T' account – that we have used so far, it is necessary to calculate the balance of each account from time-to-time, according to the needs of the business, and at the end of each financial year.

The balance of an account is the total of that account to date, eg the amount of wages paid, the amount of sales made. In this chapter we shall see how this balancing of accounts is carried out.

We shall then use the balances from each account in order to check the double-entry book-keeping by extracting a trial balance, which is a list of the balances of ledger accounts.

BALANCING THE ACCOUNTS

At regular intervals, often at the end of each month, accounts are balanced in order to show the amounts, for example:

- owing to each creditor
- owing by each debtor
- of sales
- of purchases
- of sales returns (returns in)
- of purchases returns (returns out)
- of expenses incurred by the business
- of fixed assets, eg premises, machinery, etc owned by the business
- of capital and drawings of the owner of the business
- of other liabilities, eg loans

We have already noted earlier that, where running balance accounts (see page 26) are used, there is no need to balance each account, because the balance is already calculated – either manually or by computer – after each transaction.

Method of Balancing Accounts

Set out below is an example of an account which has been balanced at the month-end:

Dr		Bank Account			Cr
20-1		£	20-1		£
1 Sep	Capital	5,000	2 Sep	Computer	1,800
5 Sep	J Jackson: loan	2,500	6 Sep	Purchases	500
10 Sep	Sales	750	12 Sep	Drawings	100
			15 Sep	Wages	200
			30 Sep	Balance c/d	5,650
		8,250			8,250
1 Oct	Balance b/d	5,650			

The steps involved in balancing accounts are:

Step 1

The entries in the debit and credit money columns are totalled; these totals are not recorded in ink on the account at this stage, but can be recorded either as sub-totals in pencil on the account, or noted on a separate piece of paper. In the example above, the debit side totals £8,250, while the credit side is £2,600.

Step 2

The difference between the two totals is the balance of the account and this is entered on the account:

- on the side of the smaller total
- on the next available line
- with the date of balancing (often the last day of the month)
- with the description 'balance c/d', or 'balance carried down'

In the bank account above, the balance carried down is £8,250 – £2,600 = £5,650, entered in the credit column.

Step 3

Both sides of the account are now totalled, including the balance which has just been entered, and the totals (the same on both sides) are entered on the same line in the appropriate column, and bold or double underlined. The bold underline indicates that the account has been balanced at this point using the figures above the total: the figures above the underline should not be added in to anything below the underline.

In the bank account above, the totals on each side of the account are £8,250.

Step 4

As we are using double-entry book-keeping, there must be an opposite entry to the 'balance c/d' calculated in Step 2. The same money amount is entered on the other side of the account below the bold underlined totals entered in Step 3. We have now completed both the debit and credit entry. The date is usually recorded as the next day after 'balance c/d', ie often the first day of the following month, and the description can be 'balance b/d' or 'balance brought down'.

In the example above, the balance brought down on the bank account on 1 October 20-1 is £5,650 debit; this means that, according to the firm's accounting records, there is £5,650 in the bank.

a practical point

When balancing accounts, use a pen and not a pencil. If any errors are made, cross them through neatly with a single line, and write the corrected version on the line below. Do not use correcting fluid: at best it conceals errors, at worst it conceals fraudulent transactions.

FURTHER EXAMPLES OF BALANCING ACCOUNTS

Dr		**Wages Account**			Cr
20-1		£	20-1		£
9 Apr	Bank	750	30 Apr	Balance c/d	2,250
16 Apr	Bank	800			
23 Apr	Bank	700			
		2,250			**2,250**
1 May	Balance b/d	2,250			

The above wages account has transactions on one side only, but is still balanced in the same way. This account shows that the total amount paid for wages is £2,250.

Dr		**B Lewis Ltd**			Cr
20-1		£	20-1		£
10 Apr	Purchases Returns	30	7 Apr	Purchases	280
26 Apr	Bank	250			
		280			**280**

This account in the name of a creditor has a 'nil' balance after the transactions for April have taken place. The two sides of the account are totalled and, as both debit and credit side are the same amount, there is nothing further to do, apart from entering the bold or double underlined total.

Dr		A Holmes			Cr
20-1		£	20-1		£
1 Apr	Balance b/d	105	10 Apr	Bank	105
11 Apr	Sales	125	11 Apr	Sales Returns	25
			30 Apr	Balance c/d	100
		230			230
1 May	Balance b/d	100			

This is the account of a debtor and, at the start of the month, there was a debit balance of £105 brought down from March. After the various transactions for April, there remains a debit balance of £100 owing at 1 May.

Dr		Office Equipment Account			Cr
20-1		£	20-1		£
12 Apr	Bank	2,000			

This account has just the one transaction and, in practice, there is no need to balance it. It should be clear that the account has a debit balance of £2,000, which is represented by the asset of office equipment.

Dr		Malvern Manufacturing Co			Cr
20-1		£	20-1		£
29 Apr	Bank	250	18 Apr	Purchases	250

This creditor's account has a 'nil' balance, with just one transaction on each side. All that is needed here is to bold or double underline the amount on both sides.

Extracting a Trial Balance

The book-keeper extracts a trial balance from the accounting records in order to check the arithmetical accuracy of the double-entry book-keeping, ie that the debit entries equal the credit entries.

A trial balance is a list of the balances of every account forming the ledger, distinguishing between those accounts which have debit balances and those which have credit balances.

A trial balance is extracted at regular intervals – often at the end of each month.

example of a trial balance

Trial balance of A-Z Suppliers as at 31 January 20-1

	Dr	Cr
Name of account	£	£
Purchases	750	
Sales		1,600
Sales returns	25	
Purchases returns		50
J Brown (debtor)	155	
T Sweet (creditor)		110
Rent paid	100	
Wages	150	
Heating and lighting	125	
Office equipment	500	
Machinery	1,000	
Cash	50	
Bank	455	
J Williams – loan		800
Capital		1,000
Drawings	250	
	3,560	3,560

Notes

- The debit and credit columns have been totalled and are the same amount. Thus the trial balance proves that the accounting records are arithmetically correct. (A trial balance does not prove the complete accuracy of the accounting records – see page 68.)
- The heading for a trial balance gives the name of the business whose accounts have been listed and the date it was extracted, ie the end of the accounting period.
- The balance for each account transferred to the trial balance is the figure brought down after the accounts have been balanced.
- As well as the name of each account, it is quite usual to show in the trial balance the account number. Most accounting systems give numbers to accounts and these can be listed in a separate 'folio' or 'reference' column.

Debit and Credit Balances – Guidelines

Certain accounts always have a debit balance, while others always have a credit balance. You should already know these, but the lists set out below will act as a revision guide, and will also help in your understanding of trial balances.

debit balances include:

- cash account
- purchases account
- sales returns account (returns in)
- fixed asset accounts, eg premises, motor vehicles, machinery, office equipment, etc
- expenses and overheads accounts, eg wages, telephone, rent paid, carriage outwards, carriage inwards, discount allowed
- drawings account
- debtors' accounts (often, for the purposes of a trial balance, the balances of individual debtors' accounts are totalled, and the total is entered in the trial balance as 'debtors')
- VAT repayable by HM Revenue & Customs (see Chapter 7)

credit balances include:

- sales account
- purchases returns account (returns out)
- income accounts, eg rent received, commission received, discount received
- capital account
- loan account
- creditors' accounts (often a total is entered in the trial balance, rather than the individual balances of each account)
- VAT due to HM Revenue & Customs (see Chapter 7)

Note: bank account can be either debit or credit – it will be debit when the business has money in the bank, and credit when it is overdrawn.

If the Trial Balance Doesn't Balance . . .

If the trial balance fails to balance, ie the two totals are different, there is an error (or errors):

- either in the addition of the trial balance
- and/or in the double-entry book-keeping

The procedure for finding the error(s) is as follows:

- check the addition of the trial balance
- check that the balance of each account has been correctly entered in the trial balance, and under the correct heading, ie debit or credit
- check that the balance of every account in the ledger has been included in the trial balance
- check the calculation of the balance on each account
- calculate the amount that the trial balance is wrong, and then look in the accounts for a transaction for this amount: if one is found, check that the double-entry book-keeping has been carried out correctly
- halve the amount by which the trial balance is wrong, and look for a transaction for this amount: if it is found, check the double-entry book-keeping
- if the amount by which the trial balance is wrong is divisible by nine, then the error may be a reversal of figures, eg £65 entered as £56, or £45 entered as £54
- if the trial balance is wrong by a round amount, eg £10, £100, £1,000, the error is likely to be in the calculation of the account balances
- if the error(s) is still not found, it is necessary to check the book-keeping transactions since the date of the last trial balance, by going back to the source documents and the subsidiary books

Errors not shown by a Trial Balance

As mentioned earlier, a trial balance does not prove the complete accuracy of the accounting records. There are six types of errors that are not shown by a trial balance.

error of omission

Here a business transaction has been completely omitted from the accounting records, ie both the debit and credit entries have not been made.

reversal of entries

With this error, the debit and credit entries have been made in the accounts but on the wrong side of the two accounts concerned. For example, a cash sale has been entered wrongly as debit sales account, credit cash account – this should have been entered as a debit to cash account, and a credit to sales account.

mispost/error of commission

Here, a transaction is entered to the wrong person's account. For example, a sale of goods on credit to A T Hughes has been entered as debit A J Hughes' account, credit sales account. Here, double-entry book-keeping has been completed but, when A J Hughes receives a statement of account, he or she will soon complain about being debited with goods not ordered or received.

error of principle

This is when a transaction has been entered in the wrong type of account. For example, the cost of petrol for vehicles has been entered as debit motor vehicles account, credit bank account. The error is that motor vehicles account represents fixed assets, and the transaction should have been debited to the expense account for motor vehicle running expenses.

error of original entry (or transcription)

Here, the correct accounts have been used, and the correct sides: what is wrong is that the amount has been entered incorrectly in both accounts. This could be caused by a 'bad figure' on an invoice or a cheque, or it could be caused by a 'reversal of figures', eg an amount of £45 being entered in both accounts as £54. Note that both debit and credit entries need to be made incorrectly for the trial balance still to balance; if one entry has been made incorrectly and the other is correct, then the error will be shown.

compensating error

This is where two errors cancel each other out. For example, if the balance of purchases account is calculated wrongly at £10 too much, and a similar error has occurred in calculating the balance of sales account, then the two errors will compensate each other, and the trial balance will not show the errors.

Correction of errors is covered fully in Chapter 13.

IMPORTANCE OF THE TRIAL BALANCE

A business will extract a trial balance on a regular basis to check the arithmetic accuracy of the book-keeping. However, the trial balance is also used as the starting point in the production of the final accounts of a business. These final accounts, which are produced once a year (often more frequently) comprise:

- **trading account**
- **profit and loss account**
- **balance sheet**

The final accounts show the owner(s) how profitable the business has been, what the business owns, and how the business is financed. The preparation of final accounts is an important aspect of your studies and one which we shall be coming to in later chapters. For the moment, we can say that extraction of a trial balance is an important exercise in the accounting process: it proves the book-keeper's accuracy, and also lists the account balances which form the basis for the final accounts of a business.

CHAPTER SUMMARY

- The traditional 'T' account needs to be balanced at regular intervals – often at the month-end.
- When balancing accounts, the book-keeper must adhere strictly to the rules of double-entry book-keeping.
- When each account in the ledger has been balanced, a trial balance can be extracted.
- A trial balance is a list of the balances of every account forming the ledger, distinguishing between those accounts which have debit balances and those which have credit balances.
- A trial balance does not prove the complete accuracy of the accounting records; errors not shown by a trial balance are:
  - error of omission
  - reversal of entries
  - mispost/error of commission
  - error of principle
  - error of original entry
  - compensating error
- The trial balance is used as the starting point for the preparation of a business' final accounts.

In the next chapter we will look at the division of the ledger into manageable sections, and we will see how an expanding accounting system uses subsidiary books to cope with large numbers of routine transactions.

QUESTIONS

NOTE: an asterisk (*) after the question number means that an answer to the question is given at the end of this book.

5.1 The following are the business transactions of Andrew Johnstone, a retailer of computer software, for the months of January and February 20-9:

Transactions for January

1 Jan	Started in business with £10,000 in the bank
4 Jan	Paid rent on premises £500, by cheque
5 Jan	Bought shop fittings £1,500, by cheque
7 Jan	Bought stock of computer software £5,000, on credit from Comp Supplies Limited
11 Jan	Software sales £1,000 paid into bank

12 Jan	Software sales £1,250 paid into bank
16 Jan	Software sales £850 on credit to Rowcester College
20 Jan	Paid Comp Supplies Limited £5,000 by cheque
22 Jan	Software sales £1,450 paid into bank
25 Jan	Bought software £6,500 on credit from Comp Supplies Limited
27 Jan	Rowcester College returns software £100

Transactions for February

2 Feb	Paid rent on premises £500 by cheque
4 Feb	Software sales £1,550 paid into bank
5 Feb	Returned faulty software, £150 to Comp Supplies Limited
10 Feb	Software sales £1,300 paid into bank
12 Feb	Rowcester College pays the amount owing by cheque
15 Feb	Bought shop fittings £850 by cheque
19 Feb	Software sales £1,600 paid into bank
22 Feb	Paid Comp Supplies Limited the amount owing by cheque
24 Feb	Bought software £5,500 on credit from Comp Supplies Limited
25 Feb	Software sales £1,100 paid into bank
26 Feb	Software sales £1,050 on credit to Rowcester College

You are to:

(a) record the January transactions in the books of account, and balance each account at 31 January 20-9

(b) draw up a trial balance at 31 January 20-9

(c) record the February transactions in the books of account, and balance each account at 28 February 20-9

(d) draw up a trial balance at 28 February 20-9

5.2

Produce the trial balance of Jane Greenwell as at 28 February 20-1. She has omitted to open a capital account.

	£
Bank overdraft	1,250
Purchases	850
Cash	48
Sales	730
Purchases returns	144
Creditors	1,442
Equipment	2,704
Van	3,200
Sales returns	90
Debtors	1,174
Wages	1,500
Capital	?

5.3* The book-keeper of Lorna Fox has extracted the following list of balances as at 31 March 20-2:

	£
Purchases	96,250
Sales	146,390
Sales returns	8,500
Administration expenses	10,240
Wages	28,980
Telephone	3,020
Interest paid	2,350
Travel expenses	1,045
Premises	125,000
Machinery	40,000
Debtors	10,390
Bank overdraft	1,050
Cash	150
Creditors	12,495
Loan from bank	20,000
Drawings	9,450
Capital	155,440

You are to:

(a) Produce the trial balance at 31 March 20-2.

(b) Take any three debit balances and any three credit balances and explain to someone who does not understand accounting why they are listed as such, and what this means to the business.

5.4* Fill in the missing words from the following sentences:

(a) "You made an error of .... when you debited the cost of diesel fuel for the van to vans account."

(b) "I've had the book-keeper from D Jones Limited on the 'phone concerning the statements of account that we sent out the other day. She says that there is a sales invoice charged that she knows nothing about. I wonder if we have done a .... and it should be for T Jones' account?"

(c) "There is a 'bad figure' on a purchases invoice – we have read it as £35 when it should be £55. It has gone through our accounts wrongly so we have an error of .... to put right."

(d) "Although the trial balance balanced last week, I've since found an error of £100 in the calculation of the balance of sales account. We will need to check the other balances as I think we may have a .... error."

(e) "Who was in charge of that trainee last week? He has entered the payment for the electricity bill on the debit side of the bank and on the credit side of electricity – a .... of ...."

(f) "I found this purchase invoice from last week in amongst the copy letters. As we haven't put it through the accounts we have an error of ...."

5.5 *"A trial balance does not prove the complete accuracy of the accounting records."*

You are to describe *four* types of error that are not shown by a trial balance.

Give an example of each type of error.

6 DIVISION OF THE LEDGER – THE USE OF SUBSIDIARY BOOKS

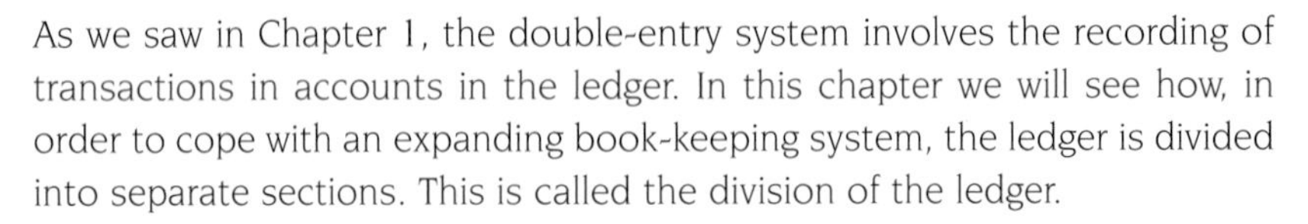

As we saw in Chapter 1, the double-entry system involves the recording of transactions in accounts in the ledger. In this chapter we will see how, in order to cope with an expanding book-keeping system, the ledger is divided into separate sections. This is called the division of the ledger.

We will also examine how a business makes use of subsidiary books to summarise business transactions before they are entered into the double-entry system.

Division of the Ledger

Double-entry book-keeping involves, as we have seen, making two entries in the ledger accounts for each business transaction. The traditional meaning of a ledger is a weighty leather-bound volume into which each account was entered on a separate page. With such a hand-written book-keeping system, as more and more accounts were opened, the point was reached where another ledger book was needed. Finally, in order to sort the accounts into a logical order, the accounting system was divided into four main sections, and this practice continues today:

- sales ledger, containing the accounts of debtors
- purchases ledger, containing the accounts of creditors
- cash books, containing the main cash book and the petty cash book
- general (or nominal) ledger, containing the nominal accounts (expenses, etc) and the real accounts (fixed assets, etc)

These four divisions comprise the ledger, and are illustrated in full on the opposite page. Most computer accounting programs (see Chapter 11) retain the four divisions of the ledger.

Use of the Divisions of the Ledger

To see how the divisions of the ledger are used, we will look at a number of business transactions and see which ledgers are used and in which accounts the transactions are recorded:

purchase of goods on credit

- general ledger – debit purchases account
- purchases ledger – credit the account of the creditor (supplier)

DIVISION OF THE LEDGER

sales ledger

Sales ledger contains the accounts of debtors, and records:

- sales made on credit to customers of the business
- sales returns (returns in) by customers
- payments received from debtors
- cash discount allowed for prompt settlement
- bad debts written off (see page 200)

Sales ledger does not record cash sales.

Sales ledger contains an account for each debtor and records the transactions with that debtor. A sales ledger control account (see Chapter 14) is often used to summarise the transactions on the accounts of debtors.

purchases ledger

Purchases ledger contains the accounts of creditors, and records:

- purchases made on credit from suppliers of the business
- purchases returns (returns out) made by the business
- payments made to creditors
- cash discount received for prompt settlement

Purchases ledger does not record cash purchases.

Purchases ledger contains an account for each creditor and records the transactions with that creditor. A purchases ledger control account (see Chapter 14) may be used to summarise the creditor account transactions.

cash books

Cash Book

– records all transactions for bank account and cash account

– cash book is also often used for listing the amounts of cash discount received and allowed, and Value Added Tax, before transfer of the totals to the relevant accounts

Petty Cash Book

– records low-value cash payments – usually for expenses – that are too small to be entered in the main cash book

general (nominal) ledger

The general (nominal) ledger contains the other accounts of the business:

Nominal Accounts

– sales account (cash and credit sales), sales returns

– purchases account (cash and credit purchases), purchases returns

– expenses and income, loans, capital, drawings

– Value Added Tax (where the business is VAT registered)

– profit and loss

Real Accounts

– fixed assets, eg computers, vehicles, machinery

– stock

purchase of goods by cheque

- general ledger – debit purchases account
- cash book – credit bank account

sale of goods on credit

- sales ledger – debit the account of the debtor (customer)
- general ledger – credit sales account

sale of goods for cash

- cash book – debit cash account
- general ledger – credit sales account

purchase of a computer for use in the business, paying by cheque

- general ledger – debit computer account (fixed asset)
- cash book – credit bank account

Note that in some accounting systems the cash book is not kept as a separate division of the ledger, but is contained within the general (or nominal) ledger.

SUBSIDIARY BOOKS

The place where a business transaction is recorded for the first time, prior to entry in the ledger, is known as the subsidiary book or book of prime entry. These comprise:

- sales day book (or sales journal)
- purchases day book (or purchases journal)
- sales returns, or returns in, day book (or sales returns journal)
- purchases returns, or returns out, day book (or purchases returns journal)
- cash book (see Chapter 8)
- petty cash book (see Chapter 9)
- general journal (see Chapter 13)

In the rest of this chapter we will see how the first four of these – the day books – fit into the accounting system. The other subsidiary books will be looked at in more detail in later chapters. We have already used cash account and bank account which, together, make up a business' cash book. In Chapter 8, we will see how the two accounts are brought together in one book. Cash book is the subsidiary book for receipts and payments in the forms of cash or cheque. Petty cash book is used mainly for small cash expenses and will be looked at in Chapter 9. General journal (often known more simply as the journal) is covered in Chapter 13.

Sales Day Book

The sales day book (which can also be called a sales journal, or sales book) is used by businesses that have a lot of separate sales transactions. The day book is simply a list of transactions, the total of which, at the end of the day, week, or month, is transferred to sales account. (When used as a weekly or monthly record, it is still called a day book.) Note that the day book is not part of double-entry book-keeping, but is used as a subsidiary book to give a total which is then entered into the accounts. By using a day book for a large number of transactions in this way, there are fewer transactions passing through the double-entry accounts. Also, the work of the accounts department can be divided up – one person can be given the task of maintaining the day book, while another can concentrate on keeping the ledger up-to-date.

The most common use of a sales day book is to record credit sales from invoices issued. We will see how it is used and will also incorporate Value Added Tax, at a rate of 17.5 per cent, into the transactions (VAT is looked at more fully in Chapter 7).

example transactions

3 Jan 20-1	Sold goods, £80 + VAT, on credit to E Doyle, invoice no 901
8 Jan 20-1	Sold goods, £200 + VAT, on credit to A Sparkes, invoice no 902
12 Jan 20-1	Sold goods, £80 + VAT, on credit to T Young, invoice no 903
18 Jan 20-1	Sold goods, £120 + VAT, on credit to A Sparkes, invoice no 904

The sales day book is written up as follows:

Sales Day Book

Date	Details	Invoice	Folio	Net	VAT	Gross
20-1				£	£	£
3 Jan	E Doyle	901	SL 58	80	14	94
8 Jan	A Sparkes	902	SL 127	200	35	235
12 Jan	T Young	903	SL 179	80	14	94
18 Jan	A Sparkes	904	SL 127	120	21	141
31 Jan	Totals for month			480	84	564

Notes

- Total net credit sales for the month are £480, and this amount is transferred to sales account in the general ledger.

- Total VAT charged on sales for the month has been totalled (£84), and is transferred to the credit side of VAT account in the general ledger. This is the amount of VAT charged by the business on sales made, and is due to HM Revenue & Customs.
- The credit sales transactions are recorded in the personal accounts of the firm's debtors in the sales ledger, the amount debited to each account being the VAT-inclusive (gross) figure.
- The sales day book incorporates a folio column which cross-references each transaction to the personal account of each debtor. In this way, an audit trail is created so that a particular transaction can be traced from source document (invoice), through the subsidiary book (sales day book), to the debtor's ledger account.
- The gross total (£564) is entered into the sales ledger control account (see Chapter 14).

The accounts to record the above transactions are:

GENERAL LEDGER

Sales Account

Dr					Cr
20-1		£	20-1		£
			31 Jan	Sales Day Book	480

Value Added Tax Account

Dr					Cr
20-1		£	20-1		£
			31 Jan	Sales Day Book	84

SALES LEDGER

E Doyle (account no 58)

Dr					Cr
20-1		£	20-1		£
3 Jan	Sales	94			

A Sparkes (account no 127)

Dr					Cr
20-1		£	20-1		£
8 Jan	Sales	235			
18 Jan	Sales	141			

T Young (account no 179)

Dr					Cr
20-1		£	20-1		£
12 Jan	Sales	94			

revision summary

Sales day book fits into the accounting system in the following way:

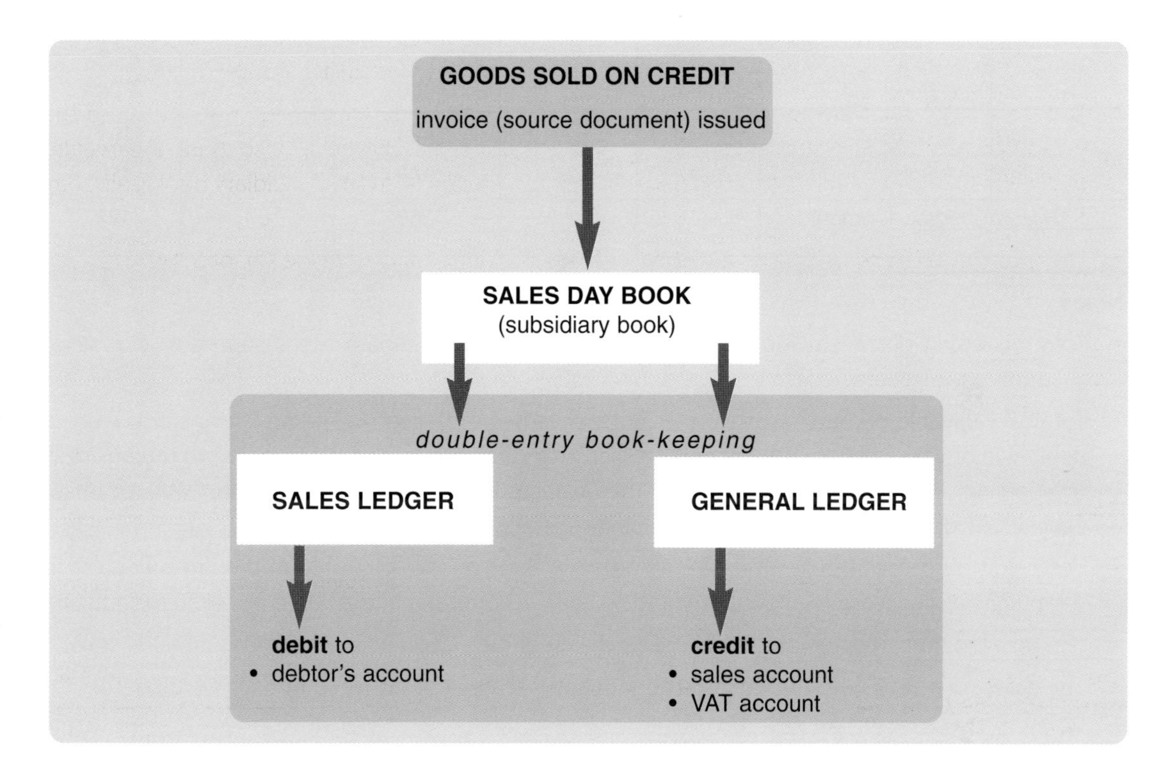

Purchases Day Book

This subsidiary book is used by businesses that have a lot of separate purchases transactions. The purchases day book lists the transactions for credit purchases from invoices received and, at the end of the day, week or month, the total is transferred to purchases account.

example transactions

2 Jan 20-1	Bought goods, £80 + VAT, on credit from P Bond, his invoice no 1234
11 Jan 20-1	Bought goods, £120 + VAT, on credit from D Webster, her invoice no A373
16 Jan 20-1	Bought goods, £160 + VAT, on credit from P Bond, his invoice no 1247
	Note: VAT is to be charged at 17.5%

The purchases day book is written up as follows:

Purchases Day Book						
Date	Details	Invoice	Folio	Net	VAT	Gross
20-1				£	£	£
2 Jan	P Bond	1234	PL 525	80	14	94
11 Jan	D Webster	A373	PL 730	120	21	141
16 Jan	P Bond	1247	PL 525	160	28	188
31 Jan	Totals for month			360	63	423

Notes

- Total net credit purchases for the month are £360, and this amount is transferred to purchases account in the general ledger.
- Total VAT payable on purchases for the month has been totalled (£63), and is transferred to the debit side of VAT account in the general ledger. This is the amount of VAT charged to the business by suppliers and can be claimed back by the business (provided it is registered for VAT), or offset against VAT due to HM Revenue & Customs (see also Chapter 7).
- The credit purchases transactions are recorded in the personal accounts of the firm's debtors in the purchases ledger, the amount credited to each account being the VAT-inclusive (gross) figure.
- The folio column gives a cross-reference to the creditors' accounts and provides an audit trail.
- The gross total (£423) is entered into the purchases ledger control account (see Chapter 14).

The accounts to record the above transactions (including a previous transaction on the VAT account) are:

GENERAL LEDGER

Dr **Purchases Account** Cr

20-1		£	20-1		£
31 Jan	Purchases Day Book	360			

Dr **Value Added Tax Account** Cr

20-1		£	20-1		£
31 Jan	Purchases Day Book	63	31 Jan	Sales Day Book	84

PURCHASES LEDGER

Dr **P Bond (account no 525)** Cr

20-1		£	20-1		£
			2 Jan	Purchases	94
			16 Jan	Purchases	188

Dr		D Webster (account no 730)			Cr
20-1		£	20-1		£
			11 Jan	Purchases	141

revision summary

Purchases day book fits into the accounting system in the following way:

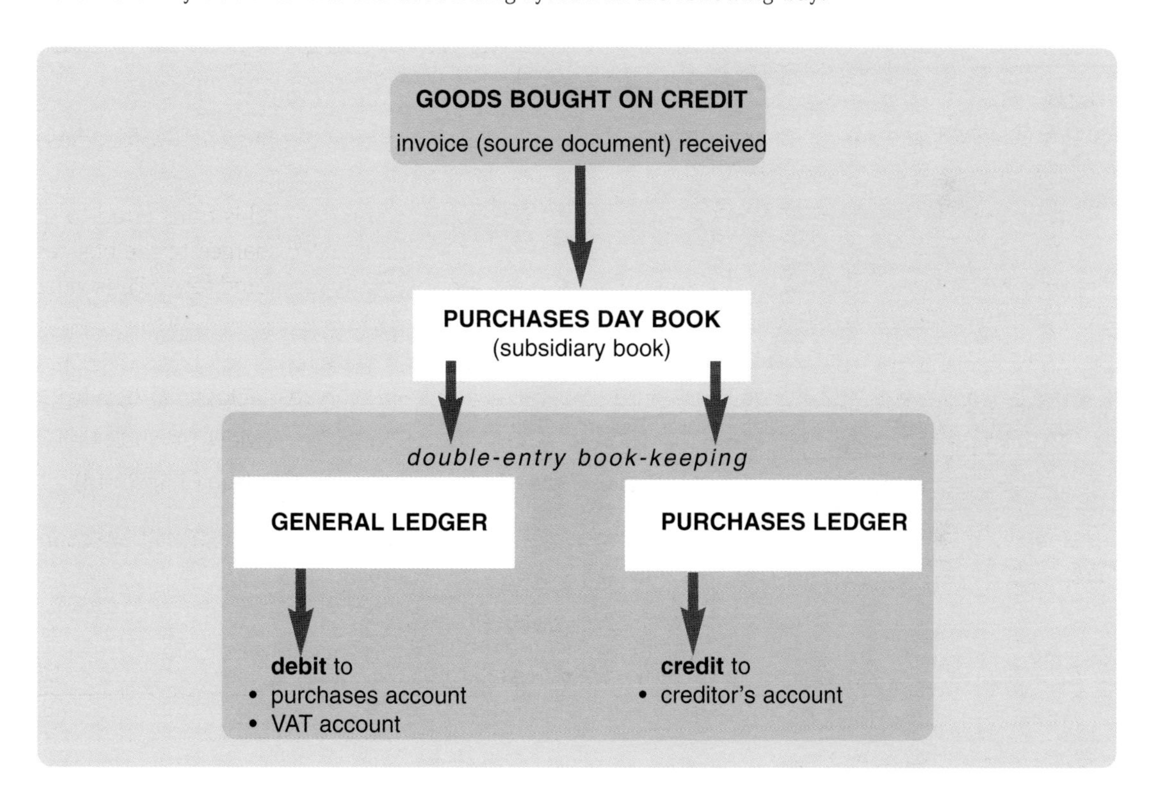

RETURNS DAY BOOKS

Where a business has a sufficient number of sales returns and purchases returns each day, week or month, it will make use of the two returns books:

- **Sales Returns (or Returns In) Day Book** – for goods previously sold on credit and now being returned to the business by its customers
- **Purchases Returns (or Returns Out) Day Book** – for goods purchased on credit by the business, and now being returned to the suppliers

The two returns day books operate in a similar way to the other day books: they are used to store information about returns until such time as it is transferred to the appropriate returns account. Note that, like all day books, the transactions are recorded from source documents (credit notes issued for sales returns, and credit notes received for purchases returns). The returns day books are subsidiary books and do not form part of the double-entry book-keeping system: the information from the day book must be transferred to the appropriate account in the ledger.

example transactions

6 Jan 20-1	Returned goods, £40 + VAT to P Bond, credit note no 406 received
15 Jan 20-1	T Young returns goods, £40 + VAT, credit note no CN702 issued
20 Jan 20-1	Returned goods, £40 + VAT to D Webster, credit note no 123 received
25 Jan 20-1	A Sparkes returns goods, £120 + VAT, credit note no CN703 issued
	Note: VAT is to be charged at 17.5 per cent

The sales returns (returns in) day book and purchases returns (returns out) day book are written up as follows:

Sales Returns Day Book

Date	Details	Credit Note	Folio	Net	VAT	Gross
20-1				£	£	£
15 Jan	T Young	CN702	SL 179	40	7	47
25 Jan	A Sparkes	CN703	SL 127	120	21	141
31 Jan	Totals for month			160	28	188

Purchases Returns Day Book

Date	Details	Credit Note	Folio	Net	VAT	Gross
20-1				£	£	£
6 Jan	P Bond	406	PL 525	40	7	47
20 Jan	D Webster	123	PL 730	40	7	47
31 Jan	Totals for month			80	14	94

Notes

- Total net sales returns and net purchases returns have been transferred to the sales returns account and purchases returns account respectively in the general ledger.
- Total VAT amounts are transferred to VAT account in the general ledger.
- The VAT-inclusive amounts of sales returns are credited to the debtors' personal accounts in the sales ledger; purchases returns are debited to the creditors' accounts in the purchases ledger.
- The gross totals will be entered into the sales ledger control account and purchases ledger control account (see Chapter 14).

The accounts to record the above transactions (including any other transactions already recorded on these accounts) are:

GENERAL LEDGER

Sales Returns Account

Dr					Cr
20-1		£	20-1		£
31 Jan	Sales Returns Day Book	160			

Purchases Returns Account

Dr					Cr
20-1		£	20-1		£
			31 Jan	Purchases Returns Day Book	80

Value Added Tax Account*

Dr					Cr
20-1		£	20-1		£
31 Jan	Purchases Day Book	63	31 Jan	Sales Day Book	84
31 Jan	Sales Returns Day Book	28	31 Jan	Purchases Returns Day Book	14

* Chapter 7 on Value Added Tax will explain the significance of the balance on this account, and how it is dealt with.

SALES LEDGER

A Sparkes (account no 127)

Dr					Cr
20-1		£	20-1		£
8 Jan	Sales	235	25 Jan	Sales Returns	141
18 Jan	Sales	141			

Dr		T Young (account no 179)			Cr
20-1		£	20-1		£
12 Jan	Sales	94	15 Jan	Sales Returns	47

PURCHASES LEDGER

Dr		P Bond (account no 525)			Cr
20-1		£	20-1		£
6 Jan	Purchases Returns	47	2 Jan	Purchases	94
			16 Jan	Purchases	188

Dr		D Webster (account no 730)			Cr
20-1		£	20-1		£
20 Jan	Purchases Returns	47	11 Jan	Purchases	141

revision summary

The two returns day books fit into the accounting system as follows:

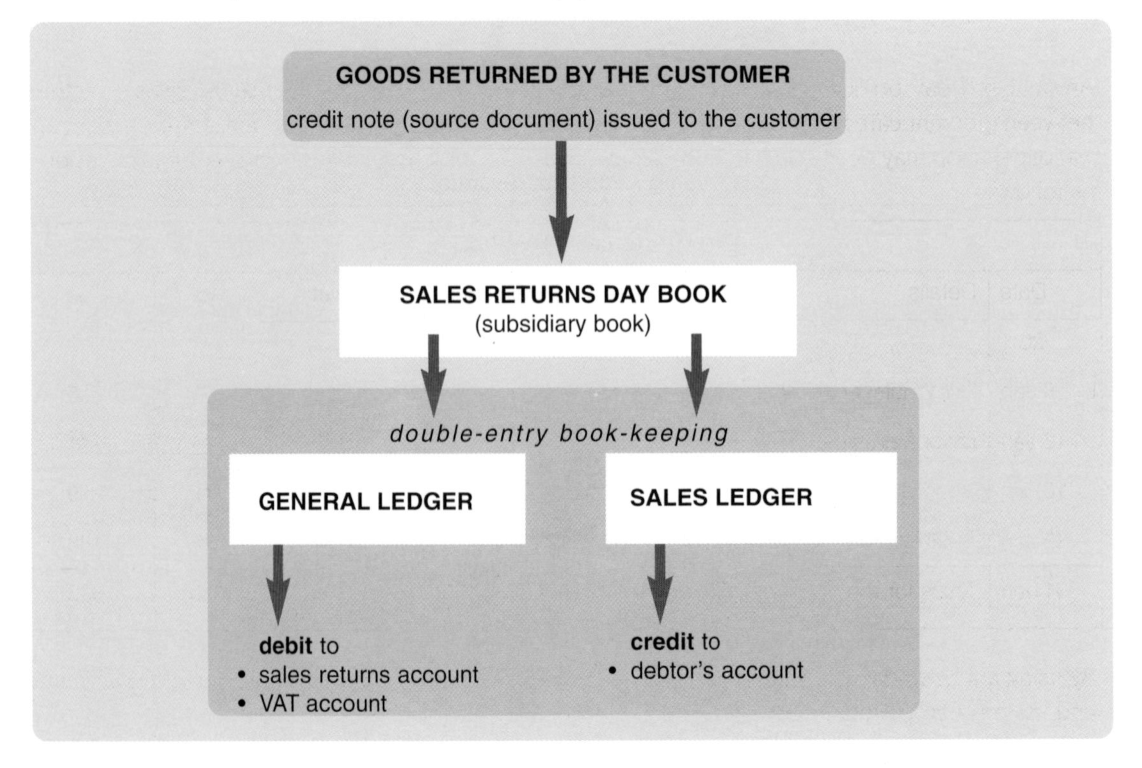

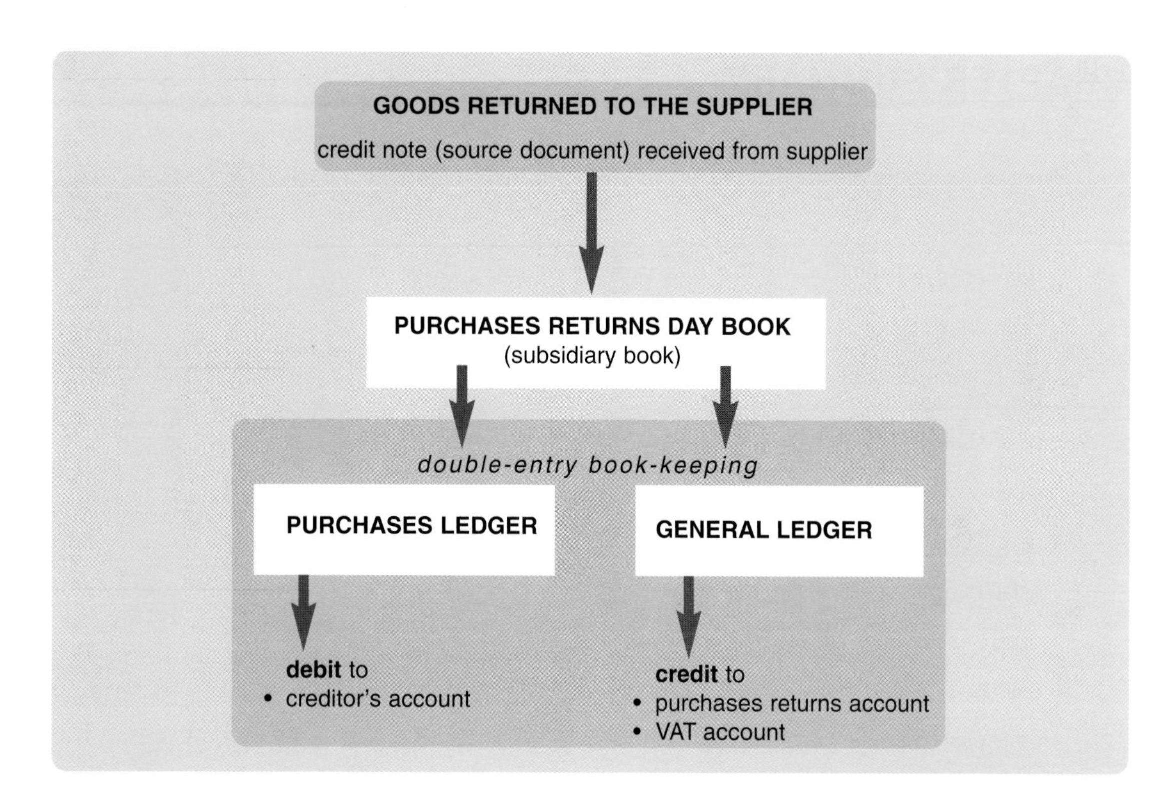

ANALYSED DAY BOOKS

An analysed day book is used whenever a business needs to split its purchases, sales or returns between different categories of products, or between different departments. For example, a paint and wallpaper shop may decide to write up its purchases day book (invoice and folio columns not shown) as follows:

Purchases Day Book						
Date	Details	Paint	Wallpaper	Net	VAT	Gross
20-1		£	£	£	£	£
8 Jan	DIY Wholesalers Ltd	75	125	200	35	235
12 Jan	Luxor Paints Ltd	120	-	120	21	141
16 Jan	Bond Supplies	180	100	280	49	329
22 Jan	Southern Manufacturing Co	60	100	160	28	188
31 Jan	Totals for month	435	325	760	133	893

By using analysed day books, a business can keep track of the purchases, sales, etc of departments and assess their performance.

CHAPTER SUMMARY

- Division of the ledger means that the accounts are divided between four sections:
  - sales ledger
  - purchases ledger
  - cash books
  - general (or nominal) ledger
- Subsidiary books include:
  - sales day book
  - purchases day book
  - sales returns, or returns in, day book
  - purchases returns, or returns out, day book
  - cash book
  - petty cash book
  - general journal
- A day book is a listing device which is used to take pressure off the main double-entry book-keeping system, and also allows the work of the accounts department to be split up amongst staff.
- Most businesses use day books for credit transactions only.
- An analysed day book is used when a business needs to know the purchases, sales, etc made by different departments or divisions of the business.

Having included Value Added Tax in the day books used in this chapter, and seen VAT applied to business documents in Chapter 4, in the next chapter we will look in more detail at this tax and how it affects businesses.

QUESTIONS

NOTE: an asterisk (*) after the question number means that an answer to the question is given at the end of this book.

6.1*

Lucinda Lamille operates a clothes wholesaling business. All the goods she buys and sells are subject to Value Added Tax (at 17.5 per cent). The following transactions are to be entered in the purchases day book or sales day book, as appropriate.

20-6

1 Feb	Bought goods from Flair Clothing Co for £520 + VAT
2 Feb	Sold goods to Wyvern Fashions for £200 + VAT
4 Feb	Bought goods from Modernwear for £240 + VAT
10 Feb	Sold goods to Zandra Smith for £160 + VAT
15 Feb	Sold goods to Just Jean for £120 + VAT
18 Feb	Bought goods from Quality Clothing for £800 + VAT
23 Feb	Sold goods to Peter Sanders Menswear for £320 + VAT
24 Feb	Sold goods to H Wilson for £80 + VAT
26 Feb	Sold goods to Mercian Models for £320 + VAT
28 Feb	Bought goods from Flair Clothing Co for £200 + VAT

You are to:

(a) write up the sales day book and the purchases day book

(b) show how the VAT account will appear in her general ledger

6.2

James Scriven started in business as a furniture wholesaler on 1 February 20-2. He has registered for Value Added Tax. During the first month of business, the following credit transactions took place (VAT is charged at 17.5%):

1 Feb	Bought furniture for resale and received invoice no 961 from Softseat Ltd, £320 + VAT
2 Feb	Bought furniture for resale and received invoice no 068 from PRK Ltd, £80 + VAT
8 Feb	Sold furniture and issued invoice no 001 to High Street Stores, £440 + VAT
14 Feb	Sold furniture and issued invoice no 002 to Peter Lounds Ltd, £120 + VAT
15 Feb	Bought furniture for resale and received invoice no 529 from Quality Furnishings, £160 + VAT
18 Feb	Sold furniture and issued invoice no 003 to Carpminster College, £320 + VAT
19 Feb	Bought furniture for resale and received invoice no 984 from Softseat Ltd, £160 + VAT
25 Feb	Sold furniture and issued invoice no 004 to High Street Stores, £200 + VAT

You are to:

(a) enter the above transactions in James Scriven's subsidiary books, and total the columns for the month

(b) record the accounting entries in James Scriven's purchases ledger, sales ledger and general ledger

6.3

Anne Green owns a shop selling paint and decorating materials; she is registered for Value Added Tax. She has two suppliers, Wyper Ltd (account no 301) and M Roper & Sons (account no 302). During the month of May 20-2 Anne received the following business documents from her suppliers:

2 May	Invoice no 562 from M Roper & Sons for £190 + VAT
4 May	Invoice no 82 from Wyper Ltd for £200 + VAT
10 May	Invoice no 86 from Wyper Ltd for £210 + VAT
18 May	Invoice no 580 from M Roper & Sons for £180 + VAT
18 May	Credit note no 82 from M Roper & Sons for £30 + VAT
21 May	Invoice no 91 from Wyper Ltd for £240 + VAT
23 May	Credit note no 6 from Wyper Ltd for £40 + VAT
25 May	Invoice no 589 from M Roper & Sons for £98 + VAT
28 May	Credit note no 84 from M Roper & Sons for £38 + VAT

Note

VAT is charged at 17.5%. Ignore fractions of a penny, ie round *down* to a whole penny.

You are to:

(a) enter the above transactions in the appropriate day books which are to be totalled at the end of May

(b) enter the transactions in the appropriate accounts in Anne Green's ledgers. (The credit balances of Wyper Ltd and M Roper & Sons at the beginning of the month were £100 and £85 respectively.)

(c) balance each account and bring down a balance on 1 June 20-2

6.4*

Lorna Pratt runs a computer software business, specialising in supplies to educational establishments. The business is registered for Value Added Tax. At the beginning of January 20-2 the balances in her ledgers were as follows:

Purchases ledger	Macstrad plc (account no 101)	£1,050.75 credit
	Amtosh plc (account no 102)	£2,750.83 credit
Sales ledger	Mereford College (account no 201)	£705.35 debit
	Carpminster College (account no 202)	£801.97 debit

During the course of the month the following business documents are issued (all plus VAT at 17.5%):

2 Jan	Invoice from Macstrad plc, M1529	£2,900.00
3 Jan	Invoice from Amtosh plc, A7095	£7,500.00
5 Jan	Invoice to Mereford College, 1093	£3,900.00
7 Jan	Invoice to Carpminster College, 1094	£8,500.00
10 Jan	Credit note from Macstrad plc, MC105	£319.75
12 Jan	Credit note from Amtosh plc, AC730	£750.18
13 Jan	Credit note to Mereford College, CN109	£850.73
14 Jan	Invoice to Carpminster College, 1095	£1,800.50
14 Jan	Invoice to Mereford College, 1096	£2,950.75
18 Jan	Invoice from Macstrad plc, M2070	£1,750.00
19 Jan	Invoice from Amtosh plc, A7519	£5,500.00
20 Jan	Invoice to Carpminster College, 1097	£3,900.75
22 Jan	Invoice to Mereford College, 1098	£1,597.85
23 Jan	Credit note from Macstrad plc, MC120	£953.07
27 Jan	Credit note to Mereford College, CN110	£593.81

Note: when calculating VAT amounts, ignore fractions of a penny, ie round down to a whole penny.

You are to:

(a) enter the above transactions in the appropriate day books which are to be totalled at the end of January

(b) record the accounting entries in Lorna Pratt's purchases ledger, sales ledger and general ledger

6.5* For each transaction shown below, state

- the source document
- the subsidiary book
- the account to be debited
- the account to be credited

(a) bought goods on credit from A Cotton

(b) sold goods on credit to D Law

(c) cheque received for cash sales

(d) returned damaged goods to A Cotton

(e) paid gas bill by cheque

(f) D Law returns damaged goods

6.6 B E Jones (Wholesale) has partially prepared the following invoice from the delivery note.

INVOICE

B E JONES (WHOLESALE)

6 Church Road, Middleton, MT4 6AQ
Tel 01687 132579 Fax 01687 123457
VAT REG 1103987654

invoice to

J C Smith
Shopping Centre
Downtown
DT6 9BJ

invoice no	**12576**
account no	**S26**
your order no	**123**
delivery note no	**0678**
date/tax point	**2 January 2002**

quantity	details	unit price	VAT rate	total amount
96	**Dresses**	**£8.50 each**	**17.5%**	
20	**Coats**	**£15 each**	**17.5%**	
			trade discount 20%	
			subtotal	
			VAT	
			total	

terms of trade
Cash discount of 5% for payment within 7 days

REQUIRED

(a) Complete the total amount column of the invoice.

(b) This invoice will be used as a source document by both J C Smith and B E Jones (Wholesale). Which subsidiary book will be used for the entry:

(i) in the books of J C Smith ....

....

(ii) in the books of B E Jones (Wholesale) ....

....

(c) Explain the terms:

(i) trade discount ....

....

....

(ii) cash discount ....

....

....

Assessment and Qualifications Alliance (AQA), 2002

6.7* In the catalogue of Wholesale Car Spares is part number 1063 which has a list price of £45.00 less a trade discount of 25%. VAT is charged at 17.5%.

J C Cross Garages, a customer, who is allowed trade discount and a cash discount of 5% for payment in 7 days, returned 23 units of part 1063, which were faulty.

REQUIRED

(a) What document will Wholesale Car Spares prepare and send to J C Cross Garages?

....

(b) Calculate the amount to be recorded on the document clearly showing all the stages in the calculation.

....

....

....

....

(c) Name the subsidiary book used by J C Cross Garages for the returned parts and show the amounts to be entered.

....

....

....

....

Assessment and Qualifications Alliance (AQA), 2001

6.8* Complete the following table by giving the source document and the subsidiary book (or book of prime entry) to be used for the transactions.

Transaction	Source Document	Subsidiary Book (or Book of Prime Entry)
(a) Goods bought on credit from a supplier		
(b) Goods sold on credit to a customer		
(c) Faulty goods returned to a supplier		
(d) Payment made by cheque to a supplier		
(e) Purchase of a new machine for use in the factory on credit		
(f) Faulty goods returned by a customer		
(g) Cheque received from a customer and paid into the bank		

6.9

Complete the following table by giving for each source document:

- the subsidiary book (or book of prime entry)
- the account to be debited
- the account to be credited

The first item has been completed as an example.

Source Document	**Subsidiary Book**	**Account to be debited**	**Account to be credited**
Invoice for goods sold on credit to V Singh	*Sales Day Book*	*V Singh*	*Sales*
(a) Invoice received for goods bought on credit from Okara Limited			
(b) Credit note issued to S Johnson			
(c) Credit note received from Roper & Company			

7 VALUE ADDED TAX

We have already seen in Chapter 4 how Value Added Tax (VAT) is added to invoices by businesses registered for VAT, and in Chapter 6 how the tax is dealt with in day books and in the book-keeping system. In this chapter we shall look at:

- the nature of VAT
- the business account that needs to be kept for VAT
- how to complete a Value Added Tax Return

REGISTERING FOR VAT

In the UK, most businesses with a significant amount of turnover (sales) must be registered for VAT. The turnover figure is normally increased annually as a part of the Chancellor of the Exchequer's budget proposals. Details of this and other aspects of VAT may be found on www.hmrc.gov.uk

Once registered, a business is issued with a VAT registration number which is quoted on invoices and on other business documents. VAT is charged at the standard rate (quoted as 17.5 per cent in this chapter) on all taxable supplies, ie whenever the business sells goods, or supplies a service. From the supplier's viewpoint, the tax charged is known as output VAT. A number of items are zero-rated and no tax is charged when they are supplied: for example, food and children's clothing are zero rated. Certain items, such as domestic fuel, are charged at a reduced rate.

Most businesses registered for VAT pay to the VAT authorities (HM Revenue & Customs):

- the amount of VAT collected on sales (output tax)
- less the amount of VAT charged to them (input tax) on all taxable supplies bought in, eg purchases, expenses, fixed assets

If the amount of input tax is larger than the output tax, the business claims a refund of the difference from HM Revenue and Customs. A VAT return (see page 99) has to be completed every three months, although some businesses submit a return on an annual basis. Payment of VAT due (if the business is not claiming a refund) is made when the VAT return is submitted.

Small businesses may alternatively use a **flat rate scheme** which allows the calculation of VAT payable as a percentage of sales – so there is no need to calculate input and output VAT or even to identify the VAT element in individual transactions. It is a very simple scheme designed to cut down on the paperwork for small businesses.

Exempt Supplies

A few types of goods and services are neither standard-rated nor zero-rated for VAT: instead they are exempt. The effect of this is that the seller of such goods cannot charge VAT on outputs (as is the case with zero-rated goods). However, unlike the seller of zero-rated goods, the seller of exempt goods cannot claim back all the tax which has been paid on inputs. Examples of exempt supplies include postal services, loans of money, and certain types of education and health care.

A Tax on the Final Consumer

VAT is a tax which is paid by the final consumer or user of the goods (except where the final user is registered for VAT). For example, a member of the public buying a computer at a total cost of £705 is paying VAT of £105 (ie 17.5 per cent of £600). This final consumer or user has to bear the cost of the VAT, but the tax is actually paid to HM Revenue and Customs by all those involved in the manufacturing and selling process. This procedure is illustrated by the flow chart on the next page. The right-hand column shows the amount of VAT paid to HM Revenue and Customs at each stage of the process. Note that, if the final consumer had been a business registered for VAT, it would be able to claim the £105 of VAT as an input tax, and would record the purchase in its books as:

– debit computer account	£600
– debit Value Added Tax account	£105
– credit bank account (or creditor's account)	£705

VAT Account

We have seen in the previous chapter how a VAT-registered business keeps a Value Added Tax Account as part of the book-keeping system in the general ledger. This records:

Debits (input tax)

- VAT on purchases
- VAT on fixed assets (except cars)
- VAT on expenses, including petty cash (see Chapter 9) payments
- VAT on sales returns

Credits (output tax)

- VAT on sales and/or services
- VAT on purchases returns
- VAT on the sale of fixed assets

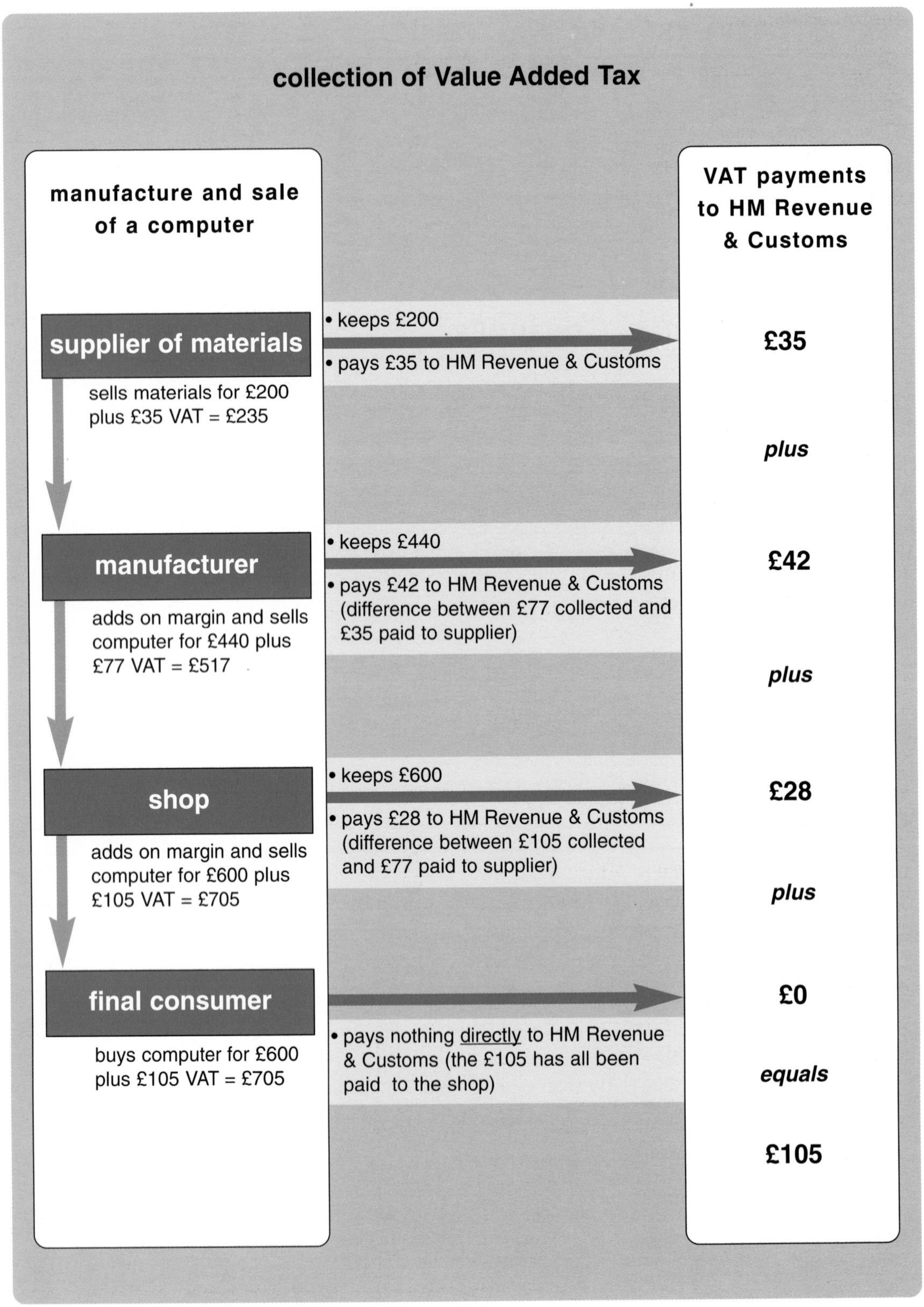

collection of Value Added Tax

manufacture and sale of a computer

supplier of materials

sells materials for £200 plus £35 VAT = £235

- keeps £200
- pays £35 to HM Revenue & Customs

manufacturer

adds on margin and sells computer for £440 plus £77 VAT = £517

- keeps £440
- pays £42 to HM Revenue & Customs (difference between £77 collected and £35 paid to supplier)

shop

adds on margin and sells computer for £600 plus £105 VAT = £705

- keeps £600
- pays £28 to HM Revenue & Customs (difference between £105 collected and £77 paid to supplier)

final consumer

buys computer for £600 plus £105 VAT = £705

- pays nothing directly to HM Revenue & Customs (the £105 has all been paid to the shop)

VAT payments to HM Revenue & Customs

£35

plus

£42

plus

£28

plus

£0

equals

£105

The VAT account shown in the previous chapter (page 83) for the month of January 20-1 is as follows:

Dr		Value Added Tax Account			Cr
20-1		£	20-1		£
31 Jan	Purchases Day Book	63	31 Jan	Sales Day Book	84
31 Jan	Sales Returns Day Book	28	31 Jan	Purchases Returns Day Book	14
31 Jan	Balance c/d	7			
		98			98
			1 Feb	Balance b/d	7

At the end of January 20-1, the account has a credit balance of £7. This amount is owing to HM Revenue and Customs and will be paid at the end of the three-month VAT period, along with the VAT due for the other two months of the VAT quarter. For example, if January is the first month of the VAT quarter, the account will be continued for a further two months until, at the end of March, the credit balance will be the amount owing to HM Revenue and Customs. The amount will be paid in April (not later than the end of the month) by making the following book-keeping transaction:

- debit Value Added Tax account
- credit bank account (cheque or BACS payment)

If, at the end of the VAT quarter, there is a debit balance on the VAT account, this represents the amount due from HM Revenue and Customs. A VAT return is completed and a payment is received (usually by BACS) from HM Revenue and Customs. This is recorded in the accounting records as:

- debit bank account
- credit Value Added Tax account

VALUE ADDED TAX RETURN

For most businesses, a Value Added Tax Return (form VAT 100) must be completed every three months. The return is then sent to HM Revenue and Customs, either with a payment for VAT due for the period, or a claim for repayment when input tax exceeds output tax.

Example

Wyvern Office Products Ltd has the following transactions, all of which are subject to VAT at 17.5%, for the three months ended 31 March 20-1:

	Purchases	Expenses	Fixed assets	Sales
20-1	£	£	£	£
January	5,000	1,000	-	10,000
February	6,000	1,400	3,000	12,000
March	7,000	1,800	-	14,000
Total	18,000	4,200	3,000	36,000

The VAT account will be written up as follows:

Dr			Value Added Tax Account		Cr
20-1		£	20-1		£
31 Jan	Purchases Day Book	875	31 Jan	Sales Day Book	1,750
	Expenses	175	28 Feb	Sales Day Book	2,100
28 Feb	Purchases Day Book	1,050	31 Mar	Sales Day Book	2,450
	Expenses	245			
	Fixed assets	525			
31 Mar	Purchases Day Book	1,225			
	Expenses	315			
		*4,410			
	Balance c/d	1,890			
		6,300			6,300
20 Apr	Bank	1,890	1 Apr	Balance b/d	1,890

* sub-totalled here for illustrative purposes (see below)

As can be seen from the account, the amount due to HM Revenue & Customs on 1 April (£1,890) has been paid on 20 April. In this way the balance of the account is reduced to 'nil', and the account is ready to be used again in recording VAT transactions for the next VAT quarter. The payment will be sent to HM Revenue & Customs, along with the firm's Value Added Tax Return (see the next page). This has been completed as follows (the notes refer to the box numbers on the VAT return):

BOX 1 This refers to the tax charged as output tax on sales invoices: here, it is £6,300.

BOX 2 This deals with VAT due to HM Revenue & Customs in respect of goods bought from VAT-registered businesses in the other member states of the European Union: there is nothing to complete on this occasion.

BOX 3 This is the total of boxes 1 and 2.

BOX 4 This is the input tax on purchases, expenses and fixed assets: the total for the quarter is £4,410.

BOX 5 This is the difference between boxes 1 and 2, ie £6,300 – £4,410 = £1,890. As tax on outputs is greater than tax on inputs, this is the amount to be paid to HM Revenue & Customs. If box 2 is greater than box 1, this indicates that a repayment is due from HM Revenue & Customs.

BOX 6 This is the value of sales made during the period covered by the VAT return. In this example, the amount is £36,000. Note that this figure excludes any VAT.

BOX 7 This is the value of purchases, and other inputs such as expenses and fixed assets, for the period; here the amount is £18,000 + £4,200 + £3,000 = £25,200. Note that this figure excludes any VAT.

BOXES 8 & 9 These are completed with the total of any sales to, and any purchases from, other European Union member states.

The box on the left-hand lower section of the form is ticked to indicate that payment is enclosed. Finally, the declaration has to be signed and dated by an authorised person within the business.

HM Customs and Excise

Value Added Tax Return

For the period

01 01 -1 to 31 03 -1

For Official Use

SPECIMEN

Registration Number 841 1160 11

Period 03 -1

WYVERN OFFICE PRODUCTS LIMITED
12 LOWER HYE STREET
MEREFORD
MR1 2JF

You could be liable to a financial penalty if your completed return and all the VAT payable are not received by the due date.

Due date: 30 04 -1

For Official Use

Before you fill in this form please read the notes on the back and the VAT leaflet *"Filling in your VAT return"*. Fill in all boxes clearly in ink, and write 'none' where necessary. Don't put a dash or leave any box blank. If there are no pence write "00" in the pence column. **Do not** enter more than one amount in any box.

For official use

	Box	£	p
VAT due in this period on **sales** and other outputs	1	6,300	00
VAT due in this period on **acquisitions** from other **EC Member States**	2	NONE	
Total VAT due **(the sum of boxes 1 and 2)**	3	6,300	00
VAT reclaimed in this period on **purchases** and other inputs (including acquisitions from the EC)	4	4,410	00
Net VAT to be paid to Customs or reclaimed by you (Difference between boxes 3 and 4)	5	1,890	00
Total value of **sales** and all other outputs excluding any VAT. **Include your box 8 figure**	6	36,000	00
Total value of **purchases** and all other inputs excluding any VAT. **Include your box 9 figure**	7	25,200	00
Total value of all **supplies** of goods and related services, excluding any VAT, to other **EC Member States**	8	NONE	00
Total value of all **acquisitions** of goods and related services, excluding any VAT, from other **EC Member States**	9	NONE	00

Retail schemes. If you have used any of the schemes in the period covered by this return, enter the relevant letter(s) in this box.

If you are enclosing a payment please tick this box. ✓

DECLARATION: You, or someone on your behalf, must sign below.

I, MATTHEW LLOYD declare that the
(Full name of signatory in BLOCK LETTERS)

information given above is true and complete.

Signature [signature] Date 20 APRIL 20-1

A false declaration can result in prosecution.

VAT 100

VAT CALCULATIONS

It is easy to calculate the VAT amount when the price of goods before the addition of VAT is known; eg using a rate of VAT of 17.5 per cent, goods costing £100 plus VAT of £17.50 gives a total cost of £117.50.

When the total cost including VAT is known, the amount of VAT is found by multiplying the amount by 17.5 and dividing by 117.5. For example:

Total cost	=	£117.50
Amount of VAT is 17.5/117.5 of £117.50	=	£ 17.50
VAT-exclusive cost	=	£100.00

The VAT-exclusive price can be found by dividing the amount by 1.175. For example:

$$\frac{£117.50}{1.175} = \text{VAT-exclusive cost of } £100$$

Note that 1.175 (the figure you divide by) applies only with a rate of VAT of 17.5%. With a rate of 10%, for example, the figure you divide by is 1.1.

When calculating VAT amounts, fractions of a penny are ignored, ie the tax is rounded down to a whole penny.

CHAPTER SUMMARY

- VAT-registered businesses charge VAT on all taxable supplies (sales).
- Most types of goods and services are taxable, but some are zero-rated, while others are exempt.
- A VAT account is used to record the amount of VAT charged on sales (output tax), and paid on purchases and expenses (input tax).
- Most VAT-registered businesses must complete a Value Added Tax Return at certain intervals, commonly every three months, and either pay over to HM Revenue & Customs the net amount of tax collected, or seek a refund where tax on inputs exceeds that on outputs.

In the next two chapters we will look at cash book and petty cash book – these are subsidiary books for cash and bank transactions.

QUESTIONS

NOTE: an asterisk (*) after the question number means that an answer to the question is given at the end of this book.

7.1* The following is a summary of purchases and sales, excluding VAT, made by Wyvern Computers for the three months ended 30 June 20-4:

Purchases	April £5,400, May £4,800, June £6,800
Sales	April £8,200, May £9,400, June £10,800

All purchases and sales are subject to Value Added Tax at a rate of 17.5 per cent.

You are to:

(a) calculate the VAT amounts for each month

(b) show the VAT account for the quarter as it will appear in the general ledger, and balance the account at 30 June 20-4

(c) explain the significance of the balance of the VAT account at 30 June 20-4 and how it will be dealt with

7.2 The following amounts include VAT at a rate of 17.5%:

- £11.75
- £10.34
- £0.94
- £14.10
- £6.50
- £2.21

You are to calculate for each amount:

(a) the amount of VAT

(b) the VAT-exclusive amount

7.3 Debbie Jones owns a fashion shop called 'Designer Labels'. She employs a book-keeper who uses a full set of double-entry accounts.

At the end of March 20-0, the book-keeper had not completed the VAT account for the month. The VAT totals from the four day books for March 20-0 were:

	£
purchases	735
sales	1,120
purchases returns	42
sales returns	28

Note: the balance on VAT account on 1 March 20-0 was £805 credit; there were no other transactions on VAT account during the month.

You are to:

(a) show the VAT account for March 20-0 in the books of Debbie Jones

(b) balance the VAT account at 31 March 20-0

(c) explain the meaning of the balance on the VAT account at 31 March 20-0

7.4* Computer Supplies Ltd issued the following sales invoices (SI) and credit notes (CN) to customers during the week commencing 19 August 20-1. All sales are subject to Value Added Tax at 17.5% and the amounts shown are the gross values.

Date	Number	Customer	Gross Amount
20-1			£
19 Aug	SI 1547	E Newman	183.30
20 Aug	SI 1548	Wyvern Traders Ltd	267.90
21 Aug	SI 1549	Teme Supplies	411.25
22 Aug	SI 1550	Lugg Brothers & Co	1,410.00
22 Aug	CN 121	Wyvern Traders Ltd	267.90
23 Aug	SI 1551	E Newman	470.00
23 Aug	CN 122	E Newman	91.65

REQUIRED

(a) Prepare Computer Supplies Ltd's sales day book and sales returns day book for the week commencing 19 August 20-1, totalling the columns on 23 August 20-1.

(b) Explain how the totals from the day books will be recorded in the double-entry book-keeping system of Computer Supplies Ltd.

(c) The balance brought down on E Newman's account as at 1 August 20-1 was £440.00. Computer Supplies Ltd received a cheque on 7 August 20-1 for this amount. There were no other transactions with E Newman during the month of August other than those detailed above.

Show E Newman's personal account for August 20-1 as it would appear in Computer Supplies Ltd's ledger. Balance the account at the end of the month.

7.5 The day books of Wholesale Car Spares show the following totals for the three months ending 31 December 2000.

Sales Day Book

Total: £47,920.02	Goods: £40,783.00	VAT: £7,137.02

Purchase Day Book

Total: £32,539.43	Goods: £27,693.13	VAT: £4,846.30

Returns Inwards Day Book

Total: £2,107.09	Goods: £1,793.27	VAT: £313.82

Returns Outwards Day Book

Total: £2,866.01	Goods: £2,439.16	VAT: £426.85

Additional information

1. The cash book shows that VAT inclusive cash sales for the period are £5,612.89.
2. The company purchased new machinery for £4,000 + £700 VAT on 31 December 2000.

REQUIRED

(a) Prepare the balance the VAT account for the quarter ended 31 December 2000.

Dr **VAT Account** Cr

2000		£ p	2000		£ p

(b) State the entries required to clear the balance with HM Revenue & Customs.

DR ....

CR ....

Assessment and Qualifications Alliance (AQA), 2001

7.6*

The following amounts appear in the books of Acme Car Fittings at 30 April 2001.

Item	£
Total VAT on goods sold	345.97
Total VAT on goods purchases	136.23
Total VAT on petty cash payments	12.86
Fixed assets purchased included total VAT	390.00

In addition, cash sales totalled £2,567.48 which included VAT at 17.5%.

REQUIRED

(a) Complete the necessary entries and balance the VAT account shown below.

Dr **VAT Account** Cr

2001		£ p	2001		£ p

(b) State what the balance of the account represents.

....

....

....

....

Assessment and Qualifications Alliance (AQA), 2001

7.7

(a) Using the figures below, complete the VAT account for the three months ended 31 March 2002 for R Masters. Bring down the balance on the account.

	£
VAT on credit sales	3,216.58
VAT on credit purchases	2,198.45
VAT on the petty cash expenses	39.27
Payments made to HM Revenue & Customs by cheque	846.39

You are also informed that the cash sales for the three months are £8,671.96 and that this figure *includes* VAT at 17.5%.

Dr **VAT Account** Cr

2002		£ p	2002		£ p
			1 Jan	Balance b/d	456 87

(b) What does the balance on the VAT account represent and in which section of the balance sheet* at 31 March 2002 will the balance be shown?

....

....

....

Assessment and Qualifications Alliance (AQA), 2002

* see Chapter 12

8 CASH BOOK

The cash book brings together the separate cash and bank transactions of a business into one 'book'.

The cash book is used to record the book-keeping transactions which involve the receipt and payment of money, for example cash, cheques and bank transfers.

The cash book forms part of the double-entry system.

Control of cash and money in the bank is very important for all businesses. A shortage of money may mean that wages and other day-to-day running expenses cannot be paid as they fall due. This could lead to the failure of the business.

THE CASH BOOK IN THE ACCOUNTING SYSTEM

For most businesses, control of cash – including both bank and cash transactions – takes place in the cash books which comprise:

- cash book, for receipts and payments in cash and by cheque and bank transfer
- petty cash book (see next chapter), for low-value expense payments

The cash books combine the roles of subsidiary books and double-entry book-keeping. Cash books are:

- subsidiary books for cash and bank transactions
- double-entry accounts for cash and bank

USES OF THE CASH BOOK

We have already used a separate cash account and bank account for double-entry book-keeping transactions. These two accounts are, in practice, brought together into one book under the title of cash book. This cash book is, therefore, used to record the money side of book-keeping transactions and is part of the double-entry system. The cash book is used for:

- **cash transactions**
  - all receipts in cash
  - most payments for cash, except for low-value expense payments (which are paid through petty cash book: see next chapter)
- **bank transactions**
  - all receipts by cheque and bank transfer (or payment of cash into the bank)
  - all payments by cheque or bank transfer (or withdrawal of cash from the bank)

The cash book is usually controlled by a **cashier** who:

- records receipts and payments by cheque and in cash
- makes cash payments, and prepares cheques and BACS payments for signature and authorisation
- pays cash and cheques received into the bank
- has control over the firm's cash, either in a cash till or cash box
- issues cash to the petty cashier who operates the firm's petty cash book (see next chapter)
- checks the accuracy of the cash and bank balances at regular intervals

It is important to note that transactions passing through the cash book must be supported by **documentary evidence**. In this way an audit trail is established which provides a link that can be checked and followed through the accounting system:

- source document
- subsidiary book
- double-entry accounts

Such an audit trail is required both as a security feature within the business (to help to ensure that fraudulent transactions cannot be made), and also for taxation purposes – both for Value Added Tax and for tax to be paid on the profits of the business.

The **cashier** has an important role to play within the accounting function of a business – most business activities will, at some point, involve cash or cheque transactions. Thus the cash book and the cashier are at the hub of the accounting system. In particular, the cashier is responsible for:

- issuing receipts for cash (and sometimes cheques) received
- making authorised payments in cash and by cheque against documents received (such as invoices and statements) showing the amounts due

At all times, payments can only be made by the cashier when authorised to do so by the appropriate person within the organisation, eg the accountant or the purchasing manager.

With so many transactions passing through the cash book, accounting procedures must include:

- security – of cash and cheque books, correct authorisation of payments
- confidentiality – that all cash/bank transactions, including cash and bank balances, are kept confidential

If the cashier has any queries about any transactions, he or she should refer them to the accounts supervisor.

Layout of the Cash Book

Although a cash book can be set out in many formats to suit the requirements of a particular business, a common format is the columnar cash book. This is set out like other double-entry accounts, with debit and credit sides, but there may be several money columns on each side. An example of a three column cash book (three money columns on each side) is shown below:

Dr					**Cash Book**						Cr
Date	Details	Folio	Discount allowed	Cash	Bank	Date	Details	Folio	Discount received	Cash	Bank
			£	£	£				£	£	£

Note the following points:

- The debit side is used for receipts.
- The credit side is used for payments.
- On both the debit and credit sides there are separate money columns for cash receipts/payments and bank receipts/payments.
- A third money column on each side is used to record cash discount (that is, an allowance offered for quick settlement of the amount due, eg 2% cash discount for settlement within seven days).
- The discount column on the debit side is for discount allowed to customers.
- The discount column on the credit side is for discount received from suppliers.
- The discount columns are not part of the double-entry book-keeping system – they are used in the cash book as a listing device or memorandum column. As we will see in the worked example which follows, the columns are totalled at the end of the week or month, and the totals are then transferred into the double-entry system.
- The folio column is used to cross-reference to the other entry in the ledger system.

WORKED EXAMPLE: TRANSACTIONS IN THE CASH BOOK

We will now look at some example transactions and then see how the three-column cash book is balanced at the month-end. The year is 20-7.
The transactions to be entered in the cash book are:

1 April	Balances at start of month: cash £300, bank £550
4 April	Received a cheque from S Wright for £98 – we have allowed her £2 cash discount
7 April	Paid a cheque to S Crane for £145 – he has allowed £5 cash discount
11 April	Paid wages in cash £275
14 April	Paid by cheque the account of T Lewis £120, deducting 2.5% cash discount
17 April	J Jones settles in cash her account of £80, deducting 5% cash discount
21 April	Withdrew £100 in cash from the bank for use in the business
23 April	Received a cheque for £45 from D Whiteman in full settlement of her account of £48
28 April	Paid cash of £70 to S Ford in full settlement of our account of £75

All cheques are banked on the day of receipt.
The cash book records these transactions (as shown below) and, after they have been entered, is balanced on 30 April. (The other part of each double-entry book-keeping transaction is not shown here, but has to be carried out in order to record the transactions correctly.)

Dr — Cash Book — Cr

Date	Details	Folio	Discount allowed	Cash	Bank	Date	Details	Folio	Discount received	Cash	Bank
			£	£	£				£	£	£
20-7						20-7					
1 Apr	Balances b/d			300	550	7 Apr	J Crane		5		145
4 Apr	S Wright		2		98	11 Apr	Wages			275	
17 Apr	J Jones		4	76		14 Apr	T Lewis		3		117
21 Apr	Bank	C		100		21 Apr	Cash	C			100
23 Apr	D Whiteman		3		45	28 Apr	S Ford		5	70	
						30 Apr	Balances c/d			131	331
			9	476	693				13	476	693
1 May	Balances b/d			131	331						

Note that the transaction on 21 April (£100 withdrawn from the bank for use in the business) involves a transfer of money between cash and bank. As each transaction is both a receipt and a payment within the cash book, it is usual to indicate both of them in the folio column with a 'C' – this stands for 'contra' and shows that both parts of the transaction are in the same book.

BALANCING THE CASH BOOK

We saw in Chapter 5 how accounts are balanced. The cash book is the ledger for cash account and bank account, and the procedure for balancing these is exactly the same as for other ledger accounts.

The cash book in the worked example on the previous page is balanced in the following way:

- add the two cash columns and subtotal in pencil (ie £476 in the debit column, and £345 in the credit column); remember to erase the subtotals afterwards
- deduct the lower total from the higher (payments from receipts) to give the balance of cash remaining (£476 – £345 = £131)
- the higher total is recorded at the bottom of both cash columns in a totals 'box' (£476)
- the balance of cash remaining (£131) is entered as a balancing item above the totals box (on the credit side), and is brought down underneath the total on the debit side as the opening balance for next month (£131)
- the two bank columns are dealt with in the same way (£693 – £362 = £331)

Notice that, in the cash book shown above, the cash and bank balances have been brought down on the debit side. It may happen that the balance at bank is brought down on the credit side: this occurs when payments exceed receipts, and indicates a bank overdraft. It is very important to appreciate that the bank columns of the cash book represent the firm's own records of bank transactions and the balance at bank – the bank statement may well show different figures (see Chapter 10).

A cash balance can only be brought down on the debit side, indicating the amount of cash held.

At the end of the month, each discount column is totalled separately – no attempt should be made to balance them. At this point, amounts recorded in the columns and the totals are not part of the double-entry system. However, the two totals are transferred to the double-entry system as follows:

- the total on the debit side (£9 in the example above) is debited to discount allowed account in the general (or nominal) ledger
- the total on the credit side (£13 in the example) is credited to discount received account, also in the general (or nominal) ledger

The opposite book-keeping entries will have already been entered in the debtors' and creditors' accounts respectively (see Chapter 4). The accounts appear as follows:

Dr		**Discount Allowed Account**			Cr
20-7		£	20-7		£
30 Apr	Cash Book	9			

Dr		**Discount Received Account**			Cr
20-7		£	20-7		£
			30 Apr	Cash Book	13

The two discount accounts represent an expense and income respectively and, at the end of the firm's financial year, the totals of the two accounts will be used in the calculation of profit. Where control accounts (see Chapter 14) are in use, the total of discount allowed is credited to the sales ledger control account, while the total of discount received is debited to the purchases ledger control account.

THE CASH BOOK AS A SUBSIDIARY BOOK

The cash book performs two functions within the accounting system:

- it is a subsidiary book for cash/bank transactions
- it forms part of the double-entry book-keeping system

The diagram below shows the flow involving:

- source documents – cash and bank receipts and payments
- the cash book as a subsidiary book
- double-entry book-keeping, involving cash book and other ledgers

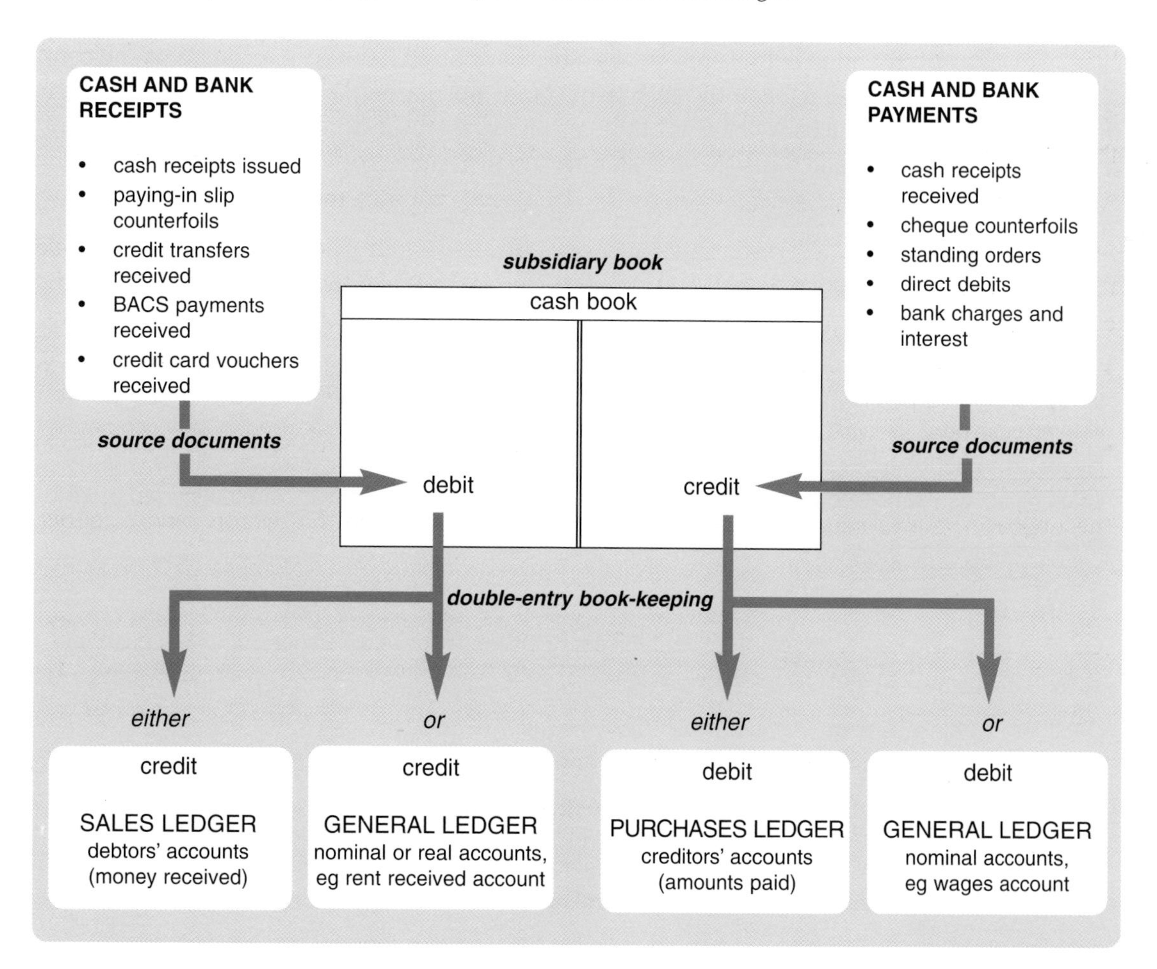

CHECKING THE CASH BOOK

As the cash book forms such an integral part of a firm's book-keeping system, it is essential that transactions are recorded accurately and that balances are calculated correctly at regular intervals, eg weekly or monthly – depending on the needs of the business. How can the cash book be checked for accuracy?

cash columns

To check the cash columns is easy. It is simply a matter of counting the cash in the cash till or box, and agreeing it with the balance shown by the cash book. In the example in the worked example on page 109, there should be £131 in the firm's cash till at 30 April 20-7. If the cash cannot be agreed in this way, the discrepancy needs to be investigated urgently.

bank columns

How are these to be checked? We could, perhaps, enquire at the bank and ask for the balance at the month-end, or we could arrange for a bank statement to be sent to us at the end of each month. However, the balance of the account at the bank may well not agree with that shown by the bank columns of the cash book. There are several reasons why there may be a difference: for example, a cheque that has been written out recently to pay a bill may not yet have been recorded on the bank statement, ie it has been entered in the cash book, but is not yet on the bank statement. To agree the bank statement and the bank columns of the cash book, it is usually necessary to prepare a bank reconciliation statement, and this topic is dealt with fully in Chapter 10.

WORKED EXAMPLE: CASH BOOK INCORPORATING VAT

A cash book can be adapted to suit the needs of a business – already we have seen how a three-column cash book uses a memorandum column for discounts allowed and received. Another common layout uses a fourth money column, for VAT, as shown in the worked example which follows. The VAT columns act as memorandum columns and, at the end of the week or month, are transferred to VAT account.

situation

On Monday, 2 June 20-7, the cash book of Eveshore Growers showed balances of £86 in cash and £248 in the bank. Transactions for the week were:

2 June	Paid insurance premium of £130 by cheque
3 June	Cash sales of £282, including Value Added Tax
3 June	Paid travel expenses in cash £47 (no Value Added Tax)
3 June	Paid an invoice for £100 from A–Z Supplies by cheque after deducting £5 cash discount
4 June	Received a cheque for £117 from a debtor, P Leech, who was settling his account balance of £120 after deducting £3 cash discount

5 June	Cash sales of £423, including Value Added Tax
6 June	Cash purchase of £188, including Value Added Tax
6 June	Paid wages of £205, partly by cheque for £105 and partly in cash £100
6 June	Transferred £250 of cash into the bank

As cashier to Eveshore Growers, you are to:

- write up the cash book for the week commencing 2 June 20-7, using separate columns for discount, VAT, cash and bank
- balance the cash book at 6 June 20-7
- explain how the totals for the discount and VAT columns will be entered in the ledger of Eveshore Growers

The rate of Value Added Tax is 17.5%. All cheques are banked on the day of receipt.

solution

Cash Book (Dr / Cr)

Date	Details	Folio	Disc't allowed	VAT	Cash	Bank	Date	Details	Folio	Disc't rec'd	VAT	Cash	Bank
20-7			£	£	£	£	20-7			£	£	£	£
2 June	Balances b/d				86	248	2 June	Insurance	GL				130
3 June	Sales	GL		42	282		3 June	Travel exp.	GL			47	
4 June	P Leech	SL	3			117	3 June	A-Z Supplies	PL	5			95
5 June	Sales	GL		63	423		6 June	Purchases	GL		28	188	
6 June	Cash	C				250	6 June	Wages	GL			100	105
							6 June	Bank	C			250	
							6 June	Balances c/d				206	285
			3	105	791	615				5	28	791	615
7 June	Balances b/d				206	285							

- The folio columns have been completed as follows:
  - GL = general ledger (or NL for nominal ledger)
  - SL = sales ledger
  - PL = purchases ledger
  - C = contra (both parts of the transaction in the same book)
- With transactions involving sales ledger (ie P Leech) and purchases ledger (ie A–Z Supplies), no amount for VAT is shown in the VAT columns. This is because VAT has been charged on invoices issued and received and was recorded in the VAT account (via the day books) when the sale or purchase was made.
- VAT on cash sales and purchases, and other transactions, is recorded in the two VAT analysis columns.

The discount and VAT columns are dealt with as follows:

- discount allowed column – the total of £3 is debited to discount allowed account (general ledger)
- discount received column – the total of £5 is credited to discount received account (general ledger)
- VAT columns – the total of £105 is credited to VAT account in the general (or nominal) ledger, while the total of £28 is debited to VAT account

BANK RECEIPTS AND PAYMENTS

In writing up the receipts and payments columns of the cash book we come across a number of banking terms that are commonly used (and also commonly examined!). These are:

- standing orders
- direct debits
- credit transfers
- bank charges

standing orders

There are regular payments – eg monthly, weekly – made from the bank account (ie they are on the credit side of the cash book, in the bank column). The payments are for the same amount each time and are made by the bank on behalf of the customer and on the written instructions of the customer.

direct debits

These are payments (ie credit side of the cash book, in the bank column) made from the bank for the customer. It is the payee, or beneficiary, who originates the payment on the written instructions of the customer. Direct debits are often used where money amounts to be paid vary, and where the payments dates alter.

credit transfers

These can be either receipts or payments – ie the debit and credit side of the cash book (bank columns) respectively. Receipts are from customers who have paid the amount due, through the banking system, directly into the bank account of the payee. Payments are to suppliers, or to employees for wages, and go into the bank account of the payees. Most credit transfers are made by BACS (Bankers Automated Clearing Services) computer transfer. In order to make these payments, it is necessary to have the bank account details – account number, sort code of bank – of the payee.

bank charges and interest

Bank charges are made by the bank for services provided. Charges are usually calculated in relation to the number of transactions – eg cheques written, amounts paid in – during the period. As a payment from bank account, bank charges are on the credit side of cash book.

In addition to bank charges, a bank will make a separate charge for interest on overdrafts and loans which have been provided to the customer.

CHAPTER SUMMARY

- The cash book records receipts (debits) and payments (credits) both in cash (except for low-value expense payments) and by cheque.
- A basic layout for a cash book has money columns for cash transactions and bank transactions on both the debit and credit sides, together with a further column on each side for discounts.
- In the discount columns are recorded cash discounts: discounts allowed (to customers) on the debit side, and discounts received (from suppliers) on the payments side.
- Another common cash book layout incorporates columns for VAT.
- Banking terms commonly used are: standing orders, direct debits, credit transfers and bank charges.

In the next chapter we will see how the petty cash book is used to record low-value expense payments.

QUESTIONS

NOTE: an asterisk (*) after the question number means that an answer to the question is given at the end of this book.

8.1* You work as the cashier for Wyvern Publishing, a company which publishes a wide range of travel and historical books. As cashier, your main responsibility is for the firm's cash book. Explain to a friend what your job involves and the qualities required of a cashier.

8.2* Walter Harrison is a sole trader who records his cash and bank transactions in a three-column cash book. The following are the transactions for June 20-2:

1 June	Balances: cash £280; bank overdraft £2,240
3 June	Received a cheque from G Wheaton for £195, in full settlement of a debt of £200
5 June	Received cash of £53 from T Francis, in full settlement of a debt of £55
8 June	Paid the amount owing to F Lloyd by cheque: the total amount due is £400 and Harrison takes advantage of a 2.5% per cent cash discount
10 June	Paid wages in cash £165
12 June	Paid A Morris in cash, £100 less 3 per cent cash discount
16 June	Withdrew £200 in cash from the bank for use in the business
18 June	Received a cheque for £640 from H Watson in full settlement of a debt of £670
20 June	Paid R Marks £78 by cheque
24 June	Paid D Farr £65 by cheque, in full settlement of a debt of £67
26 June	Paid telephone account £105 in cash
28 June	Received a cheque from M Perry in settlement of his account of £240 – he has deducted 2.5% per cent cash discount
30 June	Received cash £45 from K Willis

You are to:

(a) enter the above transactions in Harrison's three column cash book, balance the cash and bank columns, and carry the balances down to 1 July

(b) total the two discount columns and transfer them to the appropriate accounts

8.3 On 1 August 20-7, the balances in the cash book of Metro Trading Company were:

Cash	£276 debit
Bank	£4,928 debit

Transactions for the month were:

1 Aug	Received a cheque from Wild & Sons Limited, £398
5 Aug	Paid T Hall Limited a cheque for £541 in full settlement of a debt of £565
8 Aug	Paid wages in cash £254
11 Aug	Withdrew £500 in cash from the bank for use in the business
12 Aug	Received a cheque for £1,755 from A Lewis Limited in full settlement of their account of £1,775
18 Aug	Paid F Jarvis £457 by cheque
21 Aug	Received a cheque for £261 from Harvey & Sons Limited
22 Aug	Paid wages in cash £436
25 Aug	Paid J Jones a cheque for £628 in full settlement of a debt of £661
27 Aug	Paid salaries by cheque £2,043
28 Aug	Paid telephone account by cheque £276
29 Aug	Received a cheque for £595 from Wild & Sons Limited in full settlement of their account of £610
29 Aug	Withdrew £275 in cash from the bank for use in the business

All cheques are banked on the day of receipt.

REQUIRED

- Enter the above transactions in the three column cash book of Metro Trading Company.
- Balance the cash and bank columns at 31 August, and carry the balances down to September 1st.
- Total the two discount columns.

8.4

Tom Singh keeps a three-column cash book for his business. The following information relates to the month of March 2005:

2005	
1 March	Balances of cash and bank were £106 and £3,214 respectively
2 March	Drew cheque no 10674 for rent of £250
3 March	Sales £1,050. Banked £950 of this on the same day
5 March	Paid cleaning expenses of £35 from cash
8 March	Sales banked £1,680
9 March	Drew cheque no 10675 for purchases costing £1,200
11 March	Drew cheque no 10676 for £150, to replenish cash in hand
13 March	Sales banked £1,800
16 March	Paid postage of £50 from cash
18 March	Drew cheque no 10677 for £168, to pay a telephone bill
20 March	Paid Stationery of £128 from cash
22 March	Drew cheque no 10678 for £150, to replenish cash in hand
25 March	Sales banked £2,108
26 March	Paid miscellaneous expenses of £70 from cash
27 March	Drew cheque no 10679 for £2,000, to pay wages
29 March	Sales £2,200. Banked £2,000 of this on the same day
30 March	Drew cheque no 10680 for £106, to pay an electricity bill
31 March	Drew cheque no 10681 for £855 payable to Evans & Co, in settlement of a debt of £900
31 March	Drew cheque no 10682 for £494 payable to A Bennett, in settlement of a debt of £520
31 March	Received cheque for £720 from Hobbs Ltd, in settlement of an amount of £750
31 March	Received cheque for £1,160 from Pratley & Co, in settlement of an amount of £1,210

REQUIRED

Write up the three-column cash book, bringing down the balances at 1 April 2005.

8.5*

The following items have yet to be recorded in the cash book of J A Summerfield for the first week in January 2002:

		£
1 January	Balance in cash account	50.00
1 January	Overdrawn bank balance	263.67

	Cheque counterfoils show:	£	
3 January	J B Smith Ltd (cash discount taken – £4.00)	120.00	cheque amount
4 January	A E Evans Ltd	146.59	cheque amount
5 January	K L M Spares (cash discount taken – £3.96)	127.45	cheque amount
6 January	Restoring the petty cash imprest (see Chapter 9)	45.67	cheque amount
	Paying-in counterfoils show:		
3 January	M S Supplies	136.98	amount banked
4 January	J O Jones (cash discount taken – £4.67)	246.89	amount banked

The following additional items should also be recorded in the cash book:

The bank statement shows:	£
Direct debit payment Shop Insurances plc	100.00
Credit transfer received ABC Traders	120.56
Bank charges	23.98
Bank interest paid	46.97
The week's till rolls show:	
Cash receipts total of	467.23
There were cash payments of:	
Part time wages	40.00
Postage stamps	27.00

It is the business's policy to retain a cash float of £50 at the end of each week and pay the rest of the cash into the bank. This was done on 7 January 2002.

REQUIRED

(a) Record this information in the cash book below and balance the cash book at 7 January 2002.

Dr **Cash Book of J A Summerfield** Cr

Date 2002	Details	Disc't allowed £	Cash £	Bank £	Date 2002	Details	Disc't rec'd £	Cash £	Bank £
Jan					Jan				

(b) What method or technique can be used to verify:

(i) the cash balance ....

....

(ii) the bank balance* ....

....

(c) Explain the term 'petty cash imprest'** ....

....

....

Assessment and Qualifications Alliance (AQA), 2002

* see Chapter 10 ** see Chapter 9

8.6 Explain the meaning of the following items which have been found in the bank statement received by R Masters for his business and give the ledger entries for them.

(i) Standing order

Explanation ....

....

....

....

Account to be debited ....

Account to be credited ....

(ii) Credit transfer for payment by a customer

Explanation ....

....

....

....

Account to be debited ....

Account to be credited ....

Assessment and Qualifications Alliance (AQA), 2002

9 PETTY CASH BOOK

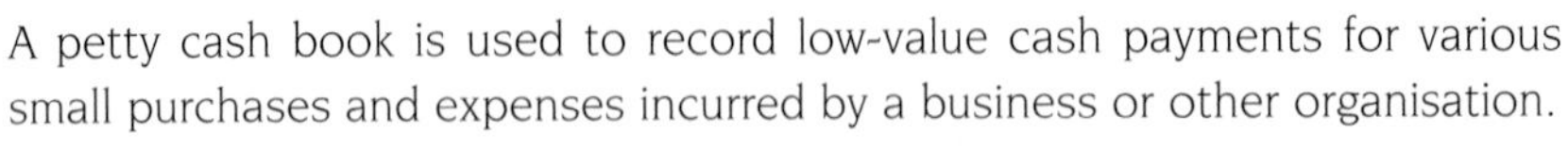

A petty cash book is used to record low-value cash payments for various small purchases and expenses incurred by a business or other organisation.

An amount of cash is handed by the main cashier to a member of staff, the petty cashier, who will be responsible for security of the money, and will make payments as appropriate against authorised petty cash vouchers.

In the context of the accounting system, the petty cash book is both

- a subsidiary book
- part of the double-entry system

THE PETTY CASH PROCEDURE

The petty cash book is used to record low-value cash payments for purchases and expenses such as small items of stationery, postages, etc, items which it would not be appropriate to enter in the main cash book. Instead, an amount of cash is handed by the main cashier to a member of staff, the petty cashier, who is responsible for control of the petty cash, making cash payments when appropriate, keeping records of payments made and balancing the petty cash book at regular intervals.

In order to operate the petty cash system, the petty cashier needs the following:

- a petty cash book in which to record transactions
- a lockable cash box in which to keep the money
- a stock of blank petty cash vouchers (see page 123) for claims on petty cash to be made
- a lockable desk drawer in which to keep these items

making a claim

An employee of a business is most likely to encounter the petty cash system when making claims for money for small purchases made. Before studying the form-filling procedures in detail, read the summary of a typical petty cash transaction set out below:

Your supervisor asks you to go and buy a box of envelopes from an office supplies shop.

You go to the shop and buy the envelopes. You pay for them in cash and keep the receipt (for £5.50) which you hand to the petty cashier on your return to the office.

The supervisor authorises a petty cash voucher which contains details of the purchase.

The petty cashier gives you £5.50 in cash.

The petty cashier attaches the receipt to the petty cash voucher and enters the details in the petty cash book.

what items can be passed through petty cash book?

Petty cash is used to make small cash payments for purchases and expenses incurred by the business. Examples of the type of payments made from petty cash include:

- stationery items
- small items of office supplies
- casual wages
- window cleaning
- bus, rail and taxi fares (incurred on behalf of the business)
- meals and drinks (incurred on behalf of the business)
- postages
- tips and donations

Note that petty cash should not be used to pay for private expenses of employees, eg tea, coffee, and milk, unless the business has agreed these in advance. Usually the petty cashier will have a list of approved expenses which can be reimbursed.

A business will also decide on the maximum value of each transaction that can be paid out of petty cash; for example, £25 is a common figure.

WORKED EXAMPLE: PETTY CASH EXPENSES

situation

You are working as an accounts clerk for Wyvern Engineering Limited. One of your duties is that of petty cashier. Which of the following expenses would you allow to be paid out of petty cash?

- envelopes for use in the office, £2.50
- postage on an urgent parcel of engineering parts, £3.75
- bus fare to work claimed by secretary £1.20
- car mileage to work of office manager called in late at night when the burglar alarm went off (false alarm!), £5.50
- tea and coffee for use in the office, £3.70
- office window cleaning, £2.80
- pot plant bought for reception area, £5.50
- computer disks, £35.00
- donation to local charity by the business, £5.00
- meal allowance paid to a member of staff required to work during the lunch hour, £3.50

solution

For most expenses it is clear whether or not they can be drawn from petty cash. However, there are points to consider for some of the expenses.

Envelopes pay from petty cash

Postage pay from petty cash

Bus fare to work this is a personal expense and cannot be drawn from petty cash

Car mileage travel to work is a personal expense, as seen with the previous item; however, as this expense was a special journey in the middle of the night in order to resolve a business problem, it can be paid from petty cash

Tea and coffee this is a personal expense of employees and cannot normally be paid out of petty cash; however, if the ingredients were used to make drinks for official visitors and customers, it can be paid from petty cash

Window cleaning pay from petty cash

Pot plant pay from petty cash (but plants for the general office cannot be bought with the company's money)

Computer disks this is a business expense but, in view of the amount (too large for petty cash), it should be paid by cheque from the cash book

Donation pay from petty cash

Meal allowance pay from petty cash, provided that it is company policy to make an allowance in these circumstances

notes on the worked example

- If the petty cashier is unable to resolve whether or not an expense can be paid from petty cash, the item should be referred to the accounts supervisor for a decision.
- Before payments can be made for petty cash expenses, they must be:
  - within the prescribed limit for petty cash expenses (for example, £25 maximum for any one expense item)
  - supported by documentary evidence, such as a receipt or a rail/bus ticket
  - authorised by the appropriate supervisor or manager

THE IMPREST SYSTEM

Most petty cash books operate on the imprest system. With this method the petty cashier starts each week (or month) with a certain amount of money – the imprest amount. As payments are made during the week (or month) the amount of money will reduce and, at the end of the period, the cash will be made up by the main cashier to the imprest amount. For example:

Started week with imprest amount	£100.00
Total of petty cash amounts paid out during week	£80.50
Cash held at end of week	£19.50
Amount drawn from cashier to restore imprest amount	£80.50
Cash at start of next week, ie imprest amount	£100.00

If, at any time, the imprest amount proves to be insufficient, further amounts of cash can be drawn from the cashier. Also, from time-to-time, it may be necessary to increase the imprest amount so that regular shortfalls are avoided.

PETTY CASH VOUCHER

Payments out of petty cash are made only against correct documentation – usually a petty cash voucher (illustrated on the next page). Petty cash vouchers are completed as follows:

- details and amount of expenditure
- signature of the person making the claim and receiving the money
- signature of the person authorising the payment to be made
- additionally, most petty cash vouchers are numbered, so that they can be controlled, the number being entered in the petty cash book
- relevant documentation, eg receipt, should be attached to the petty cash voucher

Petty cash vouchers are the source documents for the petty cash book.

petty cash voucher No. 807

date *12 May 20-7*

description	amount (£)	
C5 Envelopes	*2*	*00*
5 Marker pens	*4*	*00*
	6	*00*
VAT	*1*	*05*
	7	*05*

signature *T Harris*

authorised *R Singh*

Layout of a Petty Cash Book

The petty cash book is both the subsidiary book and part of the double-entry system for petty cash transactions. Petty cash book can be set out as follows:

Receipts	Date	Details	Voucher number	Total payment	ANALYSIS COLUMNS				
					VAT	Postages	Stationery	Travel	Ledger
£				£	£	£	£	£	£

The layout shows that:

- receipts from the main cashier are entered in the column on the extreme left
- there are columns for the date and details of all receipts and payments
- there is a column for the petty cash voucher number
- the total payment (ie the amount paid out on each petty cash voucher) is in the next column
- the analysis columns then analyse each transaction entered in the 'total payment' column (note that VAT may need to be calculated – see below)

A business will use whatever analysis columns are most suitable for it and, indeed, there may be more columns than shown in the example. It is important that expenses are analysed to the correct columns so that the contents show a true picture of petty cash expenditure.

PETTY CASH AND VAT

Value Added Tax is charged by VAT-registered businesses on their taxable supplies. Therefore, there will often be VAT included as part of the expense paid out of petty cash. However, not all expenses will have been subject to VAT. There are four possible circumstances:

- VAT has been charged at the standard rate
- VAT has not been charged because the supplier is not VAT-registered
- the zero rate of VAT applies, eg food and drink (but not meals which are standard-rated), books, newspapers, transport (but not taxis and hire cars)
- the supplies are exempt (eg financial services, postal services)

Often the indication of the supplier's VAT registration number on a receipt or invoice will tell you that VAT has been charged at the standard rate.

Where VAT has been charged, the amount of tax might be indicated separately on the receipt or invoice. However, for small money amounts it is quite usual for a total to be shown without indicating the amount of VAT. An example of a receipt which does not show the VAT content is illustrated below. The receipt is for a box of envelopes purchased from Wyvern Stationers. It shows:

- the name and address of the retailer
- the date and time of the transaction
- the VAT registration number of the retailer
- the price of the item – £4.70
- the amount of money given – a £10 note
- the amount of change given – £5.30

Wyvern Stationers
25 High St Mereford
08 10 07 16.07
VAT Reg 454 7106 34

Salesperson	**Rashid**
Stationery	**4.70**
TOTAL	**4.70**
CASH	**10.00**
CHANGE	**5.30**

What it does not show, however, is the VAT content of the purchase price – it only shows the price after the VAT has been added on.

How do you calculate purchase price before the VAT is added on?

The formula, with VAT at 17.5%, is:

price including VAT ÷ 1.175 = price before VAT is added on

in this case ...

£4.70 ÷ 1.175 = £4.00 = price before VAT is added on

The VAT content is therefore:

£4.70 less £4.00 = 70p

Here £0.70 will be entered in the VAT column in the petty cash book, £4.00 in the appropriate expense column, and the full £4.70 in the total payment column.

Remember when calculating VAT amounts that fractions of a penny are ignored, ie the tax is rounded down to a whole penny.

WORKED EXAMPLE: PETTY CASH BOOK

A business keeps a petty cash book, which is operated on the imprest system. There are a number of authorised transactions (all of which, unless otherwise indicated, include VAT at 17.5%) to be entered for the week in the petty cash book:

20-7	
7 Apr	Started the week with an imprest amount of £50.00
7 Apr	Paid stationery £3.76 on voucher no. 47
7 Apr	Paid taxi fare £2.82 on voucher no. 48
8 Apr	Paid postages £0.75 (no VAT) on voucher no. 49
9 Apr	Paid taxi fare £4.70 on voucher no. 50
9 Apr	Paid J Jones, a creditor, £6.00 (no VAT shown in petty cash book – amount will be on VAT account already) on voucher no. 51
10 Apr	Paid stationery £3.76 on voucher no. 52
10 Apr	Paid postages £2.85 (no VAT) on voucher no. 53
11 Apr	Paid taxi fare £6.11 on voucher no. 54
11 Apr	Cash received to restore imprest amount, and petty cash book balanced at the end of the week

The petty cash book is written up as follows:

Receipts	Date	Details	Voucher number	Total payment	ANALYSIS COLUMNS				
					VAT	Postages	Stationery	Travel	Ledger
£	20-7			£	£	£	£	£	£
50.00	7 April	Balance b/d							
	7 April	Stationery	47	3.76	0.56		3.20		
	7 April	Taxi fare	48	2.82	0.42			2.40	
	8 April	Postages	49	0.75		0.75			
	9 April	Taxi fare	50	4.70	0.70			4.00	
	9 April	J Jones	51	6.00					6.00
	10 April	Stationery	52	3.76	0.56		3.20		
	10 April	Postages	53	2.85		2.85			
	11 April	Taxi fare	54	6.11	0.91			5.20	
				30.75	3.15	3.60	6.40	11.60	6.00
30.75	11 April	Cash received							
	11 April	Balance c/d		50.00					
80.75				80.75					
50.00	11 April	Balance b/d							

note the following points

- The totals of the analysis columns add up to the total payment
- the amount of cash received from the main cashier to restore the imprest amount is the same as the total paid out during the week
- The petty cashier will give the firm's book-keeper details of the total of each analysis column – see below – so that the amounts can be recorded in the double-entry book-keeping system

PETTY CASH AND DOUBLE-ENTRY BOOK-KEEPING

When the petty cash book has been balanced, the petty cashier will prepare a summary which shows:

- debits to expenses accounts (and VAT account) in the general ledger in respect of each expenses column
- debits to creditors' accounts in the purchases ledger in respect of the ledger column (eg J Jones in the Worked Example)
- credit to cash book, being the amount drawn from the main cashier to restore the imprest amount of the petty cash book

For example, the postages in the Worked Example on the previous page will be debited as follows:

Dr	**Postages Account**				Cr
20-7		£	20-7		£
11 Apr	Petty cash book	3.60			

From the petty cash book, debits are passed to the general ledger accounts as follows:

- VAT account, £3.15
- postages account, £3.60
- stationery account, £6.40
- travel expenses account, £11.60

The amount in the ledger column, £6.00, is debited to the account of J Jones in the purchases ledger.

Total debits in the Worked Example are £30.75 and this is the amount that has been drawn from the main cashier on 11 April. The petty cashier will complete a cheque requisition form either for the cash itself, or for a cheque made payable to cash. The petty cashier will take the cheque to the bank and obtain the cash. An example of a cheque requisition is shown on the next page.

The cheque is credited in the firm's cash book, so completing double-entry :

– debit petty cash book £30.75

– credit cash book £30.75

If a trial balance is extracted on 11 April (after the analysis columns have been debited to the respective accounts, and a credit entered in the cash book to restore the imprest amount) the balance of petty cash, £50.00, must be included as a debit balance in the trial balance – this is because petty cash book is part of the double-entry system.

CHEQUE REQUISITION

Amount	*£30.75*
Payee	*Cash*
Date	*11 April 20-7*
Details	*Reimbursement of petty cash*
Signature	*Jane Watkins, petty cashier*
Authorised by	*Natalie Wilson, supervisor*
Cheque no	*017234*

cheque requisition form

CONTROL OF PETTY CASH

In most businesses the petty cashier is responsible to the office manager for control of the petty cash and for correct recording of authorised petty cash transactions. Many businesses will set out in writing the procedures to be followed by the petty cashier. This is of benefit not only for the petty cashier to know the extent of his or her duties, but also to help the person who takes over at holiday or other times.

The main procedures for the operation and control of petty cash are:

- On taking over, the petty cashier should check that the petty cash book has been balanced and that the amount of cash held agrees with the balance shown in the book. If there is any discrepancy, this should be referred to the office manager immediately.
- Ensure that each week is started with the imprest amount of cash which has been agreed with the office manager.
- The petty cash is to be kept securely in a locked cash box, and control kept of the keys.
- Petty cash vouchers (in number order) are to be provided on request.
- Petty cash is paid out against correctly completed petty cash vouchers after checking that:
  - the voucher is signed by the person receiving the money
  - the voucher is signed by the person authorising payment (a list of authorised signatories will be provided)
  - a receipt (whenever possible) is attached to the petty cash voucher, and that receipt and petty cash voucher are for the same amount
- The petty cash book is written up (to include calculation of VAT amounts when appropriate); it is important that the petty cash book is accurate.

- Completed petty cash vouchers are stored safely – filed in numerical order. The vouchers will need to be kept for at least six years in the company's archives. They may be needed by the firm's auditors or in the event of other queries. Completed petty cash books will also need to be retained.
- A surprise check of petty cash will be made by the office manager – at any one time the cash held plus amounts of petty cash vouchers should equal the imprest amount.
- At the end of each week (or month) the petty cash book is to be balanced and an amount of cash drawn from the cashier equal to the amount of payments made, in order to restore the imprest amount.
- Details of the totals of each analysis column are to be given to the book-keeper so that the amount of each expense can be entered into the double-entry system.
- The petty cash book and cash in hand are to be presented to the office manager for checking.
- Any discrepancies are to be dealt with promptly; these may include:
  - a receipt and petty cash voucher total differing – the matter should be queried with the person who made the purchase
  - a difference between the totals of the analysis columns and the total payments column in the petty cash book – check the addition of the columns, the figures against the vouchers, the VAT calculations (does the VAT plus the analysis column amount equal the total payment amount?)
  - a difference between the cash in the petty cash box and the balance shown in the petty cash book – if this is not an arithmetic difference it may be a case of theft, and should be reported promptly to the office manager
  - where discrepancies and queries cannot be resolved, they should be referred to the office manager
- All aspects of petty cash are confidential and should not be discussed with others.

CHAPTER SUMMARY

- The petty cash book records payments for a variety of low-value business expenses.
- The person responsible for maintaining the petty cash book is the petty cashier.
- Payment can only be made from the petty cash book against correct documentation – usually a petty cash voucher, which must be signed by the person authorising payment.
- Where a business is registered for Value Added Tax, it must record VAT amounts paid on petty cash purchases in a separate column in the petty cash book.
- At regular intervals – weekly or monthly – the petty cash book will be balanced; the main cashier will restore the imprest amount of cash and the total of each analysis column will be debited to the relevant account in the book-keeping system.

In the next chapter we will see how bank reconciliation statements are prepared in order to agree the cash book balance and bank statement balance.

QUESTIONS

NOTE: an asterisk (*) after the question number means that an answer to the question is given at the end of this book.

9.1*

You work as an accounts clerk in the office of Temeside Printers Limited. One of your duties is that of petty cashier. Which of the following expenses will you allow to be paid out of petty cash?

(a) postage on a parcel of printing sent to a customer, £3.85

(b) a rubber date stamp bought for use in the office, £4.60

(c) rail fare to work claimed by the office manager's secretary, £2.50

(d) donation to charity, £5.00

(e) tea and coffee for use by office staff, £5.50

(f) mileage allowance claimed by works foreman who had to visit a customer, £4.80

(g) meal allowance paid to assistant who had to work her lunch hour, £4.00

(h) window cleaning, £3.50

(i) purchase of shelving for the office, £55.00

(j) taxi fare claimed for delivering an urgent parcel of printing to a customer, £6.25

Explain any expenses that you will refer to the accounts supervisor.

9.2

You are going on holiday and handing your job as petty cashier to a colleague who is not familiar with the security and confidentiality aspects of the job, although she can manage the paperwork. Prepare a checklist of the security and safety aspects of the job so that she can learn them more easily. Present them as bullet points rather than as solid text – they will be more easily remembered in this format.

9.3

As petty cashier, prepare the petty cash vouchers shown on the next page under today's date for signature by the person making the claim. You are authorised to approve payments up to £10.00.

Voucher no. 851: £4.45 claimed by Jayne Smith for postage (no VAT) on an urgent parcel of spare parts sent to a customer, Evelode Supplies Limited.

Voucher no. 852: £2.35 (including VAT) claimed by Tanya Howard for air mail envelopes bought for use in the office. Show on the petty cash voucher the amount of VAT.

What documentation will you require to be attached to each voucher?

petty cash voucher No. 851

date

description	amount (£)	
VAT		

signature ....

authorised ....

petty cash voucher No. 852

date

description	amount (£)	
VAT		

signature ....

authorised ....

9.4* The business for which you work is registered for VAT. The following petty cash amounts include VAT at 17.5% and you are required to calculate the amount that will be shown in the VAT column and the appropriate expense column (remember that VAT amounts should be rounded down to the nearest penny):

(a) £9.40

(b) £4.70

(c) £2.35

(d) £2.45

(e) £5.60

(f) £3.47

(g) £8.75

(h) 94p

(i) 99p

(j) £9.41

9.5* On returning from holiday, you are told to take over the petty cash book. This is kept on the imprest system, the float being £75.00 at the beginning of each month. Analysis columns are used for VAT, travel, postages, stationery, meals, and miscellaneous.

Enter the following transactions for the month. The voucher amounts include VAT at 17.5% unless indicated. You can assume that all payments have been authorised by the office manager:

20-7	
1 Aug	Balance of cash £75.00
4 Aug	Voucher 39: taxi fare £3.80
6 Aug	Voucher 40: parcel postage £2.35 (no VAT)
7 Aug	Voucher 41: pencils £1.26
11 Aug	Voucher 42: travel expenses £5.46 (no VAT)
12 Aug	Voucher 43: window cleaner £8.50 (no VAT)
14 Aug	Voucher 44: large envelopes £2.45
18 Aug	Voucher 45: donation to charity £5 (no VAT)
19 Aug	Voucher 46: rail fare £5.60 (no VAT); meal allowance £5.00 (no VAT)
20 Aug	Voucher 47: recorded delivery postage £0.75 (no VAT)
22 Aug	Voucher 48: roll of packing tape £1.50
25 Aug	Voucher 49: excess postage paid £0.55 (no VAT)
27 Aug	Voucher 50: taxi fare £5.40
29 Aug	Petty cash book balanced and cash received from cashier to restore imprest amount to £75.00

You are to show how the following will be recorded in the double-entry book-keeping system:

- the totals of the analysis columns
- the transfer of cash from the main cashier on 29 August

9.6 Prepare a petty cash book with analysis columns for VAT, postages, travel, meals, and sundry office expenses. Enter the following authorised transactions for the week. The voucher amounts include VAT at 17.5% unless indicated.

20-7

2 June	Balance of cash £100.00
2 June	Postages £6.35 (no VAT), voucher 123
3 June	Travel expenses £3.25 (no VAT), voucher 124
3 June	Postages £1.28 (no VAT), voucher 125
4 June	Envelopes £4.54, voucher 126
4 June	Window cleaning £5.50, voucher 127
5 June	Taxi fare £4.56, meals £10.85, voucher 128
5 June	Postages £8.56 (no VAT), packing materials £3.25, voucher 129
5 June	Taxi fare £4.50, meals £7.45, voucher 130
6 June	Marker pens £2.55, envelopes £3.80, voucher 131
6 June	Petty cash book balanced and cash received from cashier to restore imprest amount to £100.00

You are to show how the following will be recorded in the double-entry book-keeping system:

- the totals of the analysis columns
- the transfer of cash from the main cashier on 6 June

9.7* Draw up a petty cash book with appropriate analysis columns and a VAT column, and enter the following transactions for the month. The voucher amounts include VAT at 17.5% unless indicated:

20-1

1 May	Balance of cash £150.00
1 May	Postages £7.00, voucher no 455, travel £2.85, voucher no 456 (no VAT on postages and travel)
2 May	Meal allowance £6.11, voucher no 457 (no VAT)
3 May	Taxi £4.70, voucher no 458
4 May	Stationery £3.76, voucher no 459
7 May	Postages £5.25, voucher no 460 (no VAT)
8 May	Travel £6.50, voucher no 461 (no VAT)
9 May	Meal allowance £6.11, voucher no 462 (no VAT)
10 May	Stationery £8.46, voucher no 463
14 May	Taxi £5.17, voucher no 464
17 May	Stationery £4.70, voucher no 465

21 May	Travel £3.50, voucher no 466, postages £4.50, voucher no 467 (no VAT on travel and postages)
23 May	Bus fares £3.80, voucher no 468 (no VAT)
26 May	Catering expenses £10.81, voucher no 469
27 May	Postages £3.50, voucher no 470 (no VAT), stationery £7.52, voucher no 471
28 May	Travel expenses £6.45, voucher no 472 (no VAT)
31 May	Cash received from cashier to restore imprest amount to £150.00

9.8 The petty cash book for The Taj Mahal Restaurant has been only partly completed for the week ended 12 January 2003.

REQUIRED

(a) Complete the petty cash book on the next page for the week from the following details:

9 January	Petrol	£12.50	(including VAT)
10 January	Postage on parcels	£8.50	(no VAT)
11 January	Saturday help	£20.00	(no VAT)

(b) Balance the petty cash book on the next page and total the analysis columns. Make the necessary entries to restore the imprest to £120.00.

(c) Explain how the balance shown in the petty cash book can be checked for accuracy.

....

....

(d) Give two benefits of using a petty cash book.

Benefit 1 ....

....

....

Benefit 2 ....

....

....

Petty Cash Book

Received £ p	Date 2003	Details	Voucher number	Total	VAT £ p	Motor expenses £ p	Stationery £ p	Postage £ p	Sundries £ p
120.00	Jan 6	Balance b/d							
	Jan 7	Petrol	27	23.00	3.43	19.57			
	Jan 8	Postage	28	15.00				15.00	
	Jan 8	Envelopes	29	10.00	1.49		8.51		
	Jan 8	Cleaner	30	15.00					15.00

Assessment and Qualifications Alliance (AQA), 2003

10 BANK RECONCILIATION STATEMENTS

Bank reconciliation statements form the link between the balance at bank shown in the cash book of a firm's book-keeping system and the balance shown on the bank statement received from the bank.

The reasons why the cash book and bank statement may differ are because:

- there are timing differences caused by:
  - unpresented cheques, ie the time delay between writing out (drawing) a cheque and recording it in the cash book, and the cheque being entered on the bank statement
  - outstanding lodgements, ie amounts paid into the bank, but not yet recorded on the bank statement
- the cash book has not been updated with items which appear on the bank statement and which should also appear in the cash book, eg bank charges

Assuming that there are no errors, both cash book and bank statement are correct, but need to be reconciled with each other, ie the closing balances need to be agreed.

TIMING DIFFERENCES

The two main timing differences between the bank columns of the cash book and the bank statement are:

- **unpresented cheques**, ie cheques drawn, not yet recorded on the bank statement
- **outstanding lodgements**, ie amounts paid into the bank, not yet recorded on the bank statement

The first of these – unpresented cheques – is caused because, when a cheque is written out, it is immediately entered on the payments side of the cash book, even though it may be some days before the cheque passes through the bank clearing system and is recorded on the bank statement. Therefore, for a few days at least, the cash book shows a lower balance than the bank statement in respect of this cheque. When the cheque is recorded on the bank statement, the difference will disappear. We have looked at only one cheque here, but a business will often be issuing many cheques each day, and the difference between the cash book balance and the bank statement balance may be considerable.

With the second timing difference – outstanding lodgements – the firm's cashier will record a receipt in the cash book as he or she prepares the bank paying-in slip. However, the receipt may not be recorded by the bank on the bank statement for a day or so, particularly if it is paid in late in the day (when the bank will put it into the next day's work), or if it is paid in at a bank branch other than the one at which the account is maintained. Until the receipt is recorded by the bank the cash book will show a higher bank account balance than the bank statement. Once the receipt is entered on the bank statement, the difference will disappear.

These two timing differences are involved in the calculation known as the bank reconciliation statement. The business cash book must not be altered for these because, as we have seen, they will correct themselves on the bank statement as time goes by.

Updating the Cash Book

Besides the timing differences described above, there may be other differences between the bank columns of the cash book and the bank statement, and these do need to be entered in the cash book to bring it up-to-date. For example, the bank might make an automatic standing order payment on behalf of a business – such an item is correctly debited by the bank, and it might be that the bank statement acts as a reminder to the business cashier of the payment: it should then be entered in the cash book.

Examples of items that show in the bank statement and need to be entered in the cash book include:

receipts

- credit transfers (BACS – Bankers Automated Clearing Services) amounts received by the bank, eg payments from debtors (customers)
- dividend amounts received by the bank
- interest credited by the bank

payments

- standing order and direct debit payments
- bank charges and interest
- unpaid cheques debited by the bank (ie cheques from debtors paid in by the business which have 'bounced' and are returned by the bank marked 'refer to drawer')

For each of these items, the cashier needs to check to see if they have been entered in the cash book; if not, they need to be recorded (provided that the bank has not made an error). If the bank has made an error, it must be notified as soon as possible and the incorrect transactions reversed by the bank in its own accounting records.

THE BANK RECONCILIATION STATEMENT

This forms the link between the balances shown in the cash book and the bank statement.

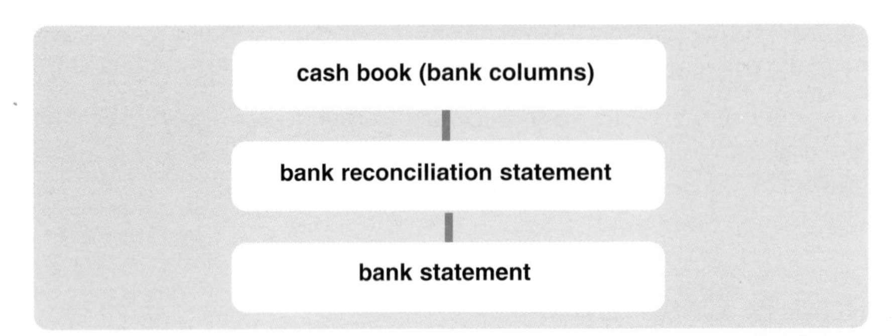

Upon receipt of a bank statement, reconciliation of the two balances is carried out in the following way:

- tick off the items that appear in both cash book and bank statement
- the unticked items on the bank statement are entered into the bank columns of the cash book to bring it up-to-date (provided none are errors made by the bank)
- the bank columns of the cash book are now balanced to find the revised figure
- the remaining unticked items from the cash book will be the timing differences
- the timing differences are used to prepare the bank reconciliation statement, which takes the following format (with example figures):

XYZ TRADING LTD
Bank Reconciliation Statement as at 31 October 20-1

			£	£
Balance at bank as per cash book				525
Add: unpresented cheques				
	J Lewis	cheque no. 0012378	60	
	ABC Ltd	cheque no. 0012392	100	
	Eastern Oil Company	cheque no. 0012407	80	
				240
				765
Less: outstanding lodgements			220	
			300	
				520
Balance at bank as per bank statement				245

Notes:

- The layout shown on the opposite page starts from the cash book balance, and works towards the bank statement balance. A common variation of this layout is to start with the bank statement balance and to work towards the cash book balance (see page 142).
- If a bank overdraft is involved, brackets should be used around the numbers to indicate this for the cash book or bank statement balance. The timing differences are still added or deducted, as appropriate.
- Once the bank reconciliation statement agrees, it should be filed because it proves that the cash book (bank columns) and bank statement were reconciled at a particular date. If, next time it is prepared, it fails to agree, the previous statement is proof that reconciliation was reached at that time.

WORKED EXAMPLE: BANK RECONCILIATION STATEMENT

The cashier of Severn Trading Co has written up the firm's cash book for the month of February 20-2, as follows (the cheque number is shown against payments):

Cash Book (Dr / Cr)

Date	Details		Cash	Bank	Date	Details		Cash	Bank
20-2			£	£	20-2			£	£
1 Feb	Balances b/d		250.75	1,340.50	3 Feb	Appleton Ltd 123456			675.25
7 Feb	A Abbott			208.50	5 Feb	Wages		58.60	
10 Feb	Sales		145.25		12 Feb	Rent 123457			125.00
13 Feb	Sales		278.30		14 Feb	Transfer to bank	C	500.00	
14 Feb	Transfer from cash	C		500.00	17 Feb	D Smith & Co 123458			421.80
20 Feb	Sales		204.35		24 Feb	Stationery		75.50	
21 Feb	D Richards Limited			162.30	25 Feb	G Christie 123459			797.55
26 Feb	Sales		353.95		27 Feb	Transfer to bank	C	500.00	
27 Feb	Transfer from cash	C		500.00	28 Feb	Balances c/d		98.50	954.00
28 Feb	P Paul Limited			262.30					
			1,232.60	2,973.60				1,232.60	2,973.60
1 Mar	Balances b/d		98.50	954.00					

The cash balance of £98.50 shown by the cash columns on 1 March has been agreed with the cash held in the firm's cash box.

The bank statement for February 20-2, which has just been received, is shown on the next page.

National Bank plc

Branch ..Bartown..............

TITLE OF ACCOUNT Severn Trading Company

ACCOUNT NUMBER 67812318

STATEMENT NUMBER 45

DATE	PARTICULARS	PAYMENTS	RECEIPTS	BALANCE
20-2		£	£	£
1 Feb	Balance brought forward			1340.50 CR
8 Feb	Credit		208.50	1549.00 CR
10 Feb	Cheque no. 123456	675.25		873.75 CR
17 Feb	Credit		500.00	1373.75 CR
17 Feb	Cheque no. 123457	125.00		1248.75 CR
24 Feb	Credit		162.30	1411.05 CR
24 Feb	BACS credit: J Jarvis Ltd		100.00	1511.05 CR
26 Feb	Cheque no. 123458	421.80		1089.25 CR
26 Feb	Direct debit: A-Z Finance	150.00		939.25 CR
28 Feb	Credit		500.00	1439.25 CR
28 Feb	Bank charges	10.00		1429.25 CR

Note that the bank statement is prepared from the bank's viewpoint: thus a credit balance shows that the customer is a creditor of the bank, ie the bank owes the balance to the customer. In the customer's own cash book, the bank is shown as a debit balance, ie an asset.

As the month-end balance at bank shown by the cash book, £954.00, is not the same as that shown by the bank statement, £1,429.25, it is necessary to prepare a bank reconciliation statement. The steps are:

1 Tick off the items that appear in both cash book and bank statement.

2 The unticked items on the bank statement are entered into the bank columns of the cash book to bring it up-to-date. These are:

• receipt	24 Feb	BACS credit, J Jarvis Limited £100.00
• payments	26 Feb	Direct debit, A-Z Finance £150.00
	28 Feb	Bank Charges, £10.00

In double-entry book-keeping, the other part of the transaction will need to be recorded in the accounts, eg in J Jarvis Ltd's account in the sales ledger, etc.

3 The cash book is now balanced to find the revised balance:

Cash Book (bank columns)

Dr					Cr
20-2		£	20-2		£
	Balance b/d	954.00	26 Feb	A-Z Finance	150.00
24 Feb	J Jarvis Ltd	100.00	28 Feb	Bank Charges	10.00
			28 Feb	Balance c/d	894.00
		1,054.00			1,054.00
1 Mar	Balance b/d	894.00			

4 The remaining unticked items from the cash book are used in the bank reconciliation statement:

- receipt 28 Feb – P Paul Limited £262.30
- payment 25 Feb – G Christie (cheque no 123459) £797.55

These items are timing differences, which should appear on next month's bank statement.

5 The bank reconciliation statement is now prepared, starting with the re-calculated cash book balance of £894.00.

SEVERN TRADING CO.
Bank Reconciliation Statement as at 28 February 20-2

	£
Balance at bank as per cash book	894.00
Add: unpresented cheque, no. 123459	797.55
	1,691.55
Less: outstanding lodgement, P Paul Limited	262.30
Balance at bank as per bank statement	1,429.25

With the above, a statement has been produced which starts with the amended balance from the cash book, and finishes with the bank statement balance, ie the two figures are reconciled.

Notes:

- The unpresented cheque is added back to the cash book balance because, until it is recorded by the bank, the cash book shows a lower balance than the bank statement.
- The outstanding lodgement is deducted from the cash book balance because, until it is recorded by the bank, the cash book shows a higher balance than the bank statement.

PREPARING A BANK RECONCILIATION STATEMENT

In order to help you with the questions at the end of the chapter, here is a step-by-step summary of the procedure. Reconciliation of the cash book balance with that shown in the bank statement should be carried out in the following way:

1 From the bank columns of the cash book tick off, in both cash book and bank statement, the receipts that appear in both.

2 From the bank columns of the cash book tick off, in both cash book and bank statement, the payments that appear in both.

3 Identify the items that are unticked on the bank statement and enter them in the cash book on the debit or credit side, as appropriate. If, however, the bank has made a mistake and debited or credited an amount in error, this should not be entered in the cash book, but should be notified to the bank for them to make the correction. The amount will need to be entered on the bank reconciliation statement – see section below, dealing with unusual items on bank statements: bank errors.

4 The bank columns of the cash book are now balanced to find the up-to-date balance.

5 Start the bank reconciliation statement with the balance brought down figure shown in the cash book.

6 In the bank reconciliation statement add the unticked payments shown in the cash book – these will be unpresented cheques.

7 In the bank reconciliation statement, deduct the unticked receipts shown in the cash book – these are outstanding lodgements.

8 The resultant money amount on the bank reconciliation statement is the balance of the bank statement.

The layout which is often used for the bank reconciliation statement is that shown on page 138. The layout starts with the cash book balance and finishes with the bank statement balance. However, there is no reason why it should not commence with the bank statement balance and finish with the cash book balance: with this layout it is necessary to:

- deduct unpresented cheques
- add outstanding lodgements

The bank reconciliation statement of Severn Trading Company (see previous page) would then appear as:

SEVERN TRADING COMPANY
Bank Reconciliation Statement as at 28 February 20-2

	£
Balance at bank as per bank statement	1,429.25
Less: unpresented cheque, no 123459	797.55
	631.70
Add: outstanding lodgement, P Paul Limited	262.30
Balance at bank as per cash book	894.00

DEALING WITH UNUSUAL ITEMS ON BANK STATEMENTS

The following are some of the unusual features that may occur on bank statements. As with other accounting discrepancies and queries, where they cannot be resolved they should be referred to a supervisor for guidance.

out-of-date cheques

These are cheques that are more than six months' old. Where a business has a number of out-of-date – or 'stale' – cheques which have not been debited on the bank statement, they will continue to appear on the bank reconciliation statement. As the bank will not pay these cheques, they can be written back in the cash book, ie debit cash book (and credit the other double-entry account involved).

returned cheques

A cheque received by a business is entered as a receipt in the cash book and then paid into the bank, but it may be returned by the drawer's (issuer's) bank to the payee's bank because:

- the drawer (the issuer) has stopped it
- the drawer has no money (the cheque may be returned 'refer to drawer') – ie it has 'bounced'

A cheque returned in this way should be entered in the book-keeping system:

- as a payment in the cash book on the credit side
- as a debit to the account of the drawer of the cheque in the sales ledger (if it is a credit sale), or sales account if it is a cash sale

On the other hand, if the business itself stops a cheque, the cheque drawn by the business will have been entered as a payment in the cash book (a credit). It should now be entered as:

- a receipt on the debit side
- a credit to the account of the payee, most probably in the purchases ledger (if it is a credit purchase)

bank errors

Errors made by the bank can include:

- A cheque debited to the bank account which has not been drawn by the business – look for a cheque number on the bank statement that is different from the current cheque series: care, though, as it could be a cheque from an old cheque book.
- A BACS payment (or other credit) shown on the bank statement for which the business is not the correct recipient. If in doubt, the bank will be able to give further details of the sender of the credit.
- Standing orders and direct debits paid at the wrong time or for the wrong amounts. A copy of all standing order and direct debit mandates sent to the bank should be kept by the business for reference purposes.

When an error is found, it should be queried immediately with the bank. The item and amount should not be entered in the firm's cash book until the issue has been resolved. If, in the meantime, a bank reconciliation statement is to be prepared, the bank error should be shown separately:

- if working from the cash book balance to the bank statement balance, deduct payments and add receipts that the bank has applied to the account incorrectly
- if working from the bank statement balance to the cash book balance, add payments and deduct receipts that the bank has applied to the account incorrectly

bank charges and interest

From time-to-time the bank will debit business customers' accounts with an amount for:

- service charges, ie the cost of operating the bank account
- interest, ie the borrowing cost when the business is overdrawn

Banks usually notify customers in writing before debiting the account.

Importance of Bank Reconciliation Statements

- A bank reconciliation statement is important because, in its preparation, the transactions in the bank columns of the cash book are compared with those recorded on the bank statement. In this way, any errors in the cash book or bank statement will be found and can be corrected (or advised to the bank, if the bank statement is wrong).
- The bank statement is an independent accounting record, therefore it will assist in deterring fraud by providing a means of verifying the cash book balance.
- By writing the cash book up-to-date, the organisation has an amended figure for the bank balance to be shown in the trial balance.
- Unpresented cheques over six months old – out-of-date cheques – can be identified and written back in the cash book (any cheque dated more than six months' ago will not be paid by the bank).
- It is good practice to prepare a bank reconciliation statement each time a bank statement is received. The reconciliation statement should be prepared as quickly as possible so that any queries – either with the bank statement or in the firm's cash book – can be resolved. Many firms will specify to their accounting staff the timescales for preparing bank reconciliation statements – as a guideline, if the bank statement is received weekly, then the reconciliation statement should be prepared within five working days.

CHAPTER SUMMARY

- A bank reconciliation statement is used to agree the balance shown by the bank columns of the cash book with that shown by the bank statement.
- Certain differences between the two are timing differences. The main timing differences are:
  - unpresented cheques
  - outstanding lodgements

  These differences will be corrected by time and, most probably, will be recorded on the next bank statement.

- Certain differences appearing on the bank statement need to be entered in the cash book to bring it up-to-date. These include:

  Receipts – credit transfers (BACS) amounts received by the bank
  – dividend amounts received by the bank
  – interest credited by the bank

  Payments – standing order and direct debit payments
  – bank charges and interest
  – unpaid cheques debited by the bank

- The bank reconciliation statement makes use of the timing differences.

- Once prepared, a bank reconciliation statement is proof that the bank statement and the cash book (bank columns) were agreed at a particular date.

The next chapter looks at the way in which computers are used to handle accounting records and the benefits they can bring.

QUESTIONS

NOTE: an asterisk (*) after the question number means that an answer to the question is given at the end of this book.

10.1* The bank columns of Tom Reid's cash book for December 20-7 are as follows:

20-7	*Receipts*	*£*	*20-7*	*Payments*		*£*
1 Dec	Balance b/d	280	9 Dec	W Smith	345123	40
12 Dec	P Jones	30	12 Dec	Rent	345124	50
18 Dec	H Homer	72	18 Dec	Wages	345125	85
29 Dec	J Hill	13	19 Dec	B Kay	345126	20
			31 Dec	Balance c/d		200
		395				395

He then received his bank statement which showed the following transactions for December 20-7:

BANK STATEMENT

		Payments	*Receipts*	*Balance*
20-7		£	£	£
1 Dec	Balance brought forward			280 CR
12 Dec	Credit		30	310 CR
15 Dec	Cheque no. 345123	40		270 CR
17 Dec	Cheque no. 345124	50		220 CR
22 Dec	Credit		72	292 CR
23 Dec	Cheque no. 345125	85		207 CR

You are to prepare a bank reconciliation statement which agrees with the bank statement balance.

10.2 The bank columns of P Gerrard's cash book for January 20-7 are as follows:

20-7	*Receipts*	£	*20-7*	*Payments*		£
1 Jan	Balance b/d	800.50	2 Jan	A Arthur Ltd	001351	100.00
6 Jan	J Baker	495.60	10 Jan	C Curtis	001352	398.50
31 Jan	G Shotton Ltd	335.75	13 Jan	Donald & Co	001353	229.70
			14 Jan	Bryant & Sons	001354	312.00
			23 Jan	P Reid	001355	176.50
			31 Jan	Balance c/d		415.15
		1,631.85				1,631.85

He received his bank statement which showed the following transactions for January 20-7:

BANK STATEMENT

		Payments	*Receipts*	*Balance*
20-7		£	£	£
1 Jan	Balance brought forward			800.50 CR
6 Jan	Cheque no. 001351	100.00		700.50 CR
6 Jan	Credit		495.60	1,196.10 CR
13 Jan	BACS credit: T K Supplies		716.50	1,912.60 CR
20 Jan	Cheque no. 001352	398.50		1,514.10 CR
23 Jan	Direct debit: Omni Finance	207.95		1,306.15 CR
24 Jan	Cheque no. 001353	229.70		1,076.45 CR

You are to:

(a) write the cash book up-to-date at 31 January 20-7

(b) prepare a bank reconciliation statement at 31 January 20-7

10.3 The bank columns of Jane Doyle's cash book for May 20-7 are as follows:

20-7	*Receipts*	*£*	*20-7*	*Payments*		*£*
1 May	Balance b/d	300	2 May	P Stone	867714	28
7 May	Cash	162	14 May	Alpha Ltd	867715	50
16 May	C Brewster	89	29 May	E Deakin	867716	110
23 May	Cash	60				
30 May	Cash	40				

She received her bank statement which showed the following transactions for May 20-7:

BANK STATEMENT

		Payments	*Receipts*	*Balance*
20-7		£	£	£
1 May	Balance brought forward			300 CR
5 May	Cheque no. 867714	28		272 CR
7 May	Credit		162	434 CR
16 May	Standing order: A-Z Insurance	25		409 CR
19 May	Credit		89	498 CR
20 May	Cheque no. 867715	50		448 CR
26 May	Credit		60	508 CR
31 May	Bank Charges	10		498 CR

You are to:

(a) write the cash book up-to-date at 31 May 20-7

(b) prepare a bank reconciliation statement at 31 May 20-7

10.4* On 4 June Milestone Motors received a bank statement which showed the following transactions for May 20-4:

BANK STATEMENT		Paid out	Paid in	Balance
20-4		£	£	£
1 May	Balance brought forward			3,652 C
10 May	Cheque no 451762	751		2,901 C
11 May	Cheque no 451763	268		2,633 C
13 May	Cheque no 451765	1,045		1,588 C
14 May	BACS credit: Perran Taxis		2,596	4,184 C
18 May	Direct debit: Wyvern Council	198		3,986 C
20 May	Direct debit: A1 Insurance	1,005		2,981 C
25 May	Direct debit: Okaro and Company	254		2,727 C
25 May	Bank charges	20		2,707 C
D = Debit C = Credit				

The cash book of Milestone Motors as at 31 May 20-4 is shown below:

CASH BOOK

Date	Details	Bank	Date	Cheque no	Details	Bank
20-4		£	20-4			£
1 May	Balance b/f	3,652	4 May	451762	Smith and Company	751
26 May	J Ackland	832	4 May	451763	Bryant Limited	268
28 May	Stamp Limited	1,119	7 May	451764	Curtis Cars	1,895
			7 May	451765	Parts Supplies	1,045

You are to:

(a) check the items on the bank statement against the items in the cash book

(b) update the cash book as needed

(c) total the cash book and show clearly the balance carried down at 31 May and brought down at 1 June

(d) prepare a bank reconciliation statement at 31 May 20-4 which agrees the bank statement balance with the cash book balance

10.5

When reconciling bank statements the adjustments will include entries in the cash book for standing orders, direct debits and credit transfers.

REQUIRED

(a) Explain what each of these terms means and whether they will be **debited** or **credited** to the bank account in the business's books.

(i) Standing orders

....

....

....

(ii) Direct debits

....

....

....

(iii) Credit transfers

....

....

....

The bank statement statement received by A Smith and Co shows a debit balance of £600 at 31 March 2001. The accountant checks it against the cash book and makes the following discoveries:

(1) The bank statement shows the following items **not** shown in the cash book:

- a standing order for £230 in favour of Planet Insurance;
- a direct debit payable to Electric Supplies £420;
- a credit transfer has been received from The Best Co for £540;
- a cheque for £265 is debited on the bank statement, which A Smith and Co are querying;
- bank charges of £46 have been levied.

(2) The cash book has an overdrawn balance of £378 and shows the following items **not** shown on the bank statement:

- unpresented cheques amounting to £469;
- uncleared bankings of £270.

REQUIRED

(b) Make any necessary entries in the cash book.

Dr **Cash Book – Bank Account** Cr

	£		£

(c) Prepare a bank reconciliation as at 31 March 2001.

Assessment and Qualifications Alliance (AQA), 2001

10.6* Wholesale Car Spares has received its bank statement for the month ending 31 October 2000 which shows a balance at the bank of £4,213 in its favour.

REQUIRED

(a) Prepare a bank reconciliation statement for Wholesale Car Spares as at 31 October 2000.

1. The bank statement shows the following items not yet in the cash book:
   - a standing order of £465.00 to Landlord Properties for rent
   - a credit transfer for £304.00 from a customer ABC Garages
2. The cash book reveals the following cheque which is unpresented:
   - A B Mechanics £67.89
3. There is a cheque paid for £500.00 on the debit of the bank statement which Wholesale Car Spares believes has been entered by the bank into this account in error.
4. There is a dishonoured cheque for £45.67, which has not been previously notified to Wholesale Car Spares. This cheque had been received from a customer.

(b) Which items will Wholesale Car Spares now enter in their cash book?

Item	Yes/No	Debit/Credit
Standing order		
Credit transfer		
Cheques: A B Mechanics		
£500.00		
£45.67		

(c) Two of the above items need further investigation. Describe what further action you would take, giving your reasons.

Assessment and Qualifications Alliance (AQA), 2001

11 INTRODUCING COMPUTER ACCOUNTING

Although some businesses, particularly small ones, still use paper-based accounting systems, an increasing number are now operating computerised accounting systems. Small and medium-sized businesses can buy 'off-the shelf' accounting programs from suppliers such as Sage while larger businesses often have custom-designed programs.

The accounting programs carry out functions such as invoicing, dealing with payments, paying wages and providing regular accounting reports such as trading and profit and loss accounts and balance sheets.

Businesses also make considerable use of computer spreadsheets, particularly for budgets. They can also be used for speeding up the processes in manual accounting systems, setting up a trial balance, for example.

The introduction of a computer accounting system can provide major advantages such as speed and accuracy of operation. There are also certain disadvantages, such as cost and training needs which the management of a business must appreciate before taking the decision to convert from a manual to a computerised accounting system.

FEATURES OF COMPUTER ACCOUNTING

facilities

A typical computer accounting program will offer a number of facilities:

- on-screen input and printout of sales invoices
- automatic updating of customer accounts in the sales ledger
- recording of suppliers' invoices
- automatic updating of supplier accounts in the purchases ledger
- recording of bank receipts
- making payments to suppliers and for expenses
- automatic updating of the general (nominal) ledger
- automatic adjustment of stock records

Payroll can also be computerised – often on a separate program.

management reports

A computer accounting program can provide instant reports for management, for example:

- aged debtors' summary – a summary of customer accounts, showing overdue amounts
- trial balance, trading and profit and loss account and balance sheet
- stock valuation
- VAT Return
- payroll analysis

computer accounting – ledger system

We have already have covered the 'Ledger' in Chapter 6. The 'Ledger' – which basically means 'the books of the business' is a term used to describe the way the accounts of the business are grouped into different sections:

- **sales ledger**, containing the accounts of debtors (customers)
- **purchases ledger**, containing the accounts of creditors (suppliers)
- **cash books**, containing the main cash book and the petty cash book
- **general ledger** (also called nominal ledger) containing the remaining accounts, eg expenses (including purchases), income (including sales), assets, loans, stock, VAT

The screens of a ledger computer accounting system are designed to be user-friendly. Look at the toolbar of the opening screen of a Sage™accounting system shown below and then read the notes printed underneath.

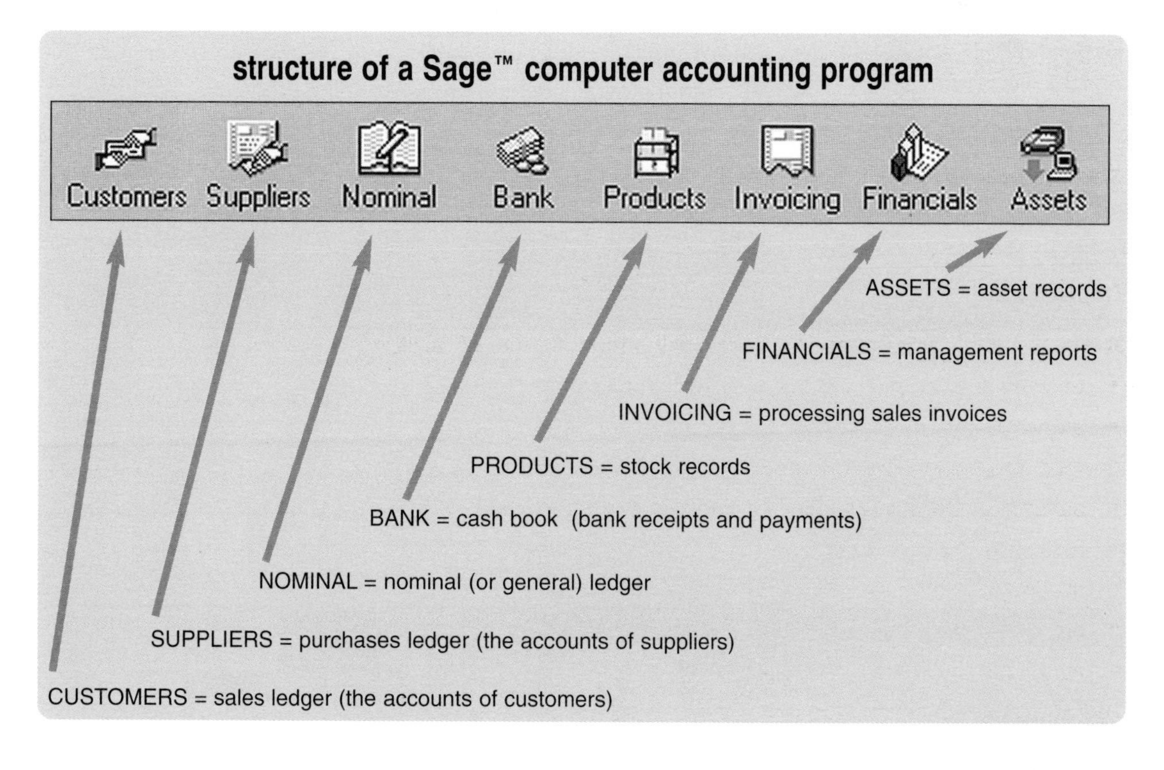

using a computer accounting system

Computer input screens are designed to be easy to use. Their main advantage is that each transaction needs only to be input once, unlike in a manual double-entry system where two or three entries are required. In the example below, payment is made for copy paper costing £45.50. The input line includes the nominal account number of bank account (1200), the date of payment, the cheque number (234234), and the nominal account code for stationery expenses (7500). The net amount of £45.50 is entered and the computer automatically calculates the VAT. The appropriate amounts are then transferred by the computer to bank account, stationery expenses account and VAT account.

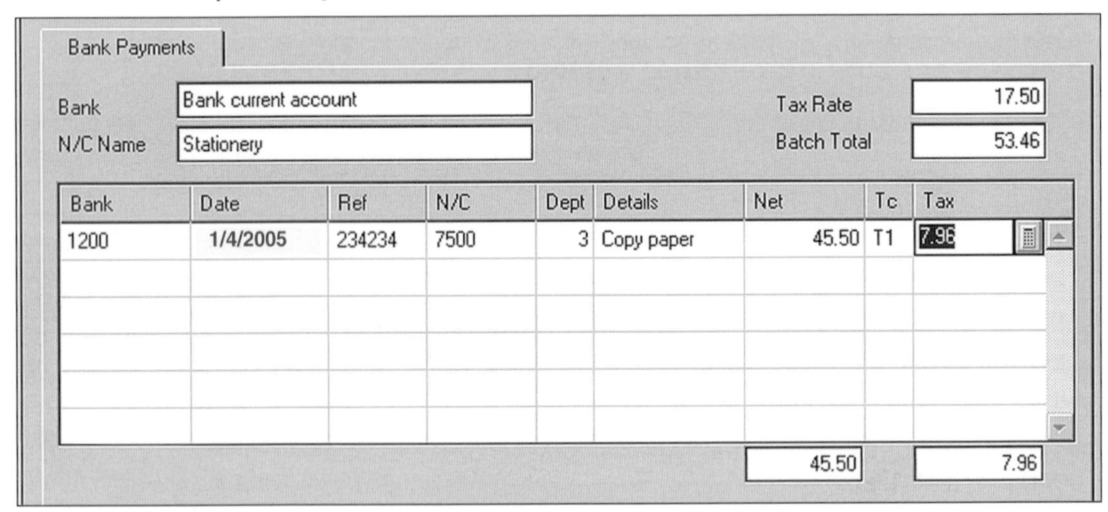

The screen below shows an invoice input screen. In this example 20 Enigma 35s are being invoiced to R Patel & Co in Salisbury. The computer will in due course print the invoice, which will contain the name of the seller as well as all the customer details held in the accounting program's database.

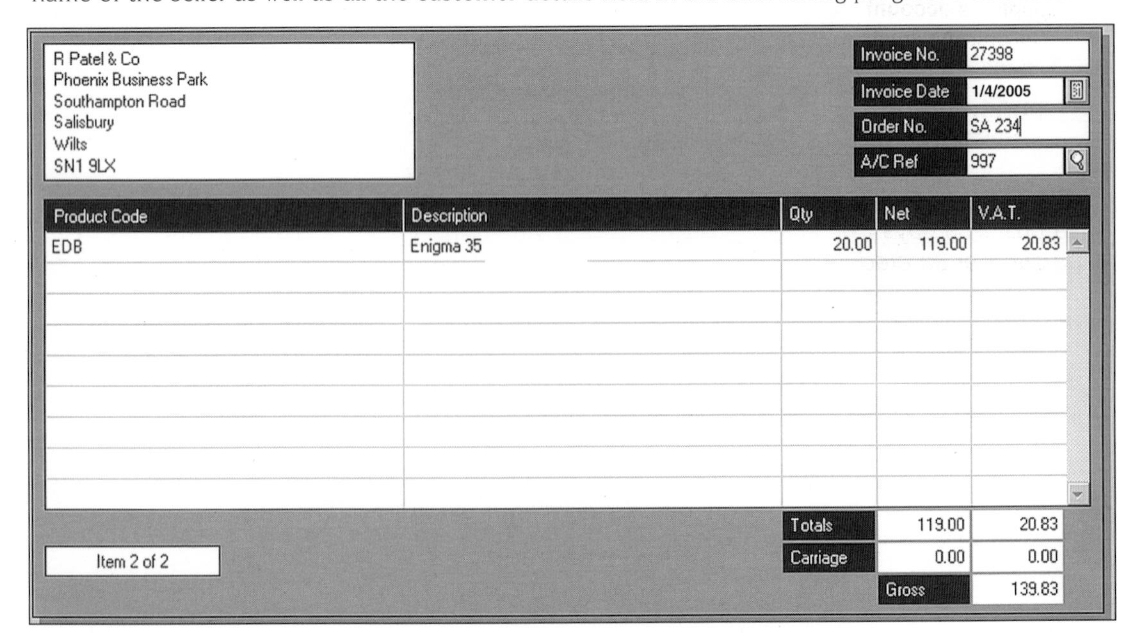

computerised ledgers – an integrated system

A computerised ledger system is **fully integrated**. This means that when a business transaction is input on the computer it is recorded in a number of different accounting records at the same time. For example, when the sales invoice on the previous page is entered on the screen and the ledgers are 'updated' an integrated program will:

- record the amount of the invoice in the customer account R Patel & Co in the sales ledger
- record the amount of the invoice in the sales account and VAT account (if appropriate) in the general ledger
- reduce the stock of goods held (in this case Enigmas) in the stock records

At the centre of an integrated program is the nominal ledger which deals with all the accounts except customers' accounts and suppliers' accounts. It is affected one way or another by most transactions.

The diagram below shows how the three 'ledgers' can link with the nominal (general) ledger. You can see how an account in the nominal ledger is affected by each of these three transactions. This is the double-entry book-keeping system at work. The advantage of the computer system is that in each case only one entry has to be made. Life is made a great deal simpler by this.

Note that VAT account is omitted from this diagram for the sake of simplicity of illustration. VAT account will be maintained in the nominal (general) ledger and will be updated by all three of the transactions shown.

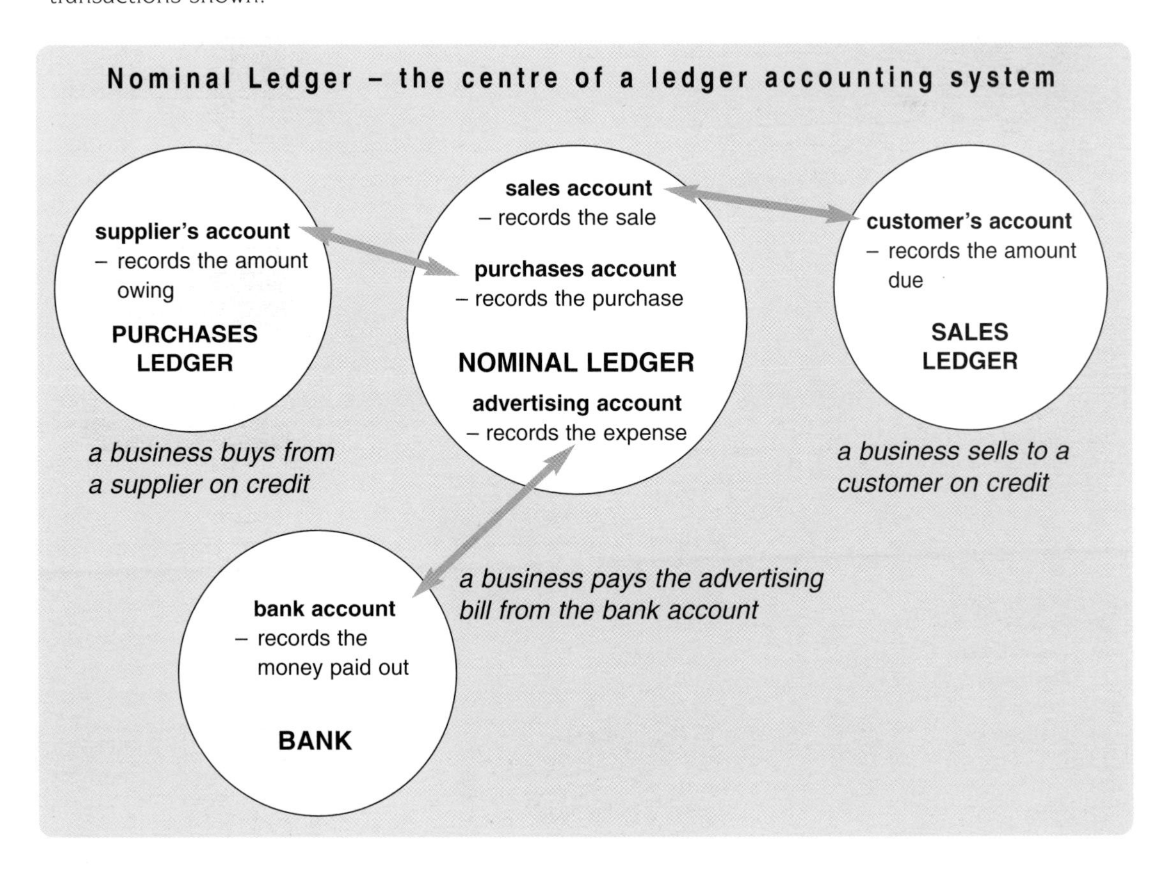

Computer Spreadsheets

A spreadsheet is a grid of boxes – 'cells' – set up on the computer, organised in rows and columns into which you can enter text and numbers. It enables you to make calculations with the figures. The computer program will work out the calculations automatically once you have entered an appropriate formula in the cell where the result of the calculations is required.

The major advantage of a spreadsheet is that if you change any of the figures the computer will automatically recalculate the total, saving you much time and effort.

Spreadsheets are used for a variety of functions in business:

- producing invoices – working out costs of products sold, calculating and adding on VAT and producing a sales total
- working out budgets for future expenditure
- working out sales figures for different products or areas

A commonly used spreadsheet program is Microsoft Excel.

Spreadsheets may be used in a wide variety of accounting functions. The first of the two examples illustrated here is very simple: it shows the two columns of a **trial balance**. The spreadsheet has been set up with columns for account names, debit balances, credit balances and totals for the columns. When the figures have been entered, they will automatically produce totals which should balance.

	A	B	C	D	E	F	G
1		Dr	Cr				
2							
3							
4	Plant and machinery	35000					
5	Office equipment	15000					
6	Furniture and fixtures	25000					
7	Debtors control account	45500					
8	Bank current account	12450					
9	Creditors control account		32510				
10	Sales tax control account		17920				
11	Purchase tax control account	26600					
12	Loans		35000				
13	Ordinary Shares		75000				
14	Hardware sales		85000				
15	Software sales		15000				
16	Computer consultancy		2400				
17	Materials purchased	69100					
18	Advertising	12400					
19	Gross wages	16230					
20	Rent	4500					
21	General rates	450					
22	Electricity	150					
23	Telephone	275					
24	Stationery	175					
25							
26							
27	Total	262830	262830				

The second example of a computer spreadsheet used in the accounting process is a form of budget known as a **cash flow forecast**. This is a projection of the cash inflows and outflows of a business over a period of months. Each month the spreadsheet calculates the total inflow (row 11) and outflow (row 23) and uses them to calculate the net cash inflow/outflow (row 24). This figure is then used to calculate the projected bank balance of the business (row 26). This figure is useful as it will show if the business needs to borrow from the bank.

The advantage of the spreadsheet in this example is that if the business wishes to change any of the receipt or payment amounts – eg if the sales receipts increase – then the cashflow figures will automatically be recalculated, potentially saving hours of work.

	A	B	C	D	E	F	G
1	**CORIANNE LIMITED**						
2	**Cash flow forecast for the six months ending June 2004**						
3		JANUARY	FEBRUARY	MARCH	APRIL	MAY	JUNE
4		£	£	£	£	£	£
5	*Receipts*						
6							
7							
8	Sales Receipts	3,000	3,000	4,000	4,000	4,000	4,000
9							
10	Capital	10,000					
11	TOTAL RECEIPTS	13,000	3,000	4,000	4,000	4,000	4,000
12	*Payments*						
13	Purchases	5,000	1,750	1,750		1,750	1,750
14	Fixed Assets	4,500	5,250				
15	Rent/Rates	575	575	575	575	575	575
16	Insurance	50	50	50	50	50	50
17	Electricity	25	25	25	25	25	25
18	Telephone	150	15	15	15	15	15
19	Stationery	10	10	10	10	10	10
20	Postage	15	15	15	15	15	15
21	Bank charges	100		75			75
22	Advertising	150	30	30	30	30	30
23	TOTAL PAYMENTS	10,575	7,720	2,545	720	2,470	2,545
24	CASHFLOW FOR MONTH	2,425	- 4,720	1,455	3,280	1,530	1,455
25	Bank Balance *brought forward*	-	2,425	- 2,295	- 840	2,440	3,970
26	Bank Balance *carried forward*	2,425	- 2,295	- 840	2,440	3,970	5,425

ADVANTAGES AND DISADVANTAGES OF COMPUTER ACCOUNTING

In this chapter so far we have stressed the advantages of the introduction of computers to carry out accounting functions in a business. There are, however, some disadvantages as well, and any business introducing computer accounting will need to weigh up carefully the 'pros and cons'. This is an area which has featured in past examinations.

The remainder of this chapter will deal with these advantages and disadvantages and provide an example in the form of a Worked Example based on the effect on employees of the introduction of a new computer accounting system.

advantages of computer accounting

The main advantages of using a computer accounting program such as Sage include:

- **speed** – data entry on the computer with its formatted screens and built-in databases of customer and supplier details and stock records can be carried out far more quickly than any manual processing
- **automatic document production** – fast and accurate invoice and credit note printing, statement runs, payroll processing
- **accuracy** – there is less room for error as only one account entry is needed for each transaction rather than the two (or three) required in a manual double-entry system
- **up-to-date information** – the accounting records are automatically updated and so account balances (eg customer accounts) will always be up-to-date
- **availability of information** – the data can be made available to different users at the same time
- **management information** – reports can be produced which will help management monitor and control the business, for example the aged debtors analysis which shows which customer accounts are overdue, trial balance, trading and profit and loss account and balance sheet
- **VAT return** – the automatic production of figures for the regular VAT return
- **legibility** – the onscreen and printed data should always be legible and so will avoid errors caused by poor figures
- **efficiency** – better use is made of resources and time; cash flow should improve through better debt collection
- **staff motivation** – the system will require staff to be trained to use new skills, which can make them feel more valued

disadvantages of computer accounting

The main disadvantages of using computer accounting programs include:

- **capital cost of installation** – the hardware and software will need to be budgeted for, not only as 'one-off' expenditure but also as recurrent costs because computers will need replacing and software updating
- **cost of training** – the staff will need to be trained in the use of the hardware and software
- **staff opposition** – motivation may suffer as some staff do not like computers, also there may be staff redundancies, all of which create bad feeling
- **disruption** – loss of work time and changes in the working environment when the computerised system is first introduced
- **system failure** – the danger of the system crashing and the subsequent loss of work when no back-ups have been made
- **back-up requirements** – the need to keep regular and secure back-ups in case of system failure
- **breaches of security** – the danger of people hacking into the system from outside, the danger of viruses, the incidence of staff fraud
- **health** dangers – the problems of bad backs, eyestrain and muscular complaints such as RSI

WORKED EXAMPLE

situation

Stitch-in-time Limited is an old-fashioned company which manufactures sewing machines. The Finance Director, Charles Cotton, is considering the introduction of a computer accounting system which will completely replace the existing manual double-entry system.

He is worried because he knows that the proposition will not go down very well with employees who have been with the company for a long time.

He asks you to prepare notes in which you are to set out:

(a) the benefits to staff of the new scheme

(b) the likely causes of staff dissatisfaction with the new scheme

solution

(a) **potential benefits to staff**

- the staff will be able to update their skills
- they will receive training
- they may get an increase in pay
- the training will increase their career prospects
- they will be motivated
- they will get job satisfaction

(b) **causes of staff dissatisfaction**

- staff prefer doing the job in a way which is familiar to them
- they do not like computers
- they may see their jobs threatened as they worry that redundancies will occur
- they do not look forward to the disruption at the time of the changeover
- they worry about the possible bad effects to their health, having heard about RSI (Repetitive Strain Injury) and radiation and eye damage from computer screens
- they will be demotivated as they consider the new system 'mechanical' – they will have to sit in front of a computer for hours at a time and not be able to communicate so well with their colleagues as they have in the past

CHAPTER SUMMARY

- Computer accounting systems save businesses time and money by automating many accounting processes, including the production of reports for management.
- Most computer accounting programs are based on the ledger system and integrate a number of different functions – one transaction will change accounting data in a number of different parts of the system.
- The different functions can include: sales ledger, purchases ledger, nominal (general) ledger, cash and bank payments, stock control, invoicing, report production
- It is common for a payroll processing program to be linked to the nominal ledger of a computer accounting program.
- Computer spreadsheets are often also used to carry out individual functions in an accounting system, for example the creation of budgets.
- A business must consider carefully all the advantages and disadvantages of computer accounting before installing a computerised system. The main advantages are speed, accuracy, availability of up-to-date information; the main disadvantages are cost, security implications and possible opposition from employees.

In the next chapter we look at how businesses present their final accounts at the end of each financial year.

QUESTIONS

NOTE: an asterisk (*) after the question number means that an answer to the question is given at the end of this book.

11.1* Explain **two** advantages to a business of using a computer accounting system to record financial transactions.

11.2* Describe **two** advantages of using a computer spreadsheet for a document such as a cash-flow forecast.

11.3* Explain how **three** different areas of the accounting system might benefit from the introduction of computer accounting.

11.4* A business is planning to introduce a computer accounting system and holds an employee meeting to explain the implications of the change. One employee asks 'I have heard that there are all sorts of risks to the computer data which could cause us to lose the lot.' Describe **two** of the main risks to the security of computer data.

11.5* You are the Accounts Manager of a large company which imports and supplies computer games to UK retailers. You want to introduce an integrated computer accounting system throughout the company.

Explain the advantages you would point out to the line manager of the Sales Ledger section to persuade her that the new system would help her staff in processing orders and producing financial documents.

11.6 Kings Products is considering the computerisation of its accounting functions.

REQUIRED

Write a report advising Kings Products on the advantages and disadvantages to the business of this proposal.

To: .... Date: ....

From: ....

Subject: ....

....

....

....

....

....

Assessment and Qualifications Alliance (AQA), 2001

11.7* Gerry Mann is the Finance Director of Colourways Limited, a design company. He wants to introduce a computer accounting system into the business, but is encountering opposition from Helen Baxill, an active trade union member who works in the Finance Department.

Describe:

(a) the objections relating to staff working conditions and welfare that Helen is likely to raise to try and block the introduction of a computer system

(b) the advantages to staff of a computer system that Gerry could use to persuade Helen to accept its introduction

12 FINAL ACCOUNTS

For most businesses, the final accounts, which are produced at the end of each financial year, comprise:

- trading account
- profit and loss account
- balance sheet

Final accounts can be presented in a vertical format, or a horizontal format. In this chapter we shall look at both. The vertical format, however, is more common nowadays and is used as the standard format in this book.

FINAL ACCOUNTS AND THE TRIAL BALANCE

So far we have looked at the format of financial accounts and the recording of different types of transactions. All that we have covered is usually carried out by the book-keeper. We will now see how the financial accountant takes to a further stage the information prepared by the book-keeper. The financial accountant will use the information from the accounting system, which is summarised in the trial balance (see Chapter 5), in order to produce the final accounts of a business.

The final accounts can be produced more often than once a year in order to give information to the owner(s) on how the business is progressing. However, it is customary to produce annual or final accounts for the benefit of the Inland Revenue, bank manager and other interested parties.

The starting point for preparing final accounts is the trial balance prepared by the book-keeper. All the figures recorded on the trial balance are used in the final accounts. The trading account and the profit and loss account are both 'accounts' in terms of double-entry book-keeping. This means that amounts recorded in these accounts must also be recorded elsewhere in the book-keeping system. By contrast, the balance sheet is not an account, but is simply a statement of account balances remaining after the trading and profit and loss accounts have been prepared.

To help us with the preparation of final accounts we will use the trial balance, shown on the next page, which has been produced by the book-keeper at the end of the firm's financial year.

TRIAL BALANCE OF WYVERN WHOLESALERS AS AT 31 DECEMBER 20-1

	Dr	Cr
	£	£
Sales		250,000
Purchases	156,000	
Sales returns	5,400	
Purchases returns		7,200
Discount received		2,500
Discount allowed	3,700	
Stock at 1 January 20-1	12,350	
Salaries	46,000	
Electricity and gas	3,000	
Rent and rates	2,000	
Sundry expenses	4,700	
Premises	100,000	
Equipment	30,000	
Vehicles	21,500	
Debtors	23,850	
Bank overdraft		851
Cash	125	
Creditors		12,041
Value Added Tax		3,475
Capital		110,000
Drawings	10,442	
Long-term loan		33,000
	419,067	419,067

Note: stock at 31 December 20-1 was valued at £16,300

You will see that the trial balance includes the stock value at the start of the year, while the end-of-year valuation is noted after the trial balance. For the purposes of financial accounting, the stock of goods for resale is valued by the business (and often verified by the auditor) at the end of each financial year, and the valuation is entered into the book-keeping system (see page 171). We will present the final accounts

- before adjustments for items such as accruals, prepayments, depreciation of fixed assets, bad debts written off, and provision for doubtful debts (each of which will be dealt with in Module 3)
- in vertical format, ie in columnar form (the alternative layout – horizontal format – is looked at on page 174)

On page 171 we will look at the double-entry book-keeping for amounts entered in the trading and profit and loss accounts.

Trading Account

The main activity of a trading business is to buy goods at one price and then to sell the same goods at a higher price. The difference between the two prices represents a profit known as *gross profit*. Instead of calculating the gross profit on each item bought and sold, we have seen how the book-keeping system stores up the totals of transactions for the year in either purchases account or sales account. Further, any goods returned are recorded in either purchases returns account or sales returns account.

At the end of the financial year (which can end at any date – it doesn't have to be the calendar year) the total of purchases and sales accounts, together with purchases returns and sales returns, are used to form the trading account. It is also necessary to take note of the value of stock of goods for resale held at the beginning and end of the financial year.

The trading account is set out as follows:

TRADING ACCOUNT OF WYVERN WHOLESALERS
FOR THE YEAR ENDED 31 DECEMBER 20-1

	£	£	£
Sales			250,000
Less Sales returns			5,400
Net sales (or turnover)			244,600
Opening stock (1 January 20-1)		12,350	
Purchases	156,000		
Carriage in	–		
Less Purchases returns	7,200		
Net purchases		148,800	
		161,150	
Less Closing stock (31 December 20-1)		16,300	
Cost of sales			144,850
Gross profit			99,750

notes on trading account

- **Sales and purchases** only include items in which the business trades – items to be kept for use in the business, such as machinery, are not included in sales and purchases but are classified as fixed assets.
- **Adjustments** are made for the value of stock in the store or warehouse at the beginning and end of the financial year. The opening stock is added to the purchases because it has been sold during the year. The closing stock is deducted from purchases because it has not been sold; it will form the opening stock for the next financial year, when it will be added to next year's figure for purchases.

- The figure for **cost of sales** (often written as 'cost of goods sold') represents the cost to the business of the goods which have been sold in this financial year. Cost of sales is:

  opening stock
  + purchases
  + carriage in (see below)
  – purchases returns
  – closing stock
  = cost of sales (or cost of goods sold)

- **Gross profit** is calculated as:

  sales
  – sales returns
  = net sales
  – cost of sales
  = gross profit

  If cost of sales is greater than net sales, the business has made a *gross loss*.

- **Carriage in** is the expense to the business of having purchases delivered (eg if you buy from a mail order company, you often have to pay the post and packing – this is the 'carriage in' cost). The cost of carriage in is added to purchases.

- **Net sales** (often described as turnover) is:

  sales
  – sales returns
  = net sales

- **Net purchases** is:

  purchases
  + carriage in
  – purchases returns
  = net purchases

Profit and Loss Account

In the profit and loss account are listed the various overheads (or expenses) of running the business. The total of overheads is deducted from gross profit to give net profit for the year. Net profit is an important figure: it shows the profitability of the business after all expenses, and how much has been earned by the business for the owner(s). It is on this profit, after certain adjustments, that the tax liability will be based.

The profit and loss account follows on from the trading account and is set out as follows:

PROFIT AND LOSS ACCOUNT OF WYVERN WHOLESALERS
FOR THE YEAR ENDED 31 DECEMBER 20-1

	£	£	£
Gross profit			99,750
Add Discount received			2,500
			102,250
Less overheads:			
Discount allowed		3,700	
Salaries		46,000	
Electricity and gas		3,000	
Rent and rates		2,000	
Sundry expenses		4,700	
			59,400
Net profit			42,850

Notes:

- The various overheads shown in the profit and loss account can be listed to suit the needs of a particular business: the headings used here are for illustrative purposes only.
- Amounts of income are also included in profit and loss account, eg discount received in the example; these are added to gross profit.
- The net profit is the amount the business earned for the owner(s) during the year; it is important to note that this is not the amount by which the cash/bank balance has increased during the year.
- If the total of overheads exceeds gross profit (and other income), the business has made a net loss.
- Drawings by the owner(s) are not listed as an overhead in profit and loss account – instead, they are deducted from capital (see balance sheet on page 168).
- If the owner of the business has taken goods for his or her own use, the amount should be deducted from purchases and added to drawings.

The trading account and the profit and loss account are usually combined together, rather than being shown as separate accounts, as shown in the 'vertical format' at the top of the next page.

The trading and profit and loss account forms part of the double-entry book-keeping system (see page 171) and can also be set out in 'horizontal' format (page 174).

service sector businesses

You should note that when preparing the final accounts of a service sector business – such as a secretarial agency, a firm of solicitors, an estate agency, a doctors' practice – a trading account will not be prepared because, instead of trading in goods, the business supplies services. Thus the final accounts will consist of a profit and loss account and balance sheet. The profit and loss account, instead of starting with gross profit, will commence with the income from the business activity, such as 'fees', 'income from clients', 'charges', 'work done'. Other items of income, such as discount received, are added, and the overheads are then listed and deducted to give the net profit, or net loss, for the accounting period. An example is shown at the bottom of the next page.

TRADING AND PROFIT AND LOSS ACCOUNT OF WYVERN WHOLESALERS
FOR THE YEAR ENDED 31 DECEMBER 20-1

	£	£	£
Sales			250,000
Less Sales returns			5,400
Net sales			244,600
Opening stock (1 January 20-1)		12,350	
Purchases	156,000		
Carriage in	–		
Less Purchases returns	7,200		
Net purchases		148,800	
		161,150	
Less Closing stock (31 December 20-1)		16,300	
Cost of sales			144,850
Gross profit			99,750
Add Discount received			2,500
			102,250
Less overheads:			
Discount allowed		3,700	
Salaries		46,000	
Electricity and gas		3,000	
Rent and rates		2,000	
Sundry expenses		4,700	
			59,400
Net profit			42,850

PROFIT AND LOSS ACCOUNT OF WYVERN SECRETARIAL AGENCY
FOR THE YEAR ENDED 31 DECEMBER 20-1

	£	£
Income from clients		110,000
Less overheads:		
Salaries	64,000	
Heating and Lighting	2,000	
Telephone	2,000	
Rent and Rates	6,000	
Sundry Expenses	3,000	
		77,000
Net profit		33,000

BALANCE SHEET

The trading and profit and loss account shows two types of profit – gross profit and net profit, respectively – for the financial year (or such other time period as may be chosen by the business). A balance sheet, by contrast, shows the state of the business at one moment in time. It lists the assets and the liabilities at a particular date, but is not part of the double-entry book-keeping system.

The balance sheet of Wyvern Wholesalers, using the figures from the trial balance on page 163, is as follows:

BALANCE SHEET OF WYVERN WHOLESALERS
AS AT 31 DECEMBER 20-1

	£	£	£
Fixed Assets			
Premises			100,000
Equipment			30,000
Vehicles			21,500
			151,500
Current Assets			
Stock		16,300	
Debtors		23,850	
Cash		125	
		40,275	
Less Current Liabilities			
Creditors	12,041		
Value Added Tax	3.475		
Bank overdraft	851		
		16,367	
Working Capital or Net Current Assets			23,908
			175,408
Less Long-term Liabilities			
Loan			33,000
NET ASSETS			142,408
FINANCED BY			
Capital			
Opening capital			110,000
Add net profit			42,850
			152,850
Less drawings			10,442
			142,408

notes on the balance sheet

- **assets**

  Assets are items or amounts owned or owed to the business, and are normally listed in increasing order of liquidity, ie the most permanent assets are listed first.

  Fixed assets are long-term assets purchased for use in the business and used over a long period (more than 12 months) to generate profits. They are divided between tangible fixed assets, which have material substance such as premises, equipment, vehicles, and intangible fixed assets, such as goodwill (see below).

  Current assets are short-term assets held for less than 12 months. They change continually from day-to-day, such as stock (which will be sold and replaced with new stock), debtors (who will pay the amounts due and will be replaced by further amounts as credit sales are made), bank (if not overdrawn) and cash. The balance of VAT account is a current asset if the account has a debit balance, ie an amount is due from HM Revenue & Customs.

- **intangible fixed assets**

  Intangible fixed assets (not shown in the balance sheet above) will appear on some balance sheets, and are listed before the tangible fixed assets. An intangible asset does not have material substance, but belongs to the business and has value. A common example of an intangible fixed asset is goodwill, which is where a business has bought another business and paid an agreed amount for the existing reputation and customer connections (the goodwill).

- **liabilities**

  Liabilities are items or amounts owed by the business.

  Current liabilities are amounts owing at the balance sheet date and due for repayment within 12 months or less (eg creditors, Value Added Tax, bank overdraft).

  Long-term liabilities are where repayment is due in more than 12 months (eg loans, bank loans).

- **capital and working capital**

  Capital is money owed by the business to the owner. It is usual practice to show on the balance sheet the owner's investment at the start of the year plus net profit for the year less drawings for the year; this equals the owner's investment at the end of the year, ie at the balance sheet date.

  Working capital – often referred to as net current assets – is the excess of current assets over current liabilities. Without working capital, a business cannot continue to operate.

significance of the balance sheet

The balance sheet shows the assets used by the business and how they have been financed:

	Fixed assets
plus	Working capital
less	Long-term liabilities
equals	Net assets
equals	Capital

The vertical presentation balance sheet agrees the figure for net assets (£142,408), with capital. An alternative style of balance sheet – the horizontal presentation – is shown on page 174.

Preparation of Final Accounts from a Trial Balance

The trial balance contains the basic figures necessary to prepare the final accounts but, as we shall see in the next section, the figures are transferred from the double-entry accounts of the business. Nevertheless, the trial balance is a suitable summary from which to prepare the final accounts. The information needed for the preparation of each of the final accounts needs to be picked out from the trial balance in the following way:

- go through the trial balance and write against the items the final account in which each appears
- 'tick' each figure as it is used – each item from the trial balance appears in the final accounts once only
- the year end (closing) stock figure is not listed in the trial balance, but is shown as a note; the closing stock appears twice in the final accounts – firstly in the trading account, and secondly in the balance sheet (as a current asset).

If this routine is followed with the trial balance of Wyvern Wholesalers, it then appears as follows:

TRIAL BALANCE OF WYVERN WHOLESALERS AS AT 31 DECEMBER 20-1

	Dr	Cr		
	£	£		
Sales		250,000	T	✔
Purchases	156,000		T	✔
Sales returns	5,400		T	✔
Purchases returns		7,200	T	✔
Discount received		2,500	P & L *(income)*	✔
Discount allowed	3,700		P & L *(expense)*	✔
Stock 1 January 20-1	12,350		T	✔
Salaries	46,000		P & L *(expense)*	✔
Electricity and gas	3,000		P & L *(expense)*	✔
Rent and rates	2,000		P & L *(expense)*	✔
Sundry expenses	4,700		P & L *(expense)*	✔
Premises	100,000		BS *(fixed asset)*	✔
Equipment	30,000		BS *(fixed asset)*	✔
Vehicles	21,500		BS *(fixed asset)*	✔
Debtors	23,850		BS *(current asset)*	✔
Bank overdraft		851	BS *(current liability)*	✔
Cash	125		BS *(current asset)*	✔
Creditors		12,041	BS *(current liability)*	✔
Value Added Tax		3,475	BS *(current liability)*	✔
Capital		110,000	BS *(capital)*	✔
Drawings	10,442		BS *(capital)*	✔
Long-term loan		33,000	BS *(long-term liability)*	✔
	419,067	419,067		
Stock at 31 December 20-1 was valued at £16,300			T	✔
			BS *(current asset)*	✔

Note: T = trading account; P & L = profit and loss account; BS = balance sheet

DOUBLE-ENTRY BOOK-KEEPING AND THE FINAL ACCOUNTS

We have already noted earlier in this chapter that the trading and profit and loss account forms part of the double-entry book-keeping system. Therefore, each amount recorded in this account must have an opposite entry elsewhere in the accounting system. In preparing the trading and profit and loss account we are, in effect, emptying each account that has been storing up a record of the transactions of the business during the course of the financial year and transferring it to the trading and profit and loss account.

trading account

In the trading account of Wyvern Wholesalers the balance of purchases account is transferred as follows (debit trading account; credit purchases account):

Purchases Account

Dr					Cr
20-1		£	20-1		£
31 Dec	Balance b/d (ie total for year)	156,000	31 Dec	Trading account	156,000

The account now has a nil balance and is ready to receive the transactions for next year.

The balances of sales, sales returns, and purchases returns accounts are cleared to nil in a similar way and the amounts transferred to trading account, as debits or credits as appropriate.

Stock account, however, is dealt with differently. Stock is valued for financial accounting purposes at the end of each year (it is also likely to be valued more regularly in order to provide management information). Only the annual stock valuation is recorded in stock account, and the account is not used at any other time. After the book-keeper has extracted the trial balance, but before preparation of the trading account, the stock account appears as follows:

Stock Account

Dr					Cr
20-1		£	20-1		£
31 Dec	Balance b/d	12,350			

This balance, which is the opening stock valuation for the year, is transferred to the trading account to leave a nil balance, as follows (debit trading account; credit stock account):

Stock Account

Dr					Cr
20-1		£	20-1		£
31 Dec	Balance b/d	12,350	31 Dec	Trading account	12,350

The closing stock valuation for the year is now recorded on the account as an asset (debit stock account; credit trading account):

Stock Account

Dr					Cr
20-1		£	20-1		£
31 Dec	Balance b/d	12,350	31 Dec	Trading account	12,350
31 Dec	Trading account	16,300	31 Dec	Balance c/d	16,300
20-2					
1 Jan	Balance b/d	16,300			

The closing stock figure is shown on the balance sheet as a current asset, and will be the opening stock in next year's trading account.

profit and loss account

Overheads and income items are transferred from the double-entry accounts to the profit and loss account. For example, the salaries account of Wyvern Wholesalers has been storing up information during the year and, at the end of the year, the total is transferred to profit and loss account (debit profit and loss account; credit salaries account):

Salaries Account

Dr					Cr
20-1		£	20-1		£
31 Dec	Balance b/d (ie total for year)	46,000	31 Dec	Profit and loss account	46,000

The salaries account now has a nil balance and is ready to receive transactions for 20-2, the next financial year.

net profit

After the profit and loss account has been completed, the amount of net profit (or net loss) is transferred to the owner's capital account. The book-keeping entries are:

- **net profit**
  - debit profit and loss account
  - credit capital account

- **net loss**
  - debit capital account
  - credit profit and loss account

A net profit increases the owner's stake in the business by adding to capital account, while a net loss decreases the owner's stake.

drawings

At the same time the account for drawings, which has been storing up the amount of drawings during the year is also transferred to capital account:

- debit capital account
- credit drawings account

Thus the total of drawings for the year is debited to capital account.

capital account

When these transactions are completed, the capital account for Wyvern Wholesalers appears as:

Dr		**Capital Account**			Cr
20-1		£	20-1		£
31 Dec	Drawings for year	10,442	31 Dec	Balance b/d	110,000
31 Dec	Balance c/d	142,408	31 Dec	Profit and loss account (net profit for year)	42,850
		152,850			152,850
20-2			20-2		
			1 Jan	Balance b/d	142,408

Note: It is the balance of capital account at the end of the year, ie £142,408, which forms the total for the capital section of the balance sheet. Whilst this figure could be shown on the balance sheet by itself, it is usual to show capital at the start of the year, with net profit for the year added, and drawings for the year deducted. In this way, the capital account is summarised on the balance sheet.

balance sheet

Unlike the trading and profit and loss account, the balance sheet is not part of the double-entry accounts. The balance sheet is made up of those accounts which remain with balances after the trading and profit and loss account transfers have been made. Thus it consists of asset and liability accounts, including capital.

HORIZONTAL PRESENTATION OF FINAL ACCOUNTS

So far in this chapter we have used the vertical presentation for setting out the final accounts of a business, ie we have started at the top of the page and worked downwards in columnar or narrative style. An alternative method is the horizontal presentation, where each of the financial statements is presented in the format of a two-sided account. The set of final accounts presented earlier would appear, in horizontal style, as follows:

TRADING ACCOUNT OF WYVERN WHOLESALERS
FOR THE YEAR ENDED 31 DECEMBER 20-1

	£	£		£
Opening stock		12,350	Sales	250,000
Purchases	156,000		Less Sales returns	5,400
Carriage in	-		Net sales	244,600
Less Purchases returns	7,200			
Net purchases		148,800		
		161,150		
Less Closing stock		16,300		
Cost of sales		144,850		
Gross profit c/d		99,750		
		244,600		244,600

PROFIT AND LOSS ACCOUNT OF WYVERN WHOLESALERS
FOR THE YEAR ENDED 31 DECEMBER 20-1

	£		£
Discount allowed	3,700	Gross profit b/d	99,750
Salaries	46,000	Discount received	2,500
Electricity and gas	3,000		
Rent and rates	2,000		
Sundry expenses	4,700		
Net profit	42,850		
	102,250		102,250

BALANCE SHEET OF WYVERN WHOLESALERS
AS AT 31 DECEMBER 20-1

	£	£		£	£
Fixed Assets			**Capital**		
Premises		100,000	Opening capital		110,000
Equipment		30,000	Add net profit		42,850
Vehicles		21,500			152,850
		151,500	Less drawings		10,442
Current Assets					142,408
Stock	16,300		**Long-term Liabilities**		
Debtors	23,850		Loan		33,000
Cash	125				175,408
		40,275	**Current Liabilities**		
			Creditors	12,041	
			Value Added Tax	3,475	
			Bank overdraft	851	
					16,367
		191,775			191,775

a choice of formats

In your study of financial accounting you will see both forms of presentation from time-to-time in the accounts of different businesses. The vertical format is far more common nowadays and is used as the standard format in this book. As you will appreciate, both forms of presentation use the same information and, after a while, you will soon be able to 'read' either version.

a 'pro-forma' vertical presentation of final accounts

Many students studying final accounts for the first time find it helpful to be able to follow a set layout, or pro-forma – certainly in the early stages. A sample layout for final accounts is available as a free download from the Resources section at www.osbornebooks.co.uk. Note that there are some items included in these final account layouts that will be covered in the later chapters of Module 3.

CHAPTER SUMMARY

- The final accounts of a business comprise:
  - trading account, which shows gross profit
  - profit and loss account, which shows net profit
  - balance sheet, which shows the assets and liabilities of the business at the year-end

  Specimen layouts for final accounts are available as free download from the Resources section at www.osbornebooks.co.uk

- The starting point for the preparation of final accounts is the summary of the information from the accounting records contained in the book-keeper's trial balance.

- Each item from the trial balance is entered into the final accounts once only.

- Any notes to the trial balance, such as the closing stock, affect the final accounts in two places.

- The trading account and profit and loss account form part of the double-entry book-keeping system – amounts entered must be recorded elsewhere in the accounts.

- The balance sheet is not part of the double-entry system; it lists the assets and liabilities at a particular date.

- Final accounts can be presented in either a vertical or a horizontal format.

There is more material in connection with final accounts in Module 3, which is covered later in this book. In particular we will be dealing with accruals and prepayments, depreciation of fixed assets, bad debts and provision for doubtful debts, and accounting concepts and stock valuation. In addition the more specialist final accounts of manufacturing businesses and limited companies will be studied. Final accounts can also be analysed and interpreted to give the user of the accounts information about the financial state of the business – this aspect of accounting is covered in Module 4.

In the next chapter we will see how the journal is used as a subsidiary book to record transfers to the final accounts, and for the correction of errors.

QUESTIONS

NOTE: an asterisk (*) after the question number means that an answer to the question is given at the end of this book.

12.1* The following information has been extracted from the business accounts of Matthew Lloyd for his first year of trading which ended on 31 December 20-8:

	£
Purchases	94,350
Sales	125,890
Stock at 31 December 20-8	5,950
Rates	4,850
Heating and lighting	2,120
Wages and salaries	10,350
Office equipment	8,500
Vehicles	10,750
Debtors	3,950
Bank balance	4,225
Cash	95
Creditors	1,750
Value Added Tax	450
Capital at start of year	20,000
Drawings for year	8,900

You are to prepare the trading and profit and loss account of Matthew Lloyd for the year ended 31 December 20-8, together with his balance sheet at that date.

12.2 Complete the table below for each item (a) to (g) indicating with a tick:

- whether the item would normally appear in the debit or credit column of the trial balance
- in which final account the item would appear at the end of the accounting period and whether as a debit or credit

	TRIAL BALANCE		FINAL ACCOUNTS			
			TRADING & P& L		BALANCE SHEET	
	Debit	Credit	Debit	Credit	Debit	Credit
(a) Salaries						
(b) Purchases						
(c) Debtors						
(d) Sales returns						
(e) Discount received						
(f) Vehicle						
(g) Capital						

12.3* You are to fill in the missing figures for the following businesses:

	Sales	Opening Stock	Purchases	Closing Stock	Gross Profit	Expenses	Net Profit/ (Loss)*
	£	£	£	£	£	£	£
Business A	20 000	5 000	10 000	3 000	....	4 000	....
Business B	35 000	8 000	15 000	5 000	....	....	10 000
Business C	....	6 500	18 750	7 250	18 500	11 750	....
Business D	45 250	9 500	....	10 500	20 750	....	10 950
Business E	71 250	....	49 250	9 100	22 750	24 450	....
Business F	25 650	4 950	13 750	....	11 550	....	(3 450)

* Note: a net loss is indicated in brackets

12.4* The following trial balance has been extracted by the book-keeper of John Adams at 31 December 20-7:

	Dr £	Cr £
Stock at 1 January 20-7	14,350	
Purchases	114,472	
Sales		259,688
Rates	13,718	
Heating and lighting	12,540	
Wages and salaries	42,614	
Vehicle expenses	5,817	
Advertising	6,341	
Premises	75,000	
Office equipment	33,000	
Vehicles	21,500	
Debtors	23,854	
Bank	1,235	
Cash	125	
Capital at 1 January 20-7		62,500
Drawings	12,358	
Loan from bank		35,000
Creditors		17,281
Value Added Tax		2,455
	376,924	376,924

Stock at 31 December 20-7 was valued at £16,280.

You are to prepare the trading and profit and loss account of John Adams for the year ended 31 December 20-7, together with his balance sheet at that date.

12.5 The following trial balance has been extracted by the book-keeper of Clare Lewis at 31 December 20-4:

	Dr £	Cr £
Debtors	18,600	
Creditors		12,140
Value Added Tax		1,210
Bank overdraft		4,610
Capital at 1 January 20-4		25,250
Sales		144,810
Purchases	96,318	
Stock at 1 January 20-4	16,010	
Salaries	18,465	
Heating and lighting	1,820	
Rent and rates	5,647	
Vehicles	9,820	
Office equipment	5,500	
Sundry expenses	845	
Vehicle expenses	1,684	
Drawings	13,311	
	188,020	188,020

Stock at 31 December 20-4 was valued at £13,735.

You are to prepare the trading and profit and loss account of Clare Lewis for the year ended 31 December 20-4, together with her balance sheet at that date.

12.6* The following balances are taken from the books of James Cadwallader showing totals for the year ended 31 December 2002.

	£
Sales	67,945
Purchases	34,981
Returns inwards	2,945
Returns outwards	1,367
Carriage inwards	679

Carriage outwards	386
Stock at 1 January 2002	5,780
Stock at 31 December 2002	6,590
Wages	12,056
Other expenses	4,650

REQUIRED

Prepare the profit and loss account for the year ended 31 December 2002.

Assessment and Qualifications Alliance (AQA), 2003

12.7 R Masters has completed his trading account for the year ended 31 March 2002.

REQUIRED

From the following information:

(a) (i) prepare the profit and loss account for the year ended 31 March 2002

	£
Gross profit	56,231
Wages	23,980
Discount received	350
Carriage outwards	3,600
Motor expenses	4,500
Bank charges	450
Drawings	12,500
Capital	36,790

(ii) prepare the capital account as at 31 March 2002

Dr **Capital Account** Cr

Date 2002	Details	£	Date 2002	Details	£

(b) Explain two possible causes of a change in the balance of the capital account over the course of a year's trading.

Assessment and Qualifications Alliance (AQA), 2002

12.8*

From the following figures complete the balance sheet for A to Z Engineering Supplies as at 31 March 2003. Clearly show the fixed and current assets and long-term and current liabilities. To complete the balance sheet calculate the proprietor's capital.

	£
Net profit for the year	23,460
Stocks at 31 March 2003	14,905
Debtors	6,500
Creditors	4,590
Premises	50,000
Motor vehicles	14,560
Bank overdraft	3,400
Petty cash	56
Drawings	13,000
Mortgage on premises	25,000

Assessment and Qualifications Alliance (AQA), 2003

12.9

The subsidiary books of Amaryllis Trading show the following totals for the month of December 2001.

Totals for the month	**Goods**	**VAT**	**Total**
	£	**£**	**£**
Sales day book	4,560.30	798.05	5,358.35
Returns inwards day book	236.91	41.46	278.37
Purchases day book	2,769.56	484.67	3,254.23
Returns outwards day book	127.50	22.31	149.81

The balances in the general ledger, made up of the totals for October and November 2001, are:

	£
Sales account	16,493.27
Returns inwards account	1,269.43
Purchases account	10,276.41
Returns outwards account	1,039.41

(a) From the information given above enter the necessary data into the following accounts. The accounts need **not** be balanced.

Dr **Sales Account** Cr

Date 2001	Details	£ p	Date 2001	Details	£ p

Dr **Returns Inwards Account** Cr

Date 2001	Details	£ p	Date 2001	Details	£ p

Dr **Purchases Account** Cr

Date 2001	Details	£ p	Date 2001	Details	£ p

Dr **Returns Outwards Account** Cr

Date	Details	£ p	Date	Details	£ p
2001			2001		

(b) The following information is also given:

	£
Stocks on 1 October 2001	2,560.87
Stocks on 31 December 2001	2,640.96
Carriage inwards for the 3 months	871.26

Prepare the trading account for the three months ended 31 December 2001.

(c) Using the figures from the trading account, state the totals of the following items:

		£
(i)	Cost of goods sold	
(ii)	Goods available for sale	
(iii)	Turnover	

Assessment and Qualifications Alliance (AQA), 2002

12.10 Mary Arbuthnot runs Mary's Doll Shop and is preparing her balance sheet but has problems with allocating four items.

Using the memorandum on the next page, advise her as to which section/sub-heading of the balance sheet the items should appear under. Give detailed reasons for your choice.

MEMORANDUM

Date ....

To ....

From ....

Subject ....

---

1. Cost of new delivery van

   Section: ....

   Reasons: ....

   ....

   ....

   ....

   ....

2. Stock of dolls for resale

   Section: ....

   Reasons: ....

   ....

   ....

   ....

   ....

continued on next page

3. Telephone bill due to be paid in one month's time

Section: ....

Reasons: ....

....

....

....

....

4. Drawings for the year

Section: ....

Reasons: ....

....

....

....

....

Assessment and Qualifications Alliance (AQA), 2003

13 THE JOURNAL AND CORRECTION OF ERRORS

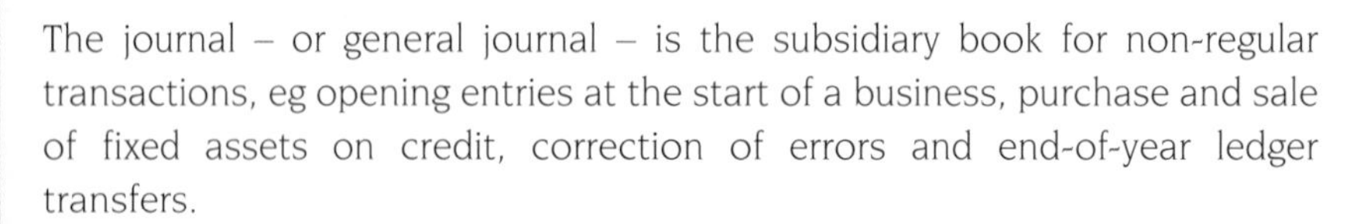

The journal – or general journal – is the subsidiary book for non-regular transactions, eg opening entries at the start of a business, purchase and sale of fixed assets on credit, correction of errors and end-of-year ledger transfers.

As a subsidiary book, the journal is not part of double-entry book-keeping; instead the journal is used to list transactions before they are entered into the accounts. In this way, the journal completes the accounting system by providing the subsidiary book for non-regular transactions.

USES OF THE JOURNAL

The journal – or general journal – completes the accounting system by providing the subsidiary book for non-regular transactions, which are not recorded in any other subsidiary book. The categories of such non-regular transactions include:

- opening entries at the start of a business
- purchase and sale of fixed assets on credit
- correction of errors
- year end ledger transfers

The reasons for using a journal are:

- to provide a subsidiary book for non-regular transactions
- to eliminate the need for remembering why non-regular transactions were put through the accounts – the journal acts as a notebook
- to reduce the risk of fraud, by making it difficult for unauthorised transactions to be entered in the accounting system
- to reduce the risk of errors, by listing the transactions that are to be put into the double-entry accounts
- to ensure that entries can be traced back to a source document, thus providing an audit trail for non-regular transactions

THE JOURNAL – A SUBSIDIARY BOOK

The journal is a subsidiary book; it is not, therefore, part of the double-entry book-keeping system. The journal is used to list the transactions that are then to be put through the accounts. The accounting system for non-regular transactions is as follows:

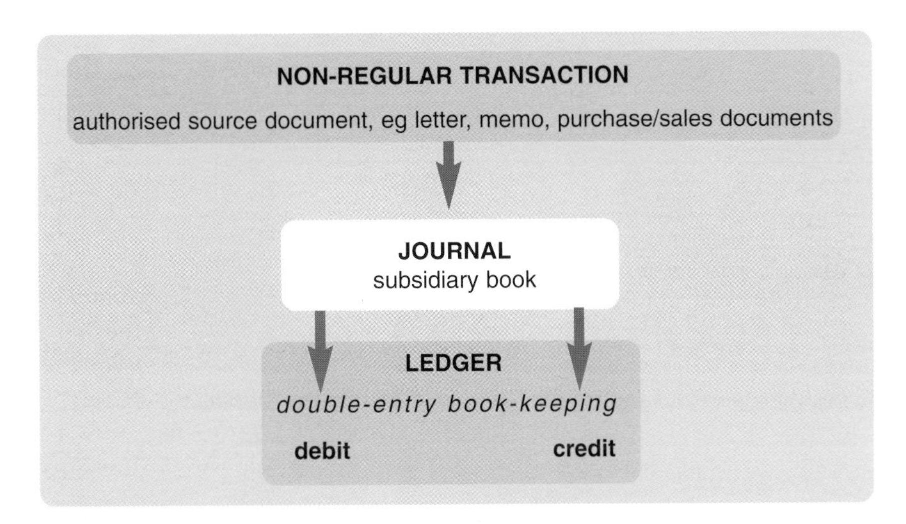

Look at the way the journal is set out with a sample transaction, and then read the notes that follow.

Date	Details	Folio	Dr	Cr
20-1			£	£
1 Jan	Bank	CB	10,000	
	Capital	GL		10,000
	Opening capital introduced			

- the names of the accounts to be debited and credited in the book-keeping system are written in the details column; it is customary to show the debit transaction first
- the money amount of each debit and credit is stated in the appropriate columns
- the folio column cross-references to the division of the ledger where each account will be found – cash book (CB), general ledger (GL), sales ledger (SL), purchases ledger (PL); an account number can also be included
- a journal entry always balances, ie debit and credit entries are for the same amount or total
- it is usual to include a brief narrative explaining why the transaction is being carried out, and making reference to the source document whenever possible (when answering questions you should always include a narrative unless specifically told otherwise)
- each journal entry is complete in itself and is ruled off to separate it from the next entry

OPENING ENTRIES

These are the transactions which open the accounts at the start of a new business. For example, a first business transaction is:

1 Jan 20-1 Started in business with £10,000 in the bank

This non-regular transaction is entered in the journal as follows:

Date	Details	Folio	Dr	Cr
20-1			£	£
1 Jan	Bank	CB	10,000	
	Capital	GL		10,000
	Opening capital introduced			

After the journal entry has been made, the transaction can be recorded in the double-entry accounts.

Here is another opening entries transaction to be recorded in the journal:

1 Feb 20-2 Started in business with cash £100, bank £5,000, stock £1,000, machinery £2,500, creditors £850

The journal entry is:

Date	Details	Folio	Dr	Cr
20-2			£	£
1 Feb	Cash	CB	100	
	Bank	CB	5,000	
	Stock account	GL	1,000	
	Machinery	GL	2,500	
	Creditors' accounts	PL		850
	Capital	GL		7,750
			8,600	8,600
	Assets and liabilities at the start of business			

Notes:

- Capital is in this example the balancing figure, ie assets minus liabilities.
- The journal is the subsidiary book for all opening entries, including cash and bank; however the normal subsidiary book for other cash/bank transactions is the cash book.
- The amounts from the journal entry will now need to be recorded in the double-entry accounts.

PURCHASE AND SALE OF FIXED ASSETS ON CREDIT

The purchase and sale of fixed assets are non-regular business transactions which are recorded in the journal as the subsidiary book. Only credit transactions are entered in the journal (because cash/bank transactions are recorded in the cash book as the subsidiary book). However, a business (or an examination question) may choose to journalise cash entries: strictly, though, this is incorrect as two subsidiary books are being used.

15 Apr 20-3 *Bought a machine for £1,000 plus VAT (at 17.5%) on credit from Machinery Supplies Limited, purchase order no 2341.*

Date	Details	Folio	Dr	Cr
20-3			£	£
15 Apr	Machinery	GL	1,000	
	VAT	GL	175	
	Machinery Supplies Limited*	PL		1,175
			1,175	1,175
	Purchase of machine, purchase order 2341			

20 May 20-4 *Car sold for £2,500 on credit to Wyvern Motors Limited (no VAT chargeable).*

Date	Details	Folio	Dr	Cr
20-4			£	£
20 May	Wyvern Motors Limited*	SL	2,500	
	Disposals	GL		2,500
	Sale of car, registration no 201 HAB			

* Instead of entering these transactions in the purchases ledger and sales ledger, an alternative treatment would be to open general ledger accounts for the creditor (Machinery Supplies Limited) and the debtor (Wyvern Motors Limited). This would avoid confusion with trade creditors (in the purchases ledger) and trade debtors (in the sales ledger).

Correction of Errors

In any book-keeping system there is always the possibility of an error. Ways to avoid errors, or ways to reveal them sooner, include:

- division of the accounting function between a number of people
- regular circulation of statements to debtors, who will check the transactions on their accounts and advise any discrepancies
- checking statements received from creditors
- extraction of a trial balance at regular intervals
- the preparation of bank reconciliation statements
- checking cash and petty cash balances against cash held
- the use of control accounts (see Chapter 14)
- the use of a computer accounting program

Despite all of these, errors will still occur from time-to-time and we shall look at:

- correction of errors not shown by a trial balance
- correction of errors shown by a trial balance, using a suspense account
- the effect of correcting errors on profit and the balance sheet

errors not shown by a trial balance

In Chapter 5, page 68, we have already seen that some types of errors in a book-keeping system are not revealed by a trial balance. These are:

- error of omission
- reversal of entries
- mispost/error of commission
- error of principle
- error of original entry (or transcription)
- compensating error

Although these errors are not shown by a trial balance, they are likely to come to light if the procedures suggested in the introduction, above, are followed. For example, a debtor will soon let you know if her account has been debited with goods she did not buy. When an error is found, it needs to be corrected by means of a journal entry which shows the book-keeping entries that have been made.

We will now look at an example of each of the errors not shown by a trial balance, and will see how it is corrected by means of a journal entry. (A practical hint which may help in correcting errors is to write out the 'T' accounts as they appear with the error; then write in the correcting entries and see if the result has achieved what was intended.) Note that the journal narrative includes document details.

Error of Omission

Credit sale of goods, £200 plus VAT (at 17.5%) on invoice 4967 to H Jarvis completely omitted from the accounting system; the error is corrected on 12 May 20-8

Date	Details	Folio	Dr	Cr
20-8			£	£
12 May	H Jarvis	SL	235	
	Sales	GL		200
	VAT	GL		35
			235	235
	Invoice 4967 omitted from the accounts.			

This type of error can happen in a very small business – often where the book-keeping is done by one person. For example, an invoice, when typed out, is 'lost' down the back of a filing cabinet. In a large business, particularly one using a computer accounting system, it should be impossible for this error to occur. Also, if documents are numbered serially, then none should be mislaid.

Reversal of Entries

A payment, on 3 May 20-8 by cheque of £50 to a creditor, S Wright, has been debited in the cash book and credited to Wright's account; this is corrected on 12 May 20-8

Date	Details	Folio	Dr	Cr
20-8			£	£
12 May	S Wright	PL	50	
	Bank	CB		50
	S Wright	PL	50	
	Bank	CB		50
			100	100
	Correction of £50 reversal of entries: cheque no. 93459			

To correct this type of error it is best to reverse the entries that have been made incorrectly (the first two journal entries), and then to put through the correct entries. This is preferable to debiting Wright £100 and crediting £100 to bank account: this is because there was never a transaction for £100 – the original transaction was for £50.

As noted earlier, it is often an idea to write out the 'T' accounts, complete with the error, and then to write in the correcting entries. As an example, the two accounts involved in this last error are shown with the error made on 3 May, and the corrections made on 12 May indicated by the shading (the opening credit balance of S Wright's account is shown as £50):

S Wright

Dr			Cr		
20-8		£	20-8		£
12 May	Bank	50	1 May	Balance b/d	50
12 May	Bank	50	3 May	Bank	50
		100			100

Cash Book (bank columns)

Dr			Cr		
20-8		£	20-8		£
3 May	S Wright	50	12 May	S Wright	50
			12 May	S Wright	50

The accounts now show a net debit transaction of £50 on S Wright's account, and a net credit transaction of £50 on bank account, which is how this payment to a creditor should have been recorded in order to clear the balance on the account.

Mispost/Error of Commission

Credit sales of £47 including VAT (at 17.5%) have been debited to the account of J Adams, instead of the account of J Adams Ltd; the error is corrected on 15 May 20-8

Date	Details	Folio	Dr	Cr
20-8			£	£
15 May	J Adams Ltd	SL	47	
	J Adams	SL		47
	Correction of mispost of invoice 5327			

This type of error can be avoided, to some extent, by the use of account numbers, and by persuading the customer to quote the account number or reference on each transaction.

Error of Principle

The cost of diesel fuel, £30 (excluding VAT), has been debited to vehicles account; the error is corrected on 20 May 20-8

Date	Details	Folio	Dr	Cr
20-8			£	£
20 May	Vehicle running expenses account	GL	30	
	Vehicles account	GL		30
	Correction of error: voucher no. 647			

This type of error is similar to a mispost except that, instead of the wrong person's account being used, it is the wrong class of account. In this example, the vehicle running costs must be kept separate from the cost of the asset (the vehicle), otherwise the expense and asset accounts will be incorrect, leading to profit for the year being overstated and the fixed asset being shown in the balance sheet at too high a figure.

Error of Original Entry (or Transcription)

Postages of £45 paid by cheque entered in the accounts as £54; the error is corrected on 27 May 20-8

Date	Details	Folio	Dr	Cr
20-8			£	£
27 May	Bank	CB	54	
	Postages	GL		54
	Postages	GL	45	
	Bank	CB		45
			99	99
	Correction of error: postages of £45 entered into the accounts as £54; cheque no. 93617			

This error could have been corrected by debiting bank and crediting postages with £9, being the difference between the two amounts. However, there was no original transaction for this amount, and it is better to reverse the wrong transaction and put through the correct one. A reversal of figures either has a difference of nine (as above), or an amount divisible by nine. An error of original entry can also be a 'bad' figure on a cheque or an invoice, entered wrongly into both accounts.

Compensating Error

Rates account is added up by £100 more than it should be (ie it is overadded or overcast); sales account is also overcast by the same amount; the error is corrected on 31 May 20-8

Date	Details	Folio	Dr	Cr
20-8			£	£
31 May	Sales account	GL	100	
	Rates account	GL		100
	Correction of overcast on rates account and sales account			

Here, an account with a debit balance – rates – has been overcast; this is compensated by an overcast on an account with a credit balance – sales. There are several permutations on this theme, eg two debit balances, one overcast, one undercast; a debit balance undercast, a credit balance undercast.

important notes to remember

We have just looked at several journal entries in connection with the correction of errors. Remember that:

- The journal is the subsidiary book for non-regular transactions. The journal entries must then be recorded in the book-keeping system.
- When a business uses control accounts (see Chapter 14) which are incorporated into the double-entry book-keeping system, the transactions from the journal must be recorded in the sales ledger or purchase ledger control accounts and in the memorandum accounts for debtors or creditors.

Trial Balance Errors: Use of Suspense Account

There are many types of errors revealed by a trial balance. Included amongst these are:

- omission of one part of the double-entry transaction
- recording two debits or two credits for a transaction
- recording a different amount for a transaction on the debit side from the credit side
- errors in the calculation of balances (not compensated by other errors)
- error in transferring the balance of an account to the trial balance
- error of addition in the trial balance

When errors are shown, the trial balance is 'balanced' by recording the difference in a suspense account, as shown in the worked example on the next page.

WORKED EXAMPLE: SUSPENSE ACCOUNT

The book-keeper of a business is unable to balance the trial balance on 31 December 20-1. As the error or errors cannot be found quickly the trial balance is balanced by recording the difference in a suspense account, as follows:

	Dr	Cr
	£	£
Trial balance totals	100,000	99,850
Suspense account		150
	100,000	100,000

A suspense account is opened in the general ledger with, in this case, a credit balance of £150:

Dr			**Suspense Account**		Cr
20-1		£	20-1		£
			31 Dec	Trial balance difference	150

A detailed examination of the book-keeping system is now made in order to find the errors. As errors are found, they are corrected by means of a journal entry. The journal entries will balance, with one part of the entry being either a debit or credit to suspense account. In this way, the balance on suspense account is eliminated by book-keeping transactions. Using the above suspense account, the following errors are found and corrected on 15 January 20-2:

- sales account is undercast by £100
- a payment to a creditor, A Wilson, for £65, has been recorded in the bank as £56
- telephone expenses of £55 have not been entered in the expenses account
- stationery expenses £48 have been debited to both the stationery account and the bank account

These errors are corrected by journal entries shown on the next page. Note that the journal narrative includes details of cheque numbers and dates taken from the records of the business.

Date	Details	Folio	Dr	Cr
20-2			£	£
15 Jan	Suspense account	GL	100	
	Sales account	GL		100
	Undercast on 23 December 20-1 now corrected			
15 Jan	Bank account	CB	56	
	Suspense account	GL		56
	Suspense account	GL	65	
	Bank account	CB		65
			121	121
	Payment to A Wilson for £65 (cheque no. 783726) on 30 December 20-1 entered in bank as £56 in error			
15 Jan	Telephone expenses account	GL	55	
	Suspense account	GL		55
	Omission of entry in expenses account: paid by cheque no 783734			
15 Jan	Suspense account	GL	48	
	Bank account	CB		48
	Suspense account	GL	48	
	Bank account	CB		48
			96	96
	Correction of error: payment by cheque no 783736 debited in error to bank account			

After these journal entries have been recorded in the accounts, suspense account appears as:

Suspense Account

Dr			Cr		
20-2		£	20-1		£
15 Jan	Sales	100	31 Dec	Trial balance difference	150
15 Jan	Bank	65	20-2		
15 Jan	Bank	48	15 Jan	Bank	56
15 Jan	Bank	48	15 Jan	Telephone expenses	55
		261			261

Thus all the errors have now been found, and suspense account has a nil balance.

Note that if final accounts have to be prepared after creating a suspense account but before the errors are found, the balance of suspense account is shown, depending on the balance, as either a current asset (debit balance) or a current liability (credit balance). Nevertheless, the error must be found at a later date and suspense account eliminated.

EFFECT ON PROFIT AND BALANCE SHEET

The correction of errors, whether shown by a trial balance or not, often has an effect on the profit figure calculated before the errors were found. For example, an undercast of sales account, when corrected, will increase gross and net profits and, of course, the profit figure shown in the balance sheet. Some errors, however, only affect the balance sheet, eg errors involving debtors' and creditor's' accounts. The diagram that follows shows the effect of errors when corrected on gross profit, net profit and the balance sheet.

TRADING ACCOUNT

Correction of error	Gross profit	Net profit	Balance sheet
sales undercast/understated	increase	increase	net profit increase
sales overcast/overstated	decrease	decrease	net profit decrease
purchases undercast/understated	decrease	decrease	net profit decrease
purchases overcast/overstated	increase	increase	net profit increase
opening stock undervalued	decrease	decrease	net profit decrease
opening stock overvalued	increase	increase	net profit increase
closing stock undervalued	increase	increase	net profit increase stock increase
closing stock overvalued	decrease	decrease	net profit decrease stock decrease

PROFIT AND LOSS ACCOUNT

Correction of error	Gross profit	Net profit	Balance sheet
expense undercast/understated	-	decrease	decrease in net profit
expense overcast/overstated	-	increase	increase in net profit
income undercast/understated	-	increase	increase in net profit
income overcast/overstated	-	decrease	decrease in net profit

BALANCE SHEET

Correction of error	Gross profit	Net profit	Balance sheet
asset undercast/understated	-	-	increase asset
asset overcast/overstated	-	-	decrease asset
liability undercast/understated	-	-	increase liability
liability overcast/overstated	-	-	decrease liability

Some examination questions on correction of errors require the preparation of a statement showing the amended profit after errors have been corrected. We will look at the errors shown on page 195 and see how their correction affects the net profit (assume the net profit before adjustments is £10,000).

Statement of corrected net profit for the year ended 31 December 20-1

	£
Net profit (unadjusted)	10,000
Add sales undercast	100
	10,100
Less additional telephone expenses	55
Adjusted net profit	10,045

Note: the other two errors do not affect net profit.

The effect on the balance sheet of correcting the errors is:

- net profit increases £45
- bank balance reduces £105 (+£56, –£65, –£48, –£48)
- the credit balance of £150 in suspense account (shown as a current liability) is eliminated

The balance sheet will now balance without the need for a suspense account – the errors have been found and corrected.

YEAR END LEDGER TRANSFERS

Any other non-regular transactions or adjustments need to be recorded in the journal. These usually take place at the end of a firm's financial year and are concerned with:

- transfers to the trading and profit and loss account
- expenses charged to the owner's drawings
- goods for the owner's use
- bad debts written off

transfers to trading and profit and loss account

As we have seen in the previous chapter, the trading and profit and loss account forms part of double-entry book-keeping. Therefore, each amount recorded in trading and profit and loss account must have an opposite entry in another account: such transfers are recorded in the journal as the subsidiary book, as shown by the entries which follow.

31 Dec 20-1 *Balance of sales account at the year-end, £155,000, transferred to trading account (debit sales account; credit trading account)*

Date	Details	Folio	Dr	Cr
20-1			£	£
31 Dec	Sales	GL	155,000	
	Trading	GL		155,000
	Transfer to trading account of sales for the year			

31 Dec 20-1 *Balance of purchases account at the year end, £105,000, transferred to trading account (debit trading account; credit purchases account)*

Date	Details	Folio	Dr	Cr
20-1			£	£
31 Dec	Trading	GL	105,000	
	Purchases	GL		105,000
	Transfer to trading account of purchases for the year			

31 Dec 20-1 *Closing stock has been valued at £12,500 and is to be entered into the accounts*

Date	Details	Folio	Dr	Cr
20-1			£	£
31 Dec	Stock	GL	12,500	
	Trading	GL		12,500
	Stock valuation at 31 December 20-1 transferred to trading account			

Remember that the closing stock valuation for the year is recorded in stock account as an asset (*debit* stock account; *credit* trading account).

31 Dec 20-1 *Balance of wages account, £23,500, transferred to profit and loss account (debit profit and loss account; credit wages account)*

Date	Details	Folio	Dr	Cr
20-1			£	£
31 Dec	Profit and loss	GL	23,500	
	Wages	GL		23,500
	Transfer to profit and loss account of expenditure for the year			

expenses charged to owner's drawings

Sometimes the owner of a business uses business facilities for private use, eg telephone, or car. The owner will agree that part of the expense shall be charged to him or her as drawings, while the other part represents a business expense. The book-keeping entry to record the adjustment is:

- debit drawings account
- credit expense account, eg telephone

31 Dec 20-1 The balance of telephone account is £600; of this, one-quarter is the estimated cost of the owner's private usage

The journal entry is:

Date	Details	Folio	Dr	Cr
20-1			£	£
31 Dec	Drawings	GL	150	
	Telephone	GL		150
	Transfer of private use to drawings account			

goods for the owner's use

When the owner of a business takes some of the goods in which the business trades for his or her own use, the double-entry book-keeping is:

- debit drawings account
- credit purchases account

15 Oct 20-1 Owner of the business takes goods for own use, £105 (no VAT)

The journal entry is:

Date	Details	Folio	Dr	Cr
20-1			£	£
15 Oct	Drawings	GL	105	
	Purchases	GL		105
	Goods taken for own use by the owner			

Note that where a business is VAT-registered, VAT must be accounted for on goods taken by the owner.

bad debts written off

A bad debt is a debt owing to a business which it considers will never be paid.

One of the problems of selling goods and services on credit terms is that, from time-to-time, some customers will not pay. As a consequence, the balances of such debtors' accounts have to be written off when they become uncollectable. This happens when all reasonable efforts to recover the amounts owing have been exhausted, ie statements and letters have been sent to the debtor requesting payment, and legal action – where appropriate – or the threat of legal action has failed to obtain payment.

In writing off a debtor's account as bad, the business is bearing the cost of the amount due. The debtor's account is written off as bad and the amount (or amounts where a number of accounts are dealt with in this way) is debited to bad debts written off account.

Towards the financial year-end it is good practice to go through the debtors' accounts to see if any need to be written off. The book-keeping entries for this are:

- debit bad debts written off account
- credit debtor's account

15 Dec 20-1 Write off the account of T Hughes, which has a balance of £25, as a bad debt

The journal entry for this non-regular transaction is:

Date	Details	Folio	Dr	Cr
20-1			£	£
15 Dec	Bad debts written off	GL	25	
	T Hughes	SL		25
	Account written off as a bad debt – see memo dated 14 December 20-1			

Note that in Module 3 we will see how bad debts written off is dealt with in the final accounts.

MAKING JOURNAL ENTRIES

As we have seen in this chapter, the journal is the subsidiary book for non-regular transactions. Because of the irregular nature of journal transactions, it is important that they are correctly authorised by the appropriate person – such as the accounts supervisor, the administration manager, the owner of the business. The authorisation will, ideally, be a source document – eg letter, memo, email or other document – but may well be verbal – eg "make the year-end ledger transfers to profit and loss account", or "find the errors and put them right".

It is good practice to ensure that journal entries are checked by an appropriate person before they are entered into the double-entry book-keeping system. It is all too easy to get a journal entry the wrong way round resulting in an error becoming twice as much as it was in the first place!

CHAPTER SUMMARY

- The journal is used to list non-regular transactions.
- The journal is a subsidiary book – it is not a double-entry account.
- The journal is used for:
  - opening entries at the start of a business
  - purchase and sale of fixed assets on credit
  - correction of errors
  - year end ledger transfers
- Correction of errors is always a difficult topic to put into practice: it tests knowledge of book-keeping procedures and it is all too easy to make the error worse than it was in the first place! The secret of dealing with this topic well is to write down – in account format – what has gone wrong. It should then be relatively easy to see what has to be done to put the error right.
- Errors not shown by a trial balance: error of omission, reversal of entries, mispost/error of commission, error of principle, error of original entry (or transcription), compensating error.
- Errors shown by a trial balance include: omission of one part of the book-keeping transaction, recording two debits/credits for a transaction, recording different amounts in the two accounts, calculating balances, transferring balances to the trial balance.
- All errors are non-regular transactions and need to be corrected by means of a journal entry: the book-keeper then needs to record the correcting transactions in the accounts.
- When error(s) are shown by a trial balance, the amount is placed into a suspense account. As the errors are found, journal entries are made which 'clear out' the suspense account.
- Correction of errors may have an effect on gross profit and net profit, and on the figures in the balance sheet. It may be necessary to restate net profit and to adjust the balance sheet.

In the next chapter we shall look at the use of control accounts which are used as a checking device for a section of the ledgers.

QUESTIONS

NOTE: an asterisk (*) after the question number means that an answer to the question is given at the end of this book.

13.1* Lucy Wallis started in business on 1 May 20-8 with the following assets and liabilities:

	£
Vehicle	6,500
Fixtures and fittings	2,800
Opening stock	4,100
Cash	150
Loan from husband	5,000

You are to prepare Lucy's opening journal entry, showing clearly her capital at 1 May 20-8.

13.2 Show the journal entries for the following transfers which relate to Trish Hall's business for the year ended 31 December 20-8:

(a) Closing stock is to be recorded in the accounts at a valuation of £22,600.

(b) Telephone expenses for the year, amounting to £890, are to be transferred to profit and loss account.

(c) Motoring expenses account shows a balance of £800; one-quarter of this is for Trish Hall's private motoring; three-quarters is to be transferred to profit and loss account.

(d) Trish has taken goods for her own use of £175 (no VAT).

(e) The sales ledger account of N Marshall, which has a debit balance of £125, is to be written off as a bad debt.

13.3* Henry Lewis is setting up the book-keeping system for his new business, which sells office stationery. He decides to use the following subsidiary books:

- Journal (or General Journal)
- Sales Day Book
- Purchases Day Book
- Sales Returns Day Book
- Purchases Returns Day Book
- Cash Book

The following business transactions take place:

(a) He receives an invoice from Temeside Traders for £956 for goods supplied on credit

(b) He issues an invoice to Malvern Models for £176 of goods

(c) He buys a computer for use in his business for £2,000 on credit from A-Z Computers Limited

(d) He issues a credit note to Johnson Brothers for £55 of goods

(e) A debtor, Melanie Fisher, settles the balance of her account, £107, by cheque

(f) He makes cash sales of £25

(g) Henry Lewis withdraws cash £100 for his own use

(h) He pays a creditor, Stationery Supplies Limited, the balance of the account, £298, by cheque

(i) A debtor, Jim Bowen, with an account balance of £35 is to be written off as a bad debt

(j) A credit note for £80 is received from a creditor, Ian Johnson

You are to take each business transaction in turn and state:

- the name of the subsidiary book
- the name of the account to be debited
- the name of the account to be credited

Note: VAT is to be ignored.

13.4 The trial balance of Thomas Wilson balanced. However, a number of errors have been found in the book-keeping system:

(a) Credit sale of £150 to J Rigby has not been entered in the accounts.

(b) A payment by cheque for £125 to H Price Limited, a creditor, has been recorded in the account of H Prince.

(c) The cost of a new delivery van, £10,000, has been entered to vehicle expenses account.

(d) Postages of £55, paid by cheque, have been entered on the wrong sides of both accounts.

(e) The totals of the purchases day book and the purchases returns day book have been undercast by £100.

(f) A payment for £89 from L Johnson, a debtor, has been entered in the accounts as £98.

You are to take each error in turn and:

- state the type of error
- show the correcting journal entry

Note: VAT is to be ignored

13.5* Jeremy Johnson extracts a trial balance from his book-keeping records on 30 September 20-8. Unfortunately the trial balance fails to balance and the difference, £19 debit, is placed to a suspense account pending further investigation.

The following errors are later found:

(a) A cheque payment of £85 for office expenses has been entered in the cash book but no entry has been made in the office expenses account.

(b) A payment for photocopying of £87 by cheque has been correctly entered in the cash book, but is shown as £78 in the photocopying account.

(c) The sales returns day book has been overcast by £100.

(d) Commission received of £25 has been entered twice in the account.

You are to:

- make journal entries to correct the errors
- show the suspense account after the errors have been corrected

13.6 R Masters has drawn up a suspense account at 31 March 2002 following the discovery of errors.

REQUIRED

(a) Name two accounting techniques which may have been used to detect the presence of errors in the books.

....

....

(b) Make the necessary entries in the journal below to correct the following errors. Narratives are not required.

(1) The sales day book has been overcast by £270.

(2) The returns inwards has been entered as a credit of £500. In fact it only totalled £300.

(3) A discount received of £400 was entered in the cash book but omitted from the general ledger.

(4) A cheque paid to J Jones of £350 was entered in the account of A Jones in error.

JOURNAL

Account	Debit £	Credit £

Assessment and Qualifications Alliance (AQA), 2002

13.7*

The trial balance of Fancy Goods Enterprises was drawn up as at 31 March 2001 but the totals did not agree. The following errors have been discovered.

1. The purchases account has been overcast by £4,500.
2. The debtors' total includes £650 which has been written off as a bad debt.
3. Discount received of £300 has been entered on the debit of the account.
4. A cheque for £673, payable to Sunshine Products Ltd, has been entered in the account of Sunmaster Products in error.
5. The credit balance in the rent payable account has been brought down as £990, it should have been £909.

REQUIRED

Make any necessary entries in the suspense account to correct these errors, and show the opening balance.

Dr **Suspense Account** **Cr**

Details	£	Details	£

Assessment and Qualifications Alliance (AQA), 2001

13.8

The trial balance of H G Patel, as at 30 April 2003, has been partially completed. The following balances have now to be included:

	£
Purchases	38,900
Sales	98,000
Returns outwards	3,698
Carriage inwards	367
Carriage outwards	450
Discount received	2,135
Drawings	6,900

REQUIRED

(a) Complete the trial balance.

(b) Total the trial balance and enter any difference in the suspense account.

H G Patel: Trial Balance as at 30 April 2003

Account	**Debit** £	**Credit** £
Wages	23,890	
Administration costs	6,000	
Capital		60,000
Premises	65,000	
Motor vehicles	5,000	
Motor expenses	1,650	
Purchases		
Sales		
Returns outwards		
Carriage inwards		
Carriage outwards		
Discount received		
Drawings		
Suspense		
TOTAL		

(c) There are many reasons for the error(s) giving rise to the suspense account.

From the following list of book-keeping errors, tick the Yes or No box to indicate whether or not the error could be responsible for the difference in the trial balance.

An example has been given.

Error	Yes	No
A balance has been entered in the wrong column of the trial balance.	✓	
An error of principle has occurred.		
The sales account has been totalled incorrectly.		
An invoice has been omitted from the books.		
A cheque has been debited in the cash book as £150 but credited in the customer's account as £105.		

Assessment and Qualifications Alliance (AQA), 2003

13.9* Barbara Smith has purchased a new computer system for her business, from JPC Computer Supplies Ltd. The computer was purchased on 1 February 2003 at a cost of £4,000 plus £665 VAT. She made full payment of 4 March 2003 and was allowed £200 trade discount.

REQUIRED

(a) Make the necessary entries for these transactions. (Journal narratives are **not** required. Do **not** balance any accounts.)

JOURNAL	Dr	Cr
	£	£

PURCHASE LEDGER

Dr **JPC Computer Supplies Ltd** **Cr**

Date 2003	Details	£	Date 2003	Details	£

GENERAL LEDGER

Dr **VAT Account** **Cr**

Date 2003	Details	£	Date 2003	Details	£

Dr **Computer Account** **Cr**

Date 2003	Details	£	Date 2003	Details	£

(b) Why will the purchase of a new computer system contribute to greater speed and accuracy in the book-keeping process?

Speed ....

....

Accuracy ....

....

Assessment and Qualifications Alliance (AQA), 2003

14 CONTROL ACCOUNTS

Control accounts are used as 'master' accounts which control a number of subsidiary ledger accounts (see the diagram below).

A control account (also known as a totals account) is used to record the totals of transactions passing through the subsidiary accounts.

In this way, the balance of the control account will always be equal (unless an error has occurred) to the total balances of the subsidiary accounts.

Two commonly-used control accounts are:

- sales ledger control account – the total of the debtors
- purchases ledger control account – the total of the creditors

In this chapter we shall look at:

- the concept of control accounts
- the layout of sales ledger and purchases ledger control accounts
- the use of control accounts as an aid to the management of a business

THE CONCEPT OF CONTROL ACCOUNTS

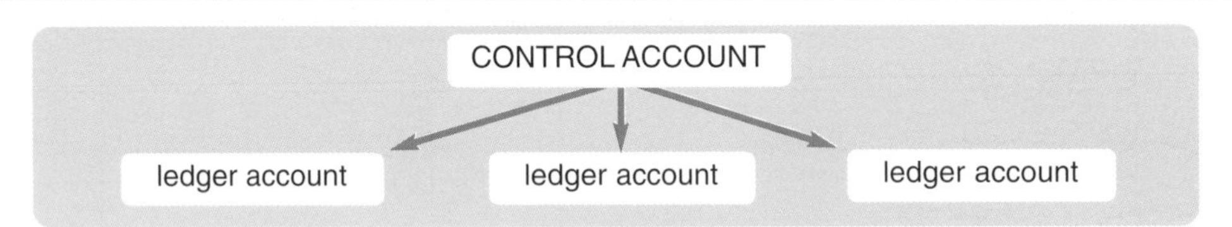

The illustration above shows how a control account acts as a master account for a number of subsidiary accounts. The principle is that, if the total of the opening balances for subsidiary accounts is known, together with the total of amounts increasing these balances, and the total of amounts decreasing these balances, then the total of the closing balances for the subsidiary accounts can be calculated.

For example:

	£
Total of opening balances	50,000
Add increases	10,000
	60,000
Less decreases	12,000
Total of closing balances	48,000

The total of the closing balances can now be checked against a separate listing of the subsidiary accounts to ensure that the two figures agree. If so, it proves that the ledgers within the section are correct (subject to any errors such as misposts and compensating errors). Let us now apply this concept to one of the divisions of the ledger – sales ledger.

The diagram on page 212 shows the personal accounts which form the entire sales ledger of a particular business (in practice there would, of course, be more than four accounts involved). The sales ledger control account acts as a totals account, which records totals of the transactions passing through the individual accounts which it controls. Notice that transactions appear in the control account on the same side as they appear in the individual accounts. It follows that the control account acts as a checking device for the individual accounts which it controls. Thus, control accounts act as an aid to locating errors: if the control account and subsidiary accounts agree, then the error is likely to lie elsewhere. In this way the control account acts as an intermediate checking device – proving the arithmetical accuracy of the ledger section.

Normally the whole of a ledger section is controlled by one control account, eg sales ledger control account and purchases ledger control account. However, it is also possible to have a number of separate control accounts for subdivisions of the sales ledger and purchases ledger, eg sales ledger control account A-K, purchases ledger control account S-Z, etc. It is for a business – the user of the accounting system – to decide what is most suitable, taking into account the number of accounts in the sales and purchases ledger, together with the type of book-keeping system – manual or computerised.

In the diagram on page 212 the sales ledger control account and subsidiary accounts are agreed at the beginning and end of the month, as follows:

Reconciliation of sales ledger control account with debtor balances

	1 January 20-1	31 January 20-1
	£	£
A Ackroyd	100	150
B Barnes	200	200
C Cox	50	180
D Douglas	150	150
Sales ledger control account	500	680

Note: The business will decide how often to reconcile the control account with the subsidiary accounts – weekly, monthly, quarterly or annually. Any discrepancy should be investigated immediately and the error(s) traced.

SALES LEDGER CONTROL ACCOUNT

Dr		£			Cr £
20-1		£	20-1		£
1 Jan	Balance b/d	500	31 Jan	Bank	443
31 Jan	Sales	700	31 Jan	Discount allowed	7
			31 Jan	Sales returns	70
			31 Jan	Balance c/d	680
		1,200			1,200
1 Feb	Balance b/d	680			

A Ackroyd

Dr					Cr
20-1		£	20-1		£
1 Jan	Balance b/d	100	10 Jan	Bank	98
6 Jan	Sales	150	10 Jan	Discount allowed	2
			31 Jan	Balance c/d	150
		250			250
1 Feb	Balance b/d	150			

B Barnes

Dr					Cr
20-1		£	20-1		£
1 Jan	Balance b/d	200	13 Jan	Bank	195
6 Jan	Sales	250	13 Jan	Discount allowed	5
			27 Jan	Sales returns	50
			31 Jan	Balance c/d	200
		450			450
1 Feb	Balance b/d	200			

C Cox

Dr					Cr
20-1		£	20-1		£
1 Jan	Balance b/d	50	20 Jan	Bank	50
15 Jan	Sales	200	29 Jan	Sales returns	20
			31 Jan	Balance c/d	180
		250			250
1 Feb	Balance b/d	180			

D Douglas

Dr					Cr
20-1		£	20-1		£
1 Jan	Balance b/d	150	30 Jan	Bank	100
20 Jan	Sales	100	31 Jan	Balance c/d	150
		250			250
1 Feb	Balance b/d	150			

Sales Ledger Control Account

The layout of a sales ledger control account (or debtors' control account) is shown below. Study the layout carefully and then read the text which explains the additional items.

Dr	Sales Ledger Control Account		Cr
	£		£
Balance b/d		Cash/cheques received from debtors	
Credit sales		Cash discount allowed	
Returned cheques		Sales returns	
Interest charged to debtors		Bad debts written off	
		Set-off/contra entries	
		Balance c/d	
Balance b/d			

- **Balance b/d**

The figure for balance b/d on the debit side of the control account represents the total of the balances of the individual debtors' accounts in the sales ledger. This principle is illustrated in the diagram on page 212. Remember that, at the end of the month (or other period covered by the control account), the account must be balanced and carried down (on the credit side) on the last day of the month, and then brought down (on the debit side) on the first day of the next month.

Note that it is possible for a debtor's account to have a credit balance, instead of the usual debit balance – see page 218. This may come about, for example, because the debtor has paid for goods and then returned them, or has overpaid in error: the business owes the amount due, ie the debtor has a credit balance for the time being.

- **Credit sales**

Only credit sales – and not cash sales – are entered in the control account because it is this transaction that is recorded in the debtors' accounts. The total sales of the business will comprise both credit and cash sales.

- **Returned cheques**

If a debtor's cheque is returned unpaid by the bank, ie the cheque has 'bounced', then entries have to be made in the book-keeping system to record this. These entries are:

– debit debtor's account

– credit cash book (bank columns)

As a transaction has been made in a debtor's account, then the amount must also be recorded in the sales ledger control account – on the debit side.

- **Interest charged to debtors**

Sometimes a business will charge a debtor for slow payment of an account. The entries are:

- debit debtor's account
- credit interest received account

As a debit transaction has been made in the debtor's account, so a debit entry must be recorded in the control account.

- **Bad debts written off**

The book-keeping entries for writing off a bad debt (see Chapter 13) are:

- debit bad debts written off account
- credit debtor's account

As you can see, a credit transaction is entered in a debtor's account. The control account 'masters' the sales ledger and so the transaction must also be recorded as a credit transaction in the control account.

- **Set-off/contra entries**

See page 217.

PURCHASES LEDGER CONTROL ACCOUNT

The specimen layout for the purchases ledger control account (or creditors' control account) is shown below. Study the format and read the notes which follow.

Dr	Purchases Ledger Control Account		Cr
	£		£
Cash/cheques paid to creditors		Balance b/d	
Cash discount received		Credit purchases	
Purchases returns		Interest charged by creditors	
Set-off/contra entries			
Balance c/d			
		Balance b/d	

- **Balance b/d**

The figure for balance b/d on the credit side of the control account represents the total of the balances of the individual creditors' accounts in the purchases ledger. This principle is illustrated in the diagram on the next page.

Note that it is possible for a creditor's account to have a debit balance, instead of the usual credit balance – see page 218. This may come about, for example, if the creditor has been paid and then goods are returned, or if the creditor has been overpaid.

- **Credit purchases**

Only credit purchases – and not cash purchases – are entered in the control account. However, the total purchases of the business will comprise both credit and cash purchases.

- **Interest charged by creditors**

If creditors charge interest because of slow payment, this must be recorded on both the creditor's account and the control account.

- **Set-off/contra entries**

See page 217.

reconciliation of purchases ledger control account

The diagram on the next page shows how a purchases ledger control account acts as a totals account for the creditors of a business.

Reconciliation of the balances on the purchases ledger control account and subsidiary accounts is made as follows:

Reconciliation of purchases ledger control account with creditor balances

	1 January 20-1	31 January 20-1
	£	£
F Francis	100	200
G Gold	200	350
H Harris	300	500
I Ingram	400	900
Purchases ledger control account	1,000	1,950

PURCHASES LEDGER CONTROL ACCOUNT

Dr			Cr		
20-1		£	20-1		£
31 Jan	Purchases returns	150	1 Jan	Balances b/d	1,000
31 Jan	Bank	594	31 Jan	Purchases	1,700
31 Jan	Discount received	6			
31 Jan	Balance c/d	1,950			
		2,700			2,700
			1 Feb	Balance b/d	1,950

F Francis

Dr			Cr		
20-1		£	20-1		£
17 Jan	Bank	98	1Jan	Balance b/d	100
17 Jan	Discount received	2	3 Jan	Purchases	200
31 Jan	Balance c/d	200			
		300			300
			1 Feb	Balance b/d	200

G Gold

Dr			Cr		
20-1		£	20-1		£
15 Jan	Purchases returns	50	1 Jan	Balance b/d	200
28 Jan	Bank	100	9 Jan	Purchases	300
31 Jan	Balance c/d	350			
		500			500
			1 Feb	Balance b/d	350

H Harris

Dr			Cr		
20-1		£	20-1		£
28 Jan	Purchases returns	100	1 Jan	Balance b/d	300
30 Jan	Bank	200	17 Jan	Purchases	500
31 Jan	Balance c/d	500			
		800			800
			1 Feb	Balance b/d	500

I Ingram

Dr			Cr		
20-1		£	20-1		£
22 Jan	Bank	196	1 Jan	Balance b/d	400
22 Jan	Discount received	4	27 Jan	Purchases	700
31 Jan	Balance c/d	900			
		1,100			1,100
			1 Feb	Balance b/d	900

SET-OFF/CONTRA ENTRIES

These entries occur when the same person or business has an account in both sales ledger and purchases ledger, ie they are both buying from, and selling to, the business whose accounts we are preparing. For example, M Patel Ltd has the following accounts in the sales and purchases ledgers:

SALES LEDGER

Dr	**A Smith**		Cr
	£		£
Balance b/d	200		

PURCHASES LEDGER

Dr	**A Smith**		Cr
	£		£
		Balance b/d	300

From these accounts we can see that:

- A Smith owes M Patel Ltd £200 (sales ledger)
- M Patel Ltd owes A Smith £300 (purchases ledger)

To save each having to write out a cheque to send to the other, it is possible (with A Smith's agreement) to set-off one account against the other, so that they can settle their net indebtedness with one cheque. The book-keeping entries for this contra transaction in M Patel's books will be:

– debit A Smith (purchases ledger) £200

– credit A Smith (sales ledger) £200

The accounts will now appear as:

SALES LEDGER

Dr	**A Smith**		Cr
	£		£
Balance b/d	200	Set-off: purchases ledger	200

PURCHASES LEDGER

Dr	**A Smith**		Cr
	£		£
Set-off: sales ledger	200	Balance b/d	300

The net result is that M Patel Ltd owes A Smith £100. The important point to note is that, because transactions have been recorded in the personal accounts, an entry needs to be made in the two control accounts:

- debit purchases ledger control account with the amount set-off
- credit sales ledger control account with the amount set-off

Set-off transactions should be appropriately documented with a journal entry (see chapter 13) authorised by the accounts supervisor.

SALES LEDGER CREDIT BALANCES AND PURCHASES LEDGER DEBIT BALANCES

sales ledger

The normal account balance of debtors in the sales ledger is debit, ie the amount is owing to the business by the debtors. As noted earlier in the chapter (page 213), it can sometimes happen that a debtor's account has a credit balance. This comes about, for example, when a debtor has paid for goods and then returns them, or has overpaid in error.

The following example shows a debtor's account with a credit balance at the end of the month:

SALES LEDGER

S Johnson

Dr			Cr		
20-1		£	20-1		£
1 Jan	Balance b/d	100	20 Jan	Bank	300
3 Jan	Sales	200	30 Jan	Sales returns	200
31 Jan	Balance c/d	200			
		500			500
			1 Feb	Balance b/d	200

This debtor's account has a credit balance at the end of January – not what we would expect to find on an account in sales ledger. Assuming that this is the only such balance, for sales ledger control account the credit balance is shown on the same side as in the debtor's account:

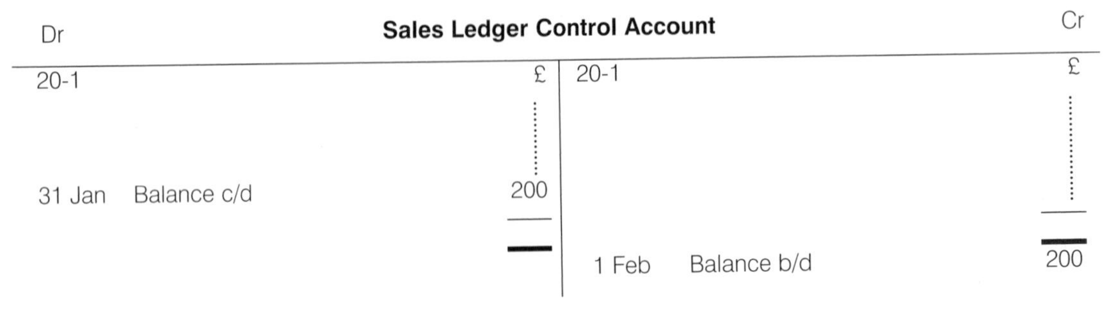

Sales Ledger Control Account

Dr			Cr		
20-1		£	20-1		£
		⋮			⋮
31 Jan	Balance c/d	200			
			1 Feb	Balance b/d	200

All other aspects of the sales ledger control account are the same as before. If there should, by chance, be more than one such credit balance in sales ledger, then they will be added together for the control account. Also note that, in a trial balance, any such credit balances must be shown on the credit side, ie separate from the main debit balances of sales ledger.

purchases ledger

In purchases ledger the normal account balance of creditors is credit, ie the amount the business owes to its creditors. As noted on page 215, it is possible for a creditor's account to have a debit balance – for example, if a creditor has been paid and then goods are returned, or if the creditor has been overpaid.

The following example shows a creditor's account with a debit balance at the end of the month.

PURCHASES LEDGER

Dr		**T Singh**			Cr
20-1		£	20-1		£
10 Jan	Bank	300	1 Jan	Balance b/d	200
20 Jan	Purchases returns	100	4 Jan	Purchases	100
			31 Jan	Balance c/d	100
		400			400
1 Feb	Balance b/d	100			

The debit balance on a creditor's account in purchases ledger is shown in purchases ledger control account as it appears on the account (assuming that this is the only such balance at the end of January):

Dr		**Purchases Ledger Control Account**			Cr
20-1		£	20-1		£
		⋮			⋮
			31 Jan	Balance c/d	100
1 Feb	Balance b/d	100			

All other aspects of purchases ledger control account are the same as before. If there is more than one such debit balance, then they will be added together for the control account. Note that, in a trial balance, any such debit balances must be shown on the debit side, ie separate from the main credit balances of sales ledger.

Sources of Information for Control Accounts

Control accounts use totals (remember that their other name is totals accounts) for the week, month, quarter or year – depending on what time period is decided upon by the business. The totals come from a number of sources in the accounting system:

sales ledger control account

- total credit sales (including VAT) – from the 'gross' column of the sales day book
- total sales returns (including VAT) – from the 'gross' column of the sales returns day book
- total cash/cheques received from debtors – from the cash book
- returned cheques – from the cash book
- total discount allowed – from the discount allowed column of the cash book, or from discount allowed account
- bad debts – from the journal, or bad debts written off account
- set-off/contra entries – from the journal

purchases ledger control account

- total credit purchases (including VAT) – from the 'gross' column of the purchases day book
- total purchases returns (including VAT) – from the 'gross' column of the purchases returns day book
- total cash/cheques paid to creditors – from the cash book
- total discount received – from the discount received column of the cash book, or from discount received account
- set-off/contra entries – from the journal

Note that when using a computer accounting system, relevant transactions are automatically recorded on the control account

Control Accounts as an Aid to Management

- **instant information**

  When the manager of a business needs to know the figure for debtors or creditors – important information for the manager – the balance of the appropriate control account will give the information immediately. There is no need to add up the balances of all the debtors' or creditors' accounts. With a computer accounting system, the control accounts can be printed at any time.

- **prevention of fraud**

  The use of a control account makes fraud more difficult – particularly in a manual accounting system. If a fraudulent transaction is to be recorded on a personal account, the transaction must also be entered in the control account. As the control account will be either maintained by a supervisor, and/or checked regularly by the manager, the control account adds another level of security within the accounting system.

- **location of errors**
  We have already seen in this chapter how control accounts can help in locating errors. Remember, though, that a control account only proves the arithmetical accuracy of the accounts which it controls – there could still be errors, such as misposts and compensating errors, within the ledger section.

- **construction of final accounts**
  A further use of control accounts is to help with the construction of final accounts when a business has not kept double-entry accounts and a trial balance cannot be extracted.

- **limitation of control accounts**
  Whilst control accounts can help in locating errors, they do have the limitation that not all errors will be revealed by them. As noted above, such errors include:
  - omission, where a transaction has been completely omitted from the accounting records
  - mispost/error of commission, where a transaction is entered in the wrong person's account, but within the same ledger section
  - original entry, where the wrong money amount has been entered into the accounting system, eg a 'bad' figure on a cheque received from a debtor is entered wrongly in both cash book and sales ledger
  - compensating error, where one error is cancelled out by another error within the same ledger section, eg the balance of one account in purchases ledger is calculated at £1,000 too much, while another account in the same ledger is calculated at £1,000 too little

Control Accounts and Book-keeping

A business must decide how to use control accounts in its book-keeping system. The commonest way of doing this is to incorporate the control accounts into double-entry book-keeping.

The control accounts therefore form part of the double-entry system: the balances of the sales ledger control account and the purchases ledger control account are recorded in the trial balance as the figures for debtors and creditors respectively. This means that the personal accounts of debtors and creditors are not part of double-entry, but are separate memorandum accounts which record how much each debtor owes, and how much is owed to each creditor. From time-to-time, the balances of the memorandum accounts are agreed with the balance of the appropriate control account.

The diagrams on the next two pages show how the sales ledger control account and the purchases ledger control account are incorporated into the double-entry book-keeping system (general ledger), with the individual debtors' and creditors' accounts kept in the form of memorandum accounts. (An alternative way is for the control accounts to be kept as memorandum accounts, with the individual debtors' and creditors' accounts being part of double-entry book-keeping.)

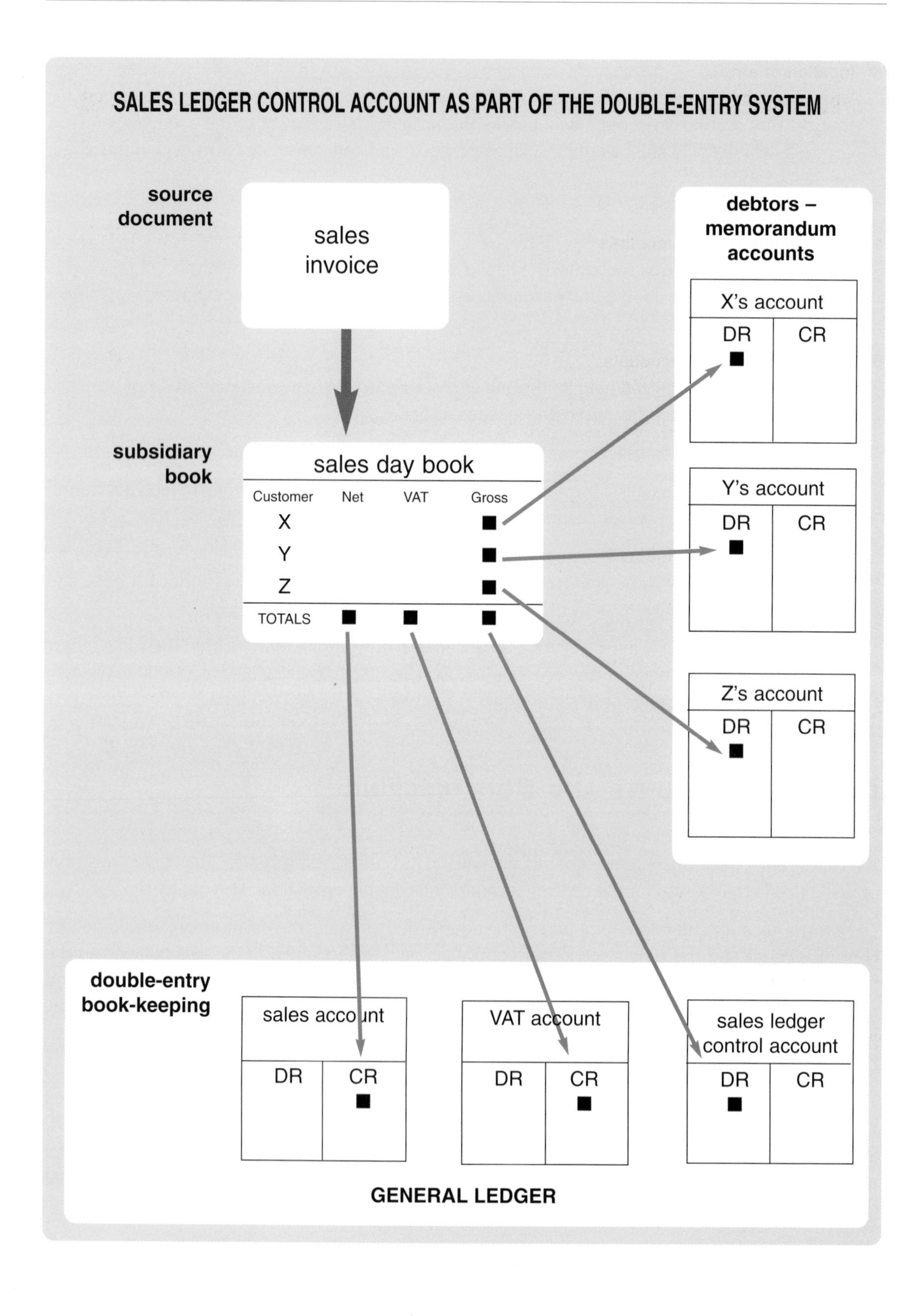

SALES LEDGER CONTROL ACCOUNT AS PART OF THE DOUBLE-ENTRY SYSTEM
source document
sales invoice
debtors – memorandum accounts
X's account
DR
CR
subsidiary book
sales day book
Customer
Net
VAT
Gross
X
Y
Z
TOTALS
Y's account
DR
CR
Z's account
DR
CR
double-entry book-keeping
sales account
DR
CR
VAT account
DR
CR
sales ledger control account
DR
CR
GENERAL LEDGER

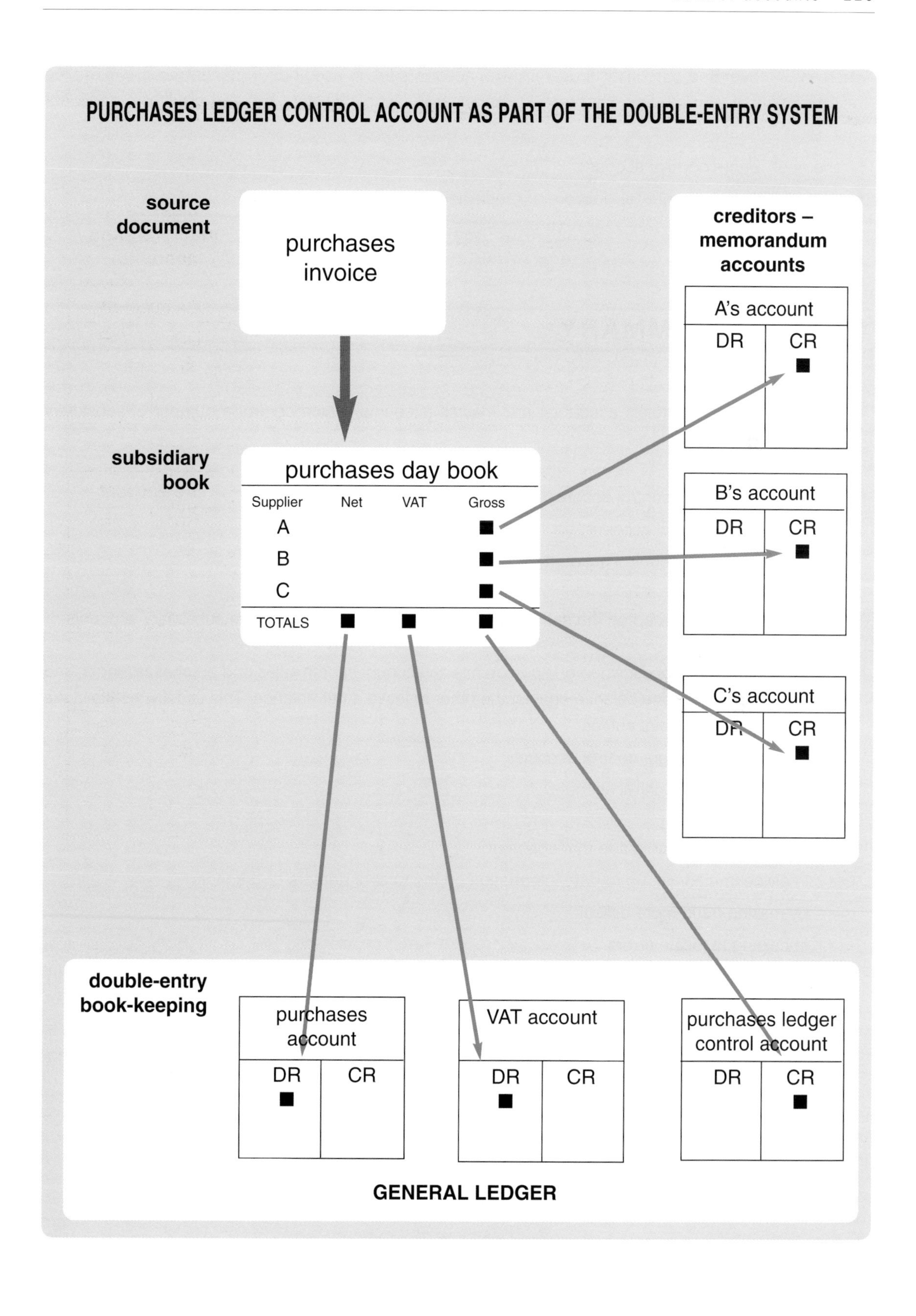
PURCHASES LEDGER CONTROL ACCOUNT AS PART OF THE DOUBLE-ENTRY SYSTEM
source document
purchases invoice
subsidiary book
purchases day book
Supplier
Net
VAT
Gross
A
B
C
TOTALS
creditors – memorandum accounts
A's account
DR
CR
B's account
DR
CR
C's account
DR
CR
double-entry book-keeping
purchases account
DR
CR
VAT account
DR
CR
purchases ledger control account
DR
CR
GENERAL LEDGER

When sales ledger and purchases ledger control accounts are in use and journal entries are made (eg for correction of errors – see Chapter 13), transactions involving debtors' and creditors' accounts must be recorded in:

- the appropriate control account
- memorandum accounts for debtors or creditors

CHAPTER SUMMARY

- Control accounts (or totals accounts) are 'master' accounts, which control a number of subsidiary accounts.

- Two commonly used control accounts are:
  - sales ledger control account
  - purchases ledger control account

- Transactions are recorded on the same side of the control account as on the subsidiary accounts.

- Set-off/contra entries occur when one person has an account in both sales and purchases ledger, and it is agreed to set-off one balance against the other to leave a net balance. This usually results in the following control account entries:

  – debit purchases ledger control account

  – credit sales ledger control account

- Control accounts are an aid to management:
  - in giving immediate, up-to-date information on the total of debtors or creditors
  - by making fraud more difficult
  - in helping to locate errors
  - in assisting with the preparation of final accounts when a business has not kept double-entry accounts

- Control accounts are normally incorporated into the double-entry book-keeping system. The subsidiary accounts are set up as separate memorandum accounts.

QUESTIONS

NOTE: an asterisk (*) after the question number means that an answer to the question is given at the end of this book.

14.1* Prepare a sales ledger control account for the month of June 20-1 from the following information:

20-1		£
1 Jun	Sales ledger balances	17,491
30 Jun	Credit sales for month	42,591
	Sales returns	1,045
	Payments received from debtors	39,024
	Cash discount allowed	593
	Bad debts written off	296

The debtors figure at 30 June is to be entered as the balancing figure.

14.2* Prepare a purchases ledger control account for the month of April 20-2 from the following information:

20-2		£
1 Apr	Purchases ledger balances	14,275
30 Apr	Credit purchases for month	36,592
	Purchases returns	653
	Payments made to creditors	31,074
	Cash discount received	1,048
	Transfer of credit balances to sales ledger	597

The creditors figure at 30 April is to be entered as the balancing figure.

14.3 The sales ledger of Rowcester Traders contains the following accounts on 1 February 20-8:

Arrow Valley Retailers	balance £826.40 debit
B Brick (Builders) Limited	balance £59.28 debit
Mereford Manufacturing Company	balance £293.49 debit
Redgrove Restorations	balance £724.86 debit
Wyvern Warehouse Limited	balance £108.40 debit

The following transactions took place during February:

3 Feb	Sold goods on credit to Arrow Valley Retailers £338.59, and to Mereford Manufacturing Company £127.48
7 Feb	Redgrove Restorations returned goods £165.38
15 Feb	Received a cheque from Wyvern Warehouse Limited for the balance of the account after deduction of 2.5% cash discount
17 Feb	Sold goods on credit to Redgrove Restorations £394.78, and to Wyvern Warehouse Limited £427.91
20 Feb	Arrow Valley Retailers settled an invoice for £826.40 by cheque after deducting 2.5% cash discount
24 Feb	Mereford Manufacturing Company returned goods £56.29
28 Feb	Transferred the balance of Mereford Manufacturing Company's account to the company's account in the purchases ledger
28 Feb	Wrote off the account of B Brick (Builders) Limited as a bad debt

You are to:

(a) write up the personal accounts in the sales ledger of Rowcester Traders for February 20-8, balancing them at the end of the month

(b) prepare a sales ledger control account for February 20-8, balancing it at the end of the month

(c) reconcile the control account balance with the debtors' accounts at 1 February and 28 February 20-8.

Note: VAT is to be ignored on all transactions and day books are not required.

14.4* (a) Advise Wholesale Car Spares of **two** benefits they would gain from keeping control accounts.

Benefit 1 ....

....

Benefit 2 ....

....

The sales ledger control account for the month ended 31 October 2000 did not agree with the sales ledger balances list total.

The following errors have been discovered.

1. The sales day book was undercast by £540.
2. The return inwards day book includes £100 which is actually for returns outwards.
3. A discount allowed of £37 has been omitted from the books completely.
4. A cheque received from J C Cross Garages for £1,479 was entered in the account of A B Cross Ltd in error.
5. The opening balance brought down should have been £25,080.

(b) Enter the necessary corrections in the control account. Balance the account.

Dr	**Sales Ledger Control Account**				Cr
2000		£	2000		£
31 Oct	Balance b/d	25,800			

(c) Explain the main limitation of control accounts using two examples to illustrate your answer.

Assessment and Qualifications Alliance (AQA), 2001

14.5

The following figures have been drawn from the books of Kings Products for the month ended 31 March 2001:

	£
Balances at 1 March 2001:	
Credit balances	23,437
Debit balances	465
Balances at 31 March 2001:	
Purchases on credit for the month	245,897
Returns to suppliers of credit purchases	4,679
Cash purchases	25,679
Purchase ledger balances set off against sales ledger	475
Cash paid to suppliers	236,498
Discounts received	3,674
Cash refunds from credit suppliers	450
Debit balance on the purchase ledger	749
Credit balances on the purchase ledger	?

Selecting from the above information, complete the control account for the month ended 31 March 2001 and calculate the credit balance at that date.

Purchase Ledger Control Account

Dr					Cr
Date 2001	Details	£	Date 2001	Details	£

Assessment and Qualifications Alliance (AQA), 2001

14.6 The following is the sales ledger control account of Wyvern Supplies for January 20-5:

Dr		**Sales Ledger Control Account**			Cr
20-5		£	20-5		£
1 Jan	Balance b/d	44,359	31 Jan	Bank	23,045
31 Jan	Sales	26,632	31 Jan	Discount allowed	1,126
31 Jan	Returned cheque	275	31 Jan	Sales returns	2,347
			31 Jan	Balance c/d	44,748
		71,266			71,266
1 Feb	Balance b/d	44,748			

The following errors have been discovered.

1. the sales day book total has been undercast by £1,000
2. the sales returns day book total should be £2,964
3. a contra entry with the purchases ledger of £247 has been omitted
4. a cheque for £685 received from a debtor, J Hampton, has been credited in error to the account of Hampton Limited

You are to redraft the sales ledger control account making the entries necessary to show the correct balance to be brought down on 1 February 20-5.

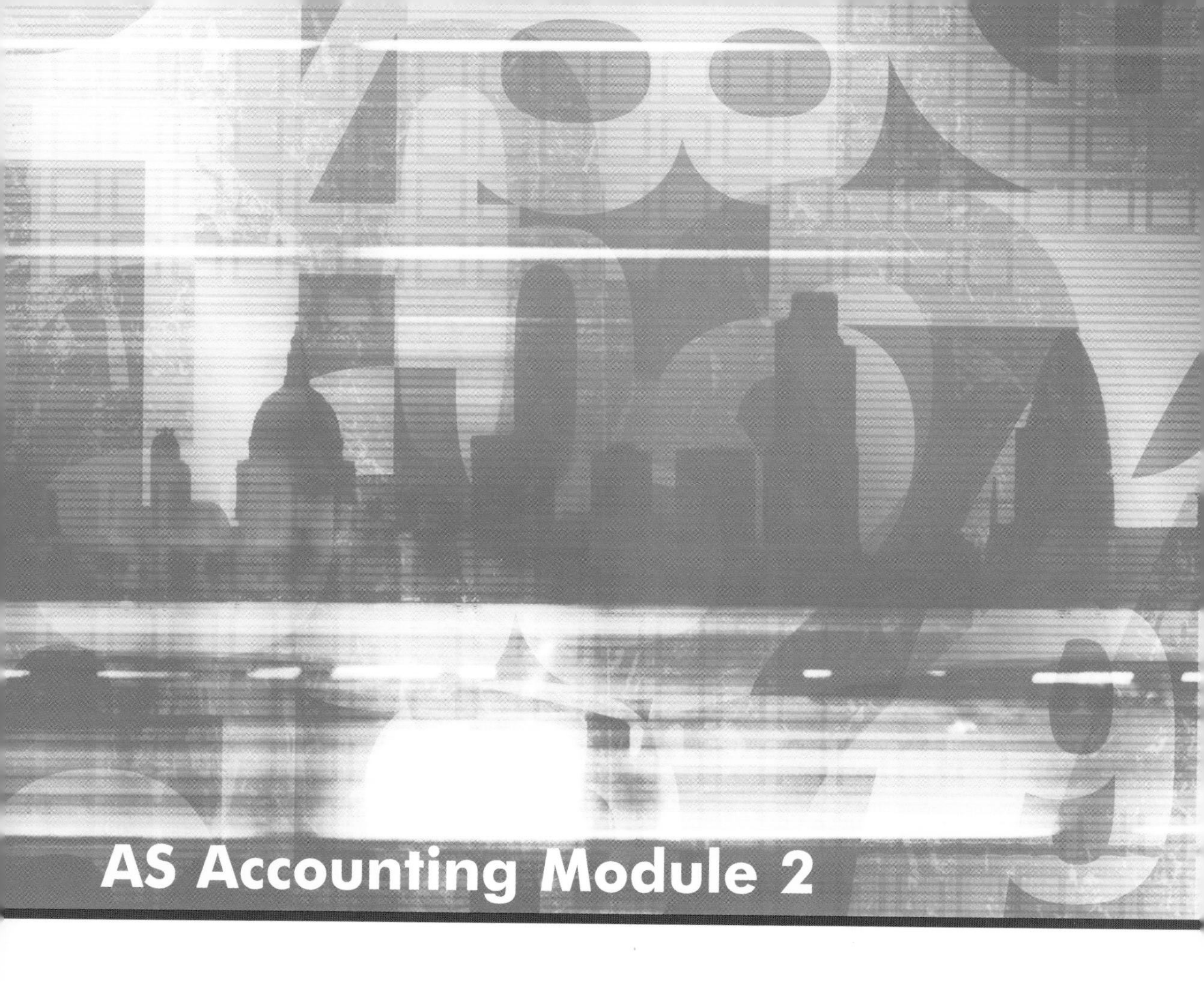

AS Accounting Module 2

Financial Accounting: Introduction to Published Accounts of Limited Companies

This Module for AQA AS Accounting is intended to be a foundation for the study of accounting, with the emphasis on the accounts of limited companies. It covers:

- trial balances
- trading, profit and loss, and profit and loss appropriation accounts, and balance sheets
- published reports and accounts of limited companies
- corporate report requirements of different user groups
- the use of computers in accounting

Note that, as an alternative to this Module, AQA offers Module 1 'The Accounting Information System', which provides a foundation for the course and covers double-entry procedures with the emphasis on the accounting systems of sole traders. Please note that AQA recommends that those wishing to complete the full A Level should study Module 1 rather than Module 2.

The series of chapters in this module is designed to be completely self-contained and therefore inevitably repeats some material from Module 1.

15 THE ACCOUNTING SYSTEM

Accounting – known as 'the language of business' – is essential to the recording and presentation of business activities in the form of accounting records and financial statements.

This chapter looks at the way in which the accounting system works and introduces you to the workings of computer accounting (covered in more detail in Chapter 17). Important reports which can be obtained from the accounting system are:

- trial balance
- trading and profit and loss account
- balance sheet

A particular focus of the chapter is on the accounting equation and how the dual aspect of business transactions affect the assets, liabilities and capital of the business.

INTRODUCTION TO ACCOUNTING

what is accounting?

Accounting is essential to the recording and presentation of business activities in the form of accounting records and financial statements. Financial accounting involves:

- recording business transactions in financial terms
- reporting financial information to the owners and managers of the business and other interested parties
- advising the owners – and other parties – how to use the financial reports to assess the past performance of the business, and to make decisions for the future

the role of the accountant

The accountant's job is to check, summarise, present, analyse and interpret the accounts for the benefit of the owners and other interested parties. There are two types of specialist accountant:

- **financial accountant**, mainly concerned with external reporting
- **management accountant**, mainly concerned with internal reporting

The function of the **financial accountant** is concerned with financial transactions, and with taking further the information produced by whoever 'keeps the books'. The financial accountant extracts information from the accounting records in order to provide a method of control, for instance over debtors, creditors, cash and bank balances. Importantly, the role requires the preparation of year end final accounts – something which we will be focusing on in this Module and again in Module 3.

The **management accountant** obtains information about costs – eg the cost of materials, labour, expenses and overheads – and interprets it and prepares reports for the owners or managers of the business. In particular, the management accountant will be concerned with financial decision-making, planning and control of the business. We will be studying the work of the management accountant in more detail in Module 4.

manual and computer accounts

Financial accounting records are kept in handwritten form and in many cases on computer. It is good practice for computer accounting systems to be backed up by handwritten records, in case of computer disasters such as the total loss of data. The main record in a handwritten system is **the ledger** which, at one time, would be a weighty leather-bound volume, neatly ruled, into which the book-keeper would write by hand each business transaction to individual accounts.

Computers are now relatively cheap and affordable. The major advantage of computer accounting is that it is a very accurate method of recording business transactions. The word 'ledger' has survived into the computer age but, instead of being a bound volume, it is used to describe data files held on a computer disk.

Whether business transactions are recorded by hand, or by using a computer, the basic principles remain the same.

THE ACCOUNTING SYSTEM

an overview

The **accounting system** as it relates to both manual and computer accounting is a series of simple stages. It starts off with business transactions such as sales and purchases, and concludes with information used by management – and other interested parties – such as the trading and profit and loss account and the balance sheet.

These four stages are summarised in the diagram that follows on the next page.

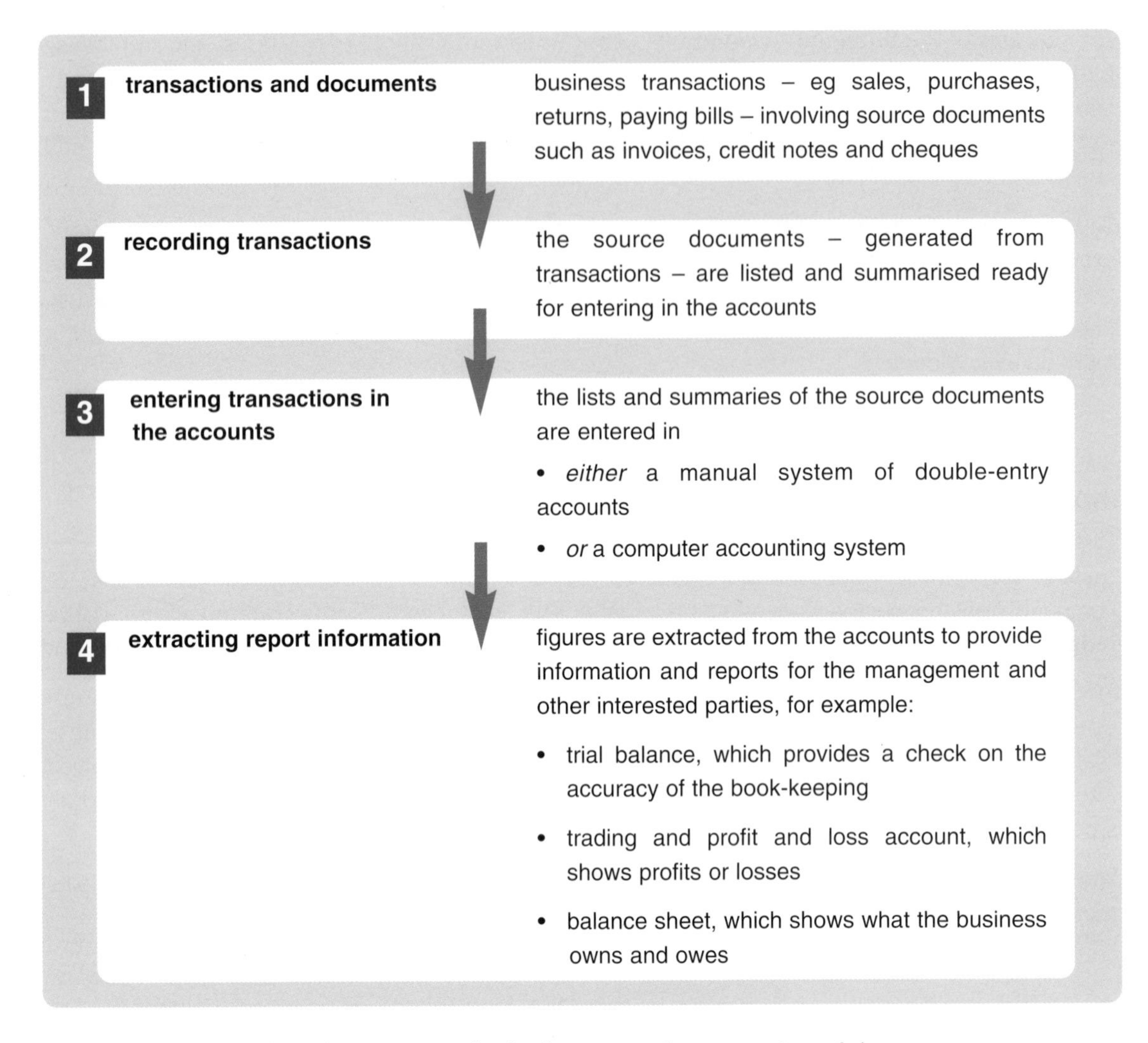

We will now look at these four stages individually to provide an overview of the system.

Stage 1 – Transactions and Documents

Two frequent business transactions involve the sale and purchase of goods or services. Immediate payment for these is described as a 'cash transaction' – even though the method of payment used may be by means other than cash, such as by cheque, by credit card or by debit card. However, many businesses buy and sell on credit terms – a 'credit transaction', where payment is made at a later date. Thus a business may have transactions for:

- cash purchases – goods bought and paid for immediately in cash, by cheque, by credit card or by debit card
- credit purchases – goods bought, with payment to be made at an agreed later date
- cash sales – goods sold, with immediate payment

- credit sales – goods sold, with payment to be received at an agreed date in the future

Business transactions involve source documents – you may already be familiar with some of these.

sales and purchases – the invoice

When a business buys or sells goods or a service, the seller prepares an invoice which sets out the details of the goods sold or the service provided, the amount owing, and the date on which it should be paid.

refunds – the credit note

If the buyer returns goods which are bought on credit or has a problem with a service supplied on credit, the seller may agree to a refund and issue a credit note which is sent to the buyer, reducing the amount of money owed.

paying-in slips and cheques

Businesses pay money into the bank account, and take out cash and make payments by using cheques and other transfers. Money can be paid in using paying-in slips or sent electronically.

Stage 2 – Recording Transactions

Businesses need to list and summarise source documents ready for entry into the accounting records. Manual systems often use **cash books** for bank and cash transactions and **day books** for listing credit transactions, such as sales, purchases and returned goods. Each day book is totalled at regular intervals – daily, weekly or monthly, depending on the needs of the business.

Computer programs often use the batch system, which is a listing of the items with an overall total to check against the computer input. It is common to find batches for sales, purchases, returns, cheques received, cheques issued.

Stage 3 – Entering Transactions in the Accounts

When the source documents have been listed in a day book or batch they are then entered in the accounts of the business. The format of a manual **double-entry account** for wages is shown at the top of the next page.

This double-entry account is only half the story – an entry has also been made in another account – here it is the bank account. This 'dual aspect' of book-keeping means that one account is debited (here wages account) and another account is credited (bank account).

A computer system, on the other hand, needs only one entry to be made for each transaction, but will require the account details of the other entry (normally a numerical code) when that single entry is made.

double-entry account recording payment of wages of £4,250, paid by cheque

Debit		Wages Account			Credit
20-5	Details	£ p	20-5	Details	£ p
1 Feb ↑ *date of the transaction*	Bank ↑ *name of the account in which the other entry is made*	4,250.00 ↑ *amount of the transaction*			

the ledger

Most accounting systems use the **ledger** system to organise the accounts. The word 'ledger' means 'book' but is used freely by both manual and computer systems to represent a section of the accounts kept on paper or on the computer. The ledgers can be summarised as follows:

- **sales ledger**

  the accounts of customers who have bought on credit (ie they have bought goods or services but will pay later) – these customers are known as 'debtors'

- **purchases ledger**

  the accounts of suppliers who have sold goods or services to the business on credit – these suppliers are known as 'creditors'

- **cash book**

  the book which records cash held by the business and bank accounts in the name of the business (note that in some ledger systems cash and bank accounts are kept in the general ledger – see below); a petty cash book is often used for recording low-value cash payments – usually for expenses – that are too small to be entered in the cash book

- **general or nominal ledger**

  all the other accounts – sales, purchases, returns, expenses, income, assets (items owned) and liabilities (items owed)

STAGE 4 – EXTRACTING REPORT INFORMATION

Financial data held in the accounts is only useful when it can be extracted and used by the management of the business or presented to owners such as shareholders. The advantage of computer accounting systems is that reports can be generated automatically from a menu and printed out. You will encounter a number of different reports in this Module, including:

- **trial balance**

  which lists the balances of the double-entry accounts in two separate columns – this is a check on the accuracy of the book-keeping

- **trading and profit and loss account**

  which shows the amount of profit or loss made by the business

- **balance sheet**

  which shows what the business owns (assets) what it owes (liabilities) and how it is financed (capital)

The diagram, below, gives a summary of the accounting system and its four stages.

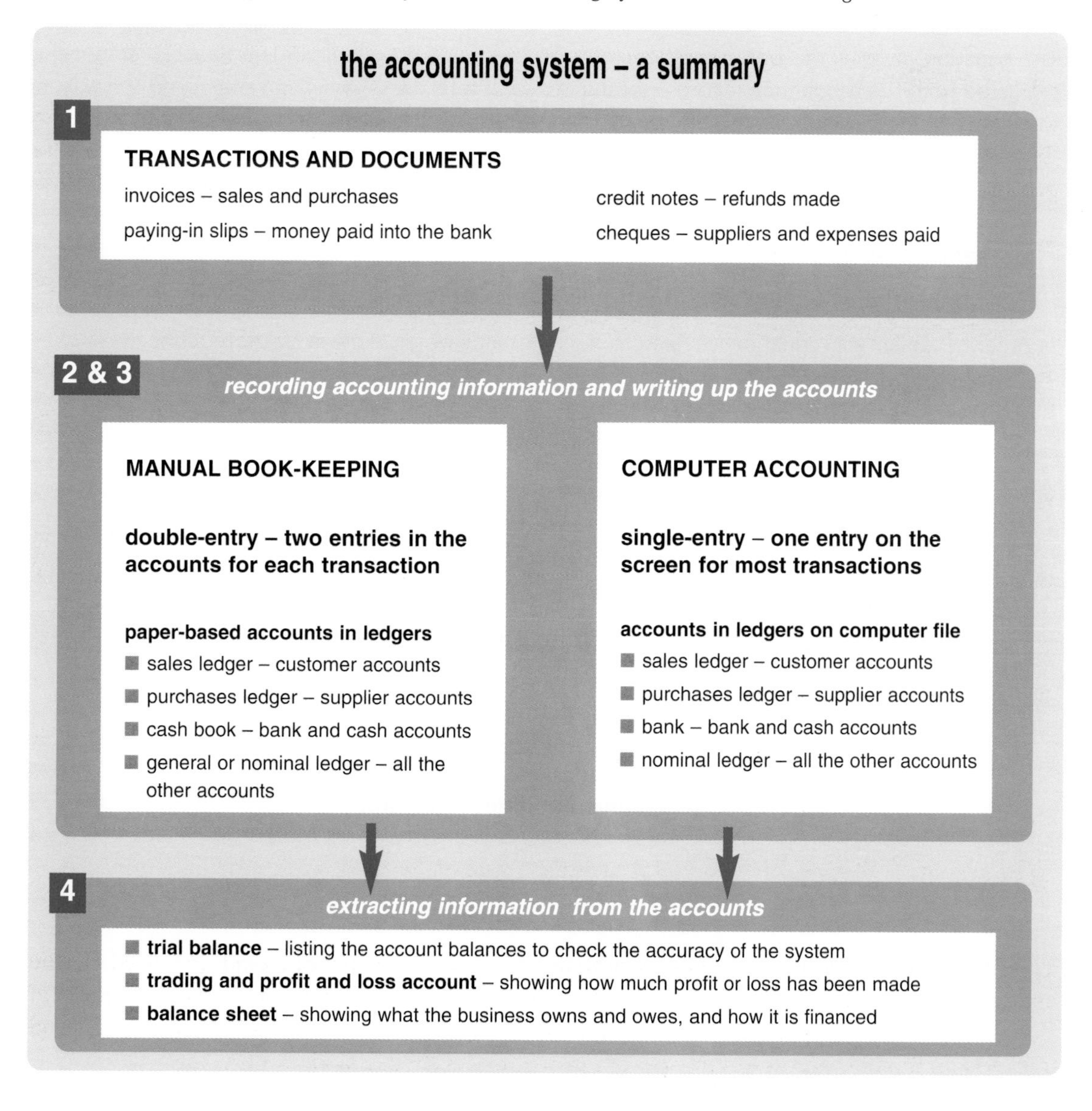

THE ACCOUNTING EQUATION

In this Module we do not study in detail the basic double-entry and other book-keeping procedures. Our starting point is the trial balance which we will be using to help in the preparation of the trading and profit and loss account and the balance sheet. Nevertheless, you do need to be aware of the book-keeping records that are kept in order to provide sources of information for the trial balance.

It is important to understand the principles of double-entry book-keeping and a way of doing this is to look at the accounting equation. Here the dual aspect of the debit and credit entries for each double-entry transaction are related to what happens in an equation. As your mathematical skills tell you, if you do something to one side of an equation you must do the same to the other side too, in order for it to remain balanced and have an equal amount on each side.

The equation involves the **balance sheet** of a business. A balance sheet, is a financial statement extracted from the accounting records, setting out what a business owns and owes, and the way in which it is financed.

Suppose you are starting a business, you will need to acquire assets and will also need to raise and invest money in order to buy them. One form of the equation is therefore:

assets (items owned)

= liabilities (money borrowed) plus capital (the owner's money)

In order to explain this equation we need to define exactly what we mean by these terms . . .

- **assets** are items the business owns such as property and equipment, money in the bank and money owed to the business by customers (debtors)
- **liabilities** are the 'other side of the coin' to assets – they are amounts that the business owes: money borrowed and amounts due to suppliers (creditors) for assets acquired
- **capital** is the money which the owner has put into the business – it is the owner's investment

Using mathematics and moving the liabilities figure onto the other side (changing the liabilities to a minus), the equation:

assets = liabilities + capital

can be restated as:

assets minus liabilities = capital

This is the basis of the balance sheet.

assets	minus	**liabilities**	equals	**capital**
what a business owns		*what a business owes*		*the owner's investment*

Let us now look at how this equation is affected as financial transactions are carried out.

workings of the accounting equation

Business transactions will have an effect on the balance sheet and the equation, as each transaction has a dual effect on the accounts. The equation will always balance. For example, if the owner of a business pays in £10,000 of new capital in the form of a cheque, the assets (bank account) will increase by this amount, and so will capital (capital account).

The diagram below shows a number of transactions which might pass through the business bank account. Note in each case:

- how the transaction has a twofold effect (the 'dual aspect')
- what those effects are from the point of view of the business
- how the equation (and hence the balance sheet) changes
- the equation always balances after the changes

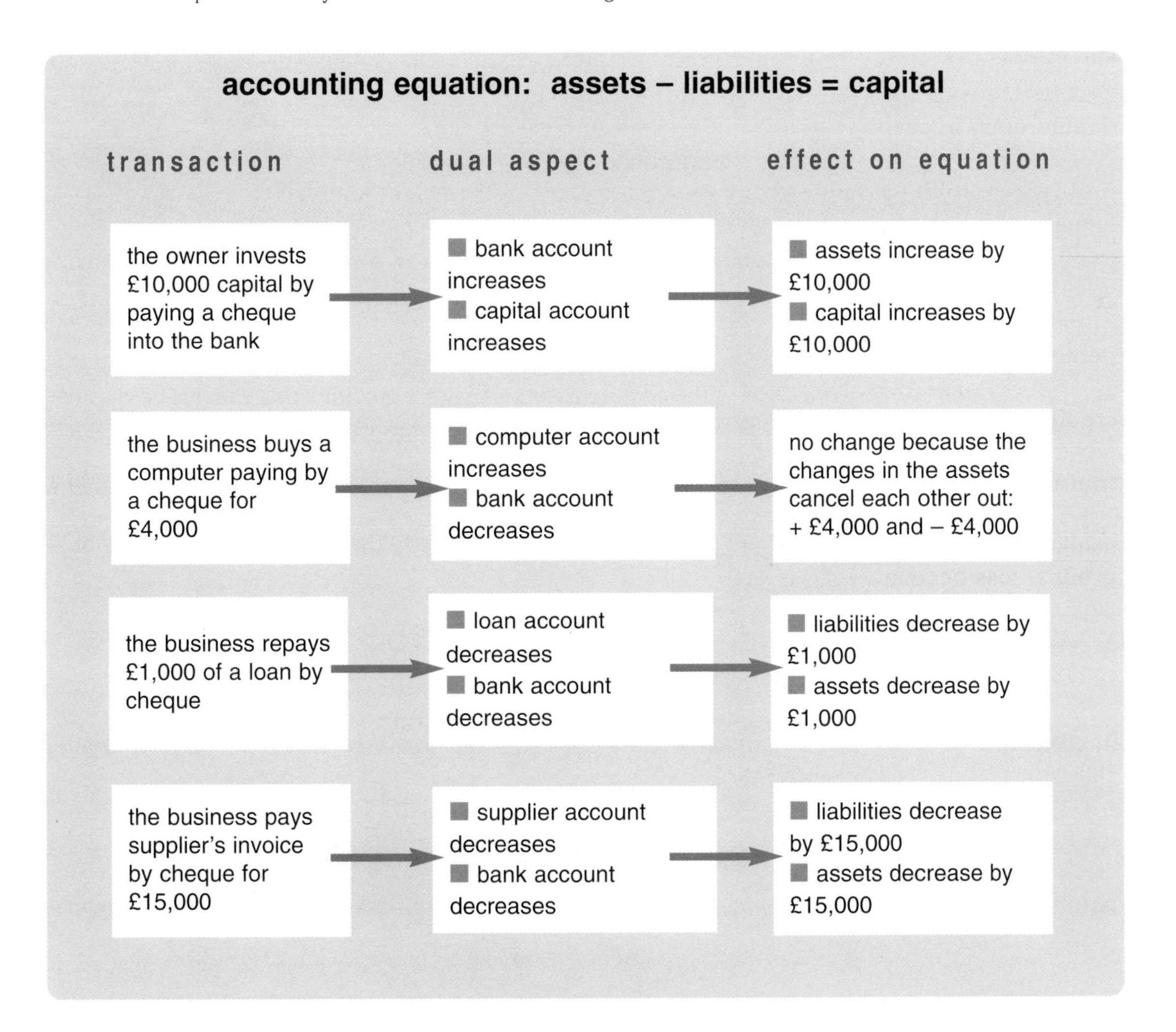

As you can see from the double-entry transactions, the equation always balances, and so will the balance sheet. It is also worth noting that the balance sheet of a business will never stay static – unless, of course, all activity ceases. It will change from day to day as the business buys and sells, pays expenses and receives income. We will be looking in detail at the balance sheets of limited companies in the later chapters of this Module.

If you wish to study double-entry book-keeping in more depth, Chapters 2 and 3 in the section of the book for Module 1 provide worked examples.

Accounting Terms

In the course of this chapter a number of specific accounting terms have been introduced. You should now study this section closely to ensure that you are clear about these definitions:

day book a listing of source documents relating to credit transactions in the accounting system ready for entry in the double-entry accounts

double-entry account an account into which business transactions are entered – entries are made in two accounts for each transaction

ledger an accounting book or section which contains specific types of account, for example the 'sales ledger' for customers who have bought on credit terms

debtors customers who have bought goods or services on credit from the business

creditors suppliers who have sold goods or services on credit to the business

trial balance list of account balances, used to check the accuracy of the ledger system

trading and profit & loss account statement which shows how much profit or loss has been made by the business

assets items which a business owns or is owed, eg vehicles or money due from customers (debtors)

liabilities items which a business owes, eg loans or money due to suppliers (creditors)

capital the investment of the owner(s) in a business

balance sheet the financial statement which 'balances' assets with liabilities and capital:

assets – liabilities = capital

CHAPTER SUMMARY

- Accounting is known as 'the language of business'.
- The accounting system comprises a series of consecutive stages: business transactions and documents, summaries of the transactions and documents, entering them into accounts kept in ledgers, using the data to produce financial reports for owners and managers. These reports include:
  - trial balance
  - trading and profit and loss account
  - balance sheet
- The accounting system can be manual (handwritten) or computerised; the same basic principles apply to both types.
- The double-entry system used by most businesses is based on the principle of there being two entries in separate accounts for each transaction – the dual aspect of accounting.
- The accounting equation is based on the balance sheet of a business and can be stated in two ways:

  assets = liabilities + capital

  assets – liabilities = capital

  The concept of the accounting equation is that for each business transaction there are two entries (the double-entry system) which means that the equation always balances.

In the next chapter we will look at how the double-entry system provides the information which goes into the trial balance.

QUESTIONS

NOTE: an asterisk (*) after the question number means that an answer to the question is given at the end of this book.

15.1* Fill in the missing words from the following sentences:

(a) The accounts of a business are organised using the .... system.

(b) A .... is a customer who has bought goods or services on credit from the business.

(c) A .... is a supplier who has sold goods or services on credit to the business.

(d) The .... contains the accounts of customers who have bought on credit terms.

(e) The .... records cash held by the business and bank accounts in the name of the business.

(f) Accounts such as assets, liabilities, expenses are kept in the ....

(g) The accounting equation is: .... minus .... equals ....

15.2 Outline the main stages of the accounting system. Describe three reports that can be found from the accounting system that will be of interest to the owners of the business.

15.3 Distinguish between:

(a) assets and liabilities

(b) debtors and creditors

(c) sales ledger and purchases ledger

(d) cash books and day books

15.4 Show the dual aspect, as it affects the accounting equation (assets – liabilities = capital), of the following transactions (which follow one another) for a particular business (ignore VAT):

(a) owner starts in business with capital of £8,000 in the bank

(b) buys a computer for £4,000, paying by cheque

(c) obtains a loan of £3,000 by cheque from a friend

(d) buys a van for £6,000, paying by cheque

15.5* Fill in the missing figures:

Assets	*Liabilities*	*Capital*
£	£	£
20,000	0	....
15,000	5,000	....
16,400	....	8,850
....	3,850	10,250
25,380	....	6,950
....	7,910	13,250

15.6* The table below sets out the assets, liabilities and capital of a business. The columns (a) to (f) show the ledger account balances resulting from a series of transactions that have taken place over time. You are to compare each set of adjacent columns, ie (a) with (b), (b) with (c), and so on and state, with figures, what accounting transactions have taken place in each case.

(Ignore VAT).

	(a) £	(b) £	(c) £	(d) £	(e) £	(f) £
Assets						
Office equipment	–	2,000	2,000	2,000	2,000	2,000
Van	–	–	–	10,000	10,000	10,000
Bank	10,000	8,000	14,000	4,000	6,000	3,000
Liabilities						
Loan	–	–	6,000	6,000	6,000	3,000
Capital	10,000	10,000	10,000	10,000	12,000	12,000

16 LEDGERS AND THE TRIAL BALANCE

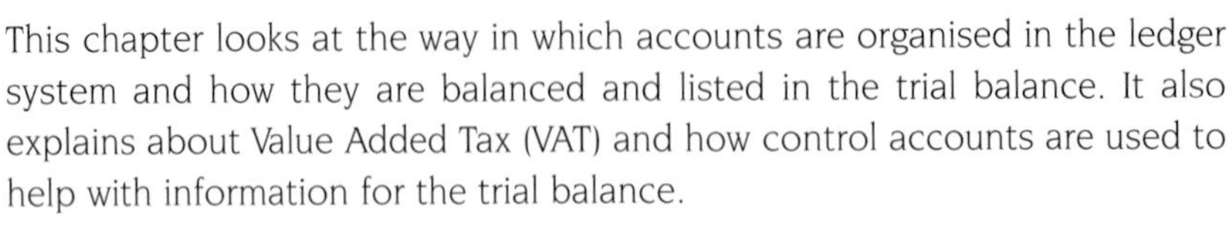

This chapter looks at the way in which accounts are organised in the ledger system and how they are balanced and listed in the trial balance. It also explains about Value Added Tax (VAT) and how control accounts are used to help with information for the trial balance.

The trial balance provides a check on the accuracy of the ledger system; however, we need to be aware that there may be errors that are not shown by a trial balance.

The trial balance is also the starting point in the preparation of final accounts – the trading and profit and loss account and the balance sheet.

Value Added Tax (VAT)

what is VAT?

Value Added Tax (VAT) is a government tax on spending paid by the person or business that buys goods or services. It is administered and collected by a government agency, HM Revenue & Customs, which was formed by the integration in 2005 of the Inland Revenue and HM Customs and Excise. VAT is charged on most sales, exceptions being items such as food, books, children's clothes and cycle helmets. If you would like further information about VAT and any other taxes, the HM Revenue & Customs website www.hmrc.gov.uk is well set out and helpful.

how does VAT affect businesses?

The main principle of VAT is that it is paid by the final consumer of a product – as you will well know when you shop. Businesses that have helped create the product you buy can claim back all the VAT they have paid – which is why accounting for VAT is so important. In other words, businesses act as tax collectors – charging their customers VAT, but keeping back the amount of VAT they pay on their purchases. This principle is illustrated in the diagram on page 96.

All businesses by law have to register with HM Revenue & Customs if their sales (or anticipated sales) of goods or services exceed a certain annual amount. This amount is known as the 'VAT threshold' and is normally increased annually in the Government's Spring Budget.

What does VAT registration involve? Once businesses are registered they are legally bound by a number of rules and regulations:

- They are given a VAT registration number which is quoted on invoices and other stationery.
- They must keep accounts for VAT.
- They must regularly send details to HM Revenue & Customs, on a VAT Return form, of the VAT they have charged to customers (on sales made) less the VAT they have paid out (on their purchases) to other businesses.

  This means that they will *either* send a payment to HM Revenue & Customs for VAT due (when they have received more VAT than they have paid) *or* they will reclaim VAT if they have paid more VAT than they have charged – if, for example they sell food, books or children's clothes.

Note that some small businesses qualify for what is known as the **flat rate scheme** which operates by calculating VAT payable by the business as a set percentage of its sales turnover. Explanations in this text will assume that the traditional VAT system described at the top of this page is used.

As you can see from all these requirements, keeping an accurate account for VAT is very important. The accounting records may be examined at any time by HM Revenue & Customs inspectors – so they have to be right!

accounting for VAT

Businesses normally keep a double-entry account for VAT charged and paid. The entries to this account come from:

- VAT amounts on purchases, eg supplier invoices and expenses
- VAT amounts on sales of goods

The balance of this account will be the amount owing to HM Revenue & Customs (or a refund due from HM Revenue & Customs). The account illustrated below shows that VAT of £1,000 (ie £3,000 less £2,000) is due to be paid:

Dr		VAT Account			Cr
20-2	**Details**	**£ p**	**20-2**	**Details**	**£ p**
30 Sep	Purchases VAT	2,000.00	30 Sep	Sales VAT	3,000.00
	VAT on purchases			**VAT on sales**	

We will return to VAT account later in the chapter when we look at the trial balance (page 249). First, however, we will look in more detail at the way in which the accounts are organised in the ledger system.

The Ledger System of Accounts

We saw in the last chapter that the double-entry accounting records of a business are divided into 'ledgers'. A ledger is a traditional word for a book. The term is used to apply to sections of a handwritten accounting system and also to divisions in some computer accounting programs (see Chapter 17). The main divisions of the ledger are:

- **sales ledger**

  the personal accounts of customers who have bought on credit (ie they have bought goods or services but will pay later) – these customers are also known as 'debtors'

- **purchases ledger**

  the personal accounts of suppliers who have sold to the business on credit – these suppliers are also known as 'creditors'

- **cash book**

  the book which records bank accounts in the name of the business, and cash held by the business; this book can be supplemented by a separate petty cash book for small cash purchases and expenses

- **general ledger (or nominal ledger)**

  all the other accounts in the accounting system, the main ones being:

  - income from sales and other sources
  - purchases of materials and stock
  - business expenses paid, eg wages, rent, insurance, advertising
  - assets (items owned) and liabilities (items owed)
  - capital (the investment of the owners)
  - VAT
  - stock (normally valued and entered in the accounts at each year end)
  - profit/loss (normally calculated for each year)
  - in some ledger systems cash and bank account are kept in the general ledger

Remember that for each double-entry transaction there will be entries in two accounts in any of the ledgers.

The ledger system can be represented diagrammatically, as shown on the next page.

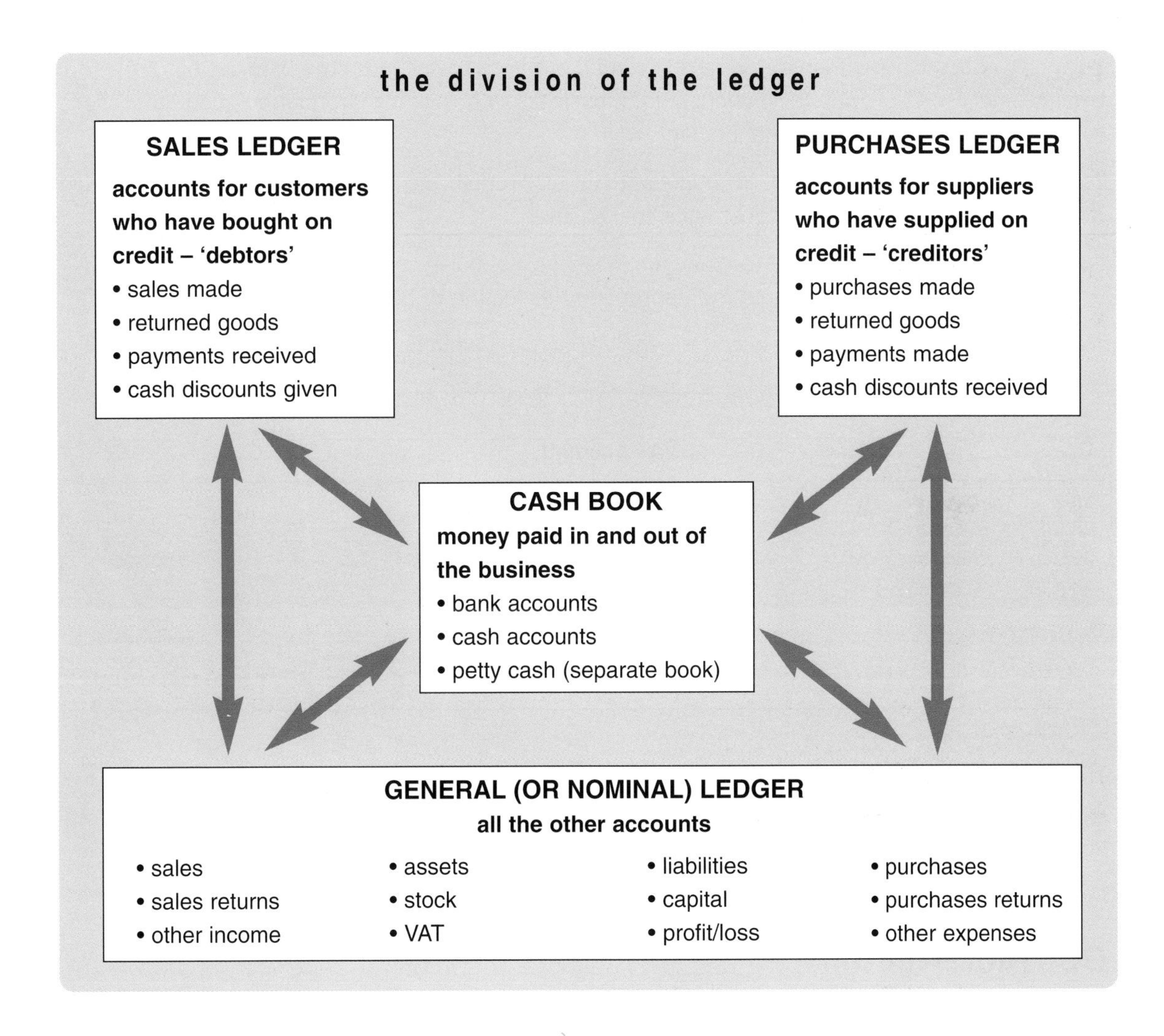

Balancing the Accounts and the Trial Balance

Double entry book-keeping involves the making of a debit entry and a credit entry for every transaction. It therefore follows that if the book-keeper has done his or her job accurately, the total of all the debit entries will equal the total of the credit entries for any given period. To test this accuracy the book-keeper will regularly, often on a monthly basis, check that the total of the debit entries equals the total of the credit entries by extracting a trial balance, which should show that these totals do, in fact, agree. A trial balance is illustrated on page 250.

balancing accounts

In order to provide the figures for a trial balance the book-keeper **balances** and calculates the running total of each account before setting out the trial balance.

Balancing of accounts is therefore regularly carried out both to speed up the preparation of the trial balance and also to provide the owner(s) of the business with valuable information about items such as sales, purchases, expenses and income.

The book-keeper will balance the accounts and, in this Module, we use the list of balances provided by the book-keeper in order to construct a trial balance.

For this purpose we do not need to study the mechanics of balancing accounts; however, if you wish to look into this topic, it is covered in Chapter 5 in the section of the book for Module 1.

To give an example of balancing accounts, the VAT account seen earlier in this chapter (page 245) is balanced at the month-end as follows:

Dr		VAT Account			Cr
20-2	Details	£ p	20-2	Details	£ p
30 Sep	Purchases VAT	2,000.00	30 Sep	Sales VAT	3,000.00
30 Sep	Balance c/d	1,000.00			
		3,000.00			3,000.00
			1 Oct	Balance b/d	1,000.00

This account has a credit balance brought down (b/d) at the start of October – this means that the business owes (ie a creditor) £1,000.00 to HM Revenue & Customs. The amount will be shown on the credit side of the trial balance when it is prepared.

Control Accounts

There is one further type of account we need to know about before looking at the accounts listed in the trial balance – a **control account.**

A control account is a summary account or master account, which records the totals of entries to a particular set of subsidiary accounts.

The sales ledger control account, for instance, shows the total of all customers' accounts in the sales ledger and tells the owner of the business how much in total is owing from debtors.

The purchases ledger control account shows the total of all the suppliers' accounts in the purchases ledger and tells the owner of the business how much in total is owing to creditors.

The individual debtor and creditor accounts are known as 'memorandum' accounts. The control accounts provide a check on the accuracy of the book-keeping in the set of accounts which they control.

control accounts and the trial balance

The trial balance (see next page) is the listing of all the account balances in two columns: debit balances on the left, credit balances on the right.

It is the balances of the control accounts which are taken to the trial balance rather than the individual debtor and creditor balances, which would clutter it up and make it very long. The description of the control accounts in the trial balance is simply 'debtors' (a debit balance on the left) and 'creditors' (a credit balance on the right). Look at the diagram below.

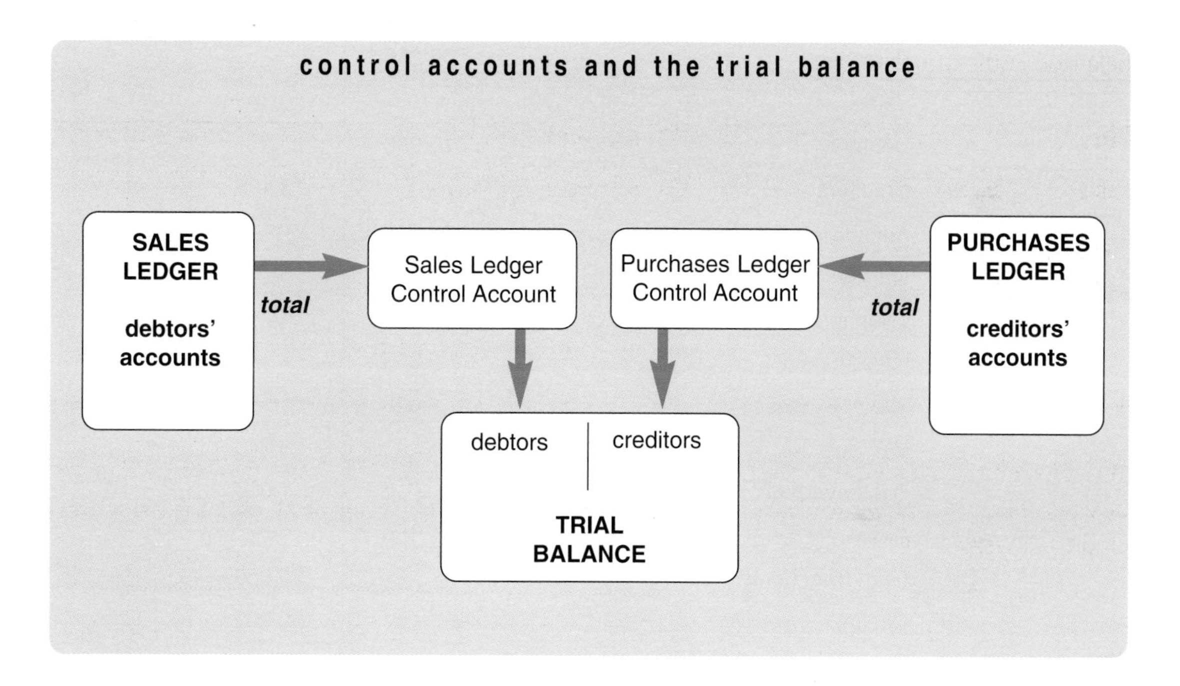

TRIAL BALANCE

When the book-keeper has balanced the accounts and totalled up the control accounts, he or she can then draw up the trial balance.

A trial balance is a summary in two columns of the balances of all the ledger accounts, listing debit balances on the left and credit balances on the right, and showing the total of each column. An example is shown on the next page.

If the book-keeper has been accurate in the day-to-day recording of transactions, the total of the two columns should agree, as they do here.

the trial balance

DOLCE LIMITED
Trial balance as at 30 June 20-2

	Dr	Cr
	£	£
Premises	125,000	
Machinery	40,000	
Purchases	96,250	
Sales		146,390
Debtors	10,390	
Creditors		12,495
Administration expenses	18,740	
Wages	38,430	
Telephone	3,020	
Interest paid	2,350	
Travel expenses	1,045	
VAT due		3,240
Bank overdraft		1,050
Cash	150	
Loan from bank		20,000
Capital		152,200
	335,375	335,375

The key to understanding a trial balance is to remember that it shows the account balances from the point of view of the business. The practical rules for debits and credits are:

debit entry

- money in the bank, cash
- purchases, expenses paid
- assets owned

credit entry

- a bank overdraft, bank loan
- sales, other income received
- liabilities owed
- capital

An easy way to remember these is to use the word 'PEARLS'.

Purchases	
Expenses	debit entries
Assets	
Receipts	
Liabilities	credit entries
Sales	

The Worked Example which follows illustrates the practicalities of drawing up a trial balance from the double-entry accounts.

WORKED EXAMPLE: THE TRIAL BALANCE

situation

The book-keeper of H Smith Limited has just completed balancing the double-entry accounts at the end of December 20-2. He has listed them as follows, identifying them as debits or credits:

	£	
Capital	50,000	Cr
Bank	1,500	Dr
Purchases	95,000	Dr
Sales	179,000	Cr
Returns out	5,000	Cr
Returns in	4,000	Dr
Wages	37,000	Dr
Equipment	35,000	Dr
Vehicles	59,000	Dr
Debtors	58,400	Dr
Creditors	25,000	Cr
VAT	21,000	Cr
Bank loan	10,000	Cr
Petty cash	100	Dr

The book-keeper shows the list to the Managing Director, who asks a number of questions:

1 'How do you know whether the bank balance is money in the bank or an overdraft?'

2 'What are returns in and returns out?'

3 'What is the VAT – is it something we have to pay, or is it being paid to us?'

4 'What are the debtors and creditors?'

5 'What is the petty cash?'

6 'How do you know whether the figures are right or not?'

solution

The book-keeper replies as follows:

1 The bank balance is a debit balance and therefore represents money in the bank. An overdraft would have been a credit balance. We do have a bank loan which is a credit balance. Remember that we look at the bank balance in the trial balance from the point of view of our business – money in the bank is an asset (ie the bank owes us our money back); by contrast with the bank loan we have a liability where we owe money to the bank.

2 'Returns in' are sales returns. The account records all the goods that have been sent back to us. It is a debit balance because the refunds to our customers are effectively a cost to the business.

'Returns out' are purchases returns. The account records all the goods that have been returned by us to our suppliers. It is a credit balance because it represents refunds made to us.

3 The VAT is the amount we have to pay. It is a liability (we owe it to HM Revenue & Customs) and so it is a credit balance.

4 Debtors is the balance of the sales ledger control account, which is the total of all the debtor accounts in the sales ledger. It is a debit balance because it is money owed to us by our customers.

Creditors is the total of the purchases ledger control account, which is the total of all the creditor accounts in the purchases ledger. It is a credit balance because it is the money we owe to our suppliers.

5 Petty cash is the float of cash we hold in the office for making low-value cash payments – usually for expenses. We use it for transactions that are too small to be entered in the cash book. When the float of petty cash runs low, we top it up by transfer of cash from the cash book. The office junior is responsible for the security of the cash and for writing up the petty cash book – I make regular checks to see that everything is ok.

6 We draw up a trial balance to show that the total of the debit balances (the left-hand column) equals the total of the credit balances (the right-hand column). As you can see we are correct here. If the columns did not have the same total we would have to investigate our arithmetic and the account entries in our ledgers. Of course, if we had a computerised accounting system I would not have to go to all this trouble – the system would produce a trial balance automatically – and it would balance!

The trial balance produced is shown below.

Trial Balance of H Smith Limited as at 31 December 20-2

	Debit (£)	*Credit (£)*
Capital		50,000
Bank	1,500	
Purchases	95,000	
Sales		179,000
Returns out		5,000
Returns in	4,000	
Wages	37,000	
Equipment	35,000	
Vehicles	59,000	
Debtors	58,400	
Creditors		25,000
VAT due		21,000
Bank loan		10,000
Petty cash	100	
	290,000	290,000

Debit and Credit Balances – Which is Which?

The trial balance is prepared from the accounts held in the ledgers. Each account is balanced by the book-keeper. Certain accounts always have a debit balance, while others always have a credit balance. You may know a number of these already, but the lists set out below will help you when doing practical exercises.

debit balances

- cash account
- purchases account
- sales returns account (returns in)
- fixed asset accounts, eg premises, motor vehicles, machinery, office equipment, etc
- expense accounts, eg wages, telephone, rent paid, carriage
- drawings account
- debtors' accounts – often shown in the trial balance as a total – the debtors control account
- VAT repayment owed by HM Revenue & Customs

credit balances

- sales account
- purchases returns account (returns out)
- income accounts, eg rent received, commission received, fees received
- capital account
- loan account
- VAT payment due to be made to HM Revenue & Customs
- creditors' accounts – often shown in the trial balance as a total – the creditors control account

bank account

Bank account can be either debit or credit – it will be debit when the business has money in the bank (an asset), and credit when it is overdrawn (a liability).

IF THE TRIAL BALANCE DOESN'T BALANCE . . .

If the trial balance fails to balance, ie the two totals are different, there is an error (or errors):

- either in the addition of the trial balance
- and/or in the double-entry book-keeping

The procedure for finding the error(s) is as follows:

- check the addition of the columns of the trial balance
- check that the balance of each account has been correctly entered in the trial balance, and under the correct heading, ie debit or credit
- check the calculation of the balance on each account
- calculate the amount that the trial balance is wrong, and then look in the accounts for a transaction for this amount: if one is found, check that the double-entry book-keeping has been carried out correctly

- if the amount by which the trial balance is wrong is divisible by nine, then the error may be a reversal of figures, eg £65 entered as £56, or £45 entered as £54
- if the error cannot be found, it will have to be placed in a suspense account (see page 321) for further investigation

Errors Not Shown by a Trial Balance

As mentioned earlier, a trial balance does not prove the complete accuracy of the ledgers. There are six types of error that are not shown by a trial balance.

error of omission

Here a business transaction has been completely omitted from the accounting records, ie both the debit and credit entries have not been made.

reversal of entries

With this error, the debit and credit entries have been made in the accounts but on the wrong side of the two accounts concerned.

mispost/error of commission

Here, a transaction is entered to the wrong person's account. For example, a sale of goods on credit to D Malfoy has been entered as debit to L Malfoy's account by mistake. The customer will soon pick up an error like this!

error of principle

This is when a transaction has been entered in the wrong type of account. For example, the cost of fuel for vehicles has been entered as a debit to motor vehicles account instead of motor vehicle expenses.

error of original entry (or transcription)

Here, the correct accounts have been used, and the correct sides. What is wrong is that the amount has been entered incorrectly in both accounts.

compensating error

This is where two errors cancel each other out. For example, if the balance of purchases account is calculated wrongly at £10 too much, and a similar error has occurred in calculating the balance of sales account, then the two errors will compensate each other, and the trial balance will not show the errors.

Later in the book (Chapter 20) we will see how to correct errors that are found in the book-keeping system.

The Trial Balance – Where Next?

The trial balance, as well as being a check on the accuracy of the book-keeping, is also the starting point in the preparation of the final accounts of a business. These final accounts, which are often prepared annually, comprise the trading and profit and loss account and balance sheet. Their preparation is made easier when a trial balance has been produced.

We will look at final accounts in Chapter 18.

CHAPTER SUMMARY

- Value Added Tax (VAT) is a government tax on spending paid by the person or business that buys goods or services.
- Businesses which reach the VAT threshold have to register for VAT.
- It is essential that a business runs an account for VAT because the tax is charged on most goods and services.
- VAT is paid in full by the final consumer – so businesses act as tax collectors, charging VAT but claiming back the VAT that they themselves have paid.
- The double-entry system of accounts is normally divided up into four ledgers or 'books': sales ledger, purchases ledger, cash book and general ledger (or nominal ledger).
- Some ledgers, such as purchases ledger and sales ledger, often contain a large number of accounts which are summarised in a control account.
- The double-entry accounts – including the control accounts – are balanced regularly to find out the 'total' of each account. These totals are then listed in a trial balance which sets out debit balances and credit balances in separate columns, the totals of which should be the same.
- The trial balance is an essential check of the accuracy of the double-entry book-keeping. If the columns of the trial balance do not agree, the error should be investigated and corrected.
- The trial balance, as well as being a check on the accuracy of the book-keeping, is also the starting point in the preparation of the final accounts.

In the next chapter we will look at the use of computers in accounting, including the advantages and disadvantages of computer accounting.

QUESTIONS

NOTE: an asterisk (*) after the question number means that an answer to the question is given at the end of this book.

16.1* VAT is a government tax on spending.

(a) Who pays all the VAT when you buy a TV from an electrical store?

(b) What happens to the VAT which the electrical store is charged by the TV manufacturer when it buys the TV in the first place?

16.2* A business registers for VAT. Describe briefly what this means for the business.

16.3* (a) Define a 'control' account.

(b) What does the balance of the sales ledger control account tell the business owner?

(c) What is the advantage of using a control account when you are drawing up a trial balance?

16.4 Which items would be transferred to the trial balance from the following:

(a) sales ledger ....

(b) purchase ledger ....

(c) the cash book ....

(d) the petty cash book ....

Assessment and Qualifications Alliance (AQA), 2001

16.5 (a) What does it imply about the ability of the book-keeper when the debit and credit totals of a trial balance are not the same figure?

(b) State two possible reasons why the debit and credit totals of a trial balance might not add up to the same total.

16.6 Produce the trial balance of Brian Montagu as at 28 February 20-1.

	£
Cash	130
Sales	3,720
VAT owing	250
Bank	720
Car	2,500
Machinery	1,500
Capital	5,000
Purchases	4,220
Debtors	192
Returns out	168
Creditors	254
Returns in	130

16.7 Produce the trial balance of Jane Greenwell as at 28 February 20-1. She has forgotten to open a capital account.

	£
Bank overdraft	1,250
Purchases	850
Cash	48
Sales	730
Returns out	144
Creditors	1,442
Equipment	2,704
Van	3,200
Returns in	90
Debtors	1,174
Wages	1,500
Capital	?

16.8 Complete the following table, which lists some items that can be found in a trial balance. State from which ledger each account is taken and whether it will be a debit or credit entry in the trial balance.

Item (a) has been completed as an example.

	Account	Ledger	Debit/Credit
(a)	*Vehicles*	*general ledger*	*debit*
(b)	Debtors		
(c)	Sales		
(d)	Returns out		
(e)	Wages		
(f)	Petty cash		
(g)	VAT owing		
(h)	Bank loan		

16.9* (a) What is the source of the figures used to construct the trial balance?

....

....

....

(b) Describe two uses of the trial balance.

....

....

....

(c) Comment on the limitations of trial balances as a means of checking the accuracy of the ledger. Use two examples to illustrate your answer.

....

....

....

....

....

Assessment and Qualifications Alliance (AQA), 2001

16.10 Write a report to the managing director of R Masters Ltd:

(i) explaining the benefits that he may obtain from using a trial balance before the preparation of the final accounts

(ii) outlining the main limitation of the procedure

(iii) describing one example to illustrate the limitation

REPORT

To: ....

From: ....

Date: ....

Subject: ....

....

....

....

....

....

....

....

Assessment and Qualifications Alliance (AQA), 2002

16.11* The book-keeper of Lorna Fox has extracted the following list of balances as at 31 March 20-2:

	£
Purchases	96,250
Sales	146,390
Sales returns	8,500
Administration expenses	10,240
Wages	28,980
Telephone	3,020
Interest paid	2,350
Travel expenses	1,045
Premises	125,000
Machinery	40,000
Debtors	10,390
Bank overdraft	1,050
Petty cash	150
Creditors	11,140
VAT owing	1,355
Loan from bank	20,000
Drawings	9,450
Capital	155,440

You are to:

(a) Produce the trial balance at 31 March 20-2.

(b) Take any three debit balances and any three credit balances and explain to someone who does not understand accounting why they are listed as such, and what this means to the business.

16.12* Fill in the missing words from the following sentences:

(a) "You made an error of .... when you recorded the cost of diesel fuel for the van in vans account."

(b) "I've had the book-keeper from D Jones Limited on the 'phone concerning the statements of account that we sent out the other day. She says that there is a sales invoice charged that she knows nothing about. I wonder if we have done a .... and it should be for T Jones' account?"

(c) "There is a 'bad figure' on a purchases invoice – we have read it as £35 when it should be £55. It has gone through our ledgers wrongly so we have an error of .... to put right."

(d) "Although the trial balance balanced last week, I've since found an error of £100 in the calculation of the balance of sales account. We will need to check the other balances as I think we may have a .... error."

(e) "Who was in charge of that trainee last week? He has done the double-entry for the payment of the electricity bill on the wrong side of both bank and electricity accounts – a .... of ...."

(f) "I found this purchase invoice from last week in amongst the copy letters. As we haven't put it through the ledgers we have an error of ...."

17 INTRODUCING COMPUTER ACCOUNTING

Although some businesses, particularly small ones, still use paper-based accounting systems, an increasing number are now operating computerised accounting systems. Small and medium-sized businesses can buy 'off-the shelf' accounting programs from suppliers such as Sage while larger businesses often have custom-designed programs.

The accounting programs carry out functions such as invoicing, dealing with payments, paying wages and providing regular management reports such as trading and profit and loss accounts and balance sheets.

Businesses also make considerable use of computer spreadsheets, particularly for budgets. They can also be used for speeding up the processes in manual accounting systems, setting up a trial balance, for example.

The introduction of a computer accounting system can provide major advantages such as speed and accuracy of operation. There are also certain disadvantages, such as cost and training needs which the management of a business must appreciate before taking the decision to convert from a manual to a computerised accounting system.

FEATURES OF COMPUTER ACCOUNTING

facilities

A typical computer accounting program will offer a number of facilities:

- on-screen input and printout of sales invoices
- automatic updating of customer accounts in the sales ledger
- recording of suppliers' invoices
- automatic updating of supplier accounts in the purchases ledger
- recording of bank receipts
- making payments to suppliers and for expenses
- automatic updating of the general (nominal) ledger
- automatic adjustment of stock records

Payroll can also be computerised – often on a separate program.

management reports

A computer accounting program can provide instant reports for management, for example:

- aged debtors' summary – a summary of customer accounts, showing overdue amounts
- trial balance, trading and profit and loss account and balance sheet
- stock valuation
- VAT Return
- payroll analysis

computer accounting – ledger system

We have already have covered the 'Ledger' in Chapter 16. The 'Ledger' – which basically means 'the books of the business' is a term used to describe the way the accounts of the business are grouped into different sections:

- **sales ledger**, containing the accounts of debtors (customers)
- **purchases ledger**, containing the accounts of creditors (suppliers)
- **cash books**, containing the main cash book and the petty cash book
- **general ledger** (also called nominal ledger) containing the remaining accounts, eg expenses (including purchases), income (including sales), assets, loans, stock, VAT

The screens of a ledger computer accounting system are designed to be user-friendly. Look at the toolbar of the opening screen of a Sage™accounting system shown below and then read the notes printed underneath.

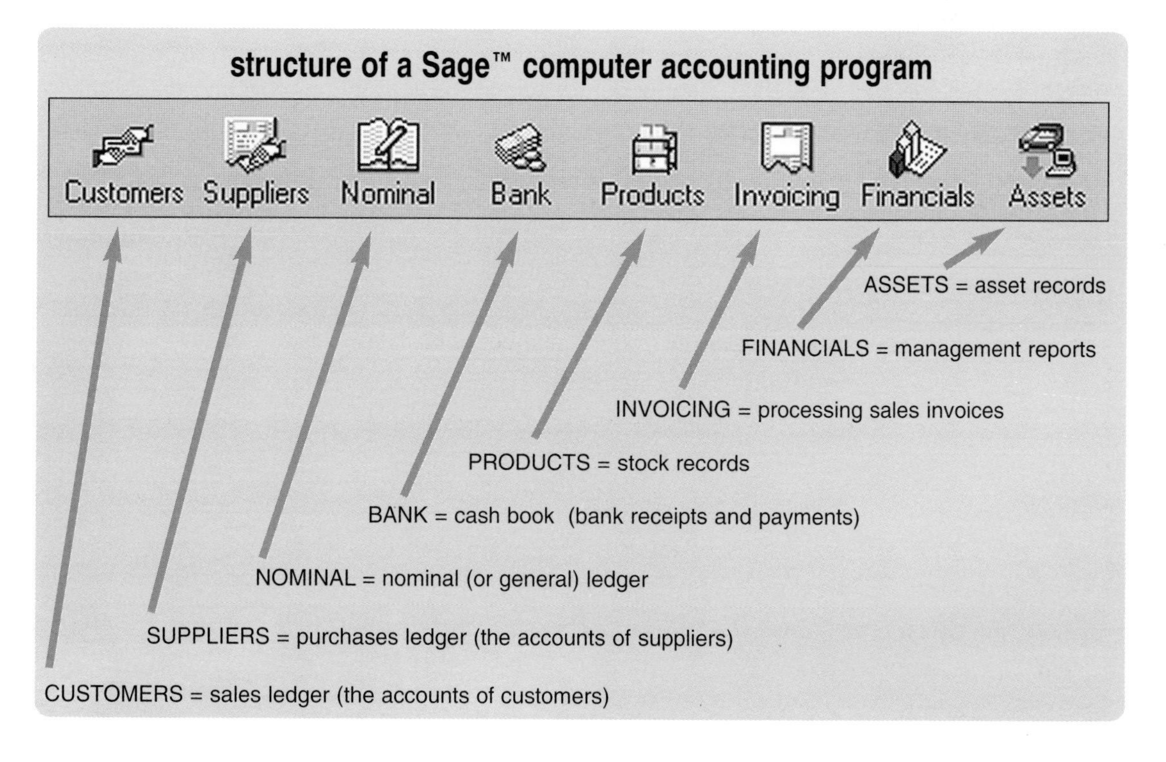

using a computer accounting system

Computer input screens are designed to be easy to use. Their main advantage is that each transaction needs only to be input once, unlike in a manual double-entry system where two or three entries are required. In the example below, payment is made for copy paper costing £45.50. The input line includes the nominal account number of bank account (1200), the date of payment, the cheque number (234234), and the nominal account code for stationery expenses (7500). The net amount of £45.50 is entered and the computer automatically calculates the VAT. The appropriate amounts are then transferred by the computer to bank account, stationery expenses account and VAT account.

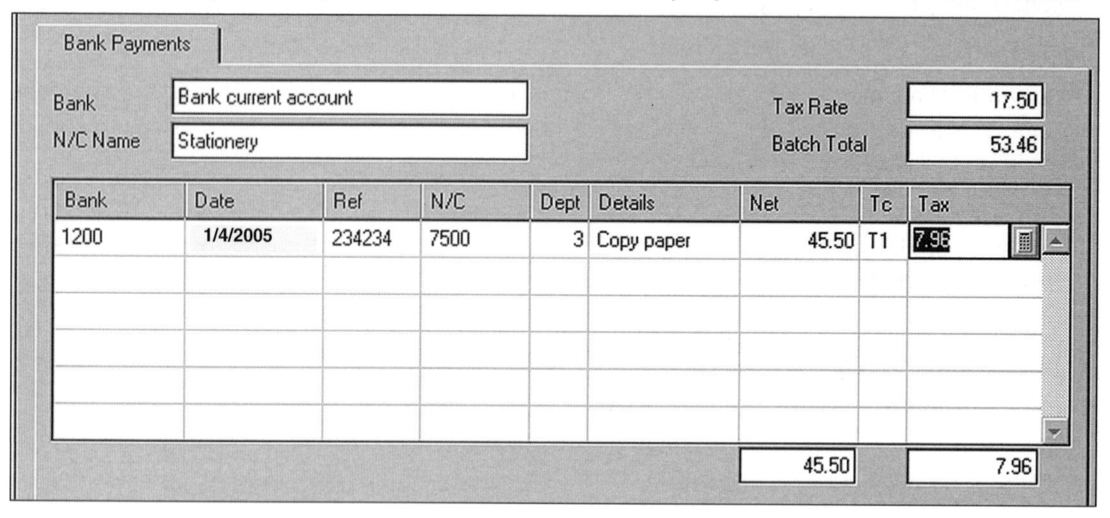

Bank Payments

Bank: Bank current account
N/C Name: Stationery
Tax Rate: 17.50
Batch Total: 53.46

Bank	Date	Ref	N/C	Dept	Details	Net	Tc	Tax
1200	1/4/2005	234234	7500	3	Copy paper	45.50	T1	7.96
						45.50		7.96

The screen below shows an invoice input screen. In this example 20 Enigma 35s are being invoiced to R Patel & Co in Salisbury. The computer will in due course print the invoice, which will contain the name of the seller as well as all the customer details held in the accounting program's database.

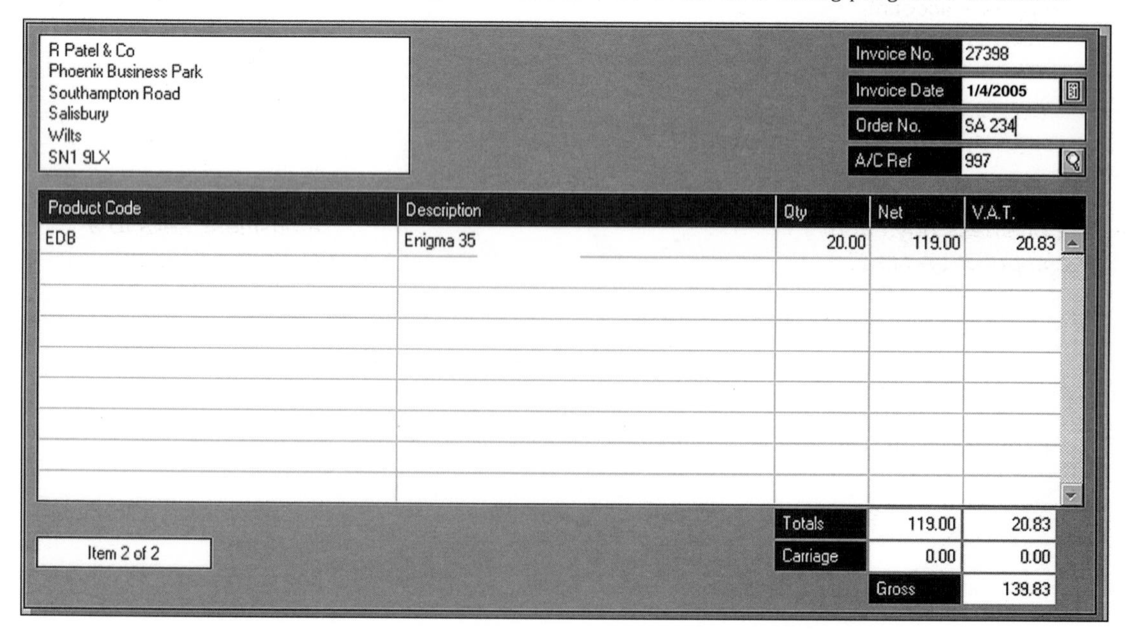

R Patel & Co
Phoenix Business Park
Southampton Road
Salisbury
Wilts
SN1 9LX

Invoice No.: 27398
Invoice Date: 1/4/2005
Order No.: SA 234
A/C Ref: 997

Product Code	Description	Qty	Net	V.A.T.
EDB	Enigma 35	20.00	119.00	20.83
		Totals	119.00	20.83
		Carriage	0.00	0.00
			Gross	139.83

Item 2 of 2

computerised ledgers – an integrated system

A computerised ledger system is **fully integrated**. This means that when a business transaction is input on the computer it is recorded in a number of different accounting records at the same time. For example, when the sales invoice on the previous page is entered on the screen and the ledgers are 'updated' an integrated program will:

- record the amount of the invoice in the customer account R Patel & Co in the sales ledger
- record the amount of the invoice in the sales account and VAT account (if appropriate) in the general ledger
- reduce the stock of goods held (in this case Enigmas) in the stock records

At the centre of an integrated program is the nominal ledger which deals with all the accounts except customers' accounts and suppliers' accounts. It is affected one way or another by most transactions.

The diagram below shows how the three 'ledgers' can link with the nominal (general) ledger. You can see how an account in the nominal ledger is affected by each of these three transactions. This is the double-entry book-keeping system at work. The advantage of the computer system is that in each case only one entry has to be made. Life is made a great deal simpler by this.

Note that VAT account is omitted from this diagram for the sake of simplicity of illustration. VAT account will be maintained in the nominal (general) ledger and will be updated by all three of the transactions shown.

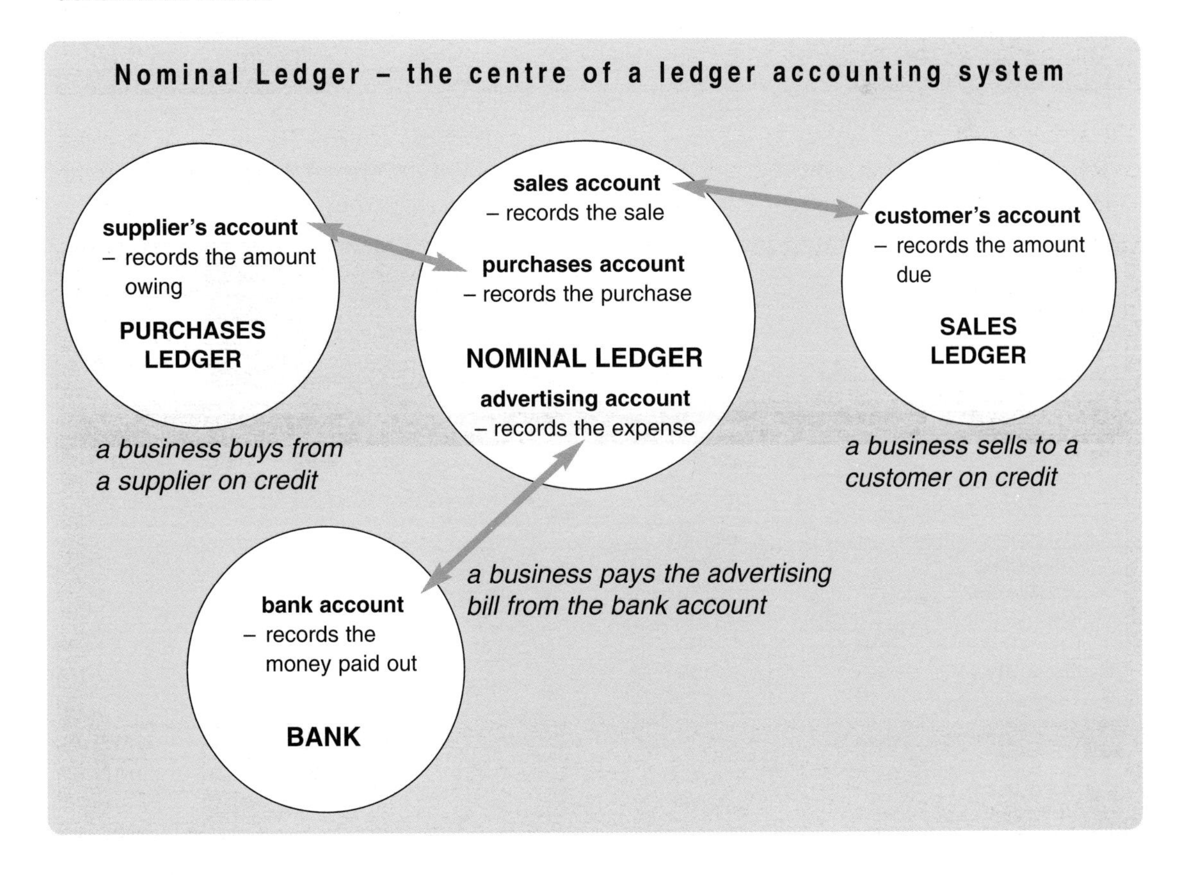

COMPUTER SPREADSHEETS

A spreadsheet is a grid of boxes – 'cells' – set up on the computer, organised in rows and columns into which you can enter text and numbers. It enables you to make calculations with the figures. The computer program will work out the calculations automatically once you have entered an appropriate formula in the cell where the result of the calculations is required.

The major advantage of a spreadsheet is that if you change any of the figures the computer will automatically recalculate the total, saving you much time and effort.

Spreadsheets are used for a variety of functions in business:

- producing invoices – working out costs of products sold, calculating and adding on VAT and producing a sales total
- working out budgets for future expenditure
- working out sales figures for different products or areas

A commonly used spreadsheet program is Microsoft Excel.

Spreadsheets may be used in a wide variety of accounting functions. The first of the two examples illustrated here is very simple: it shows the two columns of a **trial balance**. The spreadsheet has been set up with columns for account names, debit balances, credit balances and totals for the columns. When the figures have been entered, they will automatically produce totals which should balance.

	A	B	C	D	E	F	G
1		Dr	Cr				
2							
3							
4	Plant and machinery	35000					
5	Office equipment	15000					
6	Furniture and fixtures	25000					
7	Debtors control account	45500					
8	Bank current account	12450					
9	Creditors control account		32510				
10	Sales tax control account		17920				
11	Purchase tax control account	26600					
12	Loans		35000				
13	Ordinary Shares		75000				
14	Hardware sales		85000				
15	Software sales		15000				
16	Computer consultancy		2400				
17	Materials purchased	69100					
18	Advertising	12400					
19	Gross wages	16230					
20	Rent	4500					
21	General rates	450					
22	Electricity	150					
23	Telephone	275					
24	Stationery	175					
25							
26							
27	Total	262830	262830				

The second example of a computer spreadsheet used in the accounting process is a form of budget known as a **cash flow forecast**. This is a projection of the cash inflows and outflows of a business over a period of months. Each month the spreadsheet calculates the total inflow (row 11) and outflow (row 23) and uses them to calculate the net cash inflow/outflow (row 24). This figure is then used to calculate the projected bank balance of the business (row 26). This figure is useful as it will show if the business needs to borrow from the bank.

The advantage of the spreadsheet in this example is that if the business wishes to change any of the receipt or payment amounts – eg if the sales receipts increase – then the cashflow figures will automatically be recalculated, potentially saving hours of work.

	A	B	C	D	E	F	G
1	**CORIANNE LIMITED**						
2	**Cash flow forecast for the six months ending June 2004**						
3		JANUARY	FEBRUARY	MARCH	APRIL	MAY	JUNE
4		£	£	£	£	£	£
5	*Receipts*						
6							
7							
8	Sales Receipts	3,000	3,000	4,000	4,000	4,000	4,000
9							
10	Capital	10,000					
11	TOTAL RECEIPTS	13,000	3,000	4,000	4,000	4,000	4,000
12	*Payments*						
13	Purchases	5,000	1,750	1,750		1,750	1,750
14	Fixed Assets	4,500	5,250				
15	Rent/Rates	575	575	575	575	575	575
16	Insurance	50	50	50	50	50	50
17	Electricity	25	25	25	25	25	25
18	Telephone	150	15	15	15	15	15
19	Stationery	10	10	10	10	10	10
20	Postage	15	15	15	15	15	15
21	Bank charges	100		75			75
22	Advertising	150	30	30	30	30	30
23	TOTAL PAYMENTS	10,575	7,720	2,545	720	2,470	2,545
24	CASHFLOW FOR MONTH	2,425	- 4,720	1,455	3,280	1,530	1,455
25	Bank Balance *brought forward*	-	2,425	- 2,295	- 840	2,440	3,970
26	Bank Balance *carried forward*	2,425	- 2,295	- 840	2,440	3,970	5,425

Advantages and Disadvantages of Computer Accounting

In this chapter so far we have stressed the advantages of the introduction of computers to carry out accounting functions in a business. There are, however, some disadvantages as well, and any business introducing computer accounting will need to weigh up carefully the 'pros and cons'. This is an area which has featured in past examinations.

The remainder of this chapter will deal with these advantages and disadvantages and provide an example in the form of a Worked Example based on the effect on employees of the introduction of a new computer accounting system.

advantages of computer accounting

The main advantages of using a computer accounting program such as Sage include:

- **speed** – data entry on the computer with its formatted screens and built-in databases of customer and supplier details and stock records can be carried out far more quickly than any manual processing
- **automatic document production** – fast and accurate invoice and credit note printing, statement runs, payroll processing
- **accuracy** – there is less room for error as only one account entry is needed for each transaction rather than the two (or three) required in a manual double-entry system
- **up-to-date information** – the accounting records are automatically updated and so account balances (eg customer accounts) will always be up-to-date
- **availability of information** – the data can be made available to different users at the same time
- **management information** – reports can be produced which will help management monitor and control the business, for example the aged debtors analysis which shows which customer accounts are overdue, trial balance, trading and profit and loss account and balance sheet
- **VAT return** – the automatic production of figures for the regular VAT return
- **legibility** – the onscreen and printed data should always be legible and so will avoid errors caused by poor figures
- **efficiency** – better use is made of resources and time; cash flow should improve through better debt collection
- **staff motivation** – the system will require staff to be trained to use new skills, which can make them feel more valued

disadvantages of computer accounting

The main disadvantages of using computer accounting programs include:

- **capital cost of installation** – the hardware and software will need to be budgeted for, not only as 'one-off' expenditure but also as recurrent costs because computers will need replacing and software updating
- **cost of training** – the staff will need to be trained in the use of the hardware and software
- **staff opposition** – motivation may suffer as some staff do not like computers, also there may be staff redundancies, all of which create bad feeling
- **disruption** – loss of work time and changes in the working environment when the computerised system is first introduced
- **system failure** – the danger of the system crashing and the subsequent loss of work when no back-ups have been made
- **back-up requirements** – the need to keep regular and secure back-ups in case of system failure
- **breaches of security** – the danger of people hacking into the system from outside, the danger of viruses, the incidence of staff fraud
- **health** dangers – the problems of bad backs, eyestrain and muscular complaints such as RSI

WORKED EXAMPLE

situation

Stitch-in-time Limited is an old-fashioned company which manufactures sewing machines. The Finance Director, Charles Cotton, is considering the introduction of a computer accounting system which will completely replace the existing manual double-entry system.

He is worried because he knows that the proposition will not go down very well with employees who have been with the company for a long time.

He asks you to prepare notes in which you are to set out:

(a) the benefits to staff of the new scheme

(b) the likely causes of staff dissatisfaction with the new scheme

solution

(a) **potential benefits to staff**

- the staff will be able to update their skills
- they will receive training
- they may get an increase in pay
- the training will increase their career prospects
- they will be motivated
- they will get job satisfaction

(b) **causes of staff dissatisfaction**

- staff prefer doing the job in a way which is familiar to them
- they do not like computers
- they may see their jobs threatened as they worry that redundancies will occur
- they do not look forward to the disruption at the time of the changeover
- they worry about the possible bad effects to their health, having heard about RSI (Repetitive Strain Injury) and radiation and eye damage from computer screens
- they will be demotivated as they consider the new system 'mechanical' – they will have to sit in front of a computer for hours at a time and not be able to communicate so well with their colleagues as they have in the past

CHAPTER SUMMARY

- Computer accounting systems save businesses time and money by automating many accounting processes, including the production of reports for management.
- Most computer accounting programs are based on the ledger system and integrate a number of different functions – one transaction will change accounting data in a number of different parts of the system.
- The different functions can include: sales ledger, purchases ledger, nominal (general) ledger, cash and bank payments, stock control, invoicing, report production
- It is common for a payroll processing program to be linked to the nominal ledger of a computer accounting program.
- Computer spreadsheets are often also used to carry out individual functions in an accounting system, for example the creation of budgets.
- A business must consider carefully all the advantages and disadvantages of computer accounting before installing a computerised system. The main advantages are speed, accuracy, availability of up-to-date information; the main disadvantages are cost, security implications and possible opposition from employees.

In the next chapter we look at how businesses present their final accounts at the end of each financial year.

QUESTIONS

NOTE: an asterisk (*) after the question number means that an answer to the question is given at the end of this book.

17.1* Explain **two** advantages to a business of using a computer accounting system to record financial transactions.

17.2* Describe **two** advantages of using a computer spreadsheet for a document such as a cash-flow forecast.

17.3* Explain how **three** different areas of the accounting system might benefit from the introduction of computer accounting.

17.4* A business is planning to introduce a computer accounting system and holds an employee meeting to explain the implications of the change. One employee asks 'I have heard that there are all sorts of risks to the computer data which could cause us to lose the lot.' Describe **two** of the main risks to the security of computer data.

17.5* You are the Accounts Manager of a large company which imports and supplies computer games to UK retailers. You want to introduce an integrated computer accounting system throughout the company.

Explain the advantages you would point out to the line manager of the Sales Ledger section to persuade her that the new system would help her staff in processing orders and producing financial documents.

17.6 Kings Products Limited is considering the computerisation of its accounting functions.

REQUIRED

Write a report advising Kings Products Limited on the advantages and disadvantages to the company of this proposal.

To: .... Date: ....

From: ....

Subject: ....

....

....

....

....

....

Assessment and Qualifications Alliance (AQA), 2001

17.7* Gerry Mann is the Finance Director of Colourways Limited, a design company. He wants to introduce a computer accounting system into the business, but is encountering opposition from Helen Baxill, an active trade union member who works in the Finance Department.

Describe:

(a) the objections relating to staff working conditions and welfare that Helen is likely to raise to try and block the introduction of a computer system

(b) the advantages to staff of a computer system that Gerry could use to persuade Helen to accept its introduction

18 INTRODUCTION TO FINAL ACCOUNTS

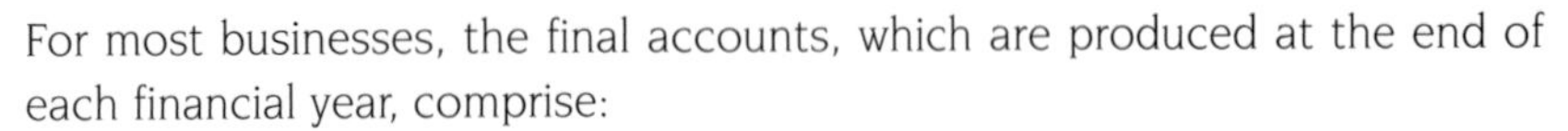

For most businesses, the final accounts, which are produced at the end of each financial year, comprise:

- trading and profit and loss account
- balance sheet

Final accounts can be presented in a vertical format, or a horizontal format. Nowadays, the vertical format is more common and is used as the standard format in this book.

In this chapter, the businesses we will use as examples and in questions are all limited companies – that is, they are owned by shareholders and run by directors. For this chapter, though, we will not be looking in detail at the structure of limited companies, instead we will focus on the form of the final accounts.

FINAL ACCOUNTS AND THE TRIAL BALANCE

final accounts

The final accounts of a business comprise:

- a **trading and profit and loss account** which shows the profit or loss of the business
- a **balance sheet**, which shows the assets and liabilities of the business together with the capital invested by the owners (ordinary shareholders in a limited company)

These final accounts can be produced more often than once a year in order to give information to the owners and managers on how the business is progressing. However, it is customary to produce annual accounts for the benefit of the Inland Revenue, lenders and other interested parties. In this way the trading and profit and loss account covers an accounting period of a financial year (which can end at any date – it doesn't have to be the calendar year), and the balance sheet shows the state of the business at the end of the accounting period.

trading and profit and loss account

income less **expenses** equals **net profit (or loss)**

The trading and profit and loss account shows the income a business has received over a given period for goods sold or services provided (together with any small amounts of other income, eg rent received). It also sets out the expenses incurred – the cost of the product or service, and the overheads (eg wages, administration expenses, rent, and so on). The difference between income and expenses is the net profit of the business. If expenses are greater than income, then a loss has been made. The net profit of a limited company belongs to the ordinary shareholders. Companies often pay dividends to their shareholders from the net profit.

balance sheet

assets less **liabilities** equals **capital**

A balance sheet gives a 'snapshot' of the business at a particular date – the end of the financial year. A typical business balance sheet will show:

assets What the business owns:

- fixed assets, eg premises, vehicles, computers
- current assets, eg stock of goods for resale, debtors (money owed by customers), bank and cash balances

liabilities What the business owes:

- current liabilities, eg creditors, overdrafts, VAT due
- long-term liabilities, eg long-term bank loans

net assets The total of fixed and current assets, less current and long-term liabilities. The net assets are financed by the owners of the business, in the form of capital. Net assets therefore equal the total of the 'financed by' section – the balance sheet 'balances'.

capital Where the money to finance the business has come from, eg the ordinary shareholders, business profits.

TRIAL BALANCE

The starting point for preparing final accounts is the trial balance: all the figures recorded on the trial balance are used in the final accounts. The trading account and the profit and loss account are both 'accounts' in terms of double-entry book-keeping. By contrast, the balance sheet is not an account, but is simply a statement of account balances remaining after the trading and profit and loss accounts have been prepared.

To help us with the preparation of final accounts we will use the trial balance, shown in the Worked Example on the next page. The trial balance has been produced at the end of the financial year. In the

Worked Example we will present the final accounts before adjustments for items such as accruals, prepayments, bad debts and depreciation – these will be covered in later chapters of this book, in the section for Module 3.

The accounts are presented in vertical format, ie in the column format used by accountants. Final accounts can also be presented in a horizontal format, although this is comparatively rare.

WORKED EXAMPLE: FINAL ACCOUNTS FROM THE TRIAL BALANCE

Boulton Limited owns a kitchen and cookware shop. The company's accountant has used the year-end trial balance, shown below, to draft provisional final accounts for discussion with the directors.

Note that the trial balance includes the stock value at the start of the year, while the end-of-year stock valuation is given after the trial balance. For the purposes of financial accounting, the stock of goods for resale is valued by the business at the end of each financial year, and the valuation is subsequently entered into the book-keeping system.

Trial balance of Boulton Limited, as at 31 December 20-2

	Dr	Cr
	£	£
Stock at 1 January 20-2	50,000	
Purchases	420,000	
Sales		557,500
Shop expenses	6,200	
Wages	33,500	
Rent paid	750	
Telephone expenses	500	
Interest paid	4,500	
Travel expenses	550	
Premises	200,000	
Shop fittings	40,000	
Debtors	10,100	
Bank	5,850	
Cash	50	
Capital		75,000
Loan from bank		123,000
Creditors		14,500
Value Added Tax		2,000
	772,000	772,000

Note: stock at 31 December 20-2 was valued at £42,000

preparation of final accounts from a trial balance

The trial balance contains the basic figures necessary in order to prepare the final accounts, and is often used as the starting point. The information needed for the preparation of each of the final accounts needs to be picked out from the trial balance in the following way:

- go through the trial balance and write against the items the final account in which each appears
- 'tick' each figure as it is used – each item from the trial balance appears in the final accounts once only
- the year end (closing) stock figure is not listed in the trial balance, but is shown as a note; the closing stock appears twice in the final accounts – firstly in the trading account, and secondly in the balance sheet (as a current asset)

If this routine is followed with the trial balance of Boulton Limited, it appears as follows . . .

Trial balance of Boulton Limited as at 31 December 20-2

	Dr	Cr		
	£	£		
Stock at 1 January 20-2	50,000		T	✔
Purchases	420,000		T	✔
Sales		557,500	T	✔
Shop expenses	6,200		P & L (*expense*)	✔
Wages	33,500		P & L (*expense*)	✔
Rent paid	750		P & L (*expense*)	✔
Telephone	500		P & L (*expense*)	✔
Interest paid	4,500		P & L (*expense*)	✔
Travel expenses	550		P & L (*expense*)	✔
Premises	200,000		BS (*fixed asset*)	✔
Shop fittings	40,000		BS (*fixed asset*)	✔
Debtors	10,100		BS (*current asset*)	✔
Bank	5,850		BS (*current asset*)	✔
Cash	50		BS (*current asset*)	✔
Capital		75,000	BS (*capital*)	✔
Loan from bank		123,000	BS (*long-term liability*)	✔
Creditors		14,500	BS (*current liability*)	✔
Value Added Tax		2,000	BS (*current liability*)	✔
	772,000	772,000		

Note: stock at 31 December 20-2 was valued at £42,000 — T ✔; BS (*current asset*) ✔

Note: T = trading account; P & L = profit and loss account; BS = balance sheet

Trading account shows gross profit for the accounting period. **Profit and loss account** shows net profit for the accounting period. Note that 'profit and loss account' is often used as a general heading which includes both of these financial statements.

The amounts for **sales** and **purchases** include only items in which the business trades – eg a clothes shop buying clothes from the manufacturer and selling to the public. Note that items bought for use in the business, such as a new till for the shop, are not included with purchases but are shown as assets on the balance sheet.

Cost of sales represents the cost to the business of the goods which have been sold in this financial year. Cost of sales is:

	opening stock	(stock bought previously)
plus	purchases	(purchased during the year)
minus	closing stock	(stock left unsold at the end of the year)
equals	cost of sales	(cost of what has actually been sold)

Gross profit is calculated as:

sales – cost of sales = gross profit

If cost of sales is greater than sales, the business has made a gross loss.

Overheads, or expenses are the running costs of the business – known as *revenue expenditure*. The categories of overheads or expenses used vary according to the needs of each business.

Net profit is calculated as:

gross profit – overheads = net profit

If overheads are more than gross profit, the business has made a net loss.

The net profit is the amount the company earned for the shareholders during the year. From the profit, companies often pay dividends to their shareholders (this aspect of limited company accounts will be studied in more detail in the next chapter). Part of the profit might well be kept in the business in order to help build up the company for the future.

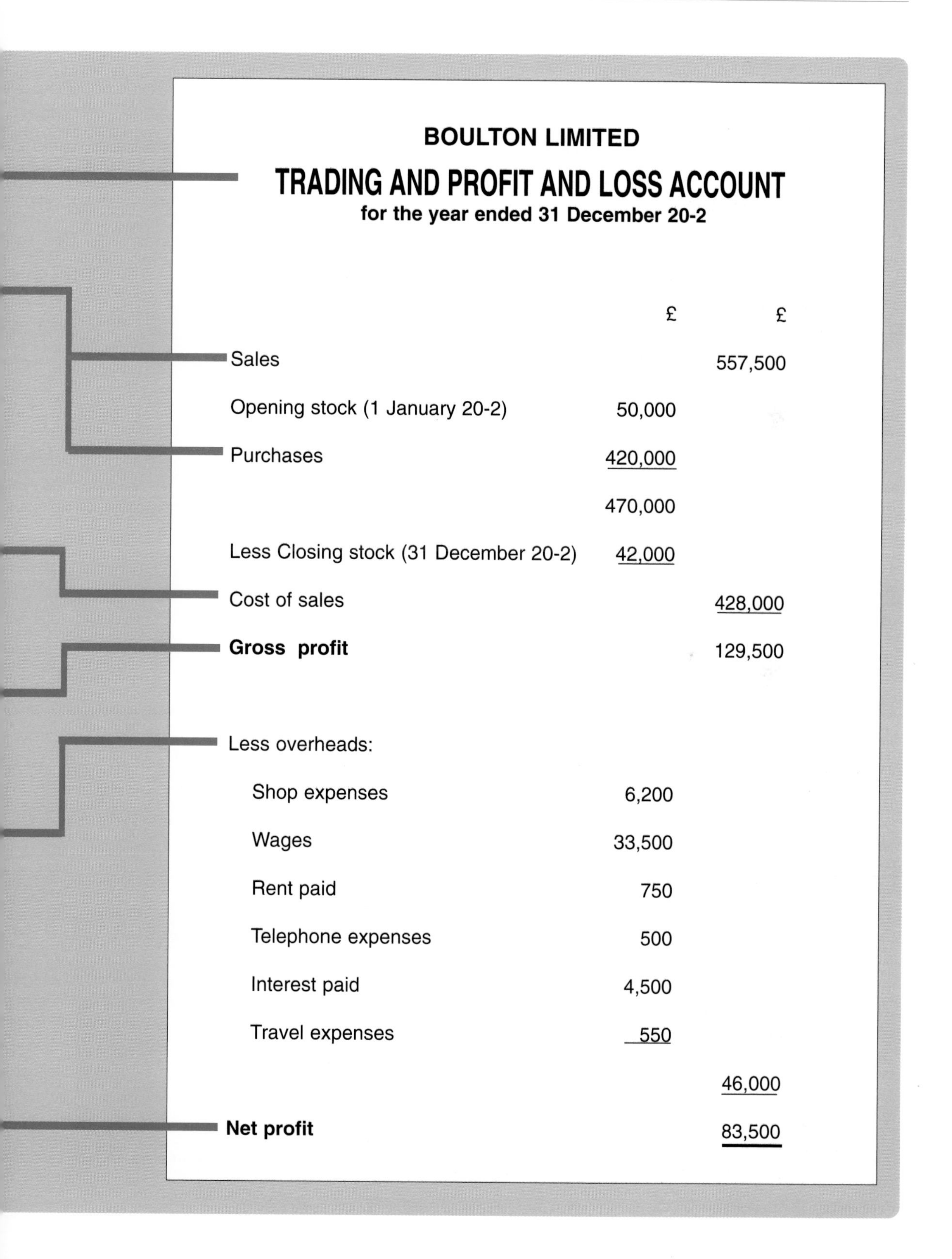

BOULTON LIMITED

TRADING AND PROFIT AND LOSS ACCOUNT

for the year ended 31 December 20-2

	£	£
Sales		557,500
Opening stock (1 January 20-2)	50,000	
Purchases	420,000	
	470,000	
Less Closing stock (31 December 20-2)	42,000	
Cost of sales		428,000
Gross profit		129,500
Less overheads:		
Shop expenses	6,200	
Wages	33,500	
Rent paid	750	
Telephone expenses	500	
Interest paid	4,500	
Travel expenses	550	
		46,000
Net profit		83,500

Fixed assets comprise the long-term items owned by a business which are not bought with the intention of selling them off in the near future, eg premises, machinery, motor vehicles, office equipment, shop fittings, etc.

Current assets comprise short-term assets which change regularly, eg stock of goods for resale, debtors, bank balances and cash. These items will alter as the business trades, eg stock will be sold, or more will be bought; debtors will make payment to the business, or sales on credit will be made; the cash and bank balances will alter with the flow of money paid into the bank account, or as withdrawals are made. VAT owed by HM Revenue & Customs is also listed as a current asset.

Current liabilities are due for repayment within twelve months of the date of the balance sheet, eg creditors, expenses owing, and bank overdraft (which is technically repayable on demand, unlike a bank loan repayable over a period of years). VAT due to HM Revenue & Customs is also listed as a current liability.

Working capital (or **net current assets**) is the excess of current assets over current liabilities, ie current assets minus current liabilities = working capital. Without adequate working capital, a business will find it difficult to continue to operate.

Long-term liabilities are where repayment is due in more than one year from the date of the balance sheet; they are often described by terms such as 'bank loan', 'long-term loan', 'debenture', or 'mortgage'.

Net assets is the total of fixed and current assets, less current and long-term liabilities. The net assets are financed by the shareholders of the company, in the form of capital. Net assets therefore equals the total of the 'financed by' section – the balance sheet 'balances'.

Capital is the shareholders' investment, and is a liability of a company, ie it is what the company owes the shareholders. In the next chapter we will look in detail at the types of shares issued by limited companies.

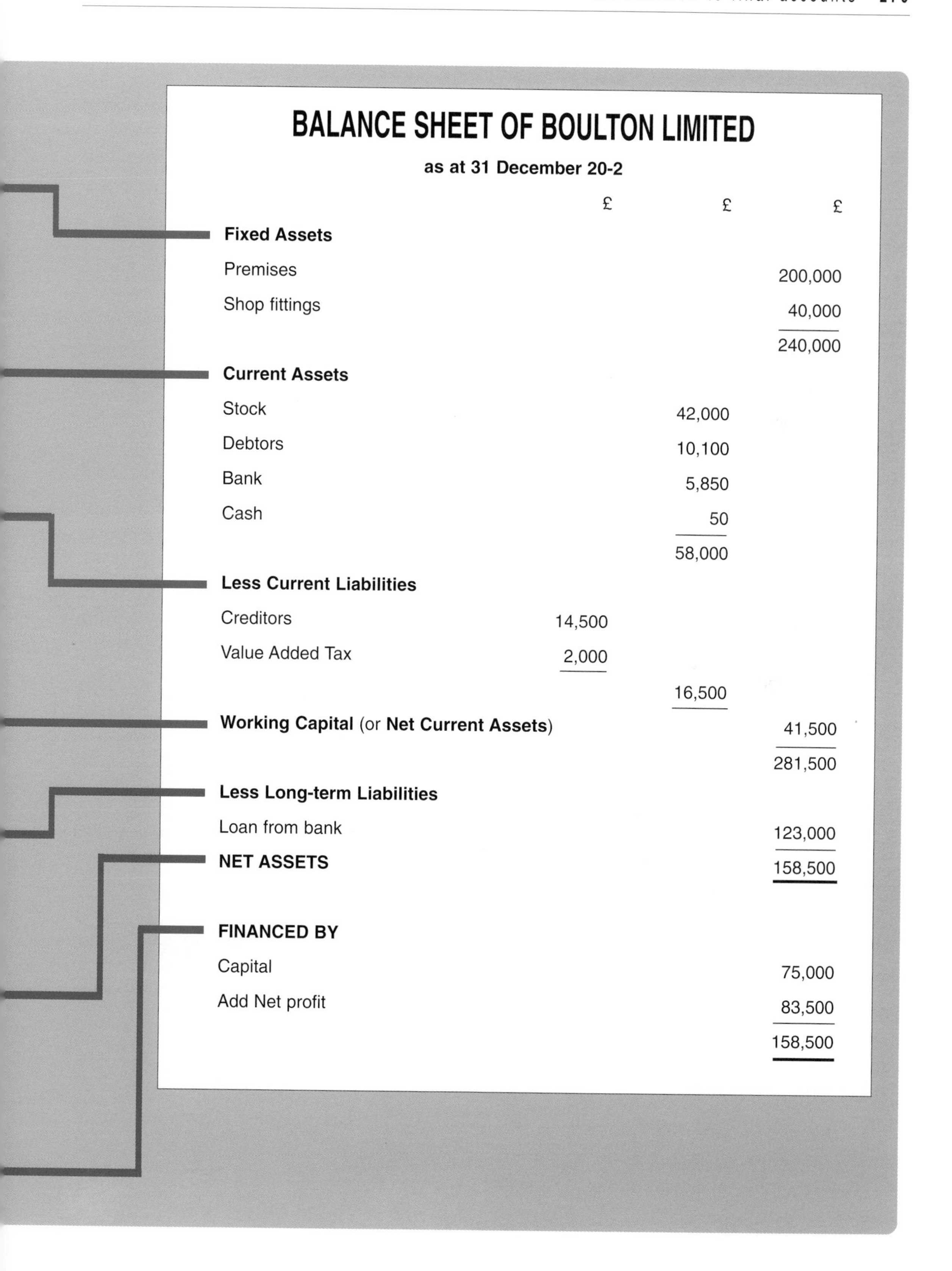

BALANCE SHEET OF BOULTON LIMITED

as at 31 December 20-2

	£	£	£
Fixed Assets			
Premises			200,000
Shop fittings			40,000
			240,000
Current Assets			
Stock		42,000	
Debtors		10,100	
Bank		5,850	
Cash		50	
		58,000	
Less Current Liabilities			
Creditors	14,500		
Value Added Tax	2,000		
		16,500	
Working Capital (or **Net Current Assets**)			41,500
			281,500
Less Long-term Liabilities			
Loan from bank			123,000
NET ASSETS			158,500
FINANCED BY			
Capital			75,000
Add Net profit			83,500
			158,500

Additional Items in Final Accounts

There are a number of additional items that are shown in the trading and profit and loss account. These include:

- carriage in
- carriage out
- sales returns
- purchases returns
- discount received
- discount allowed
- bad debts written off

carriage in

This is the expense to a buyer of the carriage (transport) costs. For example, if an item is purchased by mail order, the buyer usually has to pay the additional cost of delivery.

In the trading account, the cost of carriage in is added to the cost of purchases. The reason for doing this is so that all purchases are at a 'delivered to your door' price.

carriage out

This is where the seller pays the expense of the carriage charge. For example, an item is sold to the customer and described as 'post free'.

In the profit and loss account, the cost of carriage out incurred on sales is shown as an expense of the business.

sales returns

Sales returns (or returns in) is where a debtor (a customer who has bought on credit) returns goods to the business. In final accounts, the amount of sales returns is deducted from the figure for sales in trading account.

purchases returns

Purchases returns (or returns out) is where a business returns goods to a creditor (a supplier).

In final accounts, the amount of purchases returns is deducted from the figure for purchases in trading account.

discount received

Discount received is an allowance offered by creditors on purchases invoice amounts for quick settlement, eg 2% cash discount for settlement within seven days.

In final accounts, the amount of discount received is shown in profit and loss account as income received.

discount allowed

This is an allowance offered to debtors on sales invoice amounts for quick settlement.

In final accounts, the amount of discount allowed is shown in profit and loss account as an expense.

bad debts written off

A bad debt is a debt owing to a business which it considers will never be paid. One of the problems of selling goods and services on credit terms is that, from time-to-time, some customers will not pay. As a consequence, the balances of such debtors' accounts have to be written off when they become uncollectable. This happens when all reasonable efforts to recover the amounts owing have been exhausted.

In the profit and loss account, the amount of bad debts written off is shown as an expense of the business.

Note that, in Module 3, we will be looking in more detail at the topic of bad debts.

WORKED EXAMPLE: ADDITIONAL ITEMS IN THE FINAL ACCOUNTS

situation

An extract from the trial balance of Morgan Limited is as follows:

Trial balance (extract) as at 30 June 20-3

	Dr	Cr
	£	£
Stock at 1 July 20-2	12,350	
Sales		250,000
Purchases	156,000	
Sales returns	5,400	
Purchases returns		7,200
Carriage in	1,450	
Carriage out	3,250	
Discount received		2,500
Discount allowed	3,700	
Bad debts written off	500	
Other expenses	78,550	

Note: stock at 30 June 20-3 was valued at £16,300

How do these items affect the preparation of the trading and profit and loss account?

solution

There are a number of additional items to be incorporated into the layout of the trading and profit and loss account. In particular, the calculation of cost of sales is made in the following way:

opening stock
+ purchases
+ carriage in
– purchases returns
– closing stock
= cost of sales

For Morgan Limited, the trading and profit and loss account is as follows (note the use of three money columns):

MORGAN LIMITED
TRADING AND PROFIT AND LOSS ACCOUNT
for the year ended 30 June 20-3

	£	£	£
Sales			250,000
Less Sales returns			5,400
Net sales			244,600
Opening stock (1 July 20-2)		12,350	
Purchases	156,000		
Add Carriage in	1,450		
	157,450		
Less Purchases returns	7,200		
Net purchases		150,250	
		162,600	
Less Closing stock (30 June 20-3)		16,300	
Cost of sales			146,300
Gross profit			98,300
Add Discount received			2,500
			100,800
Less overheads:			
Discount allowed		3,700	
Bad debts written off		500	
Other expenses		78,550	
Carriage out		3,250	
			86,000
Net profit			14,800

SERVICE SECTOR BUSINESSES

The final accounts of a service sector business – such as a secretarial agency, firm of solicitors, estate agency, doctors' practice – do not normally include a trading account. This is because the business, instead of trading in goods, supplies services. The final accounts of a service business consist of:

- profit and loss account
- balance sheet

The profit and loss account, instead of starting with gross profit from the trading account section, commences with the income from the business activity – such as 'fees', 'income from clients', 'charges', 'work done'. Other items of income – such as discount received – are added, and the overheads are then listed and deducted to give the net profit, or net loss, for the accounting period. An example of a service sector profit and loss account is shown below:

WYVERN SECRETARIAL AGENCY LIMITED
PROFIT AND LOSS ACCOUNT
for the year ended 31 December 20-2

	£	£
Income from clients		110,000
Less overheads:		
Salaries	64,000	
Heating and lighting	2,000	
Telephone	2,000	
Rent and rates	6,000	
Sundry expenses	3,000	
		77,000
Net profit		33,000

The balance sheet layout of a service sector business is identical to that seen earlier (page 279); the only difference is that there is unlikely to be much stock, if any, in the current assets section.

CHAPTER SUMMARY

- Final accounts are accounting statements which are produced at least once a year in order to give information to the owners, managers, and other interested parties in how the business is progressing.

- The final accounts of a business comprise:
  - trading account, which shows gross profit
  - profit and loss account, which shows net profit (or loss)
  - balance sheet, which shows the assets and liabilities of the business at the year end together with the capital

- The starting point for the preparation of final accounts is the summary of the information from the accounting records contained in the trial balance.

- Each balance shown by the trial balance is entered into the final accounts once only.

- Any notes to the trial balance, such as the closing stock, affect the final accounts in two places.

- Final accounts can be presented in either a vertical or horizontal format – the former is more commonly used.

This chapter has provided an introduction to final accounts. In the next chapter we focus on the detail of the final accounts of limited companies, including the types of shares and loans which may be issued. Later on in this Module, in Chapter 21, we will look at the published accounts of limited companies, such as are distributed to shareholders.

There will be more material to cover in connection with final accounts in Module 3, where we shall deal with accruals and prepayments, depreciation of fixed assets, bad debts and provision for doubtful debts, and accounting concepts. In Module 4 we shall be analysing and interpreting final accounts in order to give the users of the accounts information about the financial state of the business.

QUESTIONS

NOTE: an asterisk (*) after the question number means that an answer to the question is given at the end of this book.

18.1 Identify the main financial statements which comprise the final accounts of a business. Explain the main sections contained within the statements.

18.2 Distinguish between:

(a) gross profit and net profit

(b) fixed assets and current assets

(c) long-term liabilities and current liabilities

(d) capital and loans

18.3* The following information has been extracted from the business accounts of Lloyd Limited for the first year of trading which ended on 31 December 20-8:

	£
Purchases	94,350
Sales	125,890
Rates	4,850
Heating and lighting	2,120
Wages and salaries	10,350
Office equipment	8,500
Vehicles	10,750
Debtors	12,850
Bank balance (money at bank)	4,225
Petty cash	95
Creditors	1,750
Value Added Tax due	450
Capital	20,000

REQUIRED

(i) construct a trial balance from the list of balances given above.

(ii) prepare the trading and profit and loss account of Lloyd Limited for the year ended 31 December 20-8, together with a balance sheet at that date (note that stock at 31 December 20-8 was valued at £5,950)

18.4 Complete the table below for each item (a) to (g) indicating with a tick:

- whether the item would normally appear in the debit or credit column of the trial balance
- in which final account the item would appear at the end of the accounting period

	TRIAL BALANCE		FINAL ACCOUNTS	
			TRADING & P& L	BALANCE SHEET
	Debit	Credit		
(a) Salaries				
(b) Purchases				
(c) Debtors				
(d) Sales returns				
(e) Discount received				
(f) Vehicle				
(g) Capital				

18.5* You are to fill in the missing figures for the following businesses:

	Sales	Opening Stock	Purchases	Closing Stock	Gross Profit	Overheads	Net Profit/ (Loss)*
	£	£	£	£	£	£	£
Business A	20 000	5 000	10 000	3 000	....	4 000	....
Business B	35 000	8 000	15 000	5 000	....	....	10 000
Business C	....	6 500	18 750	7 250	18 500	11 750	....
Business D	45 250	9 500	....	10 500	20 750	....	10 950
Business E	71 250	....	49 250	9 100	22 750	24 450	....
Business F	25 650	4 950	13 750	....	11 550	....	(3 450)

* Note: a net loss is indicated in brackets

18.6* The following trial balance has been extracted by the book-keeper of Adams Limited at 31 December 20-7:

	Dr	Cr
	£	£
Stock at 1 January 20-7	14,350	
Purchases	114,472	
Sales		259,688
Rates	13,718	
Heating and lighting	12,540	
Wages and salaries	42,614	
Vehicle expenses	5,817	
Advertising	6,341	
Premises	75,000	
Office equipment	33,000	
Vehicles	21,500	
Debtors	23,854	
Bank	1,235	
Cash	125	
Capital		62,500
Loan from bank		22,642
Creditors		17,281
Value Added Tax		2,455
	364,566	364,566

Stock at 31 December 20-7 was valued at £16,280.

REQUIRED

Prepare the trading and profit and loss account of Adams Limited for the year ended 31 December 20-7, together with a balance sheet at that date.

18.7

The following trial balance has been extracted by the book-keeper of Lewis Limited at 31 December 20-4:

	Dr	Cr
	£	£
Debtors	31,811	
Creditors		12,140
Value Added Tax		1,210
Bank		4,610
Capital		25,150
Sales		144,810
Purchases	96,318	
Stock at 1 January 20-4	16,010	
Salaries	18,465	
Heating and lighting	1,820	
Rent and rates	5,647	
Vehicles	9,820	
Office equipment	5,500	
Sundry expenses	845	
Vehicle expenses	1,684	
	187,920	187,920

Stock at 31 December 20-4 was valued at £13,735.

REQUIRED

Prepare the trading and profit and loss account of Lewis Limited for the year ended 31 December 20-4, together with a balance sheet at that date.

18.8*

At 30 June 20-6 the ledger accounts of Wyvern Traders Limited show the following balances:

	£
Purchases	146,850
Sales	298,300
Purchases returns (returns out)	2,850
Sales returns (returns in)	4,620
Carriage in	3,860
Carriage out	12,590
Discount allowed	1,870
Discount received	2,310
Bad debts written off	250
Stock at 1 July 20-5	27,820
Stock at 30 June 20-6	33,940

REQUIRED

Prepare the trading account of Wyvern Traders Limited from the relevant items of information given above.

18.9

The following balances are taken from the books of James Cadwallader Ltd showing totals for the year ended 31 December 2002.

	£
Sales	67,945
Purchases	34,981
Returns inwards	2,945
Returns outwards	1,367
Carriage inwards	679
Carriage outwards	386
Stock at 1 January 2002	5,780
Stock at 31 December 2002	6,590
Wages	12,056
Other expenses	4,650

REQUIRED

Prepare the trading and profit and loss account for the year ended 31 December 2002.

Assessment and Qualifications Alliance (AQA), 2003

19 LIMITED COMPANY ACCOUNTS

In the last chapter we looked at an introductory layout of final accounts. In this chapter we look in detail at limited companies and their final accounts, including:

- the reasons for forming a limited company
- the differences between a private limited company, a public limited company, and a company limited by guarantee
- the information contained in a company's Memorandum of Association and its Articles of Association
- the differences between ordinary shares and preference shares
- the concept of reserves, and the differences between capital reserves and revenue reserves
- the layout of a company's trading, profit and loss, and profit and loss appropriation accounts, and balance sheet for internal use

WHY FORM A LIMITED COMPANY?

A limited company is a separate legal entity, owned by shareholders and run by directors.

The limited company is often chosen as the legal status of a business for a number of reasons:

limited liability

The shareholders (members) of a company can only lose the amount of their investment, being the money paid already, together with any money unpaid on their shares (unpaid instalments on new share issues, for example). Thus, if the company became insolvent (went 'bust'), shareholders would have to pay any unpaid instalments to help pay the creditors. As this happens very rarely, shareholders are usually in a safe position: their personal assets are not available to the company's creditors – they have **limited liability**.

separate legal entity

A limited company is a separate legal entity from its owners. Anyone taking legal action proceeds against the company and not the individual shareholders.

ability to raise finance

A limited company can raise substantial funds from outside sources by the issue of shares:

- for the larger public company – from the public and investing institutions on the Stock Exchange or similar markets
- for the smaller company – privately from venture capital companies, relatives and friends

Companies can also raise finance by means of debentures (see page 296).

membership

A member of a limited company is a person who owns at least one share in that company. A member of a company is the same as a shareholder.

other factors

A limited company may be a much larger business unit than a sole trader, ie one person in business on their own. This gives the company a higher standing and status in the business community, allowing it to benefit from economies of scale, and making it of sufficient size to employ specialists for functions such as production, marketing, finance and human resources.

The Companies Act

Limited companies are regulated by the Companies Act 1985, as amended by the Companies Act 1989.

Under the terms of the 1985 Act there are two main types of limited company: the larger **public limited company** (abbreviated to 'Plc'), which is defined in the Act, and the smaller company, traditionally known as a **private limited company** (abbreviated to 'Ltd'), which is any other limited company. A further type of company is limited by guarantee.

public limited company (Plc)

A company may become a public limited company if it has:

- issued share capital of over £50,000
- at least two members (shareholders) and at least two directors

A public limited company may raise capital from the public on the Stock Exchange or similar markets – the new issues and privatisations of recent years are examples of this. A public limited company does not have to issue shares on the stock markets, and not all do so.

private limited company (Ltd)

The private limited company is the most common form of limited company. The term private is not set out in the Companies Act 1985, but it is a traditional description, and well describes the smaller company, often in family ownership. A private limited company has:

- no minimum requirement for issued share capital
- at least one member (shareholder) and at least one director who may be the sole shareholder

The shares are not traded publicly, but are transferable between individuals, although valuation will be more difficult for shares not quoted on the stock markets.

company limited by guarantee

A company limited by guarantee is not formed with share capital, but relies on the guarantee of its members to pay a stated amount in the event of the company's insolvency. Examples of such companies include charities, and artistic and educational organisations.

GOVERNING DOCUMENTS OF COMPANIES

There are a number of documents required by the Companies Act in the setting-up of a company. Two essential governing documents are the Memorandum of Association and the Articles of Association.

The **Memorandum of Association**, the constitution of the company, regulates the affairs of the company to the outside world and contains five main clauses:

1. the name of the company (together with the words 'public limited company' or 'limited', as appropriate)
2. capital of the company (the amount that can be issued in shares: the authorised share capital)
3. 'objects' of the company, ie what activities the company can engage in; under the Companies Act the objects can be stated as being those of 'a general commercial company', ie the company can engage in any commercial activity
4. registered office of the company (not the address, but whether it is registered in England and Wales, or in Scotland)
5. a statement that the liability of the members is limited

The **Articles of Association** regulate the internal administration of the company, including the powers of directors and the holding of company meetings.

ACCOUNTING REQUIREMENTS OF THE COMPANIES ACT

The Companies Act 1985 (as amended by the Companies Act 1989) requires that companies produce sets of accounts. The Act seeks to protect the interests of shareholders, creditors, and lenders by requiring accounts to be presented in a standardised layout. This enables comparisons to be made with other companies so that users of accounts can understand and assess the progress being made. The Act also states the detailed information that must be disclosed.

For larger companies the accounts are audited by external auditors – this is a costly and time-consuming exercise (smaller companies are often exempt from audit). Nevertheless, the audit process enhances the reliability of the accounts for users.

The accounts must be sent to Companies House, where they are available for public inspection. The accounts are available to all shareholders, together with a report on the company's activities during the year.

In this chapter we will study the 'internal use' accounts, rather than being concerned with the accounting requirements of the Companies Act. Chapter 21 will look at such 'published accounts', as they are often known.

Before we examine the final accounts in detail we will look first at the principal ways in which a company raises finance: shares. There are different types of shares which appear in a company's balance sheet as the company's share capital.

Types of Shares Issued by Limited Companies

authorised and issued share capital

Before looking at the types of shares issued by companies we need to distinguish between the authorised share capital and the issued share capital:

- the **authorised share capital** is stated in the Memorandum of Association and is the maximum share capital that the company is allowed to issue
- the **issued share capital** is the amount of share capital that the company has issued, which cannot exceed the amount authorised; another name for issued share capital is **called up share capital**

The authorised share capital may be higher than that which has been issued. However, where a company has already issued the full extent of its authorised share capital (ie both authorised and issued are the same amount) and it wishes to make an increase, it must first pass the appropriate resolution at a general meeting of the shareholders.

The authorised share capital is shown on the balance sheet (or as a note to the accounts) 'for information', but is not added into the balance sheet total, as it may not be the same amount as the issued share capital. By contrast, the issued share capital – showing the classes and numbers of shares that have been issued – forms a part of the 'financed by' section of the balance sheet of a limited company.

The authorised and issued share capital may be divided into a number of classes or types of share; the main types are **ordinary shares** and, less commonly, **preference shares.**

ordinary (equity) shares

Ordinary shares – often called 'equities' – are the most commonly issued class of share which carry the main 'risks and rewards' of the business. The risks are of losing part or all of the value of the shares if the business loses money or becomes insolvent; the rewards are that they take a share of the profits

– in the form of **dividends** – after allowance has been made for all expenses of the business, including loan and debenture interest (see page 296), taxation, and after preference dividends (if any). Amounts paid as dividends to ordinary shareholders will vary: when a company makes large profits, it will have the ability to pay higher dividends to the ordinary shareholders; when losses are made, the ordinary shareholders may receive no dividend.

Often dividends are paid twice a year to shareholders. An **interim dividend** is paid just over half-way through the company's financial year and is based on the profits made during the first half of the year. A **final dividend** is paid early in the next financial year and is based on the profits made for the full year.

Companies rarely pay out all of their profits in the form of dividends; most retain some profits as reserves. These can always be used to enable a dividend to be paid in a year when the company makes little or no profit, always assuming that the company has sufficient cash in the bank to make the payment. Ordinary shareholders, in the event of the company becoming insolvent, will be the last to receive any repayment of their investment: other creditors will be paid off first.

Ordinary shares carry voting rights – thus shareholders have a say at the annual general meeting and at any other shareholders' meetings.

preference shares

Whereas ordinary share dividends will vary from year-to-year, preference shares usually carry a fixed percentage rate of dividend – for example, "10 per cent preference shares" will receive a dividend of ten per cent of nominal value (see next page). Their dividends are paid in preference to those of ordinary shareholders; but they are only paid if the company makes profits. In the event of the company ceasing to trade, the preference shareholders will also receive repayment of capital before the ordinary shareholders. Sometimes preference shares are issued as **redeemable** – this means that they are repayable at some date in the future.

Preference shares do not carry voting rights.

advantages and disadvantages of shares

To the company raising finance, the advantages and disadvantages of issuing ordinary and preference shares need to be considered.

advantages to the company – ordinary shares:

- a variable dividend is paid, which is dependent on profits
- if profits are low and a dividend is not paid in one year, the dividend is not carried forward
- in the event of insolvency of the company, ordinary shareholders will be paid off last

disadvantage to the company – ordinary shares:

- ordinary shareholders can speak and vote at the annual general meeting of the company, and each share carries one vote

advantages to the company – preference shares:

- the dividend is fixed so, if profits of the company increase, more profit is retained in the company
- preference shareholders cannot vote at meetings of the company, so they have little control over the company

disadvantages to the company – preference shares:

- preference dividends are usually cumulative, that is they must be paid each year; if not, they have to be carried forward to the next year
- shareholders can attend meetings of the company (but cannot vote)
- preference shares may be redeemable (repayable) in the future
- in the event of insolvency of the company, preference shareholders must be repaid in full before any money can be paid to ordinary shareholders

nominal value of shares

Each share has a nominal value – or face value – which is entered in the accounts. Shares may be issued with nominal values of 5p, 10p, 25p, 50p or £1, or indeed for any amount. Thus a company with an authorised share capital of £100,000 might state in its Memorandum of Association that this is divided up into:

100,000 ordinary shares of 50p each	£50,000
50,000 ten per cent preference shares of £1 each	£50,000
	£100,000

market value of shares

The market value is the price at which issued – or 'secondhand' – shares are traded. Share prices of a quoted public limited company may be listed in the *Financial Times*. Note that the market value usually bears little relationship to the nominal value.

issue price

This is the price at which shares are issued to shareholders by the company – either when the company is being set up, or at a later date when it needs to raise more funds. The issue price is either 'at par' (ie the nominal value), or above nominal value. In the latter case, the amount of the difference between issue price and nominal value is known as a **share premium** (see page 302): for example – nominal value £1.00; issue price £1.50; therefore share premium is 50p per share.

Loans and Debentures

In addition to money provided by shareholders, who are the owners of the company, further funds can be obtained by borrowing in the form of loans or debentures:

- **Loans** are money borrowed by companies from lenders – such as banks – on a medium or long-term basis. Generally repayments are made throughout the period of the loan, but can often be tailored to suit the needs of the borrower. Invariably lenders require security for loans so that, if the loan is not repaid, the lender has an asset – such as property – that can be sold.

  Smaller companies are sometimes also financed by directors' loans.

- **Debentures** are formal certificates issued by companies raising long-term finance from lenders and investors. Debenture certificates issued by large public limited companies are often traded on the Stock Exchange. Most debentures state the date they will be repaid, for example, "debentures 2015-2020" means that repayment will be made by the issuer between the years 2015 and 2020, at the date to be decided by the issuer. Debentures are commonly secured against assets such as property that, in the event of the company ceasing to trade, could be sold and used to repay the debenture holders.

Loans and debentures usually carry fixed rates of interest – for example, "8 per cent debentures" – that must be paid, just like other business overheads, whether a company makes profits or not. As loan and debenture interest is a business expense, this is shown in the profit and loss account along with all other overheads. In the event of the company ceasing to trade, loan and debenture-holders would be repaid before any shareholders.

A major advantage to a company of raising finance by means of loans and debentures is that the lender receives interest payments at an agreed rate and, if profits increase, more profit is retained in the company.

Trading and Profit and Loss Account

In the previous chapter we studied the general layout of final accounts. There are two specialist overhead items commonly found in the profit and loss account of a limited company:

- **directors' remuneration** – ie amounts paid to directors; as directors are employed by the company, their pay appears amongst the overheads of the company
- **debenture interest** – as already noted, when debentures are issued by companies, the interest is shown as an overhead in the profit and loss account

A limited company follows the profit and loss account with an appropriation section (or profit and loss appropriation account). This shows how the net profit has been distributed and includes a deduction for dividends proposed – on ordinary and preference shares. This is the amount to be distributed to the shareholders as a final dividend, ie it is proposed at the end of the year and paid early in the next financial year.

The diagram on pages 298 and 299 shows the internal use trading and profit and loss account of Max Music Limited as an example (published accounts are covered in Chapter 21).

BALANCE SHEET

Balance sheets of limited companies follow the same layout as those we have seen earlier, but the capital section is more complex because of the different classes of shares that may be issued, and the various reserves. The diagram on pages 300 and 301 shows the internal use balance sheet of Max Music Limited as an example (published accounts are covered in Chapter 21).

EXAMPLE OF FINAL ACCOUNTS

As mentioned above, on pages 298-301 are set out the trading and profit and loss account and balance sheet for Max Music Limited, a private limited company. Note that these are the 'internal use' accounts – the detailed accounting requirements of the Companies Act are covered in Chapter 21.

Explanations of the financial statements are set out on the left-hand page.

Please study carefully the example accounts on pages 298-301 and then continue reading the text below.

RESERVES IN THE BALANCE SHEET

A limited company rarely distributes all its profits to its shareholders. Instead, it will often keep part of the profits earned each year in the form of reserves. There are two types of reserve:

- capital reserves, which are created as a result of a non-trading profit, or may be unrealised profits
- revenue reserves, which are retained profits from profit and loss account

capital reserves

Examples of capital reserves (which cannot be used to fund dividend payments) include:

- **Revaluation reserve.** This occurs when a fixed asset, most probably property, is revalued (in an upwards direction) in the balance sheet. The amount of the revaluation is placed in a revaluation reserve where it increases the value of the shareholders' investment in the company. Note, however, that this is purely a 'book' adjustment – no cash has changed hands.

Turn now to page 302 and study an example in which a company revalues its property upwards by £250,000 from £500,000 to £750,000.

The appropriation section (or profit and loss appropriation account) is the part of the profit and loss account which shows how net profit is distributed – here the final dividends to shareholders. (There is more detail on the use of appropriation account in Chapter 27.)

The **overheads** of a limited company include directors' remuneration and interest paid on debentures (if debentures have been issued).

The company has recorded a **net profit** of £43,000 in its profit and loss account.

The company proposes to pay **final dividends** on the two classes of shares it has in issue (ordinary shares and preference shares): these will be paid in the early part of the next financial year. Note that a dividend is often expressed as an amount per share, based on the nominal value, eg 5p per £1 nominal value share (which is the same as a five per cent dividend).

Added to **net profit** is a **balance** of £41,000. This represents profits of the company from previous years that have not been distributed as dividends. Note that the appropriation section shows a balance of retained profits at the year end of £60,000. Such retained profits form a revenue reserve of the company.

MAX MUSIC LIMITED

TRADING AND PROFIT AND LOSS ACCOUNT

for the year ended 31 December 20-8

	£	£
Sales		725,000
Opening stock	45,000	
Purchases	381,000	
	426,000	
Less closing stock	50,000	
Cost of sales		376,000
Gross profit		349,000
Less overheads:		
Directors' remuneration	75,000	
Debenture interest	6,000	
Other overheads	225,000	
		306,000
Net profit		43,000
Less final dividends proposed		
ordinary shares	20,000	
preference shares	4,000	
		24,000
Retained profit for year		19,000
Add balance of retained profits at beginning of year		41,000
Balance of retained profits at end of year		60,000

Limited company balance sheets usually distinguish between:

intangible fixed assets, which do not have material substance but belong to the company and have value, eg goodwill (the amount paid for the reputation and connections of a business that has been taken over), patents and trademarks.

tangible fixed assets, which have material substance, such as premises, equipment, machinery, vehicles, fixtures and fittings.

Note that fixed assets, such as property, may be revalued (reval'n) upwards (with an effect on revaluation reserve); other assets may be reduced in value by depreciation (dep'n) – depreciation is covered in more detail in Chapter 24.

The **current liabilities** section includes the amount of proposed dividends to be paid shortly.
Note that, in company balance sheets, current liabilities are often described as "creditors: falling due within one year."

Long-term liabilities are those that are due to be repaid more than twelve months from the date of the balance sheet, eg loans and debentures.
Note that long-term liabilities are often described as "creditors: falling due after more than one year."

Authorised share capital is included on the balance sheet 'for information', but is not added into the balance sheet total, as it may not be the same amount as the issued share capital.

Issued share capital shows the classes and number of shares that have been issued. In this balance sheet, the shares are described as being fully paid, meaning that the company has received the full amount of the value of each share from the shareholders. Sometimes shares will be partly paid, eg ordinary shares of £1, but 75p paid. This means that the company can make a call on the shareholders to pay the extra 25p to make the shares fully paid.

Capital reserves are created as a result of non-trading profit, or may be unrealised profit.

Revenue reserves are retained profits from profit and loss account.

The total for **shareholders' funds** represents the stake of the shareholders in the company. It comprises share capital (ordinary and preference shares), plus reserves (capital and revenue reserves).

MAX MUSIC LIMITED
BALANCE SHEET AS AT 31 DECEMBER 20-8

Fixed Assets	*Cost/Reval'n*	*Dep'n to date*	*Net*
	£	£	£
Intangible			
Goodwill	50,000	20,000	30,000
Tangible			
Freehold land and buildings	410,000	110,000	300,000
Fixtures and fittings	100,000	25,000	75,000
	560,000	155,000	405,000
Current Assets			
Stock		50,000	
Debtors		23,000	
Bank		29,000	
Cash		2,000	
		104,000	
Less Current Liabilities			
Creditors	25,000		
Proposed dividends	24,000		
		49,000	
Working Capital (or **Net Current Assets**)			55,000
			460,000
Less Long-term Liabilities			
10% debentures, 2015-2020			60,000
NET ASSETS			400,000
FINANCED BY			
Authorised Share Capital			
100,000 10% preference shares of £1 each			100,000
600,000 ordinary shares of £1 each			600,000
			700,000
Issued Share Capital			
40,000 10% preference shares of £1 each, fully paid			40,000
200,000 ordinary shares of £1 each, fully paid			200,000
			240,000
Capital Reserve			
Revaluation reserve			100,000
Revenue Reserve			
Profit and loss account			60,000
SHAREHOLDERS' FUNDS			400,000

BALANCE SHEET (EXTRACTS)	
Before revaluation	£
Fixed asset: property at cost	500,000
Share capital: ordinary shares of £1 each	500,000
After revaluation	
Fixed asset: property at revaluation	750,000
Share capital: ordinary shares of £1 each	500,000
Capital reserve: revaluation reserve	250,000
	750,000

- **Share premium account.** An established company may issue additional shares to the public at a higher amount than the nominal value. For example, a company seeks finance for further expansion by issuing additional ordinary shares. The shares have a nominal value of £1 each, but, because it is a well-established company, the shares are issued at £1.50 each. Of this amount, £1 is recorded in the issued share capital section, and the extra 50p is the share premium.

revenue reserves

Revenue reserves are profits generated from trading activities; they have been retained in the company to help build the company for the future. Revenue reserves include the balance of the appropriation section of the profit and loss account after proposed dividends have been deducted: this balance is commonly described as 'profit and loss account balance' or 'balance of retained profits'.

reserves: profits not cash

It should be noted that reserves – both capital and revenue – are not cash funds to be used whenever the company needs money, but are in fact represented by assets shown on the balance sheet. The reserves record the fact that the assets belong to the shareholders via their ownership of the company.

COMPLETING THE TRIAL BALANCE

In this chapter we have dealt with a number of specialist items to be found on the final accounts of limited companies. These items will feature in the trial balance, including retained profits, proposed dividends, revaluation reserve, and share capital. In the trial balance, all of these appear on the credit side, ie they are amounts which the company owes to the shareholders. However, apart from proposed dividends, none is likely to be paid to the shareholders in the immediate future – for example, if the share capital was repaid, the company would cease to exist. In other words they are items that are technically liabilities of the company but, in reality, are unlikely to be paid in the near future. Debentures are also liabilities of the company and are shown on the credit side of the trial balance; the repayment date may be stated as part of the description, eg "8% debentures, 2015 – 2020".

There are two possible debit entries for the trial balance:

- retained losses, where the company has made losses: these are a reduction in the shareholders' funds
- dividends paid, where the company has paid dividends during the financial year – an interim dividend, for example

Note that dividends paid are transferred from the trial balance to profit and loss account where they are deducted, together with proposed dividends, from net profit to give the figure for retained profits. Dividends paid do not show on the balance sheet because, at the balance sheet date, there is no liability to record – this contrasts with proposed dividends which are a current liability.

The Worked Example which follows shows how to complete the trial balance for a number of the specialist items to be found on limited company final accounts. Note that no dividends paid are shown – any such items will have already been transferred from the trial balance to be deducted from net profit in order to calculate retained profits, which is the profit figure given.

WORKED EXAMPLE: COMPLETING THE TRIAL BALANCE

situation

The book-keeper of Vanessa's Garden Centre Limited has completed the trading and profit and loss account for the year ended 30 April 20-3. She has the following items to enter into the trial balance but is unsure whether they are on the debit or credit side:

	£
Retained profits	5,470
Final ordinary dividend proposed	12,000
Revaluation reserve	50,000
Ordinary shares of £1 each	240,000
6% Preference shares of £1 each	30,000
8% Debentures, 2015-2020	25,000

Trial Balance as at 30 April 20-3

	£	£
Land and buildings	300,000	
Vehicles	55,000	
Office equipment	15,000	
Debtors and creditors	5,050	10,850
Bank loan		22,600
Bank		8,480
Stock at 30 April 20-3	29,350	
Retained profits		
Final ordinary dividend proposed		
Revaluation reserve		
Ordinary shares of £1 each		
6% Preference shares of £1 each		
8% Debentures, 2015-2020		

The book-keeper asks you for help in completing the trial balance and then to prepare the balance sheet as at 30 April 20-3.

solution

The trial balance is completed as follows:

Trial Balance as at 30 April 20-3

	£	£
Land and buildings	300,000	
Vehicles	55,000	
Office equipment	15,000	
Debtors and creditors	5,050	10,850
Bank loan		22,600
Bank		8,480
Stock at 30 April 20-3	29,350	
Retained profits		5,470
Final ordinary dividend proposed		12,000
Revaluation reserve		50,000
Ordinary shares of £1 each		240,000
Preference shares of £1 each		30,000
8% Debentures, 2015-2020		25,000
	404,400	404,400

Tutorial notes:

- Retained profits belong to the ordinary shareholders and are shown on the credit side – the company owes this amount to the ordinary shareholders. As the figure is for retained profits – rather than net profit – this tells us that dividends (paid and proposed) have already been deducted.
- The final ordinary dividend is proposed; until it is paid it is a current liability, ie a credit balance.
- Revaluation reserve belongs to the ordinary shareholders and is shown on the credit side.
- The share capital, ordinary and preference, is shown on the credit side – the company owes this amount to the ordinary shareholders.
- The debentures are shown on the credit side – the company owes this amount to the lenders, with a repayment date, here, of between 2015 and 2020.

The balance sheet is completed as follows:

VANESSA'S GARDEN CENTRE LIMITED

BALANCE SHEET AS AT 30 APRIL 20-3

	£	£	£
Fixed Assets			
Land and buildings			300,000
Vehicles			55,000
Office equipment			15,000
			370,000
Current Assets			
Stock		29,350	
Debtors		5,050	
		34,400	
Less Current Liabilities			
Creditors	10,850		
Bank	8,480		
Proposed dividends	12,000		
		31,330	
Working Capital (or **Net Current Assets**)			3,070
			373,070
Less Long-term Liabilities			
Bank loan		22,600	
8% Debentures, 2015-2020		25,000	
			47,600
NET ASSETS			325,470
FINANCED BY			
Issued Share Capital			
240,000 Ordinary shares of £1 each			240,000
30,000 6% Preference shares of £1 each			30,000
			270,000
Capital Reserve			
Revaluation reserve			50,000
Revenue Reserve			
Profit and loss account			5,470
SHAREHOLDERS' FUNDS			325,470

CHAPTER SUMMARY

- A limited company is a separate legal entity owned by shareholders and run by directors.
- A company is regulated by the Companies Act 1985 (as amended by the Companies Act 1989), and is owned by shareholders and managed by directors.
- A limited company may be either a public limited company or a private limited company.
- The liability of shareholders is limited to any money unpaid on their shares.
- The main types of shares that may be issued by companies are ordinary shares and preference shares.
- Borrowings in the form of loans and debentures are a further source of finance.
- The final accounts of a company include an appropriation section (or profit and loss appropriation account).
- The balance sheet of a limited company includes a capital and reserves section which reflects the ownership of the company by its shareholders:
  - a statement of the authorised and issued share capital
  - details of capital reserves and revenue reserves

In the next chapter we look at errors within the accounting system and how they are corrected.

QUESTIONS

NOTE: an asterisk (*) after the question number means that an answer to the question is given at the end of this book.

19.1 Distinguish between:

(a) a public limited company and a private limited company

(b) the Memorandum of Association and the Articles of Association

(c) authorised share capital and issued share capital

(d) ordinary shares and preference shares

(e) nominal value and market value of shares

(f) capital reserves and revenue reserves

19.2* Paging Systems plc wishes to prepare a handout for new staff explaining some facts about limited companies.

REQUIRED

(a) Who owns Paging Systems plc?

(b) Who is responsible for the day-to-day running of Paging Systems plc?

(c) What is the meaning of limited liability?

Assessment and Qualifications Alliance (AQA), 2003

19.3 Prepare a five-minute talk on the types of companies and the advantages of forming a limited company. The talk is to form part of your local radio station's business programme entitled 'Business Matters'. To accompany your talk, prepare a handout which can be distributed to listeners who contact the station.

19.4 Explain where the following items appear in a limited company's year end financial statements:

(a) debenture interest

(b) directors' remuneration

(c) dividends proposed

(d) revaluation reserve

(e) goodwill

19.5 Mason Motors Limited is a second-hand car business. The following information is available for the year ended 31 December 20-1:

- balance of retained profits from previous years stands at £100,000
- net profit for the year was £75,000
- it has been agreed that a dividend of 10% is to be paid on the issued share capital of £500,000

REQUIRED

(a) Set out the appropriation section of the profit and loss account for Mason Motors Limited for the year ended 31 December 20-1.

(b) State how you would reply to one of the directors of the company who asks if the retained profits could be used to rebuild the garage forecourt.

19.6* R Masters Ltd has completed the trading account for the year ended 31 March 2002.

REQUIRED

From the following information

(a) prepare the profit and loss account for the year ended 31 March 2002

	£
Gross profit	56,231
Wages	23,980
Discount received	350
Carriage outwards	3,600
Motor expenses	4,500
Bank charges	450
Dividends proposed	12,500
Profit and loss balance at 1 April 2001	36,790

(b) set out a detailed calculation of the profit and loss account balance at 1 April 2002

Assessment and Qualifications Alliance (AQA), 2002

19.7 From the following figures, complete the balance sheet for A to Z Engineering Supplies Ltd as at 31 March 2003. Clearly show the fixed and current assets and long-term and current liabilities. To complete the balance sheet, calculate the issued share capital.

	£
Profit and loss account at 31 March 2003	19,031
Stocks at 31 March 2003	14,905
Debtors	6,500
Creditors	4,590
Premises	50,000
Motor vehicles	14,560
Bank overdraft	3,400
Petty cash	56
Dividends proposed	13,000
10% Debentures (2020)	25,000

Assessment and Qualifications Alliance (AQA), 2003

19.8*

The following figures are taken from the accounting records of Jobseekers Limited, a recruitment agency, at the end of the financial year on 31 December 20-6:

	£
Issued share capital (£1 ordinary shares)	150,000
Premises	175,000
Office equipment	85,000
Stock at 31 December 20-6	750
Debtors	42,500
Creditors	7,250
Bank overdraft	15,450
Long-term bank loan	55,000
Net profit	68,200
Final ordinary dividend proposed	40,000
Retained profit at 1 January 20-6	7,350

You are to prepare the appropriation section of the profit and loss account (starting with net profit) for the year ended 31 December 20-6, together with a balance sheet at that date.

19.9

Mary Arbuthnot manages Mary's Doll Shop Ltd and is preparing the balance sheet but has problems with allocating four items.

REQUIRED

Using the memorandum below, advise her as to which section/sub-heading of the balance sheet the items should appear under. Give detailed reasons for your choice.

MEMORANDUM

Date ....

To ....

From ....

Subject ....

1. Cost of new delivery van

Section: ....

Reasons: ....

....

....

....

2. Stock of dolls for resale

Section: ....

Reasons: ....

....

....

....

....

3. Telephone bill due to be paid in one month's time

Section: ....

Reasons: ....

....

....

....

....

4. Retained profits

Section: ....

Reasons: ....

....

....

....

....

Assessment and Qualifications Alliance (AQA), 2003

19.10* A detailed examination of the books of Olympus Heights plc has revealed the following figures at 31 December 2001.

The list contains the balances for all of the company's capital, reserves and liabilities.

	£
Profit and loss account	56,000
Revaluation reserve	nil
Long-term liabilities	150,000
Current liabilities	30,000
Ordinary shares	340,000

Before the balance sheet for 31 December 2001 can be completed the following adjustments need to be taken into account:

(1) the net profit for the year before dividends were paid was £148,000

(2) dividends amounting to £34,000 were proposed

(3) the buildings have been revalued from £400,000 to £550,000

(4) £50,000 worth of new debentures have been issued

(5) £100,000 worth of ordinary shares have been issued

REQUIRED

(a) Calculate the balances as at 31 December 2001, clearly showing all workings, for:

(i) profit and loss account

(ii) revaluation reserve

(iii) long-term liabilities/creditors due after more than one year

(iv) ordinary share capital

(v) current liabilities/creditors due within one year

(b) Calculate the balance sheet value of the total assets held by the company, clearly showing all workings.

(c) Explain the difference between capital reserves and revenue reserves, using examples to illustrate your answer.

Assessment and Qualifications Alliance (AQA), 2002

19.11* Details of the share capital of Okaro Limited are as follows:

	Authorised	Issued	
	£	£	
Share capital			
Ordinary shares of 25p each	2,000,000	1,500,000	fully paid
7% preference shares of £1 each	500,000	300,000	fully paid

The directors have decided to pay:

- a dividend of 2p per share on the ordinary shares, and
- the full annual dividend due on the preference shares.

The interest is also due for the full year on £100,000 8% Debentures.

REQUIRED

(a) For each item calculate the payments to be made.

	£
Ordinary share dividend	
Preference share dividend	
Debenture interest	

(b) State three differences between ordinary share dividends and debenture interest.

(c) State two differences between ordinary and preference shares.

19.12 Joe's Supplies Ltd has retained profits of £4,373 and proposed dividends of £12,000 for the year ended 28 February 2001.

REQUIRED

(a) Using the above information

(i) complete the trial balance

(ii) calculate the ordinary share capital
(*Note*: all of the share capital is in £1 ordinary shares.)

Joe's Supplies Ltd
Trial Balance as at 28 February 2001

	DR £	CR £
Vehicles	14,600	
Buildings	120,000	
Office furniture	13,000	
Bank loan		46,000
Bank		4,600
Debtors and Creditors	27,500	34,000
Stock at 28 February	15,873	

(b) Prepare the balance sheet from this trial balance to show clearly: fixed assets, current assets, current liabilities, long-term liabilities and capital and reserves.

Assessment and Qualifications Alliance (AQA), 2001

19.13

REQUIRED

(a) In the following trial balance for the month ended 30 September 2000 enter, where necessary, the remaining balances given and calculate the profit and loss account balance.

	£
Returns inwards	4,783
Returns outwards	3,791
Carriage outwards	4,796
Carriage inwards	396
Salaries	16,894
Stock at 1 September 2000	4,792
Stock at 30 September 2000	2,289
Petty cash	94
Bank overdraft	3,671

Wholesale Car Spares plc
Trial balance as at 30 September 2000

	£	£
Sales		102,578
Purchases	56,453	
Trade creditors		5,239
Trade debtors	7,824	
Discount allowed	452	
Discount received		896
Rent and rates	11,889	
Interest paid	800	
Fixtures and fittings	20,000	
Motor vehicles	13,000	
Buildings	80,000	
Motor expenses	3,568	
Share capital		12,000
Revaluation reserve		60,000
Share premium		20,000
Profit and loss account		
8% Debentures		10,000
Returns inwards		
Returns outwards		
Carriage outwards		
Carriage inwards		
Salaries		
Stock		
Petty cash		
Bank overdraft		

(b) Prepare a balance sheet extract as at 30 September 2000 to show the total net assets. (The section showing capital and reserves is **not** required.)

Assessment and Qualifications Alliance (AQA), 2001

19.14*

REQUIRED

Wholesale Car Spares plc has paid no interim dividend this year. A concerned shareholder has written a letter containing the following queries. Give a brief answer to each of his queries.

(a) "I notice that the balance sheet shows:

(i) a revaluation reserve; and

(ii) a share premium.

Can you explain how these reserves have arisen.

....

....

....

....

....

....

....

....

(b) Why have dividends not been distributed from these reserves?

....

....

....

....

....

(c) Why were the debenture holders paid interest when the ordinary shareholders did not get any dividend?"

....

....

....

....

....

Assessment and Qualifications Alliance (AQA), 2001

20 CORRECTION OF ERRORS

In this chapter, we will look at:

- correction of errors not shown by a trial balance
- correction of errors shown by a trial balance, using a suspense account
- the effect of correcting errors on profit and the balance sheet

In any book-keeping system there is always the possibility of an error. Ways to avoid errors, or ways to reveal them sooner, include:

- division of the accounting function between a number of people
- regular circulation of statements to debtors, who will check the transactions on their accounts and advise any discrepancies
- checking statements received from creditors
- extraction of a trial balance at regular intervals
- checking bank transactions against bank statements received
- checking cash and petty cash balances against cash held
- the use of control accounts for sales ledger and purchases ledger
- the use of a computer accounting program

Despite all of these, errors will still occur from time-to-time.

ERRORS NOT SHOWN BY A TRIAL BALANCE

In Chapter 16, page 255, we have already seen that some types of errors in a book-keeping system are not revealed by a trial balance. These are:

- error of omission
- reversal of entries
- mispost/error of commission
- error of principle
- error of original entry (or transcription)
- compensating error

Although these errors are not shown by a trial balance, they are likely to come to light if the procedures suggested above are followed. For example, a debtor will soon let you know if her account has been debited with goods she did not buy. When an error is found, it needs to be corrected as quickly as possible by a member of the accounting staff who is authorised to make adjustments.

We will now look at an example of each of the errors not shown by a trial balance, and will see how it is corrected. (Take great care when correcting errors – it is all too easy to make the error twice as bad!)

error of omission

Credit sale of goods, £200 to H Jarvis, a debtor, completely omitted from the accounting system. (Ignore VAT)

To correct this error we must:

- increase the figure for debtors by £200 (on the debit side of the trial balance)
- increase the figure for sales by £200 (on the credit side of the trial balance)

This type of error can happen in a very small business – often where the book-keeping is done by one person, for example, an invoice 'lost' down the back of a filing cabinet. In a large business, particularly one using a computer accounting system, it should be impossible for this error to occur. Also, if documents are numbered serially, then none should be mislaid.

reversal of entries

A payment by cheque of £50 to S Wright, a creditor, has been debited to bank and credited to Wright's account.

This cheque payment should be recorded on the payments (credit) side of bank, and debited to the creditor's account so as to reduce the amount owing. The first step is to reverse the wrong entries:

- decrease the figure for bank by £50 (assuming that bank is on the debit side of the trial balance)
- decrease the figure for creditors by £50 (on the credit side of the trial balance)

Now we can put through the correct transaction as follows:

- decrease the figure for bank by £50
- decrease the figure for creditors by £50

To correct this type of error it is better to reverse the entries that have been made incorrectly and then to record the correct entries. This is preferable to adjusting by £100 because there never was a transaction for this amount – the original transaction was for £50.

mispost/error of commission

Credit sales of £47 to J Adams Limited have been entered in the account of J Adams.

This error affects two accounts within the sales ledger but will not affect the figure for debtors in the trial balance. Within the sales ledger we must:

- decrease the account of J Adams by £47
- increase the account of J Adams Limited by £47

There is no change to the trial balance because the total of debtors is unchanged.

This type of error can be avoided, to some extent, by the use of account numbers, and by persuading the customer to quote the account number or reference on each transaction. All computer accounting systems use numbers/references to identify accounts, but it is still possible to post a transaction to the wrong account.

error of principle

The cost of diesel fuel, £30, has been entered in vehicles account.

To correct this error we must:

- increase vehicle running expenses by £30 (on the debit side of the trial balance)
- decrease vehicles account by £30 (on the debit side of the trial balance)

This type of error is similar to a mispost except that, instead of the wrong person's account being used, it is the wrong class of account. In this example, the vehicle running costs must be kept separate from the cost of the asset (the vehicle), otherwise the expense and asset accounts will be incorrect, leading to profit for the year being overstated and the fixed asset being shown in the balance sheet at too high a figure.

error of original entry (or transcription)

Postages of £45 paid by cheque entered in the accounts as £54.

Here the amount has been entered wrongly in the accounting system. The first step is to take out the wrong entries:

- increase bank by £54 (assuming that bank is on the debit side of the trial balance)
- decrease postages by £54 (on the debit side of the trial balance)

Now we can put through the correct amount of the transaction as follows:

- increase postages by £45
- decrease bank by £45

This error could have been corrected by adjusting bank and postages accounts by £9, being the difference between the two amounts. However, there was no original transaction for this amount, and it is better to reverse the wrong transaction and put through the correct one. A reversal of figures either has a difference of nine (as above), or an amount divisible by nine. An error of original entry can also be a 'bad' figure on a cheque or an invoice, entered wrongly into the accounting system.

compensating error

Rates is added up by £100 more than it should be (ie it is overadded or overcast); sales is also overcast by the same amount.

To correct this error we must:

- decrease rates by £100 (on the debit side of the trial balance)
- decrease sales by £100 (on the credit side of the trial balance)

Here, an account with a debit balance – rates – has been overcast; this is compensated by an overcast on an account with a credit balance – sales. There are several permutations on this theme, eg two debit balances, one overcast, one undercast; a debit balance undercast, a credit balance undercast.

TRIAL BALANCE ERRORS: USE OF SUSPENSE ACCOUNT

There are many types of errors revealed by a trial balance. Included amongst these are:

- omission of one part of the double-entry transaction
- recording two entries on the same side of an account (eg two debits) for a transaction
- recording a different amount for a transaction on the debit side from that shown on the credit side of the account
- errors in the calculation of balances (not compensated by other errors)
- error in transferring the balance of an account to the trial balance
- error of addition in the trial balance

When errors are shown, the trial balance is 'balanced' by recording the difference in a suspense account, as shown in the Worked Example below.

WORKED EXAMPLE: SUSPENSE ACCOUNT

situation

The book-keeper of a business is unable to balance the trial balance on 31 December 20-1. As the error or errors cannot be found quickly, the trial balance is balanced by recording the difference in a suspense account, as follows:

	Dr	Cr
	£	£
Trial balance totals	100,000	99,096
Suspense account		904
	100,000	100,000

A suspense account is opened with, in this case, a credit balance of £904:

Dr	Suspense Account		Cr
	£		£
		Trial balance difference	904

Note that the balance is recorded in suspense account on the same side as it is shown in the trial balance.

A detailed examination of the book-keeping system is now made in order to find the errors. As errors are found, one part of the correction will be to suspense account. Using the above suspense account, the following errors are found and corrected:

- the sales total is undercast by £1,000
- general expenses of £65 should be £56
- a payment of £105 for telephone expenses has not been recorded in telephone expenses account

solution

These errors are corrected as follows:

- increase sales by £1,000 (on the credit side of the trial balance) and debit suspense account with £1,000
- decrease general expenses by £65 (on the debit side of the trial balance) and debit suspense account with £65; also ...
- increase general expenses by £56 (on the debit side of the trial balance) and credit suspense account with £56
- increase telephone expenses by £105 (on the debit side of the trial balance) and credit suspense account with £105

After these errors have been corrected, suspense account appears as:

Dr	Suspense Account		Cr
	£		£
Sales	1,000	Trial balance difference	904
General expenses	65	General expenses	56
		Telephone expenses	105
	1,065		1,065

Note that if final accounts have to be prepared after creating a suspense account but before the errors are found, the balance of suspense account is shown, depending on the balance, as either a current asset (debit balance) or a current liability (credit balance). Nevertheless, the error must be found at a later date and suspense account eliminated.

The adjustments for the errors can also be shown directly on the trial balance as follows:

	Dr	Cr
	£	£
Trial balance totals	100,000	99,096
Sales		1,000
General expenses		65
General expenses	56	
Telephone expenses	105	
Corrected totals	100,161	100,161

Effect on Profit and Balance Sheet

The correction of errors, whether shown by a trial balance or not, often has an effect on the profit figure calculated before the errors were found. For example, an undercast of sales account, when corrected, will increase gross and net profits and, of course, the profit figure shown in the balance sheet. Some errors, however, only affect the balance sheet, eg errors involving debtors and creditors. The diagram that follows shows the effect of errors when corrected on gross profit, net profit and the balance sheet.

TRADING ACCOUNT

Correction of error	Gross profit	Net profit	Balance sheet
sales undercast/understated	increase	increase	net profit increase
sales overcast/overstated	decrease	decrease	net profit decrease
purchases undercast/understated	decrease	decrease	net profit decrease
purchases overcast/overstated	increase	increase	net profit increase
opening stock undervalued	decrease	decrease	net profit decrease
opening stock overvalued	increase	increase	net profit increase
closing stock undervalued	increase	increase	net profit increase stock increase
closing stock overvalued	decrease	decrease	net profit decrease stock decrease

PROFIT AND LOSS ACCOUNT

Correction of error	Gross profit	Net profit	Balance sheet
expense undercast/understated	-	decrease	decrease in net profit
expense overcast/overstated	-	increase	increase in net profit
income undercast/understated	-	increase	increase in net profit
income overcast/overstated	-	decrease	decrease in net profit

BALANCE SHEET

Correction of error	Gross profit	Net profit	Balance sheet
asset undercast/understated	-	-	increase asset
asset overcast/overstated	-	-	decrease asset
liability undercast/understated	-	-	increase liability
liability overcast/overstated	-	-	decrease liability

Some examination questions on correction of errors require the preparation of a statement showing the amended profit after errors have been corrected. We will look at the errors shown on page 322 and see how their correction affects the net profit (assume the net profit before adjustments is £10,000).

Statement of corrected net profit for the year ended 31 December 20-1

	£
Net profit (unadjusted)	10,000
Add sales undercast	1,000
Add general expenses decreased by £65 – £56	9
	11,009
Less additional telephone expenses	105
Adjusted net profit	10,904

The effect on the balance sheet of correcting the errors is:

- net profit increases £904
- the credit balance of £904 in suspense account (shown as a current liability) is eliminated

The balance sheet will now balance without the need for a suspense account – the errors have been found and corrected.

CHAPTER SUMMARY

- Correction of errors is always a difficult topic to put into practice: it tests knowledge of accounting procedures and it is all too easy to make the error worse than it was in the first place!
- Errors not shown by a trial balance: error of omission, reversal of entries, mispost/error of commission, error of principle, error of original entry (or transcription), compensating error.
- Errors shown by a trial balance include: omission of one part of the book-keeping transaction, recording two entries on the same side for a transaction, recording different amounts in the two accounts, calculating balances, transferring balances to the trial balance.
- When error(s) are shown by a trial balance, the amount is placed into a suspense account. When the errors are found, entries are made which 'clear out' the suspense account.
- Correction of errors may have an effect on gross profit and net profit, and on the figures in the balance sheet. It may be necessary to restate net profit and to adjust the balance sheet.

In the next chapter we shall look at the published accounts of limited companies – the form in which large companies report their results to shareholders and other interested parties.

QUESTIONS

NOTE: an asterisk (*) after the question number means that an answer to the question is given at the end of this book.

20.1 The book-keeper of Johnson Limited extracts a trial balance on 30 September 20-8. Unfortunately the trial balance fails to balance by £12.

The following errors are later found:

(a) A payment of £85 for office expenses has not been recorded in office expenses account.

(b) The sales return total has been overcast by £100.

(c) Commission received of £52 should be £25.

(d) A cheque paid to Harvey Limited for £1,310 has been entered in the account of Harry Limited in error.

The totals of the trial balances are given on the next page. Write in the adjustments you would make for the errors and recalculate the total.

Trial Balance as at 30 September 20-8

	Dr £	Cr £
Incorrect totals	40,378	40,390
Corrected totals		

20.2* Wholesale Car Spares plc is a leading supplier of vehicle parts.

REQUIRED

(a) Advise Wholesale Car Spares plc of **two** benefits of drawing up a trial balance.

(b) The trial balance for the month ended 31 October 2000 has been drawn up and the following errors have been discovered.

1. The sales total was undercast by £540
2. The returns inwards total includes £100 which is actually for returns outwards.
3. A cheque received from J C Cross Garages for £1,479 was entered in the account of A B Cross Ltd in error.
4. The debtors' total has been entered as £25,080, it should have been £25,800.

The totals of the trial balance are given below. Write in the adjustments you would make for the errors and recalculate the total.

Trial Balance as at 31 October 2000

	£	£
Incorrect totals	20,280	20,260
Corrected totals		

(c) Explain the main limitation of preparing a trial balance, using **two** examples to illustrate your answer.

Assessment and Qualifications Alliance (AQA), 2001

20.3 The trial balance of H G Patel Ltd, as at 30 April 2003, has been partially completed. The following balances have now to be included:

	£
Purchases	38,900
Sales	98,000
Returns outwards	3,698
Carriage inwards	367
Carriage outwards	450
Discount received	2,135
Dividends paid	6,900

REQUIRED

(a) Enter these figures into the trial balance provided below.

(b) Total the trial balance and enter any difference in the suspense account.

H G Patel Ltd: Trial Balance as at 30 April 2003

Account	**Debit** £	**Credit** £
Wages	23,890	
Administration costs	6,000	
Share capital		60,000
Premises	65,000	
Motor vehicles	5,000	
Motor expenses	1,650	
Purchases		
Sales		
Returns outwards		
Carriage inwards		
Carriage outwards		
Discount received		
Dividends paid		
Suspense		
TOTAL		

(c) There are many reasons for the error(s) giving rise to the suspense account.

From the following list of book-keeping errors, tick the Yes or No box to indicate whether or not the error could be responsible for the difference in the trial balance.

An example has been given.

	Error	Yes	No
1.	*A balance has been entered in the wrong column of the trial balance.*	✓	
2.	An error of principle has occurred.		
3.	The sales account has been totalled incorrectly.		
4.	An invoice has been completely omitted.		
5.	A cheque has been debited in the cash book as £150 but credited in the customer's account as £105.		

Assessment and Qualifications Alliance (AQA), 2003

20.4* Northern Lights Ltd drew up the following trial balance. When it was totalled it revealed errors, which resulted in a suspense account being opened.

Northern Lights Ltd

Trial Balance as at 31 December 2001

	Dr £	Cr £
Sales		400,000
Purchases	350,000	
Returns inwards		5,000
Returns outwards	6,200	
Stock at 1 January 2001	100,000	
Carriage outwards	800	
Wages	32,000	

Rates	6,000	
Carriage inwards		1,000
Fixed assets		70,000
Debtors		9,800
Creditors	7,000	
Bank balance (overdrawn)	3,000	
Dividends paid	18,000	
Share capital and reserves		106,400
10% Debentures	70,000	
Suspense account		800
Total	593,000	593,000

REQUIRED

Draw up the corrected trial balance, using the grid below.

Northern Lights Ltd
Trial Balance as at 31 December 2001

	Dr £	Cr £
Sales		
Purchases		
Returns inwards		
Returns outwards		
Stock at 1 January 2001		
Carriage outwards		
Wages		
Rates		
Carriage inwards		
Fixed assets		
Debtors		
Creditors		
Bank balance (overdrawn)		
Dividends paid		
Share capital and reserves		
10% Debentures		
Total		

Assessment and Qualifications Alliance (AQA), 2002

20.5*

The trial balance of Fancy Goods Enterprises was drawn up as at 31 March 2001 but the totals did not agree. The following errors have been discovered.

(1) The purchases account has been overcast by £4,500.

(2) The debtors' total includes £650 which has been written off as a bad debt.

(3) Discount received of £300 has been entered on the debit of the account.

(4) A cheque for £673, payable to Sunshine Products Ltd, has been entered in the account of Sunmaster Products in error.

(5) The credit balance in the rent payable account has been brought down as £990. It should have been £909.

REQUIRED

Make any necessary entries in the suspense account to correct these errors, and show the opening balance.

Dr **Suspense Account** Cr

Details	£	Details	£

Assessment and Qualifications Alliance (AQA), 2001

20.6

R Masters has drawn up a suspense account at 31 March 2002 following the discovery of errors.

REQUIRED

(a) From the following list of errors make the necessary entries in the suspense account and calculate the opening balance.

(1) The sales day book has been overcast by £270.

(2) The returns inwards has been entered as a credit of £500. It in fact totalled £300.

(3) A discount received of £400 was entered in the cash book but omitted from the general ledger.

(4) A cheque paid to J Jones of £350 was entered in the account of A Jones in error.

Dr **Suspense Account** Cr

Date 2002	Details	£	Date 2002	Details	£

(b) The profit for the year ended 31 March 2002, before the errors were discovered, was £17,690. Set out a detailed calculation of the correct net profit **after** the adjustments for the above errors have been made.

Assessment and Qualifications Alliance (AQA), 2002

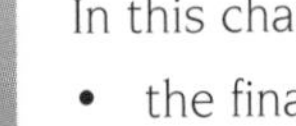

21 PUBLISHED ACCOUNTS OF LIMITED COMPANIES

In this chapter we look at:

- the financial statements required by the Companies Act
- the reasons for, and the layout of, published accounts
- interpretation of the auditors' report
- the accounting policies followed by a particular company
- the differences between earnings per share and dividends per share
- the different user groups of the corporate report

The chapter includes extracts from the annual report and accounts of Tesco PLC. To help with your studies you should obtain a set of published accounts from a public limited company that is of interest to you.

COMPANY 'ACCOUNTS'

Every limited company, whether public or private, is required by law to produce financial statements, which are also available for anyone to inspect if they so wish. We need to distinguish between the statutory accounts and the report and accounts. The **statutory accounts** are those which are required to be produced under company law, and a copy of these is filed with the Registrar of Companies. The **report and accounts** – often referred to as the **corporate report** – is available to every shareholder and contains:

- directors' report
- auditors' report (where required)
- profit and loss account (which includes a trading account, where required)
- balance sheet
- cash flow statement (where required)
- notes to the accounts, including a statement of the company's accounting policies

Company law not only requires the production of financial statements, but also states the detailed information that must be disclosed. The legal requirements are detailed in the relevant sections of the Companies Act 1985 (as amended by the Companies Act 1989).

Responsibilities of Directors

The directors of a limited company are responsible for ensuring that the provisions of the Companies Act 1985 which relate to accounting records and statements are followed. This requires directors to produce accounts in the correct form and at the proper time. The directors are responsible for ensuring that the company keeps supporting accounting records. They must ensure that the annual accounts comply with company law and the accounting standards (see below).

Statements Required by the Companies Act

The financial statements required by the Companies Act are:

- profit and loss account
- balance sheet
- directors' report
- auditors' report
- consolidated accounts, where appropriate

When producing financial statements, companies also have to take note of the requirements of the accounting standards – Statements of Standard Accounting Practice (SSAPs) and Financial Reporting Standards (FRSs). These are issued by the Accounting Standards Board and set out acceptable accounting methods for various topics. Of particular note is FRS 1, which requires larger limited companies to include a cash flow statement (see Chapter 22) as part of the published accounts.

Profit and Loss Account

The published profit and loss account does not, by law, have to detail every single overhead incurred by the company – to do so would be to disclose important management information to competitors. Instead, the main items are summarised; however, the Companies Act requires that certain items must be detailed either in the profit and loss account itself, or in separate notes to the accounts (see page 343).

The profit and loss account must follow one of two standard formats set out in the Act, and the example on the next page shows the one that is most commonly used by trading companies. On page 335 is shown the profit and loss account for the Tesco group of companies.

As mentioned above, much of the detail shown in profit and loss account is summarised. For example:

- turnover incorporates the figures for sales and sales returns
- cost of sales includes opening stock, purchases, purchases returns, carriage inwards and closing stock

continued on page 336

DURNING PLC

Profit and Loss Account for the year ended 31 December 20-2

	£000s	£000s
Turnover		
Continuing operations	22,000	
Acquisitions	3,000	
	25,000	
Discontinued operations	2,000	27,000
Cost of sales		16,500
Gross profit		10,500
Distribution costs		4,250
Administrative expenses		4,000
Operating profit		
Continuing operations	2,000	
Acquisitions	200	
	2,200	
Discontinued operations	50	2,250
Profit on disposal of discontinued operations		250
		2,500
Other operating income		250
Income from shares in group undertakings		–
Income from participating interests		–
Income from other fixed asset investments		100
Other interest receivable and similar income		–
Amounts written off investments		–
Profit on ordinary activities before interest		2,850
Interest payable and similar charges		200
Profit on ordinary activities before taxation		2,650
Tax on profit on ordinary activities		725
Profit on ordinary activities after taxation		1,925
Extraordinary items		–
Profit for the financial year		1,925
Dividends		1,125
Retained profit for the financial year		800

TESCO PLC

group profit and loss account

52 weeks ended 22 February 2003

	note	Continuing operations 2003 £m	Acquisitions 2003 £m	2003 £m	2002 £m
Sales at net selling prices	1	28,352	261	28,613	25,654
Turnover including share of joint ventures		26,300	230	26,530	23,804
Less: share of joint ventures' turnover		(193)	–	(193)	(151)
Group turnover excluding value added tax	1/2	26,107	230	26,337	23,653
Operating expenses					
– Normal operating expenses		(24,558)	(219)	(24,777)	(22,273)
– Employee profit-sharing	3	(51)	–	(51)	(48)
– Integration costs		–	(4)	(4)	–
– Goodwill amortisation	11	(10)	(11)	(21)	(10)
Operating profit	1/2	1,488	(4)	1,484	1,322
Share of operating profit of joint ventures and associates		70	–	70	42
Net loss on disposal of fixed assets		(13)	–	(13)	(10)
Profit on ordinary activities before interest and taxation		1,545	(4)	1,541	1,354
Net interest payable	7			(180)	(153)
Profit on ordinary activities before taxation	4			1,361	1,201
Underlying profit before net loss on disposal of fixed assets, integration costs and goodwill amortisation				1,401	1,221
Net loss on disposal of fixed assets				(13)	(10)
Integration costs				(4)	–
Goodwill amortisation				(21)	(10)
Goodwill amortisation in joint ventures and associates				(2)	–
Tax on profit on ordinary activities	8			(415)	(371)
Profit on ordinary activities after taxation				946	830
Minority interests				–	–
Profit for the financial year				946	830
Dividends	9			(443)	(390)
Retained profit for the financial year	24			503	440
				Pence	Pence
Earnings per share	10			13.54	12.05
Adjusted for net loss on disposal of fixed assets after taxation				0.18	0.14
Adjusted for integration costs after taxation				0.06	–
Adjusted for goodwill amortisation				0.32	0.14
Underlying earnings per share†	10			14.10	12.33
Diluted earnings per share	10			13.42	11.86
Adjusted for net loss on disposal of fixed assets after taxation				0.18	0.14
Adjusted for integration costs after taxation				0.06	–
Adjusted for goodwill amortisation				0.32	0.14
Underlying diluted earnings per share†	10			13.98	12.14
Dividend per share	9			6.20	5.60
Dividend cover (times)				2.25	2.17

Accounting policies and notes forming part of these financial statements are on pages 28 to 53.

† Excluding net loss on disposal of fixed assets, integration costs and goodwill amortisation.

Profit and loss account for the Tesco group of companies

(note that, for comparison, figures for both the current year and last year are shown)

- distribution costs include warehouse costs, post and packing, delivery drivers' wages, running costs of vehicles, depreciation of vehicles, etc
- administrative expenses include office costs, rent and rates, heating and lighting, depreciation of office equipment, etc.

A profit and loss account for Tesco PLC is shown on the previous page. This gives the consolidated (or group) profit and loss account, together with the figures for the previous year. Consolidated accounts are explained on page 343.

continuing and discontinued operations

Limited company profit and loss accounts are also required to show the financial results of any changes to the structure of the company, eg the purchase of another company, or the disposal of a section of the business. To this end the profit and loss account must distinguish between:

- results of continuing operations, ie from those parts of the business that have been kept throughout the year
- results of acquisitions, ie from businesses bought during the year
- results of discontinued operations, ie from parts of the business that have been sold or terminated during the year
- exceptional items of which the following are to be disclosed:
  - profits or losses on the sale or termination of an operation
  - costs of fundamental reorganisation
  - profits or losses on the disposal of fixed assets

The objective of these requirements is to give more information to users of accounts.

Balance Sheet

The Companies Act 1985 sets out the standard formats for balance sheets. The example on the next page is presented in the layout most commonly used. As with the profit and loss account, extra detail is often shown in the notes to the balance sheet (see page 343).

The layout of the balance sheet follows that which we have used for limited companies in Chapter 19. However, some of the terms used need further explanation:

- **intangible fixed assets** – those assets which do not have material substance but belong to the company, eg goodwill (the amount paid for the reputation and connections of a business that has been taken over), patents and trademarks
- **tangible fixed assets** – those assets which have material substance, such as premises, equipment and vehicles

continued on page 339

DURNING PLC

Balance Sheet as at 31 December 20-2

	£000s	£000s
Fixed assets		
Intangible assets		50
Tangible assets		6,750
Investments		1,000
		7,800
Current assets		
Stock	1,190	
Debtors	1,600	
Investments	–	
Cash at bank and in hand	10	
	2,800	
Creditors: amounts falling due within one year	1,800	
Net current assets		1,000
Total assets less current liabilities		8,800
Creditors: amounts falling due after more than one year		1,500
Provisions for liabilities and charges		100
		7,200
Capital and reserves		
Called up share capital		2,800
Share premium		400
Revaluation reserve		1,500
Profit and loss account		2,500
		7,200

A balance sheet for the Tesco group of companies is shown on the next page.

TESCO PLC

balance sheets

22 February 2003

	note	£m	2003 £m	£m	Group 2002 £m	Company 2003 £m	Company 2002 £m
Fixed assets							
Intangible assets	11		890		154	–	–
Tangible assets	12		12,828		11,032	–	–
Investments	13		59		69	7,820	6,704
Investments in joint ventures	13						
Share of gross assets		1,708		1,480		–	–
Less: share of gross liabilities		(1,459)		(1,266)		–	–
Goodwill		17		18		–	–
			266		232	158	156
Investments in associates	13		18		16	–	–
			14,061		11,503	7,978	6,860
Current assets							
Stocks	14		1,140		929	–	–
Debtors	15		662		454	1,012	3,060
Investments	16		239		225	–	5
Cash at bank and in hand			399		445	–	–
			2,440		2,053	1,012	3,065
Creditors: falling due within one year	17		(5,372)		(4,809)	(1,961)	(4,707)
Net current liabilities			(2,932)		(2,756)	(949)	(1,642)
Total assets less current liabilities			11,129		8,747	7,029	5,218
Creditors: falling due after more than one year	18		(4,049)		(2,741)	(3,772)	(2,609)
Provisions for liabilities and charges	21		(521)		(440)	–	–
Net assets			6,559		5,566	3,257	2,609
Capital and reserves							
Called up share capital	23		362		350	362	350
Share premium account	24		2,465		2,004	2,465	2,004
Other reserves	24		40		40	–	–
Profit and loss account	24		3,649		3,136	430	255
Equity shareholders' funds			6,516		5,530	3,257	2,609
Minority interests			43		36	–	–
Total capital employed			6,559		5,566	3,257	2,609

Accounting policies and notes forming part of these financial statements are on pages 28 to 53.

Terry Leahy
Andrew Higginson
Directors
Financial statements approved by the Board on 7 April 2003.

Balance sheet for the Tesco group of companies

(note that both the 'group' and 'company' balance sheets are shown – see also consolidated accounts on page 343)

- **investments** – shares held in other companies (for example, suppliers and customers), or government securities: classed as fixed asset investments if there is the intention to hold them for a long time, and as current asset investments where they are likely to be sold, probably at a profit, within twelve months of the balance sheet date

- **creditors: amounts falling due within one year** – the term used in company balance sheets for current liabilities, ie amounts that are due to be paid within twelve months of the balance sheet date

- **creditors: amounts falling due after more than one year** – the term used for long-term liabilities, ie amounts that are due to be paid more than twelve months from the balance sheet date, eg loans and debentures

- **provisions for liabilities and charges** – an estimate of possible liabilities to be paid in the future.

Note that, on the balance sheet, a distinction may be made between **equity funds** and **non equity funds**. As we have seen in Chapter 19 (page 293), ordinary shares are often known as 'equities' (because they share equally in the profits of the company). Equity funds are the ordinary shares, plus all of the reserves (capital reserves and revenue reserves), ie the amount of the ordinary shareholders' stake in the company. Non equity funds consist of the preference shares, the holders of which are not entitled to any of the reserves. As we saw when we looked at the differences between ordinary and preference shares (page 294), preference shares rank above ordinary shares in terms of both dividends and repayment of capital. However, ordinary shares are entitled to all remaining profits and reserves after the non equity shares have been settled.

Directors' Report

The directors' report contains details of the following:

- review of the activities of the company over the past year and of likely developments in the future, including research and development activity
- directors' names and their shareholdings
- proposed dividends
- significant differences between the book value and market value of land and buildings
- political and charitable contributions
- policy on employment of disabled people
- health and safety at work of employees
- action taken on employee involvement and consultation
- policy on payment of creditors

TESCO PLC

group cash flow statement

52 weeks ended 22 February 2003

	note	2003 £m	2002 £m
Net cash inflow from operating activities	31	2,375	2,038
Dividends from joint ventures and associates			
Income received from joint ventures and associates		11	15
Returns on investments and servicing of finance			
Interest received		37	44
Interest paid		(253)	(232)
Interest element of finance lease rental payments		(2)	(4)
Net cash outflow from returns on investments and servicing of finance		(218)	(192)
Taxation			
Corporation tax paid		(366)	(378)
Capital expenditure and financial investment			
Payments to acquire tangible fixed assets		(2,032)	(1,877)
Receipts from sale of tangible fixed assets		32	42
Purchase of own shares		(52)	(85)
Net cash outflow from capital expenditure and financial investment		(2,052)	(1,920)
Acquisitions and disposals			
Purchase of subsidiary undertakings		(419)	(31)
Net cash at bank and in hand acquired with subsidiaries		33	–
Invested in joint ventures		(43)	(46)
Invested in associates and other investments		(7)	(19)
Net cash outflow from acquisitions and disposals		(436)	(96)
Equity dividends paid		(368)	(297)
Cash outflow before management of liquid resources and financing		(1,054)	(830)
Management of liquid resources			
(Increase)/decrease in short-term deposits		(14)	27
Financing			
Ordinary shares issued for cash		73	82
Increase in other loans		774	916
New finance leases		249	–
Capital element of finance leases repaid		(73)	(24)
Net cash inflow from financing		1,023	974
(Decrease)/increase in cash		(45)	171
Reconciliation of net cash flow to movement in net debt			
(Decrease)/increase in cash		(45)	171
Cash inflow from increase in debt and lease financing		(950)	(892)
Increase/(decrease) in liquid resources		14	(27)
Loans and finance leases acquired with subsidiaries		(172)	–
Amortisation of 4% unsecured deep discount loan stock, RPI and LPI bonds		(8)	(14)
Other non-cash movements		(19)	(12)
Foreign exchange differences		3	18
Increase in net debt		(1,177)	(756)
Opening net debt	32	(3,560)	(2,804)
Closing net debt	32	(4,737)	(3,560)

Accounting policies and notes forming part of these financial statements are on pages 28 to 53.

Cash flow statement for Tesco PLC

CASH FLOW STATEMENTS

All but the smaller limited companies must include, as part of their published accounts, a cash flow statement, which we will study in the next chapter. Such a statement shows where the funds (money) have come from during the course of a financial year, and how such funds have been used. The statement also provides a direct link between the previous year's balance sheet and the current one. A recent cash flow statement for Tesco PLC is shown on the previous page.

AUDITORS' REPORT

Larger companies must have their accounts audited by external auditors, who are appointed by the shareholders to check the accounts. The auditors' report, which is printed in the published accounts, is the culmination of their work. The three main sections of the auditors' report are:

- **respective responsibilities of directors and auditors** – the directors are responsible for preparing the accounts, while the auditors are responsible for forming an opinion on the accounts
- **basis of opinion** – the framework of Auditing Standards (issued by the Auditing Practices Board) within which the audit was conducted, other assessments, and the way in which the audit was planned and performed
- **opinion** – the auditors' view of the company's accounts

An 'unqualified' auditors' opinion will read as follows:

> *'In our opinion the financial statements give a true and fair view of the state of affairs of the Company at .... 20.., and of the profit, and cash flows of the Company for the year then ended, and have been properly prepared in accordance with the Companies Act 1985.'*

A 'qualified' auditors' report will raise points that the auditors consider have not been dealt with correctly in the accounts. Where such points are not too serious, the auditors will use phrases such as 'except for ...' or 'subject to ... the financial statements give a true and fair view'. Much more serious is where the auditors' statement says that the accounts 'do not show a true and fair view' or 'we are unable to form an opinion ...'. These indicate a major disagreement between the company and the auditors, and a person involved with the company – such as an investor or creditor – should take serious note.

Note that smaller private companies are exempt from audit requirements if their turnover (sales) for the year is below a certain figure.

8 TESCO PLC

accounting policies

BASIS OF PREPARATION OF FINANCIAL STATEMENTS
These financial statements have been prepared under the historical cost convention, in accordance with applicable accounting standards and the Companies Act 1985.

As in the prior year, the Group has continued to account for pensions and other post-employment benefits in accordance with SSAP 24 but has complied with the transitional disclosure requirements of FRS 17. These transitional disclosures are presented in note 26.

BASIS OF CONSOLIDATION The Group financial statements consist of the financial statements of the parent company, its subsidiary undertakings and the Group's share of interests in joint ventures and associates. The accounts of the parent company's subsidiary undertakings are prepared to dates around 22 February 2003 apart from Global T.H., Tesco Polska Sp. z o.o., Tesco Stores ČR a.s., Tesco Stores SR a.s., Samsung Tesco Co. Limited, Tesco Malaysia Sdn Bhd, Tesco Taiwan Co. Limited and Ek-Chai Distribution System Co. Ltd which prepared accounts to 31 December 2002. In the opinion of the Directors it is necessary for the above named subsidiaries to prepare accounts to a date earlier than the rest of the Group to enable the timely publication of the Group financial statements.

The Group's interests in joint ventures are accounted for using the gross equity method. The Group's interests in associates are accounted for using the equity method.

TURNOVER Turnover consists of sales through retail outlets and sales of development properties excluding value added tax.

STOCKS Stocks comprise goods held for resale and properties held for, or in the course of, development and are valued at the lower of cost and net realisable value. Stocks in stores are calculated at retail prices and reduced by appropriate margins to the lower of cost and net realisable value.

MONEY MARKET DEPOSITS Money market deposits are stated at cost. All income from these investments is included in the profit and loss account as interest receivable and similar income.

FIXED ASSETS AND DEPRECIATION Fixed assets are carried at cost and include amounts in respect of interest paid on funds specifically related to the financing of assets in the course of construction. Interest is capitalised on a gross basis.

Depreciation is provided on a straight-line basis over the anticipated useful economic lives of the assets.

The following rates applied for the Group and are consistent with the prior year:

- Land premia paid in excess of the alternative use value – at 2.5% of cost.
- Freehold and leasehold buildings with greater than 40 years unexpired – at 2.5% of cost.
- Leasehold properties with less than 40 years unexpired are amortised by equal annual instalments over the unexpired period of the lease.
- Plant, equipment, fixtures and fittings and motor vehicles – at rates varying from 10% to 33%.

GOODWILL Goodwill arising from transactions entered into after 1 March 1998 is capitalised and amortised on a straight-line basis over its useful economic life, up to a maximum of 20 years.

All goodwill arising from transactions entered into prior to 1 March 1998 has been written off to reserves.

IMPAIRMENT OF FIXED ASSETS AND GOODWILL Fixed assets and goodwill are subject to review for impairment in accordance with FRS 11, 'Impairment of Fixed Assets and Goodwill'. Any impairment is recognised in the profit and loss account in the year in which it occurs.

LEASING Plant, equipment and fixtures and fittings which are the subject of finance leases are dealt with in the financial statements as tangible fixed assets and equivalent liabilities at what would otherwise have been the cost of outright purchase.

Rentals are apportioned between reductions of the respective liabilities and finance charges, the latter being calculated by reference to the rates of interest implicit in the leases. The finance charges are dealt with under interest payable in the profit and loss account.

Leased assets are depreciated in accordance with the depreciation accounting policy over the anticipated working lives of the assets which generally correspond to the primary rental periods. The cost of operating leases in respect of land and buildings and other assets is expensed as incurred.

Extract from the accounting policies of Tesco PLC

Accounting Policies

Accounting policies are the accounting techniques that the directors of a company choose to follow in the accounts. Examples include the way in which a company values its stock, how it deals with goodwill and other intangible assets, how it deals with fixed assets such as land and buildings, vehicles.

Companies include a statement of their accounting policies in the published accounts. An extract from the accounting policies of Tesco PLC is shown on the previous page.

Notes to the Accounts

The Companies Act 1985, as well as requiring the presentation of financial statements in a particular layout, also requires additional information to be provided. These **notes to the accounts** include:

- disclosure of accounting policies (see previous section)
- details of authorised and allotted share capital
- movements on fixed assets
- details of listed investments
- movements on reserves
- provision for deferred tax
- analysis of indebtedness
- details of charges and contingent liabilities
- details of interest or similar charges on loans and overdrafts
- basis of computation of UK Corporation Tax and details of tax charge
- directors' emoluments including Chairman's emoluments where necessary
- auditor's remuneration

Consolidated Accounts

In recent years many companies have been taken over by other companies to form groups. Each company within a group maintains its separate legal entity, and so a group of companies may take the form of the diagram on the next page. One way in which this happens is where one company buys more than half of the shares in another company which then becomes a subsidiary company of the parent company.

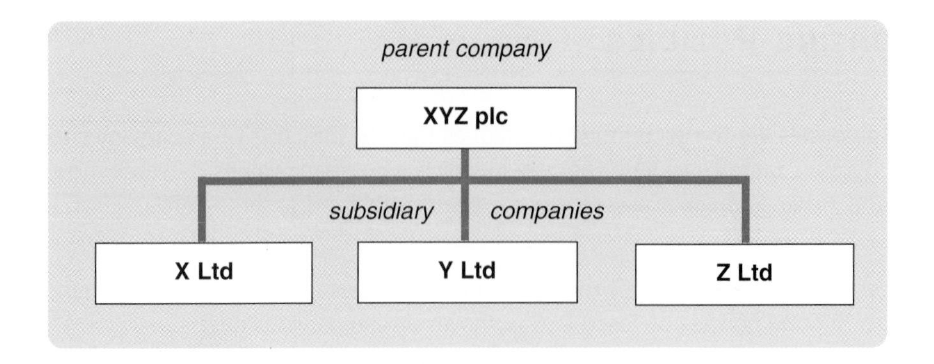

Earnings per Share and Dividends per Share

These are two important calculations, both of which are often stated at the bottom of a published profit and loss account. They are calculations of importance for a number of users of accounts (see next section) who wish to assess the stability of the company.

Earnings per share (or EPS) measures the amount of profit – usually expressed in pence per share – earned by each ordinary share, after corporation tax and preference dividends. It is calculated as follows:

$$\frac{\text{Net profit} - \text{corporation tax} - \text{preference dividend (if any)}}{\text{Number of issued ordinary shares}}$$

Note that corporation tax and preference dividends (but not ordinary dividends) are deducted, before dividing by the number of ordinary shares in issue.

EPS shows the amount earned by each share and guides ordinary shareholders as to the profitability of the shares, as well as enabling comparisons with previous years or other shares.

Dividends per share (or total dividend per share) shows the amount of dividend – expressed in pence per share – paid by the company on each ordinary share. It is calculated as follows:

$$\frac{\text{Total ordinary dividend}}{\text{Number of issued ordinary shares}}$$

Note that dividends per share may relate to the current dividend only, or it may relate to the whole year – in which case it will often include both an interim and a final dividend.

Dividends per share tells shareholders how much they are receiving as the dividend for each share owned. From this the shareholders can look at earnings per share and see if the company is distributing a reasonable amount of the earnings as dividends.

The shareholders can also see how much of the earnings is being retained by the company to invest for the future, for example:

	45p	earnings per share
less	20p	dividend per share
	25p	retained by the company for investment

In this example, while a reasonable dividend is being paid, more than half of the EPS amount is retained for future investment. This is a good indicator for ordinary shareholders because it shows that there is the potential for growth in the company.

Dividends per share shows the amount of dividend paid on each share and guides ordinary shareholders to to the amount of cash they are receiving from the company. Comparisons can also be made with previous years or other shares.

The Corporate Report: User Groups

A number of people are interested in reading the annual report and accounts – the corporate report – of a company, especially those of large public limited companies. These user groups include actual or potential:

- shareholders
- loan providers/debenture holders
- creditors (suppliers)
- employees

Each of these user groups is interested in different aspects, as summarised in the diagram on the next page.

There are a number of other user groups interested more generally in the report and accounts of companies. Examples include:

- the Government and government agencies – interested in the tax and VAT due
- the public – interested in the contribution of the company to the economy
- pressure groups, such as environmentalists – interested in the company's stance on social issues and environmental issues

the Corporate Report: user groups

Who is interested?	What are they interested in?	Why are they interested?
Shareholders	• Dividends • Profits	• To see how much cash they are receiving in dividends from their investment and to enable comparison with previous years/other investments • To see how much profit is being retained by the company for investment, and to assess the future prospects of the company in terms of long-term profitability and the security of their investment
Loan providers, debenture holders	• Total loans • Interest paid • Profits	• To check if there are other lenders who need to be repaid, so reducing the ability of the company to repay its lending • To ensure that interest is paid to date • To see how much profit is being made in order to assess the likelihood of receiving interest payments and loan repayments
Creditors (suppliers)	• Current assets, net current assets (working capital) • Profits	• To assess whether the current assets and net current assets provide sufficient liquidity (ie the stability of the company on a short-term basis) for the company to pay its creditors as they fall due • To see how much profit is being made in order to assess its ability to pay creditors; to see if the company is expanding, so creating an increased level of purchases from its suppliers; to make comparison of profits with previous years
Employees	• Profits • Net assets	• To assess whether the company is making profits to be able to afford pay rises; to make comparison of profits with previous years • To consider the net assets of the company, which show its financial strength and indicate its ability to continue in business, so assuring future employment prospects

CHAPTER SUMMARY

- The Companies Act 1985 (as amended by the Companies Act 1989) requires a considerable amount of detail to be disclosed in the published accounts of limited companies.
- The Act requires all limited companies to produce:
  - a profit and loss account
  - a balance sheet
  - a directors' report
  - an auditors' report
- The Act lays down formats for profit and loss account and balance sheet.
- Most companies also include in their published accounts a cash flow statement which shows where the funds (money) has come from during the course of the financial year, and how it has been used.
- For larger companies, external auditors report to the shareholders on the state of affairs of the company.
- The directors establish the accounting policies which the company will follow.
- Consolidated accounts are prepared for groups of companies.
- Earnings per share measures the amount of profit earned by each ordinary share.
- Dividends per share (or total dividend per share) shows the amount of dividend paid by the company on each ordinary share.
- User groups interested in the corporate report of companies include actual or potential:
  - shareholders
  - loan providers/debenture holders
  - creditors (suppliers)
  - employees

The next chapter focuses on the cash flow statement – this uses information from the profit and loss account and balance sheet to show the effect on the cash of the business.

QUESTIONS

NOTE: an asterisk (*) after the question number means that an answer to the question is given at the end of the book.

21.1 Explain what is contained within the report and accounts – or corporate report – of a public limited company.

21.2* List four items that have to be included in a directors' report.

21.3 From a set of published accounts, give an example of an unqualified auditors' report.

21.4

Select a public limited company of your choice and obtain the latest set of published accounts. (Write to the company asking for a set or look on the company's website; alternatively some financial newspapers offer a 'report and accounts service' whereby accounts for the larger plcs can be sent on request.)

Read the report and accounts and, from the final accounts, extract the following information for the current and previous year (if there is a choice of figures, use those from the consolidated accounts):

profit and loss account

- turnover
- profit on ordinary activities before taxation
- profit for the financial year
- earnings per share

balance sheet

- total of fixed assets
- total of current assets
- total of current liabilities (often shown as 'creditors: amounts falling due within one year')
- total of long-term liabilities (often shown as 'creditors: amounts falling due after one year')
- capital employed

cash flow statement (see also chapter 22)

- cash flow from operating activities
- cash flow from
  - returns on investments and servicing of finance
  - taxation
  - capital expenditure and financial investment
  - financing

auditors' report (current year only)

- does it state that the financial statements show a 'true and fair view'?
- are there any 'qualifications' to the report

accounting policies (current year only)

- state two accounting policies followed by the plc

You are to compile a short report – from the point of view of a private investor – which contains:

- an introduction to the selected plc; its structure, size, products, position in its own industry
- the information extracted from the published accounts
- a portfolio of your observations from the report and accounts, eg
  - is the company expanding/declining/remaining static?
  - have the shareholders received higher/lower dividends?

21.5* The following is an extract from the balance sheet of Great Traders plc as at 30 November 2001:

	£m
Fixed assets	
Intangible assets: Goodwill	10.6
Tangible assets	340.9
Investments	45.0
	396.5
Current assets	
Stocks	23.0
Debtors	123.0
Investments	23.0
Cash at bank and in hand	10.0
	179.0
Creditors: amounts falling due within one year	
Loans	6.0
Other creditors	135.0
	141.0

REQUIRED

(a) Explain why some of the investments are shown as fixed assets and some as current assets.

(b) Give **two** examples of items that might be found included in the heading 'other creditors' contained in the section 'creditors falling due within one year'.

(c) State the meaning of the following:

(i) the share premium account

(ii) revaluation reserve

(d) What is the difference between equity funds and non equity funds?

Assessment and Qualifications Alliance (AQA), 2002

21.6* Extract from the balance sheet of D Austin plc as at 31 March 2002.

Fixed assets	**£000**	**£000**	**£000**
Tangibles			4,000
Intangibles			2,000
Investments			1,500
			7,500
Current assets			
Stocks	500		
Debtors	600		
Balance at bank	250	1,350	
Creditors due in less than one year		1,200	150
Total assets less current liabilities			7,350
Creditors due after more than one year			
8% Debentures 2015-2020			1,000
			6,350

REQUIRED

(a) Explain the following terms used in the above extract.

(i) Fixed Assets: Investments

(ii) 8% Debentures 2015-2020 £1,000,000

(b) State **two** items of information which could be gained from the directors' report.

(c) The company's annual report shows:

(i) Earnings per share 23.9p

(ii) Dividend per share 14.6p

Explain the significance of these two figures for the ordinary shareholder of the company.

Assessment and Qualifications Alliance (AQA), 2002

21.7 A to Z Spares Ltd has an authorised capital of:

3 million ordinary shares of £1 each

1 million 6% preference shares of 25p each

The company issued:

2 million ordinary shares at a premium of 50p each and

500,000 6% preference shares at par

All shares were fully paid.

REQUIRED

(a) Complete the following table to show the amount to be entered in each account.

Account	Amount £
Ordinary share capital	
Preference share capital	
Share premium	
Bank	

(b) On 31 March 2003 there was profit available for distribution of £750,000. The directors therefore propose that the annual dividend is paid on the preference shares and a dividend of 10p per share is paid on the ordinary shares.

Calculate

(i) the total preference share dividend

(ii) the total ordinary share dividend

(iii) the total of retained profit after distribution

(c) List **three** items which will be included in the Directors' Report.

Assessment and Qualifications Alliance (AQA), 2003

21.8 An extract from the published accounts of Tesco PLC for 2003 showed the following information.

CALLED UP SHARE CAPITAL

	ordinary shares of 5p each	
	Number (millions)	£m
Authorised at 22 February 2003	9,632	482
Issued at 22 February 2003	7,238	362

(a) Explain the meaning of the following terms as used in the above extract:

(i) Authorised share capital

(ii) Issued share capital

(iii) Called up share capital

The Directors' Report stated that earnings per share was 13.98p and that the total dividend per share was 6.2p.

(b) How much would a holder of 1,000 ordinary shares receive for the year?

(c) Explain the meaning of the terms:

(i) earnings per share

(ii) total dividend per share

21.9* (a) Define the following terms used in published accounts, giving an example for each:

(i) intangible fixed assets

(ii) tangible fixed assets

(iii) current assets

(b) Published accounts also include a directors' report and an auditors' report.

(i) Identify **three** areas you would expect the directors' report to cover.

(ii) What is the difference between the duties of directors and auditors with regard to the published accounts?

21.10* The four main groups of users of published accounts are

- shareholders
- loan providers
- creditors
- employees

For each user group:

(i) state two items from the final accounts which would be of particular interest to them

(ii) give reasons for your choice

21.11 The Chairman's statement in the accounts of Great Traders plc contained the following:

> "I am pleased to report that the total operating profit for the year to 30 November 2001 was £143 million. These good results were achieved despite higher costs. After interest of £19.5 million the profit before tax of £123.5 million was 12 per cent up on the same period in 2000. Future investment will be concentrated on those areas offering the highest returns and the greatest growth prospects."

This reported profit would have pleased the following interested groups but for different reasons.

REQUIRED

Give reasons why the following groups would be pleased to hear of the increase in the profits of Great Traders plc.

(a) Shareholders

(b) Debenture holders

(c) Employees

Assessment and Qualifications Alliance (AQA), 2002

22 CASH FLOW STATEMENTS

The cash flow statement links profit from the profit and loss account with changes in assets and liabilities in the balance sheet, and shows the effect on the cash of the business.

In this chapter we will cover:

- an appreciation of the need for a cash flow statement
- the layout of a cash flow statement
- the cash flows for the main sections of the statement
- reading the cash flow statement
- users of the cash flow statement

Note that Module 2 does not require you to be able to prepare a cash flow statement from given information; however, you will be required to comment on aspects of the statement.

WHAT ARE CASH FLOWS?

By using the term 'cash' accountants don't just mean cash in the form of notes and coin; instead they mean money in a wider sense – cash, money in the bank, bank overdraft, together with any money on deposit which can be withdrawn on demand. Cash flows are receipts and payments of money flowing in and out of a business during an accounting period.

With most business transactions it is easy to identify the cash flow and we will soon be able to see how they fit into the cash flow statement. For example:

- cash purchase of goods, paid for by cheque – here there is a cash outflow (note that the term 'cash purchase' means that the buyer is paying for the goods immediately)
- purchase of a new fixed asset, paying by cheque – clearly this is another cash outflow (as we will see later, we need to note that this is for the purchase of fixed assets)
- raising a loan by issuing debentures, receiving a cheque – this is a cash inflow for a loan raised
- paying dividends by cheque – a cash outflow (which is paid to the shareholders)

It is important to note that some business transactions do not have an effect on cash, for example:

- selling goods on credit – this is a 'non-cash' transaction, with payment to be made at a later date (but note that the profit on the goods sold will be taken to the trading and profit and loss account)
- allowing for depreciation of fixed assets – this is a non-cash transaction (because the fall in value of fixed assets does not directly affect the cash of a business, eg a car depreciating over time, does not cause a cash outflow)

FUNCTION OF THE CASH FLOW STATEMENT

As we saw in the last chapter, the three main financial statements in the published accounts of limited companies comprise:

- profit and loss account
- balance sheet
- cash flow statement

These three statements together provide users of published accounts with most of the information they need to understand the financial performance of the company.

It is the cash flow statement that links profit from the profit and loss account with changes in assets and liabilities in the balance sheet, and shows the effect on the cash of the business.

A cash flow statement uses information from the accounting records (including profit and loss account and balance sheet) to show an overall view of money flowing in and out of a business during an accounting period.

Such a statement explains to the shareholders why, after a year of good profits for example, there is a reduced balance at the bank or a larger bank overdraft at the year end than there was at the beginning of the year. The cash flow statement concentrates on the liquidity of the business: it is often a lack of cash (a lack of liquidity) that causes most businesses to fail.

To show why cash flow statements are important, look at the following figures taken from last year's accounts of a business.

	£	
Bank balance at the start of the year	20,000	
Bank balance at the end of the year	10,000	overdrawn
Profit for year	7,500	

What has caused the change in the bank? – an outflow of cash of £30,000 (from £20,000 in the bank to £10,000 overdraft)? A cash flow statement is needed to explain why, after a profit of £7,500, there has been a fall in the bank balance during the year.

The importance of the cash flow statement is such that all but smaller limited companies have to include the statement as a part of their published accounts. For smaller companies, the information that the statement contains is of considerable interest to the directors and to a lender, such as a bank.

The diagram which follows shows the links between the three main financial statements of published accounts, and the place of the cash flow statement:

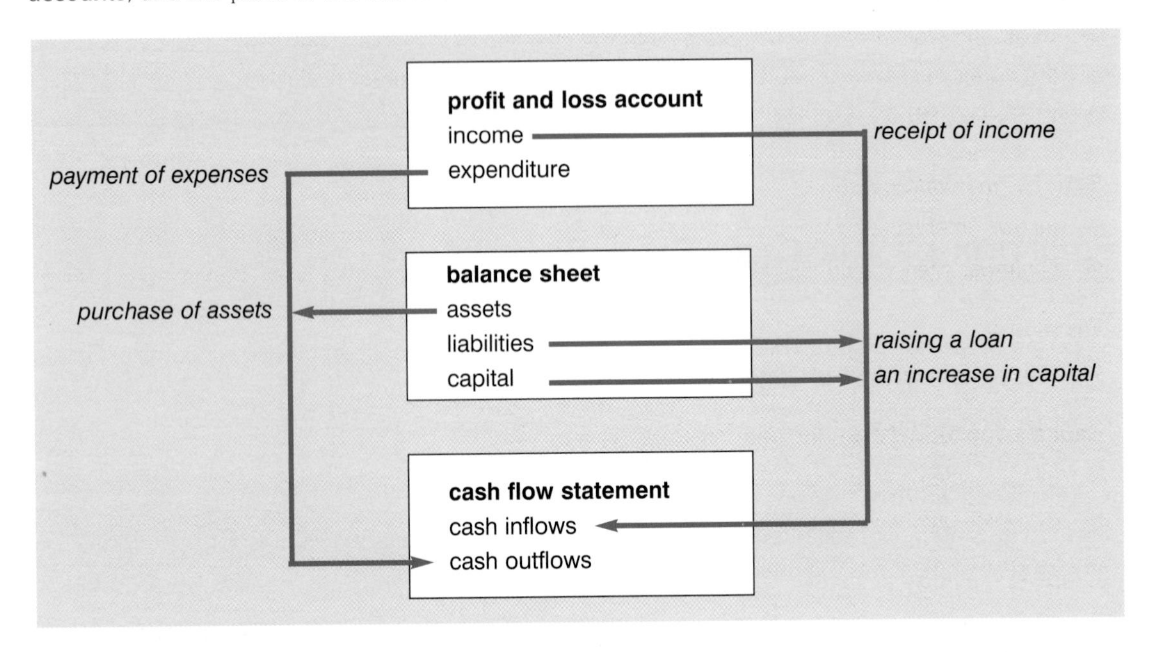

Format of the Cash Flow Statement

Cash flow statements are divided into eight sections:

1. Operating activities
2. Returns on investments and servicing of finance
3. Taxation
4. Capital expenditure and financial investment
5. Acquisitions and disposals
6. Equity dividends paid
7. Management of liquid resources
8. Financing

Note: this format follows the guidelines set out in Financial Reporting Standard No.1 'Cash flow statements'.

The cash flows for the year affecting each of these main areas of business activity are shown in the statement, although not every business will have cash flows under each of the eight sections. The final figure at the bottom of the cash flow statement shows the net cash inflow or outflow for the period.

The illustration on the next page shows the main cash inflows and outflows under each heading, and indicates the content of the cash flow statement. Each of these sections should be read in conjunction with the explanation of the headings which follows.

CASH FLOW STATEMENT

Operating activities

- Operating profit (ie net profit, before deduction of interest)
- Depreciation charge for the year
- Changes in stock, debtors and creditors

Returns on investments and servicing of finance

- Inflows: interest received, dividends received
- Outflows: interest paid, dividends paid on preference shares (but not ordinary shares – see below)

Taxation

- Outflow: corporation tax paid during the year

Capital expenditure and financial investment

- Inflows: sale proceeds from fixed assets and investments
- Outflows: purchase cost of fixed assets and investments

Acquisitions and disposals

- This section deals with acquisitions and disposals of investments and interests in other companies and businesses (note that this aspect of cash flow statements is outside the scope of the AQA AS level syllabus)

Equity dividends paid

- Outflow: the amount of dividends paid to equity (ordinary) shareholders during the year

Management of liquid resources

- Inflows: sale proceeds from short-term investments that are almost equal to cash – such as treasury bills (a form of government debt), and term deposits of up to a year with a bank
- Outflows: purchase of short-term liquid investments

Financing

- Inflows: receipts from increase in share capital, raising/increase of loans
- Outflows: repayment of share capital/loans

operating activities

The operating activities section is the main source of cash inflows for most businesses. It is calculated by using figures from the profit and loss account and balance sheet.

The starting point is the operating profit which is the profit from the normal trading activities of the business – without any exceptional (or 'one-off') items, such as the closure costs of a factory. Note that the operating profit is the profit before interest charges are deducted in profit and loss account.

The next step is to add back depreciation for the year. (Depreciation is the estimate of the fall in value of fixed assets – the topic is covered in more detail in Module 3.) This is because depreciation is a non-cash expense – ie no cash has left the business – which is charged to profit and loss account.

We then pick up the movements, or the change, in stock, debtors and creditors by comparing the balance sheet figures at the start and end of the year. The rules are:

- add a decrease in stock
- deduct an increase in stock
- add a decrease in debtors
- deduct an increase in debtors
- add an increase in creditors
- deduct a decrease in creditors

To explain these:

- For example, if stocks increase by £5,000, there is a cash outflow to pay for them so the amount is deducted from operating profit. If stock reduces then there is a cash inflow (one of the reasons why shops have sales so often) which is added to operating profit.
- For example, if credit sales are £200,000, but debtors have increased by £20,000, then the business must have received £180,000 cash from its customers, but has financed an extra £20,000 of debtors. This increase in debtors is deducted from operating profit. A decrease in debtors is added because the business has, overall, collected in debts, ie a cash inflow.
- For example, if credit purchases are £100,000, but creditors have increased by £10,000, then the business must have paid £90,000 to its suppliers. The increase in creditors is added to operating profit. A decrease in creditors is deducted because the business has, overall, paid off creditors, ie a cash outflow.

The operating activities section is summarised below. Note that companies often set out the detail of this section as a note to the cash flow statement, with just the figure for net cash flow from operating activities being shown on the statement.

operating profit (ie net profit, before deduction of interest paid)

add depreciation for the year

add decrease in stock, or *deduct* increase in stock

add decrease in debtors, or *deduct* increase in debtors

add increase in creditors, or *deduct* decrease in creditors

The Worked Example on page 361 shows how this section of the cash flow statement is calculated.

returns on investments and servicing of finance

This section shows cash received as returns from investments owned by the company, together with cash paid as interest to lenders. It includes interest received, dividends received, interest paid, and dividends paid on preference shares. Note that dividends paid on ordinary shares do not appear in this section – see 'equity dividends paid' (below).

taxation

Under this heading is shown the amount of corporation tax paid by a company during the year on its profits. Note that, for cash flow statements, there is often a time lag between earning profits and paying corporation tax – some part of the tax bill on the current year's profits will be paid in the next financial year.

capital expenditure and financial investment

This section deals with transactions in fixed assets – cash outflows are payments made to purchase fixed assets, while cash inflows are receipts from the sale of fixed assets. This section also deals with the purchase and sale of investments where they are not dealt with under 'management of liquid resources' (see below).

acquisitions and disposals

This section deals with acquisitions and disposals of investments and interests in other companies and businesses. This aspect of cash flow statements is outside the scope of the AQA AS level syllabus.

equity dividends paid

This shows the amount of dividends paid to equity (ordinary) shareholders during the year. Note that, for cash flow statements, there is often a time lag between proposing a dividend and the payment being made – proposed dividends at the year end will be paid in the early months of the next financial year.

management of liquid resources

Liquid resources are short-term investments that are almost equal to cash. Examples include treasury bills (a form of government debt), and term deposits of up to a year with a bank. Cash inflows come from the sale of liquid resources, while cash outflows show their purchase.

financing

The financing section shows the cash inflows from the issue of shares and debentures, together with borrowing (except for overdrafts, which are included with cash). Cash outflows show the repayment of shares, loans and borrowing.

Layout of a Cash Flow Statement

A cash flow statement uses a common layout which can be amended to suit the particular needs of the business for which it is being prepared. The example layout shown on the next page (with specimen figures included) is commonly used – see also the cash flow statement for Tesco PLC shown on page 340.

ORION LIMITED
CASH FLOW STATEMENT FOR THE YEAR ENDED 31 DECEMBER 20-2

	£	£
Net cash inflow from operating activities		89,000
Returns on investments and servicing of finance:		
Interest and dividends received	10,000	
Interest paid	(5,000)	
		5,000
Taxation:		
Corporation tax paid (note: amount paid during year)		(6,000)
Capital expenditure and financial investment:		
Payments to acquire fixed assets	(125,000)	
Receipts from sales of fixed assets	15,000	
		(110,000)
Acquisitions and disposals:		–
Equity dividends paid: (note: amount paid during year)		(22,000)
Cash outflow before use of liquid resources and financing		(44,000)
Management of liquid resources:		
Purchase of treasury bills	(250,000)	
Sale of treasury bills	200,000	
		(50,000)
Financing:		
Issue of share capital	275,000	
Repayment of capital/share capital	(–)	
Increase in loans	–	
Repayment of loans	(90,000)	
		185,000
Increase in cash		91,000

Reconciliation of operating profit to net cash inflow from operating activities	
Operating profit (note: before tax and interest)	75,000
Depreciation for year	10,000
Decrease in stock	2,000
Increase in debtors	(5,000)
Increase in creditors	7,000
Net cash inflow from operating activities	89,000

notes on the cash flow statement

- The separate amounts shown for each section can, if preferred, be detailed in a note to the cash flow statement. The operating activities section is invariably set out in detail as a note below the cash flow statement (see example opposite), with just the figure for net cash flow from operating activities being shown on the statement (see blue line).
- Money amounts shown in brackets indicate a deduction or, where the figure is a sub-total, a negative figure.
- The changes in the main working capital items of stock, debtors and creditors have an effect on cash balances. For example, a decrease in stock increases cash, while an increase in debtors reduces cash.
- The cash flow statement concludes with a figure for the increase or decrease in cash for the period. This is calculated from the subtotals of each of the eight sections of the statement.

WORKED EXAMPLE: CASH FLOW FROM OPERATING ACTIVITIES

situation

You are helping the accountant of Chatsala Limited to prepare the company's cash flow statement for the year ended 30 April 20-8. The following information is available to you:

	£
Net profit (after deducting interest paid of £2,500)	137,200
Depreciation of fixed assets for the year	15,000
Decrease in stock during the year	3,500
Increase in debtors during the year	5,000
Increase in creditors during the year	4,000

The accountant asks you to calculate the net cash flow from operating activities.

solution

Operating profit is calculated by adding back interest to the net profit, ie £2,500 + £137,200 = £139,700 operating profit. This is because operating profit is profit before interest is deducted:

	£	
Operating profit	139,700	
Less interest paid	2,500	*add back interest*
Net profit	137,200	

Interest paid is shown as an outflow of cash in the section of the cash flow statement for 'returns on investments and servicing of finance'.

The cash flow from operating activities is now calculated:

	£
Operating profit	139,700
Depreciation for year	15,000
Decrease in stock	3,500
Increase in debtors	(5,000)
Increase in creditors	4,000
Net cash inflow from operating activities	157,200

Note that:

- depreciation is a non-cash expense, so it is added back to profit
- a decrease in stock is a cash inflow – because stock is being sold for cash – and is added to profit
- an increase in debtors is a cash outflow – because the company is financing additional debtors – and is deducted from profit
- an increase in creditors is a cash inflow – because the company has increased the amount it owes – and is added to profit

REVALUATION OF FIXED ASSETS

From time-to-time some fixed assets are revalued upwards and the amount of the revaluation is recorded in the balance sheet. The most common assets to be treated in this way are land and buildings. The value of the fixed asset is increased and the amount of the revaluation is placed to a revaluation reserve (see page 297) in the 'financed by' section of the balance sheet where it increases the value of the shareholders' investment in the company. As a revaluation is purely a 'book' adjustment, ie no cash has changed hands, it does not feature in a cash flow statement.

READING THE CASH FLOW STATEMENT

The cash flow statement is important because it identifies the sources of cash flowing into the business and shows how they have been used. We need to read the statement in conjunction with the other two main financial statements – profit and loss account and balance sheet – and also in the context of the previous year's statements. The following points should also be borne in mind when reading a cash flow statement:

- Look for a reasonable cash flow from operating activities each year – this is the cash from the trading activities of the business.
- Changes in the working capital items of stock, debtors and creditors need to be put into context. For example, it would be a warning sign if there were large increases in these items in a business with a falling operating profit, and such a trend would put a strain on the liquidity of the business.
- The statement will show the amount of investment made during the year (eg the purchase of fixed assets). In general there should be a link between the cost of the investment and an increase in loans and/or capital – it isn't usual to finance fixed assets from short-term sources, such as a bank overdraft.
- Where there has been an increase in loans and/or capital, look to see how the cash has been used. Was it to buy fixed assets or other investments, or to finance stocks and debtors, or other purposes?
- The statement, as a whole, links profit with changes in cash. Both of these are important: without profits the business cannot generate cash (unless it sells fixed assets), and without cash it cannot pay bills as they fall due.

USERS OF CASH FLOW STATEMENTS

As cash flow statements are included in the published accounts of all but smaller companies, they are widely available to be read by a number of interested users.

shareholders

Shareholders will read the statement because:

- it demonstrates the ability of the company to generate cash from trading activities
- it shows the liquidity of the business
- it shows clearly the sources and uses of cash over the year
- it shows the investment of the company in capital expenditure, which should flow through into increasing profits and share price
- it shows the amount of dividends paid to shareholders

loan providers/debenture holders

The cash flow statement shows:

- the cash available at the year-end, thus demonstrating the security of loans and debentures
- the 'financed by' section shows additional loans raised, or repayment of lending
- interest paid to lenders, in the 'returns on investments and servicing of finance' section

managers and employees

The cash flow statement is useful because:

- it highlights further information on the state of the company's finances that is not readily available from the profit and loss account and balance sheet
- it shows clearly the sources and uses of cash over the year
- it shows the cash available at the year end for future development of the company and, therefore, security of employment
- it may help managers with decision-making
- a surplus of cash for the year may indicate to employees that the company can afford pay increases

creditors (suppliers)

Creditors will be interested in the cash flow statement because:

- it shows the liquidity of the company and, therefore, the likelihood of being paid for the goods or services they have supplied
- it shows the cash available at the year end for future development which should lead to suppliers doing more business with the company
- it shows whether the company is financing itself through lending (which is usually repaid ahead of creditors in the event of the company 'going bust') or through shareholders (which rank after creditors)
- as it shows flows of cash, it is considered to be the most objective of the three main financial statements – thus it gives a good picture of the state of the company's finances

CHAPTER SUMMARY

- The objective of a cash flow statement is to show an overall view of money flowing in and out of a business during an accounting period
- A cash flow statement is divided into eight sections:
  1 operating activities
  2 returns on investments and servicing of finance
  3 taxation
  4 capital expenditure and financial investment
  5 acquisitions and disposals
  6 equity dividends paid
  7 management of liquid resources
  8 financing

- *Cash flow from operating activities* is the operating profit (before interest and tax), plus depreciation for the year, together with changes in the working capital items (stock, debtors and creditors)
- *Returns on investments and servicing of finance* is interest received and paid; dividends received; dividends paid on preference shares
- *Capital expenditure and financial investment* is the purchase and/or sale of fixed assets and investments
- *Liquid resources* are short-term investments that are almost equal to cash
- *Financing* is the issue or repayment of loans or share capital
- Financial Reporting Standard No. 1 'Cash flow statements' provides a specimen layout.
- Larger limited companies are required to include a cash flow statement as a part of their published accounts. They are also useful statements for smaller limited companies.
- Users of cash flow statements include:
  - shareholders
  - loan providers/debenture holders
  - managers and employees
  - creditors (suppliers)

QUESTIONS

NOTE: an asterisk (*) after the question number means that an answer to the question is given at the end of this book.

22.1* Complete the following table to show the effect on cash – inflow, outflow, or no effect – of the transactions.

The first item has been completed as an example.

Transaction	Inflow of cash	Outflow of cash	No effect on cash
Cash sales	✓		
(a) Cash purchases			
(b) Sold goods on credit			
(c) Bought goods on credit			
(d) Bought new fixed asset, paying by cheque			
(e) Received a cheque from a debtor			
(f) Paid expenses in cash			
(g) Paid a creditor by cheque			

22.2 Explain why depreciation is added back to the operating profit in the operating activities section of a cash flow statement?

22.3 Raven Limited has an operating profit of £30,000 for 20-5, and there were the following movements in the year:

	£
depreciation charge	10,000
increase in stock	5,000
decrease in debtors	4,000
increase in creditors	6,000

Calculate the net cash flow from operating activities.

22.4 Meadow Limited has an operating loss of £10,000 for 20-6, and there were the following movements in the year:

	£
depreciation charge	8,000
decrease in stock	4,000
increase in debtors	5,000
decrease in creditors	3,000

Calculate the net cash flow from operating activities.

22.5 Explain five points that you would look for when reading the cash flow statement of a business.

22.6* (a) The cash flow statement is an integral part of the published accounts. What information will this provide for shareholders?

(b) Name two other financial statements which published accounts must contain.

Assessment and Qualifications Alliance (AQA), 2001

22.7 Set out below is an extract from the published accounts of Tesco PLC showing the cash flow statement.

group cash flow statement
52 weeks ended 22 February 2003

	2003 £m	2002 £m
Net cash inflow from operating activities	2,375	2,038
Dividends from joint ventures and associates	11	15
Returns on investments and servicing of finance	(218)	(192)
Taxation	(366)	(378)
Capital expenditure and financial investment	(2,052)	(1,920)
Acquisitions and disposals	(436)	(96)
Equity dividends paid	(368)	(297)
Cash outflow before management of liquid resources and financing	**(1,054)**	**(830)**
Management of liquid resources	(14)	27
Financing	1,023	974
(Decrease)/increase in cash	(45)	171

REQUIRED

(a) Explain the following terms:

(i) equity dividends paid

(ii) net cash inflow from operating activities

(iii) returns on investments

(b) Explain the value of the information contained in the cash flow statement to:

(i) managers

(ii) shareholders

(iii) debenture holders

22.8* The following extract is taken from the cash flow statement of Durning Limited for the year ended 31 December 20-8. It gives the reconciliation of operating profit to net cash flow from operating activities.

	£
Operating profit	71,250
Depreciation	6,500
Increase in stock	(7,500)
Increase in debtors	(6,000)
Increase in creditors	2,400
Net cash inflow from operating activities	66,650

(a) Explain the terms:

(i) operating profit

(ii) net cash inflow from operating activities

(b) Explain why the following adjustments have been made to operating profit:

(i) depreciation – added

(ii) increase in stock – subtracted

(iii) increase in debtors – subtracted

(iv) increase in creditors – added

AS Accounting Module 3

Financial Accounting: Determination of Income

This Module for AQA AS Accounting develops the ability to produce final accounts and balance sheets for sole traders as well as limited companies. It covers:

- accounting principles, concepts and conventions
- final accounts and balance sheets, capital and revenue income and expenditure, depreciation, disposal of fixed assets
- stock valuation
- final accounts and balance sheets of manufacturing organisations
- limited liability, capital structure of limited companies
- internal final accounts, balance sheets of limited companies

23 ACCRUALS AND PREPAYMENTS

Module 3 of AQA AS level in Accounting is entitled 'Financial Accounting: Determination of Income'. We will see how, having prepared the final accounts of trading and profit and loss account and balance sheet, a number of adjustments are made at the year end in order to show a more realistic view of the state of the business.

This chapter is concerned with the adjustments for accruals and prepayments. Further adjustments will be covered in Chapters 24 and 25. Also covered in this chapter are the treatment of the owner's private expenses and goods for the owner's use.

The difference between income and expenditure accounting and receipts and payments accounting is discussed towards the end of the chapter.

To illustrate the effect of adjustments we shall in this, and the next two chapters, be referring to the final accounts of Wyvern Wholesalers (see pages 372 and 373).

Introduction to Adjustments to Final Accounts

By making adjustments to final accounts we can improve the relevance and reliability of accounts in determining the income and expenditure, and showing the profit, and the assets and liabilities of the business.

The six adjustments to final accounts are as follows:

- **closing stock** – incorporating the value of stock held at the financial year end into the final accounts (this adjustment has been made already in the final accounts we have prepared in earlier studies; there is more on stock valuation in Chapter 26)
- **adjusting for accruals** – expenses due in an accounting period which have not been paid for at the end of that period
- **adjusting for prepayments** – payments made in advance of the accounting period to which they relate
- **depreciation of fixed assets** – writing down the value of fixed assets over their useful economic lives
- **bad debts written off** – removing from the sales ledger the accounts of debtors who will not pay, or cannot pay
- **provision for doubtful debts** – making provision for debtors who may not pay

Each of these adjustments is based on a number of accounting concepts – which we will look at in more detail in Chapter 26. For the moment, we can say that the two main accounting concepts which form the basis of these adjustments are:

- the **accruals concept** – which is the matching of expenses and revenues to the same goods or services and the same time period – applies to closing stock, accruals, prepayments
- the **prudence concept** – which requires that final accounts should always, where there is any doubt, report a conservative (ie lower) figure for profit or the valuation of assets – applies to depreciation, and the treatment of bad and doubtful debts

To illustrate the effect of adjustments on final accounts we shall in this, and the next two chapters, be referring to the final accounts of Wyvern Wholesalers, which are shown on the next two pages (the trial balance – if you wish to refer to it – is on page 170).

Tutorial note

Wyvern Wholesalers is a sole trader business, ie it is run by one person. If you have previously studied Module 1, you will be familiar with the layout of sole trader final accounts. If you have previously studied Module 2, you will be familiar with the layout of limited company accounts. The points to note are that, for sole traders:

- all of the net profit is added to the owner's capital in the 'financed by' section of the balance sheet
- drawings – where the owner takes money from the business – are deducted in the 'financed by' section of the balance sheet

Limited company accounts will be studied later in this module (Chapter 27). The adjustments we shall be making in this and the next two chapters do not affect the layout of the final accounts that you have studied previously.

Accrual of Expenses

An accrual is an amount due in an accounting period which is unpaid at the end of that period.

In the final accounts, accrued expenses are:

- added to the expense from the trial balance before listing it in the profit and loss account
- shown as a current liability in the year end balance sheet

The reason for dealing with accruals in this way is to ensure that the profit and loss account records the cost that has been incurred for the year, instead of simply the amount that has been paid. In other words, the expense is adjusted to relate to the time period covered by the profit and loss account. The year end balance sheet shows a liability for the amount that is due, but unpaid.

example of an accrual expense

The trial balance of Wyvern Wholesalers (see page 170) shows a debit balance for electricity and gas of £3,000. Before preparing the final accounts, an electricity bill for £250 is received on 1st January 20-2, ie on the first day of the new financial year. As this bill is clearly for electricity used in 20-1, an adjustment needs to be made in the final accounts for 20-1 to record this accrued expense.

continued on page 374

TRADING AND PROFIT AND LOSS ACCOUNT OF WYVERN WHOLESALERS
FOR THE YEAR ENDED 31 DECEMBER 20-1

	£	£	£
Sales			250,000
Less Sales returns			5,400
Net sales			244,600
Opening stock (1 January 20-1)		12,350	
Purchases	156,000		
Carriage in	–		
Less Purchases returns	7,200		
Net purchases		148,800	
		161,150	
Less Closing stock (31 December 20-1)		16,300	
Cost of sales			144,850
Gross profit			99,750
Add Discount received			2,500
			102,250
Less overheads (expenses):			
Discount allowed		3,700	
Salaries		46,000	
Electricity and gas		3,000	
Rent and rates		2,000	
Sundry expenses		4,700	
			59,400
Net profit			42,850

BALANCE SHEET OF WYVERN WHOLESALERS
AS AT 31 DECEMBER 20-1

	£	£	£
Fixed Assets			
Premises			100,000
Equipment			30,000
Vehicles			21,500
			151,500
Current Assets			
Stock		16,300	
Debtors		23,850	
Cash		125	
		40,275	
Less Current Liabilities			
Creditors	12,041		
Value Added Tax	3.475		
Bank overdraft	851		
		16,367	
Working Capital or Net Current Assets			23,908
			175,408
Less Long-term Liabilities			
Loan			33,000
NET ASSETS			142,408
FINANCED BY			
Capital			
Opening capital			110,000
Add net profit			42,850
			152,850
Less drawings			10,442
			142,408

In the profit and loss account, the total cost of £3,250 (ie £3,000 from the trial balance, plus £250 accrued) will be recorded as an expense. In the balance sheet, £250 will be shown as a separate current liability of 'accruals'.

effect on profit

Taking note of the accrual of an expense has the effect of reducing a previously reported net profit. As the expenses have been increased, net profit is less (but there is no effect on gross profit). Thus, the net profit of Wyvern Wholesalers reduces by £250 from £42,850 to £42,600.

PREPAYMENT OF EXPENSES

A prepayment is a payment made in advance of the accounting period to which it relates.

A prepayment is, therefore, the opposite of an accrual: with a prepayment of expenses, some part of the expense has been paid in advance of the next accounting period.

In the final accounts, prepaid expenses are:

- deducted from the expense amount of the trial balance before listing it in the profit and loss account
- shown as a current asset in the year end balance sheet

As with accruals, the reason for dealing with prepaid expenses in this way is to ensure that the profit and loss account records the cost incurred for the year, and not the amount that has been paid – the profit and loss account expense relates to the time period covered by the profit and loss account. The year end balance sheet shows an asset for the amount that has been prepaid.

example of a prepaid expense

The owner of Wyvern Wholesalers tells you that the trial balance (see page 170) figure for rent and rates of £2,000, includes £100 of rent paid in advance for January 20-2. An adjustment needs to be made in the final accounts for 20-1 to record this prepaid expense.

In the profit and loss account, the cost of £1,900 (ie £2,000 from the trial balance, less £100 prepaid) will be recorded as an expense. In the balance sheet, £100 will be shown as a separate current asset of 'prepayments'.

effect on profit

Taking note of the prepayment of an expense has the effect of increasing a previously reported net profit – expenses have been reduced, so net profit is greater.

stocks of office supplies

At the end of a financial year most businesses have stocks of office supplies which have been recorded as expenses during the year, such as stationery, postage stamps (or a balance held in a franking machine). Technically, at the end of each year, these items should be valued and treated as a prepayment for next year, so reducing the expense in the current year's profit and loss account. However, in practice, this is done only when the stock of such items is substantial enough to affect the accounts in a material way. The firm's accountant will decide at what level the prepayment will apply.

To give an example of office stocks, the trial balance total for postages of a business at the year-end is £1,050; stocks of postage stamps at the same date are £150. The business will record an expense of £900 (£1,050, less £150) in the profit and loss account, while £150 is listed on the balance sheet as a current asset 'stocks of postage stamps'.

ACCRUALS AND PREPAYMENTS IN FINAL ACCOUNTS

We have looked at the separate effect of dealing with accruals and prepayments. Let us now see how they are presented in the final accounts of Wyvern Wholesalers (see pages 372 and 373). Remember that we are taking note of the following items at 31 December 20-1:

- electricity accrued £250
- rent prepaid £100

trading and profit and loss account

As there is no effect on gross profit, the details of the trading account are not shown here. The profit and loss section appears as shown below. Note that the calculations for accruals and prepayments do not appear in the final accounts; they are presented here for illustrative purposes only.

PROFIT AND LOSS ACCOUNT OF WYVERN WHOLESALERS
FOR THE YEAR ENDED 31 DECEMBER 20-1

		£	£	£
Gross profit				99,750
Add Discount received				2,500
				102,250
Less overheads (expenses):				
Discount allowed			3,700	
Salaries			46,000	
Electricity and gas	3,000 + 250		3,250	
Rent and rates	2,000 – 100		1,900	
Sundry expenses			4,700	
				59,550
Net profit				42,700

The effect of taking note of accruals and prepayments is to alter net profit:

	£
Net profit (before adjustments)	42,850
Add rent prepaid	100
	42,950
Less electricity accrued	250
Net profit (after adjustments)	42,700

balance sheet

The balance sheet is shown below with the accruals and prepayments shaded for illustrative purposes. These items do appear in the final accounts, (but not the shading).

BALANCE SHEET OF WYVERN WHOLESALERS
AS AT 31 DECEMBER 20-1

	£	£	£
Fixed Assets			
Premises			100,000
Equipment			30,000
Vehicles			21,500
			151,500
Current Assets			
Stock		16,300	
Debtors		23,850	
Prepayments		100	
Cash		125	
		40,375	
Less Current Liabilities			
Creditors	12,041		
Value Added Tax	3,475		
Accruals	250		
Bank	851		
		16,617	
Working Capital or Net Current Assets			23,758
			175,258
Less Long-term Liabilities			
Loan			33,000
NET ASSETS			142,258
FINANCED BY			
Capital			
Opening capital			110,000
Add net profit			*42,700
			152,700
Less drawings			10,442
			142,258

* see net profit calculations at top of page

Accruals and Prepayments of Income

Just as expenses can be accrued or prepaid at the end of a financial year, income amounts can also be accrued or prepaid also.

accrual of income

Here, income of a business is due but unpaid at the end of the financial year. For example, commission receivable might have been earned, but the payment is received after the end of the financial year to which it relates. In the final accounts, accrual of income is:

- added to the income amount from the trial balance before listing it in the profit and loss account
- shown as a current asset (eg commission receivable) in the year end balance sheet

prepayment of income

Here, the income of a business has been paid in advance by the payer. For example, the rent receivable account for the financial year could include an advance payment received from a tenant in respect of the next financial year.

In the final accounts, prepayment of income is:

- deducted from the income amount from the trial balance before listing it in the profit and loss account
- shown as a current liability (eg rent receivable prepaid) in the year end balance sheet

As with expenses, the objective of taking note of accruals and prepayments of income is to ensure that the amount stated in the profit and loss account relates to the period covered by that account.

WORKED EXAMPLE: DEALING WITH ACCRUALS AND PREPAYMENTS

So far in this chapter, we have looked at adjustments which take place at the end of a financial year. But what happens if there are also accruals and prepayments at the *beginning* of the year? In this Worked Example, we see how to calculate the correct amount of income or expense for profit and loss account.

situation

The book-keeper of Corley Carpets asks for your assistance in calculating the amount of income or expense for the profit and loss account for the year ended 30 June 20-8. The following information is available:

	£
Payments to National Telecom for telephone expenses during the year	830
Payments to landlord for rent of premises during the year	5,650
Receipts from Zelah Limited for commission receivable during the year	700

Details of accruals and prepayments are:

	year ended 30 June 20-7		year ended 30 June 20-8	
		£		£
Payment to National Telecom	in arrears	50	in arrears	120
Payment to landlord	in advance	150	in arrears	100
Commission receivable from Zelah Limited	in arrears	40	in advance	20

solution

To calculate the correct amount of income or expense for profit and loss, we must take account of accruals and prepayments at both the beginning and end of the year. Calculations are as follows:

Telephone expenses	£
Paid in year	830
Less accrual at start of year	(50)
Add accrual at end of year	120
Expense to profit and loss account	900

Rent expense	
Paid in year	5,650
Add prepayment at start of year	150
Add accrual at end of year	100
Expense to profit and loss account	5,900

Commission income	
Received in year	700
Less accrual at start of year	(40)
Less prepayment at end of year	(20)
Receipt to profit and loss account	640

The rules are quite simple: for both accruals and prepayments:

- start of year
  - \+ prepayments
  - – accruals
- end of year
  - – prepayments
  - \+ accruals

Note that it is the end of year adjustments that are shown in the closing balance sheet.

Private Expenses and Goods for Own Use

Adjustments also have to be made in the final accounts for the amount of any business facilities that are used by the owner for private purposes. These adjustments are for private expenses and goods for own use.

private expenses

Sometimes the owner of a business uses business facilities for private purposes, eg telephone, or car. The owner will agree that part of the expense shall be charged to him or her as drawings, while the other part represents a business expense.

For example, telephone expenses for the year amount to £600, and the owner agrees that this should be split as one-quarter private use, and three-quarters to the business. This is recorded in the final accounts as:

- £450 (three-quarters) in profit and loss account as a business expense
- £150 (one-quarter) is added to the owner's drawings

goods for own use

When the owner of a business takes some of the goods in which the business trades for his or her own use, the amount is:

- deducted from purchases
- added to the owner's drawings

Insurance Claims

When a business loses stock as a result of causes such as fire, theft, water damage, a claim is made to the insurance company for the cost of the insured stock. The insurance company will then need to agree the amount of the claim and will make payment to the business.

In the final accounts of a business that has agreed an insurance claim, but where payment has not yet been received from the insurance company, the adjustments are:

- reduce the figure for purchases in the trading account by the amount of the claim
- show the amount of the agreed claim due from the insurance company as a current asset in the balance sheet

Income and Expenditure Accounting

In this chapter we have made adjustments for accruals and prepayments to ensure that the profit and loss account shows the correct amount of income and expenses for the financial year, ie what should have been paid, instead of what has actually been paid. In doing this we are adopting the principle of income and expenditure accounting. If we simply used the trial balance figures, we would be following the principle of receipts and payments accounting, ie comparing money coming in, with money going out: this would usually give a false view of the net profit for the year.

The principle of income and expenditure accounting is applied in the same way to purchases and sales, although no adjustments are needed because of the way in which these two are handled in the accounting records. For purchases, the amount is entered into the accounts when the supplier's invoice is received, although the agreement to buy will be contained in the legal contract which exists between buyer and seller. From the accounting viewpoint, it is receipt of the supplier's invoice that causes an accounting entry to be made; the subsequent payment is handled as a different accounting transaction. A business could have bought goods, not paid for them yet, but will have a purchases figure to enter into the trading account. Doubtless the creditors will soon be wanting payment!

Sales are recorded in a similar way – when the invoice for the goods is sent, rather than when payment is made. This applies the principle of income and expenditure accounting. In this way, a business could have made a large amount of sales, which will be entered in the trading account, but may not yet have received any payments.

The way in which accounts are adjusted to take note of accruals and prepayments is formally recognised in the accruals (or matching) concept, which is discussed in more detail in Chapter 26.

CHAPTER SUMMARY

- Final accounts are prepared on the income and expenditure basis, rather than the receipts and payments basis.
- An adjustment should be made at the end of the financial year in respect of accruals and prepayments.
- In the final accounts, accrued expenses are:
  - added to the expense from the trial balance
  - shown as a current liability in the balance sheet
- In the final accounts, prepaid expenses are:
  - deducted from the expense from the trial balance
  - shown as a current asset in the balance sheet
- In the final accounts, an accrual of income is:
  - added to the income amount from the trial balance
  - shown as a current asset in the balance sheet
- In the final accounts, a prepayment of income is:
  - deducted from the income amount from the trial balance
  - shown as a current liability in the balance sheet

- Adjustments also need to be made in the final accounts for:
  - private expenses
  - goods for own use

Accruals and prepayments are just one type of adjustment made at the end of a financial year in order to present the final accounts more accurately. The next chapter continues the theme by considering depreciation of fixed assets.

QUESTIONS

NOTE: an asterisk (*) after the question number means that an answer to the question is given at the end of the book.

23.1 Explain how the following would be dealt with in the profit and loss account, and balance sheet of a business with a financial year end of 31 December 20-2:

(a) Wages and salaries paid to 31 December 20-2 amount to £55,640. However, at that date, £1,120 is owing: this amount is paid on 4 January 20-3.

(b) Rates totalling £3,565 have been paid to cover the period 1 January 20-2 to 31 March 20-3.

(c) A computer is rented at a cost of £150 per month. The rental for January 20-3 was paid in December 20-2 and is included in the total payments during 20-2 which amount to £1,950.

23.2 The following information has been extracted from the accounts of Southtown Supplies, a wholesaling business, for the year ended 31 December 20-9:

	£
Sales	420,000
Purchases	280,000
Stock at 1 January 20-9	70,000
Stock at 31 December 20-9	60,000
Rent and rates	10,250
Electricity	3,100
Telephone	1,820
Salaries	35,600
Vehicle expenses	13,750

Notes: at 31 December 20-9:

- rent prepaid is £550
- salaries owing are £450

You are to prepare the trading and profit and loss account of Southtown Supplies for the year ended 31 December 20-9.

23.3* Jock McIntyre has produced a draft profit and loss account for the year ended 31 March 2003. As yet no entries have been made in the profit and loss account for the following information.

	£
Payments to local authority for business rates during the year	1,950
Payments to landlord for rent of premises during the year	4,200
Receipts from Qualwen plc for commission receivable during the year	600

Additional information	*Year ended 31 March 2002*		*Year ended 31 March 2003*	
		£		£
Payment to local authority	in advance	70	in arrears	80
Payment to landlord	in arrears	60	in advance	120
Commission received from Qualwen plc	in arrears	50	in arrears	40

REQUIRED

Calculate the amounts to be entered in the profit and loss account for the year ended 31 March 2003. Indicate in the table below the amount and whether it should be subtracted from or added to the profit of the business.

	Amount to be subtracted from draft net profit £	*Amount to be added to draft net profit* £
Business rates		
Rent of premises		
Commission receivable		

Assessment and Qualifications Alliance (AQA), 2003

23.4* The following trial balance has been extracted by the book-keeper of Don Smith, who runs a wholesale stationery business, at 31 December 20-8:

	Dr	Cr
	£	£
Debtors	24,325	
Creditors		15,408
Value Added Tax		4,276
Capital		30,000
Bank		1,083
Rent and rates	10,862	
Electricity	2,054	
Telephone	1,695	
Salaries	55,891	
Vehicles	22,250	
Office equipment	7,500	
Vehicle expenses	10,855	
Drawings	15,275	
Discount allowed	478	
Discount received		591
Purchases	138,960	
Sales		257,258
Stock at 1 January 20-8	18,471	
	308,616	308,616

Notes at 31 December 20-8:

- stock was valued at £14,075
- rates are prepaid £250
- electricity owing £110
- salaries are owing £365

REQUIRED

You are to prepare the trading and profit and loss account of Don Smith for the year ended 31 December 20-8, together with his balance sheet at that date.

23.5

The following trial balance has been extracted by the book-keeper of John Barclay at 30 June 20-9:

	Dr	Cr
	£	£
Sales		864,321
Purchases	600,128	
Sales returns	2,746	
Purchases returns		3,894
Office expenses	33,947	
Salaries	122,611	
Vehicle expenses	36,894	
Discounts allowed	3,187	
Discounts received		4,951
Debtors and creditors	74,328	52,919
Value Added Tax		10,497
Stock at 1 July 20-8	63,084	
Vehicles	83,500	
Office equipment	23,250	
Land and buildings	100,000	
Bank loan		75,000
Bank	1,197	
Capital		155,000
Drawings	21,710	
	1,166,582	1,166,582

Notes at 30 June 20-9:

- stock was valued at £66,941
- motor vehicle expenses owing £1,250
- office expenses prepaid £346
- goods costing £250 were taken by John Barclay for his own use

REQUIRED

You are to prepare the trading and profit and loss account of John Barclay for the year ended 30 June 20-9, together with his balance sheet at that date.

23.6* The following list of balances has been extracted by the book-keeper of Southtown Supplies, a wholesaling business, at 31 December 20-4:

	£
Opening stock	70,000
Purchases	280,000
Sales	420,000
Sales returns	6,000
Purchases returns	4,500
Discount received	750
Discount allowed	500
Electricity	13,750
Salaries	35,600
Post and packing	1,400
Premises	120,000
Fixtures and fittings	45,000
Debtors	55,000
Creditors	47,000
Bank balance	5,000
Capital	195,000
Drawings	41,000
Value Added Tax (amount due)	6,000

Notes at 31 December 20-4:

- stock was valued at £60,000; this figure excludes goods which were damaged by a burst water pipe and have been scrapped (no sale proceeds); Wyvern Insurance has agreed to cover the loss of £500 incurred in writing off the goods
- electricity owing £350
- salaries prepaid £400

REQUIRED

You are to prepare the trading and profit and loss account of Southtown Supplies for the year ended 31 December 20-4, together with a balance sheet at that date.

24 DEPRECIATION OF FIXED ASSETS

Fixed assets, for example machinery and vehicles, fall in value as time goes by, largely as a result of wear and tear. This reduction in value is measured by what is known as depreciation.

In this chapter we will:

- define depreciation
- consider the methods of calculating depreciation
- apply depreciation to the final accounts
- investigate the calculations when a fixed asset is sold
- see how a revaluation of assets is recorded in the final accounts

When preparing final accounts it is important to distinguish between capital expenditure and revenue expenditure. Towards the end of the chapter we will look at the differences between these, and why they are important to final accounts.

WHAT IS DEPRECIATION?

Depreciation is a way of measuring the amount of the fall in value of fixed assets over a period of time.

Most fixed assets fall in value over time and, in accounting, it is necessary, in order to present a realistic view of the business, to measure the amount of the fall in value. This is done by showing an expense – called 'depreciation of fixed assets' – in the profit and loss account, and recording the asset at a lower value than cost price in the balance sheet. The expense of depreciation is an estimate of both the fall in value of the fixed asset and the time period; the estimate is linked to the cost price of the asset. Depreciation is a further application of the accruals concept, because we are recognising the timing difference between payment for the fixed asset and the asset's fall in value.

The main factors which cause fixed assets to depreciate are:

- wearing out through use, eg vehicles, machinery, etc
- passage of time, eg the lease on a building
- using up, eg extraction of stone from a quarry

- economic reasons
  - obsolescence, eg a new design of machine which does the job better and faster makes the old machine obsolete
  - inadequacy, eg a machine no longer has the capacity to meet the demand for its goods

Fixed assets – even buildings – are depreciated over their useful economic life. The only exception is land which, because it is a non-wasting asset, does not normally depreciate (unless it is a quarry or a mine, when it will have a limited useful economic life). Land and buildings are sometimes increased in value from time-to-time, ie a revaluation takes place, and this is recorded in the accounts (see page 397).

METHODS OF CALCULATING DEPRECIATION

There are several different ways in which we can allow for the fall in value of fixed assets. All of these are estimates, and it is only when the asset is sold or scrapped that we will know the accuracy of the estimate (see page 395). The two most common methods of calculating depreciation are:

- straight-line method
- reducing balance method

For the calculations of depreciation amounts we will use the following data:

MACHINE	
Cost price on 1 January 20-1	£2,000
Estimated life	4 years
Estimated scrap value at end of four years	£400

straight-line method

With this method, a fixed percentage is written off the original cost of the asset each year. For this example, twenty-five per cent will be written off each year by the straight-line method. The depreciation amount (ignoring for the moment any residual or scrap value) for each year is:

$$£2{,}000 \times 25\% = £500 \text{ per year}$$

The depreciation percentage will be decided by a business on the basis of what it considers to be the useful economic life of the asset. Thus, twenty-five per cent each year gives a useful economic life of four years (assuming a nil residual value at the end of its life).

Different classes of fixed assets are often depreciated at different rates, eg motor vehicles may be depreciated at a different rate to office equipment. It is important that, once a particular method and rate of depreciation has been selected, depreciation should be applied consistently, ie methods and rates are not changed from year-to-year without good reason.

The method of calculating straight-line depreciation, taking into account the asset's estimated sale proceeds at the end of its useful economic life, is:

$$\frac{\text{cost of asset} - \text{estimated residual (scrap or salvage) sale proceeds}}{\text{number of years' expected use of asset}}$$

For example, the machine is expected to have a residual (scrap or salvage) value of £400, so the depreciation amount will be:

$$\frac{£2{,}000 - £400}{4 \text{ years}} = £400 \text{ per year (ie 20\% per annum on cost)}$$

reducing (or diminishing) balance method

With this method, a fixed percentage is written off the reduced balance each year. The reduced balance is cost of the asset less depreciation to date. For example, the machine is to be depreciated by 33.3% (one-third) each year, using the reducing balance method. The depreciation amounts for the four years of ownership are:

Original cost	£2,000
20-1 depreciation: 33.3% of £2,000	£667
Value at end of 20-1	£1,333
20-2 depreciation: 33.3% of £1,333	£444
Value at end of 20-2	£889
20-3 depreciation: 33.3% of £889	£296
Value at end of 20-3	£593
20-4 depreciation: 33.3% of £593	£193
Value at end of 20-4	£400

Note that the figures have been rounded to the nearest £, and year 4 depreciation has been adjusted by £5 to leave a residual value of £400.

Although you will not need to use it in your examination, you may be interested in the formula to calculate the percentage of reducing balance depreciation:

$$r = 1 - \sqrt[n]{\frac{s}{c}}$$

In this formula:

r = percentage rate of depreciation

n = number of years

s = salvage (residual) value

c = cost of asset

In the example above the 33.3% is calculated as:

$$r = 1 - \sqrt[4]{\frac{400}{2,000}}$$

$$r = 1 - \sqrt[4]{0.2}$$

(to find the fourth root press the square root key on the calculator twice)

$$r = 1 - 0.669$$

r = 0.331 or 33.1% (which is close to the 33.3% used above)

straight-line and reducing balance methods compared

The following tables use the depreciation amounts calculated above.

straight-line depreciation				
Year	*1* Original cost	*2* Depreciation for year	*3* Depreciation to date	*4* Net book value (ie column 1-3)
	£	£	£	£
20-1	2,000	400	400	1,600
20-2	2,000	400	800	1,200
20-3	2,000	400	1,200	800
20-4	2,000	400	1,600	400

Note: Net book value is cost, less depreciation to date, ie column 1, less column 3.

These calculations will be used in the final accounts (see page 393) as follows: taking 20-2 as an example, the profit and loss account will be charged with £400 (column 2) as an expense, while the balance sheet will record £1,200 (column 4) as the net book value.

reducing balance depreciation				
Year	*1* Original cost	*2* Depreciation for year	*3* Depreciation to date	*4* Net book value (ie column 1-3)
	£	£	£	£
20-1	2,000	667	667	1,333
20-2	2,000	444	1,111	889
20-3	2,000	296	1,407	593
20-4	2,000	193	1,600	400

In the final accounts, using 20-3 as an example, £296 (column 2) will be charged as an expense in profit and loss account, while £593 (column 4) is the net book value that will be shown in the balance sheet.

Using these tables, we will now see how the two methods compare:

	straight-line method	**reducing balance method**
depreciation amount	Same money amount each year – see chart below	Different money amounts each year: more than straight-line in early years, less in later years – see chart below
depreciation percentage	Lower depreciation percentage required to achieve same residual value	Higher depreciation percentage required to achieve same residual value – but can never reach a nil value
suitability	Best used for fixed assets likely to be kept for the whole of their expected lives, eg machinery, office equipment, fixtures and fittings	Best used for fixed assets which depreciate more in early years and which are not kept for the whole of expected lives, eg vehicles

The year-by-year depreciation amounts of the machine in the example are shown on the following bar chart:

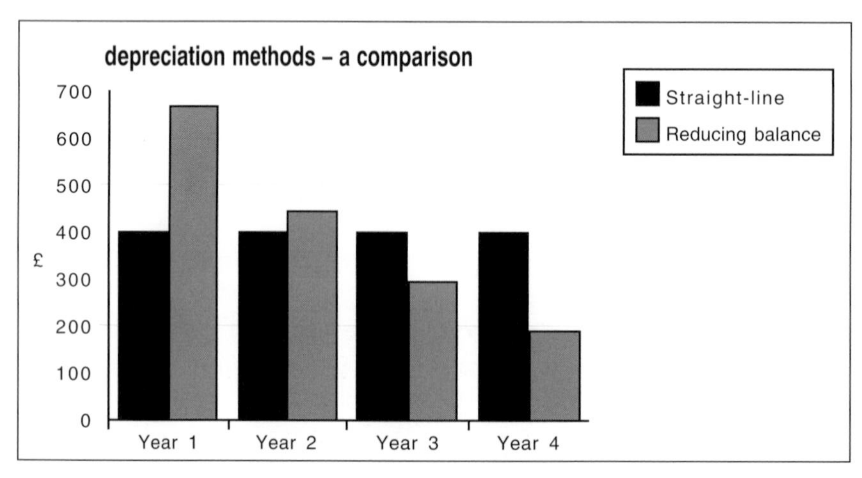

Depreciation and Final Accounts

profit and loss account

The depreciation amount calculated for each class of asset is listed amongst the expenses as the allowance for depreciation for that particular class of asset.

For example, for the machine being depreciated by the straight-line method (see table on page 389), the profit and loss account will show 'depreciation: machinery £400' as an expense for each of the years 20-1 to 20-4. If the machine is being depreciated by the reducing balance method, the profit and loss account for 20-1 will show 'depreciation: machinery £667' as an expense. In subsequent years the amounts will be £444 in 20-2, £296 in 20-3, and £193 in 20-4.

balance sheet

Each class of fixed asset should be shown at cost price (or revaluation – see page 397), less the amount of provision for depreciation to date (ie this year's depreciation, plus depreciation from previous years if any). The resulting figure is the net book value of the fixed asset.

The usual way of setting these out in a balance sheet (using the first year figures for the machine being depreciated by the straight-line method) is:

Balance sheet (extract) .... as at 31 December 20-1

	£ Cost	£ Prov for dep'n	£ Net book value
Fixed Assets			
Machinery	2,000	400	1,600
Vehicles, etc	X	X	X
	X	X	X

Note that the figures for the balance sheet come from columns 1, 3 and 4 from the table in page 389. Where there is only one class of fixed asset, eg machinery, the balance sheet extract can be set out in a simpler layout, as follows:

Balance sheet (extract) .... as at 31 December 20-1

	£
Fixed Assets	
Machinery at cost	2,000
Less provision for depreciation	400
Net book value	1,600

At the end of the second year, the machine is shown in the balance sheet as follows:

Balance sheet (extract) .... as at 31 December 20-2

	£	£	£
	Cost	Prov for dep'n	Net book value
Fixed Assets			
Machinery	2,000	800	1,200
Vehicles, etc	x	x	x
	x	x	x

Notice, from the above, how provision for depreciation increases with the addition of each further year's depreciation. At the same time, the net book value figure reduces – it is this net book value figure which is added to the other fixed assets to give a sub-total for this section of the balance sheet.

trial balance figures

When preparing final accounts from a trial balance, the trial balance often gives separate figures for the cost of an asset and its provision for depreciation at the start of the year. For example:

Trial Balance of .... as at 31 December 20-3

	Dr	Cr
	£	£
Machinery at cost	2,000	
Provision for depreciation: machinery		800

If a note to the trial balance then says, for example, to "depreciate machinery for the year at twenty per cent on cost", this indicates that the trial balance figure is at the start of the year. Accordingly, depreciation of £400 for 20-3 must be calculated and shown as an expense in profit and loss account.

The balance sheet will then show:

Balance sheet (extract) .... as at 31 December 20-3

	£	£	£
	Cost	Prov for dep'n	Net book value
Fixed Assets			
Machinery	2,000	1,200	800
Vehicles, etc	x	x	x
	x	x	x

depreciation policies of a business

In examination questions, information will be given – where it is needed – on the depreciation policies of the business whose accounts you are preparing. In particular, the information will be given on what to do when a fixed asset is bought part of the way through a firm's financial year. The choices here will be to allocate depreciation for the part of the year that it is owned; alternatively the firm may choose to provide for depreciation for the whole year on assets held at the end of the year.

SHOWING DEPRECIATION IN THE FINAL ACCOUNTS

We will now focus on how the depreciation amounts are shown in the profit and loss account and balance sheet. We will continue with the final accounts of Wyvern Wholesalers (see pages 372 and 373) and include depreciation for the year of:

- premises: 2 per cent straight-line, ie £2,000
- equipment: 10 per cent straight-line, ie £3,000
- vehicles: 20 per cent reducing balance, ie £4,300 (note that, as this is the first year in which depreciation has been calculated, reducing balance is calculated on cost price)

trading and profit and loss account

There is no effect on gross profit, so the details of the trading account are not shown here. The profit and loss account appears as shown below, with the depreciation amounts for the year included amongst the overheads, where they are shaded for illustrative purposes. Note that it is usual to show the separate amount of depreciation for each class of fixed asset (as below), rather than the total amount of depreciation.

PROFIT AND LOSS ACCOUNT OF WYVERN WHOLESALERS
FOR THE YEAR ENDED 31 DECEMBER 20-1

	£	£	£
Gross profit			99,750
Add Discount received			2,500
			102,250
Less overheads (expenses):			
Discount allowed		3,700	
Salaries		46,000	
Electricity and gas		3,250	
Rent and rates		1,900	
Sundry expenses		4,700	
Depreciation:			
premises		2,000	
equipment		3,000	
vehicles		4,300	
			68,850
Net profit			33,400

The effect of taking note of depreciation is to reduce net profit:

	£	
Net profit (before adjustment for depreciation)	42,700	(see page 376)
Less depreciation £2,000 + £3,000 + £4,300	9,300	
Net profit (after adjustment for depreciation)	33,400	

balance sheet

The balance sheet is shown below with the depreciation amounts shaded for illustrative purposes. Note that the deduction in the balance sheet is the amount of provision for depreciation to date (ie this year's depreciation, plus depreciation from previous years, if any). Cost, less provision for depreciation, equals the net book value (NBV) of the fixed asset. It is good practice when preparing balance sheets to total the first two columns and to sub-total the third, as illustrated below.

BALANCE SHEET OF WYVERN WHOLESALERS
AS AT 31 DECEMBER 20-1

	£	£	£
Fixed Assets	*Cost*	*Prov for dep'n*	*Net book value*
Premises	100,000	2,000	98,000
Equipment	30,000	3,000	27,000
Vehicles	21,500	4,300	17,200
	151,500	9,300	142,200
Current Assets			
Stock		16,300	
Debtors		23,850	
Prepayments		100	
Cash		125	
		40,375	
Less Current Liabilities			
Creditors	12,041		
Value Added Tax	3,475		
Accruals	250		
Bank	851		
		16,617	
Working Capital or Net Current Assets			23,758
			165,958
Less Long-term Liabilities			
Loan			33,000
NET ASSETS			132,958
FINANCED BY			
Capital			
Opening capital			110,000
Add net profit			*33,400
			143,400
Less drawings			10,442
			132,958

* see net profit calculations at top of page

Depreciation: a Non-cash Expense

It is very important to realise that depreciation is a non-cash expense: unlike most of the other expenses in the profit and loss account, no cheque is written out, or cash paid, for depreciation. In cash terms, depreciation causes no outflow of money. Nevertheless, it is correct, in the final accounts of a business, to show an allowance for depreciation in the profit and loss account, and to reduce the value of the fixed asset in the balance sheet. This is because the business has had the use of the asset, and needs to record the fall in value as an expense in order to present a true picture of its financial state. Thus we are led back to the definition of depreciation as 'a way of measuring the amount of the fall in value of fixed assets over a period of time', ie it is an accounting adjustment. As depreciation is shown as an expense in profit and loss account, it reduces net profit – a lower profit figure may discourage the owner from drawing too much cash from the business. The non-cash effect of depreciation is shown in the following diagram:

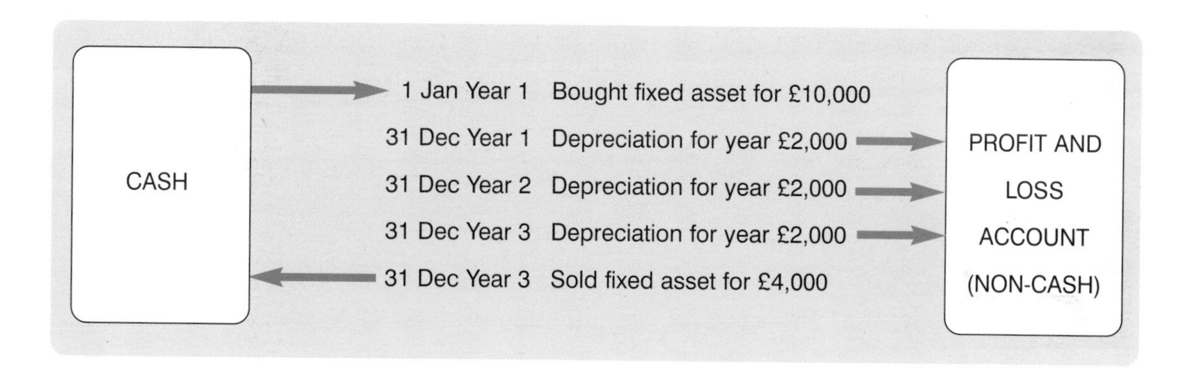

As depreciation is a non-cash expense, it should be noted that depreciation is not a method of providing a fund of cash which can be used to replace the asset at the end of its life. In order to do this, it is necessary to create a separate fund into which cash is transferred at regular intervals. This technique is often known as a sinking fund, and it needs to be represented by a separate bank account, eg a deposit account, which can be drawn against when the new fixed asset is to be purchased. This, however, is not a common practice.

Sale of Fixed Assets

When a fixed asset is sold or disposed, it is necessary to bring together:

- the original cost of the fixed asset
- provision for depreciation over the life of the fixed asset
- sale proceeds

These figures are obtained from the ledger system. They will enable us to calculate the 'profit' or 'loss' on sale of the asset (more correctly the terms are 'over-provision' and 'under-provision' of depreciation, respectively).

The calculations are:

	original cost of the fixed asset
less	provision for depreciation to date*
less	sale proceeds
equals	profit on sale (a negative number), or loss on sale (a positive number)

* Take care to ensure that the provision for depreciation to date is calculated for the correct period, eg if the disposal takes place part of the way through a financial year and the firm's policy is to charge part-years.

Any profit or loss on sale is shown in the profit and loss account of the year of sale: a loss is shown as an expense; a profit is shown as income. Small adjustments to profit and loss account for under-provision (loss on sale) and over-provision (profit on sale) of depreciation will usually be needed because it is impossible, at the start of an asset's life, to predict exactly what it will sell for in a number of years' time.

WORKED EXAMPLE: SALE OF ASSET

situation

To illustrate the calculation of profit or loss on sale, we will use the machine purchased for £2,000 on 1 January 20-1, which is depreciated at twenty per cent each year, using the straight-line depreciation method. On 31 December 20-3, the machine is sold for £600; the company's accounting policy is to depreciate assets in the year of sale.

solution

The calculations are		£
	original cost of machine	2,000
less	provision for depreciation to date	1,200
equals	net book value at date of sale	800
less	sale proceeds (or part-exchange – see next page)	600
equals	loss on sale	200

In profit and loss account, the loss on sale of £200 is shown amongst the expenses of the business, together with depreciation, if any, for the year (here it is £400):

Profit and loss account (extract) .... for the year ended 31 December 20-3

	£	£
Gross profit		x
Less overheads:		
Depreciation: machinery	400	
Loss on sale of machinery	200	

A profit on sale would be added to gross profit, so increasing the income of the business.

Part-exchange of an Asset

Instead of selling an old fixed asset for cash, it is quite common to part-exchange it, or trade it in, for a new asset. This is exactly the same as if a person trades in an old car for a new (or newer) one. Once the part-exchange allowance has been agreed, the disposal calculations are as detailed earlier except that, instead of sale proceeds, there will be the amount of the part-exchange (see previous page).

The part-exchange allowance is a way of providing part of the purchase cost of a new fixed asset. The remainder of the purchase cost will need to be met from other sources, eg payment by cheque. Note that the cost price of the new asset is the full amount before deducting the part-exchange allowance, and it is on this full amount that depreciation on the new asset will be calculated.

Revaluation of a Fixed Asset

From time-to-time fixed assets are revalued at a higher value. In practice, the most likely asset to be revalued is property. After an asset has been revalued, depreciation is calculated on the revalued amount. When a fixed asset is revalued, a reserve is created which adds to the value of the owner's capital.

WORKED EXAMPLE: REVALUATION OF A FIXED ASSET

situation

A business owns premises which is shown in the accounts on 1 January 20-1 at the original cost of £100,000. The premises have been revalued on 31 December 20-1 at £150,000 and it has been decided to record this value in the final accounts. The owner's capital account is £200,000 before the revaluation is recorded.

solution

The balance sheet extracts are as follows:

Before revaluation	£
Fixed asset: premises at cost	100,000
Other net assets	100,000
	200,000
Capital	200,000
After revaluation	
Fixed asset: premises at revaluation	150,000
Other net assets	100,000
	250,000
Capital	*250,000

* £200,000 + revaluation reserve £50,000

Notes:

- The 'other net assets' of £100,000 are shown on the balance sheet in order to balance assets against capital.
- Both premises and the owner's capital have been increased by the amount of the revaluation. The owner's stake in the business is now £250,000.
- There is no new cash in the business – a non-cash book-keeping entry has recorded the increase in value. If the premises were sold for the revalued amount, cash would be received.
- The revaluation transaction has not been recorded in profit and loss account because it is a capital transaction rather than a revenue transaction (see next page for more on capital and revenue expenditure).
- In limited company final accounts (see Chapter 27), a revaluation reserve is placed in a separate account which is grouped under the heading of 'capital reserves'.

FRS 15: Tangible Fixed Assets

Financial Reporting Standard (FRS) no. 15, entitled Tangible Fixed Assets, is the accounting standard which sets out the rules for dealing with depreciation in financial accounts. FRS 15 states that:

- fixed assets having a known useful economic life must be depreciated
- any acceptable depreciation method can be used to spread the cost of the fixed asset consistently over its useful economic life
- depreciation amounts are normally based on the cost of the fixed assets

Capital Expenditure and Revenue Expenditure

When preparing final accounts it is important to distinguish between capital expenditure and revenue expenditure.

capital expenditure

Capital expenditure can be defined as expenditure incurred on the purchase, alteration or improvement of fixed assets. For example, the purchase of a car for use in the business is capital expenditure. Included in capital expenditure are such costs as:

- delivery of fixed assets
- installation of fixed assets
- improvement (but not repair) of fixed assets
- legal costs of buying property

revenue expenditure

Revenue expenditure is expenditure incurred on running expenses. For example, the cost of petrol or diesel for the car (above) is revenue expenditure. Included in revenue expenditure are the costs of:

- maintenance and repair of fixed assets
- administration of the business
- selling and distributing the goods or products in which the business trades

capital expenditure and revenue expenditure – the differences

Capital expenditure is shown on the balance sheet, while revenue expenditure is an expense in the profit and loss account. It is important to classify these types of expenditure correctly in the accounting system. For example, if the cost of the car was shown as an expense in profit and loss account, then net profit would be reduced considerably, or a net loss recorded; meanwhile, the balance sheet would not show the car as a fixed asset – clearly this is incorrect as the business owns the asset.

Study the following examples and the table on the next page; they both show the differences between capital expenditure and revenue expenditure.

- **cost of building an extension to the factory £30,000, which includes £1,000 for repairs to the existing factory**
  - capital expenditure, £29,000
  - revenue expenditure, £1,000 (because it is for repairs to an existing fixed asset)

- **a plot of land has been bought for £20,000, the legal costs are £750**
  - capital expenditure £20,750 (the legal costs are included in the capital expenditure, because they are the cost of acquiring the fixed asset, ie the legal costs are capitalised)

- **the business' own employees are used to install a new air conditioning system: wages £1,000, materials £1,500**
  - capital expenditure £2,500 (an addition to the property); note that, in cases such as this, revenue expenditure, ie wages and materials purchases, will need to be reduced to allow for the transfer to capital expenditure

- **own employees used to repair and redecorate the premises: wages £500, materials £750**
  - revenue expenditure £1,250 (repairs and redecoration are running expenses)

- **purchase of a new machine £10,000, payment for installation and setting up £250**
  - capital expenditure £10,250 (costs of installation of a fixed asset are capitalised)

Only by allocating capital expenditure and revenue expenditure correctly between the balance sheet and the profit and loss account can the final accounts reflect accurately the financial state of the business. The chart on the next page shows the main items of capital expenditure and revenue expenditure associated with three major fixed assets – buildings, vehicles and computers.

	capital expenditure	revenue expenditure
buildings	• cost of building • cost of extension • carriage on raw materials used • legal fees • labour cost of own employees used on improving the building • installation of utilities, eg gas, water, electricity	• general maintenance • repairs • redecoration
vehicles	• net cost, including any optional extras • delivery costs • number plates • changes to the vehicle	• fuel • road fund licence • extended warranty • painting company logo • insurance • servicing and repairs
computers	• net cost • installation and testing • modifications, including memory upgrades, to meet specific needs of business • installation of special wiring • cost of air conditioning to computer room • staff training (where directly related to new equipment) • computer programs (but can be classified as revenue expenditure if cost is low and will have little impact on final accounts)	• data storage discs • printer paper and other consumables • insurance • computer programs (or can be classified as capital expenditure if cost is high and will have a large impact on final accounts)

CHAPTER SUMMARY

- Depreciation is a measure of the amount of the fall in value of fixed assets over a time period.
- Two common methods of calculating depreciation are the straight-line method and the reducing (diminishing) balance method.
- The depreciation amount for each class of fixed asset is included amongst the expenses in profit and loss account, while the value of the asset, as shown in the balance sheet, is reduced by the same amount.
- Depreciation is a non-cash expense.

- When a fixed asset is sold, it is necessary to make an adjustment in respect of any under-provision (loss on sale) or over-provision (profit on sale) of depreciation during the life of the asset. The amount of the profit or loss is calculated, and is then transferred to profit and loss account.
- When assets are revalued at a higher value, the owner's stake in the business is increased. This is a capital transaction (rather than revenue) and does not pass through profit and loss account.
- FRS 15, 'Tangible Fixed Assets', sets out the accounting standard for depreciation
- Capital expenditure is expenditure incurred on the purchase, alteration or improvement of fixed assets.
- Revenue expenditure is expenditure incurred on running expenses.

In the next chapter we look at another expense to be shown in profit and loss account: bad debts, and provision for doubtful debts.

QUESTIONS

NOTE: an asterisk (*) after the question number means that an answer to the question is given at the end of this book.

24.1* Martin Hough, sole owner of Juicyburger, a fast food shop, operating from leased premises in the town, is suspicious of his accountant, Mr S Harris, whom he claims doesn't really understand the food business. On the telephone he asks Mr Harris why depreciation is charged on a rigid formula, as surely no-one really knows how much his equipment is worth, and in fact he might not get anything for it. Draft a reply to Mr Hough from Mr Harris explaining the importance of depreciation and its application to final accounts.

24.2 Cindy Fireplace wishes to improve her reported business profits and cash balances. She has purchased a new computer system for her business at a cost of £6,000. She will use the system for two years and then replace it. At the end of the two years the system will have no scrap value.

She will depreciate her computer system by using
either the straight-line method
or the reducing-balance method using 60% per annum

She is unsure which method will increase her reported profits and her cash balances over the two years.

REQUIRED

(a) Calculate the charge to the profit and loss account for each year for each method.

	Straight-line method £	Reducing-balance method £
Year 1		
Year 2		

(b) Discuss how charging depreciation will affect Cindy's cash flow.

Assessment and Qualifications Alliance (AQA), 2003

24.3* David Evans started in business on 1 July 20-1 with a financial year end of 30 June. On 1 July 20-1 he bought fixed assets at a cost of £50,000. The fixed assets have an expected useful life of 10 years at the end of which they will have a nil scrap value.

For the year ended 30 June 20-2, David used the straight-line method of depreciating his fixed assets at an annual rate of 10%. For the year ended 30 June 20-3 David changed to the reducing balance method of depreciating his fixed assets; he has increased the annual rate to 20%.

David's profits for the two years *before* depreciation of fixed assets were £18,700 for 20-2 and £33,100 for 20-3.

REQUIRED

(a) Calculate David's net profit after depreciation of fixed assets.

	year ended 30 June 20-2 £	year ended 30 June 20-3 £
Net profit before depreciation	18,700	33,100
Depreciation on fixed assets	....	....
Net profit after depreciation	....	....

(b) Prepare a balance sheet extract showing David's fixed assets after allowing for provision for depreciation.

	as at 30 June 20-2 £	as at 30 June 20-3 £
Fixed assets at cost	50,000	50,000
Less provision for depreciation to date	....	....
Net book value	....	....

24.4

On 1 January 20-4 the following information is taken from the accounting system of Lisa Hall.

	£
• Motor vehicle (registration number T787 KAB) at cost	20,000
• Provision for depreciation of motor vehicle T787 KAB	12,500

Lisa purchased a new vehicle (registration number VK04 PZV) on 15 March 20-4 at a cost of £25,000. The garage gave Lisa a trade in allowance of £4,000 on vehicle T787 KAB.
Lisa's financial year ends on 31 December. She depreciates motor vehicles at 12.5% per annum using the straight-line method. Depreciation is calculated on vehicles held at the end of the financial year.

REQUIRED

(a) Calculate the profit or loss made on the disposal of vehicle T787 KAB.

(b) Prepare the balance sheet extract as at 31 December 20-4 of Lisa Hall, showing entries arising from the above transactions.

24.5*

Howard and Son, a joinery business, depreciates its machinery at the rate of 10% per annum, using the straight line method. Depreciation is calculated on assets held at the end of the financial year.
The following information was extracted from Howard and Son's general ledger.

	1 January 2000
	£
Machinery at cost	100,000
Provision for depreciation of machinery	60,000

On 2 January 2000 an additional machine was purchased at a cost of £30,000.
In November 2000 machine VM/3, which had been purchased on 1 January 1994 at a cost of £18,000, was sold for £4,000 cash. The aggregate depreciation on the machine amounted to £10,800.

REQUIRED

(a) Calculate the profit or loss made on the sale of machine VM/3.

(b) Prepare an extract from the balance sheet as at 31 December 2000, of Howard and Son, showing entries arising from the above transactions.

Assessment and Qualifications Alliance (AQA), 2001

24.6* The book-keeper of Shahida Rashid has extracted the following trial balance *after* preparing the trading account of the business:

Trial balance as at 31 December 20-5

	Dr	Cr
	£	£
Gross profit		135,400
Discount received		730
Discount allowed	1,040	
Wages and salaries	84,270	
Provision for depreciation of fixed assets		15,000
General expenses	23,860	
Rent received		4,290
Fixed assets at cost	60,000	
Current assets	45,310	
Current liabilities		29,870
Capital		29,190
	214,480	214,480

Note: depreciation is to be provided for on fixed assets at a rate of 25% using the reducing balance method.

REQUIRED

You are to prepare:

(a) the profit and loss account of Shahida Rashid for the year ended 31 December 20-5.

(b) the balance sheet extract showing Shahida's fixed assets as at 31 December 20-5, after charging depreciation

24.7

The following trial balance was extracted from the books of Abel Brown as at 31 December 2001.

	Dr	Cr
	£	£
Capital 1 January 2001		78,570
Fixed assets	150,000	
Provision for depreciation of fixed assets 1 January 2001		90,000
Purchases	153,900	
Sales		278,400
Wages	74,750	
Rent	2,500	
Other expenses	25,120	
Debtors	16,100	
Creditors		8,400
Bank balance	1,700	
Drawings	18,600	
Stock 1 January 2001	12,700	
	455,370	455,370

At 31 December 2001 the following additional information was available:

- stock in trade was valued at £14,100
- one week's wages £650 was owed to staff
- two weeks' rent amounting to £220 had been paid in advance
- depreciation is provided on fixed assets at the rate of 10% per annum on cost using the straight line method

REQUIRED

(a) Prepare a trading and profit and loss account for the year ended 31 December 2001 for Abel Brown.

(b) Abel is considering changing his method of providing depreciation on fixed assets from the straight line method to the reducing (diminishing) balance method.
What would Abel's net profit for the year ended 31 December 2001 have been if he had used the reducing balance method of providing for depreciation on fixed assets at 20% per annum instead of using the straight line method?

Assessment and Qualifications Alliance (AQA), 2002

24.8

Tara Kassir has bought a new delivery van for use in her business. The invoice received from the garage for the van includes the following items:

	£
Cost of van	11,650
Air conditioning	550
Fitted shelving	350
Road fund licence	165
Cost of extended warranty	220
Tank of fuel	40
Insurance premium	450

REQUIRED

(a) calculate the total amount of capital expenditure incurred by Tara

(b) calculate the total amount of revenue expenditure incurred by Tara

24.9

The following list of balances has been extracted from the books of John Henson at 31 December 20-8:

	£
Purchases	71,600
Sales	122,000
Stock at 1 January 20-8	6,250
Vehicle running expenses	1,480
Rent and rates	5,650
Office expenses	2,220
Discount received	285
Wages and salaries	18,950
Office equipment	10,000
Vehicle	12,000
Debtors	5,225
Creditors	3,190
Value Added Tax	1,720
Capital	20,000
Drawings for the year	13,095
Cash at bank	725

REQUIRED

You are to prepare the trading and profit and loss account of John Henson for the year ended 31 December 20-8, together with his balance sheet at that date, taking into account:

- closing stock of £8,500
- depreciation of office equipment for the year £1,000
- depreciation of vehicle for the year £3,000

24.10* The following trial balance has been extracted by the book-keeper of Hazel Harris at 31 December 20-4:

	Dr	Cr
	£	£
Bank loan		75,000
Capital		125,000
Purchases and sales	465,000	614,000
Building repairs	8,480	
Vehicles at cost	12,000	
Provision for depreciation on vehicles		2,400
Vehicle expenses	2,680	
Land at cost	100,000	
Bank overdraft		2,000
Furniture and fittings at cost	25,000	
Provision for depreciation on furniture and fittings		2,500
Wages and salaries	86,060	
Discounts	10,610	8,140
Drawings	24,000	
Rates and insurance	6,070	
Debtors and creditors	52,130	38,730
Value Added Tax		3,120
General expenses	15,860	
Stock at 1 January 20-4	63,000	
	870,890	870,890

Notes at 31 December 20-4:

- Stock was valued at £88,000
- Wages and salaries outstanding: £3,180
- Rates and insurance paid in advance: £450
- Depreciate vehicles at 20 per cent using the straight-line method
- Depreciate furniture and fittings at 10 per cent using the straight-line method
- Land is not to be depreciated

REQUIRED

You are to prepare her trading and profit and loss accounts for the year ended 31 December 20-4, together with her balance sheet at that date.

25 BAD DEBTS AND PROVISION FOR DOUBTFUL DEBTS

Most businesses selling their goods and services to other businesses do not receive payment immediately. Instead, they often have to allow a period of credit and, until the payment is received, they have a current asset of debtors. Unfortunately, it is likely that not all debtors will eventually settle the amount they owe, ie the amounts are bad debts which have to be written off. At the same time a business needs to make a provision for doubtful debts, which allows for debtors who may not pay.

In this chapter we will:

- distinguish between bad debts and provision for doubtful debts
- see how bad debts are recorded in the final accounts
- see how provision for doubtful debts is recorded in the final accounts
- look at the procedures a business may use in order to minimise the risk of bad debts

BAD DEBTS AND PROVISION FOR DOUBTFUL DEBTS

A bad debt is a debt owing to a business which it considers will never be paid.

Let us consider a business with debtors of £10,000. This total will, most probably, be made up of a number of debtors' accounts. At any one time, a few of these accounts will be bad, and therefore the amount is uncollectable: these are bad debts, and they need to be written off, ie the business will give up trying to collect the debt and will accept the loss.

Provision for doubtful debts is the estimate by a business of the likely percentage of its debtors which may go bad during any one accounting period.

There are likely to be some debtors' accounts which, although they are not yet bad, may be giving some concern as to their ability to pay: a provision for doubtful debts needs to be made in respect of these. The one thing the business with debtors of £10,000 cannot do is to show this debtors' amount as a current asset in the balance sheet: to do so would be to imply to the user of the balance sheet that the full £10,000 is collectable. Instead, this gross debtors' figure might be reduced in two stages, for example:

- debtors' accounts with balances totalling £200 are to be written off as bad
- a general provision for doubtful debts is to be made amounting, in this case, to two per cent of remaining debtors

Thus the debtors' figure becomes:

Gross debtors	£10,000
Less: bad debts	£200
	£9,800
Less: provision for doubtful debts at 2%	£196
Net debtors (recorded in balance sheet)	£9,604

The amount of the provision for doubtful debts (here 2%) will vary from business to business, depending on the past experience of receiving payment, the nature of the business and the current economic climate.

Bad debts and provision for doubtful debts is an application of the accounting concept of prudence (see Chapter 26). By reducing the debtors' figure, through the profit and loss account and balance sheet, a more realistic view is shown of the amount that the business can expect to receive.

Treatment of Bad Debts

Bad debts are written off when they become uncollectable. This means that all reasonable efforts to recover the amount owing have been exhausted, ie statements and letters have been sent to the debtor requesting payment, and legal action, where appropriate, or the threat of legal action has failed to obtain payment.

In writing off a debtor's account as bad, the business is bearing the cost of the amount due. The debtor's account is closed and the amount (or amounts, where a number of debtors' accounts are dealt with in this way) is charged as an expense – described as 'bad debts' – to profit and loss account. The effect of this is to reduce profit by the amount of the write off.

When preparing final accounts in examination questions, there are two ways in which you can be given information about bad debts:

- if the figure for bad debts is shown in the trial balance (debit side), you will simply record the amount as an expense in profit and loss account – the debtors' figure has been reduced already
- if the bad debts figure is not already shown in the trial balance, and a note tells you to write off a certain debt as bad, you will need to list the amount as an expense in profit and loss account and reduce the debtors' figure for the balance sheet

bad debts recovered

If, by chance, a former debtor whose account has been written off as bad, should make a payment, the effect on final accounts is to record the amount as income added to gross profit, describing it as 'bad debts recovered'. (The payment will, separately, have been recorded in either the cash or bank accounts upon receipt so, unless you are told in an examination question that this has not happened, you do not need to adjust for this.)

Having recovered payment from the former debtor, if the customer now wishes to buy goods or services, it is prudent to insist on cash payment for some time to come!

TREATMENT OF PROVISION FOR DOUBTFUL DEBTS

Provision for doubtful debts is different from writing off a bad debt because there is the possibility – not the certainty – of future bad debts. The debtors' figure (after writing off bad debts) is reduced either by totalling the balances of the accounts that may not pay or, more likely, by applying a percentage to the total figure for debtors. The percentage chosen will be based on past experience and will vary from business to business – for example, a hire purchase company may well use a higher percentage than a bank.

initial creation of a provision for doubtful debts

The procedure for the provision for doubtful debts comes after writing off bad debts (if any). The steps are:

1. A business, at the end of the financial year, estimates the percentage of its debtors which may go bad, say two per cent
2. The provision is calculated (eg £9,800 x 2% = £196)
3. In the final accounts, the amount of the provision is:
   - listed in the profit and loss account as an expense described as 'increase in provision for doubtful debts'
   - deducted from the debtors' figure in the current assets section of the balance sheet, eg:

	£	£	£
Current Assets			
Stock		x	
Debtors	9,800		
Less provision for doubtful debts	196		
		9,604	
Prepayments		x	
Bank		x	
Cash		x	
		x	

Note that the business, in creating a provision for doubtful debts, is presenting a realistic and prudent estimate of its debtor position.

ADJUSTMENTS TO PROVISION FOR DOUBTFUL DEBTS

Once a provision for doubtful debts has been created, the only adjustments that need to be made to the provision for doubtful debts are as a result of:

- a policy change in the provision, eg an increase in the fixed percentage from 2% to 5%
- an arithmetic adjustment in the provision as a result of a change in the total of debtors, eg increase in debtors of £5,000 will require a higher provision

When either of these two situations arises, the adjustment to the existing position will be:

- either upwards (increase in provision percentage, or increase in debtor figure)
- or downwards (decrease in provision percentage, or decrease in debtor figure)

In the final accounts an **increase in the provision** is:

- listed in the profit and loss account as an expense described as 'increase in provision for doubtful debts'
- shown in the balance sheet where the amount of the increase is added to the existing provision to give a new figure for provision for doubtful debts (which is deducted from the debtors' figure)

In the final accounts a **decrease in the provision** is:

- listed in the profit and loss account as income, described as 'reduction in provision for doubtful debts'
- shown in the balance sheet at the lower amount, ie the existing provision less amount of decrease

Note that provision for doubtful debts and bad debts written off are completely separate adjustments: the two should not be confused. It is quite usual to see in a profit and loss account entries for both bad debts (written off) and provision for doubtful debts (the creation or adjustment of provision for bad debts).

WORKED EXAMPLE: PROVISION FOR DOUBTFUL DEBTS

A business decides to create a provision for doubtful debts of five per cent of its debtors. After writing off bad debts, the debtors figures at the end of each of three years are:

20-1	£10,000
20-2	£15,000
20-3	£12,000

calculations

20-1 creating the provision

- £10,000 x 5% = £500

20-2 increasing the provision

- new provision is £15,000 x 5% = £750
- existing provision is £500
- therefore increase in provision is £250

20-3 decreasing the provision

- new provision is £12,000 x 5% = £600
- existing provision is £750
- therefore decrease in provision is £150

the final accounts

The effect on the final accounts is shown in the following table:

Year	Profit and loss account		Balance sheet		
	Overhead	Income	Debtors	Less provision for doubtful debts	Net debtors
	£	£	£	£	£
20-1	500	-	10,000	500	9,500
20-2	250	-	15,000	750	14,250
20-3	-	150	12,000	600	11,400

The profit and loss account and balance sheet extracts for each year are as follows:

20-1 **Profit and loss account (extract) for the year ended 31 December 20-1**

	£	£
Gross profit		x
Less overheads:		
Increase in provision for doubtful debts	500	

Balance sheet (extract) as at 31 December 20-1

	£	£	£
Current Assets			
Stock		x	
Debtors	10,000		
Less provision for doubtful debts	500		
		9,500	

20-2

Profit and loss account (extract) for the year ended 31 December 20-2

	£	£
Gross profit		x
Less overheads:		
Increase in provision for doubtful debts	250	

Balance sheet (extract) as at 31 December 20-2

	£	£	£
Current Assets			
Stock		x	
Debtors	15,000		
Less provision for doubtful debts	750		
		14,250	

20-3

Profit and loss account (extract) for the year ended 31 December 20-3

	£	£
Gross profit		x
Add income:		
Decrease in provision for doubtful debts		150

Balance sheet (extract) as at 31 December 20-3

	£	£	£
Current Assets			
Stock		x	
Debtors	12,000		
Less provision for doubtful debts	600		
		11,400	

Note:

When preparing final accounts in an examination question, there will be a note to the trial balance telling you to make an adjustment to the provision for doubtful debts. Sometimes you will be told a percentage figure, eg 'provision for doubtful debts is to be maintained at five per cent of debtors'; alternatively, you may be told the new provision figure (be careful of the wording – distinguish between 'increase the provision **to** £750' and 'increase the provision **by** £750').

Showing Bad and Doubtful Debts in the Final Accounts

We will now focus on how the amounts for bad and doubtful debts are shown in the profit and loss account and balance sheet. We will continue with the final accounts of Wyvern Wholesalers (see pages 372 and 373) and include adjustments for the year for:

- bad debts of £250 written off
- provision for doubtful debts of 2% of debtors to be created (note that there is no existing provision)

trading and profit and loss account

There is no effect on gross profit, so the details of the trading account are not shown here. The profit and loss account appears as shown below, with the bad debt and provision for doubtful debt amounts for the year included amongst the overheads, where they are shaded for illustrative purposes.

The amount of the provision for doubtful debts is calculated after deducting bad debts written off from the debtors figure. The provision to be created is:

£23,850 debtors – £250 written off = £23,600 x 2% = £472 provision

PROFIT AND LOSS ACCOUNT OF WYVERN WHOLESALERS
FOR THE YEAR ENDED 31 DECEMBER 20-1

	£	£	£
Gross profit			99,750
Add Discount received			2,500
			102,250
Less overheads (expenses):			
Discount allowed		3,700	
Salaries		46,000	
Electricity and gas		3,250	
Rent and rates		1,900	
Sundry expenses		4,700	
Depreciation:			
premises		2,000	
equipment		3,000	
vehicles		4,300	
Bad debts		250	
Increase in provision for doubtful debts		472	
			69,572
Net profit			32,678

The effect of taking note of bad and doubtful debts is to reduce net profit:

Net profit (before adjustment for bad and doubtful debts)	£33,400	(see page 393)
Less bad debts written off	£250	
Less increase in provision for doubtful debts	£472	
Net profit (after adjustment for bad and doubtful debts)	£32,678	

balance sheet

The balance sheet is shown below with the debtors and provision for doubtful debts amounts shaded for illustrative purposes. The amount of bad debts of £250 has been deducted before debtors are recorded in the balance sheet, ie £23,850 – £250 written off = £23,600. The amount of provision for doubtful debts – here £472 – is deducted from the debtors figure of £23,600 to give net debtors of £23,128; it is this latter amount that is added in to current assets.

BALANCE SHEET OF WYVERN WHOLESALERS
AS AT 31 DECEMBER 20-1

	£	£	£
Fixed Assets	*Cost*	*Prov for dep'n*	*Net book value*
Premises	100,000	2,000	98,000
Equipment	30,000	3,000	27,000
Vehicles	21,500	4,300	17,200
	151,500	9,300	142,200
Current Assets			
Stock		16,300	
Debtors	23,600		
Less provision for doubtful debts	472		
		23,128	
Prepayments		100	
Cash		125	
		39,653	
Less Current Liabilities			
Creditors	12,041		
Value Added Tax	3,475		
Accruals	250		
Bank	851		
		16,617	
Working Capital or Net Current Assets			23,036
			165,236
Less Long-term Liabilities			
Loan			33,000
NET ASSETS			132,236
FINANCED BY			
Capital			
Opening capital			110,000
Add net profit			*32,678
			142,678
Less drawings			10,442
			132,236

* see net profit calculations at top of page

MINIMISING THE RISK OF BAD DEBTS

Having studied the technicalities of accounting for bad debts, and creating a provision for doubtful debts, it is appropriate to look at ways in which businesses selling on credit can minimise the risks. The following are some of the procedures that can be followed:

- When first approached by an unknown business wishing to buy goods on credit, the seller should ask for references. One of these should be the buyer's bank, and the others should be from traders (at least two) with whom the buyer has previously done business.
- The seller, before supplying goods on credit, should take up the references and obtain satisfactory replies.
- Once satisfactory replies have been received, a credit limit for the customer should be established, and an account opened in the sales ledger. The amount of the credit limit will depend very much on the expected amount of future business – for example, £1,000 might be appropriate. The credit limit should not normally be exceeded – the firm's credit controller or financial accountant will approve any transactions above the limit.
- Invoices and month-end statements of account should be sent out promptly; invoices should state the terms of trade and statements should analyse the balance to show how long it has been outstanding, eg 'over 30 days, over 60 days, over 90 days' – computer-produced statements can show this automatically.
- If a customer does not pay within a reasonable time, the firm should follow established procedures in order to chase up the debt promptly. These procedures are likely to include 'chaser' letters, the first of which points out that the account is overdue, with a later letter threatening legal action. Whether or not legal action is taken will depend on the size of the debt – for a small amount the costs and time involved in taking legal action may outweigh the benefits of recovering the money.

the use of an aged schedule of debtors

To help with credit control, many firms produce an aged schedule of debtors at the end of each month. This analyses individual debtor balances into the time that the amount has been owing. Thus it shows the long outstanding debts that are, potentially, bad debtors, against whom early action is necessary. An aged schedule is easily produced using a computer accounting system.

An aged schedule of debtors can also be used to calculate the provision for doubtful debts. For example, a business has the following schedule of debtors at the end of its financial year:

Days outstanding	*Debtors*
	£
Current (up to 30 days)	50,000
31 to 60	26,000
61 to 90	10,000
91 and over	4,000
	90,000

Provision for doubtful debts is to be calculated by providing for 25% on debts which have been outstanding for 91 days and over, 10% on debts outstanding for 61-90 days, and 2% on debts outstanding for 31-60 days. No provision is to be made on current debts.

Provision for doubtful debts is calculated as:

			£
Current	£50,000 (no provision)	=	nil
31-60 days	£26,000 x 2%	=	520
61-90 days	£10,000 x 10%	=	1,000
91 days and over	£4,000 x 25%	=	1,000
Provision for doubtful debts to be created (or adjusted) to			2,520

CHAPTER SUMMARY

- A bad debt is a debt owing to a business which it considers will never be paid.

- A provision for doubtful debts is the estimate by a business of the likely percentage of its debtors which may go bad during any one accounting period.

- The specific order for dealing with bad debts and provisions should be followed:
  - write off bad debts (if any)
  - create (or adjust) provision for doubtful debts

- In profit and loss account:
  - a bad debt written off is charged as an expense
  - a bad debt recovered is recorded as income

- In the final accounts:
  - an increase or decrease in provision for doubtful debts is listed in the profit and loss account
  - the provision for doubtful debts is deducted from the debtors' figure in the current assets section of the balance sheet

- Having created a provision for doubtful debts, it will be either increased or decreased in later years in line with the change in the level of debtors.

- A business should follow set procedures when opening new accounts in order to minimise the risk of bad debts.

Having looked, in the last few chapters, at adjustments to final accounts to take note of accruals and prepayments, depreciation, bad debts and provision for doubtful debts, the next chapter considers the basic framework – or concepts – within which final accounts are prepared, and looks at stock valuation.

QUESTIONS

NOTE: an asterisk (*) after the question number means that an answer to the question is given at the end of this book.

25.1 You are the book-keeper at Waterston Plant Hire. At 31 December 20-8, the end of the financial year, the business has gross debtors of £20,210. The owner decides to:

(a) write off, as bad debts, the accounts of:

P Ross	£55
J Ball	£105
L Jones	£50

(b) make a provision for doubtful debts of 2.5% of debtors (after writing off the above bad debts)

You are to explain how these transactions will be recorded in the final accounts at the end of the financial year.

25.2* Ross Engineering has an existing provision for doubtful debts of £300, based on 5 per cent of debtors. After writing off bad debts, the amounts of debtors at the end of the next two financial years are found to be:

30 June 20-1	£8,000
30 June 20-2	£7,000

The business continues to keep the provision for doubtful debts equal to 5 per cent of debtors.

As an accounts assistant at Ross Engineering, you are to show:

(a) the adjustments to the provision for doubtful debts at the end of the financial years ended 30 June 20-1 and 30 June 20-2

(b) how the provision for doubtful debts will be recorded in the final accounts at the end of each of the two financial years.

25.3 You are the book-keeper at Enterprise Trading Company. The following information is available for the financial years ending 31 December 20-5, 20-6, 20-7:

	£
• Debtor balances at 31 December 20-5, before writing off bad debts	105,200
• Bad debts written off on 31 December 20-5	1,800
• 2.5% provision for doubtful debts created at 31 December 20-5	
• Debtor balances at 31 December 20-6, before writing off bad debts	115,600
• Bad debts written off on 31 December 20-6	2,400

- 2.5% provision for doubtful debts adjusted in line with the change in the level of debtors at 31 December 20-6
- Bad debt recovered on 15 June 20-7 — 150
- Debtor balances at 31 December 20-7, before writing off bad debts — 110,200
- Bad debts written off on 31 December 20-7 — 1,400
- 2.5% provision for doubtful debts adjusted in line with the change in the level of debtors at 31 December 20-7

You are to record the effect of these transactions in the appropriate columns of the following table:

YEAR	PROFIT AND LOSS ACCOUNT				BALANCE SHEET		
	Overhead		Income				
	Bad debts	Increase in provision for doubtful debts	Bad debts recovered	Decrease in provision for doubtful debts	Debtors	Less prov for doubtful debts	Net debtors
	£	£	£	£	£	£	£
20-5							
20-6							
20-7							

25.4* The following balances were extracted from the books of account of Josh Porter, a trader, as at 31 March 2001.

	Dr	Cr
	£	£
Provision for doubtful debts		700
Debtors	10,000	
Bad debts written off during the year	178	
Bad debts recovered during the year		261

It has always been Josh's policy to provide for doubtful debts at the rate of 5% on debtors outstanding at his financial year end.
The net profit earned in the year ended 31 March 2001 was £18,090.
The net profit and the debtors' figures have been arrived at *before* taking into account any bad debts, any bad debts recovered and any adjustments to the provision for doubtful debts.

REQUIRED

Analyse the effect that the information outlined above would have had on Josh's:

(a) net profit

(b) working capital

(c) bank balance

Assessment and Qualifications Alliance (AQA), 2001

25.5 The following trial balance has been extracted by the book-keeper of Beth Davis, a shopkeeper, after the preparation of her trading account for the year ended 31 December 20-8.

	Dr	Cr
	£	£
Gross profit		95,374
Wages and salaries	55,217	
Heating and lighting	1,864	
Rent and rates	5,273	
Advertising	2,246	
Bad debts written off	395	
General expenses	783	
Shop fittings at cost	12,000	
Provision for depreciation on shop fittings		4,320
Stock at 31 December 20-8	28,176	
Debtors	3,641	
Creditors		10,290
Bank		3,084
Cash	163	
Capital		18,886
Drawings	22,196	
	131,954	131,954

Notes at 31 December 20-8:

- rent prepaid £310
- accrued general expenses £85
- depreciate shop fittings at 20% per annum, using the reducing balance method
- a debt of £155 written off as bad in 20-5 was recovered in full on 12 December 20-8; no entries have been made to record recovery of the bad debt, and Beth has the cash received in an envelope at home

You are to prepare the profit and loss account of Beth Davis for the year ended 31 December 20-8, together with her balance sheet at that date.

25.6* The following trial balance has been extracted by the book-keeper of James Jenkins, who owns a patisserie and coffee lounge, as at 30 June 20-9:

	Dr	Cr
	£	£
Capital		36,175
Drawings	19,050	
Purchases and sales	105,240	168,432
Stock at 1 July 20-8	9,427	
Debtors and creditors	3,840	5,294
Value Added Tax		1,492
Returns	975	1,237
Discounts	127	243
Wages and salaries	30,841	
Vehicle expenses	1,021	
Rent and rates	8,796	
Heating and lighting	1,840	
Telephone	355	
General expenses	1,752	
Bad debts written off	85	
Vehicle at cost	8,000	
Provision for depreciation on vehicle		3,500
Shop fittings at cost	6,000	
Provision for depreciation on shop fittings		2,400
Provision for doubtful debts		150
Cash	155	
Bank	21,419	
	218,923	218,923

Notes at 30 June 20-9:

- stock was valued at £11,517
- vehicle expenses owing £55
- rent prepaid £275
- depreciate the vehicle at 25 per cent per annum, using the reducing balance method
- depreciate shop fittings at 10 per cent per annum, using the straight-line method
- the provision for doubtful debts is to be equal to 2.5 per cent of debtors

You are to prepare the trading and profit and loss account of James Jenkins for the year ended 30 June 20-9, together with his balance sheet at that date.

26 ACCOUNTING CONCEPTS AND STOCK VALUATION

In this chapter we will explain the 'rules' of accounting which are to be followed when preparing final accounts. These rules take the form of:

- accounting concepts
- accounting standards

If the same rules are followed, then comparisons can be made between the final accounts of different businesses.

Later in the chapter we will see how the accounting 'rules' relating to the valuation of stock are applied.

ACCOUNTING CONCEPTS

There are a number of generally accepted **accounting concepts** – or 'rules' of accounting – which underlie the preparation of final accounts. These concepts help to make final accounts relevant and reliable to users, and also enable them to be comparable and understandable.

The accounting concepts are illustrated in the diagram below.

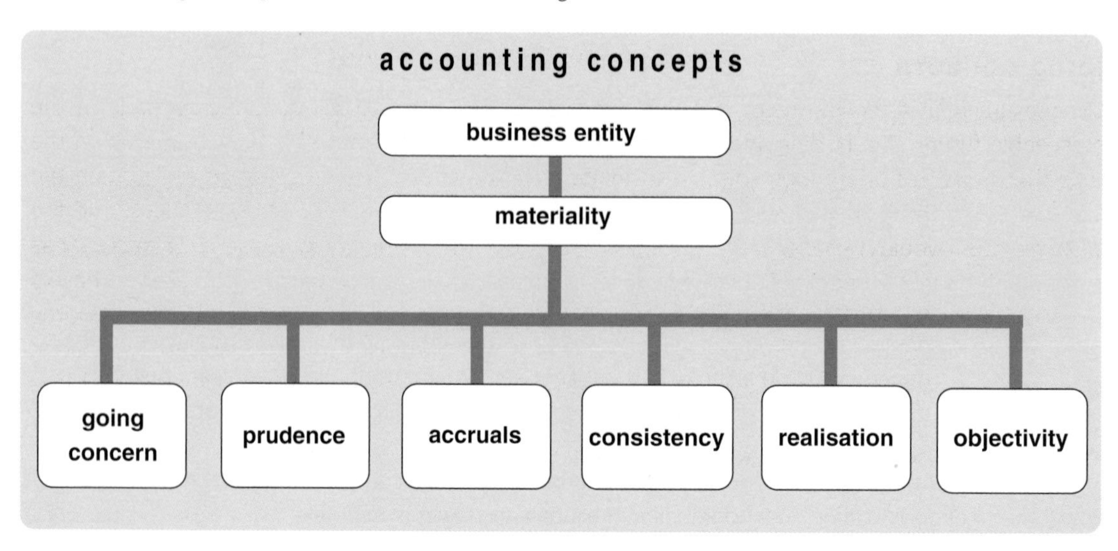

business entity

This refers to the fact that final accounts record and report on the activities of one particular business. They do not include the assets and liabilities of those who play a part in owning or running the business. Thus the owner's personal assets and liabilities are kept separate from those of the business: the main links between the business and the owner's personal funds are capital and drawings.

materiality

Some items in accounts have such a low monetary value that it is not worthwhile recording them separately, ie they are not 'material'. Examples of this include:

- Small expense items, such as donations to charities, the purchase of plants for the office, window cleaning, etc, do not justify their own separate expense account; instead they are grouped together in a sundry expenses account.
- End-of-year stocks of office stationery, eg paper clips, staples, photocopying paper, etc, are often not valued for the purpose of final accounts, because the amount is not material and does not justify the time and effort involved. This does mean, however, that the cost of all stationery purchased during the year is charged as an expense to profit and loss account – technically wrong, but not material enough to affect the final accounts.
- Low-cost fixed assets are often charged as an expense in profit and loss account, instead of being classed as capital expenditure, eg a stapler, waste-paper basket, etc. Strictly, these should be treated as fixed assets and depreciated each year over their estimated life; in practice, because the amounts involved are not material, they are treated as profit and loss account expenses.

Materiality depends very much on the size of the business. A large company may consider that items of less than £1,000 are not material; a small company will usually use a much lower figure. What is material, and what is not becomes a matter of judgement.

going concern

This presumes that the business to which the final accounts relate will continue to trade in the foreseeable future. The trading and profit and loss account and balance sheet are prepared on the basis that there is no intention to reduce significantly the size of the business or to liquidate the business. If the business was not a going concern, assets would have very different values, and the balance sheet would be affected considerably. For example, a large, purpose-built factory has considerable value to a going concern business but, if the factory had to be sold, it is likely to have a limited use for other industries, and therefore will have a lower market value. The latter case is the opposite of the going concern concept and would be described as a *gone concern*. Also, in a gone concern situation, extra depreciation would need to be charged as an expense to profit and loss account to allow for the reduced value of fixed assets. Stock valuation (see page 429), which is usually on a going concern basis, would normally be much lower on a gone concern basis.

accruals (or matching)

This means that expenses and revenues for goods and services must be matched to the same time period. We have already put this concept into practice in Chapter 23, where expenses and revenues were adjusted to take note of prepayments and accruals. The trading and profit and loss account should always show the amount of the expense that should have been incurred, ie the expenditure for the year, whether or not it has been paid. This is the principle of income and expenditure accounting, rather than using receipts and payments as and when they fall due.

Further examples of the accruals concept are:

- debtors
- creditors
- depreciation
- bad debts
- provision for doubtful debts
- opening and closing stock adjustments in profit and loss account

consistency

This requires that, when a business adopts particular accounting methods, it should continue to use such methods consistently. For example, a business that decides to make a provision for depreciation on machinery at ten per cent per annum, using the straight-line method, should continue to use that percentage and method for future final accounts for this asset. Of course, having once chosen a particular method, a business is entitled to make changes provided there are good reasons for so doing, and a note to the final accounts would explain what has happened. By applying the consistency concept, direct comparison between the final accounts of different years can be made. Further examples of the use of the consistency concept are:

- stock valuation (see page 429)
- the application of the materiality concept

prudence

This concept, also known as conservatism in accounting, requires that final accounts should always, where there is any doubt, report a conservative (lower) figure for profit or the valuation of assets. To this end, profits are not to be anticipated and should only be recognised when it is reasonably certain that they will be realised; at the same time all known liabilities should be provided for. A good example of the prudence concept is where a provision is made for doubtful debts (see Chapter 25) – the debtors have not yet gone bad, but it is expected, from experience, that a certain percentage will eventually need to be written off as bad debts. The valuation of stock (see later in this chapter) also follows the prudence concept. 'Anticipate no profit, but anticipate all losses' is a summary of the concept which, in its application, prevents an over-optimistic presentation of a business through the final accounts.

realisation

This concept states that business transactions are recorded in the final accounts when the legal title passes between buyer and seller. This may well not be at the same time as payment is made, eg credit sales are recorded when the sale is made, but payment will be made at a later date

objectivity

This requires that the presentation of final accounts should be objective, rather than subjective, and should not be influenced by the opinions or personal expectations of the owner of the business concerned, or the accountant preparing the accounts. As far as possible, objectivity is supported by business documents. As an example, the owner of a business says that she has just invented a new product that will make 'millions of pounds of profit' and wants to put it on the balance sheet as an asset of £5m, the concept of objectivity says that this cannot be done – only time will tell what the effect will be on profits.

ACCOUNTING POLICIES

Accounting policies are the methods used by an individual business to show the effect of transactions, and to record assets and liabilities, in its accounts. For example, straight-line and reducing balance are two ways of recording depreciation in the accounts – a business will select, as its accounting policy, a particular method for each class of fixed asset to be depreciated. A business selects its accounting policies to fit in with the objectives of:

- relevance – the financial information is useful to users of accounts
- reliability – the financial information can be depended upon by users
- comparability – financial information can be compared with that from previous accounting periods
- understandability – users can understand the financial information provided

An accounting standard (see next section), Financial Reporting Standard No 18, entitled *Accounting policies*, sets out how businesses are to select and report their accounting policies.

ACCOUNTING STANDARDS

Over the last thirty years or so, accounting standards have been developed to provide the rules, or framework, of accounting. The intention has been to reduce the variety of alternative accounting treatments. This framework for accounting is represented by **Statements of Standard Accounting Practice** (SSAPs) and **Financial Reporting Standards** (FRSs). The Accounting Standards Board is the organisation responsible for these rules of accounting. Its aims are to establish and improve standards of financial accounting and reporting.

Note that, from 2005, large companies in the European Union are required to prepare their final accounts in accordance with International Financial Reporting Standards (IFRSs). Over time, it is expected that IFRSs will apply to all company final accounts.

The main accounting standards relevant to topics covered in Module 3 are set out below:

SSAP 5 Accounting for Value Added Tax

VAT is a tax on the supply of goods and services, which is borne by the final consumer but is collected at each stage of the production and distribution chain.

Most businesses with a turnover (sales) above a certain figure must be registered for VAT.

At regular intervals, businesses pay HM Revenue & Customs (which collects VAT):

- the amount of output tax collected on sales made
- less the amount of input tax on goods and services purchased

If the amount of input tax is greater than output tax, the business claims a refund of the difference from HM Revenue & Customs.

A VAT-registered business does not normally include VAT in the income and expenditure of the business – whether for capital or revenue items. For example, the purchase of goods for £100 plus VAT is recorded as purchases of £100 (the VAT is recorded separately). By contrast, a business not registered for VAT records the cost as £117.50 (current VAT rate of 17.5%).

Some goods and services (such as postal services, loans of money, sales or lettings of land) are exempt from VAT – the effect of this is that the supplier cannot charge output tax, and can claim back only a proportion of input tax as agreed with the VAT authorities.

Irrecoverable VAT is where a business registered for VAT cannot reclaim input tax (for example on cars, other than for resale); thus the total cost, including VAT, is entered into the accounts as the expenditure.

A VAT-registered business does not normally include VAT in the financial statements – whether for capital or revenue items. A business not registered for VAT will include input VAT as a cost in the final accounts.

SSAP 9 Stocks and long-term contracts

This sets out the broad rule that stock should be valued at cost or, where lower, net realisable value (selling price) – see next page.

FRS 15 Tangible fixed assets

This requires that fixed assets having a known useful economic life are to be depreciated (note that land is not depreciated – unless it is a mine or a quarry). See Chapter 24.

Any acceptable depreciation method can be used to spread the cost of the fixed asset consistently over its useful economic life.

Depreciation amounts are normally based on the cost of the fixed assets (straight-line depreciation), or on the net book value (reducing balance depreciation).

FRS 18 Accounting policies

The objective of this standard is to ensure that for all material items:

- a business selects the accounting policies most appropriate to its particular circumstances for the purpose of giving a true and fair view
- the accounting policies are reviewed regularly to ensure that they remain appropriate, and are changed when necessary
- sufficient information is disclosed in the financial statements to enable users to understand the accounting policies adopted and how they have been implemented

VALUATION OF STOCK

The control and valuation of stock is an important aspect in the efficient management of a business. Manual or computer records are used to show the amount of stock held and its value at any time during the year. However, at the end of the financial year it is essential for a business to make a physical stock-take for use in the final accounts. This involves stock control personnel going into the stores, the shop, or the warehouse and counting each item. The counted stock for each type of stock held is then valued as follows:

number of items held x stock valuation per item = stock value

The auditors of a business may make random checks to ensure that the stock value is correct.

The value of stock at the beginning and end of the financial year is used in the calculation for cost of sales. Therefore, the stock value has an effect on profit for the year.

Stock is valued at:

- either what it cost the business to buy the stock (including additional costs to bring the product or service to its present location and condition, such as delivery charges)
- or the net realisable value – the actual or estimated selling price (less any further costs, such as selling and distribution)

The stock valuation is often described as being **at the lower of cost and net realisable value**. This valuation is taken from SSAP 9 and applies the prudence concept. It is illustrated as follows:

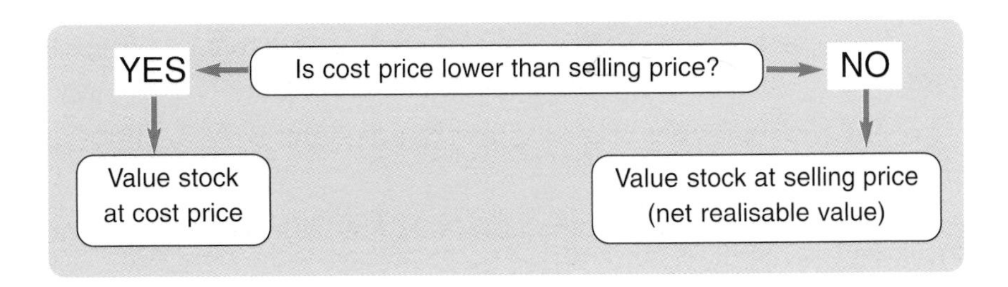

Thus two different stock values are compared:

- cost, including additional costs such as delivery charges
- net realisable value, which is the selling price of the goods, less any expenses incurred in getting the stock into a saleable condition, such as repairs and replacements, selling and distribution costs

Sometimes very large businesses use replacement cost – the cost of replacing stock that has been sold – as a further stock value. However, replacement cost applies only to raw materials – such as oil – that are traded on world markets. Unless you are told otherwise, the stock valuation rule of the lower of cost and net realisable value should be used at all times.

Note that some businesses will have stock in a number of different forms, eg a manufacturing business (see Chapter 28) will have stocks of raw materials, work-in-progress and finished goods.

WORKED EXAMPLE: STOCK VALUATION

situation

Andrew Williams runs an electrical shop. He asks for your advice on the valuation of the following items of stock:

item	*cost*	*net realisable value*	*comments*
	£	£	
washing machine	220	350	
dishwasher	300	280	the replacement cost is £290
television	250	325	the case is badly scratched and will need to be replaced at a cost of £90 before the television can be sold
DVD player	75	125	the remote control has been lost; a new one will cost £20

You are to advise Andrew of the valuations for each item.

solution

The principle of lower of cost and net realisable value applies here as follows:

- *washing machine*
  - the cost price of £220 is used, being lower than the net realisable value of £350
- *dishwasher*
  - the net realisable value of £280 is used, being lower than cost price
  - replacement cost of £290 is not used as it does not apply to the stock values of this type of business

- *television*
  - replacement parts are needed before the item can be sold
  - the rule to follow is to deduct the cost of replacement parts/repairs from net realisable value, and then to compare with cost
  - here it is £325 – £90 = £235, compared with cost of £250
  - the net realisable value of £235 is used, being lower than cost price of £250
- *DVD player*
  - as with the television, money needs to be spent before this item can be sold
  - £125 – £20 = £105, compared with cost of £75
  - the cost price of £75 is used, being lower than the net realisable value less expenses, of £105

CHAPTER SUMMARY

- Accounting concepts are part of the 'rules' of accounting.
- Business entity concept – final accounts record and report on the activities of one particular business.
- Materiality concept – items with a low value are not worthwhile recording in the accounts separately.
- Going concern concept – the presumption that the business to which the final accounts relate will continue to trade in the foreseeable future.
- Accruals concept – expenses and revenues for goods and services must be matched to the same time period.
- Prudence concept – final accounts should always, where there is any doubt, report a conservative figure for profit or the valuation of assets.
- Consistency concept – when a business adopts particular accounting methods, it should continue to use such methods consistently.
- Realisation concept – business transactions are recorded in the final accounts when the legal title passes between buyer and seller.
- Objectivity concept – the presentation of final accounts should be objective rather than subjective.
- Accounting standards comprise SSAPs and FRSs (and, from 2005, for larger EU companies, IFRSs).
- The usual valuation for stock is at the lower of cost and net realisable value (SSAP 9).
- Net realisable value is the selling price of the goods, less any expenses incurred in getting the stock into a saleable condition.

In the last four chapters we have looked at the preparation of final accounts, and a number of adjustments, in some detail. In the next two chapters we turn our attention to the final accounts of limited companies (Chapter 27) and manufacturing businesses (Chapter 28).

QUESTIONS

NOTE: an asterisk (*) after the question number means that an answer to the question is given at the end of this book.

26.1 The accounting concepts applied when preparing accounts include:

- the going concern concept
- the accruals concept
- the consistency concept
- the prudence concept

You are to explain each of these concepts, giving in each case an example to illustrate an application of the concept.

26.2* A discussion is taking place between Jane Smith, a sole trader, who owns a furniture shop, and her husband, John, who solely owns an engineering business. The following points are made:

(a) John says that, having depreciated his firm's machinery last year on the reducing balance method, for this year he intends to use the straight-line method. By doing this he says that he will deduct less depreciation from profit and loss account, so his net profit will be higher and his bank manager will be impressed. He says he might revert back to reducing balance method next year.

(b) At the end of her financial year, Jane comments that the stock of her shop had cost £10,000. She says that, as she normally adds 50 per cent to cost price to give the selling price, she intends to put a value of £15,000 for closing stock in the final accounts.

(c) John's car is owned by his business but he keeps referring to it as my car. Jane reminds him that it does not belong to him, but to the firm. He replies that of course it belongs to him and, furthermore, if the firm went bankrupt, he would be able to keep the car.

(d) John's business has debtors of £30,000. He knows that, included in this figure is a bad debt of £2,500. He wants to show £30,000 as debtors in the year-end balance sheet in order to have a high figure for current assets.

(e) On the last day of her financial year, Jane sold a large order of furniture, totalling £3,000, to a local hotel. The furniture was invoiced and delivered from stock that day, before year-end stocktaking commenced. The payment was received early in the new financial year and Jane now asks John if she will be able to put this sale through the accounts for the new year, instead of the old, but without altering the figures for purchases and closing stock for the old year.

(f) John says that his accountant talks of preparing his accounts on a going concern basis. John asks Jane if she knows of any other basis that can be used, and which it is usual to follow.

You are to take each of the points and state the correct accounting treatment, referring to appropriate accounting concepts.

26.3* Given below are three *unconnected* proposals for three *different* businesses.

1. Ben Chan has always depreciated his fixed assets at the rate of 20% on cost. He thinks that he may sell his business next year so he has proposed changing the rate of depreciation to 5% this year as this will increase his profits.

2. Lotte Betz's drawings have increased this year to £36,000. Lotte's drawings normally average £18,000 per annum. She is proposing to charge the usual £18,000 to drawings and include £18,000 as business expenses.

3. Harry Jones has his financial year end on 30 June 2001. He has been negotiating to supply ski jackets to Pierre Duval in August 2001. Pierre will sign the contract on 5 July 2001 when he returns from a business trip to Austria. Harry proposes to include the selling price of the jackets, £9,700, in his sales figure for the year ending 30 June 2001.

REQUIRED

Identify which generally accepted accounting concepts should have been applied and the correct treatment for each proposal. Proposal 1 has been answered for you.

Proposal	Concept	Action
1.	*Consistency*	*Continue to depreciate at 20%*
2.		
3.		

Assessment and Qualifications Alliance (AQA), 2001

26.4

Bert's profits are less than they have been in previous years. In order to improve his profitability he has included the following in this year's final accounts.

1. Bert delayed paying the annual rent of £4,000 on his premises until after his financial year end. He has not recorded this in any way.
2. Bert has always calculated his depreciation on equipment at 25% per annum on cost. This year he has charged £10,000 depreciation which is only 10% on cost.
3. The closing stock at the financial year end cost £30,000. Bert has valued this stock at £48,000 which is cost plus 60% to increase his profits.
4. The anticipated increase in profits meant that Bert was able to take a family holiday cruise in the Caribbean. The holiday which cost £13,000 has been charged to his profit and loss account. "The rest did me good and made me more effective in my business", he said.

REQUIRED

Using the table below, identify the concept involved in each of the notes above. Show the effect that any corrective treatment will have. The first one has been done for you as an example.

	Concept	Gross Profit	Net Profit	Current Assets	Current Liabilities	Capital
1.	Accruals	no change	decrease £4,000	no change	increase £4,000	decrease £4,000
2.						
3.						
4.						

Assessment and Qualifications Alliance (AQA), 2001

26.5* The accountant of Wyvern Garden Centre has valued the year end stock at £35,500. The three items below have not been included in the stock valuation and the accountant provides you with the following information:

item	*cost*	*net realisable value*	*replacement cost*
	£	£	£
lawnmower	220	430	200
conservatory	800	750	850
greenhouse	300	290	320

The accountant explains that he has not included the above items in the stock valuation as he was not sure which value to use for each.

REQUIRED

(a) You are to calculate the total value of Wyvern Garden Centre's stock at the year-end.

(b) Which concept should be used in the valuation of the three items listed above?

(c) What is meant by the term 'net realisable value'?

26.6 Roger Dunn runs a clothes and accessories shop. He asks you for advice on the valuation of the following items of stock:

item	**cost**	**net realisable value**	**comments**
	£	£	
jacket	40	75	the replacement cost is £35
shirt	30	25	
suit	80	150	there is a fault in the material, so Roger will sell the suit for £120
trousers	20	35	the stitching needs repairing at a cost of £10, after which the trousers will be sold for £25
electric trouser press	80	155	the electric plug and wiring is damaged and replacements will cost £15, after which the press will be sold for £130

REQUIRED

(a) Advise Roger on the value of each item of stock.

(b) How is the concept of prudence applied to stock valuation and why is it necessary to apply it?

27 LIMITED COMPANY ACCOUNTS

In the last few chapters we have looked at adjustments for a wide range of matters in the final accounts. In this chapter we look in detail at limited companies and their final accounts, including:

- the reasons for forming a limited company
- the differences between a private limited company, a public limited company, and a company limited by guarantee
- the information contained in a company's Memorandum of Association and its Articles of Association
- the differences between ordinary shares and preference shares
- the concept of reserves, and the differences between capital reserves and revenue reserves
- the layout of a company's trading, profit and loss, and profit and loss appropriation accounts, and balance sheet for internal use

TUTORIAL NOTE

If you have previously studied Module 2, you will already have an understanding of limited company accounts. Nevertheless, in this Module, you will need to develop your knowledge of the use of the profit and loss appropriation account, together with a greater knowledge of the use of capital and revenue reserves, and an understanding of the needs of investors. You will also need to practise the range of questions asked in this Module.

WHY FORM A LIMITED COMPANY?

A limited company is a separate legal entity, owned by shareholders and run by directors.

Many people in business as sole traders, ie one person in business on their own, often consider converting to a limited company. Read the following about a sole trader business and the discussions between the trader and her accountant:

Veta Bix has been trading very successfully for the last three years running her bodycare products business as a sole trader. At the moment she has three shops and a mail order business trading under the 'BodyZone' name. She has plans, as she says to her accountant:

'I've big plans for expansion and have identified suitable sites for new shops in the south east, nearer to London. My problem, though, is finance; I will need a lot more capital. As a sole trader, it is difficult to see how I can raise the money I will need. I am also concerned about my unlimited liability for the debts of the business.'

Veta's accountant suggests that she consider forming a private limited company which will enable her to issue shares to family, friends and to local investors. As the accountant says:

'We aren't talking about a company quoted on the Stock Market – although some small businesses have made it to that stage. Instead, forming a private limited company should enable you to raise the finance you need and you will still be able to retain control of the business.'

The accountant suggests she calls the company BodyZone Limited. He comments:

'Forming a company is a big change from a sole trader business. The company will have to produce formal annual accounts, which have to be filed at Companies House. The way you draw income from the company will also be different – a mix of salary and dividend payments. In terms of cost, it is quite an expensive option, but it would give you the added protection of limited liability. You may also find that your tax bill is reduced.'

The limited company is often chosen as the legal status of a business for a number of reasons:

limited liability

The shareholders (members) of a company can only lose the amount of their investment, being the money paid already, together with any money unpaid on their shares (unpaid instalments on new share issues, for example). Thus, if the company became insolvent (went 'bust'), shareholders would have to pay any unpaid instalments to help pay the creditors. As this happens very rarely, shareholders are usually in a safe position: their personal assets are not available to the company's creditors – they have **limited liability**.

separate legal entity

A limited company is a separate legal entity from its owners. Anyone taking legal action proceeds against the company and not the individual shareholders.

ability to raise finance

A limited company can raise substantial funds from outside sources by the issue of shares:

- for the larger public company – from the public and investing institutions on the Stock Exchange or similar markets

- for the smaller company – privately from venture capital companies, relatives and friends

Companies can also raise finance by means of debentures (see page 443).

membership

A member of a limited company is a person who owns at least one share in that company. A member of a company is the same as a shareholder. All ordinary shareholders have voting rights, so a sole trader who has converted to limited company status may lose some control of the business.

other factors

A limited company may be a much larger business unit than a sole trader. This gives the company a higher standing and status in the business community, allowing it to benefit from economies of scale, and making it of sufficient size to employ specialists for functions such as production, marketing, finance and human resources. There may also be tax benefits of a limited company over a sole trader business.

On the negative side, there is more documentation – eg the preparation of formal annual accounts – for a company to produce than for a sole trader business.

THE COMPANIES ACT

Limited companies are regulated by the Companies Act 1985, as amended by the Companies Act 1989.

Under the terms of the 1985 Act there are two main types of limited company: the larger **public limited company** (abbreviated to 'Plc'), which is defined in the Act, and the smaller company, traditionally known as a **private limited company** (abbreviated to 'Ltd'), which is any other limited company. A further type of company is limited by guarantee.

public limited company (Plc)

A company may become a public limited company if it has:

- issued share capital of over £50,000
- at least two members (shareholders) and at least two directors

A public limited company may raise capital from the public on the Stock Exchange or similar markets – the new issues and privatisations of recent years are examples of this. A public limited company does not have to issue shares on the stock markets, and not all do so.

private limited company (Ltd)

The private limited company is the most common form of limited company. The term private is not set out in the Companies Act 1985, but it is a traditional description, and well describes the smaller company, often in family ownership. A private limited company has:

- no minimum requirement for issued share capital
- at least one member (shareholder) and at least one director who may be the sole shareholder

The shares are not traded publicly, but are transferable between individuals, although valuation will be more difficult for shares not quoted on the stock markets.

company limited by guarantee

A company limited by guarantee is not formed with share capital, but relies on the guarantee of its members to pay a stated amount in the event of the company's insolvency. Examples of such companies include charities, and artistic and educational organisations.

GOVERNING DOCUMENTS OF COMPANIES

There are a number of documents required by the Companies Act in the setting-up of a company. Two essential governing documents are the Memorandum of Association and the Articles of Association.

The **Memorandum of Association**, the constitution of the company, regulates the affairs of the company to the outside world and contains five main clauses:

1. the name of the company (together with the words 'public limited company' or 'limited', as appropriate)
2. capital of the company (the amount that can be issued in shares: the authorised share capital)
3. 'objects' of the company, ie what activities the company can engage in; under the Companies Act the objects can be stated as being those of 'a general commercial company', ie the company can engage in any commercial activity
4. registered office of the company (not the address, but whether it is registered in England and Wales, or in Scotland)
5. a statement that the liability of the members is limited

The **Articles of Association** regulate the internal administration of the company, including the powers of directors and the holding of company meetings.

ACCOUNTING REQUIREMENTS OF THE COMPANIES ACT

The Companies Act 1985 (as amended by the Companies Act 1989) requires that companies produce sets of accounts. The Act seeks to protect the interests of shareholders, creditors, and lenders by requiring accounts to be presented in a standardised layout. This enables comparisons to be made with other companies so that users of accounts can understand and assess the progress being made. The Act also states the detailed information that must be disclosed.

For larger companies the accounts are audited by external auditors – this is a costly and time-consuming exercise (smaller companies are often exempt from audit). Nevertheless, the audit process enhances the reliability of the accounts for users.

The accounts must be sent to Companies House, where they are available for public inspection. The accounts are available to all shareholders, together with a report on the company's activities during the year.

In this chapter we will study the 'internal use' accounts, rather than being concerned with the accounting requirements of the Companies Act. 'Published accounts', as they are often known, are covered in Chapter 21 as a part of Module 2.

Before we examine the final accounts in detail we will look first at the principal ways in which a company raises finance: shares. There are different types of shares which appear in a company's balance sheet as the company's share capital.

TYPES OF SHARES ISSUED BY LIMITED COMPANIES

authorised and issued share capital

Before looking at the types of shares issued by companies we need to distinguish between the authorised share capital and the issued share capital:

- the **authorised share capital** is stated in the Memorandum of Association and is the maximum share capital that the company is allowed to issue
- the **issued share capital** is the amount of share capital that the company has issued, which cannot exceed the amount authorised; another name for issued share capital is **called up share capital**

The authorised share capital may be higher than that which has been issued. However, where a company has already issued the full extent of its authorised share capital (ie both authorised and issued are the same amount) and it wishes to make an increase, it must first pass the appropriate resolution at a general meeting of the shareholders.

The authorised share capital is shown on the balance sheet (or as a note to the accounts) 'for information', but is not added into the balance sheet total, as it may not be the same amount as the issued share capital. By contrast, the issued share capital – showing the classes and number of shares that have been issued – forms a part of the 'financed by' section of the balance sheet of a limited company.

The authorised and issued share capital may be divided into a number of classes or types of share; the main types are **ordinary shares** and, less commonly, **preference shares.**

ordinary (equity) shares

Ordinary shares – often called 'equities' – are the most commonly issued class of share which carry the main 'risks and rewards' of the business. The risks are of losing part or all of the value of the shares if the business loses money or becomes insolvent; the rewards are that they take a share of the profits – in the form of **dividends** – after allowance has been made for all expenses of the business, including loan and debenture interest (see page 443), taxation, and after preference dividends (if any). Amounts paid as dividends to ordinary shareholders will vary: when a company makes large profits, it will have the ability to pay higher dividends to the ordinary shareholders; when losses are made, the ordinary shareholders may receive no dividend.

Often dividends are paid twice a year to shareholders. An **interim dividend** is paid just over half-way through the company's financial year and is based on the profits made during the first half of the year. A **final dividend** is paid early in the next financial year and is based on the profits made for the full year. Until the final dividend is paid, it is shown as a current liability in the balance sheet.

Companies rarely pay out all of their profits in the form of dividends; most retain some profits as reserves. These can always be used to enable a dividend to be paid in a year when the company makes little or no profit, always assuming that the company has sufficient cash in the bank to make the payment. Ordinary shareholders, in the event of the company becoming insolvent, will be the last to receive any repayment of their investment: other creditors will be paid off first.

Ordinary shares carry voting rights – thus shareholders have a say at the annual general meeting and at any other shareholders' meetings.

preference shares

Whereas ordinary share dividends will vary from year-to-year, preference shares usually carry a fixed percentage rate of dividend – for example, "10 per cent preference shares" will receive a dividend of ten per cent of nominal value (see next page). Their dividends are paid in preference to those of ordinary shareholders; but they are only paid if the company makes profits. In the event of the company ceasing to trade, the preference shareholders will also receive repayment of capital before the ordinary shareholders. Sometimes preference shares are issued as **redeemable** – this means that they are repayable at some date in the future.

Preference shares do not carry voting rights.

advantages and disadvantages of shares

To the company raising finance, the advantages and disadvantages of issuing ordinary and preference shares need to be considered.

ordinary shares

advantages to the company:

- a variable dividend is paid, which is dependent on profits
- if profits are low and a dividend is not paid in one year, the dividend is not carried forward
- in the event of insolvency of the company, ordinary shareholders will be paid off last

disadvantage to the company:

- ordinary shareholders can speak and vote at the annual general meeting of the company, and each share carries one vote

preference shares

advantages to the company:

- the dividend is fixed so, if profits of the company increase, more profit is retained in the company
- preference shareholders cannot vote at meetings of the company, so they have little control over the company

disadvantages to the company:

- preference dividends are usually cumulative, that is they must be paid each year; if not, they have to be carried forward to the next year
- shareholders can attend meetings of the company (but cannot vote)
- preference shares may be redeemable (repayable) in the future
- in the event of insolvency of the company, preference shareholders must be repaid in full before any money can be paid to ordinary shareholders

nominal value of shares

Each share has a nominal value – or face value – which is entered in the accounts. Shares may be issued with nominal values of 5p, 10p, 25p, 50p or £1, or indeed for any amount. Thus a company with an authorised share capital of £100,000 might state in its Memorandum of Association that this is divided up into:

100,000 ordinary shares of 50p each	£50,000
50,000 ten per cent preference shares of £1 each	£50,000
	£100,000

market value of shares

The market value is the price at which issued – or 'secondhand' – shares are traded. Share prices of a quoted public limited company may be listed in the *Financial Times*. Note that the market value usually bears little relationship to the nominal value.

issue price

This is the price at which shares are issued to shareholders by the company – either when the company is being set up, or at a later date when it needs to raise more funds. The issue price is either 'at par' (ie the nominal value), or above nominal value. In the latter case, the amount of the difference between issue price and nominal value is known as a **share premium** (see page 450): for example – nominal value £1.00; issue price £1.50; therefore share premium is 50p per share.

Loans and Debentures

In addition to money provided by shareholders, who are the owners of the company, further funds can be obtained by borrowing in the form of loans or debentures:

- **Loans** are money borrowed by companies from lenders – such as banks – on a medium or long-term basis. Generally repayments are made throughout the period of the loan, but can often be tailored to suit the needs of the borrower. Invariably lenders require security for loans so that, if the loan is not repaid, the lender has an asset – such as property – that can be sold.

  Smaller companies are sometimes also financed by directors' loans.

- **Debentures** are formal certificates issued by companies raising long-term finance from lenders and investors. Debenture certificates issued by large public limited companies are often traded on the Stock Exchange. Most debentures state the date they will be repaid, for example, "debentures 2015-2020" means that repayment will be made by the issuer between the years 2015 and 2020, at the date to be decided by the issuer. Debentures are commonly secured against assets such as property that, in the event of the company ceasing to trade, could be sold and used to repay the debenture holders.

Loans and debentures usually carry fixed rates of interest – for example, "8 per cent debentures" – that must be paid, just like other business overheads, whether a company makes profits or not. As loan and debenture interest is a business expense, this is shown in the profit and loss account along with all other overheads. In the event of the company ceasing to trade, loan and debenture-holders would be repaid before any shareholders.

A major advantage to a company of raising finance by means of loans and debentures is that the lender receives interest payments at an agreed rate and, if profits increase, more profit is retained in the company.

Shares or Debentures – Which does the Investor Choose?

A person who has money to invest in a company is faced with the dilemma of whether to buy ordinary shares, preference shares, or debentures. To make the decision, much depends on the 'risk profile' of the investor – is he/she prepared to take risks (a risk taker), or is he/she a more cautious person (risk averse)? Then there is the question of how much income the investor wants from the shares or debentures, and whether he/she wants to receive a regular income.

Bearing these points in mind, the main advantages and disadvantages to the investor of ordinary shares, preference shares, and debentures are:

ordinary shares

advantages to the investor:

- ordinary shareholders can speak and vote at the annual general meeting of the company, and each share carries one vote

- if the company prospers, there is the potential for shares to increase in value giving the shareholder capital growth
- if the company makes high profits, there is the possibility of the shareholder receiving high dividends

disadvantages to the investor:

- there is the risk of losing some or all of the money invested if the share price falls
- the dividend will vary, being dependent on profits
- if a dividend is not paid in one year, it is not carried forward
- in the event of insolvency of the company, ordinary shareholders will be paid off last

preference shares

advantages to the investor:

- the dividend is paid at a fixed rate which will not go down if the general level of interest rates falls
- preference dividends are usually cumulative, that is they must be paid each year or, if not, they have to be carried forward to the next year
- less risky than ordinary shares
- in the event of insolvency of the company, preference shareholders must be repaid in full before any money can be paid to ordinary shareholders
- preference shareholders can attend meetings of the company (but, generally, cannot vote)

disadvantages to the investor:

- generally, preference shareholders do not have voting rights
- the dividend rate is fixed, so there can be no growth in dividends if the company prospers
- there are fewer capital growth prospects than with ordinary shares

debentures

advantages to the investor:

- a fixed rate of interest is paid, which will not go down if the general level of interest rates falls
- the interest must be paid by the company each year
- debentures are loans rather than shares, and are a much safer investment than shares because they are often backed by the security of the company's assets
- in the event of insolvency of the company, debenture holders will look firstly to their security backing; in any case, they must be repaid in full before anything is paid to shareholders
- altogether, debentures are a much safer investment than shares

disadvantages to the investor:

- a fixed rate of interest is paid, whatever may happen to the general level of interest rates
- there are no prospects for capital growth

Trading and Profit and Loss Account

A limited company uses the same form of financial statements as a sole trader or partnership. However there are two overhead items commonly found in the profit and loss account of a limited company that are not found in those of other business types:

- **directors' remuneration** – ie amounts paid to directors; as directors are employed by the company, their pay appears amongst the overheads of the company
- **debenture interest** – as already noted, when debentures are issued by companies, the interest is shown as an overhead in the profit and loss account

A limited company follows the profit and loss account with an **appropriation section**. This shows how net profit has been distributed and includes:

- corporation tax – the tax payable on company profits
- dividends paid and proposed – on both ordinary and preference shares, including interim dividends (usually paid just over half-way through the financial year) and final dividends (proposed at the end of the year, and paid early in the next financial year)
- transfers to and from reserves – see below

The diagram on pages 446 and 447 shows an example of the internal use trading and profit and loss account of a limited company. Explanations are set out on the left-hand page.

Balance Sheet

Balance sheets of limited companies follow the same layout as those we have seen earlier, but the capital section is more complex because of the different classes of shares that may be issued, and the various reserves. The diagram on pages 448 and 449 shows an example of the internal use balance sheet of a limited company. Explanations are set out on the left-hand page. Note that proposed dividends and corporation tax due are shown as current liabilities.

Reserves

A limited company rarely distributes all its profits to its shareholders. Instead, it will often keep part of the profits earned each year in the form of reserves. There are two types of reserves:

- capital reserves, which are created as a result of a non-trading profit, or may be unrealised profits
- revenue reserves, which are retained profits from profit and loss account

capital reserves

Capital reserves are created as a result of a non-trading profit, or may be unrealised profit. Note that capital reserves cannot be used to fund dividend payments.

continued on page 450

The **appropriation section** (or account) is the part of the profit and loss account which shows how net profit is distributed. It includes corporation tax, dividends paid and proposed, and transfers to and from reserves.

The **overheads** of a limited company include directors' remuneration and interest paid on debentures (if debentures have been issued).

The company has recorded a **net profit** of £43,000 in its profit and loss account – this is brought into the appropriation section.

Corporation tax, the tax that a company has to pay, based on its profits, is shown in the appropriation section. We shall not be studying the calculations for corporation tax in this book. It is, however, important to see how the tax is recorded in the financial statements.

The company has already paid **interim dividends** on the two classes of shares it has in issue (ordinary shares and preference shares); these would, most probably, have been paid just over half-way through the company's financial year. The company also proposes to pay a **final dividend** to its shareholders: these will be paid in the early part of the next financial year. Note that a dividend is often expressed as an amount per share, based on the nominal value, eg 5p per £1 nominal value share (which is the same as a five per cent dividend).

Part of the profit is transferred to **general reserve**, which is a revenue reserve of the company.

Added to profit is a **balance of retained profits** of £41,000. This represents profits of the company from previous years that have not been distributed as dividends. Note that the appropriation section shows a balance of retained profits at the year-end of £45,000. Such retained profits form a revenue reserve of the company.

MAX MUSIC LIMITED

TRADING AND PROFIT AND LOSS ACCOUNT

for the year ended 31 December 20-8

	£	£
Sales		725,000
Opening stock	45,000	
Purchases	381,000	
	426,000	
Less closing stock	50,000	
Cost of sales		376,000
Gross profit		349,000
Less overheads:		
Directors' remuneration	75,000	
Debenture interest	6,000	
Other overheads	225,000	
		306,000
Net profit for year before taxation		43,000
Less corporation tax		15,000
Profit for year after taxation		28,000
Less interim dividends paid		
ordinary shares	5,000	
preference shares	2,000	
final dividends proposed		
ordinary shares	10,000	
preference shares	2,000	
		19,000
		9,000
Transfer to general reserve		5,000
Retained profit for year		4,000
Add balance of retained profits at beginning of year		41,000
Balance of retained profits at end of year		45,000

Limited company balance sheets usually distinguish between:

intangible fixed assets, which do not have material substance but belong to the company and have value, eg goodwill (the amount paid for the reputation and connections of a business that has been taken over), patents and trademarks; intangible fixed assets are amortised (depreciated) in the same way as tangible fixed assets.

tangible fixed assets, which have material substance, such as premises, equipment, machinery, vehicles, fixtures and fittings.

Note that fixed assets, such as property, may be revalued (reval'n) upwards (with an effect on revaluation reserve); other assets may be reduced in value by depreciation (dep'n).

As well as the usual **current liabilities**, for limited companies, this section also contains the amount of proposed dividends (but not dividends that have been paid in the year) and the amount of corporation tax to be paid within the next twelve months. The amounts for both of these items are also included in the appropriation section of the profit and loss account.
Note that, in company balance sheets, current liabilities are often described as "creditors: falling due within one year".

Long-term liabilities are those that are due to be repaid more than twelve months from the date of the balance sheet, eg loans and debentures.
Note that long-term liabilities are often described as "creditors: falling due after more than one year".

Authorised share capital is included on the balance sheet 'for information', but is not added into the balance sheet total, as it may not be the same amount as the issued share capital.

Issued share capital shows the classes and number of shares that have been issued. In this balance sheet, the shares are described as being fully paid, meaning that the company has received the full amount of the value of each share from the shareholders. Sometimes shares will be partly paid, eg ordinary shares of £1, but 75p paid. This means that the company can make a call on the shareholders to pay the extra 25p to make the shares fully paid.

Capital reserves are created as a result of non-trading profit, or may be unrealised profit.

Revenue reserves are profits generated from trading activities.

The total for **shareholders' funds** represents the stake of the shareholders in the company. It comprises share capital (ordinary and preference shares), plus reserves (capital and revenue reserves).

MAX MUSIC LIMITED
BALANCE SHEET AS AT 31 DECEMBER 20-8

Fixed Assets	*Cost/Reval'n*	*Dep'n to date*	*Net*
	£	£	£
Intangible			
Goodwill	50,000	20,000	30,000
Tangible			
Freehold land and buildings	410,000	110,000	300,000
Fixtures and fittings	100,000	25,000	75,000
	560,000	155,000	405,000
Current Assets			
Stock		50,000	
Debtors		23,000	
Bank		32,000	
Cash		2,000	
		107,000	
Less Current Liabilities			
Creditors	25,000		
Proposed dividends	12,000		
Corporation tax	15,000		
		52,000	
Working Capital (or **Net Current Assets**)			55,000
			460,000
Less Long-term Liabilities			
10% debentures, 2015-2020			60,000
NET ASSETS			400,000
FINANCED BY			
Authorised Share Capital			
100,000 10% preference shares of £1 each			100,000
600,000 ordinary shares of £1 each			600,000
			700,000
Issued Share Capital			
40,000 10% preference shares of £1 each, fully paid			40,000
300,000 ordinary shares of £1 each, fully paid			300,000
			340,000
Capital Reserve			
Share premium account			10,000
Revenue Reserves			
General reserve			5,000
Profit and loss account			45,000
SHAREHOLDERS' FUNDS			400,000

Examples of capital reserves include:

- **Revaluation reserve.** This occurs when a fixed asset, most probably property, is revalued (in an upwards direction) in the balance sheet. The amount of the revaluation is placed in a revaluation reserve where it increases the value of the shareholders' investment in the company. Note, however, that this is purely a 'book' adjustment – no cash has changed hands.

In the example below a company revalues its property upwards by £250,000 from £500,000 to £750,000.

BALANCE SHEET (EXTRACTS)

Before revaluation	£
Fixed asset: property at cost	500,000
Share capital: ordinary shares of £1 each	500,000
After revaluation	
Fixed asset: property at revaluation	750,000
Share capital: ordinary shares of £1 each	500,000
Capital reserve: revaluation reserve	250,000
	750,000

- **Share premium account.** An established company may issue additional shares to the public at a higher amount than the nominal value. For example, a company seeks finance for further expansion by issuing additional ordinary shares. The shares have a nominal value of £1 each, but, because it is a well-established company, the shares are issued at £1.50 each. Of this amount, £1 is recorded in the issued share capital section, and the extra 50p is the share premium.

revenue reserves

Revenue reserves are profits generated from trading activities; they have been retained in the company to help build the company for the future. Revenue reserves include the balance of the appropriation section of the profit and loss account: this balance is commonly described as 'profit and loss account balance' or 'balance of retained profits'. Alternatively, a transfer may be made from the appropriation section to a named revenue reserve account, such as general reserve, or a revenue reserve for a specific purpose, such as reserve for the replacement of machinery. Transfers to or from these named revenue reserve accounts are made in the appropriation section of the profit and loss account.

A feature of revenue reserves is that, as they have been created from the trading activities of the company, they are available to fund dividend payments (as we have seen on page 445, dividends are deducted in the appropriation section of the profit and loss account).

reserves: profits not cash

It should be noted that reserves – both capital and revenue – are not cash funds to be used whenever the company needs money, but are in fact represented by assets shown on the balance sheet. The reserves record the fact that the assets belong to the shareholders via their ownership of the company.

CHAPTER SUMMARY

- A limited company is a separate legal entity owned by shareholders and run by directors.
- A company is regulated by the Companies Act 1985 (as amended by the Companies Act 1989), and is owned by shareholders and managed by directors.
- A limited company may be either a public limited company or a private limited company.
- The liability of shareholders is limited to any money unpaid on their shares.
- The main types of shares that may be issued by companies are ordinary shares and preference shares.
- Borrowings in the form of loans and debentures are a further source of finance.
- The final accounts of a company include an appropriation section, which follows the profit and loss account.
- The balance sheet of a limited company includes a capital and reserves section which reflects the ownership of the company by its shareholders:

  – a statement of the authorised and issued share capital

  – details of capital reserves and revenue reserves
- Capital reserves are created as a result of a non-trading profit, or may be unrealised profits, and cannot be used to fund dividend payments.
- Revenue reserves are profits generated from trading activities.

In the next chapter we look at the final accounts of manufacturing businesses – firms that buy in raw materials and manufacture products which are then sold as finished goods.

QUESTIONS

NOTE: an asterisk (*) after the question number means that an answer to the question is given at the end of this book.

27.1 Distinguish between:

(a) a public limited company and a private limited company

(b) the Memorandum of Association and the Articles of Association

(c) authorised share capital and issued share capital

(d) ordinary shares and preference shares

(e) nominal value and market value of shares

(f) capital reserves and revenue reserves

27.2 Prepare a five-minute talk on the types of companies and the advantages of forming a limited company. The talk is to form part of your local radio station's business programme entitled 'Business Matters'. To accompany your talk, prepare a handout which can be distributed to listeners who contact the station.

27.3 Explain where the following items appear in a limited company's year end financial statements:

(a) debenture interest

(b) directors' remuneration

(c) corporation tax

(d) dividends proposed

(e) revaluation reserve

(f) goodwill

27.4* Chapelporth Limited has made a pre-tax profit of £135,000 for the year ended 30 June 20-8. The following interim dividends for the half-year ended 31 December 20-7 were paid in February 20-8:

	£
interim ordinary dividend	21,000
interim preference dividend	8,000

The directors of Chapelporth Limited wish to provide for the following at the year end on 30 June 19-8:

	£
corporation tax	48,000
final ordinary dividend	29,000
final preference dividend	8,000

You are to prepare the profit and loss appropriation account of Chapelporth Limited for the year ended 30 June 20-8.

27.5 Mason Motors Limited is a second-hand car business. The following information is available for the year ended 31 December 20-1:

- balance of retained profits from previous years stands at £100,000
- net profit for the year was £75,000
- it has been agreed that a transfer to a general reserve of £20,000 is to be made
- corporation tax of £20,050 is to be paid on the year's profit
- it has been agreed that a dividend of 10% is to be paid on the issued share capital of £100,000

You are to

(a) Set out the appropriation section of the profit and loss account for Mason Motors Limited for the year ended 31 December 20-1.

(b) State how you would reply to one of the directors of the company who asks if the £20,000 being transferred to general reserve could be used to rebuild the garage forecourt.

27.6* The following figures are taken from the accounting records of Jobseekers Limited, a recruitment agency, at the end of the financial year on 31 December 20-6:

	£
Issued share capital (£1 ordinary shares)	100,000
Premises at cost	175,000
Depreciation of premises to date	10,500
Office equipment at cost	25,000
Depreciation of office equipment to date	5,000
Goodwill at cost	20,000
Amortisation* of goodwill to date	6,000
Stock at 31 December 20-6	750
Debtors	42,500
Creditors	7,250
Bank overdraft	13,950
Bank loan	55,000
Net profit for year before taxation	68,200
Corporation tax for the year	14,850
Interim ordinary dividend paid	10,000
Final ordinary dividend proposed	40,000
Retained profit at 1 January 20-6	7,350

* amortisation is similar to depreciation

You are to prepare the appropriation section of the profit and loss account (starting with net profit) for the year ended 31 December 20-6, together with a balance sheet at that date.

27.7*

Jill and her brother Jack have recently inherited £10,000 each. They wish to invest all of their inheritance in Multar plc.

They could invest in one of the following:

ordinary shares

7% preference shares

6% debentures

Jill does not mind taking risks with any money she has whereas her brother is a much more cautious person. He is looking for an investment which will give him a steady income.

REQUIRED

(a) State **one** advantage **and one** disadvantage of each type of investment.

Ordinary shares

Advantage ....

....

Disadvantage ....

....

7% preference shares

Advantage ....

....

Disadvantage ....

....

6% debentures

Advantage ....

....

Disadvantage ....

....

(b) Advise Jill which type of investment she should choose.

....

....

....

....

(c) Advise Jack which type of investment he should choose.

....

....

....

....

Assessment and Qualifications Alliance (AQA), 2003

27.8

(a) The draft profit for the year ended 31 May 2003 of Srian plc is £12,000,000. The following information for the year has not been taken into account.

	£
Ordinary dividends – paid	800,000
proposed	1,300,000
Directors' fees	1,500,000
Provision for corporation tax	2,600,000
Debenture interest	1,200,000
Transfer to general reserve	1,000,000

REQUIRED

Prepare the profit and loss appropriation account for the year ended 31 May 2003.

(b) The following has been extracted from the balance sheet of Srian plc as at 31 May 2003.

	£
Ordinary shares of £1 each fully paid	25,000,000
6% Debentures	20,000,000

The directors have seen an opportunity to expand the company's operation. They need to raise £30,000,000.

The directors are considering raising the whole amount by

either an issue of 20,000,000 ordinary shares at £1.50 each

or an issue of £30,000,000 6% debentures.

REQUIRED

Evaluate the two methods of raising finance being considered by the directors of the company.

Assessment and Qualifications Alliance (AQA), 2003

27.9* The following is the summarised draft balance sheet of Vlasmin plc as at 31 March 2002.

	Cost	*Depreciation*	*Net*
	£000	*£000*	*£000*
Fixed assets	1,000	620	380
Current assets		420	
Less Current liabilities		360	60
			440
Ordinary share capital			200
Profit and loss account			240
			440

Depreciation has been charged on all fixed assets at 20% per annum using the straight-line method.

After preparing the draft balance sheet the directors of Vlasmin plc have decided to incorporate the following changes in the final accounts.

(a) Wages due but unpaid at the year end amounted to £12,000.

(b) Depreciation on all fixed assets is to be charged at 15% per annum using the straight-line method.

(c) A transfer of £25,000 to a general reserve.

(d) A final dividend on the ordinary share capital of £43,000.

REQUIRED

Using the table below show the effect that any amendments resulting from notes (a) to (d) above will have on the balance sheet of Vlasmin plc.

If you believe that there is no amendment necessary write *no change*.

Note (a) has been completed as an example.

Note	Net profit before appropriations	Retained profits	Shareholders' funds	Current assets	Current liabilities
(a)	decrease £12,000	decrease £12,000	decrease £12,000	no change	increase £12,000
(b)					
(c)					
(d)					

Assessment and Qualifications Alliance (AQA), 2002

27.10 The following is the summarised draft balance sheet as at 31 December 2002 for David Mark Ltd.

	£	£
Fixed assets		700,000
Current assets		
Stock	85,000	
Debtors	60,000	
Bank	17,000	
	162,000	
Less Current liabilities		
Trade creditors	37,000	125,000
		825,000
Share capital and reserves		
Ordinary shares of 50 pence each		250,000
8% preference shares of £1 each		100,000
Profit and loss account		400,000
General reserve		75,000
		825,000

The company's retained profit for the year, before appropriations, was £150,000, which has been included in the profit and loss account figure shown in the balance sheet above.

Additional information:

The following have **not** yet been taken into consideration

- Transfer from profit and loss account to the general reserve £45,000
- A proposed final dividend on preference shares of £4,000
- A proposed final dividend on ordinary shares of 7 pence per share
- An issue of 200,000 ordinary shares of 50 pence each at 75 pence per share. (*Note*: these shares are not eligible for dividend in the year ended 31 December 2002)

REQUIRED

(a) Starting with the retained profit of £150,000 from the draft accounts, calculate the retained profit for the year ended 31 December 2002 after appropriations.

(b) Prepare the summarised balance sheet as at 31 December 2002 as it would appear, after taking into account the additional information listed above.

(c) State the type of business ownership that would have "Ltd" as part of its name.

(d) Assess the importance of the term "Ltd" to an ordinary shareholder in David Mark Ltd.

Assessment and Qualifications Alliance (AQA), 2003

27.11* The following draft balance sheet has been prepared (in horizontal format) from a correct trial balance by an inexperienced clerk.

Grift Ltd
Balance Sheet as at 28 February 2002

	£		£
Premises	270,000	Debtors	8,500
Stock 28 February 2002	17,000	Stock 1 March 2001	21,000
Bank balance (Dr)	1,500	Vehicles	170,000
Trade creditors	6,000	Authorised ordinary shares	1,000,000
Proposed ordinary dividend	18,000	Retained earnings	93,000
Issued ordinary shares	500,000	Machinery	150,000
"Balancing figure"	630,000		
	1,442,500		1,442,500

REQUIRED

(a) Explain the difference between the authorised share capital and the issued share capital of a limited company.

(b) Prepare a redrafted balance sheet for the company presented in good form.*

* **Tutorial note**: 'in good form' means using the correct headings, with items included in their proper place, set out either in vertical or in horizontal format

Roger Grift had been in business as a sole trader for many years. On 1 January 2000 he turned his business into Grift Ltd, a limited company.

REQUIRED

(c) Discuss one factor that Roger Grift should have considered before changing his business into a limited company.

Assessment and Qualifications Alliance (AQA), 2002

27.12

The following information has been extracted from the books of account of Leroy McDade plc as at 31 December 2001.

	£
Issued share capital:	
ordinary shares of 50p each, fully paid	1,600,000
7% debentures (2020 - 2025)	200,000
Share premium account	800,000
Profit and loss account balance 1 January 2001	612,000
General reserve	150,000
Interim ordinary dividend paid 4 August 2001	40,000
Trade creditors	78,200
Directors' fees	117,000
Provision for corporation tax due	180,000

Additional information:

- Net profit for the year after interest but before taxation was £546,000.
- Debenture interest is payable half-yearly to 30 June and 31 December. It is paid to debenture holders on 27 July and 27 January each year.
- The directors propose a transfer to general reserve of £50,000 and a final ordinary dividend of 5p per share.

REQUIRED

(a) Prepare the profit and loss appropriation account for the year ended 31 December 2001 of Leroy McDade plc.

(b) Prepare balance sheet extracts as at 31 December 2001 for Leroy McDade plc showing the sections for:

(i) the capital and reserves, and

(ii) creditors falling due within one year (ie current liabilities).

(c) Discuss the advantages and disadvantages that an investor should consider when deciding whether to invest in debentures or ordinary shares.

Assessment and Qualifications Alliance (AQA), 2002

27.13* Forall Ltd had the following credit balances in the general ledger on 31 March 2000.

	£
Profit and loss account	72,350
General reserve	28,000
Share premium account	40,000
Revaluation reserve	100,000

During the year ended 31 March 2001 the following occurred:

1. Forall Ltd issued a further 100,000 ordinary shares of £1 each.

   The issue price was £1.75

2. Forall Ltd made a net profit before interest and taxation of £321,000

3. The company paid an interim dividend of £35,000.

4. The directors propose:

   (i) a final dividend of £50,000

   (ii) a transfer to general reserve of £25,000

   (iii) to provide £80,000 for corporation tax

REQUIRED

(a) Prepare a profit and loss appropriation account for the year ended 31 March 2001 for Forall Ltd.

(b) State the balance to be shown on the balance sheet for the profit and loss account.

(c) State the balance to be shown on the balance sheet for the share premium account.

(d) Explain the difference between a capital reserve and a revenue reserve. Give one example of each from the question.

Assessment and Qualifications Alliance (AQA), 2001

28 MANUFACTURING ACCOUNTS

In previous chapters we have concerned ourselves with the accounts of businesses that trade, ie buy and sell goods without carrying out a manufacturing process. However, many firms buy raw materials and manufacture products which are then sold as finished goods. The final accounts for a manufacturer include a manufacturing account which brings together all the elements of cost making up the production cost. In this chapter we will:

- consider the manufacturing process
- study the elements of cost
- prepare a manufacturing account

THE MANUFACTURING PROCESS AND ELEMENTS OF COST

The diagram below shows, in outline, the manufacturing process and the costs incurred at each stage.

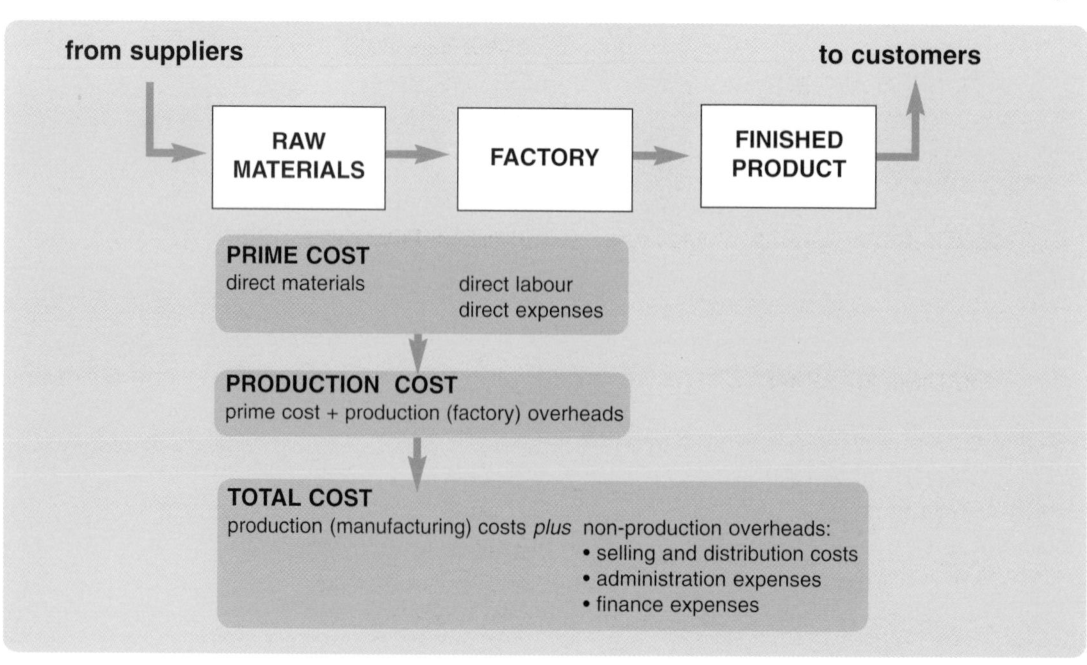

Note that there are four main elements of cost which make up the manufacturing (or production) cost:

1 **direct materials** – the raw materials that are required in manufacturing the finished product
2 **direct labour** – this is the cost of the workforce engaged in production, eg machine operators (note that the wages of factory supervisors are a production overhead and are usually described as 'indirect labour')
3 **direct expenses** – these include any special costs that can be identified with each unit produced, eg a royalty payable for the use of patents or copyrights for each unit made, or the hire of specialist machinery to carry out a particular manufacturing task
4 **production (factory) overheads** – all the other costs of manufacture, eg wages of supervisors, rent of factory, depreciation of factory machinery, heating and lighting of factory

Prime cost is the basic cost of manufacturing a product before the addition of production overheads. It consists of the first three costs, ie

direct materials + direct labour + direct expenses = prime cost

Production cost is the factory cost of making the product after the addition of production overheads, and is:

prime cost + production (factory) overheads = production (or manufacturing) cost

Final Accounts of a Manufacturer

The final accounts of a manufacturer are structured as follows:

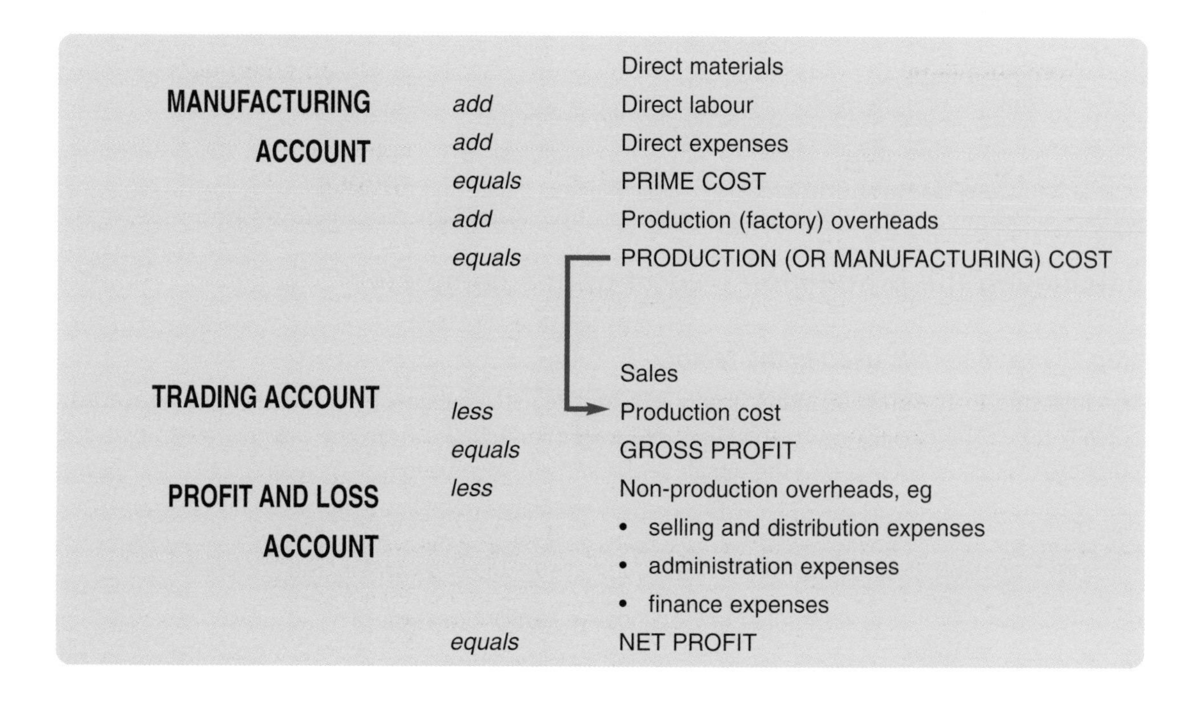

Note that a manufacturing business also prepares a balance sheet.

We will now study the manufacturing account, and the trading and profit and loss account in more detail.

MANUFACTURING ACCOUNT

A manufacturing account must be prepared at the end of the financial year for a manufacturing business.

The bottom line of a manufacturing account provides **the production cost of goods completed for the period**. Total production cost is defined as:

direct costs (prime cost) + production overheads = production cost

The manufacturing account includes all the **direct costs** (prime cost) of making the products, together with the **production overheads**. Finished goods are sent from the factory to the warehouse, from which they are sold to customers. The accounts reflect this movement: the cost of producing the finished goods – adjusted for the value of any work-in-progress (partly finished goods) not yet completed – is carried forward from the manufacturing account to the trading account. The calculations are explained step by step below.

manufacturing account calculation

	cost of raw materials used (or consumed)
add	direct labour costs
add	direct expenses
equals	prime cost
add	production (factory) overheads
adjust for	value of any work-in-progress
equals	production cost of goods completed

calculating the production cost of goods completed

step 1 raw materials used in the factory

The first step in the manufacturing account is to calculate the direct cost of the **raw materials** actually used. The closing stock (the stock not used) is deducted from the opening stock plus the purchases, and so it follows that the remainder must have been used (see diagram on the next page):

opening stock of raw materials + purchases – closing stock of raw materials

= cost of raw materials used (or consumed)

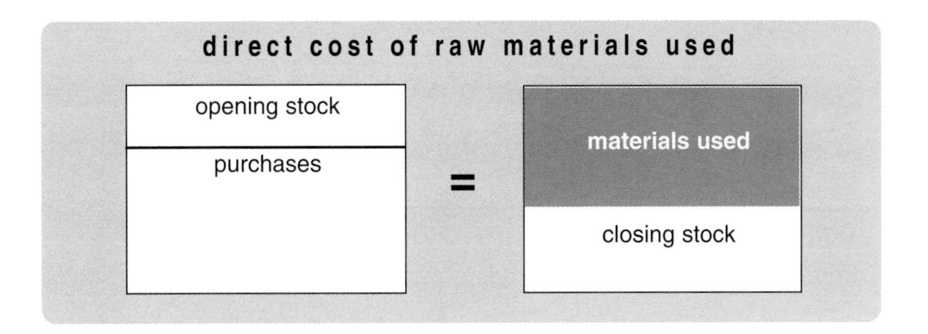

step 2 calculating prime cost

In addition to the direct cost of materials used, the cost of direct labour and any direct expenses, eg royalties, must be added. The total of all the direct costs is the prime cost.

step 3 adding production (factory) overheads

Production overheads are added to the prime cost to give the **production cost**. Production overheads are the overheads relating to the factory.

Note that some overheads – eg rent and rates – may be split between the factory and the office. The factory part of the total figure is included in the manufacturing account at this stage and the office part will be included in the profit and loss account.

step 4 adjusting for work-in-progress

Work-in-progress – or partly finished goods in course of manufacture – remains in the factory: it cannot be sold because it is not complete. Therefore there is an adjustment at the end of the manufacturing account to ensure that the cost of closing work-in-progress is removed from the total of all production costs, leaving just the cost of producing the finished (completed) goods.

Note also that if there is any work-in-progress brought forward at the start of the period, its value must be included in the manufacturing account. The calculation for the production cost of goods completed is:

	production cost
add	opening stock of work-in-progress
less	closing stock of work-in-progress
equals	production cost of goods completed

This figure (production cost of goods completed) is the bottom line of the manufacturing account and is passed to the trading account. However, manufacturing businesses may add a factory profit before making the transfer to the trading account – this aspect of manufacturing accounts is covered on page 473.

The work-in-progress adjustment is illustrated as follows:

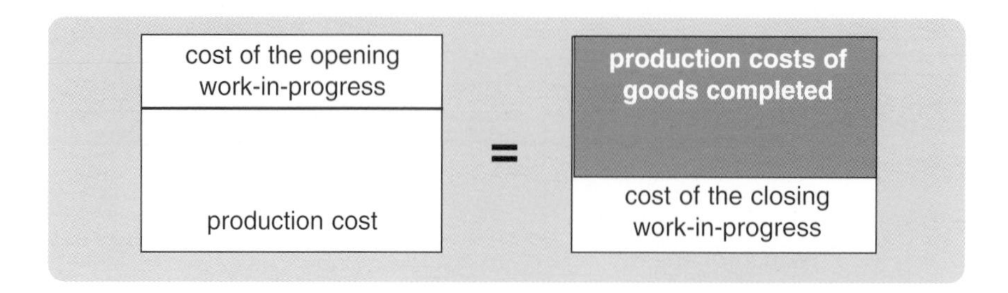

Trading and Profit and Loss Accounts

The trading and profit and loss accounts follow on from the manufacturing account.

the trading account

In the trading account the manufacturer sells its manufactured goods to its customers. It is also in effect 'buying' the finished goods from its own factory. Instead of 'purchases' of goods from outside suppliers, we now have the 'production cost' of goods completed coming from the factory. This figure is brought forward from the manufacturing account as explained above.

The cost of sales (or 'cost of goods sold') is therefore calculated in the trading account as:

	opening stock of finished goods
add	production cost of goods completed
less	closing stock of finished goods
equals	cost of sales

the profit and loss account

The profit and loss account of a manufacturing business is prepared in exactly the same way as for any other business. Notice that the **factory** costs have already been dealt with in the manufacturing account, so the profit and loss account deals only with **non-production** (usually warehouse and office) costs.

summary so far . . .

The diagram opposite illustrates how the manufacturing, trading and profit and loss accounts are constructed and shows where the three stock adjustments – for raw materials, work-in-progress and finished goods – are made in the accounts.

The two Worked Examples that follow put these principles into practice.

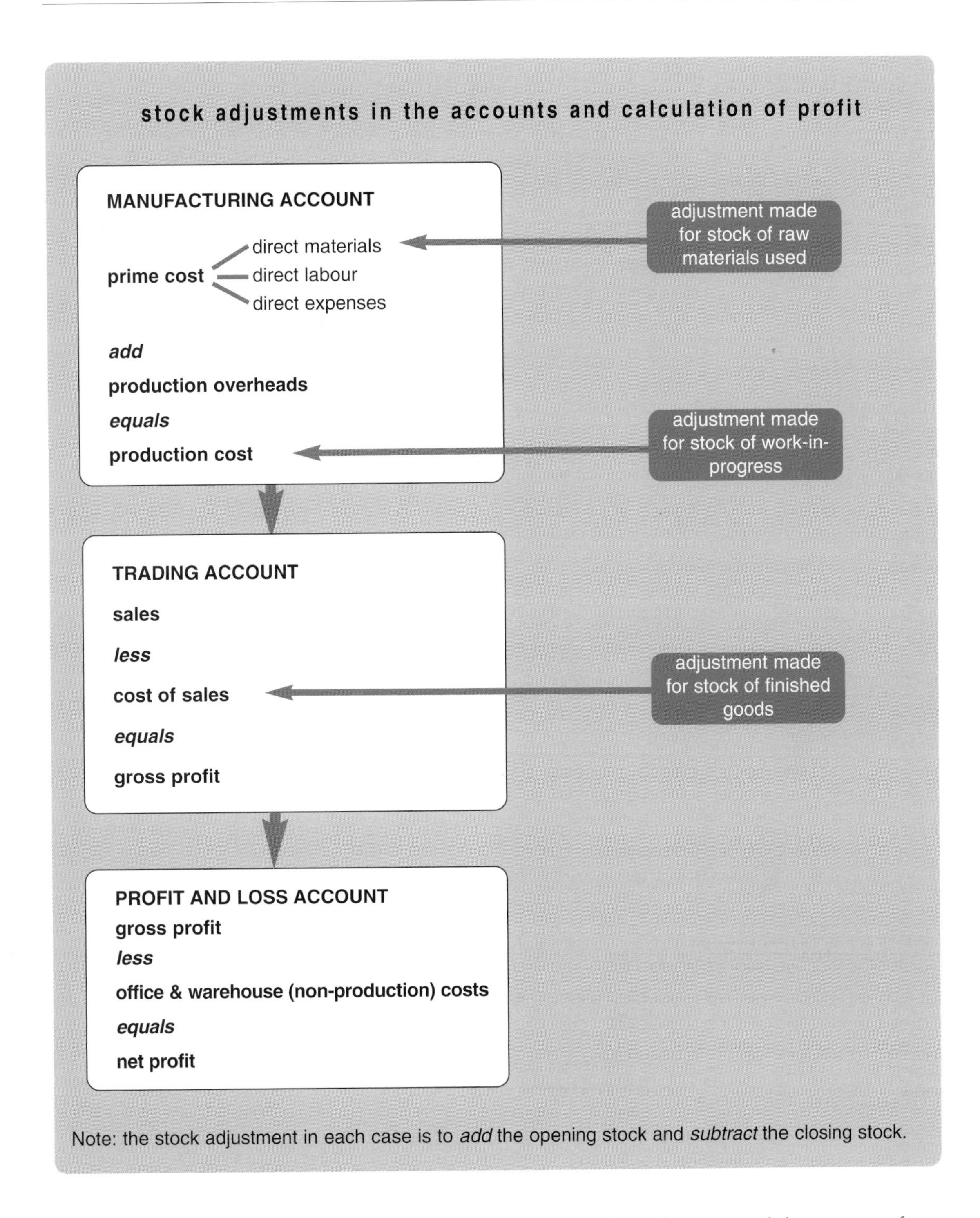

Now study the two Worked Examples that follow. We will first show the layout of the accounts for a manufacturing business, together with notes highlighting important points. We will then illustrate the calculations required in order to prepare the accounts for a manufacturing business.

WORKED EXAMPLE 1: MANUFACTURING ACCOUNTS

Alpha Manufacturing Company makes paving slabs. The layout of its manufacturing, trading, and profit and loss account for the year 20-2 is as follows:

ALPHA MANUFACTURING COMPANY
MANUFACTURING, TRADING AND PROFIT AND LOSS ACCOUNT
for the year ended 31 December 20-2

	£	£
Opening stock of raw materials		5,000
Add Purchases of raw materials		50,000
		55,000
Less Closing stock of raw materials		6,000
COST OF RAW MATERIALS USED (OR CONSUMED)		49,000
Direct labour		26,000
Direct expenses		2,500
PRIME COST		77,500
Add Production (factory) overheads:		
Indirect materials	2,000	
Indirect labour	16,000	
Rent of factory	5,000	
Depreciation of factory machinery	10,000	
Factory light and heat	4,000	
		37,000
		114,500
Add Opening stock of work-in-progress		4,000
		118,500
Less Closing stock of work-in-progress		3,000
PRODUCTION (OR MANUFACTURING) COST OF GOODS COMPLETED		115,500
Sales		195,500
Opening stock of finished goods	6,500	
Production (or manufacturing) cost of goods completed	115,500	
	122,000	
Less Closing stock of finished goods	7,500	
COST OF SALES		114,500
Gross profit		81,000
Less Non-production overheads:		
Selling and distribution expenses	38,500	
Administration expenses	32,000	
Finance expenses	3,500	
		74,000
Net profit		7,000

BALANCE SHEET EXTRACT as at 31 December 20-2

		£	£	£
Current Assets				
Stock	– raw materials	6,000		
	– work-in-progress	3,000		
	– finished goods	7,500		
			16,500	

points to note

1. The first step in the manufacturing account is to calculate the cost of **raw materials used**.
2. The next step is to calculate the **prime cost** of production.
3. The manufacturing account collects together all 'factory' costs, ie prime cost plus production overheads.
4. If there is any work-in-progress, an adjustment is made at the end of the manufacturing account. This ensures that the figure carried forward is the **production cost of the goods completed** in the period.
5. The figure for 'sales' goes into the top line of the trading account as usual.
6. **Cost of sales** is calculated in the normal way, except that the production or 'factory' cost replaces the 'purchases' of goods for sale. The production cost of goods completed is transferred from the manufacturing account.
7. **Gross profit = sales – cost of sales,** as usual.
8. The profit and loss account shows all **non-production** (non-factory) ie **warehouse and office costs**.
9. In the balance sheet, all three forms of stock – raw materials, work-in-progress, finished goods – held at the end of the year are listed in the current assets section.

unit cost of goods manufactured

When the production cost has been ascertained, the unit cost can be calculated as follows:

$$\textit{Unit cost} = \frac{\textit{Production cost of goods completed}}{\textit{Number of units completed}}$$

For example, if the manufacturing account of Alpha Manufacturing Company, on the previous page, represented production of 200,000 units, the unit cost for the year was:

$$\textit{Unit cost} = \frac{£115,500}{200,000} = £0.58 \textit{ per unit}$$

WORKED EXAMPLE 2: MANUFACTURING ACCOUNTS

situation

Trevellas Manufacturing is a small business which makes surf boards. The following figures relate to the year ended 31 December 20-2.

	Opening stock	*Closing stock*
	1 January 20-2	*31 December 20-2*
	£	£
Stock of raw material (at cost)	15,275	14,385
Stock of work-in-progress (valued at factory cost)	3,800	3,250
Stock of finished goods	27,350	26,000

	£
Purchases of raw materials	43,850
Factory wages (direct)	22,725
Factory indirect expenses	12,500
Depreciation of factory machinery	1,500
Rent and rates*	4,000
General administration expenses	13,250
Sales of finished goods	168,000
Depreciation of vehicles	1,400
Vehicle running expenses	2,550
Selling expenses	13,090

Note: at 31 December 20-2, rent of £2,000 is owing.

**Rent and rates are three-quarters for the factory and one-quarter for buildings housing the warehouse and office.*

You are to prepare the manufacturing, trading and profit and loss account for Trevellas Manufacturing, for the year ended 31 December 20-2, together with the balance sheet extract showing stock.

solution

When preparing these accounts from given data, it is useful to mark against each item where it will go. Remember that the stocks of raw materials and work-in-progress are dealt with in the manufacturing account. The finished goods stocks appear in the trading account.

Purchases of raw materials and all 'factory' expenditure go into the manufacturing account. In the case of rent and rates, the factory part must be calculated.

Factory rent and rates = (£4,000 + £2,000) x three-quarters = £4,500 → manufacturing account

Non-production rent and rates = £6,000 x one-quarter = £1,500 → profit and loss account

Note: always adjust for accruals and prepayments before calculating the appropriate costs for manufacturing account and profit and loss account.

All other costs relating to the office (administration) and selling and distribution (including vehicles) are entered in profit and loss account.

Sales are part of the trading account.

TREVELLAS MANUFACTURING

MANUFACTURING ACCOUNT for the year ended 31 December 20-2

	£	£
Opening stock of raw materials	15,275	
Add Purchases of raw materials	43,850	
	59,125	
Less Closing stock of raw materials	14,385	
COST OF RAW MATERIALS USED (OR CONSUMED)		44,740
Direct labour (factory wages)		22,725
PRIME COST		67,465
Add Production (factory) overheads		
Factory indirect expenses	12,500	
Factory machinery depreciation	1,500	
Factory rent and rates	4,500	18,500
		85,965
Add Opening stock of work-in-progress		3,800
		89,765
Less Closing stock of work-in-progress		3,250
PRODUCTION COST OF GOODS COMPLETED		86,515

TREVELLAS MANUFACTURING

TRADING AND PROFIT AND LOSS ACCOUNT

for the year ended 31 December 20-2

	£	£
Sales		168,000
Opening stock of finished goods	27,350	
Production cost of goods completed	86,515	
	113,865	
Less: Closing stock of finished goods	26,000	
COST OF SALES		87,865
Gross profit		80,135
Less Non-production overheads:		
Selling and distribution costs (see note 1, below)	17,040	
Administration costs (see note 2, below)	14,750	
		31,790
Net profit		48,345

Note 1: Selling and distribution costs include:

Depreciation of vehicles	1,400
Vehicle running expenses	2,550
Selling expenses	13,090
	17,040

Note 2: Administration costs include

Rent and rates (one-quarter)	1,500
General administration expenses	13,250
	14,750

BALANCE SHEET EXTRACT as at 31 December 20-2

		£	£	£
Current Assets				
Stock	– raw materials	14,385		
	– work-in-progress	3,250		
	– finished goods	26,000		
			43,635	

Transfer Prices and Factory Profit

Often manufacturing businesses transfer completed goods from the factory to the warehouse at, for example, 'factory cost plus ten per cent' (the transfer price). The objective in doing this is for the factory to make a notional profit which is added into net profit at a later stage. This might enable the unit cost of goods manufactured to be compared with the cost of buying in completed goods from an outside source. Also, by showing a factory profit, the profit (or loss) from trading activities (as distinct from manufacturing) can be identified separately.

Referring back to the manufacturing account on page 468 and amending the figures to allow for a factory 'profit' of ten per cent, the final part of the manufacturing account, and the trading and profit and loss account appear as follows:

	£	£
PRODUCTION COST		115,500
Factory profit of ten per cent		11,550
PRODUCTION COST OF GOODS COMPLETED (including profit)		127,050
Sales		195,500
Opening stock of finished goods	6,500	
Production (or manufacturing) cost of goods completed	127,050	
	133,550	
Less Closing stock of finished goods	7,500	
COST OF SALES		126,050
Gross profit		69,450
Less Non-production overheads:		
Selling and distribution expenses	38,500	
Administration expenses	32,000	
Finance expenses	3,500	
		74,000
Loss from trading		(4,550)
Add Factory profit		11,550
Net profit		7,000

Note that the final net profit is unchanged, but the manufacturing cost is higher, and gross profit is lower. The factory profit is added back in the profit and loss account, after showing separately the profit or loss from trading. The reason for doing this is to make the factory and the warehouse into separate profit centres.

provision for unrealised profit on finished goods stocks

A business using the 'factory profit' method may choose to value stocks of finished goods at manufacturing cost plus manufacturing profit. For example, the business whose manufacturing account is shown on the previous page, might value finished goods stocks as:

Opening stock at 1 January 20-2

manufacturing cost £6,500 + manufacturing profit of 10 per cent £650 = £7,150

Closing stock at 31 December 20-2

manufacturing cost £7,500 + manufacturing profit of 10 per cent £750 = £8,250

The logic behind valuing finished goods stocks in this way is to show more clearly the profit from the separate sections of the business, ie manufacturing and trading. It will apply particularly where goods are both manufactured and bought in as finished goods from outside manufacturers. The trading account now compares 'like with like', ie own-manufactured goods are priced to include a profit, while the bought-in goods include the supplier's profit. At the end of the financial year the closing stock of own-manufactured goods includes an element of unrealised profit.

Statement of Standard Accounting Practice No 9 (Stocks and long-term contracts) – see Chapter 26 – requires that stocks should be shown in the balance sheet at cost price if purchased, or cost of production if manufactured. (Note that if realisable value is lower than cost, then this will be used instead.) In order to comply with SSAP 9, it is necessary to account for the element of unrealised profit included in the finished goods stock valuation. This is done by calculating the provision for unrealised profit, which is used to adjust downwards the closing stock figure in the balance sheet to cost price.

For example, using the adjusted finished goods opening and closing stock figures of £7,150 (above) and £8,250 (which include manufacturing profits of £650 and £750 respectively), the calculation of the change in unrealised profit is as follows:

	£
Unrealised profit at start of year	650
Unrealised profit at end of year	750
Increase in provision for unrealised profit	100

Here the unrealised profit has increased by £100. This increase is shown as a deduction from factory profit shown in the profit and loss account, eg

	£	£
Factory profit	11,550	
Less increase in provision for unrealised profit	100	
		11,450

Alternatively, the increase can be shown as an expense in profit and loss account.

If there is a fall in the value of finished goods stock during the year, then there will be a decrease in the provision for unrealised profit, and this will be added to the factory profit shown in the profit and loss account, or shown separately as income.

In the balance sheet, the figure for finished goods stocks at 31 December 20-2 shows the net value, ie:

Current Assets	£	£
Stock of finished goods	8,250	
Less Provision for unrealised profit	750	
Net value		7,500

As can be seen this reduces the closing stock value of finished goods to cost price, and enables the balance sheet valuation to comply with SSAP 9 and the concept of prudence.

calculating the figures for unrealised profit

When we are told a figure for stock which includes unrealised profit, how do we work out the amount of unrealised profit?

The calculation is as follows:

$$\textit{stock figure (including unrealised profit)} \quad \times \quad \frac{\textit{profit percentage}}{100 + \textit{profit percentage}}$$

For example, stock of £7,150 includes a manufacturing profit of 10 per cent:

$$£7{,}150 \times \frac{10}{100 + 10} = £650 \textit{ unrealised profit}$$

Thus the stock without the manufacturing profit is

$$£7{,}150 - £650 = £6{,}500$$

This can, of course, be calculated as follows:

$$£7{,}150 \times \frac{100}{100 + 10} = £6{,}500$$

CHAPTER SUMMARY

- A manufacturing account brings together all the elements of cost which make up production (or manufacturing) cost.

- A manufacturing account shows prime cost and the production (or manufacturing) cost:
  - the prime cost is the total of all direct costs.
  - the production (or manufacturing) cost is the total of direct costs and production overheads, ie prime cost plus production overheads.

- Manufacturing businesses usually have three types of stock:
  - raw materials
  - work-in-progress
  - finished goods

- The total value of all three kinds of stock is shown on the balance sheet of a manufacturing business.

- Raw materials and work-in-progress remain in the factory and are therefore dealt with in the manufacturing account:

opening stock of raw materials + purchases – closing stock of raw materials
= cost of raw materials used

total production cost + cost of the opening work-in-progress – cost of the closing work-in-progress
= production cost of finished goods

- Finished goods are transferred from the factory to the warehouse: their cost of production is similarly transferred from the manufacturing account to the trading account. A transfer price can be used to enable a factory to earn a notional profit.

- In the trading account, the cost of sales or 'cost of goods sold' is calculated as follows:

	opening stock of finished goods
add	*production cost of finished goods*
less	*closing stock of finished goods*

- The profit and loss account deals with non-production costs, such as warehouse and office costs.

QUESTIONS

NOTE: an asterisk (*) after the question number means that an answer to the question is given at the end of this book.

28.1* Allocate the following costs to

- manufacturing account
- profit and loss account

(a) factory rent

(b) production supervisors' wages

(c) insurance of factory buildings

(d) depreciation of office photocopier

(e) sales commission

(f) raw materials purchased

(g) advertising

28.2* The following figures relate to the accounts of Barbara Francis, who operates a furniture manufacturing business, for the year ended 31 December 20-8:

	£
Stocks of raw materials, 1 January 20-8	31,860
Stocks of raw materials, 31 December 20-8	44,790
Stocks of finished goods, 1 January 20-8	42,640
Stocks of finished goods, 31 December 20-8	96,510
Purchases of raw materials	237,660
Sale of finished goods	796,950
Rent and rates	32,920
Manufacturing wages	234,630
Manufacturing power	7,650
Manufacturing heat and light	2,370
Manufacturing sundry expenses and maintenance	8,190
Salaries	138,700
Advertising	22,170
Office expenses	7,860
Depreciation of manufacturing plant and machinery	7,450

Rent and rates are to be 75% to manufacturing and 25% to administration.

You are to prepare manufacturing and profit and loss accounts for the year-ended 31 December 20-8, to show clearly:

- cost of raw materials used
- prime cost
- cost of production (factory) overheads
- production cost of goods completed
- cost of sales
- gross profit for the year
- net profit for the year

Explain, by memorandum, to Miss Francis why you have presented the accounts in such a form, and what they show.

28.3* Noriv plc is a manufacturing business. The following figures have been extracted from the company's ledgers as at 31 May 2003.

		£
Stocks as at 1 June 2002:	raw materials	21,450
	work-in-progress	14,780
	finished goods	58,620
Sales		657,000
Purchases of raw materials		234,090
Direct labour costs		260,000
Indirect labour costs		82,800
Factory overheads (excluding labour costs)		138,000
Manufacturing royalties		6,560
Returns inwards		1,000
Returns outwards		980
Carriage inwards		750
Carriage outwards		1,340

Additional information:

- At 31 May 2003 stocks were valued as follows:

	£
Raw materials	22,170
Work-in-progress	13,750
Finished goods	60,650

- At 31 May 2003 factory wages accrued and unpaid amounted to £8,000. One-quarter of this was for indirect labour and the remainder was for direct labour.
- Depreciation of factory machinery for the year was £25,000.

REQUIRED

(a) Selecting from the information given, prepare an extract from the manufacturing account for the year ended 31 May 2003 to show prime cost.

(b) Explain what is meant by 'work-in-progress'.

Assessment and Qualifications Alliance (AQA), 2003

28.4

Jacqui King plc is a manufacturing business. The following figures have been extracted from the company's books of account as at 30 November 2001.

		£
Stocks as at 1 December 2000:	raw materials	47,600
	work-in-progress	23,000
	finished goods	76,400
Sales		3,780,000
Purchases of raw materials		498,000
Factory overheads (excluding labour costs)		548,000
Factory labour costs		959,400
Office salaries		365,000
Royalties		17,000
Provisions for depreciation:	factory machinery	48,000
	delivery vehicles	56,000
	office equipment	11,000

Additional information:

- At 30 November 2001 stocks were valued as follows:

	£
Raw materials at cost	50,900
Work-in-progress at cost	24,100
Finished goods at cost	79,200

- Factory labour costs are apportioned:
  2/3 to direct labour, and
  1/3 to indirect labour

REQUIRED

(a) Prepare the manufacturing account for the year ended 30 November 2001 for Jacqui King plc, selecting from the information given.

The account should show clearly the totals for raw materials consumed, prime cost and total production cost.

(b) Explain the term 'royalties'.

Assessment and Qualifications Alliance (AQA), 2002

28.5*

Cheung Lee runs a business which manufactures garden chairs. He transfers the production cost of completed chairs from the manufacturing account to the trading account at cost plus 25%.

Cheung provides you with the following information for the year ended 31 December 20-8:

	1 January 20-8	*31 December 20-8*
Stock of finished goods at cost plus 25%	£56,000	£60,500

Provision for unrealised profit at 1 January 20-8 was £11,200.

REQUIRED

(a) Calculate the adjustment to the provision for unrealised profit to be shown in the profit and loss account for the year ended 31 December 20-8.

(b) Draw up a balance sheet extract at 31 December 20-8 which shows the treatment of the provision for unrealised profit calculated in (a).

(c) Explain why Cheung Lee makes a provision for unrealised profit in the final accounts.

28.6

Malcolm plc is a manufacturing company producing bathroom and kitchen tiles.

The tiles are transferred from the manufacturing account to the trading account at cost plus 25%.

The cost of finished goods at 31 December 2000 was £680,000.

Transfer price was £850,000.

Factory gross profit for the year was £170,000.

All stocks of finished goods are valued at the transfer price shown below.

	31 December 1999	*31 December 2000*
Stocks of finished goods	£20,000	£24,000

REQUIRED

(a) Calculate the provision for unrealised profit at

(i) 31 December 1999

(ii) 31 December 2000

(b) From your calculations, complete the entries for the year ended 31 December 2000.

Malcolm plc

Profit and loss account for the year ended 31 December 2000

	£
Factory gross profit	170,000
Provision for unrealised profit	______
Adjusted factory gross profit	______

Malcolm plc

Balance sheet as at 31 December 2000

	£
Current asset	
Stock of finished goods	
Provision for unrealised profit	______
Adjusted stock of finished goods	______

Assessment and Qualifications Alliance (AQA), 2001

28.7

Dewray plc manufactures bedroom furniture.

All completed furniture is transferred to the trading account at cost plus 20%.

The following figures have been extracted from the trial balance of the company as at 31 December 2002 after calculating prime cost.

		Dr	Cr
		£000	£000
Prime cost		1,207	
Factory overheads		915	
Factory machinery at cost		150	
Office equipment at cost		60	
Provision for depreciation	– factory machinery		90
	– office equipment		18
Provision for unrealised profit			26
Stocks as at 1 January 2002			
work-in-progress at cost		34	
finished goods at cost plus 20%		156	
Sales			3,460

Additional information:

- All fixed assets are depreciated at 10% per annum on cost.

		£000
• Stocks as at 31 December 2002 –	raw materials at cost	75
	work-in-progress at cost	36
	finished goods at cost plus 20%	192

REQUIRED

(a) Starting with the prime cost of £1,207,000, prepare a summarised manufacturing account for the year ended 31 December 2002.

(b) Prepare a trading account for the year ended 31 December 2002.

(c) Calculate the amount of the adjustment to the provision for unrealised profit to be shown in the profit and loss account for the year ended 31 December 2002.

The amount of the adjustment to the provision for unrealised profit to be shown in the profit and loss account is: £............................

(d) Explain how the amount calculated in (c) should be shown in the profit and loss account.

(e) Complete the following extract from the balance sheet.

Dewray plc

Balance sheet extract as at 31 December 2002

Current assets

Stock – raw materials ....

– work-in-progress ....

– finished goods ....

Assessment and Qualifications Alliance (AQA), 2003

28.8

Cathy Yow manufactures garden furniture. The following balances have been extracted from her books of account as at 31 December 2001.

		£
Stocks as at 1 January 2001:	raw materials at cost	9,000
	work-in-progress at cost	3,000
	finished goods at cost plus 25%	8,750
Purchases of raw materials		63,600
Direct labour costs		146,800
Factory overhead costs		106,790
Administrative expenses		140,500
Manufacturing royalties		8,140
Sales		568,720
Plant and machinery at cost		400,000
Provision for depreciation of plant and machinery 1 January 2001		160,000
Office equipment at cost		115,000
Provision for depreciation of office equipment 1 January 2001		75,000
Provision for unrealised profit 1 January 2001		1,750

Additional information:

- Factory output is transferred to the trading account at factory cost plus 25%.
- Stocks as at 31 December 2001 were valued as follows:

	£
raw materials at cost	9,400
work-in-progress at cost	3,100
finished goods at cost plus 25%	9,250

- Direct labour costs accrued at 31 December 2001 amounted to £3,450.

REQUIRED

(a) Prepare the prime cost section **only** of the manufacturing account for the year ended 31 December 2001 for Cathy Yow, selecting from the information given.

(b) Calculate the amount to be charged to the profit and loss account for the adjustment to the provision for unrealised gross profit.

The adjustment is £............................

(c) Explain why Cathy needs to make provision for unrealised profit in her final accounts.

Assessment and Qualifications Alliance (AQA), 2002

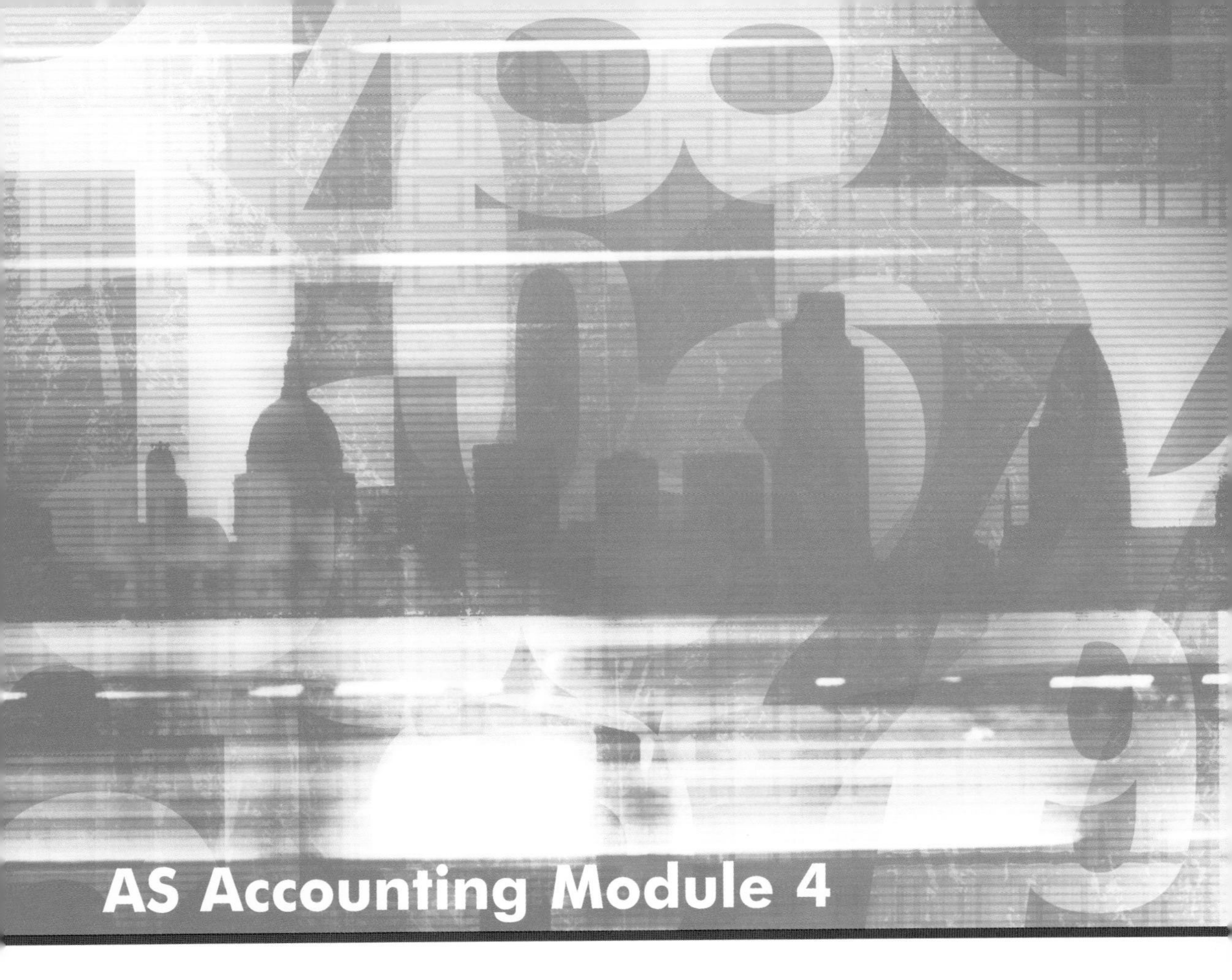

AS Accounting Module 4

Introduction to Accounting for Management and Decision-making

This Module for AQA AS Accounting introduces some of the ways in which accounting information can provide valuable information for measuring and monitoring business performance, and for planning and decision-making. It covers:

- ratio analysis and the assessment of business performance
- types of costs, marginal costing, contribution
- break-even analysis
- budgeting and budgetary control
- factors affecting decision-making and social accounting

29 RATIO ANALYSIS

Ratio analysis is the technique of interpreting the final accounts of businesses in order to assess strengths and weaknesses. A business needs to be performing well in areas of profitability, liquidity, and asset utilisation.

In this chapter we examine:

- the importance of interpretation of final accounts
- the main accounting ratios and performance indicators
- the difference between profit and cash
- a commentary on trends shown by the main accounting ratios
- how to report on the overall financial situation of a business
- limitations in the interpretation of accounts

Interested Parties

The use of ratio analysis to interpret accounts is not always made by an accountant; interested parties include:

- managers or owners of the business, who need to make financial decisions affecting the future development of the business
- the bank manager, who is being asked to lend money to finance the business
- creditors, who wish to assess the likelihood of receiving payment
- customers, who wish to be assured of continuity of supplies in the future
- shareholders of a limited company, who wish to be assured that their investment is sound
- prospective investors in a limited company, who wish to compare comparative strengths and weaknesses
- the owner of a business, who wishes to make comparisons with other businesses
- employees and trade unions, who wish to check on the financial prospects of the business
- HM Revenue & Customs, that wishes to check it is receiving the amount due for VAT and the tax payable on the profits of the business

In all of these cases, the interested party will be able to calculate the main ratios, percentages and performance indicators. By doing this, the strengths and weaknesses of the business will be highlighted and appropriate conclusions can be drawn.

The diagram on page 346, in Module 2, shows some of the users of accounts and what they are interested in.

TYPES OF ACCOUNTING RATIOS AND PERFORMANCE INDICATORS

The general term 'accounting ratios' is usually used to describe the calculations aspect of interpretation of accounts. The term ratio is, in fact, partly misleading because the performance indicators include percentages, time periods, as well as ratios in the strict sense of the word.

The main themes covered by ratio analysis are:

- profitability, the relationship between profit and sales turnover, assets and capital employed
- liquidity, which considers the stability of the business on a short-term basis
- asset utilisation, the effective and efficient use of assets

MAKING USE OF RATIO ANALYSIS

It is important when examining a set of final accounts and using ratio analysis to relate them to reference points or standards. These points of reference might be to:

- establish trends from past years, so providing a standard of comparison
- compare against other businesses in the same industry
- compare with standards assumed to be satisfactory by the interested party, eg a bank

Above all, it is important to understand the relationships between ratios: one ratio may give an indication of the state of the business but, before drawing conclusions, this needs to be supported by other ratios. Ratios can indicate symptoms, but the cause will then need to be investigated.

Another use of ratios is to estimate forward the likely profit or balance sheet of a business. For example, it might be assumed that the same gross profit percentage as last year will also apply next year; thus, given an estimated increase in sales, it is a simple matter to estimate gross profit. In a similar way, by making use of ratios, net profit and the balance sheet can be forecast.

Look first at the illustration on the next two pages. It shows the ways in which the profitability of a business is assessed. Then read the section 'Profitability' which follows on page 490.

PROFITABILITY RATIOS

Gross profit margin = $\frac{\text{Gross profit}}{\text{Sales turnover}} \times \frac{100}{1}$

Gross profit mark-up = $\frac{\text{Gross profit}}{\text{Cost of sales}} \times \frac{100}{1}$

Overheads/sales margin = $\frac{\text{Overheads}}{\text{Sales turnover}} \times \frac{100}{1}$

Net profit margin = $\frac{\text{Net profit}}{\text{Sales turnover}} \times \frac{100}{1}$

Return on capital employed = $\frac{\text{Net profit}}{\text{Capital employed*}} \times \frac{100}{1}$

* limited companies: ordinary share capital + reserves + preference share capital + debentures/long-term loans

sole traders: the owner's capital in the business

Mithian Trading Company Limited

TRADING AND PROFIT AND LOSS ACCOUNT

for the year ended 31 December 20-7

	£000s	£000s
Sales		1,430
Opening stock	200	
Purchases	1,000	
	1,200	
Less Closing stock	240	
Cost of sales		960
Gross profit		470
Less **overheads**:		
Selling expenses	160	
Administration expenses	140	
		300
Net profit for year before taxation		170
Less: Corporation tax		50
Profit for year after taxation		120
Less:		
preference dividend paid	25	
ordinary dividend proposed	75	
		100
Retained profit for the year		20
Add balance of retained profits at beginning of year		180
Balance of retained profits at end of year		200

BALANCE SHEET (extract)

Capital employed (share capital + reserves + long-term liabilities)	1,550

Notes: Items used in the ratios on the opposite page are shown in bold type on a blue background

PROFITABILITY

One of the main objectives of a business is to make a profit. Profitability ratios examine the relationship between profit and sales turnover, and capital employed. Before calculating the profitability ratios, it is important to read the profit and loss account in order to review the figures.

The key profitability ratios are illustrated on the previous two pages. We will be calculating the accounting ratios from these figures in the Worked Example (pages 499 - 503).

gross profit margin

$$\frac{\textit{Gross profit}}{\textit{Sales turnover}} \times \frac{100}{1}$$

This ratio expresses, as a percentage, the gross profit (sales minus cost of sales) in relation to sales turnover. For example, a gross profit margin of 20 per cent means that for every £100 of sales made, the gross profit is £20.

The gross profit margin should be similar from year-to-year for the same business. It will vary between different types of businesses, eg the gross profit margin on jewellery is considerably higher than that on food. A significant change from one year to the next, particularly a fall in the percentage, requires investigation into the buying and selling prices.

Gross profit margin and mark-up (see below) – and also net profit margin (see next page) – need to be considered in context. For example, a supermarket may well have a lower gross profit margin than a small corner shop but, because of the supermarket's much higher sales turnover, the amount of profit will be much higher. Whatever the type of business, gross profit – both as an amount and a percentage – needs to be sufficient to cover the overheads (expenses), and then to give an acceptable return on capital employed (see page 492).

gross profit mark-up

$$\frac{\textit{Gross profit}}{\textit{Cost of sales}} \times \frac{100}{1}$$

This ratio expresses, as a percentage, the gross profit in relation to cost of sales. For example, a gross profit mark-up of 25 per cent means that for every £100 of purchases made, the gross profit is £25. Gross profit mark-up should be similar from year-to-year for the same business, although it will vary between different types of businesses. Any significant change needs investigation into the buying and selling prices.

It is quite common for a business to establish its selling price by reference to either a margin or a mark-up. The difference between the two is that:

- margin is a percentage profit based on the selling price
- mark-up is a profit percentage added to buying or cost price

For example, a product is bought by a retailer for £100; the retailer sells it for £125, ie

cost price	+	gross profit	=	selling price
£100	+	£25	=	£125

The **margin** is:

$$\frac{\text{gross profit}}{\text{selling price}} \times \frac{100}{1} = \frac{£25}{£125} \times \frac{100}{1} = \mathbf{20\%}$$

The **mark-up** is:

$$\frac{\text{gross profit}}{\text{cost price}} \times \frac{100}{1} = \frac{£25}{£100} \times \frac{100}{1} = \mathbf{25\%}$$

Notice here that gross profit margin and mark-up look at the same information, but from a different viewpoint: with margin, it is the gross profit related to the selling price; with mark-up, it is the gross profit related to the buying price (cost of sales).

overheads/sales margin

$$\frac{\textit{Overheads}}{\textit{Sales turnover}} \times \frac{100}{1}$$

Here the overheads (expenses) of a business are expressed as a percentage of sales turnover. The ratio should fall as sales turnover increases – this is because not all overheads are variable, ie increase in direct proportion to the increase in sales turnover. As we will see in the next chapter each overhead or expense falls into one of three categories of cost:

- fixed costs, or
- variable costs, or
- semi-variable costs

Fixed costs remain constant despite other changes. Variable costs alter with changed circumstances, such as increased output or sales. Semi-variable costs combine both a fixed and a variable element, eg hire of a car at a basic (fixed) cost, with a variable cost per mile. It is important to appreciate the nature of costs when interpreting accounts: for example, if sales this year are twice last year's figure, not all expenses will have doubled.

Any large overhead item from profit and loss account can be expressed as a percentage of sales turnover. For example, if advertising is £50,000 and turnover is £500,000 then the percentage is 10 per cent; if it is found to be 20 per cent next year then this could indicate that an increase in advertising has failed to produce a proportionate increase in sales.

net profit margin

$$\frac{\textit{Net profit}}{\textit{Sales turnover}} \times \frac{100}{1}$$

As with gross profit margin, the net profit margin should be similar from year-to-year for the same business, and should also be comparable with other firms in the same line of business. Net profit margin should, ideally, increase from year-to-year, which indicates that the profit and loss account costs are being kept under control. Any significant fall should be investigated to see if it has been caused by

- a fall in gross profit margin
- and/or an increase in one particular expense, eg wages and salaries, advertising, etc

return on capital employed (ROCE)

This expresses the profit of a business in relation to the amount of capital invested in the business by the owner. The percentage return is best thought of in relation to other investments, eg a bank might offer a return of five per cent on a savings account. A person running a business is investing a sum of money in that business, and the profit is the return that is achieved on that investment. However, it should be noted that the risks in running a business are considerably greater than depositing the money with a bank, and an additional return to allow for the extra risk is needed.

For limited companies, the calculation of return on capital employed must take note of their methods of financing. It is necessary to distinguish between the ordinary shareholders' investment (the equity) and the capital employed by the company, which includes preference shares and debentures/long-term loans:

	Ordinary share capital
add	*Reserves (capital and revenue)*
equals	*Equity*
add	*Preference share capital*
add	*Debentures/long-term loans*
equals	*Capital Employed*

The reason for including preference shares and debentures/long-term loans in the capital employed is that the company has the use of the money from these contributors for the foreseeable future, or certainly for a fixed time period.

The calculation of return on capital employed is:

$$\frac{\text{Net profit}}{\text{Capital employed*}} \times \frac{100}{1}$$

* *limited companies: ordinary share capital + reserves + preference share capital + debentures/long-term loans*

sole traders: the amount of the owner's capital in the business

the difference between profit and cash

This section has looked at the profitability of a business, ie the ability of the business to generate profit. Many people who use accounts are also interested in cash flows, ie the ability to generate cash. There is an important difference between profit and cash – it is possible to have a highly profitable company that is using more cash than it is generating so that its bank balance is falling (or its overdraft is increasing). Liquidity (which we shall be looking at in the next section) is important: it is often a lack of cash (a lack of liquidity) that causes most businesses to fail.

To distinguish between cash and profit:

- **cash** is the actual amount of money held in the bank or as cash
- **profit** is a calculated figure which shows the surplus of income over expenditure for the year; it takes note of adjustments for accruals and prepayments and non-cash items such as depreciation and provision for doubtful debts.

Various transactions have an unequal effect on cash and profit as shown in the following diagram:

Effect on profit		**Transaction**	**Effect on cash**	
increase	decrease		increase	decrease
		• purchase of fixed assets		✓
	✓	• depreciation of fixed assets		
	✓	• increase in provision for doubtful debts		
✓		• reduction in provision for doubtful debts		
		• issue of new shares	✓	
		• repayment of a loan		✓
		• raising of a loan	✓	
		• payment of dividends		✓

LIQUIDITY

Liquidity ratios measure the financial stability of the business, ie the ability of the business to pay its way on a short-term basis. For this we focus our attention on the current assets and current liabilities sections of the balance sheet.

The key liquidity ratios are shown linked to the balance sheet of Mithian Trading Company Limited on pages 494 and 495. The ratios are calculated in the Worked Example (pages 499 - 503).

continued on page 496

LIQUIDITY RATIOS

Working capital ratio* = $\frac{\text{Current assets}}{\text{Current liabilities}}$

* also known as the current ratio, or net current asset ratio

Liquid capital ratio* = $\frac{\text{Current assets} - \text{Stock}}{\text{Current liabilities}}$

* also known as the quick ratio, or acid test

ASSET UTILISATION RATIOS

Stock turnover (days) = $\frac{\text{Average stock*}}{\text{Cost of sales}} \times 365 \text{ days}$

* usually taken as: (opening stock + closing stock) ÷ 2; alternatively, if opening stock figure not available, use closing stock from the balance sheet in the calculation

Debtors' collection period (days) = $\frac{\text{Debtors}}{\text{Credit sales}} \times 365 \text{ days}$

Creditors' payment period (days) = $\frac{\text{Trade creditors}}{\text{Credit purchases}} \times 365 \text{ days}$

Fixed asset turnover ratio = $\frac{\text{Sales turnover}}{\text{Fixed assets}}$

Net current asset turnover ratio = $\frac{\text{Sales turnover}}{\text{Net current assets*}}$

* or working capital

Mithian Trading Company Limited

BALANCE SHEET

as at 31 December 20-7

	Cost	Prov for dep'n	Net book value
Fixed Assets	£000s	£000s	£000s
Premises	850	–	850
Fixtures and fittings	300	120	180
Vehicles	350	100	250
	1,500	220	1,280
Current Assets			
Stock		240	
Debtors		150	
Bank/cash		135	
		525	
Less **Current Liabilities**			
Creditors	130		
Proposed ordinary dividend	75		
Corporation tax	50		
		255	
Working Capital/Net Current Assets			270
			1,550
Less Long-term Liabilities			
10% Debentures			100
NET ASSETS			1,450
FINANCED BY			
Authorised and Issued Share Capital			
1,000,000 ordinary shares of £1 each, fully paid			1,000
250,000 10% preference shares of £1 each, fully paid			250
			1,250
Revenue Reserve			
Profit and loss account			200
SHAREHOLDERS' FUNDS			1,450

PROFIT AND LOSS ACCOUNT (extract)

Cost of sales	960
Credit sales	1,430
Credit purchases	1,000

Note: Items used in ratios are shown in bold type with a blue background.

working capital

Working capital = Current assets – Current liabilities

Working capital, or net current assets, is needed by all businesses in order to finance day-to-day trading activities. Sufficient working capital enables a business to hold adequate stocks, allow a measure of credit to its customers (debtors), and to pay its suppliers (creditors) as payments fall due.

working capital ratio (or current ratio, or net current asset ratio)

Working capital ratio = Current assets : Current liabilities

Working capital ratio uses figures from the balance sheet and measures the relationship between current assets and current liabilities. Although there is no ideal working capital ratio, an acceptable ratio is about 2:1, ie £2 of current assets to every £1 of current liabilities. However, a business in the retail trade may be able to work with a lower ratio, eg 1.5:1 or even less, because it deals mainly in sales for cash and so does not have a large figure for debtors. A working capital ratio can be too high: if it is above 3:1 an investigation of the make-up of current assets and current liabilities is needed: eg the business may have too much stock, too many debtors, or too much cash at the bank.

liquid capital ratio (or quick ratio, or acid test)

$$\text{Liquid capital ratio} = \frac{\text{Current assets} - \text{Stock}}{\text{Current liabilities}}$$

The liquid capital ratio uses the current assets and current liabilities from the balance sheet, but stock is omitted. This is because stock is the most illiquid current asset: it has to be sold, turned into debtors, and then the cash has to be collected from the debtors. Thus the liquid capital ratio provides a direct comparison between debtors/cash/bank and short-term liabilities. The balance between liquid assets, that is debtors and cash/bank, and current liabilities should, ideally, be about 1:1, ie £1 of liquid assets to each £1 of current liabilities. This means that a business is expected to be able to pay its current liabilities from its liquid assets; a figure below 1:1, eg 0.75:1, indicates that the firm would have difficulty in meeting pressing demands from creditors. However, as with the working capital ratio, some businesses are able to operate with a lower liquid capital ratio than others.

Asset Utilisation

Asset utilisation measures how effectively management controls the current aspects of the business – principally stock, debtors and creditors. Like all accounting ratios, comparison needs to be made either with figures for the previous year, or with a similar firm.

stock turnover

$$\frac{\text{Average stock}}{\text{Cost of sales}} \times 365 \text{ days}$$

Stock turnover is the number of days' stock held on average. This figure will depend on the type of goods sold by the business. For example, a market trader selling fresh flowers, who finishes each day when sold out, will have a stock turnover of one day. By contrast, a jewellery shop – because it may hold large stocks of jewellery – will have a much slower stock turnover, perhaps sixty or ninety days, or longer. Nevertheless, stock turnover must not be too long, bearing in mind the type of business. A business which is improving will seek to reduce the number of days' stock it holds, when comparing one year with the previous one, or with the stock turnover of similar businesses. This indicates that it is more efficient at managing its stocks.

Stock turnover can also be expressed as number of times per year:

$$\text{Stock turnover (times per year)} = \frac{\text{Cost of sales}}{\text{Average stock}}$$

A stock turnover of, say, twelve times a year means that about thirty days' stock is held. Note that stock turnover can only be calculated where a business buys and sells goods; it cannot be used for a business that provides a service.

debtors' collection period

$$\frac{\text{Debtors}}{\text{Credit sales}} \times 365 \text{ days}$$

This calculation shows how many days, on average, debtors take to pay for goods sold to them by the business. The figure of credit sales for the year may not be disclosed in the trading account, in which case the sales figure should be used. Some businesses make the majority of their sales on credit but others, such as shops, will have a considerably lower proportion of credit sales.

The debt collection time can be compared with that for the previous year, or with that of a similar business. In Britain, most debtors should make payment within about 30 days; however, sales made abroad will take longer for the proceeds to be received. Over time, a business will seek to reduce the debtors' collection period, showing that it is more efficient at collecting the money that is due to it.

creditors' payment period

$$\frac{\text{Trade creditors}}{\text{Credit purchases}} \times 365 \text{ days}$$

This calculation is the opposite aspect to that of debtors: here we are measuring the speed it takes to pay creditors. While creditors can be a useful temporary source of finance, delaying payment too long may cause problems. This ratio is most appropriate for businesses that buy and sell goods; it cannot be used for a business that provides a service; it is also difficult to interpret when a business buys in some goods and, at the same time, provides a service, eg an hotel. Generally, though, we would expect to see the creditor days period longer than the debtor days, ie money is being received from debtors before it is paid out to creditors. Over time, a business should seek to maintain the same creditors' payment period, and possibly increase it slightly if better terms can be negotiated with the creditors.

Tutorial note: Instead of in days, stock turnover, debtors' collection and creditors' payment periods can also be calculated in weeks or months. Instead of multiplying by 365, use 52 for weeks, or 12 for months.

asset turnover ratios

fixed asset turnover ratio

$$\frac{\textit{Sales turnover}}{\textit{Fixed assets}}$$

This ratio measures the efficiency of the use of fixed assets in generating sales turnover. An increasing ratio from one year to the next indicates greater efficiency. A fall in the ratio may be caused either by a decrease in sales, or an increase in fixed assets – as a result of the purchase or revaluation of fixed assets.

Different types of businesses may well have very different fixed asset turnover ratios. For example a supermarket, with high sales and relatively few fixed assets, will have a very high figure; by contrast, an engineering business, with lower sales and a substantial investment in fixed assets, will have a much lower figure.

net current asset turnover ratio

$$\frac{\textit{Sales turnover}}{\textit{Net current assets}}$$

This ratio measures the efficiency of the use of net current assets (or working capital) in generating sales turnover. As with the fixed asset turnover ratio, an increasing ratio from one year to the next indicates greater efficiency. A fall in the ratio may be caused by either a decrease in sales, or an increase in net current assets – perhaps as a result of a build-up of stock or increase in debtors (because of poor debtors' collection). Different businesses may well have different ratios – the supermarket and the engineering firm, mentioned in the previous paragraph, for example.

WORKED EXAMPLE: RATIO ANALYSIS

Ratio analysis is the calculation of a number of accounting ratios. Interpretation of accounts involves the analysis of the relationships between the figures in the accounts and the presentation of the information gathered in a meaningful way to interested parties.

In the example which follows, we will look at the set of accounts of a limited company. For clarity, one year's accounts are given although, in practice, more than one year's accounts should be used. The comments given indicate what should be looked for when analysing and interpreting a set of accounts.

situation

The following are the accounts of Mithian Trading Company Limited. The business trades in office supplies and sells to the public through three retail shops in its area; it also delivers direct to businesses in the area from its modern warehouse on a local business park.

Mithian Trading Company Limited
TRADING AND PROFIT AND LOSS ACCOUNT
for the year ended 31 December 20-7

	£000s	£000s
Sales		1,430
Opening stock	200	
Purchases	1,000	
	1,200	
Less Closing stock	240	
Cost of sales		960
Gross profit		470
Less overheads:		
Selling expenses	160	
Administration expenses	140	
		300
Net profit for year before taxation		170
Less: Corporation tax		50
Profit for year after taxation		120
Less:		
preference dividend paid	25	
ordinary dividend proposed	75	
		100
Retained profit for the year		20
Add balance of retained profits at beginning of year		180
Balance of retained profits at end of year		200

Mithian Trading Company Limited
BALANCE SHEET
as at 31 December 20-7

Fixed Assets	*Cost*	*Prov for dep'n*	*Net book value*
	£000s	£000s	£000s
Premises	850	–	850
Fixtures and fittings	300	120	180
Vehicles	350	100	250
	1,500	220	1,280
Current Assets			
Stock		240	
Debtors		150	
Bank/cash		135	
		525	
Less Current Liabilities			
Creditors	130		
Proposed ordinary dividend	75		
Corporation tax	50		
		255	
Working Capital/Net Current Assets			270
			1,550
Less Long-term Liabilities			
10% debentures			100
NET ASSETS			1,450
FINANCED BY			
Authorised and Issued Share Capital			
1,000,000 ordinary shares of £1 each, fully paid			1,000
250,000 10% preference shares of £1 each, fully paid			250
			1,250
Revenue Reserve			
Profit and loss account			200
SHAREHOLDERS' FUNDS			1,450

solution

We will now use ratio analysis to analyse the accounts from the point of view of a potential investor. All figures shown are in £000s.

PROFITABILITY

Gross profit margin

$$\frac{£470}{£1,430} \times \frac{100}{1} = 32.87\%$$

Gross profit mark-up

$$\frac{£470}{£960} \times \frac{100}{1} = 48.96\%$$

Overheads/sales margin

$$\frac{£300}{£1,430} \times \frac{100}{1} = 20.98\%$$

Net profit margin

$$\frac{£170}{£1,430} \times \frac{100}{1} = 11.89\%$$

Return on capital employed

$$\frac{£170}{£1,000 + £250 + £200 + £100} \times \frac{100}{1} = 10.97\%$$

The gross profit margin and mark-up, and net profit margin seem to be acceptable figures for the type of business, although comparisons should be made with those of the previous accounting period. A business should always aim at least to hold its margins and mark-up with, ideally, a small improvement. A significant fall may indicate a poor buying policy, poor pricing (perhaps caused by competition), and the causes should be investigated.

Overheads seem to be quite a high percentage of sales – comparisons need to be made with previous years to see if they are increasing. As they are likely to be a relatively fixed cost, it would seem that the business could increase sales turnover without a corresponding increase in sales overheads.

Return on capital employed is satisfactory, but could be better. At 10.97% return on capital employed is less than one percentage point above the ten per cent cost of the preference shares and debentures.

LIQUIDITY

Working capital ratio

$$\frac{£525}{£255} = 2.06:1$$

Liquid capital ratio

$$\frac{(£525 - £240)}{£255} = 1.12:1$$

The working capital and liquid capital ratios are excellent: they are slightly higher than the expected 'norms' of 2:1 and 1:1 respectively (although many companies operate successfully with lower ratios); however, they are not too high which would be an indication of inefficient use of assets.

All-in-all, the company is very liquid, with no problems in this area.

ASSET UTILISATION

Stock turnover

$$\frac{(£200 + £240) \div 2 \times 365}{£960} = 83.6 \text{ days (or 4.36 times per year)}$$

Debtors' collection period

$$\frac{£150 \times 365}{£1,430} = 38.3 \text{ days}$$

Creditors' payment period

$$\frac{£130 \times 365}{£1,000} = 47.5 \text{ days}$$

Fixed asset turnover ratio

$$\frac{£1,430}{£1,280} = 1.12:1$$

Net current asset turnover ratio

$$\frac{£1,430}{£270} = 5.30:1$$

This group of ratios shows the main weakness of the company: not enough business is passing through for the size of the company. Stock turnover is very low for an office supplies business: the stock is turning over only every 83 days – surely it should be faster than this. Debtors' collection period is acceptable on the face of it – 30 days would be better – but quite a volume of the sales will be made through the retail outlets in cash. This amount should, if known, be deducted from the sales turnover before calculating the debtors' collection period: thus the collection period is, in reality, longer than that calculated. Creditors' payment period is quite leisurely for this type of business – long delays could cause problems with suppliers in the future.

The asset turnover ratios show the value of sales generated by each £1 of fixed assets and net current assets. Both seem very low, particularly where each £1 of fixed assets provides just £1.12 of sales. This type of business should be able to obtain much better figures than this.

CONCLUSION

This appears to be a profitable business, although there may be some scope for cutting down somewhat on the profit and loss account overheads. The business offers a reasonable return on capital employed, although things could be improved.

The company is liquid and has good working capital and liquid capital ratios.

The main area of weakness is in asset utilisation. It appears that the company could do much to reduce the days for stock turnover and the debtors' collection period; at the same time creditors could be paid faster. Asset turnover ratios are very low for this type of business. It does seem that there is much scope for expansion within the structure of the existing company. As the benefits of expansion flow through to the final accounts, the ratios will show an improvement from their present leisurely performance.

LIMITATIONS IN THE USE OF RATIO ANALYSIS

Although ratio analysis can usefully highlight strengths and weaknesses, it should always be considered as a part of the overall assessment of a business, rather than as a whole. We have already seen the need to place ratios in context and relate them to a reference point or standard. The limitations of ratio analysis should always be borne in mind.

retrospective nature of ratio analysis

Accounting ratios are usually retrospective, based on previous performance and conditions prevailing in the past. They may not necessarily be valid for making forward projections: for example, a large customer may become insolvent, so threatening the business with a bad debt, and also reducing sales in the future.

differences in accounting policies

When the accounts of a business are compared, either with previous years' figures, or with figures from a similar business, there is a danger that the comparative accounts are not drawn up on the same basis as those currently being worked on. Different accounting policies, in respect of depreciation and stock valuation for instance, may well result in distortion and invalid comparisons.

inflation

Inflation may prove a problem, as most financial statements are prepared on an historic cost basis, that is, assets and liabilities are recorded at their original cost. As a result, comparison of figures from one year to the next may be difficult. In countries where inflation is running at high levels any form of comparison becomes practically meaningless.

reliance on standards

We have already mentioned guideline standards for some accounting ratios, for instance 2:1 for the working capital ratio. There is a danger of relying too heavily on such suggested standards, and ignoring other factors in the balance sheet. An example of this would be to criticise a business for having a low current ratio when the business sells the majority of its goods for cash and consequently has a very low debtors figure: this would in fact be the case with many well-known and successful retail companies. Large manufacturing businesses are able to operate with lower working capital ratios because of their good reputation and creditworthiness.

other considerations

Economic: The general economic climate and the effect this may have on the nature of the business, eg in an economic downturn retailers are usually the first to suffer, whereas manufacturers feel the effects later.

State of the business: The chairman's report for a limited company should be read in conjunction with the final accounts to ascertain an overall view of the state of the business. Of great importance are the products of the company and their stage in the product life cycle, eg is a car manufacturer relying on old models, or is there an up-to-date product range which appeals to buyers?

Comparing like with like: Before making comparisons between 'similar' businesses we need to ensure that we are comparing 'like with like'. Differences, such as the acquisition of assets – renting premises compared with ownership, leasing vehicles compared with ownership – will affect the profitability of the business and the structure of the balance sheet; likewise, the long-term financing of a business – the balance between share capital/owner's capital and loans – will also have an effect.

CHAPTER SUMMARY

The key accounting ratios are summarised in this chapter on pages 488 and 494.

- Ratio analysis uses numerical values – percentages, time periods, ratios – extracted from the final accounts of businesses.
- Accounting ratios can be used to measure:
  - profitability
  - liquidity
  - asset utilisation
- Comparisons need to be made with previous final accounts, or those of similar companies.
- There are a number of limitations to be borne in mind when drawing conclusions from accounting ratios:
  - retrospective nature, based on past performance
  - differences in accounting policies
  - effects of inflation when comparing year-to-year
  - reliance on standards
  - economic and other factors

QUESTIONS

NOTE: an asterisk (*) after the question number means that an answer to the question is given at the end of this book.

29.1* The following information is taken from the profit and loss accounts of two plcs:

	Amero plc	Britz plc
	£m	£m
Sales	55.7	32.3
Cost of sales	(49.1)	(20.2)
GROSS PROFIT	6.6	12.1
Overheads	(5.0)	(7.4)
NET PROFIT BEFORE TAX	1.6	4.7
Note: Capital employed	£8.8m	£34.3m

You are to calculate, for each company:

- gross profit margin
- gross profit mark-up
- net profit margin
- return on capital employed

29.2* The following is taken from the balance sheets of two plcs:

	Cawston plc	Dunley plc
	£m	£m
Stock	3.8	4.1
Debtors	4.5	0.7
Bank/(bank overdraft)	(0.4)	6.3
Creditors	5.1	10.7
Long-term loans	3.2	2.1
Ordinary share capital	4.5	8.4
Reserves	1.4	4.7
Notes:		
Sales for year	43.9	96.3
Purchases for year	32.4	85.1
Cost of sales for year	33.6	84.7

You are to calculate, for each company:

- working capital ratio
- liquid capital ratio
- debtors' collection period

- creditors' payment period
- stock turnover

One company runs department stores, the other is a chemical manufacturer. Which is which? Why is this?

29.3

The following information relates to two businesses, Exton and Frimley:

	Exton	Frimley
	£000s	£000s
PROFIT AND LOSS ACCOUNT (EXTRACTS)		
Sales	3,057	1,628
Cost of sales	2,647	911
Gross profit	410	717
Overheads	366	648
Net profit	44	69

	Exton		Frimley	
	£000s	£000s	£000s	£000s
SUMMARISED BALANCE SHEETS				
Fixed Assets		344		555
Current Assets				
Stock	242		237	
Debtors	6		269	
Bank	3		1	
	251		507	
Less Current Liabilities	195		212	
Working Capital/Net Current Assets		56		295
NET ASSETS		400		850
FINANCED BY				
Capital		400		850

One business operates a supermarket; the other is an engineering company. You are to calculate the following accounting ratios for both businesses:

(a) gross profit margin

(b) gross profit mark-up

(c) net profit margin

(d) stock turnover (use balance sheet figure as average stock)

(e) working capital ratio

(f) liquid capital ratio

(g) debtors' collection period

(h) return on capital employed

Indicate which business you believe to be the supermarket and which the engineering company. Briefly explain the reasons for your choice based on the ratios calculated and the accounting information.

29.4 Distinguish between the following terms:

(a) gross profit margin and gross profit mark-up

(b) working capital and liquid capital

(c) fixed asset turnover ratio and net current asset turnover ratio

(d) cash and profit

29.5* The following figures are extracted from the trial balance of Haque Limited as at 31 December 20-8:

	Dr	Cr
	£	£
Credit sales		96,000
Credit purchases	56,000	
Stock at 1 January 20-8	8,400	
Debtors	10,250	
Trade creditors		6,000
Bank		1,865
Cash	450	

Notes:

- Stock at 31 December 20-8 was valued at £5,200
- A debtor who owes £2,450 has gone into liquidation and is not expected to be able to pay off any of the debt. No adjustment has been made for this in the above figures.

REQUIRED

(a) Define the terms:

- working capital
- liquid capital

(b) State the formula to be used for:
- working capital ratio
- acid test ratio
- debtors' collection period
- creditors' payment period

(c) Calculate the following for Haque Limited (showing your workings to two decimal places):
- working capital ratio
- acid test ratio
- debtors' collection period
- creditors' payment period

(d) Assess the effect on the liquidity and liquidity ratios of Haque Limited of
- writing off the debt for £2,450
- reducing the value of stock over the year

29.6 Season Suppliers Ltd sell Christmas gifts. The following information is available for the last two years.

	As at 31 October 2001	**As at 31 October 2002**
	£	£
Trade debtors	43,000	32,550
Trade creditors	28,500	38,500
	For the year ended 31 October 2001	**For the year ended 31 October 2002**
Credit sales	680,000	660,000
Credit purchases	520,000	540,000

REQUIRED

(a) State the formula for the debtor collection period.

(b) State the formula for the creditor payment period.

(c) Calculate the debtor collection periods in days for the years ended 31 October 2001 and 31 October 2002. Show your workings.

(d) Calculate the creditor payment periods in days for the years ended 31 October 2001 and 31 October 2002. Show your workings.

(e) Briefly evaluate Season Suppliers Ltd's management of credit control. Base your answers on your calculations from (c) and (d).

Assessment and Qualifications Alliance (AQA), 2003

29.7 The following accounting ratios have been calculated for two different businesses for the year ended 30 June 20-7:

	Green Ltd	Hawke Ltd
Working capital ratio	1.1:1	1.8:1
Acid test ratio	0.6:1	0.9:1
Net profit margin	3%	12%
Stock turnover	20 times	5 times
Return on capital employed	3%	6%

One business is a supermarket; the other is a furniture store.

REQUIRED

(a) State the formula used to calculate each accounting ratio.

(b) Indicate which business you believe to be the supermarket and which the furniture store. Briefly explain the reasons for your choice based on the ratio analysis.

(c) Write a note to the owner of Green Limited suggesting two ways in which the performance of the business could be improved.

30 COSTS AND CONTRIBUTION

In this chapter and the next three chapters we focus on a different type of accounting from that which we have studied so far. Until now this book has concentrated on financial accounting, which processes financial information through the accounting records to produce final accounts. In this chapter we begin to study cost accounting, which produces reports for managers and directors to help with making decisions, and planning and control of the business.

In the chapter we shall cover:

- the purpose of cost accounting
- the differences between cost accounting and financial accounting
- the terms direct costs and indirect costs
- the nature of costs – fixed, semi-variable and variable
- marginal costing
- the calculation of contribution and how it can be used in management decision-making

PURPOSE OF COST ACCOUNTING

Cost accounting, as its name implies, enables the managers of a business to know the cost of the firm's output – whether a product or a service – and the revenues from sales. Once costing information is available, managers can use it to assist with

- decision-making
- planning for the future
- control of expenditure

Cost accounting is widely used by all types of businesses – the cost of a hospital operation, the cost of building a new hospital ward, the cost of tuition to a student, the cost of a swim at a sports centre, the cost of a passenger's bus journey, the cost of a new road are all just as important as the cost of making a product. A business – whether it provides a service or makes a product – needs to keep its costs under review; in order to do this it needs accurate cost information. Thus cost accounting will provide answers to questions such as:

What does it cost us to provide a student with a day's accountancy course?

What does it cost us to carry out a hip replacement operation?

What does it cost us to make a pair of trainers?

What does it cost us to serve a cheeseburger and fries?

What does it cost us to provide a week's holiday in the Canaries?

Cost accounting helps managers with production planning and decision-making, such as:

- short-term decisions, eg "how many do we need to make and sell in order to break-even?"
- long-term decisions, eg "we need to buy a new machine for the factory – shall we buy Machine Exe or Machine Wye?"

COST ACCOUNTING AND FINANCIAL ACCOUNTING

Cost accounting and financial accounting are two types of accounting which, although they produce different reports and statements, obtain their information from the same set of transactions carried out by the business over a given period. The following diagram illustrates these two types of accounting.

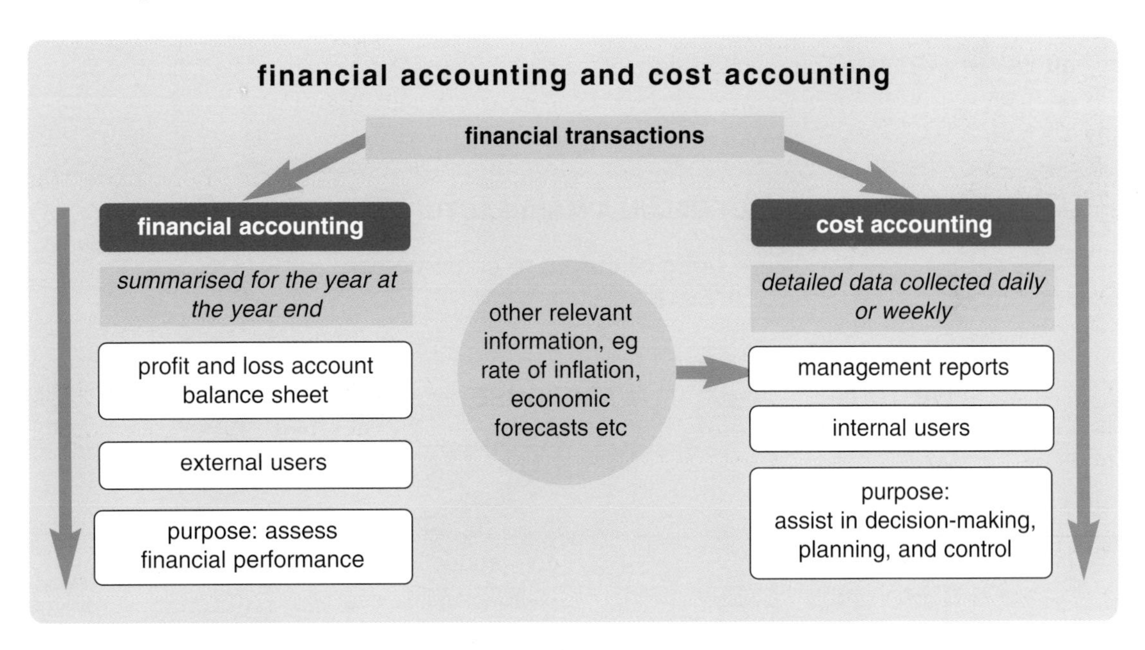

Financial accounting uses the financial information relating to transactions carried out over a period of time. The information is processed through the accounting records and extracted in the form of final accounts – trading and profit and loss account, and balance sheet. The statements are often required to be produced by law, eg the Companies Act, and are available to external users such as shareholders, creditors, bank, Inland Revenue, Companies House.

Cost accounting uses the same data to produce reports containing financial information on the recent past and projections for the future. The reports are available to internal users only, such as managers, directors, and owners (but not to shareholders generally). There is no legal requirement to produce this information and the content of the report and the principles used can be suited to the activities of the business and the requirements of its managers. The information is prepared as frequently as it is required, and speed is often vital as the information may go out-of-date very quickly.

CLASSIFICATION OF COSTS

Within any business, whether it manufactures a product or provides a service, there are certain costs involved at various stages to produce the units of output. The diagram below shows the costs of a manufacturing business (see also Chapter 28) which are incurred by the three main sections or 'areas' of a manufacturing business.

These three separate sections are:

- **factory** – where production takes place and the product is 'finished' and made ready for selling
- **warehouse** – where finished goods are stored and from where they are despatched when they are sold
- **office** – where the support functions take place – marketing, sales, administration, finance and so on

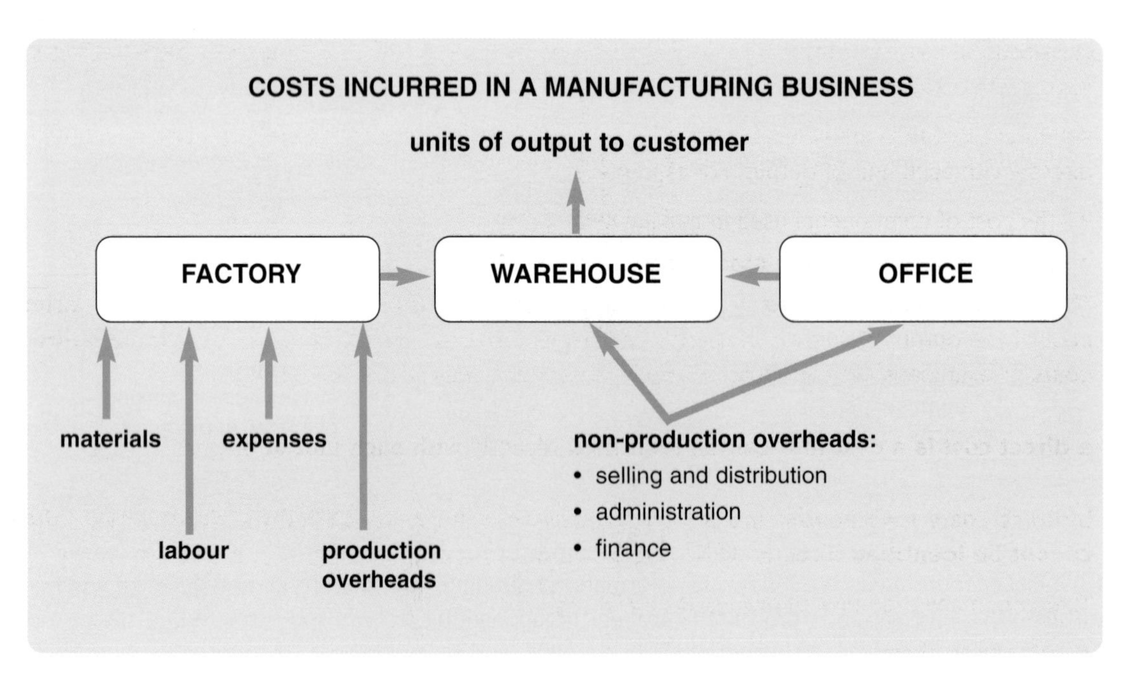

Note that while the diagram above shows the costs of a manufacturing business, it can be adapted easily to fit non-manufacturing businesses and organisations, such as a shop, a hospital, a school or college, a church, a club. While the units of output of these organisations differ from those of a manufacturer, nevertheless they still incur costs at various stages of the 'production' process.

In order to prepare information for the managers of a business, costs must be **classified**, ie organised into sets in a way which the managers will find useful. We will look at how costs can be classified in two ways:

- by element, which focuses on direct costs and indirect costs
- by nature, which focuses on fixed costs, semi-variable costs and variable costs

CLASSIFICATION OF COSTS BY ELEMENT

Businesses and organisations incur many different kinds of cost in the production of goods or 'output', including costs of the warehouse and the office. The most basic way of splitting up costs is according to the type of expenditure under the headings:

- **materials**, eg the components to make a car
- **labour**, eg wages of an employee
- **expenses**, eg rent and rates, telephone charges, insurance

Note: materials, labour, and expenses are often referred to as the three elements of cost.

Splitting costs into these three elements applies to both manufacturing and service businesses. The classification provides important information to managers as they can see the breakdown of the total into different kinds of cost.

Within each of the three elements of materials, labour and expenses, some costs can be identified directly with each unit of output. For example:

- the cost of components used in making cars
- the wages of workers on a production line in a factory

These are termed **direct costs**. In manufacturing, the total of all the direct costs is called the **prime cost** of the output. Costs which cannot be identified directly with each unit of output are **indirect costs** or overheads. We can therefore define these two types of cost as follows:

a direct cost is a cost that can be identified directly with each unit of output

indirect costs (overheads) are all costs other than those identified as 'direct costs'; they cannot be identified directly with specific units of output

There are many examples of overheads, including:

- telephone charges
- insurance premiums
- cost of wages of non-production staff, such as managers, secretaries, cost accountants and so on
- running costs of delivery vehicles
- depreciation charge for fixed assets

Note particularly the last two examples. In cost accounting, as in financial accounting, we distinguish between capital and revenue expenditure. In our analysis of costs we are referring to revenue expenditure, and therefore include the running costs and depreciation of fixed assets, rather than the capital cost of their purchase.

The direct and indirect costs for a manufacturing business are illustrated in the table below.

	DIRECT COSTS	INDIRECT COSTS
MATERIALS	The cost of raw materials from which the finished product is made.	The cost of all other materials, eg grease for machines, cleaning materials.
LABOUR	Wages paid to those who work the machinery on the production line or who are involved in assembly or finishing of the product.	Wages and salaries paid to all other employees, eg managers and supervisors, maintenance staff, administration staff.
EXPENSES	Any expenses which can be attributed to particular units of output, eg royalties payable to the designer of a product, fees linked directly to specific output and paid to people who are not employees.	All other expenses, eg rent, rates, telephone, lighting and heating costs, depreciation of fixed assets, insurance, advertising, etc. These are costs which cannot be linked directly with units of output.
TOTAL	**TOTAL DIRECT COST = PRIME COST**	**TOTAL INDIRECT COST = TOTAL OVERHEADS**

Classification of Costs by Nature

In cost accounting, it is important to appreciate the nature of costs – in particular to understand that not all costs increase or decrease directly in line with increases or decreases in output or activity. By nature, costs are:

- fixed, or
- semi-variable, or
- variable

The diagram on the next page shows the differences between these.

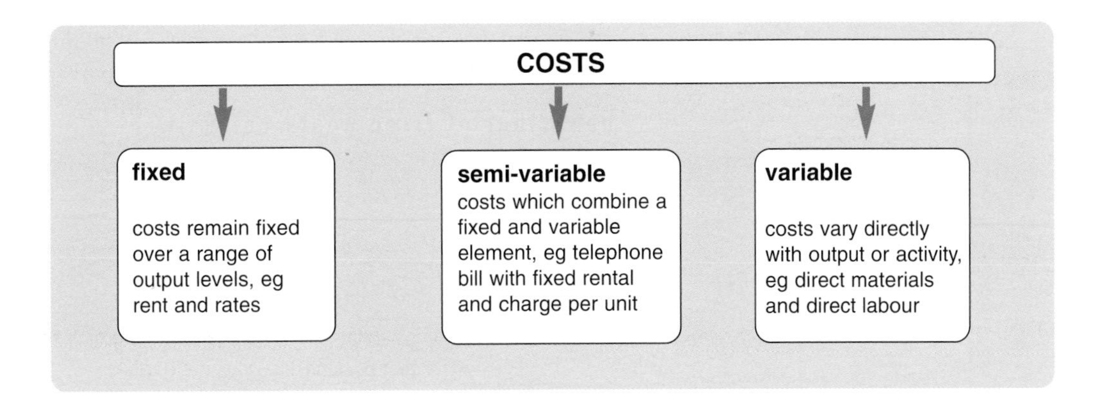

It is important to know the nature of costs and how they are affected by changes in the level of output. For example, a business decides to increase its output by 25% – will all costs increase by 25%? Fixed costs, such as rent and rates, are likely to remain unchanged, provided that there is capacity for the increased output within the existing building. Variable costs, such as direct materials and direct labour, are likely to increase by 25% as they generally vary directly with output (unless any economies of scale can be achieved). Semi-variable costs, such as the telephone bill, will increase as the extra business generates more 'phone calls; however, the increase should certainly be much less than 25%.

We shall be studying the relationship between fixed and variable costs in detail in the next chapter. In particular, we will be looking at the technique of break-even analysis – the point at which costs are exactly equal to income. For the moment we will see how the differing nature of costs is shown in the form of a graph.

fixed costs

These are costs that do not normally change when the level of output or activity changes. For example, the cost of insuring a car factory against business risks will not vary in line with the number of cars produced – it is a fixed cost.

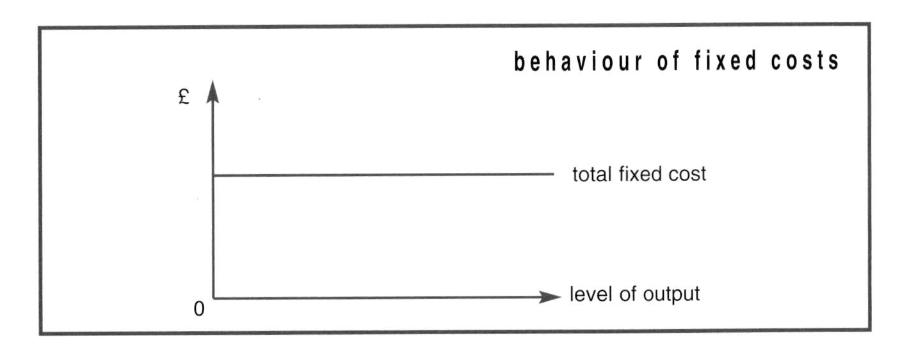

Note that money amounts are shown on the vertical axis and the level of output or activity on the horizontal axis.

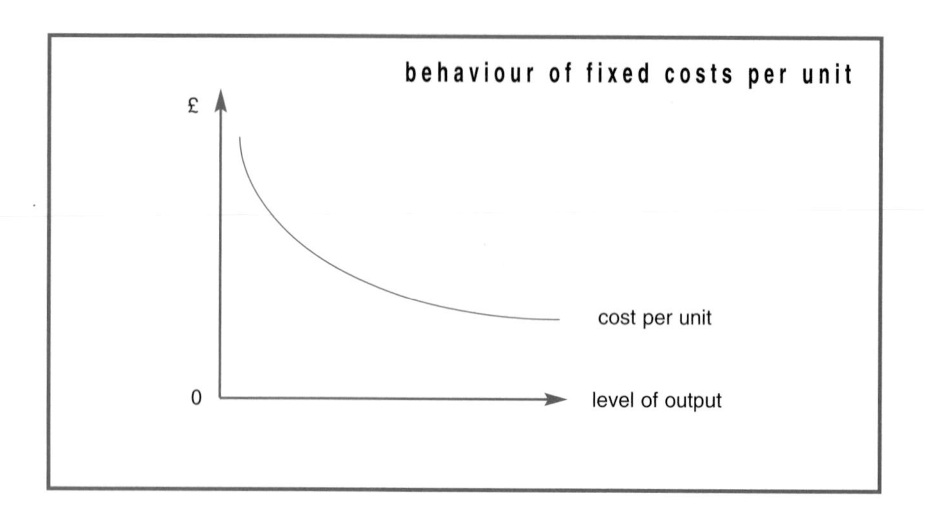

For fixed costs, the *cost per unit* falls as output increases, as follows:

For example, with rent of £40,000 per year:

- at output of 4,000 units, equals £10 per unit
- at output of 10,000 units, equals £4 per unit

Whilst it is sensible to seek to achieve maximum output in order to reduce the cost per unit, fixed costs do not remain fixed at all levels of production. For example, a decision to double production is likely to increase the fixed costs – an increase in factory rent, for example, because an additional factory may need to be rented. Fixed costs are often described as *stepped fixed costs*, because they increase by a large amount all at once; graphically, the cost behaviour is shown as a step:

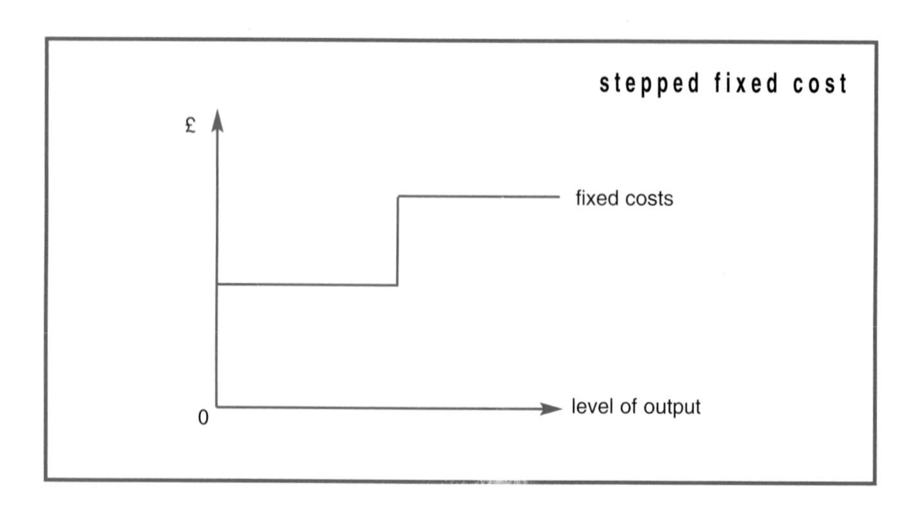

semi-variable costs

These are costs where a part of the cost acts as a variable cost, and a part acts as a fixed cost. For example, some fuel bills are semi-variable: there is a fixed 'standing charge' and a variable 'unit charge'.

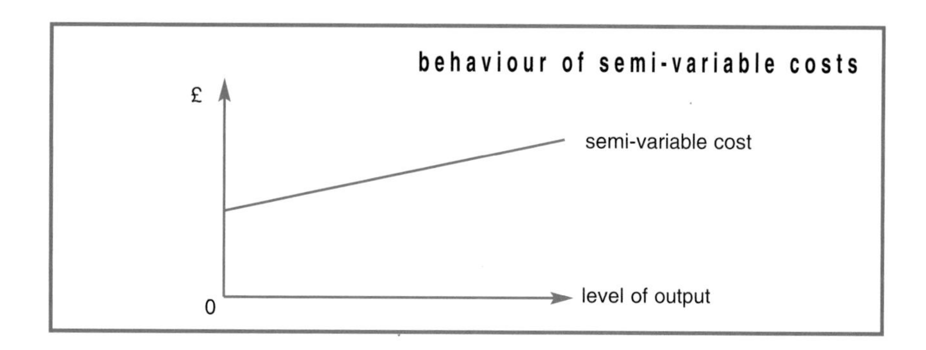

variable costs

These are the costs where the the cost varies in proportion to the level of output or activity. For example, if a car manufacturer makes more cars it will use more metal – a variable cost. Note however that the cost per unit remains constant at all levels of output.

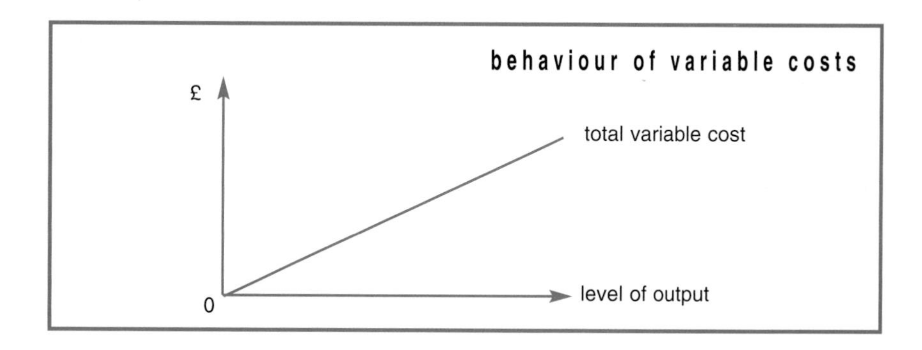

fixed and variable costs in decision-making

Identifying costs as being fixed, semi-variable or variable helps with decision-making – the business might be able to alter the balance between fixed and variable costs in order to increase profits. A product could be made:

- either, by using a labour-intensive process, with a large number of employees supported by basic machinery
- or, by using expensive machinery in an automated process with very few employees

In the first case, the cost structure will be high variable costs (direct labour) and low fixed costs (depreciation of machinery). In the second case, there will be low variable costs, and high fixed costs.

Management will need to examine the relationship between the costs – together with the likely sales figures, and the availability of finance with which to buy the machinery – before making a decision.

More specifically, a knowledge of the nature of costs can be used to help management to identify the point at which costs are exactly equal to income – known as the break-even point (covered in the next chapter).

MARGINAL COSTING, CONTRIBUTION AND PROFIT

To help with decision-making, costs are classified as either variable costs or fixed costs (semi-variable costs are divided into their fixed and variable components). For example, a car manufacturer will need to identify:

- the variable costs of each car
- the total fixed costs of running the business over a period of time

The classification of costs as fixed or variable is used in the technique of **marginal costing** to work out how much it costs to produce each extra unit of output.

marginal cost is the cost of producing one extra unit of output

The marginal cost for a car manufacturer is therefore the cost of producing one extra car.

Marginal cost is often – but not always – the total of the variable costs of producing a unit of output. For most purposes, marginal costing is not concerned with fixed costs (such as the rent of a factory); instead it is concerned with variable costs – direct materials, direct labour, direct expenses, and variable production overheads – which increase as output increases. For most decision-making, the marginal cost of a unit of output is, therefore, the variable cost of producing one more unit.

Knowing the marginal cost of a unit of output enables the management of a business to focus their attention on the **contribution** provided by each unit. The contribution is the amount of money coming in from sales after marginal/variable costs have been paid. The formula for calculating contribution is:

selling price per unit less variable cost per unit = contribution per unit

Contribution can be calculated on a per unit basis (as here), or for a batch of output (eg 1,000 units), or for a whole business.

It follows that the difference between the sales income and the variable costs of the units sold in a period is the **total contribution** that the sales of all the units in the period make towards the fixed costs of the business. Once these are covered, the remainder of the contribution is profit.

Thus a business can work out its profit for any given period from the total contribution and fixed costs figures:

total contribution less total fixed costs = profit

A profit statement can be prepared in the following format:

	sales revenue
less	variable costs
equals	contribution
less	fixed costs
equals	profit

Note from the profit statement how the contribution goes firstly towards the fixed costs and, when they have been covered, secondly contributes to profit.

The relationship between marginal costing, contribution and profit is shown in the Worked Example which follows.

WORKED EXAMPLE: COSTS, CONTRIBUTION AND PROFIT

situation

The Wyvern Bike Company makes 100 bikes each week and its costs are as follows:

Direct materials	£3,000
Direct labour	£2,500
Indirect costs	£3,500

Investigations into the behaviour of costs has revealed the following information:

- direct materials are variable costs
- direct labour is a variable cost
- of the indirect costs, £1,500 is a fixed cost, and the remainder is a variable cost

The selling price of each bike is £120.

You are to:

- calculate the marginal cost of producing each bike
- show the expected contribution per bike
- prepare a statement to show clearly the total contribution and the total profit each week.

solution

Marginal cost per bike

Variable costs per unit:	£
direct materials (£3,000 ÷ 100)	30
direct labour (£2,500 ÷ 100)	25
indirect costs (£2,000* ÷ 100)	20
marginal cost per bike	75

* £3,500 – £1,500 fixed costs

Contribution per bike

	selling price per bike	120
less	variable cost per bike	75
equals	contribution per bike	45

Total contribution and total profit each week

		£	£
	sales £120 x 100 bikes		12,000
less	variable costs:		
	direct materials	3,000	
	direct labour	2,500	
	indirect costs	2,000	
			7,500
equals	total contribution		4,500
less	fixed costs (indirect costs)		1,500
equals	profit for the week		3,000

CHAPTER SUMMARY

- Cost accounting provides information for managers of a business in order to assist with decision-making, planning and control.

- The main elements of cost are
  - materials
  - labour
  - expenses

  Each of these can be direct or indirect.

- Direct costs can be identified directly with each unit of output.

- Indirect costs (overheads) cannot be identified directly with specific units of output.

- By nature, costs are fixed, or semi-variable, or variable.

- A fixed cost remains fixed over a range of output levels.

- A variable cost varies directly with output.

- A semi-variable cost combines a fixed and variable element.

- The marginal cost is the cost of producing one extra unit of output.

- Knowing the marginal cost of a unit of output enables the management of a business to focus their attention on the contribution of each unit.

- Contribution per unit = selling price per unit *less* variable costs per unit.

- A business can work out its profit for any given period from the total contribution and fixed cost figures:

  total contribution *less* total fixed costs = profit

In the next chapter we develop the relationship between fixed and variable costs in the form of break-even analysis.

QUESTIONS

NOTE: an asterisk (*) after the question number means that an answer to the question is given at the end of this book.

30.1* (a) Explain how costs are classified (i) by element, and (ii) by nature.

(b) Analyse each of the following costs by nature (ie fixed, or semi-variable, or variable):

- raw materials
- factory rent
- telephone bill with fixed rental and charge per call unit
- direct labour, eg production workers paid on the basis of work done
- indirect labour, eg supervisors' salaries
- commission paid to sales staff

Taking the costs in turn, explain to a friend, who is about to set up a furniture manufacturing business, why you have analysed each as fixed, or semi-variable, or variable. Answer the comment, "What difference does it make anyway, they are all costs that have to be paid."

30.2* Explain the nature of the costs shown by the following graphs. (Study the graphs and read the notes that follow on the next page).

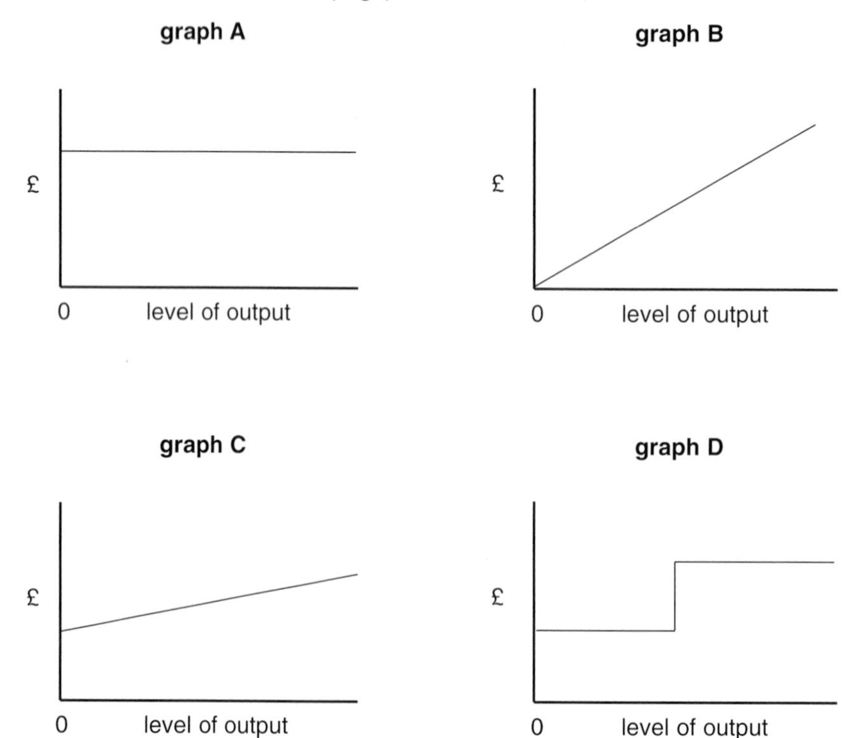

notes to the graphs

Graph A shows the cost of factory rent.

Graph B shows the wages of production-line employees who are paid on a piecework basis (ie on the basis of goods produced).

Graph C shows the cost of a photocopier with a fixed rental and a cost per unit copied.

Graph D shows the cost of factory rent in an expanding business.

30.3* Classify the following costs (tick the appropriate column):

		fixed	**semi-variable**	**variable**
(a)	rates of business premises			
(b)	royalty paid to designer for each unit of output			
(c)	car hire with fixed rental and charge per mile			
(d)	employees paid on piecework basis (ie on the basis of goods produced)			
(e)	straight-line depreciation			
(f)	direct materials			
(g)	telephone bill with fixed rental and charge per call unit			
(h)	office salaries			

30.4

Each of the following types of costs is incurred by Seedy Limited, a company that makes music CDs:

(a) factory rates

(b) CD cases

(c) production workers paid a basic wage plus a bonus per CD made

(d) production supervisors paid a fixed salary

(e) blank CDs

(f) factory rent

(g) cellophane for packaging individual CDs

(h) royalties paid to recording artists for each CD made

You are to state whether each of the above costs behaves as a fixed, semi-variable, or variable cost.

30.5

You have been asked to organise a day of lectures on costing techniques for students. You will need to advertise the event, and hire a suitable room in a local hotel, and speakers. You will also need to provide lunch and course materials for each person who books a place, and decide how much to charge them each for the day.

Using your own estimates for the relevant costs and price, you are to:

(a) calculate the total fixed costs for the event

(b) calculate the total variable costs per delegate

(c) decide the price to be charged per delegate and then calculate the contribution per delegate

(d) assuming that thirty delegates attend, prepare a statement to show clearly the total contribution and the profit or loss for the event

30.6*

Newman Electronics Ltd manufactures one product which sells for £32 per unit.

The company plans to manufacture 40,000 units.

Annual costs are expected to be:

	£
variable costs	360,000
semi-variable costs of which £80,000 are fixed	280,000
other fixed costs	340,000

In the year ended 31 March 2003 46,000 units were produced and sold.

REQUIRED

(a) Define the following:

  (i) fixed costs

  (ii) variable costs

  (iii) semi-variable costs

(b) Calculate the expected contribution per unit. State the formula used.

(c) Prepare a statement for Newman Electronics Ltd for the year ended 31 March 2003 to show clearly the total contribution and the total profit for the year.

Assessment and Qualifications Alliance (AQA), 2003

30.7

John Walker Limited manufactures high quality trainers. The management of the company is considering next year's production and has asked you to help with certain financial decisions.

The following information is available:

wholesale selling price (per pair)	£40
direct materials (per pair)	£15
direct labour (per pair)	£12
overheads (fixed)	£245,000 per year

The company is planning to manufacture 25,000 pairs of trainers next year.

You are to:

(a) calculate the marginal cost per pair of trainers

(b) calculate the contribution per pair of trainers

(c) prepare a profit statement to show the profit or loss if 25,000 pairs of trainers are sold

30.8

Pinder Ltd manufactures parachutes.

The cost of producing one parachute is:

	£
materials (£4 per metre)	10
labour (£8 per hour)	16
other variable costs	8

Total fixed costs for the year are expected to be £134,000.

Each parachute sells for £44. The company expects to sell 22,000 parachutes each year.

The production manager intends to purchase new advanced machinery, which will reduce the time taken to produce one parachute by 25%.

In order to operate the machinery the workforce must be retrained for two months at a cost of £32,000. If the retraining is completed satisfactorily the workforce will receive a 12.5% pay rise.

It is expected that not all the workforce will wish to be retrained.

REQUIRED

(a) Define the term "contribution".

(b) Calculate the contribution per unit:

 (i) before the proposed purchase of the machinery

 (ii) after the proposed purchase of the machinery

(c) Assess the effect the proposed purchase of the machinery will have on the profitability of Pinder Ltd.

Assessment and Qualifications Alliance (AQA), 2002

30.9* Perpend plc manufactures and sells electrical heat pumps.

It is expected that 600 pumps will be produced in August 2001. At this level of production the following costs would arise:

	£
Materials: Unassembled pump kit	20
Labour: 3 employees working in the Assembly Dept at £5 per hour	15
Other variable costs (one-fifth of labour cost per pump)	3
Total fixed costs are expected to be £2,400	
Each pump is sold at a 20% mark-up on cost	

In order to increase production the Production Manager has introduced a bonus scheme within the Assembly Department. It will be paid in September for each pump manufactured in excess of the expected production level of 600 pumps.

The bonus is valued at £3 per pump, but this figure is not to be included in the calculation for the variable overhead cost.

The Purchasing Manager has also negotiated a 10% discount on pump materials. The discount will take effect from 1 September and will only apply to each pump kit purchased in excess of 400 kits.

REQUIRED

(a) Distinguish between fixed costs and variable costs. State one example of each.

(b) Calculate the total cost if 650 pumps are manufactured in September.

Total cost of 650 pumps:	£
Materials:	
Labour:	
Other variable costs:	
Fixed costs:	
Total costs:	

Assessment and Qualifications Alliance (AQA), 2001

31 BREAK-EVEN ANALYSIS

This chapter looks at the relationship between fixed costs and variable costs: the nature of these costs has been examined already in Chapter 30. We shall now study the relationship between them in break-even analysis, which is the point at which a business makes neither a profit nor a loss.

In this chapter we look at:

- the nature of fixed and variable costs
- break-even point
- break-even analysis, by calculation, by table, by graph
- interpretation of break-even
- limitations of break-even analysis
- margin of safety, ie the amount by which sales exceed the break-even point
- target profit, and the contribution sales ratio
- use of break-even analysis

FIXED AND VARIABLE COSTS

In Chapter 30 we have seen that the main elements of cost for most businesses comprise:

- materials
- labour
- expenses (overheads)

We know that, by nature, costs are:

- fixed, or
- semi-variable, or
- variable

In brief, fixed costs remain fixed over a range of output levels, despite other changes. Variable costs vary directly with changes in output levels. Semi-variable costs combine both a fixed and variable element, eg the telephone bill comprises the fixed rental for the line, together with the variable element of call charges.

Do remember that the nature of costs can change as the business changes. For example, a fixed cost, such as factory rent, is only likely to be fixed at or near current production levels: if output is doubled or trebled, then it is likely that an additional factory will need to be rented. In this way, the fixed cost becomes a stepped fixed cost.

For the purposes of break-even analysis we need to distinguish between fixed and variable costs, and to be able to pick out from semi-variable costs the amounts of the fixed and variable elements.

BREAK-EVEN POINT

Break-even is the point at which neither a profit nor a loss is made.

The break-even point (bep) is the output level (units manufactured or services provided) at which the income from sales is just enough to cover all the costs. Break-even is the point at which the profit (or loss) is zero. The output level can be measured in a way that is appropriate for the particular business; it is commonly measured in units of output.

The formula for break-even in units of output is:

$$\frac{\textit{fixed costs (£)}}{\textit{*contribution per unit (£)}} = \textit{break-even point (in units of output)}$$

* selling price – variable costs

In order to use break-even analysis, we need to know:

- selling price (per unit)
- costs of the product
  - variable costs (such as materials, labour) per unit
  - overhead costs, and whether these are fixed or variable
- limitations, such as maximum production capacity, maximum sales

The Worked Example of Fluffy Toys Limited which follows shows how the break-even point can be determined.

WORKED EXAMPLE: BREAK-EVEN

situation

Fluffy Toys Limited manufactures soft toys, and is able to sell all that can be produced. The variable costs (materials and direct labour) for producing each toy are £10 and the selling price is £20 each. The fixed costs of running the business are £5,000 per month. How many toys need to be produced and sold each month for the business to cover its costs, ie to break-even?

solution

This problem can be solved by calculation, by constructing a table, or by means of a graph. Which method is used depends on the purpose for which the information is required:

- the **calculation method** is quick to use and is convenient for seeing the effect of different cost structures on break-even point
- the **table method** shows the amounts of fixed and variable costs, sales revenue, and profit at different levels of production
- the **graph method** is used for making presentations – for example, to the directors of a company – because it shows in a visual form the relationship between costs and sales revenue, and the amount of profit or loss at different levels of production

Often the calculation or table methods are used before drawing a graph. By doing this, the break-even point is known and suitable scales can be selected for the axes of the graph in order to give a good visual presentation.

calculation method

The contribution per unit is:

	selling price per unit	£20
less	variable costs per unit	£10
equals	contribution per unit	£10

Each toy sold gives a contribution (selling price, less variable costs) of £10. This contributes towards the fixed costs and, in order to break-even, the business must have sufficient £10 'lots' to meet the fixed costs. Thus, with fixed costs of £5,000 per month, the break-even calculation is:

$$\frac{\textit{fixed costs (£)}}{\textit{contribution per unit (£)}} = \frac{\textit{£5,000}}{\textit{£10}} = \textit{500 toys each month}$$

The break-even point (in units of output) is 500 toys each month.

table method

units of output	*fixed costs*	*variable costs*	*total cost*	*sales revenue*	*profit/(loss)*
	A	B	C	D	
			A + B		D – C
	£	£	£	£	£
100	5,000	1,000	6,000	2,000	(4,000)
200	5,000	2,000	7,000	4,000	(3,000)
300	5,000	3,000	8,000	6,000	(2 000)
400	5,000	4,000	9,000	8,000	(1,000)
500	5,000	5,000	10,000	10,000	nil
600	5,000	6,000	11,000	12,000	1,000
700	5,000	7,000	12,000	14,000	2,000

graph method

A graphical presentation uses money amounts as the common denominator between fixed costs, variable costs, and sales revenue.

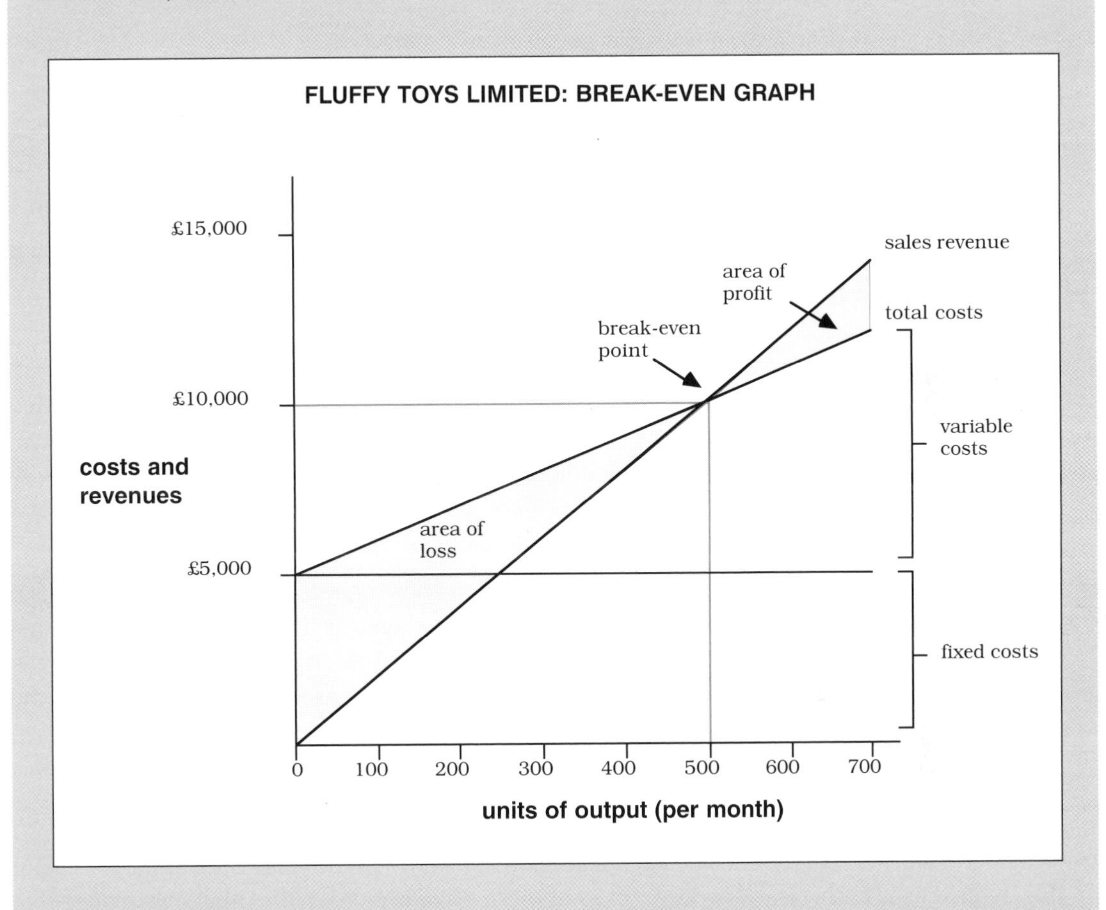

notes to the graph

- With a break-even graph, it is usual for the vertical axis to show money amounts; the horizontal axis shows units of output/sales.
- The fixed costs are unchanged at all levels of output, in this case they are £5,000.
- The variable costs commence, on the vertical axis, *from the fixed costs amount*, not from 'zero'. This is because the cost of producing zero units is the fixed costs.
- The fixed costs *and* the variable costs form the *total costs line.*
- The point at which the total costs and sales revenue lines cross is the break-even point.
- From the graph we can read off the break-even point both in terms of units of output, 500 units on the horizontal axis, and in sales value, £10,000 on the vertical axis.

- The 'proof' of the break-even chart is:

		£
	sales revenue (500 units at £20 each)	10,000
less	variable costs (500 units at £10 each)	5,000
equals	contribution	5,000
less	fixed costs	5,000
equals	profit/loss	nil

Hints for Drawing a Break-even Graph

- In most break-even charts all lines are straight. This means that only two points need be plotted for each line; for example, with sales, choose a number that is fairly near to the maximum expected, multiply by the selling price per unit, and this is the point to be marked on the graph. As the sales line always passes through zero, there are now two points along which to draw a straight line.
- When drawing a break-even graph it is often difficult to know what total value to show on each axis, ie how many units, and/or how much in costs and revenues. As a guide, look for a maximum output or sales level that will not be exceeded: this will give the horizontal axis. Multiply the maximum sales, if known, by the unit selling price to give the maximum sales revenue for the vertical axis. If the figure for maximum sales is not known, it is recommended that the break-even point is calculated before drawing the graph so that the extent of the graph can be established.
- A common error is to start the variable costs from the zero point instead of the fixed costs line.
- Although fixed costs are likely to be unchanged within a fairly narrow range of outputs, watch out for stepped fixed costs (see page 516). For example, a major expansion of output may require that additional premises are rented: thus the fixed cost of rent will increase at a particular point (and is shown graphically as a step). Such a stepped fixed cost has a direct effect on total costs.

Interpretation of Break-even

When interpreting break-even, it is all too easy to concentrate solely on the break-even point. The graph, for example, tells us much more than this: it also shows the profit or loss at any level of output/sales contained within the graph. To find this, simply measure the gap between sales revenue and total costs at a chosen number of units, and read the money amounts off on the vertical axis (above break-even point it is a profit; below, it is a loss). For example, the graph in the Worked Example shows a profit or loss at:

- 650 units = £1,500 profit
- 600 units = £1,000 profit
- 400 units = £1,000 loss

Break-even analysis, whether by calculation, by table, or by graph, can be used by all types of businesses, as well as other organisations. For example, a shop will wish to know the sales it has to make each week to meet costs; a sports centre will wish to know the ticket sales that have to be made to meet costs; a club or society might wish to know how many raffle tickets it needs to sell to meet the costs of prizes and of printing tickets.

Once the break-even point has been reached, the additional contribution forms the profit. For example, if the business considered in the Worked Example was selling 650 toys each month, it would have a total contribution of 650 x £10 = £6,500; of this the first £5,000 will be used to meet fixed costs, and the remaining £1,500 represents the profit (which can be read off the break-even graph). This can be shown by means of a profit statement as follows:

		£
	sales revenue (650 units at £20 each)	13,000
less	variable costs (650 units at £10 each)	6,500
equals	contribution (to fixed costs and profit)	6,500
less	monthly fixed costs	5,000
equals	profit for month	1,500

A quick way of calculating the profit is to use the following formula:

(selling price – variable costs) per unit x volume – fixed costs = profit*

* the level of output or activity

ie (£20 – £10) x 650 – £5,000 = £6,500 – £5,000 = £1,500 profit

Limitations of Break-even Analysis

The problem of break-even analysis is the assumption that the relationship between sales revenue, variable costs and fixed costs, remains the same at all levels of production. This is a rather simplistic view because, for example, in order to increase sales, a business will often need to offer bulk discounts, so reducing the sales revenue per unit at higher levels. The limitations of break-even analysis can be summarised as follows:

- The assumption is made that all output is sold. There is no point in preparing the cost data, calculating the break-even point, and estimating the profits to be made if the product will not sell in sufficient quantities. However, break-even analysis is useful for a new business in order to establish the level of sales that must be achieved to reach break-even point. The feasibility of reaching that level of sales must then be considered by the owner.

- The presumption is made that there is only one product. While separate break-even analysis can be made for different products, it is difficult to make the calculations for a mix of products.
- All costs and revenues are expressed in terms of straight lines. However, this relationship is not always so. As indicated above selling prices may vary at different quantities sold; in a similar way, variable costs alter at different levels as advantage is taken of the lower prices to be gained from bulk buying, and/or more efficient production methods.
- Fixed costs do not remain fixed at all levels of output; instead, there may be stepped fixed costs (see page 516).
- It is not possible to *extrapolate* the graph or calculation; by extrapolation is meant extending the lines on the graph beyond the limits of the activity on which the graph is based. For example, in the Worked Example, the graph cannot be extended to, say, 1,000 units of output and the profit read off at this point. The relationship between sales revenues and costs will be different at much higher levels of output – different methods of production might be used, for example.
- The profit or loss shown by the graph or calculations is probably only true for figures close to current output levels – the further away from current figures, the less accurate will be the expected profit or loss.
- External factors – such as the state of the economy, interest rates, the rate of inflation, etc – are not considered by break-even analysis.
- A further disadvantage of break-even analysis is that it concentrates too much attention on the break-even point. While this aspect is important, other considerations such as ensuring that the output is produced as efficiently as possible, and that costs are kept under review, are just as important.

Break-even: Margin of Safety

The **margin of safety** is the amount by which sales exceed the break-even point. Margin of safety can be expressed as:

- a number of units, ie sales volume – break-even point (units)
- a sales revenue amount, ie sales volume – break-even point (units) x selling price
- a percentage, using the following formula

$$\frac{\textit{current output} - \textit{break-even output}}{\textit{current output}} \times \frac{100}{1}$$

WORKED EXAMPLE: MARGIN OF SAFETY

Referring back to the Fluffy Toys Limited Worked Example (pages 529 - 532), if current output is 700 units, while the break-even point is 500 units, the margin of safety is:

- 200 units (ie 700 – 500)
- £4,000 of sales revenue (ie 200 units at £20 each)
- 29 per cent, ie $\frac{700 - 500}{700} \times \frac{100}{1}$

In interpreting this margin of safety we can say that production/sales can fall by these values before the business reaches break-even point and ceases to make a profit.

Margin of safety is especially important in times of recession as it expresses to management the amount of the 'cushion' which current production/sales gives beyond the break-even point. Where there is a comparison to be made between two or more products, each with different margins of safety, the product with the highest margin of safety is looked on favourably; however, margin of safety is only one factor in decision-making.

BREAK-EVEN: TARGET PROFIT

A further development of break-even is to calculate the output that needs to be sold in order to give a certain amount of profit – the **target profit**. This is calculated as follows:

$$\frac{\textit{fixed costs (£) + target profit (£)}}{\textit{contribution per unit (£)}} = \textit{number of units of output}$$

WORKED EXAMPLE: TARGET PROFIT

If Fluffy Toys Limited (pages 529 - 532) required a profit of £2,000 per month, the calculation is:

$$\frac{£5,000 + £2,000}{£10} = \text{700 units, with a sales value of £14,000*}$$

* 700 units at £20 each = £14,000

This target profit can then be shown by means of a profit statement as follows:

		£
	sales revenue (700 units at £20 each)	14,000
less	variable costs (700 units at £10 each)	7,000
equals	contribution (to fixed costs and profit)	7,000
less	monthly fixed costs	5,000
equals	target profit for month	2,000

Alternatively, it can be calculated as follows:

(selling price – variable costs) per unit x volume – fixed costs = profit

ie (£20 – £10) x 700 – £5,000 = £7,000 – £5,000 = £2,000

Note that target profit can also be calculated by making use of the contribution sales ratio (see below).

CONTRIBUTION SALES RATIO

The contribution sales (CS) ratio – also known as the profit volume (PV) ratio – expresses the amount of contribution in relation to the amount of the selling price:

$$\frac{\textit{contribution (£)}}{\textit{selling price (£)}} = \textit{contribution to sales ratio}$$

The ratio, or percentage, can be calculated on the basis of a single unit of production or for the whole business.

In break-even analysis, if fixed costs are known, we can use the CS ratio to find the sales value at which the business breaks-even, or the sales value to give a target amount of profit.

WORKED EXAMPLE: CONTRIBUTION SALES RATIO

Referring back to Fluffy Toys Limited, the CS ratio (per unit) is:

$$\frac{\text{contribution (£)}}{\text{selling price (£)}} = \frac{\text{£10*}}{\text{£20}} = 0.5 \text{ or } 50\%$$

* selling price £20 – variable costs £10 = contribution £10

Fixed costs are £5,000 per month, so the sales revenue needed to break-even is:

$$\frac{\text{fixed costs (£)}}{\text{CS ratio}} = \frac{\text{£5,000}}{\text{0.5 (see above)}} = \text{£10,000}$$

As the selling price is £20 per toy, we can get back to the break-even in units of output as follows:
£10,000 ÷ £20 = 500 units

If the directors of Fluffy Toys Limited wish to know the sales revenue that must be made to achieve a target profit of £2,000 per month, the CS ratio is used as follows:

$$\frac{\text{fixed costs + target profit}}{\text{CS ratio}} = \text{required level of sales}$$

$$\frac{£5{,}000 + £2{,}000}{0.5} = \underline{£14{,}000}$$

As the selling price is £20 per toy, we can get to the units of output as follows:

£14,000 ÷ £20 = 700 units to achieve a target profit of £2,000.

When to use Break-even Analysis

Break-even analysis is used by businesses in a variety of situations:

before starting a new business

The calculation of break-even point is important in order to see the level of sales needed by the new business in order to cover costs, or to make a particular level of profit. The feasibility of achieving the level can then be considered by the owner of the business, and other parties such as the bank manager.

when making changes within a business

The costs of a major change will need to be considered by the owners and/or managers. For example, a large increase in production will, most likely, affect the balance between fixed and variable costs. Break-even analysis will be used as part of the planning process to ensure that the business remains profitable.

to measure profits and losses

Within the limitations of break-even analysis, profits and losses can be estimated at different levels of output from current production. (Remember that this can be done only where the new output is close to current levels and where there is no major change to the structure of costs – ie it is not possible to extrapolate.)

to answer 'what if?' questions

Questions such as 'what if sales fall by 10 per cent?' and 'what if fixed costs increase by £1,000?' can be answered – in part at least – by break-even analysis. The effect on the profitability of the business can be seen, subject to the limitations noted earlier. A question such as 'what if sales increase by 300 per cent?' is such a fundamental change that it can only be answered by examining the effect on the nature of the fixed and variable costs and then re-calculating the break-even point.

to evaluate alternative viewpoints

There are often different ways of production; this is particularly true of a manufacturing business. For example, a product could be made:

- either, by using a labour-intensive process, with a large number of employees supported by basic machinery
- or, by using expensive machinery in an automated process with very few employees.

In the first case, the cost structure will be high variable costs (labour) and low fixed costs (depreciation of machinery). In the second case, there will be low variable costs and high fixed costs. Break-even analysis can be used to examine the relationship between the costs which are likely to show a low break-even point in the first case, and a high break-even point in the second. In this way, the management of the business is guided by break-even analysis; management will also need to know the likely sales figures, and the availability of money with which to buy the machinery.

CHAPTER SUMMARY

- Break-even analysis distinguishes between fixed costs and variable costs.
- Break-even is the point at which neither a profit nor a loss is made.
- The relationship between sales revenue, and fixed costs and variable costs is used to ascertain the break-even point, by means of a calculation, a table, or a graph.
- The break-even calculation is:

$$\frac{\textit{fixed costs (£)}}{\textit{contribution per unit (£)}} = \textit{break-even point (number of units)}$$

- Break-even analysis can show:
  - break-even point in units of output
  - break-even point in value of sales
  - profit or loss at a given level of output/sales

- The limitations of break-even analysis are that:
  - the assumption is made that all output is sold
  - the presumption is that there is only one product
  - costs and revenues are expressed in straight lines
  - fixed costs do not remain fixed at all levels of output
  - it is not possible to extrapolate the break-even graph or calculation
  - the profit or loss is probably only true for figures close to current output levels
  - external factors are not considered
  - it concentrates too much on break-even point

- Margin of safety is the amount by which sales exceed the break-even point.

- Target profit uses break-even analysis to calculate the output that needs to be sold in order to give a certain amount of profit.

- The contribution sales ratio – also known as the profit volume ratio – expresses the amount of contribution in relation to the amount of the selling price.

- Break-even analysis is often used:
  - before starting a new business
  - when making changes to a business
  - to measure profits or losses
  - to answer 'what if?' questions
  - to evaluate alternative viewpoints

In the next chapter we look at how costs and revenues can be incorporated into the budget of a business, the preparation of budgets, and their uses in the control of a business.

QUESTIONS

NOTE: an asterisk (*) after the question number means that an answer to the question is given at the end of this book.

31.1 Bright Limited estimates that costs and revenue for next month will be:

selling price	£10 per unit
variable cost	£5 per unit
fixed costs for the month	£7,500

Maximum output is 3,000 units per month

You are to complete the following table:

units of output	*fixed costs*	*variable costs*	*total cost*	*sales revenue*	*profit/(loss)*
	£	£	£	£	£
0					
500					
1,000					
1,500					
2,000					
2,500					
3,000					

31.2* Cuddly Toys Limited manufactures a popular children's teddy bear. At present production is limited by the capacity of the factory to 50 bears each week. The following information is available:

Selling price per teddy bear	£20
Materials per teddy bear	£4
Direct labour per teddy bear	£5
Weekly fixed expenses	
• factory rent and rates	£100
• fuel and power	£20
• other costs	£34

You are to find the weekly break-even point by the graphical method, and to check your answer by calculation.

31.3* Mike Etherton, a manufacturer of cricket bats, has the following monthly costs:

Material cost	£8 per bat
Labour cost	£12 per bat
Selling price	£35 per bat
Overheads (fixed)	£12,000

You are to:

(a) Prepare a table showing costs, sales revenue, and profit or loss for production of bats in multiples of 100 up to 1,200.

(b) Draw a graph showing the break-even point.

(c) Prove your answer by calculation.

(d) Read off the graph the profit or loss if 200 bats, and 1,200 bats are sold each month: prove the answer by calculation.

(e) If production is currently 1,000 bats per month, what is the margin of safety, expressed as a percentage and in units?

31.4 Riley Limited has made the following estimates for next month:

Selling price	£25 per unit
Variable cost	£10 per unit
Fixed costs for the month	£300,000
Forecast output	30,000 units
Maximum output	40,000 units

You are to carry out the following tasks:

Task 1

Calculate:

- the contribution sales ratio
- the break-even point in units
- the break-even point in sales revenue
- the margin of safety at the forecast output
- the number of units to generate a profit of £100,000

Task 2

Calculate the profit at:

- the forecast output
- the maximum output

Task 3

One of the managers has suggested that, if the selling price were reduced to £20 per unit, then sales would be increased to the maximum output.

- For this new strategy, you are to calculate:
  - the contribution sales ratio
  - the break-even point in units
  - the break-even point in sales revenue
  - the margin of safety
  - the forecast profit
- Write a memorandum to the general manager advising whether you believe that the new strategy should be implemented.

31.5

Melvin Books Ltd manufactures bookmarks, which sell for £1.00 each.

The bookmarks are made by people working at home, who are paid 20p for every bookmark they produce. The raw materials bought to make one bookmark cost 30p. Salespeople sell the bookmarks and are paid 10p for each bookmark which they sell. The administration costs £42,000 per year. Business rates of £20,400 are also paid annually.

REQUIRED

(a) Classify each cost by completing the following table and total each column:

	Total fixed costs £	Variable costs per unit in pence
Wages		
Raw materials		
Salespeople's wages		
Administration costs		
Business rates		
Total		

(b) (i) State the formula used to calculate the contribution per unit.

(ii) Calculate the contribution per unit.

(iii) Why is the amount of contribution per unit important?

(c) Calculate:

(i) The number of bookmarks which must be manufactured and sold per year for the business to break-even. State the formula used.

(ii) The total revenue at this level of sales.

(iii) The profit or loss achieved by Melvin Books Ltd if 150,000 bookmarks are sold.

Assessment and Qualifications Alliance (AQA), 2002

31.6* Suddley Ltd manufactures a single product.

For the year ending 31 March 2002 each unit is expected to sell for £50.

The expected costs per unit for the year ended 31 March 2002 are:

	£
Materials	12
Labour	16
Variable overheads	7

The annual fixed overheads are expected to be £450,000.

Suddley Ltd has a maximum annual production capacity of 37,500 units.

REQUIRED

(a) Define and calculate:

(i) the contribution per unit

(ii) the break-even point in £s and units.

State the formula used in each case.

(i) Formula: ....

Definition: ....

....

Calculation: ....

....

(ii) Formula: ....

Definition: ....

....

Calculation: ....

....

31.6* continued

(b) In the graph below, the letters **A, B, C** and **D** have been used to identify particular lines or terms used in accounting.

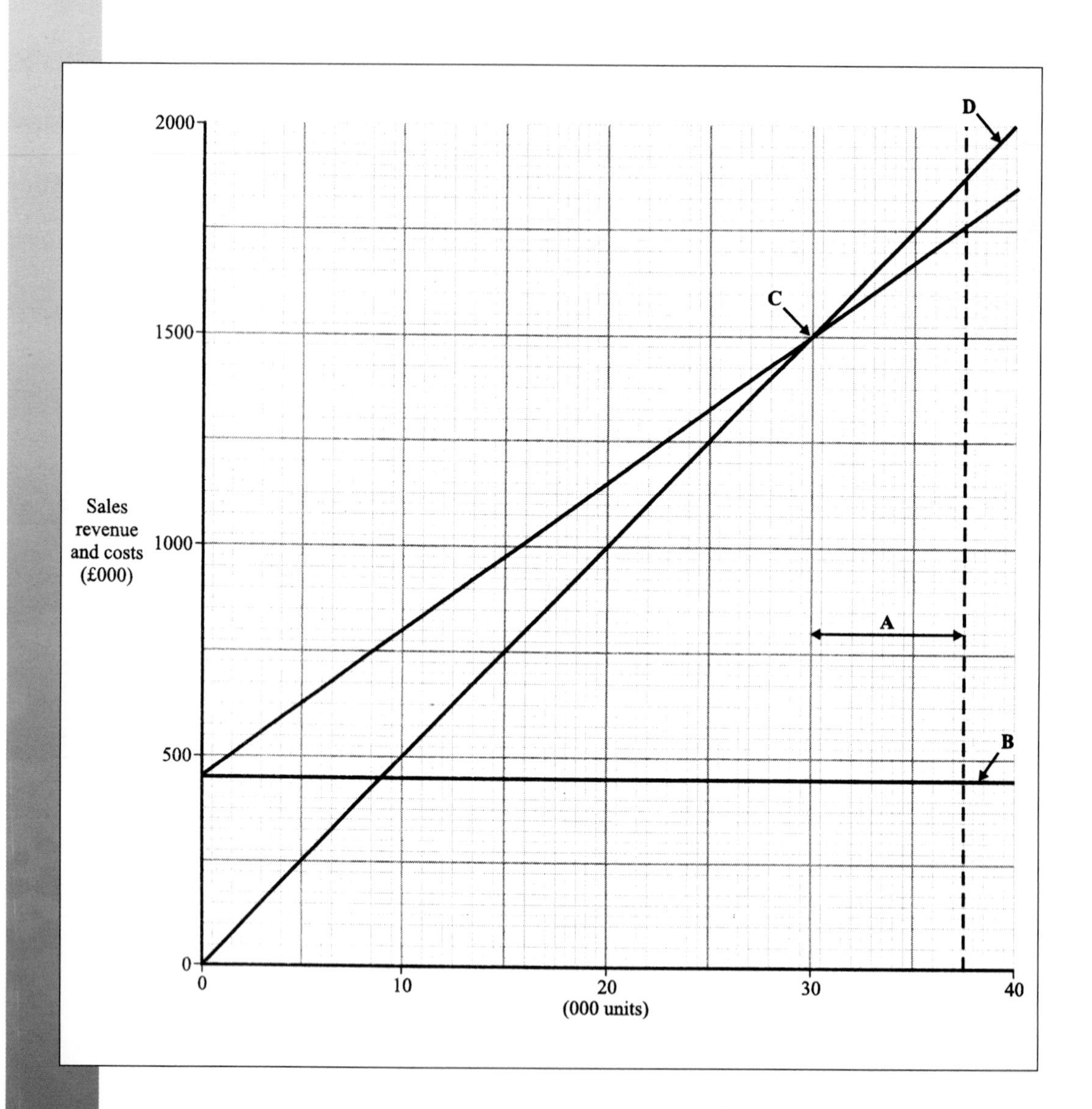

In the table below, match each line or term against the correct letter.

Line or term	A, B, C or D
Fixed costs	
Total sales revenue	
Break-even point	
Margin of safety	

31.6* continued

(c) From the graph, calculate the profit made from the sale of 35,000 units.

(d) Explain two possible consequences for Suddley Ltd if the selling price is reduced to £47 per unit.

Assessment and Qualifications Alliance (AQA), 2001

31.7*

"Break-even analysis has its limitations in decision-making."

Discuss four limitations of break-even analysis.

32 BUDGETING AND BUDGETARY CONTROL

Budgeting is used by businesses as a method of financial planning for the future. Budgets are prepared for important aspects of the business – sales, production, purchases, debtors, creditors, cash – which give detailed plans of the business for the next three, six or twelve months. The budgets are brought together in a forecast operating statement – a forecast trading and profit and loss account – and a balance sheet.

In this chapter we shall be looking at:

- the benefits and limitations of budgets
- budgets for sales, production, purchases, debtors, creditors and cash
- how the budgets link into the master budget of forecast operating statements
- how budgets can be used to control the business by means of budgetary control

INTRODUCTION TO BUDGETS

Businesses need to plan for the future. In large businesses such planning, usually known as **corporate planning**, is very formal while, for smaller businesses, it will be less formal. Planning for the future falls into three time scales:

- **long-term**: from about three years up to, sometimes, as far as twenty years ahead
- **medium-term**: one to three years ahead
- **short-term**: for the next year

Clearly, planning for these different time scales needs different approaches: the further on in time, the less detailed are the plans. In the medium and longer term, a business will establish broad **business objectives**. Such objectives do not have to be formally written down, although in a large business they are likely to be; for smaller businesses, objectives will certainly be thought about by the owners or managers.

In this chapter we are concerned with planning for the more immediate future, ie the next financial year. Such planning takes note of the broader business objectives and sets out how these are to be achieved in the form of detailed plans known as **budgets**.

What is a Budget?

A budget is a financial plan for a business, prepared in advance.

A budget may be set in money terms, eg a sales budget of £500,000, or it can be expressed in terms of units, eg a production budget of 5,000 units.

Budgets can be **income** budgets for money received, eg a sales budget, or **expenditure** budgets for money spent, eg a purchases budget.

Most budgets are prepared for the next financial year (the **budget period**), and are usually broken down into shorter time periods, commonly four-weekly or monthly. This enables control to be exercised over the budget: the actual results can be monitored against the budget, and discrepancies between the two can be investigated and corrective action taken where appropriate.

Benefits of Budgets

Budgets provide benefits both for the business, and also for its managers and other staff:

the budget assists planning

By formalising objectives through a budget, a business can ensure that its plans are achievable. It will be able to decide what resources are required to produce the output of goods and services, and to make sure that they will be available at the right time.

the budget communicates and coordinates

Because a budget is agreed by the business, all the relevant managers and staff will be working towards the same end.

When the budget is being set any anticipated problems should be resolved and any areas of potential confusion clarified. All departments should be in a position to play their part in achieving the overall goals.

the budget helps with decision-making

By planning ahead through budgets, a business can make decisions on how much output – in the form of goods or services – can be achieved. At the same time, the cost of the output can be planned and changes can be made where appropriate.

the budget can be used to monitor and control

An important reason for producing a budget is that management is able to monitor and compare the actual results against the budget (see diagram on the next page). This is so that action can be taken to modify the operation of the business as time passes, or possibly to change the budget if it becomes unachievable.

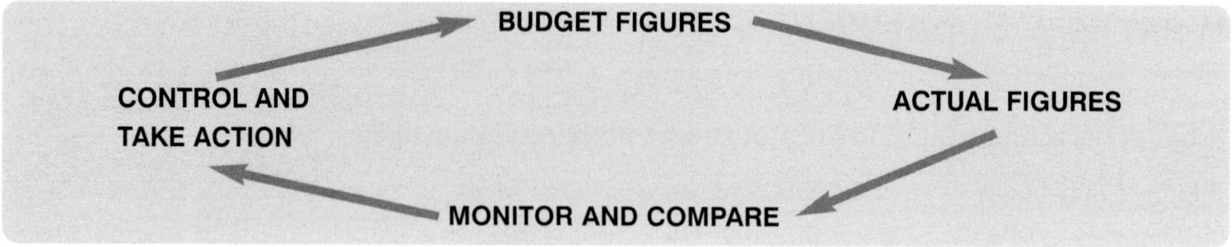

the budget can be used to motivate

A budget can be part of the techniques for motivating managers and other staff to achieve the objectives of the business. The extent to which this happens will depend on how the budget is agreed and set, and whether it is thought to be fair and achievable. The budget may also be linked to rewards (for example, bonuses) where targets are met or exceeded.

LIMITATIONS OF BUDGETS

Whilst most businesses will benefit from the use of budgets, there are a number of limitations of budgets to be aware of:

the benefit of the budget must exceed the cost

Budgeting is a fairly complex process and some businesses – particularly small ones – may find that the task is too much of a burden, with only limited benefits. Nevertheless, many lenders – such as banks – often require the production of budgets as part of the business plan. As a general rule, the benefit of producing the budget must exceed its cost.

budget information may not be accurate

It is essential that the information going into budgets should be as accurate as possible. Anybody can produce a budget, but the more inaccurate it is, the less use it is to the business as a planning and control mechanism. Great care needs to be taken with estimates of sales – often the starting point of the budgeting process – and costs. Budgetary control is the technique that is used to compare the budget against what actually happened – the budget may need to be changed if it becomes unachievable.

the budget may demotivate

Employees who have had no part in agreeing and setting a budget which is imposed upon them, will feel that they do not own it. As a consequence, the staff may be demotivated. Another limitation is that employees may see budgets as either a 'carrot' or a 'stick', ie as a form of encouragement to achieve the targets set, or as a form of punishment if targets are missed.

budgets may lead to disfunctional management

A limitation that can occur is that employees in one department of the business may over-achieve against their budget and create problems elsewhere. For example, a production department might achieve extra output that the sales department finds difficult to sell. To avoid such disfunctional management, budgets need to be set at realistic levels and linked across all departments within the business.

budgets may be set at too low a level

Where the budget is too easy to achieve it will be of no benefit to the business and may, in fact, lead to lower levels of output and higher costs than before the budget was established. Budgets should be set at realistic levels, which make the best use of the resources available.

WHAT BUDGETS ARE PREPARED?

Budgets are planned for specific sections of the business: these budgets can then be controlled by a **budget holder**, who may be the manager or supervisor of the specific section. Such budgets include:

- sales budget
- production budget
- purchases budget
- creditor budget
- debtor budget
- cash budget

The end result of the budgeting process is often the production of a **master budget**, which takes the form of forecast operating statements – forecast trading and profit and loss account – and forecast balance sheet. The master budget is the 'master plan' which shows how all the other budgets 'work together'. The diagram on the next page shows how all the budgets are linked to each other.

The starting point for the budgeting process is generally the **sales budget**. Consequently the order in which the budgets will be prepared is usually:

- **sales budget** – what can the business sell in the next 12 months?
- **production budget** – how can the business make/supply all the items which it plans to sell?
- **purchases budget** – what does the business need to buy to make/supply the goods it expects to sell?
- **creditor budget** – how much will the business have to pay for purchases?
- **debtor budget** – how much will the business receive from sales?
- **cash budget** – what money will be flowing in and out of the bank account? – will an overdraft be needed?
- **master budget** – a summary of all the budgets to provide a forecast operating statement – forecast trading and profit and loss account – and a forecast balance sheet

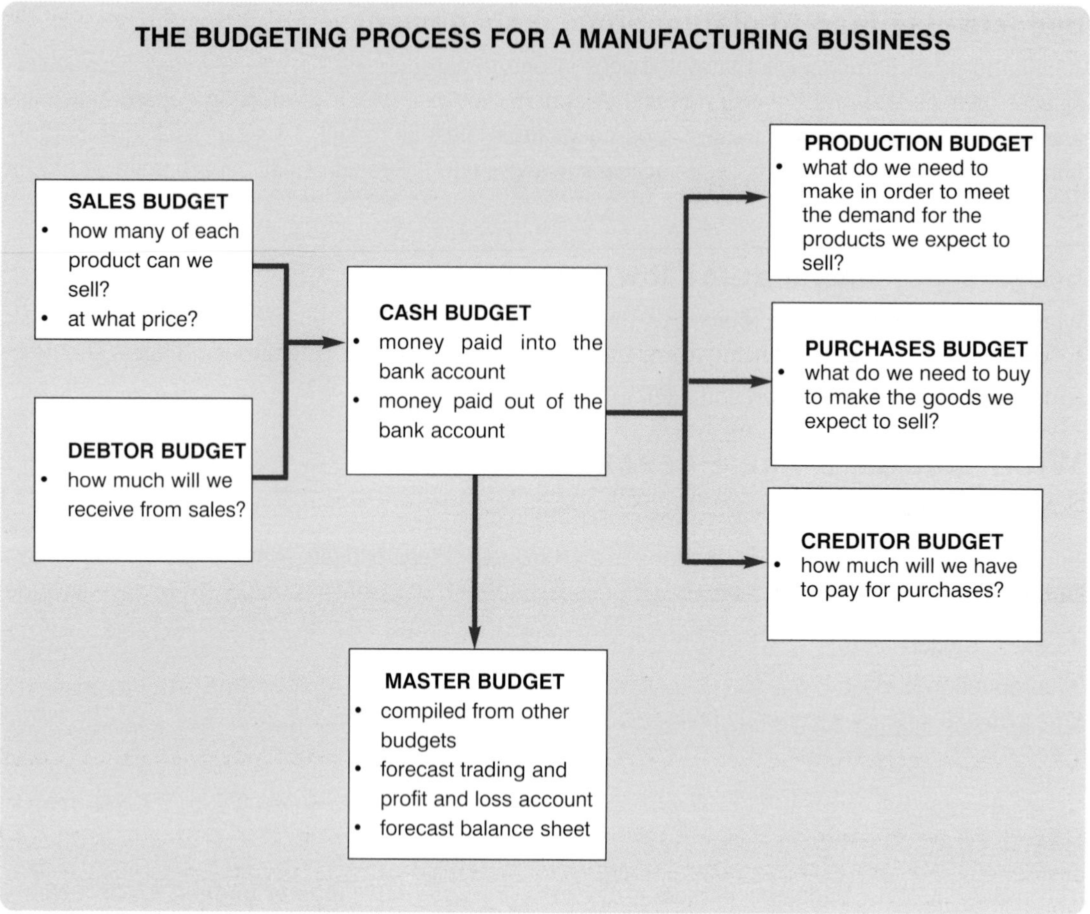

THE BUDGETING PROCESS FOR A MANUFACTURING BUSINESS

SALES BUDGET
- how many of each product can we sell?
- at what price?

DEBTOR BUDGET
- how much will we receive from sales?

CASH BUDGET
- money paid into the bank account
- money paid out of the bank account

PRODUCTION BUDGET
- what do we need to make in order to meet the demand for the products we expect to sell?

PURCHASES BUDGET
- what do we need to buy to make the goods we expect to sell?

CREDITOR BUDGET
- how much will we have to pay for purchases?

MASTER BUDGET
- compiled from other budgets
- forecast trading and profit and loss account
- forecast balance sheet

BUDGETARY PLANNING

Many large businesses take a highly formal view of planning the budget and make use of:

- a **budget manual**, which provides a set of guidelines as to who is involved with the budgetary planning and control process, and how the process is to be conducted
- a **budget committee**, which organises the process of budgetary planning and control; comprises representatives from the main functions of the business – eg production, sales, administration – together with a budget co-ordinator whose job is to administer and oversee the activities of the committee

In smaller businesses, the process of planning the budget may be rather more informal, with the owner or manager taking charge.

Whatever the size of the business it is important, though, that the planning process begins well before the start of the budget period; this then gives time for budgets to be prepared, reviewed, redrafted, and reviewed again before being finally agreed and submitted to the directors or owners for approval.

For example, the planning process for a budget which is to start on 1 January might commence in the previous June, as follows:

- June — Budget committee meets to plan next year's budgets
- July — First draft of budgets prepared
- August — Review of draft budgets
- September — Draft budgets amended in light of review
- October — Further review and redrafting to final version
- November — Budgets submitted to directors or owners for approval
- December — Budgets for next year circulated to managers
- January — Budget period commences

SALES BUDGET AND PRODUCTION BUDGET

planning the sales budget

The sales budget is often the starting point for budgetary planning in any type of business. It is the plan which will project the sales of:

- products made by a **manufacturing** business, eg cars, CDs, breakfast cereals
- services provided by a **service** business, eg holidays, educational courses, bus and train journeys

The accuracy of the sales budget is critical for the success of the business. If a business overestimates sales, it will be left with unsold goods or under-utilised services; if sales are underestimated, then customers will be lost to competitors. Both overestimating and underestimating sales can lose money. While budgeting is not an exact science, and is unlikely to be 100% accurate, it is essential that as much accurate information as possible is gathered; this can include:

- details of past sales performance – available within the business
- present sales figures – up-to-date figures from sales representatives
- what the competition is doing – estimates of market share
- assessment of whether the market is expanding or declining
- forecasts made – by sales representatives and market researchers
- trading conditions and the economic climate

A sales budget will start off by estimating the number of units to be sold over the next year and then applying a selling price to produce an estimate of the income figure in money terms. There is no laid-down format for a sales budget: it can project sales in a number of different ways:

- by product
- by customer
- by geographical area

An example of a product-based sales budget follows:

sales budget by product

	January	February	March	April	May	June	Total
	£	£	£	£	£	£	£
product A	1,000	1,000	1,000	1,000	1,000	1,000	6,000
product B	1,500	1,500	1,500	1,500	1,500	1,500	9,000
product C	2,500	2,500	2,500	2,500	2,500	2,500	15,000
etc ...							

Note how the budget uses:

budget periods – the subdivision of the budget into monthly, four-weekly (which divides a 52-week year into 13 four-weekly periods), or weekly

budget headings – the subdivision of the budget by product (or other category of income or expense).

planning the production/operating budget

When a business has established its sales budget it is then in a position to work out its production budget (for a manufacturing business), or its operating budget (for a service). Note that production/operating budgets are normally prepared using units of output (rather than money amounts).

When planning a production/operating budget, management must gather together information about the business' resources and consider a range of external factors in order to assess what can and cannot be achieved. These include:

- *timing* When during the year are the products required? Are there any seasonal fluctuations (Christmas cards, fireworks) which will produce uneven demands on production facilities? Will the business need to hold stocks of products in advance?
- *capacity* Can the existing production facilities cope with the expected demand? Will new fixed assets be needed? Should some work be subcontracted to other businesses?
- *labour cost* Does the business have the right number of staff with the necessary skills? Will more staff be needed? Will there need to be training? Will overtime need to be worked, or is an additional shift required?
- *materials* Can the right quality and quantity of materials be obtained at the right price?

When all of this information has been gathered and analysed, the business should then be in a position to prepare the production budget, taking into account:

- the projected monthly sales (in units)
- the number of units of finished products in stock at the beginning and end of each month

The production budget is usually prepared in terms of units of production. Some of the factors listed above will need to be considered, for example:

- there may be a maximum level of stocks that can be held in the warehouse/stores
- management may require that each month's closing stock is a set percentage of next month's sales

WORKED EXAMPLE 1: PRODUCTION BUDGET

This production budget (in units) has been prepared where there are the following constraints:

- each month's closing stock is to be 20% of the following month's sales units
- the maximum capacity of the warehouse is 100 units

production budget

	January	February	March	April	May	June	Total
	units	units	units	units	units	units	units
sales	250	300	280	600	325	300	2,055
opening stock	50	60	56	100	65	60	50
closing stock	60	56	*100	65	60	**65	65
production	260	296	324	565	320	305	2,070

* maximum capacity of the warehouse

** sales in July are estimated to be 325 units, so closing stock at the end of June is budgeted to be 65 units

Tutorial notes:

- To calculate the production units for each month, deduct the opening stock from sales and add the closing stock. For example, in January:

		Units
	sales	250
less	opening stock	50
add	closing stock	60
equals	production	260

- The total column, on the right-hand side of the budget, can be used as a cross-check of the monthly figures.

We will now look at a more complex Worked Example of a production budget.

WORKED EXAMPLE 2: PRODUCTION BUDGET

situation

Jim Lewis is the production manager of Fitta Homegym Limited, manufacturers of the Fitta De Luxe Exercise Cycle. The sales manager has just presented Jim with the budgeted sales for the forthcoming twelve months, as follows:

January	150 units
February	150 "
March	200 "
April	400 "
May	400 "
June	400 "
July	500 "
August	300 "
September	200 "
October	200 "
November	700 "
December	425 "

Stock in the warehouse on 1 January at the start of the year is budgeted to be 100 units. Jim's problem is that the factory, working at normal capacity, can produce 350 units each month. More units can be made if overtime is paid, but the directors are not keen to see this happen, just as they do not like to see too much under-utilisation of the factory. Jim has to work out an even production budget – set in terms of units of production – which will keep the factory working at near or full capacity, but without incurring too much overtime. He has three other constraints:

- month-end stock must never fall below 100 units
- the warehouse is fairly small and cannot hold more than 600 units
- the factory is closed for half of August

solution

Jim plans the production budget as follows:

production budget for next year

UNITS	Jan	Feb	Mar	Apr	May	Jun	Jul	Aug	Sep	Oct	Nov	Dec
sales	150	150	200	400	400	400	500	300	200	200	700	425
opening stock	100	275	450	600	550	500	450	300	175	325	475	125
closing stock	275	450	600	550	500	450	300	175	325	475	125	100
production	325	325	350	350	350	350	350	175	350	350	350	400

Note that Jim has been successful in meeting all of the constraints, except that:

- the factory could produce another 25 units in both January and February; however, the effect of this would be to take the warehouse beyond its capacity in March
- overtime will have to be paid for the production of 50 units in December

advantages of a production budget

The use of a production budget enables a business to:

- identify the production capacity available
- schedule resources – eg cash, materials, labour – effectively
- meet sales demand
- make best use of spare capacity

PURCHASES BUDGET

This budget is a development of the sales and production budgets. It is used to work out the level of purchases that will have to be made:

- either, to meet the requirements for materials in the production process of a manufacturing business
- or, to provide the goods to be sold in a shop

Purchases budget may be expressed in terms of units of goods (eg a manufacturing business buying in components), or it may be in terms of money (eg a shop buying in stock for resale). It is for the business preparing the budget to decide which is the more appropriate budget for its needs.

purchases budget in units

The layout for this budget is very similar to that for production, using sales, opening stock and closing stock to calculate purchases. As with the production budget, there may be factors to consider when preparing the purchases budget, for example:

- there may be a maximum level of stocks that can be held in the warehouse/stores
- management may require that each month's closing stock is a set percentage of next month's sales

WORKED EXAMPLE: PURCHASES BUDGET IN UNITS

This purchases budget has been prepared where there are the following constraints:

- each month's closing stock is to be 50% of the following month's sales units
- the maximum capacity of the warehouse is 350 units

purchases budget

	January	February	March	April	May	June	Total
	units	units	units	units	units	units	units
sales	500	550	600	780	570	620	3,620
opening stock	250	275	300	350	285	310	250
closing stock	275	300	*350	285	310	**320	320
purchases	525	575	650	715	595	630	3,690

* maximum capacity of the warehouse

** sales in July are estimated to be 640 units, so closing stock at the end of June is budgeted to be 320 units

Tutorial notes:

- To calculate the number of units to be purchased each month, deduct the opening stock from sales and add the closing stock.
- The total column, on the right-hand side of the budget, can be used as a cross-check of the monthly figures.

purchases budget in £s

This budget starts with the sales figures (expressed in money amounts) and then deducts the gross profit margin or the gross profit mark-up – see page 490 – to calculate the amount of purchases to be made. This method of budgeting for purchases is quite common for shops and other businesses which establish their selling prices by reference to a profit margin or mark-up.

WORKED EXAMPLE: PURCHASES BUDGET IN £S

This purchases budget has been prepared (in £000) where:

- the business has a gross profit margin of 20%
- there are no closing stocks at the month-end, ie the business buys in the goods during the same month in which it expects to sell them

purchases budget

	January	February	March	April	May	June	Total
	£000	£000	£000	£000	£000	£000	£000
sales	20	28	30	26	32	36	172
profit margin	4	5.6	6	5.2	6.4	7.2	34.4
purchases	16	22.4	24	20.8	25.6	28.8	137.6

Tutorial notes:

- To calculate the profit margin, multiply the sales figure by the percentage profit margin. For example, in January £20,000 x 20% = £4,000.
- Deduct the profit margin from sales to give the figure for purchases.
- If using a profit mark-up – see page 490 – and working from budgeted sales figures, care needs to be taken with the calculations for purchases. This is because mark-up is based on the purchase price. Thus the selling price is:

	purchase price	+ profit mark-up	= selling price
eg	£100	+ £25	= £125

Here, with a 25% mark-up, the purchase price is 100/125* of the selling price.

* 100 + percentage mark-up

DEBTOR BUDGET AND CREDITOR BUDGET

These two budgets are prepared in a similar way and calculate the amount of debtors or creditors expected to be outstanding at the end of each month.

planning the debtor budget

The information needed to plan the debtor budget is:

- the amount of credit sales (from the sales budget)
- the expected receipts from debtors (from the cash budget)

- the expected cash discount allowed to debtors (from the cash budget)
- the normal trade terms under which credit sales are made (eg 30 days net, 2% cash discount for settlement within 7 days)
- the debtors' collection period (see page 497)
- details of any bad debts written off

WORKED EXAMPLE: DEBTOR BUDGET

This debtor budget has been prepared from the following information:

- credit sales are budgeted to be £30,000 per month for January to March, and £40,000 for April to June
- receipts from debtors are budgeted to be £28,000 per month for January and February, £35,000 per month for March and April, and £39,000 per month for May and June
- cash discount allowed is budgeted to be £500 per month
- bad debts of £500 per month are to be written off in January and February
- the figure for debtors at 1 January is £33,000

debtor budget

	January	February	March	April	May	June	Total
	£000	£000	£000	£000	£000	£000	£000
opening debtors	33	34	35	29.5	34	34.5	33
credit sales	30	30	30	40	40	40	210
receipts	28	28	35	35	39	39	204
discount allowed	0.5	0.5	0.5	0.5	0.5	0.5	3
bad debts written off	0.5	0.5	–	–	–	–	1
closing debtors	34	35	29.5	34	34.5	35	35

Tutorial notes:

- The figure for closing debtors is calculated as follows:

  opening debtors + credit sales – receipts – discount allowed – bad debts

- The total column can be used as a cross-check of the monthly figures

planning the creditor budget

The information needed to plan the creditor budget is:

- the amount of credit purchases (from the purchases budget)
- the expected payments to creditors (from the cash budget)
- the expected cash discount received from creditors (from the cash budget)
- the normal trade terms under which credit purchases are made
- the creditors' payment period (see page 497)

WORKED EXAMPLE: CREDITOR BUDGET

This creditor budget has been prepared from the following information:

- credit purchases are budgeted to be £25,000 per month in July and August, £30,000 per month in September and October, and £35,000 per month in November and December
- payments to creditors are budgeted to be £26,000 per month for July to September, and £33,000 per month for October to December
- cash discount received is budgeted to be £300 per month
- the figure for creditors at 1 July is £29,000

creditor budget

	July	Aug	Sep	Oct	Nov	Dec	Total
	£000	£000	£000	£000	£000	£000	£000
opening creditors	29	27.7	26.4	30.1	26.8	28.5	29
credit purchases	25	25	30	30	35	35	180
payments	26	26	26	33	33	33	177
discount received	0.3	0.3	0.3	0.3	0.3	0.3	1.8
closing creditors	27.7	26.4	30.1	26.8	28.5	30.2	30.2

Tutorial notes:

- The figure for closing creditors is calculated as follows:

  opening creditors + credit purchases – payments – discount received

- The total column can be used as a cross-check of the monthly figures

CASH BUDGET

A cash budget details the expected cash/bank receipts and payments, usually on a month-by-month basis, for the next three, six or twelve months, in order to show the estimated bank balance at the end of each month throughout the period.

From the cash budget, the managers of a business can decide what action to take when a surplus of cash is shown to be available or, as is more likely, when a bank overdraft needs to be arranged.

A suitable format for a cash budget, with sample figures, is set out below:

Name ....Cash Budget for the .... months ending				
	Jan	Feb	Mar	Apr
	£000	£000	£000	£000
Receipts				
eg from debtors	150	150	161	170
cash sales	70	80	75	80
Total receipts for month (A)	220	230	236	250
Payments				
eg to creditors	160	165	170	170
expenses	50	50	50	60
fixed assets		50		
Total payments for month (B)	210	265	220	230
Net cash flow (Receipts less Payments, ie A–B)	10	(35)	16	20
Add bank balance at beginning of month	10	20	(15)	1
Bank balance (overdraft) at end of month	20	(15)	1	21

A cash budget consists of three main sections:

- receipts for the month
- payments for the month
- summary of bank account

The receipts are analysed to show the amount of money that is expected to be received from cash sales, debtors, sale of fixed assets, issue of shares, loans received etc.

Payments show how much money is expected to be paid in respect of cash purchases, creditors, expenses, purchases of fixed assets, repayment of shares and loans. Note that non-cash expenses (such as depreciation and doubtful debts) are not shown in the cash budget.

The summary at the bottom of the cash budget shows **net cash flow** (total receipts less total payments) added to the bank balance at the beginning of the month, and resulting in the estimated closing bank balance at the end of the month. An overdrawn bank balance is shown in brackets.

The main difficulty in the preparation of cash budgets lies in the **timing** of receipts and payments – for example, debtors may pay two months after date of sale, or creditors may be paid one month after date of purchase: it is important to ensure that such receipts and payments are recorded correctly. Note too that the cash budget, as its name suggests, deals only in cash/bank transactions; thus non-cash items, such as depreciation, are never shown. Similarly, where cash discounts are allowed or received, only the actual amount of cash expected to be received or paid is recorded.

WORKED EXAMPLE: CASH BUDGET

situation

A friend of yours, Mike Anderson, has recently been made redundant from his job as a sales representative for an arts and crafts company. Mike has decided to set up in business on his own selling art supplies to shops and art societies. He plans to invest £20,000 of his savings into the new business. He has a number of good business contacts, and is confident that his firm will do well. He thinks that some additional finance will be required in the short term and plans to approach his bank for this.

Mike asks for your assistance in producing estimates for his new business for the next six months. He provides the following information:

- The business, which is to be called 'Art Supplies' will commence in January 20-8.
- Fixed assets costing £8,000 will be bought in early January. These will be paid for immediately and are expected to have a five-year life, at the end of which they will be worthless.
- An initial stock of goods costing £5,000 will be bought and paid for at the beginning of January.
- Monthly purchases of stocks will then be made at a level sufficient to replace forecast sales for that month, ie the goods he expects to sell in January will be replaced by purchases made in January, and so on.
- Forecast monthly sales are:

January	February	March	April	May	June
£3,000	£6,000	£6,000	£10,500	£10,500	£10,500

- The selling price of goods is fixed at the cost price plus 50 per cent.
- To encourage sales, he will allow two months' credit to customers; however, only one month's credit will be received from suppliers of stock (but the initial stock will be paid for immediately).
- Running expenses of the business, including rent of premises, but excluding depreciation of fixed assets, are estimated at £1,600 per month.
- Mike intends to draw £1,000 each month in cash from the business.

You are asked to prepare a cash budget for the first six months of the business.

solution

Mike Anderson, trading as 'Art Supplies'
Cash budget for the six months ending 30 June 20-8

	Jan	Feb	Mar	Apr	May	Jun
	£	£	£	£	£	£
Receipts						
Capital introduced	20,000					
Debtors	–	–	3,000	6,000	6,000	10,500
Total receipts for month	20,000	–	3,000	6,000	6,000	10,500
Payments						
Fixed assets	8,000					
Stock	5,000					
Creditors	–	2,000	4,000	4,000	7,000	7,000
Running expenses	1,600	1,600	1,600	1,600	1,600	1,600
Drawings	1,000	1,000	1,000	1,000	1,000	1,000
Total payments for month	15,600	4,600	6,600	6,600	9,600	9,600
Net cash flow	4,400	(4,600)	(3,600)	(600)	(3,600)	900
Add bank balance (overdraft) at beginning of month	–	4,400	(200)	(3,800)	(4,400)	(8,000)
Bank balance (overdraft) at end of month	4,400	(200)	(3,800)	(4,400)	(8,000)	(7,100)

Reminder: No depreciation – a non-cash expense – is shown in the cash budget.

Notes:

- purchases are two-thirds of the sales values (because selling price is cost price plus 50 per cent)
- customers pay two months after sale, ie debtors from January settle in March
- suppliers are paid one month after purchase, ie creditors from January are paid in February

The cash budget shows that there is a need, in the first six months at least, for some bank finance. An early approach to the bank needs to be made.

On the next page, we will see how the master budget is prepared for this business.

advantages of a cash budget

The use of a cash budget enables a business to:

- identify any possible bank overdraft in advance and take steps to minimise the borrowing (so saving interest payable)
- consider rescheduling payments to avoid bank borrowing, eg delay purchase of fixed assets, agreement to pay rises, payment of drawings/dividends

- arrange any possible bank finance well in advance
- identify any possible cash surpluses in advance and take steps to invest the surplus on a short-term basis (so earning interest)

The Master Budget

A cash budget does not indicate the profits (or losses) being made by a business. It does not follow that a cash budget which reveals an increasing bank balance necessarily indicates a profitable business. A **master budget** is the next logical step once all other budgets, including the cash budget, have been prepared.

A master budget takes the form of a forecast operating statement – forecast trading and profit and loss account – and a forecast balance sheet.

WORKED EXAMPLE: MASTER BUDGET

situation

Before visiting the bank to arrange finance, you help Mike Anderson (see Worked Example on the previous two pages) to prepare a master budget for the first six months of his business.

solution

Mike Anderson, trading as 'Art Supplies'

Forecast trading and profit and loss account for the six months ending 30 June 20-8

	£	£
Sales		46,500
Opening stock	5,000	
Purchases £46,500 x 2/3	31,000	
	36,000	
Less Closing stock	5,000	
Cost of sales		31,000
Gross profit		15,500
Less overheads:		
Running expenses	9,600	
Depreciation of fixed assets		
(68,000 ÷ 5 years) ÷ 2, ie six months	800	
		10,400
Net profit		5,100

Mike Anderson, trading as 'Art Supplies'
Forecast balance sheet as at 30 June 20-8

	£	£
Fixed Assets		
At cost		8,000
Less provision for depreciation		800
Net book value		7,200
Current Assets		
Stock	5,000	
Debtors £10,500 x 2 months	21,000	
	26,000	
Less Current Liabilities		
Creditors	7,000	
Bank overdraft	7,100	
	14,100	
Working Capital or Net Current Assets		11,900
NET ASSETS		19,100
FINANCED BY		
Capital		
Opening capital		20,000
Add net profit		5,100
		25,100
Less Drawings		6,000
		19,100

Points to note when preparing forecast final accounts:

- The sales figure used is the total amount of goods sold, whether paid for or not (sales made, but not yet paid for, are recorded as debtors in the balance sheet).
- Likewise, the figure for purchases is the total of goods bought, with amounts not yet paid for recorded as creditors in the balance sheet.
- Depreciation, which *never* appears in the cash budget, is shown amongst the overheads in the profit and loss account, and deducted from the cost of the fixed asset in the balance sheet. (Note that, in the example above, depreciation is for a period of six months.)

Budgetary Control

Once the budgetary planning process has been completed, and the budget is approved by the owner or directors, the budget becomes the official plan of the business. During the period of the budget the process of **budgetary control** uses the budget as a control mechanism to compare actual results with what was planned to happen in the budget. As the budget period progresses, separate budget reports are prepared monthly. The 'actual' and 'variance' columns are completed and the cumulative figures for the year-to-date are recorded. An example of a budget report is shown below (the owner/directors should be pleased with the results shown).

Fitta Homegym Limited – sales budget report

	Income: December			*Income: Year-to-date*		
	budget	actual	variance	budget	actual	variance
	£	£	£	£	£	£
Retail sales	200,000	250,000	50,000 FAV	2,750,000	3,125,000	375,000 FAV
Mail order	225,000	200,000	25,000 ADV	1,275,000	1,350,000	75,000 FAV
Total sales	425,000	450,000	25,000 FAV	4,025,000	4,475,000	450,000 FAV

The management of a business will be monitoring the budget during the year and will be watching closely for differences between the budgeted and actual figures – the *variances*. There are two types of variance:

- a **favourable variance** (FAV), where the results are better than expected
- an **adverse variance** (ADV), where the results are worse than expected

Details of variances are used to:

- **feed back** information to budget holders so that, where necessary, corrective action can be taken
- **feed forward** into the planning process for the next period's budgets

benefits of budgetary control

- planning – the formal framework of budgets is used to predict future activities of the business, and potential problems will be highlighted
- co-ordination – individual budgets, eg sales, production, purchases, debtor, creditor, are integrated into the master budget
- control – comparison is made of actual results against the budget
- communication – between managers and other staff in order to achieve the objectives of the business

- motivation – of staff to ensure that budgets are met
- evaluation of performance – to compare the budget against the actual results, and to see where improvements can be made
- decision-making – about production, sales and costs

limitations of budgetary control

- costs and benefits – the benefit must exceed the cost
- accuracy – some information used in the budgets may be inaccurate
- demotivation – of staff who have not been involved in planning the budget, or who are set too high a level to achieve
- disfunctional management – where different sections of the business are not co-ordinated
- set too easy – where budgets are set at too low a level they will not enable the business to use its resources to best advantage

CHAPTER SUMMARY

- Budgets are used to plan and control the business.
- Budgets – for income or expenditure – are prepared for each section of the business, eg sales, production, purchases, debtors, creditors, cash
- Budgetary planning is the process of setting the budget for the next period.
- Responsibility for budgets is given to managers and supervisors – the budget holders.
- The master budget is compiled from the budgets of a business.
- The master budget comprises:
  - forecast trading and profit and loss account
  - forecast balance sheet
- Budgetary control uses the budgets to monitor actual results with budgeted figures.
- Variances – the difference between actual and budgeted figures – should be investigated so that, where necessary, corrective action can be taken.

In the next chapter we turn our attention to the way in which businesses make decisions. As well as the requirement for profitability, we will consider the role of social accounting in decision-making, eg the effects of decisions on the workforce, the local economy and the environment.

QUESTIONS

NOTE: an asterisk (*) after the question number means that an answer to the question is given at the end of this book.

32.1*

Davidson Reproductions Ltd produces tables. The production manager has collected the following information in order to produce a production budget for the next four months.

1. Demand is expected to be 1,200 tables in month 1. This should reduce by 10% in month 2, but thereafter increase by 5% each month, based on the demand for the previous month.
2. The stock at the end of each month is to be maintained at a level of 20% of the following month's sales but due to a storage constraint should not exceed 240 tables.
3. The stock at the start of month 1 is 100 tables.

REQUIRED

Produce a production budget for the next four months. Round up to the nearest whole table.

	Month 1 (tables)	Month 2 (tables)	Month 3 (tables)	Month 4 (tables)
Sales	....	....	....	....
Opening stock	....	....	....	....
Closing stock	....	....	....	....
Production	....	....	....	....

Assessment and Qualifications Alliance (AQA), 2003

32.2

Lee's Landscapes Ltd supplies plants for residential gardens.

The results for the year ended 31 March 2003 are:

	£
Sales	150,000
Purchases	110,000
Trade debtors	12,000
Trade creditors	11,000

All sales and purchases are on credit terms.

Total sales for the year ending 31 March 2004 are expected to be:

April – June	£20,000 per month
July – October	£15,000 per month
November – March	£5,000 per month

As at 31 March 2004 trade debtors and trade creditors are expected to be £14,000 and £10,000 respectively.

There is no closing stock. The profit margin is 25%.

The business prepares budgets on a two-monthly basis.

REQUIRED

(a) Prepare a purchases budget for the year ending 31 March 2004.

	April and May £000	June and July £000	August and September £000	October and November £000	December and January £000	February and March £000
Sales						
Margin						
Purchases						

(b) (i) Calculate the debtors' collection period for each of the last two years. State the formula used.

Formula ....

....

Year ending 31 March 2003	Year ending 31 March 2004
....	....
....	....
....	....

(ii) Calculate the creditors' payment period for each of the last two years. State the formula used.

Formula ....

....

Year ending 31 March 2003	Year ending 31 March 2004
....	....
....	....
....	....

(c) Comment on the results from (b). Give one recommendation to improve the credit control at Lee's Landscapes Ltd.

Debtors' collection period ....

....

Creditors' payment period ....

....

Recommendation ....

....

Assessment and Qualifications Alliance (AQA), 2003

32.3 Classic Furniture is a manufacturer of reproduction antique furniture. It is owned by Helen Sutton as a sole trader business. There are four employees and annual turnover is approximately £200,000 per year.

REQUIRED

(a) Explain two benefits of budgetary control to Helen Sutton.

(b) Suggest three budgets which Helen could use in the business to provide an adequate system of budgetary control.

(c) Advise Helen of the relevant factors to consider when implementing budgetary control.

32.4 Wyvern (Medical) Limited is a manufacturer of specialist equipment used in hospitals. The accounts assistant has collected the following information in order to prepare the debtor and creditor budgets for the six months to 30 June 20-5.

- On 1 January 20-5 the figures for debtors and creditors are £65,500 and £42,400 respectively.
- For the six months to 30 June 20-5, the following transactions are forecast:

	January	February	March	April	May	June
	£	£	£	£	£	£
credit purchases	19,500	22,300	22,500	24,000	22,600	23,400
credit sales	38,300	39,500	42,400	45,000	47,400	44,700
cash discount allowed	350	400	450	500	500	400
cash discount received	170	200	220	280	260	270
receipts from debtors	42,400	38,100	37,400	40,600	43,200	45,800
payments to creditors	22,600	20,500	21,600	22,300	24,300	23,200
bad debts written off	500	500	–	–	–	–

REQUIRED

(a) Prepare the debtor budget of Wyvern (Medical) Limited for the six months to 30 June 20-5.

debtor budget

	January	February	March	April	May	June	Total
	£	£	£	£	£	£	£

creditor budget

	January	February	March	April	May	June	Total
	£	£	£	£	£	£	£

(b) Prepare the creditor budget of Wyvern (Medical) Limited for the six months to 30 June 20-5.

32.5* N Kayali, the assistant accountant at Strudwick Stationers Ltd, has obtained the following information for the seven months ending 30 September 2002. This information is to be used to prepare a cash budget for the four months ending 31 August 2002.

1. Actual sales were £44,000 and £46,000 for March and April 2002 respectively.
2. Total forecast sales at the end of each of the next five months are expected to be:

		2002		
May	June	July	Aug	Sep
£	£	£	£	£
44,000	46,000	42,000	44,000	48,000

80% of each month's total forecast sales are expected to be for cash. The debtors are expected to pay one month in arrears.

3. Purchases are expected to be 70% of the following month's total forecast sales value and are paid for two months in arrears.
4. The following costs are expected to be paid for in the month in which they occur:

   Wages £9,000 per month to 31 July 2002 and £9,500 per month thereafter

   Fixed Costs £3,000 per month

   Variable costs being 10% of each month's total forecast sales
5. The bank balance as at 1 May 2002 was £12,100.

REQUIRED

(a) Prepare a cash budget for each of the four months ending 31 August 2002.

Strudwick Stationers Ltd

Cash Budget for four months ending 31 August 2002

Details	**May** £000	**June** £000	**July** £000	**Aug** £000
....	....	....	....	....
....	....	....	....	....
....	....	....	....	....
....	....	....	....	....
....	....	....	....	....
....	....	....	....	....
....	....	....	....	....
....	....	....	....	....
....	....	....	....	....
....	....	....	....	....
....	....	....	....	....
....	....	....	....	....
....	....	....	....	....

(b) N Kayali is unsure of the benefits of producing a cash budget for a four month period. Explain one benefit to Strudwick Stationers Ltd of completing a four month cash budget.

....

....

....

....

Assessment and Qualifications Alliance (AQA), 2002

32.6* Peversal Papers Ltd manufactures reams of paper. Each ream is sold for £22 and costs £12 to manufacture.

The company's policy is to maintain stock levels at the end of each month at 20% of the next month's expected sales.

Sales for 2002 are expected to be:

February	March	April	May	June
£88,000	£99,000	£110,000	£121,000	£110,000

Customers are allowed one month's credit. Only 5% pay immediately and receive a 2% discount for prompt payment.

Stock as at 1 March 2002 is expected to be 900 units.

Administration and distribution costs which are paid in the month in which they occur are expected to be:

February	March	April	May	June
£26,000	£28,000	£34,000	£38,000	£36,000

The bank balance on 1 March 2002 is expected to be £6,000.

Production costs are paid in the month in which they occur.

REQUIRED

(a) (i) Complete the following cash budget for the 3 months ending 31 May 2002.

Cash Budget for Peversal Papers Ltd
for the three months ending 31 May 2002

	March £000	April £000	May £000
Sales – cash			
– credit			
Production costs			
Admin/distribution			
Net inflow/outflow			
Opening balance			
Closing balance			

(ii) Complete the following production budget for the 3 months ending 31 May 2002.

Production Budget for Peversal Papers Ltd
for the three months ending 31 May 2002

	March units	April units	May units
Sales			
Opening stock			
Closing stock			
Production			

(b) The Managing Director of Peversal Papers Ltd believes that a cash budget is all that is required, however the Production Manager disagrees. He believes that the production budget is vital too. Assess three advantages to Peversal Papers Ltd of using both a cash budget and a production budget.

....

....

....

....

....

....

....

....

....

....

....

Assessment and Qualifications Alliance (AQA), 2002

32.7 Sunshine Ltd sells beach buckets and spades.

The forecast information for the six months ending 31 October 2002 is:

	May	June	July	August	September	October
	£000	£000	£000	£000	£000	£000
Sales	16	20	26	28	24	20
Purchases	12	16	18	14	12	10
Overheads	4	8	8	8	8	4

Additional information

1. On average 20% of each month's sales is expected to be for cash. A further 60% will be given one month's credit. The rest will be given two months' credit. All monies should be received when due.
2. The increase in overheads arises from the employment of casual staff. The overheads are paid in the month in which they occur.
3. Suppliers are expected to allow one month's credit.
4. The cash at bank balance as at 1 July 2002 is £7,200 overdrawn.

REQUIRED

(a) Prepare a detailed forecast month by month cash budget for the four months ending 31 October 2002.

Sunshine Ltd

Cash budget for four months ending 31 October 2002

	July £000	Aug £000	Sept £000	Oct £000
Sales – cash				
– 1 month				
– 2 months				
Purchases				
Overheads				
Net inflow/outflow				
Opening balance				
Closing balance				

(b) (i) Assess the cash position of Sunshine Ltd as at 31 October 2002.

(ii) Recommend one way the company could improve its cash position.

Assessment and Qualifications Alliance (AQA), 2001

32.8* You are preparing the cash budget of Wilkinson Limited for the first six months of 20-8. The following budgeted figures are available:

	Sales	*Purchases*	*Wages and salaries*	*Other expenses*
	£	£	£	£
January	65,000	26,500	17,500	15,500
February	70,000	45,000	18,000	20,500
March	72,500	50,000	18,250	19,000
April	85,000	34,500	18,500	18,500
May	65,000	35,500	16,500	20,500
June	107,500	40,500	20,000	22,000

The following additional information is available:

- Sales income is received in the month after sale, and sales for December 20-7 amounted to £57,500
- 'Other expenses' each month includes an allocation of £1,000 for depreciation; all other expenses are paid for in the month in which they are incurred
- Purchases, and wages and salaries are paid for in the month in which they are incurred
- The bank balance at 1 January 20-8 is £2,250
- Stock at 1 January 20-8 is valued at £15,500 and, at 30 June 20-8, is expected to have a value of £17,350

REQUIRED

You are to prepare:

(a) a month-by-month cash budget for the first six months of 20-8

(b) a forecast trading and profit and loss account for the six months ending 30 June 20-8

32.9

Jim Smith has recently been made redundant; he has received a redundancy payment and this, together with his accumulated savings, amounts to £10,000. He has decided to set up his own business selling computer stationery and this will commence trading with an initial capital of £10,000 on 1 January. On this date he will buy a van for business use at a cost of £6,000. He has estimated his purchases, sales, and expenses for the next six months as follows:

	Purchases	*Sales*	*Expenses*
	£	£	£
January	4,500	1,250	750
February	4,500	3,000	600
March	3,500	4,000	600
April	3,500	4,000	650
May	3,500	4,500	650
June	4,000	6,000	700

He will pay for purchases in the month after purchase; likewise, he expects his customers to pay for sales in the month after sale. All expenses will be paid for in the month they are incurred.

Jim realises that he may need bank overdraft facilities before his business becomes established. He asks you to help him with information for the bank and, in particular, he asks you to prepare:

(a) a month-by-month cash budget for the first six months

(b) a forecast trading and profit and loss account for the first six months – for this he tells you that his closing stock at 30 June is expected to have a value of £3,250, and that he wishes to depreciate the van at 20% per annum

(c) a forecast balance sheet as at 30 June

33 DECISION-MAKING AND SOCIAL ACCOUNTING

In this book we have looked at various aspects of financial accounting and cost accounting. Accounting information is useful in helping the managers of a business to make decisions – for example, we need to replace our existing machinery, so which new machine shall we buy? However, such decisions cannot be made in isolation – a business is part of a wider community, with responsibilities to its employees, the local economy and the environment.

In this chapter we look at the accounting factors, including social accounting factors, which affect decision-making.

DECISION-MAKING IN CONTEXT

A business does not operate in isolation where it can do what it wishes with no thought for others. Even small businesses have responsibilities to others, while large businesses must take great care to consider the effect of their decisions – the public and the media (in the form of television, radio, newspapers) will certainly scrutinise their every move.

The diagram on the next page shows some of the factors which affect decision-making. This shows that, while the effect on profit and cash is important, other factors need to be considered. These other factors are often referred to as 'social accounting' and we shall be looking at the impact of a variety of social accounting factors later in the chapter.

When we talk about making decisions, there are a variety of levels at which decisions are made. More decisions are made at lower levels than at higher levels – although it is the latter that get most attention in the media. Look at some of these decisions:

- higher level decisions
  - we have decided to close our factory in Scotland
  - our call centre will be transferred to India
  - we will only buy furniture which uses timber from managed forests

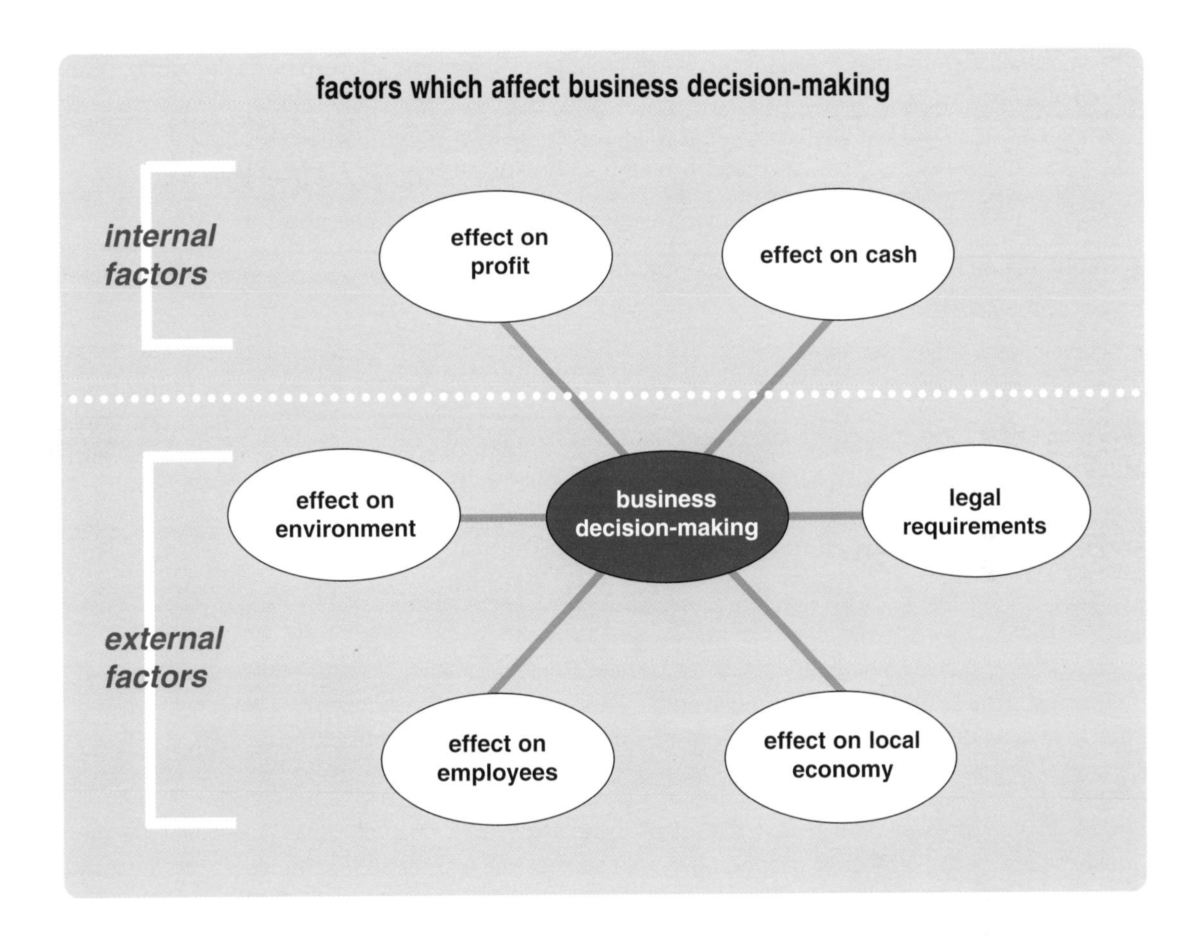

- lower level decisions
  - we have instituted a first-aid training programme
  - all our photocopying is done on recycled paper
  - the tea used in our canteen comes from 'fairtrade' suppliers

The conclusion to draw is that we all make decisions – whether at work or in our personal lives. We need to consider not only the financial implications of our decisions, but other factors as well.

Decision-making: the Effect on Profit and Cash

- **cash** is the actual amount of money held in the bank or as cash
- **profit** is a calculated figure which shows the surplus of income over expenditure for the year

In Chapter 29 (page 493) we looked in detail at the differences between profit and cash. We saw that some transactions often have an unequal effect on profit and cash – for example, depreciation is a non-cash expense which reduces profit, but has no effect on cash.

A business will wish to know the extent to which profit and cash will be affected by its decisions. Often the effects need to be calculated over more than one year, as there could well be initial costs – eg redundancy costs paid to employees – that will not recur in later years. Thus decisions should not be taken on the basis of first year calculations only, but should consider the effect of later years.

The rules to be followed when considering the effect on profit and cash are that:

- profit should be maximised
- costs should be minimised
- cash inflows should be maximised
- cash outflows should be minimised

However, as we have seen, decisions should not be taken entirely on the basis of profit and cash – other social accounting factors are important, and we will discuss these later in this chapter.

WORKED EXAMPLE: DECISION-MAKING

situation

John Cazalet is the Managing Director of Cazalet Printers Limited, a large printer of books and magazines. The printing presses are getting old and are prone to breakdown, and John has decided that they need to be replaced with new presses. John is considering the following two options:

Option 1

Invest in new presses, which use the latest technology, at a cost of £1 million. Currently the manufacturer of the presses is offering buyers an interest-free loan of 80% of the cost, with the loan repayable at the end of five years. The new presses will require fewer staff to operate them and the cost of redundancies and early retirement will be £140,000 in the first year. After the first year there will be staff cost savings of £60,000 a year. A training programme will have to be set up for remaining staff at a cost of £60,000 spread over the first three years. The new presses will only be able to use paper which is 100% brand new – even a small percentage of recycled content in the paper will cause the presses to break down.

Option 2

Invest in new presses of a lower specification at a cost of £600,000. These presses are able to cope with paper which contains up to 50% of recycled paper. The new presses will be financed with a loan of £400,000, which will be repayable at the end of five years. Interest will be paid annually on the loan at 5%. No staff will need to be made redundant. Retraining costs of £20,000 will be payable in the first year.

Note: under both options the new presses will have a life of ten years and will be depreciated using the straight-line method.

You are to help John Cazalet to evaluate these options by calculating the effect of each on profit and cash for the next financial year. Are there any other factors which John should consider before making a recommendation to the company's board of directors?

solution

	Profit	Cash
	£	£
Option 1		
new presses	–	(1,000,000)
loan	–	800,000
redundancies/early retirement	(140,000)	(140,000)
retraining	(20,000)	(20,000)
depreciation	(100,000)	–
net effect	(260,000)	(360,000)
Option 2		
new presses	–	(600,000)
loan	–	400,000
interest on loan	(20,000)	(20,000)
retraining	(20,000)	(20,000)
depreciation	(60,000)	–
net effect	(100,000)	(240,000)

Note that depreciation is a non-cash expense which affects profit only.

discussion points

- For this first year, option 2 has the smaller effect on both profit and cash.
- If redundancy costs could be avoided in option 1, the effect on profit would be (£120,000), which is £20,000 more than option 2 at (£100,000). The effect on cash would be (£220,000), which is £20,000 less than option 2 at (£240,000).
- For years 2 and 3, the effects on profit will be:

	Option 1		Option 2	
	Year 2	Year 3	Year 2	Year 3
	£	£	£	£
retraining	(20,000)	(£20,000)	–	–
staff cost savings	60,000	60,000	–	–
interest on loan	–	–	(20,000)	(20,000)
depreciation	(100,000)	(100,000)	(60,000)	(60,000)
net effect	(60,000)	(60,000)	(80,000)	(80,000)

- For years 2 and 3, the effects on cash will be:

	Option 1		Option 2	
	Year 2	Year 3	Year 2	Year 3
	£	£	£	£
retraining	(20,000)	(20,000)	–	–
staff cost savings	60,000	60,000	–	–
interest on loan	–	–	(20,000)	(20,000)
net effect	40,000	40,000	(20,000)	(20,000)

- The company must decide how the loan is to be repaid – either £800,000 for option 1, or £600,000 for option 2.
- There are social factors to consider:
  - redundancy (effect on workforce and local economy)
  - recycling (customers may be lost under option 1 if only non-recycled paper can be used; customers may be gained under option 2 if recycled paper can be used)
- Option 2 is preferred in the short-term because there is less effect on profit and cash. In the longer-term, option 1 is preferable, although the social factors need to be considered. The method of repaying the loan under each option needs to be decided.

THE IMPORTANCE OF SOCIAL ACCOUNTING

This chapter so far has concentrated on business decision-making from the point of view of the internal factors of the need to maximise profit and cash. A typical choice has been shown in the Worked Example on the last few pages, where the need for decision-making also raised the issue of social accounting.

what is social accounting?

The word 'social' is often used but rarely defined. It has a variety of attributes which include:

- living in a group of people
- groups of people that depend on each other
- treating people equally and fairly

Hence the phrases 'social conscience' and 'social work'.

The word 'accounting' can relate in a very specific sense to the processes described in the rest of this book, ie financial accounting, management accounting, and so on. It can also relate to 'being accountable', ie being responsible to others for what you do.

Social accounting in business can therefore be defined as:

the need for a business to be accountable for its actions to a variety of groups of people

This need is recognised by businesses generally. In the case of larger limited companies, solutions to the need – ie 'what we have done to help Society' – are formalised in publications and on websites. The term given to this sense of social responsibility is 'Corporate Responsibility'. To see examples, visit the websites www.ba.com and www.rbs.co.uk and carry out a search on 'corporate responsibility'.

the demands of society: areas of social accounting

As we saw at the beginning of this chapter, social accounting involves a potential conflict of interest within businesses between:

- internal pressures – the need to maximise cash and profit
- external pressures – social accounting – the need to 'take account' of the demands of society

The external pressures involved in social accounting are very wide and varied. They include the requirements of law, the environment, economic well-being, technological improvements, politics and ethics. The diagram below shows the main external pressures that are placed on the business decision-making process. Study this diagram and then read the text and Discussion Points that follow. You may wish to debate the issues raised by these Discussion Points with others.

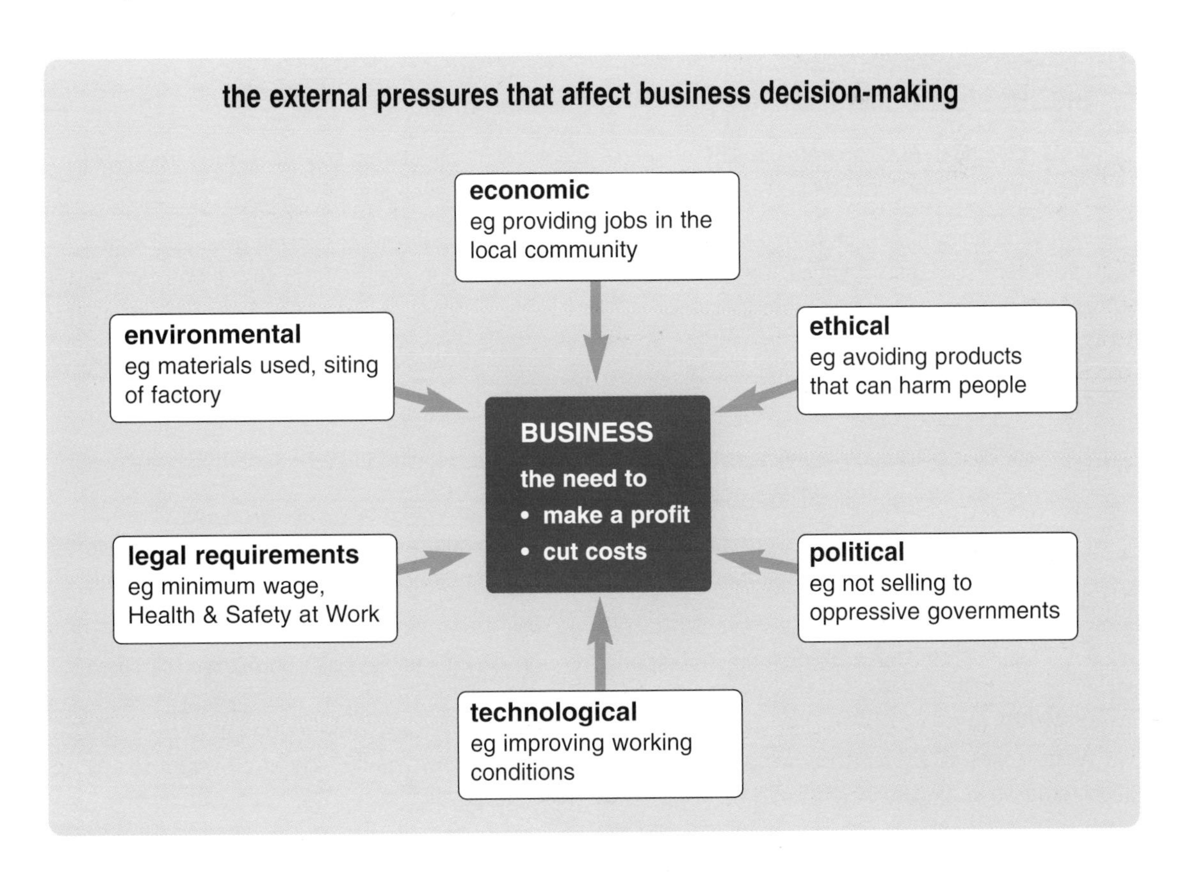

Social Accounting in Action

The business aim of cash and profit maximisation may get in the way of the'social' needs mentioned previously. In the pages that follow you should read the text and subjects for discussion and write notes on the issues that they raise. These can then be discussed in preparation for the exam.

Note that the individual discussion topics may well involve more than one of the external pressures, and you should look out for this. The first, for example, involves a question of technology in addition to the need to help the Government's economic policy and to benefit local communities.

the demands of economic pressures

The UK Government is committed to maintaining a healthy economy which will provide, as well as price stability and low interest rates:

- full employment of a skilled workforce
- support for the less prosperous areas of the country

There are a number of ways in which businesses can help to support this aim. The Government provides through the Department of Trade and Industry (DTI) a wide range of incentives and grants to encourage employment in areas of higher unemployment. It also encourages the development of skills training through the Department for Education and Skills.

DISCUSSION POINT: Volta Electrical – a question of closure

Volta Electrical PLC operates a UK chain of electrical retail stores selling a wide range of household electrical goods such as TVs, DVD players, microwaves and freezers.

Last year the company launched www.voltadirect.com an online discount shopping website which offers very competitive prices. This enabled the company to cut labour and distribution costs by centralising its warehousing and logistics.

Voltadirect.com has been a huge success and now accounts for 30% of the company's turnover.

The board is meeting today to hear a presentation which will recommend:

- a 25% increase in marketing spend on the online shop, resulting in a projected 30% increase in sales through the online shop
- the closure of fifteen smaller retail sites in city and town centres in areas of the UK which have a high rate of unemployment and do not have as much disposable income for spending on electrical goods
- financing the increase on marketing spend through job cuts achieved through these closures

question

What issues of social accounting should be discussed at the meeting? Can you suggest any alternative strategies which could be adopted by the company?

the demands of political pressures

Sometimes businesses may be restricted in their commercial operations by political factors. Are there any restrictions, for example, in exporting goods and services to a country which has an oppressive government? Are there any trade sanctions in place which will restrict exports?

In the example that follows the social and political conscience of a company is put to the test.

DISCUSSION POINT: ICO Chemicals PLC – a question of conscience

ICO Chemicals PLC produces a wide range of chemical products, including pharmaceuticals, plastics and paints.

The company has exported raw chemical products to the Government of Maribia for a number of years. Last year there was a military coup in the capital Melba, and the country was taken over by a military dictatorship which operates an autocratic regime and has threatened the neighbouring states with invasion.

The sales director of ICO Chemicals has asked for an urgent board meeting following an order from a Maribian government agency for a large consignment of raw chemicals. The order will be very profitable for ICO Chemicals. Maribia pays cash up front for its orders. The problem is that the chemicals are not only used for fertilisers (Maribia is highly dependent on agriculture), they can also be used in the production of highly effective chemical weapons.

question

What issues are likely to be discussed at the ICO Chemicals meeting? What do you consider to be the right decision?

the demands of the law

All businesses are regulated by the law. By 'law' we mean Statute Law (ie Act of Parliament) and other regulations, some of them required by European Union directives. Areas of law include:

- employment law – anti-discrimination law, for example
- Health and Safety at Work legislation – ensuring a safe and healthy workplace
- law relating to the sale of goods and services
- data protection law – protecting personal details of individuals held on file

Some of these areas are likely to involve business expenditure and may therefore reduce profit.

DISCUSSION POINT: Arbor Sawmills Limited – a question of safety

Arbor Sawmills Limited is a small family-run timber company situated in Dorset. The company has made losses over the last two years and lacks the funds to invest in the new equipment it needs to remain competitive. Its run of bad luck continued last month when as part of a 'risk assessment' required under Health & Safety legislation it was discovered that two of the electric saws operated by the company lacked the necessary guard rail and safety equipment. A supplier has quoted the sum of £25,000 for supply and installation of this equipment. 'It goes against the grain to have to borrow all this', commented Giles Oak, Managing Director. 'We can hardly afford the wages, let alone all this stuff!'

question

What issues are raised here, and how would you advise Mr Oak?

the technological issue

One of the aims of new technology is to improve the working environment, making it cleaner and more efficient. Many manufacturing and service environments have been transformed beyond recognition by the introduction of computing and electronic communications. But technology has its downside and has brought its problems:

- staff redundancies and increased unemployment as technology replaces jobs, eg robotics in manufacturing, computer applications used for accounting
- health problems such as eyestrain, headaches and Repetitive Strain Injury (RSI) through operation of computers

In the Discussion Point that follows, the problems of technological advance are clearly highlighted.

DISCUSSION POINT: Mercia Finance PLC – a question of customer service

Mercia Finance PLC is a Midlands-based finance company which offers finance products (loans, leasing and hire purchase) to a wide range of personal and business customers. Currently all its main functions – including sales and customer service – operate from a central office in Wolverhampton. The Marketing Director has recently been researching the possibility of transferring its sales and customer service operations to a call centre in India. He has calculated that he will be able to cut forty jobs in Wolverhampton, resulting in savings of £250,000 a year.

question

The Marketing Director will have to 'sell' his idea to the Board at a meeting next week. What opposition is he likely to encounter, and what arguments could he use to counter this opposition?

the demands of the environmental lobby

The demands on business practice by environmental pressure groups have become so well known that business has even turned them to advantage – the marketing of organic food, for example. Traditionally, environmental concerns have concentrated on a number of defined needs:

- energy conservation
- restrictions on pollution
- the use of recycled materials
- the use of biodegradable materials
- the use of materials which are not harmful to wildlife

A number of these environmental issues are raised in the Discussion Point that follows.

DISCUSSION POINT: Premier Packaging Limited – a question of going 'green'

Premier Packaging Limited manufactures packaging and labelling for a number of the major UK food producers. The company has recently commissioned a review of its manufacturing processes and the materials it uses. The Report produced has highlighted the following issues:

- the plastic wrapping currently used is imported cheaply from overseas, and has been found to contain a substance which has been rumoured (but not proved) to cause cancer when it comes into contact with food
- this imported plastic wrapping is non-biodegradable and can be toxic to animals
- an alternative recycled plastic wrapping is available, but it is more expensive and will add 10% to production costs

question

What issues does this Report raise which the management of the company will have to discuss and decide upon?

CHAPTER SUMMARY

- Businesses cannot make decisions in isolation – they need to consider their responsibilities to others.
- There may be a conflict between internal factors (what the business wants to do) and external factors (what other people want the business to do).
- Internal factors affecting decision-making include the need to maximise profitability and the advisability of maximising cash.
- External pressures influencing business decision-making include
  - environmental pressures, eg the choice of materials used, the siting of a manufacturing plant
  - the needs of the local economy, eg the need to support local employment
  - the opportunities offered by new technology, eg improving working conditions and efficiency
  - legal requirements such as the Health & Safety at Work regulations
  - ethical issues such as making profits from the sale of tobacco and alcohol which may cause damage to health
  - political issues such as selling goods and services to countries which are known to have oppressive governments

QUESTIONS

NOTE: an asterisk (*) after the question number means that an answer to the question is given at the end of this book.

33.1* Jack Smart is the manager of a factory which produces cardboard boxes from recycled paper. The current production process needs to be replaced. Jack has the following two options.

Option 1. Invest in new recycling machinery at a cost of £450,000. In order to finance this purchase a loan of £600,000 will need to be taken out. This will be repayable at the end of five years. Interest is paid annually at 10%. Also 15% of the staff will no longer be needed and will have to be made redundant or take early retirement in the first year at a cost of £160,000. Most of the remaining staff will need to be retrained to use the new machinery, which is expected to cost £60,000 and is payable over 2 years.

Option 2. To make cardboard boxes from paper which has not been recycled. This will involve investing in new machinery at a cost of £250,000. This will be financed by a loan of £300,000, repayable at the end of five years. Interest is paid annually at 10%. No staff will need to be made redundant. The retraining costs are expected to be £80,000 and are payable in the first year. Jack is unsure how customers will react to boxes which are not made from recycled paper. However, he believes that this is the better option as it will have less of an effect on cash resources and therefore profitability.

Both machines will be depreciated using the straight-line method over 10 years.

REQUIRED

(a) Explain the difference between profit and cash.

(b) Calculate the effect of each option on profit and cash for the next financial year.

(c) State which option you would recommend. Justify your choice.

Assessment and Qualifications Alliance, (AQA), 2003

33.2* Sid Porter is the manager of Last Minute Shop, the only supermarket in a small town. Sid is considering introducing checkout scanners, which will cost £40,000 and will be replaced after 2 years. These scan the bar codes of goods and send data through to a central computer. As well as controlling stock the computer data will be used to manage the checkout staff, as a record will be made of how fast they scan products and take payment for goods.

Sid expects that additional staff training will be required at a yearly cost of £1,840. He employs 28 part-time staff at a rate of £5 per hour. Each employee completes a daily 4 hour shift. The supermarket is open daily from 6 am to 10 pm, 365 days a year. Sid believes that the new scanners will be faster and that the surplus staff will have to be made redundant.

REQUIRED

(a) Advise Sid Porter of three benefits to Last Minute Shop of introducing the checkout scanners.

(b) (i) Calculate the weekly cost of the scanners.

(ii) Calculate the number of weekly shifts which will need to be cut in order to cover the weekly cost of the scanners.

(iii) Advise Sid Porter of how many employees will need to be made redundant if the scanners are introduced.

(c) Evaluate the adverse effects the new system will have on:

(i) the current employees

(ii) the local community

Assessment and Qualifications Alliance, (AQA), 2002

33.3

Sanderson Sheds Supplies has been trading for many years. The business is expected to manufacture 12,000 sheds a year. Each shed is sold for £190 and costs £140 to make.

In an attempt to reduce costs the business has changed its supplier of paint. This will save £22 per shed. The new paint is rumoured to be harmful to wildlife.

REQUIRED

(a) Calculate the increase in total contribution which will result from the change in paint supplier.

(b) Discuss whether Sanderson Sheds Supplies should have changed its paint supplier.

Assessment and Qualifications Alliance, (AQA), 2003

33.4

Smarts Trading Ltd has three large branches, one of which is unprofitable. Each branch produces a different product. Each is located in an economically deprived rural area.

T Jones, the financial controller, believes that the only factor to be considered when making business decisions is profitability. Therefore, the unprofitable branch should be closed. 20% of its staff should be offered redeployment to the other two branches.

REQUIRED

Write a report to T Jones explaining three factors, other than profitability, which need to be considered before closing a branch.

REPORT

To ....

From ....

Date ....

Subject ....

....

....

....

....

....

....

....

....

....

....

Assessment and Qualifications Alliance, (AQA), 2002

Answers to Chapter Questions

Answers to asterisked (*) questions follow in chapter order over the next thirty eight pages. Answers are given in fully displayed form; this will assist by showing the correct layouts, which is important in accounting.

Where answers are given to questions from the past examination papers, these answers are the responsibility of the author and not of the examining board. They have not been provided by or approved by AQA and may not necessarily constitute the only possible solutions.

Answers to the remaining questions are given in a separate *Tutor Pack*. Please telephone Osborne Books (01905 748071) for further details.

CHAPTER 1 What is financial accounting?

1.1

(a) ledger
(b) debtor
(c) creditor
(d) sales day book
(e) cash book
(f) general (or nominal) ledger
(g) assets – liabilities = capital
(h) business entity
(i) auditors

1.7

capital	£20,000
capital	£10,000
liabilities	£7,550
assets	£14,100
liabilities	£18,430
assets	£21,160

1.8

(a) Owner started in business with capital of £10,000 in the bank
(b) Bought office equipment for £2,000, paying by cheque
(c) Received a loan of £6,000 by cheque
(d) Bought a van for £10,000, paying by cheque
(e) Owner introduces £2,000 additional capital by cheque
(f) Loan repayment of £3,000 made by cheque

CHAPTER 2 Double-entry book-keeping: first principles

2.2

Bank Account

Dr					Cr
20-2		£	20-2		£
1 May	Capital	6,000	4 May	Machinery	3,500
12 May	L Warner: loan	1,000	6 May	Office equipment	2,000
17 May	Commission rec'd	150	10 May	Rent paid	350
			15 May	Wages	250
			20 May	Drawings	85
			25 May	Wages	135

Capital Account

Dr					Cr
20-2		£	20-2		£
			1 May	Bank	6,000

Machinery Account

Dr					Cr
20-2		£	20-2		£
4 May	Bank	3,500			

Office Equipment Account

Dr					Cr
20-2		£	20-2		£
6 May	Bank	2,000			

Rent Paid Account

Dr					Cr
20-2		£	20-2		£
10 May	Bank	350			

Lucy Warner: Loan Account

Dr					Cr
20-2		£	20-2		£
			12 May	Bank	1,000

Wages Account

Dr					Cr
20-2		£	20-2		£
15 May	Bank	250			
25 May	Bank	135			

Commission Received Account

Dr					Cr
20-2		£	20-2		£
			17 May	Bank	150

Drawings Account

Dr					Cr
20-2		£	20-2		£
20 May	Bank	85			

2.4

Bank Account

Dr					Cr
20-2		£	20-2		£
1 Mar	Capital	6,500	4 Mar	Office equipment	1,000
5 Mar	Bank loan	2,500	7 Mar	Wages	250
8 Mar	Commission rec'd	150	10 Mar	Rent paid	200
			12 Mar	Drawings	175
			15 Mar	Van	6,000

Capital Account

Dr					Cr
20-2		£	20-2		£
			1 Mar	Bank	6,500

Office Equipment Account

Dr					Cr
20-2		£	20-2		£
4 Mar	Bank	1,000			

Bank Loan Account

Dr					Cr
20-2		£	20-2		£
			5 Mar	Bank	2,500

Wages Account

Dr					Cr
20-2		£	20-2		£
7 Mar	Bank	250			

Commission Received Account

Dr		£			Cr £
20-2		£	20-2		£
			8 Mar	Bank	150

Rent Paid Account

Dr					Cr
20-2		£	20-2		£
10 Mar	Bank	200			

Drawings Account

Dr					Cr
20-2		£	20-2		£
12 Mar	Bank	175			

Van Account

Dr					Cr
20-2		£	20-2		£
15 Mar	Bank	6,000			

CHAPTER 3 Double-entry book-keeping: further transactions

3.2

Bank Account

Dr					Cr
20-1		£	20-1		£
1 Feb	Capital	3,000	3 Feb	Purchases	100
2 Feb	Sales	250	5 Feb	Wages	150
7 Feb	Sales	300	12 Feb	Purchases	200
15 Feb	J Walters: loan	1,000	20 Feb	Computer	1,950
25 Feb	Sales	150	27 Feb	Wages	125

Capital Account

Dr					Cr
20-1		£	20-1		£
			1 Feb	Bank	3,000

Sales Account

Dr					Cr
20-1		£	20-1		£
			2 Feb	Bank	250
			7 Feb	Bank	300
			25 Feb	Bank	150

Purchases Account

Dr					Cr
20-1		£	20-1		£
3 Feb	Bank	100			
12 Feb	Bank	200			

Wages Account

Dr					Cr
20-1		£	20-1		£
5 Feb	Bank	150			
27 Feb	Bank	125			

J Walters: Loan Account

Dr					Cr
20-1		£	20-1		£
			15 Feb	Bank	1,000

Computer Account

Dr					Cr
20-1		£	20-1		£
20 Feb	Bank	1,950			

3.3

Bank Account

		Debit	Credit	Balance
20-1		£	£	£
1 Feb	Capital	3,000		3,000 Dr
2 Feb	Sales	250		3,250 Dr
3 Feb	Purchases		100	3,150 Dr
5 Feb	Wages		150	3,000 Dr
7 Feb	Sales	300		3,300 Dr
12 Feb	Purchases		200	3,100 Dr
15 Feb	J Walters: loan	1,000		4,100 Dr
20 Feb	Computer		1,950	2,150 Dr
25 Feb	Sales	150		2,300 Dr
27 Feb	Wages		125	2,175 Dr

3.4

Purchases Account

Dr					Cr
20-1		£	20-1		£
4 Jan	AB Supplies Ltd	250			
20 Jan	Bank	225			

AB Supplies Ltd

Dr					Cr
20-1		£	20-1		£
15 Jan	Bank	250	4 Jan	Purchases	250

Sales Account

Dr					Cr
20-1		£	20-1		£
			5 Jan	Bank	195
			7 Jan	Cash	150
			17 Jan	L Lewis	145

Bank Account

Dr					Cr
20-1		£	20-1		£
5 Jan	Sales	195	15 Jan	AB Supplies Ltd	250
10 Jan	J Johnson: loan	1,000	20 Jan	Purchases	225
29 Jan	L Lewis	145	31 Jan	Mercia Office Supplies Ltd	160

Cash Account

Dr					Cr
20-1		£	20-1		£
7 Jan	Sales	150	22 Jan	Wages	125

J Johnson: Loan Account

Dr					Cr
20-1		£	20-1		£
			10 Jan	Bank	1,000

L Lewis

Dr					Cr
20-1		£	20-1		£
17 Jan	Sales	145	29 Jan	Bank	145

Wages Account

Dr					Cr
20-1		£	20-1		£
22 Jan	Cash	125			

Office Equipment Account

Dr					Cr
20-1		£	20-1		£
26 Jan	Mercia O S Ltd	160			

Mercia Office Supplies Ltd

Dr					Cr
20-1		£	20-1		£
31 Jan	Bank	160	26 Jan	Office equipment	160

CHAPTER 4 Business documents

4.1 (a) purchase order
(b) invoice
(c) cash discount
(d) trade discount
(e) net
(f) Value Added Tax
(g) credit note
(h) statement of account

4.6 (a) (i) Trade discount is given, if prearranged:
- to businesses in the same trade (but not to the general public)
- for buying in bulk
- as a discount off list price to retailers by wholesalers

(ii) Cash discount is given, if prearranged, and shown on the invoice, for prompt payment

(b) Invoice total: £466.50

Workings:

£500 – 20% = £400 x 0.95 = £380 x 0.175 VAT = £66.50

Total is £400 + £66.50 = £466.50

CHAPTER 5 Balancing accounts – the trial balance

5.3 (a)

LORNA FOX
Trial balance as at 31 March 20-2

	Dr	Cr
	£	£
Purchases	96,250	
Sales		146,390
Sales returns	8,500	
Administration expenses	10,240	
Wages	28,980	
Telephone	3,020	
Interest paid	2,350	
Travel expenses	1,045	
Premises	125,000	
Machinery	40,000	
Debtors	10,390	
Bank overdraft		1,050
Cash	150	
Creditors		12,495
Loan from bank		20,000
Drawings	9,450	
Capital		155,440
	335,375	335,375

(b) See Chapters 2 and 3 and page 65. The explanation should be appropriate for someone who does not understand accounting.

5.4 (a) principle
(b) mispost
(c) original entry
(d) compensating
(e) reversal of entries
(f) omission

6.1

Sales Day Book

Date	Details	Invoice	Folio	Net	VAT	Gross
20-6				£	£	£
2 Feb	Wyvern Fashions			200	35	235
10 Feb	Zandra Smith			160	28	188
15 Feb	Just Jean			120	21	141
23 Feb	Peter Sanders			320	56	376
24 Feb	H Wilson			80	14	94
26 Feb	Mercian Models			320	56	376
28 Feb	Totals for month			1,200	210	1,410

Purchases Day Book

Date	Details	Invoice	Folio	Net	VAT	Gross
20-6				£	£	£
1 Feb	Flair Clothing			520	91	611
4 Feb	Modernwear			240	42	282
18 Feb	Quality Clothing			800	140	940
28 Feb	Flair Clothing			200	35	235
28 Feb	Totals for month			1,760	308	2,068

GENERAL LEDGER
Value Added Tax Account

Dr					Cr
20-6		£	20-6		£
28 Feb	Purchases Day Book	308	28 Feb	Sales Day Book	210
			28 Feb	Balance c/d	98
		308			308
1 Mar	Balance b/d	98			

6.4

Sales Day Book

Date	Details	Invoice	Folio	Net	VAT	Gross
20-2				£	£	£
5 Jan	Mereford College	1093	SL 201	3,900.00	682.50	4,582.50
7 Jan	Carpminster College	1094	SL 202	8,500.00	1,487.50	9,987.50
14 Jan	Carpminster College	1095	SL 202	1,800.50	315.08	2,115.58
14 Jan	Mereford College	1096	SL 201	2,950.75	516.38	3,467.13
20 Jan	Carpminster College	1097	SL 202	3,900.75	682.63	4,583.38
22 Jan	Mereford College	1098	SL 201	1,597.85	279.62	1,877.47
31 Jan	Totals for month			22,649.85	3,963.71	26,613.56

Purchases Day Book

Date	Details	Invoice	Folio	Net	VAT	Gross
20-2				£	£	£
2 Jan	Macstrad plc	M1529	PL 101	2,900.00	507.50	3,407.50
3 Jan	Amtosh plc	A7095	PL 102	7,500.00	1,312.50	8,812.50
18 Jan	Macstrad plc	M2070	PL 101	1,750.00	306.25	2,056.25
19 Jan	Amtosh plc	A7519	PL 102	5,500.00	962.50	6,462.50
31 Jan	Totals for month			17,650.00	3,088.75	20,738.75

Sales Returns Day Book

Date	Details	Credit Note	Folio	Net	VAT	Gross
20-2				£	£	£
13 Jan	Mereford College	CN109	SL 201	850.73	148.87	999.60
27 Jan	Mereford College	CN110	SL 201	593.81	103.91	697.72
31 Jan	Totals for month			1,444.54	252.78	1,697.32

Purchases Returns Day Book

Date	Details	Credit Note	Folio	Net	VAT	Gross
20-2				£	£	£
10 Jan	Macstrad plc	MC105	PL 101	319.75	55.95	375.70
12 Jan	Amtosh plc	AC 730	PL 102	750.18	131.28	881.46
23 Jan	Macstrad plc	MC120	PL 101	953.07	166.78	1,119.85
31 Jan	Totals for month			2,023.00	354.01	2,377.01

SALES LEDGER
Mereford College (account no 201)

Dr					Cr
20-2		£	20-2		£
1 Jan	Balance b/d	705.35	13 Jan	Sales Returns	999.60
5 Jan	Sales	4,582.50	27 Jan	Sales Returns	697.72
14 Jan	Sales	3,467.13	31 Jan	Balance c/d	8,935.13
22 Jan	Sales	1,877.47			
		10,632.45			10,632.45
1 Feb	Balance b/d	8,935.13			

Carpminster College (account no 202)

Dr					Cr
20-2		£	20-2		£
1 Jan	Balance b/d	801.97	31 Jan	Balance c/d	17,488.43
7 Jan	Sales	9,987.50			
14 Jan	Sales	2,115.58			
20 Jan	Sales	4,583.38			
		17,488.43			17,488.43
1 Feb	Balance b/d	17,488.43			

PURCHASES LEDGER

Macstrad plc (account no 101)

Dr					Cr
20-2		£	20-2		£
10 Jan	Purchases Returns	375.70	1 Jan	Balance b/d	1,050.75
23 Jan	Purchases Returns	1,119.85	2 Jan	Purchases	3,407.50
31 Jan	Balance c/d	5,018.95	18 Jan	Purchases	2,056.25
		6,514.50			6,514.50
			1 Feb	Balance b/d	5,018.95

Amtosh plc (account no 102)

Dr					Cr
20-2		£	20-2		£
12 Jan	Purchases Returns	881.46	1 Jan	Balance b/d	2,750.83
31 Jan	Balance c/d	17,144.37	3 Jan	Purchases	8,812.50
			19 Jan	Purchases	6,462.50
		18,025.83			18,025.83
			1 Feb	Balance b/d	17,144.37

GENERAL LEDGER

Sales Account

Dr					Cr
20-2		£	20-2		£
			31 Jan	Sales Day Book	22,649.85

Purchases Account

Dr					Cr
20-2		£	20-2		£
31 Jan	Purchases Day Book	17,650.00			

Sales Returns Account

Dr					Cr
20-2		£	20-2		£
31 Jan	Sales Returns Day Book	1,444.54			

Purchases Returns Account

Dr					Cr
20-2		£	20-2		£
			31 Jan	Purchases Returns Day Book	2,023.00

Value Added Tax Account

Dr					Cr
20-2		£	20-2		£
31 Jan	Purchases Day Book	3,088.75	31 Jan	Sales Day Book	3,963.71
31 Jan	Sales Returns Day Book	252.78	31 Jan	Purchases Returns Day Book	354.01
31 Jan	Balance c/d	976.19			
		4,317.72			4,317.72
			1 Feb	Balance b/d	976.19

6.5

	Source document	Subsidiary Book	Account to be debited	Account to be credited
(a)	invoice received	purchases day book	purchases	A Cotton
(b)	invoice issued	sales day book	D Law	sales
(c)	paying in slip counterfoil	cash book	bank	sales
(d)	credit note received	purchases returns day book	A Cotton	purchases returns
(e)	cheque counterfoil	cash book	gas	bank
(f)	credit note issued	sales returns day book	sales returns	D Law

6.7

(a) Credit note

(b) 23 x £45 = £1,035 – £258.75 (trade discount) = £776.25

less cash discount = £38.81 = £737.44 x 17.5% = VAT £129.05

Credit note total = £776.25 + £129.05 = £905.30

(c) Returns outwards day book

Net £776.25 VAT £129.05 Gross £905.30

6.8

Transaction	Source Document	Subsidiary Book (or Book of Prime Entry)
(a) Goods bought on credit from a supplier	Purchase invoice	Purchases Day Book
(b) Goods sold on credit to a customer	Sales invoice	Sales Day Book
(c) Faulty goods returned to a supplier	Credit note received	Purchases Returns (Returns Out) Day Book
(d) Payment made by cheque to a supplier	Cheque counterfoil	Cash Book
(e) Purchase of a new machine for use in the factory on credit	Purchase invoice	General Journal, or Analysed Purchases Day Book
(f) Faulty goods returned by a customer	Credit note issued	Sales Returns (Returns In) Day Book
(g) Cheque received from a customer and paid into the bank	Paying-in slip counterfoil	Cash Book

CHAPTER 7 Value Added Tax

7.1 (a)

Month	*Purchases* £	*VAT* £	*Sales* £	*VAT* £
April	5,400	945	8,200	1,435
May	4,800	840	9,400	1,645
June	6,800	1,190	10,800	1,890

(b)

Value Added Tax Account

Dr.		£			Cr. £
20-4			20-4		
30 Apr	Purchases Day Book	945	30 Apr	Sales Day Book	1,435
31 May	Purchases Day Book	840	31 May	Sales Day Book	1,645
30 Jun	Purchases Day Book	1,190	30 Jun	Sales Day Book	1,890
30 Jun	Balance c/d	1,995			
		4,970			4,970
			1 Jul	Balance b/d	1,995

(c) VAT account has a credit balance of £1,995: this means that Wyvern Computers owes the amount to HM Revenue & Customs. The amount is payable not later than 31 July 20-4. The book-keeping entries for payment will be
– debit Value Added Tax Account
– credit Bank Account

If Wyvern Computers prepares a balance sheet at 30 June 20-4, the amount owing to HM Revenue & Customs will be listed as a creditor.

7.4 (a)

Sales Day Book

Date	Details	Invoice	Folio	Net	VAT	Gross
20-1				£	£	£
19 Aug	E Newman	SI 1547		156.00	27.30	183.30
20 Aug	Wyvern Traders Ltd	SI 1548		228.00	39.90	267.90
21 Aug	Teme Supplies	SI 1549		350.00	61.25	411.25
22 Aug	Lugg Brothers & Co	SI 1550		1,200.00	210.00	1,410.00
23 Aug	E Newman			400.00	70.00	470.00
23 Aug	Totals for week			2,334.00	408.45	2,742.45

Sales Returns Day Book

Date	Details	Credit Note	Folio	Net	VAT	Gross
20-1				£	£	£
22 Aug	Wyvern Traders Ltd	CN 121		228.00	39.90	267.90
23 Aug	E Newman	CN 122		78.00	13.65	91.65
23 Aug	Totals for week			306.00	53.55	359.55

(b) *Sales Day Book:*
- The total of net sales is credited to sales account in the general ledger.
- The total of the VAT column is credited to the VAT account in the general ledger.
- The individual gross amounts for each customer are debited to the debtors' personal accounts in the sales ledger.

Sales Returns Day Book:
- The total of net sales returns is debited to sales returns account in the general ledger.
- The total of the VAT column is debited to the VAT account in the general ledger.
- The individual gross amounts for each customer are credited to the debtors' personal accounts in the sales ledger.

(c)

E Newman

Dr		£			Cr £
20-1			20-1		
1 Aug	Balance b/d	440.00	7 Aug	Bank	440.00
19 Aug	Sales	183.30	23 Aug	Sales returns	91.65
23 Aug	Sales	470.00	31 Aug	Balance c/d	561.65
		1,093.30			1,093.30
1 Sep	Balance b/d	561.65			

7.6 (a)

VAT Account

Dr | | | | | Cr

Date 2000	Details	£ p	Date 2000	Details	£ p
30 Apr	Purchases	136.23	30 Apr	Sales	345.97
	Petty cash	12.86		Cash sales	382.39
	Fixed assets	390.00			
	Balance c/d	189.27			
		728.36			728.36
			1 May	Balance b/d	189.27

(b) The total amount of VAT owed by Acme Car Fittings to HM Revenue & Customs.

CHAPTER 8 Cash book

8.1 *Main responsibilities of the cashier*

- Recording receipts and payments by cheque and in cash in the firm's cash book
- Issuing receipts for cash (and sometimes cheques) received
- Making authorised cash payments (except for low-value expenses payments which are paid by the petty cashier)
- Preparing cheques and BACS payments for signature and authorisation
- Paying cash and cheques received into the bank
- Controlling the firm's cash, either in a cash till or cash box
- Issuing cash to the petty cashier who operates the firm's petty cash book
- Ensuring that all transactions passing through the cash book are supported by documentary evidence
- Checking the accuracy of the cash and bank balances at regular intervals
- Liaising with the other accounts staff – accounts clerks and petty cashier

Qualities of a cashier

- Accuracy – in writing up the cash book, in cash handling, and in ensuring that payments are made only against correct documents and appropriate authorisation
- Security – of cash and cheque books, and correct authorisation of payments
- Confidentiality – that all cash/bank transactions, including cash and bank balances, are kept confidential

8.2

Cash Book

Dr | | | | | Cr

Date	Details	Folio	Discount allowed	Cash	Bank	Date	Details	Folio	Discount received	Cash	Bank
20-2			£	£	£	20-2			£	£	£
1 Jun	Balance b/d			280		1 Jun	Balance b/d				2,240
3 Jun	G Wheaton		5		195	8 Jun	F Lloyd		10		390
5 Jun	T Francis		2	53		10 Jun	Wages			165	
16 Jun	Bank	C		200		12 Jun	A Morris		3	97	
18 Jun	H Watson		30		640	16 Jun	Cash	C			200
28 Jun	M Perry		6		234	20 Jun	R Marks				78
30 Jun	K Willis			45		24 Jun	D Farr		2		65
30 Jun	Balance c/d				1,904	26 Jun	Telephone			105	
						30 Jun	Balance c/d			211	
			43	578	2,973				15	578	2,973
1 Jul	Balance b/d			211		1 Jul	Balance b/d				1,904

Discount Allowed Account

Dr | | | Cr

20-2		£	20-2		£
30 Jun	Cash Book	43			

Discount Received Account

Dr | | | Cr

20-2		£	20-2		£
			30 Jun	Cash Book	15

8.5

Cash Book

Dr | | | | Cr

Date	Details	Discount allowed	Cash	Bank	Date	Details	Discount received	Cash	Bank
2002		£	£	£	2002		£	£	£
1 Jan	Balance b/d		50.00		1 Jan	Balance b/d			263.67
3 Jan	M S Supplies			136.98	3 Jan	J B Smith Ltd	4.00		120.00
4 Jan	J O Jones	4.67		246.89	4 Jan	A E Evans Ltd			146.59
7 Jan	Cash sales		467.23		5 Jan	K L M Spares	3.96		127.45
7 Jan	ABC Traders			120.56	6 Jan	Petty cash			45.67
7 Jan	Cash			400.23	7 Jan	Insurance			100.00
					7 Jan	Bank charges			23.98
					7 Jan	Bank interest			46.97
					7 Jan	Wages		40.00	
					7 Jan	Postage		27.00	
					7 Jan	Bank		400.23	
					7 Jan	Balance		50.00	30.33
		4.67	517.23	904.66			7.96	517.23	904.66
8 Jan	Balance b/d		50.00	30.33					

(b (i) Count the cash float or cash in the till and check to the book total.

(ii) Prepare a bank reconciliation statement (see Chapter 10)

(c) The imprest is the amount in the petty cash float at the beginning of the accounting period which is restored to the original total at the period end (see Chapter 9).

CHAPTER 9 Petty cash book

9.1 *Allow:* (a), (b), (d), (f), (g), (h), (j) – all subject to an appropriate receipt being attached to the petty cash voucher, and payment being in accordance with the company's policies – eg amount, authorisation.

Refer:

(c) travel to work – not normally a business expense, except for emergency call-outs

(e) staff tea and coffee – check if it is company policy to pay for this personal expense of the office staff

(i) shelving for the office – this expense is, most probably, too large to be put through petty cash; check with the accounts supervisor who is likely to say that it should go through the main cash book

9.4

	Expense (excluding VAT)	*VAT*	*Total*
	£	£	£
(a)	8.00	1.40	9.40
(b)	4.00	0.70	4.70
(c)	2.00	0.35	2.35
(d)	2.09	0.36	2.45
(e)	4.77	0.83	5.60
(f)	2.96	0.51	3.47
(g)	7.45	1.30	8.75
(h)	0.80	0.14	0.94
(i)	0.85	0.14	0.99
(j)	8.01	1.40	9.41

9.5 **Petty Cash Book**

Receipts	Date	Details	Voucher No	Total Payment	Analysis columns VAT	Travel	Postages	Stationery	Meals	Misc
£	20-7			£	£	£	£	£	£	£
75.00	1 Aug	Balance b/d								
	4 Aug	Taxi fare	39	3.80	0.56	3.24				
	6 Aug	Parcel post	40	2.35			2.35			
	7 Aug	Pencils	41	1.26	0.18			1.08		
	11 Aug	Travel expenses	42	5.46		5.46				
	12 Aug	Window cleaner	43	8.50						8.50
	14 Aug	Envelopes	44	2.45	0.36			2.09		
	18 Aug	Donation	45	5.00						5.00
	19 Aug	Rail fare/meal allow	46	10.60		5.60			5.00	
	20 Aug	Postage	47	0.75			0.75			
	22 Aug	Tape	48	1.50	0.22			1.28		
	25 Aug	Postage	49	0.55			0.55			
	27 Aug	Taxi fare	50	5.40	0.80	4.60				
				47.62	2.12	18.90	3.65	4.45	5.00	13.50
47.62	29 Aug	Cash received								
	29 Aug	Balance c/d		75.00						
122.62				122.62						
75.00	1 Sep	Balance b/d								

GENERAL LEDGER

Value Added Tax Account

Dr			Cr		
20-7		£ p	20-7		£ p
29 Aug	Petty Cash Book	2.12			

Travel Expenses Account

Dr			Cr		
20-7		£ p	20-7		£ p
29 Aug	Petty Cash Book	18.90			

Postages Account

Dr			Cr		
20-7		£ p	20-7		£ p
29 Aug	Petty Cash Book	3.65			

Stationery Account

Dr			Cr		
20-7		£ p	20-7		£ p
29 Aug	Petty Cash Book	4.45			

Meals Account

Dr			Cr		
20-7		£ p	20-7		£ p
29 Aug	Petty Cash Book	5.00			

Miscellaneous Expenses Account

Dr					Cr
20-7		£ p	20-7		£ p
29 Aug	Petty Cash Book	13.50			

CASH BOOK

Cash book

Dr		Cash	Bank			Cash	Bank Cr
20-7		£ p	£ p	20-7		£ p	£ p
				29 Aug	Petty Cash Book	47.62	

9.7

Receipts	Date	Details	Voucher No.	Total P'm't	Analysis columns: VAT	Postages	Travel	Meals	Stationery
£	20-1			£					
150.00	1 May	Balance b/d							
	1 May	Postages	455	7.00		7.00			
	1 May	Travel	456	2.85			2.85		
	2 May	Meal allowance	457	6.11				6.11	
	3 May	Taxi	458	4.70	0.70		4.00		
	4 May	Stationery	459	3.76	0.56				3.20
	7 May	Postages	460	5.25		5.25			
	8 May	Travel	461	6.50			6.50		
	9 May	Meal allowance	462	6.11				6.11	
	10 May	Stationery	463	8.46	1.26				7.20
	14 May	Taxi	464	5.17	0.77		4.40		
	17 May	Stationery	465	4.70	0.70				4.00
	21 May	Travel	466	3.50			3.50		
	21 May	Postages	467	4.50		4.50			
	23 May	Bus fares	468	3.80			3.80		
	26 May	Catering	469	10.81	1.61			9.20	
	27 May	Postages	470	3.50		3.50			
	27 May	Stationery	471	7.52	1.12				6.40
	28 May	Travel	472	6.45			6.45		
				100.69	6.72	20.25	31.50	21.42	20.80
100.69	31 May	Cash received							
	31 May	Balance c/d		150.00					
250.69				250.69					
150.00	1 Jun	Balance b/d							

10.1

TOM REID
BANK RECONCILIATION STATEMENT AS AT 31 DECEMBER 20-7

	£
Balance at bank as per cash book	200
Add: unpresented cheque	
B Kay cheque no. 345126	20
	220
Less: outstanding lodgement	
J Hill	13
Balance at bank as per bank statement	207

10.4 (a) - (c)

CASH BOOK

Date	Details	Bank	Date	Cheque no	Details	Bank
20-4		£	20-4			£
1 May	Balance b/f	3,652	4 May	451762	Smith and Company	751
26 May	J Ackland	832	4 May	451763	Bryant Limited	268
28 May	Stamp Limited	1,119	7 May	451764	Curtis Cars	1,895
14 May	*Perran Taxis*	*2,596*	7 May	451765	Parts Supplies	1,045
			18 May		*Wyvern Council*	*198*
			20 May		*A1 Insurance*	*1,005*
			25 May		*Okaro and Company*	*254*
			25 May		*Bank charges*	*20*
			31 May		*Balance c/d*	*2,763*
		8,199				*8,199*
1 Jun	*Balance b/d*	*2,763*				

(d)

MILESTONE MOTORS

Bank Reconciliation Statement as at 31 May 20-4

		£	£
Balance at bank as per bank statement			2,707
Less:	unpresented cheque no 451764		1,895
			812
Add:	outstanding lodgements		
	J Ackland	832	
	Stamp Limited	1,119	
			1,951
Balance at bank as per cash book			2,763

10.6 (a)

Bank Reconciliation Statement of
Wholesale Car Spares as at 31 October 2000

		£	£
Balance at bank as per bank statement			4,213.00
Add:	standing order	465.00	
	queried cheque	500.00	
	returned cheque	45.67	1,010.67
			5,223.67
Less:	credit transfer	304.00	
	A B Mechanics	67.89	371.89
Balance at bank as per cash book			4,851.78

(b)

Item		Yes/No	Debit/Credit
Standing order		Yes	CR
Credit transfer		Yes	DR
Cheques:	A B Mechanics	No	
	£500	No	
	£45.67	Yes	CR

(c) Any two from:

- Dishonoured cheque for £45.67
  - reason for the return of the cheque to be investigated
  - is it a simple error, eg date, or is the customer unable to pay?
- Item for £500
  - query item with the bank
  - whose error is it, our's or the bank's?
  - enquire on whom the item is drawn
- Unpresented cheque
  - investigate the length of time involved and the reason why it has not been presented
  - contact the supplier to see if a replacement cheque is needed

CHAPTER 11 Introducing computer accounting

11.1 Explanation of two advantages out of the list on page 158. The most obvious advantages are speed of input, accuracy of transaction recording, accessibility of up-to-date information and document printing (eg invoices, credit notes and statements).

11.2 The main two advantages are that a spreadsheet saves time in calculation and secondly that if any of the figures should alter, the remaining dependent figures will automatically be recalculated.

11.3 Three from: ledger accounting, eg sales ledger, purchases ledger, cash book; payroll processing; management reports, eg aged debtors analysis, trial balance, profit and loss account and balance sheet. Other areas could include stock control and job costing.

11.4 Two from: hacking in from outside, hacking from the inside, theft from outside (or inside), computer breakdown when periodic back-ups have not been made, viruses, inefficient back-up policy.

11.5 The sales ledger function would benefit from: accuracy of input, up-to-date balances of account available to all authorised staff, aged debtors analysis produced automatically, automatic production of invoices, credit notes and statements.

11.7 (a) Objections might include dislike of change, dislike of computers, fear of redundancies, worries about health issues such as RSI, back strain and eye strain.

(b) Advantages include opportunities for staff training and promotion, motivation, job satisfaction and possibly higher pay

12.1

MATTHEW LLOYD
TRADING AND PROFIT AND LOSS ACCOUNT
FOR THE YEAR ENDED 31 DECEMBER 20-8

	£	£
Sales		125,890
Opening stock	–	
Purchases	94,350	
Less Closing stock	5,950	
Cost of sales		88,400
Gross profit		37,490
Less overheads:		
Rates	4,850	
Heating and lighting	2,120	
Wages and salaries	10,350	
		17,320
Net profit		20,170

BALANCE SHEET AS AT 31 DECEMBER 20-8

	£	£	£
Fixed Assets			
Office equipment			8,500
Vehicles			10,750
			19,250
Current Assets			
Stock		5,950	
Debtors		3,950	
Bank		4,225	
Cash		95	
		14,220	
Less Current Liabilities			
Creditors	1,750		
Value Added Tax	450		
		2,200	
Working Capital or Net Current Assets			12,020
NET ASSETS			31,270
FINANCED BY			
Capital			
Opening capital			20,000
Add Net profit			20,170
			40,170
Less Drawings			8,900
			31,270

12.3

Business A: gross profit £8,000, net profit £4,000
Business B: gross profit £17,000, expenses £7,000
Business C: sales £36,500, net profit £6,750
Business D: purchases £25,500, expenses £9,800
Business E: opening stock £8,350, net loss £1,700
Business F: closing stock £4,600, expenses £15,000

12.4

JOHN ADAMS
TRADING AND PROFIT AND LOSS ACCOUNT
FOR THE YEAR ENDED 31 DECEMBER 20-7

	£	£
Sales		259,688
Opening stock	14,350	
Purchases	114,472	
	128,822	
Less Closing stock	16,280	
Cost of sales		112,542
Gross profit		147,146
Less overheads:		
Rates	13,718	
Heating and lighting	12,540	
Wages and salaries	42,614	
Vehicle expenses	5,817	
Advertising	6,341	
		81,030
Net profit		66,116

BALANCE SHEET AS AT 31 DECEMBER 20-7

		£	£
Fixed Assets			
Premises			75,000
Office equipment			33,000
Vehicles			21,500
			129,500
Current Assets			
Stock		16,280	
Debtors		23,854	
Bank		1,235	
Cash		125	
		41,494	
Less Current Liabilities			
Creditors	17,281		
Value Added Tax	2,455		
		19,736	
Working Capital or Net Current Assets			21,758
			151,258
Less Long-term Liabilities			
Loan from bank			35,000
NET ASSETS			116,258
FINANCED BY			
Capital			
Opening capital			62,500
Add Net profit			66,116
			128,616
Less Drawings			12,358
			116,258

12.6

JAMES CADWALLADER

TRADING AND PROFIT AND LOSS ACCOUNT FOR THE YEAR ENDED 31 DECEMBER 2002

	£	£	£
Sales			67,945
Less Returns inwards			2,945
Turnover/net sales			65,000
Opening stock		5,780	
Purchases	34,981		
Carriage inwards	679		
Less Returns outwards	1,367		
		34,293	
Less Closing stock		6,590	
Cost of sales			33,483
Gross profit			31,517
Less overheads:			
Wages		12,056	
Carriage out		386	
Other expenses		4,650	
			17,092
Net profit			14,425

12.8

A to Z ENGINEERING SUPPLIES
BALANCE SHEET AS AT 31 MARCH 2003

	£	£	£
Fixed Assets			
Premises			50,000
Motor vehicles			14,560
			64,560
Current Assets			
Stock		14,905	
Debtors		6,500	
Petty cash		56	
		21,461	
Less Current Liabilities			
Creditors	4,590		
Overdraft	3,400	7,990	13,471
			78,031
Less Long-term Liabilities			25,000
			53,031
Capital			42,571
Add net profit			23,460
Less drawings			13,000
			53,031

13.1

Date	Details	Folio	Dr	Cr
20-8			£	£
1 May	Vehicle	GL	6,500	
	Fixtures and fittings	GL	2,800	
	Stock	GL	4,100	
	Cash	CB	150	
	Loan from husband	GL		5,000
	Capital	GL		8,550
			13,550	13,550
	Assets and liabilities at the start of business			

13.3

	subsidiary book	*debit*	*credit*
(a)	purchases day book	purchases account	Temeside Traders
(b)	sales day book	Malvern Models	sales account
(c)	journal	office equipment account	A-Z Computers Ltd
(d)	sales returns day book	sales returns account	Johnson Bros
(e)	cash book	bank account	Melanie Fisher
(f)	cash book	cash account	sales account
(g)	cash book	drawings account	cash account
(h)	cash book	Stationery Supplies Ltd	bank account
(i)	journal	bad debts written off account	J Bowen
(j)	purchases returns day book	I Johnson	purchases returns account

13.5

	Date	Details	Folio	Dr	Cr
				£	£
(a)		Office expenses	GL	85	
		Suspense	GL		85
		Omission of entry in office expenses account – payment made by cheque no .... on ....(date)			
(b)		Suspense	GL	78	
		Photocopying	GL		78
		Photocopying	GL	87	
		Suspense	GL		87
				165	165
		Payment for photocopying £87 (cheque no .... on ....) entered in photocopying account as £78 in error			
(c)		Suspense	GL	100	
		Sales returns	GL		100
		Overcast on ...(date)... now corrected			
(d)		Commission received	GL	25	
		Suspense	GL		25
		Commission received on .... entered twice in commission received account, now corrected			

Suspense Account

Dr		£	Cr		£
20-8			20-8		
30 Sep	Trial balance difference	19	(a)	Office expenses	85
(b)	Photocopying	78	(b)	Photocopying	87
(c)	Sales returns	100	(d)	Commission received	25
		197			197

13.7

Suspense Account

Dr Details	£	Cr Details	£
Purchases	4,500	Opening balance (error)	5,669
Debtors	650	Rent payable	81
Discount received	300		
Discount received	300		
	5,750		5,750

Tutorial note: The mispost between Sunshine Products Ltd and Sunmaster Products needs to be corrected in the sales ledger, but has no effect on suspense account.

13.9 (a)

JOURNAL	DR	CR
Computers (£4,000 – £200 trade discount)	3,800	
VAT	665	
JPC Computer Supplies Ltd		4,465

PURCHASE LEDGER

DR **JPC Computer Supplies Ltd** CR

2003	Details	£	2003	Details	£
4 Mar	Bank	4,465	1 Feb	Journal	4,465

GENERAL LEDGER

DR **VAT Account** CR

2003	Details	£	2003	Details	£
1 Feb	Journal	665			

DR **Computer Account** CR

2003	Details	£	2003	Details	£
1 Feb	Journal	3,800			

(b) **Speed**

- when the entry is keyed in it is automatically entered in every account
- the totals are calculated automatically
- accounts can be printed out if required
- the trial balance, final accounts, etc are prepared by the program
- error correction may be speedier

Accuracy

- only one entry is made and so there are likely to be fewer errors
- the totalling is automatic and accurate
- the entries can be batched for control purposes

CHAPTER 14 Control accounts

14.1

Sales Ledger Control Account

Dr					Cr
20-1		£	20-1		£
1 Jun	Balances b/d	17,491	30 Jun	Sales returns	1,045
30 Jun	Credit sales	42,591	30 Jun	Payments received	39,024
			30 Jun	Cash discount allowed	593
			30 Jun	Bad debts written off	296
			30 Jun	Balances c/d	19,124
		60,082			60,082
1 Jul	Balances b/d	19,124			

14.2

Purchases Ledger Control Account

Dr					Cr
20-2		£	20-2		£
30 Apr	Purchases returns	653	1 Apr	Balances b/d	14,275
30 Apr	Payments made to creditors	31,074	30 Apr	Credit purchases	36,592
30 Apr	Cash discount received	1,048			
30 Apr	Set-off: sales ledger	597			
30 Apr	Balances c/d	17,495			
		50,867			50,867
			1 May	Balances b/d	17,495

14.4 (a) Benefits include:

- enabling the arithmetical accuracy of the ledgers to be checked
- making the preparation of final accounts easier
- disclosing errors
- supplying a figure of debtors' or creditors' totals quickly

(b)

Sales Ledger Control Account

Dr					Cr
2000		£	2000		£
31 Oct	Balance b/d	25,800	31 Oct	Discount	37
31 Oct	Sales	540	31 Oct	Adjustment to balance	720
31 Oct	Returns	100	31 Oct	Balance c/d	25,683
		26,440			26,440
1 Nov	Balance b/d	25,683			

(c) Certain errors are not revealed so users may believe it to be correct.

Examples include errors of omission, commission, compensating errors, original entry.

CHAPTER 15 The accounting system

15.1

(a) ledger
(b) debtor
(c) creditor
(d) sales ledger
(e) cash book
(f) general (or nominal) ledger
(g) assets – liabilities = capital

15.5

capital	£20,000
capital	£10,000
liabilities	£7,550
assets	£14,100
liabilities	£18,430
assets	£21,160

15.6

(a) Owner started in business with capital of £10,000 in the bank
(b) Bought office equipment for £2,000, paying by cheque
(c) Received a loan of £6,000 by cheque
(d) Bought a van for £10,000, paying by cheque
(e) Owner introduces £2,000 additional capital by cheque
(f) Loan repayment of £3,000 made by cheque

CHAPTER 16 Ledgers and the trial balance

16.1 (a) You, the final purchaser, pay the whole VAT amount.

(b) It pays the VAT on the TV charged by the manufacturer and then claims this amount back by setting it off against the VAT it charges you (which will be more) when it settles up with HM Revenue & Customs.

16.2 Issue of a VAT registration number; use of number on invoices, letterheads, etc; an account must be kept for VAT; VAT must be charged on sales; VAT can be reclaimed on purchases; the difference to be accounted for to HM Revenue & Customs on VAT Return; VAT records can be inspected at any time.

16.3 (a) a control account is a summary account or master account for a number of subsidiary accounts

(b) the total amount of money owing by debtors

(c) it means that only the control account balance needs to be shown in the trial balance – not the balances of all the subsidiary accounts – this makes the trial balance clearer and more concise

16.9 (a)
- sales ledger
- purchases ledger
- cash book*
- general ledger

* note that, in some ledger systems, cash and bank account are kept in the general ledger

(b)
- ensures the arithmetical accuracy of the ledgers
- ensures that the debit and credit totals are equal
- collects the balances into a list to make the preparation of final accounts easier

(c) The trial balance does not prove the complete accuracy of the ledgers as there are some errors it does not reveal.

Errors not shown by a trial balance:
- omission
- reversal of entries
- mispost/error of commission
- principle
- original entry (or transcription)
- compensating

Any two of the above, together with a description

16.11 (a)

LORNA FOX
Trial balance as at 31 March 20-2

	Dr	Cr
	£	£
Purchases	96,250	
Sales		146,390
Sales returns	8,500	
Administration expenses	10,240	
Wages	28,980	
Telephone	3,020	
Interest paid	2,350	
Travel expenses	1,045	
Premises	125,000	
Machinery	40,000	
Debtors	10,390	
Bank overdraft		1,050
Cash	150	
Creditors		12,495
Loan from bank		20,000
Drawings	9,450	
Capital		155,440
	335,375	335,375

(b) See Chapter16, pages 252 and 254. The explanation should be appropriate for someone who does not understand accounting.

16.12 (a) principle
(b) mispost
(c) original entry
(d) compensating
(e) reversal of entries
(f) omission

CHAPTER 17 Introducing computer accounting

17.1 Explanation of two advantages out of the list on page 268. The most obvious advantages are speed of input, accuracy of transaction recording, accessibility of up-to-date information and document printing (eg invoices, credit notes and statements).

17.2 The main two advantages are that a spreadsheet saves time in calculation and secondly that if any of the figures should alter, the remaining dependent figures will automatically be recalculated.

17.3 Three from: ledger accounting, eg sales ledger, purchases ledger, cash book; payroll processing; management reports, eg aged debtors analysis, trial balance, profit and loss account and balance sheet. Other areas could include stock control and job costing.

17.4 Two from: hacking in from outside, hacking from the inside, theft from outside (or inside), computer breakdown when periodic back-ups have not been made, viruses, inefficient back-up policy.

17.5 The sales ledger function would benefit from: accuracy of input, up-to-date balances of account available to all authorised staff, aged debtors analysis produced automatically, automatic production of invoices, credit notes and statements.

17.7 (a) Objections might include dislike of change, dislike of computers, fear of redundancies, worries about health issues such as RSI, back strain and eye strain.
(b) Advantages include opportunities for staff training and promotion, motivation, job satisfaction and possibly higher pay

CHAPTER 18 Introduction to final accounts

18.3 (i) **Trial Balance of Lloyd Limited, as at 31 December 20-8**

	Dr	Cr
	£	£
Purchases	94,350	
Sales		125,890
Rates	4,850	
Heating and lighting	2,120	
Wages and salaries	10,350	
Office equipment	8,500	
Vehicles	10,750	
Debtors	12,850	
Bank	4,225	
Petty cash	95	
Creditors		1,750
Value Added Tax		450
Capital		20,000
	148,090	148,090

(ii)

LLOYD LIMITED
TRADING AND PROFIT AND LOSS ACCOUNT
FOR THE YEAR ENDED 31 DECEMBER 20-8

	£	£
Sales		125,890
Opening stock	–	
Purchases	94,350	
Less Closing stock	5,950	
Cost of sales		88,400
Gross profit		37,490
Less overheads:		
Rates	4,850	
Heating and lighting	2,120	
Wages and salaries	10,350	
		17,320
Net profit		20,170

BALANCE SHEET AS AT 31 DECEMBER 20-8

	£	£	£
Fixed Assets			
Office equipment			8,500
Vehicles			10,750
			19,250
Current Assets			
Stock		5,950	
Debtors		12,850	
Bank		4,225	
Petty cash		95	
		23,120	
Less Current Liabilities			
Creditors	1,750		
Value Added Tax	450		
		2,200	
Working Capital or Net Current Assets			20,920
NET ASSETS			40,170
FINANCED BY			
Capital			20,000
Add Net profit			20,170
			40,170

18.5 Business A: gross profit £8,000, net profit £4,000
Business B: gross profit £17,000, expenses £7,000
Business C: sales £36,500, net profit £6,750
Business D: purchases £25,500, expenses £9,800
Business E: opening stock £8,350, net loss £1,700
Business F: closing stock £4,600, expenses £15,000

18.6

ADAMS LIMITED
TRADING AND PROFIT AND LOSS ACCOUNT
FOR THE YEAR ENDED 31 DECEMBER 20-7

	£	£
Sales		259,688
Opening stock	14,350	
Purchases	114,472	
	128,822	
Less Closing stock	16,280	
Cost of sales		112,542
Gross profit		147,146
Less overheads:		
Rates	13,718	
Heating and lighting	12,540	
Wages and salaries	42,614	
Vehicle expenses	5,817	
Advertising	6,341	
		81,030
Net profit		66,116

BALANCE SHEET AS AT 31 DECEMBER 20-7

		£	£
Fixed Assets			
Premises			75,000
Office equipment			33,000
Vehicles			21,500
			129,500
Current Assets			
Stock		16,280	
Debtors		23,854	
Bank		1,235	
Cash		125	
		41,494	
Less Current Liabilities			
Creditors	17,281		
Value Added Tax	2,455		
		19,736	
Working Capital or Net Current Assets			21,758
			151,258
Less Long-term Liabilities			
Loan from bank			22,642
NET ASSETS			128,616
FINANCED BY			
Capital			62,500
Add Net profit			66,116
			128,616

18.8

WYVERN TRADERS LIMITED
TRADING ACCOUNT FOR THE YEAR ENDED 30 JUNE 20-6

	£	£	£
Sales			298,300
Less Sales returns			4,620
Net sales			293,680
Opening stock (1 July 20-5)		27,820	
Purchases	146,850		
Add Carriage in	3,860		
	150,710		
Less Purchases returns	2,850		
Net purchases		147,860	
		175,680	
Less Closing stock (30 June 20-6)		33,940	
Cost of sales			141,740
Gross profit			151,940

CHAPTER 19 Limited company accounts

19.2
(a) The shareholders
(b) The directors
(c) If the company becomes insolvent (goes 'bust') the most the shareholders can lose is the amount of their investment, together with any money unpaid on their shares (unpaid instalments on new share issues, for example).

19.6 (a)

R MASTERS
PROFIT AND LOSS ACCOUNT FOR THE YEAR ENDED 31 MARCH 2002

	£	£
Gross profit		56,231
Add Discount received		350
		56,581
Less overheads:		
Wages	23,980	
Carriage outwards	3,600	
Motor expenses	4,500	
Bank charges	450	
		32,530
Net profit		24,051

(b)

	£
Net profit	24,051
Less dividends proposed	12,500
Retained profit for year	11,551
Add balance of retained profits at beginning of year	36,790
Balance of retained profits at end of year	48,341

19.8 **JOBSEEKERS LIMITED**

PROFIT AND LOSS ACCOUNT FOR THE YEAR ENDED 31 DECEMBER 20-6

	£
Net profit	68,200
Less final ordinary dividend proposed	40,000
Retained profit for year	28,200
Add balance of retained profits at beginning of year	7,350
Balance of retained profits at end of year	35,550

BALANCE SHEET AS AT 31 DECEMBER 20-6

	£	£	£
Fixed Assets			
Premises			175,000
Office equipment			85,000
			260,000
Current Assets			
Stock		750	
Debtors		42,500	
		43,250	
Less Current Liabilities			
Creditors	7,250		
Bank	15,450		
Proposed dividend	40,000		
		62,700	
Working Capital or Net Current Assets			(19,450)
			240,550
Less Long-term Liabilities			
Bank loan			55,000
NET ASSETS			185,550
FINANCED BY			
Issued Share Capital			
150,000 ordinary shares of £1 each			150,000
Revenue Reserve			
Profit and loss account			35,550
SHAREHOLDERS' FUNDS			185,550

19.10 (a)

(i) profit and loss account
£56,000 + £148,000 – £34,000 = £170,000

(ii) revaluation reserve
£150,000 (£550,000 – £400,000)

(iii) long-term liabilities/creditors due after more than one year
£150,000 + £50,000 = £200,000

(iv) ordinary share capital
£340,000 + £100,000 = £440,000

(v) current liabilities/creditors due within one year
£30,000 + £34,000 = £64,000

(b) Balance sheet value of total assets
£170,000 + £150,000 + £200,000 + £440,000 + £64,000 = £1,024,000

(c) **Capital reserves** arise from non-trading activities

– revaluation reserve

– share premium account

Capital reserves cannot be used to fund dividend payments

Revenue reserves arise from trading activities

– balance of retained profits/profit and loss account/general reserve

Revenue reserves can be used to fund dividend payments

19.11 (a)

	£	
Ordinary share dividend	120,000	(6,000,000 shares x 2p)
Preference share dividend	21,000	(£300,000 x 7%)
Debenture interest	8,000	(£100,000 x 8%)

(b)

Ordinary share dividends	*Debenture interest*
• Variable amount	• Fixed percentage
• Paid on shares	• Paid on loans
• Reduce retained profit	• Reduce net profit
• Do not have to be paid	• Must be paid
• Reward to owners	• Reward to lenders

(c)

Ordinary shares	*Preference shares*
• Equity shares	• Non-equity shares
• Variable dividend paid	• Fixed dividend paid
• Voting rights	• No voting rights
• Dividend paid after preference shares	• Dividend paid before ordinary shares
• Dividend need not be paid	• If dividend is cumulative and is not paid in one year, it must be carried forward
• In event of insolvency, are repaid after preference shares	• In event of insolvency, are repaid before ordinary shares

19.14 (a) (i) Revaluation reserve has come about as a result of the revaluation upwards of a fixed asset, such as buildings.

(ii) Share premium has come about as a result of the issue of shares at above par value.

(b) These reserves are capital reserves and cannot be distributed as dividends.

(c) Debenture interest has to be paid, but ordinary dividends do not have to be paid, being dependent on profits.

CHAPTER 20 Correction of errors

20.2 (a) The benefits of drawing up a trial balance are:

- to enable a check to be made of the arithmetical accuracy of the accounting system
- to eliminate or disclose errors
- to make the preparation of final accounts easier

(b) **Trial Balance as at 31 October 2000**

	£	£
Incorrect totals	20,280	20,260
1. Sales		540
2. Returns inwards	(100)	
Returns outwards		100
3. No adjustment		
4. Debtors	*720	
Corrected totals	20,900	20,900

* £25,800 – £25,080

(c) The trial balance does not prove the complete accuracy of the ledgers as there are some errors it does not reveal.

Errors not shown by a trial balance:

- omission
- reversal of entries
- mispost/error of commission
- principle
- original entry (or transcription)
- compensating

Any two of the above, together with a description

20.4

Northern Lights Ltd
Trial Balance as at 31 December 2001

	Dr £	Cr £
Sales		400,000
Purchases	350,000	
Returns inwards	5,000	
Returns outwards		6,200
Stock at 1 January 2001	100,000	
Carriage outwards	800	
Wages	32,000	
Rates	6,000	
Carriage inwards	1,000	
fixed assets	70,000	
Debtors	9,800	
Creditors		7,000
Bank balance (overdrawn)		3,000
dividends paid	18,000	
Share capital and reserves		106,400
10% Debentures		70,000
TOTAL	592,600	592,600

20.5

Dr **Suspense Account** Cr

Details	£	Details	£
Purchases	4,500	Opening balance (error)	5,669
Debtors	650	Rent payable	81
Discount received	300		
Discount received	300		
	5,750		5,750

Tutorial note: The mispost between Sunshine Products Ltd and Sunmaster Products needs to be corrected in the sales ledger, but has no effect on suspense account.

CHAPTER 21 Published accounts of limited companies

21.2 Items to be included in a directors' report (four items required for the question):

- review of the activities of the company over the past year and of likely developments in the future, including research and development activity
- directors' names and their shareholdings
- proposed dividends
- significant differences between the book value and market value of land and buildings
- political and charitable contributions
- policy on employment of disabled people
- health and safety at work of employees
- action taken on employee involvement and consultation
- policy on payment of creditors

21.5 (a) The fixed asset investments are held for the long-term. They may be investments in a company or companies closely linked to GT plc. They are held for a profit or for the influence GT plc might exert.

The current asset investments are held for the short-term. They are likely to be sold within the next year, with the aim of making a profit.

(b) Corporation tax and VAT due, trade creditors, accrued expenses, dividends due, bank overdraft.

(c) (i) share premium account arises on an issue of shares at above par value

(ii) revaluation reserve is a reserve equal to the increase in property values (or other fixed asset) recorded in the fixed assets, but not yet realised

(d)
- Equity funds are ordinary shares plus all of the reserves
- Non-equity funds are preference shares (which are not entitled to any of the reserves)
- Non-equity shares rank above equity shares for dividends and repayment, but equity shares are entitled to all remaining profits after non-equity shares have been settled

21.6 (a) (i) *Fixed assets: investments*

These are amounts invested in other businesses (such as suppliers and customers of D Austin plc) with the aim of maintaining a long-term stake in the business. They are held for a profit or for the influence D Austin plc might exert.

(ii) *8% Debenture 2015-2020 £1,000,000*

D Austin plc has issued £1,000,000 of debentures. This is money the company has borrowed at an interest rate of 8% pa. The company will have to repay them between the years 2015 and 2020. It is a long-term liability of D Austin plc.

(b) Dividends; activities; review of business; list of directors and their shareholdings; employees; charity/political contributions; health and safety; creditors, etc

(c) (i) Earnings per share is the net profit after tax before ordinary dividends, divided by the number of ordinary shares. It shows the amount earned by each share and guides the ordinary shareholder as to the profitability of the shares and enables comparison with other shares.

(ii) Dividends per share shows the amount paid out/proposed in dividends to the ordinary shareholder for each share owned. This guides them when comparing with other shares and they can see if the company is distributing a fair amount per share but keeping some profits for future investment.

21.9 (a) (i) *Intangible fixed assets* eg goodwill, patents, etc

Assets which do not have material substance but which belong to the company.

(ii) *Tangible fixed assets* eg premises, equipment, vehicles, etc

Assets which have a material substance and are retained in the long-term for use in the business.

(iii) *Current assets* eg stock, trade debtors, bank balance, cash, petty cash, etc

Assets which are held in the short-term, and change from day-to-day – the working capital of the business.

(b) (i) Dividends; activities; review of business; list of directors and their shareholdings; employees; charity/political contributions; health and safety; creditors, etc.

(ii) The directors are responsible for producing the accounts in the correct form, at the proper time, with regard to company law and accounting standards, and maintaining the supporting accounting records.

Auditors are responsible for ensuring that the accounts give a true and fair view and comply with the Companies Acts

21.10

- *shareholders*
  - dividends
  - profits

Dividends enable shareholders to see how much cash they are receiving from their investment and to enable comparison with previous years/other investments.

Profits enable shareholders to see how much was retained in the company for investment and to assess the future prospects of the company.

- *loan providers*
  - total loans
  - profits

There may be other lenders which need to be repaid, so reducing the ability of the company to repay its lending.

Profits enable the loan providers to assess the likelihood of receiving their interest payments and loan repayments.

- *creditors*
  - current assets, net current assets (working capital)
  - profits

The current assets/net current assets will enable creditors to look at the liquidity of the company (ie the stability of the company on a short-term basis) and to assess its ability to pay creditors as they fall due.

A company that is generating profits is likely to be able to pay its creditors. Also, the company may be expanding, so creating an increased level of purchases from its suppliers; comparison of profits with previous years.

- *employees*
  - profits
  - net assets

A profitable company may be able to afford pay rises; comparison of profits with previous years.

The net assets show the financial strength of the company and indicate its ability to continue in business, so assuring future employment prospects.

CHAPTER 22 Cash flow statements

22.1

Transaction of cash	Inflow of cash	Outflow on cash	No effect
(a) Cash purchases		✓	
(b) Sold goods on credit			✓
(c) Bought goods on credit			✓
(d) Bought new fixed asset paying by cheque		✓	
(e) Received a cheque from a debtor	✓		
(f) Paid expenses in cash		✓	
(g) Paid a creditor by cheque		✓	

22.6 (a)

- Cash flow statement links profit from the profit and loss account with changes in assets and liabilities in the balance sheet and the cash flows of the company over a period of time.

* It gives information that is not found in the profit and loss account and balance sheet, eg the *change* in stocks, debtors, creditors.

- It is an objective accounting statement which shows the exact sources and uses of cash.
- For the current year it shows:
  - tax paid
  - dividends paid
  - interest paid and received
  - fixed assets purchased and sold
  - loans received and repaid
  - shares issued

(b)

- profit and loss account
- balance sheet

22.8 (a) (i) *operating profit*

Profit from the normal trading activities of the company, before deduction of interest. Does not include any profit from exceptional – one-off – items.

(ii) *net cash inflow from operating activities*

Amount of cash generated by the trading activities of the company, taking into account non-cash items, and changes in stocks, debtors and creditors

(b) (i) *depreciation – added*

Depreciation is a non-cash item and is added back as the cash has not left the company.

(ii) *increase in stock – subtracted*

An increase in stock uses cash, ie the company spends money, so it is subtracted

(iii) *increase in debtors – subtracted*

An increase in debtors means that the company is allowing its debtors longer to pay, or has increased its credit sales business. Either way, the company is financing the increase and therefore has less cash available, so it is subtracted.

(iv) *increase in creditors – added*

An increase in creditors means that the company is paying its creditors more slowly, or has increased its credit purchases. Either way, the company has more cash available, so it is added.

CHAPTER 23 Accruals and prepayments

23.3

	Amount to be subtracted from draft net profit £	*Amount to be added to draft net profit* £
Business rates	2,100	
Rent of premises	4,020	
Commission receivable		590

Workings:

Rates: £1,950 + £70 + £80

Rent: £4,200 – £60 – £120

Commission received: £600 – £50 + £40

23.4

DON SMITH

TRADING AND PROFIT AND LOSS ACCOUNT FOR THE YEAR ENDED 31 DECEMBER 20-8

	£	£
Sales		257,258
Opening stock (1 January 20-8)	18,471	
Purchases	138,960	
	157,431	
Less Closing stock (31 December 20-8)	14,075	
Cost of sales		143,356
Gross profit		113,902
Add Discount received		591
		114,493
Less overheads:		
Rent and rates	10,612	
Electricity	2,164	
Telephone	1,695	
Salaries	56,256	
Vehicle expenses	10,855	
Discount allowed	478	
		82,060
Net profit		32,433

BALANCE SHEET AS AT 31 DECEMBER 20-8

	£	£	£
Fixed Assets			
Vehicles			22,250
Office equipment			7,500
			29,750
Current Assets			
Stock		14,075	
Debtors		24,325	
Prepayment		250	
		38,650	
Less Current Liabilities			
Creditors	15,408		
Value Added Tax	4,276		
Bank overdraft	1,083		
Accruals	475	21,242	
Working Capital or Net Current Assets			17,408
NET ASSETS			47,158
FINANCED BY			
Capital			
Opening capital			30,000
Add net profit			32,433
			62,433
Less drawings			15,275
			47,158

23.6

SOUTHTOWN SUPPLIES

TRADING AND PROFIT AND LOSS ACCOUNT
FOR THE YEAR ENDED 31 DECEMBER 20-4

	£	£	£
Sales			420,000
Less Sales returns			6,000
			414,000
Opening stock		70,000	
Purchases 280,000 – 500*	279,500		
Less Purchases returns	4,500		
		275,000	
		345,000	
Less Closing stock		60,000	
Cost of sales			285,000
Gross profit			129,000
Add income: Discount received			750
			129,750
Less overheads:			
Discount allowed		500	
Electricity 13,750 + 350		14,100	
Salaries 35,600 – 400		35,200	
Post and packing		1,400	
			51,200
Net profit			78,550

* goods scrapped

BALANCE SHEET AS AT 31 DECEMBER 20-4
4

	£	£	£
Fixed Assets			
Premises			120,000
Fixtures and fittings			45,000
			165,000
Current Assets			
Stock (closing)		60,000	
Debtors		55,000	
Prepayment		400	
Insurance claim*		500	
Bank		5,000	
		120,900	
Less Current Liabilities			
Creditors	47,000		
Accrual	350		
Value Added Tax	6,000		
		53,350	
Working Capital or Net Current Assets			67,550
NET ASSETS			232,550
FINANCED BY			
Capital			
Opening capital			195,000
Add net profit			78,550
			273,550
Less drawings			41,000
			232,550

* for goods scrapped

24.1 A letter incorporating the following points:

- Depreciation is a measure of the amount of the fall in value of fixed assets over a time period.
- It is a systematic method of charging against profits over the life of an asset.
- When the asset is sold, adjustments are made for over-provision or under-provision of depreciation.
- A recognised system which fits with the accounting concepts (see Chapter 26) of going concern, accruals, consistency and prudence.

24.3 (a)

	year ended 30 June 20-2	*year ended 30 June 20-3*
	£	£
Net profit before depreciation	18,700	33,100
Depreciation on fixed assets	5,000	9,000
Net profit after depreciation	13,700	24,100

(b)

	as at 30 June 20-2	*as at 30 June 20-3*
	£	£
Fixed assets at cost	50,000	50,000
Less provision for depreciation to date	5,000	14,000
Net book value	45,000	36,000

24.5 (a)

	£
Net book value (£18,000 – £10,800)	7,200
Selling price	4,000
Loss on sale	3,200

(b) **BALANCE SHEET (EXTRACT) AS AT 31 DECEMBER 2000**

Fixed Assets	**£**	
Machinery at cost	112,000	(£100,000 – £18,000 + £30,000)
Less prov for depreciation	60,400	(£60,000 – £10,800 + £11,200)
Net book value	51,600	

24.6 (a) **SHAHIDA RASHID**

PROFIT AND LOSS ACCOUNT FOR THE YEAR ENDED 31 DECEMBER 20-5

	£	£
Gross profit		135,400
Add other income:		
Discount received	730	
Rent received	4,290	
		5,020
		140,420
Less overheads:		
Discount allowed	1,040	
Wages and salaries	84,270	
General expenses	23,860	
Depreciation of fixed assets	*11,250	
		120,420
Net profit		20,000

* 25% x (£60,000 – £15,000)

(b) **BALANCE SHEET (EXTRACT) AS AT 31 DECEMBER 20-5**

	£
Fixed Assets	
At cost	60,000
Less provision for depreciation	**26,250
Net book value	33,750

** £15,000 + this year's depreciation of £11,250

24.10

HAZEL HARRIS

TRADING AND PROFIT AND LOSS ACCOUNT FOR THE YEAR ENDED 31 DECEMBER 20-4

	£	£
Sales		614,000
Opening stock	63,000	
Purchases	465,000	
	528,000	
Less Closing stock	88,000	
Cost of sales		440,000
Gross profit		174,000
Add Discount received		8,140
		182,140
Less overheads:		
Building repairs	8,480	
Vehicle expenses	2,680	
Wages and salaries	89,240	
Discount allowed	10,610	
Rates and insurance	5,620	
General expenses	15,860	
Depreciation: vehicles	2,400	
furniture and fittings	2,500	
		137,390
Net profit		44,750

BALANCE SHEET AS AT 31 DECEMBER 20-4

	£	£	£
Fixed Assets	*Cost*	*Prov for dep'n*	*Net book value*
Land	100,000	–	100,000
Vehicles	12,000	4,800	7,200
Furniture and fittings	25,000	5,000	20,000
	137,000	9,800	127,200
Current Assets			
Stock		88,000	
Debtors		52,130	
Prepayment		450	
		140,580	
Less Current Liabilities			
Creditors	38,730		
Value Added Tax	3,120		
Accrual	3,180		
Bank	2,000		
		47,030	
Working Capital or Net Current Assets			93,550
			220,750
Less Long-term Liabilities			
Bank loan			75,000
NET ASSETS			145,750
FINANCED BY			
Capital			
Opening capital			125,000
Add Net profit			44,750
			169,750
Less Drawings			24,000
			145,750

CHAPTER 25 Bad debts and provision for doubtful debts

25.2 (a) *20-1 increasing the provision*

- new provision is £8,000 x 5% = £400
- existing provision is £300
- therefore increase in provision is £100

20-2 decreasing the provision

- new provision is £7,000 x 5% = £350
- existing provision is £400
- therefore decrease in provision is £50

(b) *20-1 Extracts from final accounts produced for year ended 30 June:*

- profit and loss account: expense of £100
- balance sheet: debtors £8,000 - £400 = £7,600

20-2 Extracts from final accounts produced for year ended 30 June:

- profit and loss account: income of £50
- balance sheet: debtors £7,000 - £350 = £6,650

25.4 (a) *net profit*

	£
Reduction in provision for doubtful debts	200
Bad debts written off	(178)
Bad debts recovered	261
Change in net profit	283
∴ Net profit is now	18,373

(b) *working capital*

	£
Debtors increase £200 – £178	22
Bank increase	261
∴ Working capital increase	283

(c) *bank balance*

Bank balance increases by £261 from the bad debts recovered

25.6

JAMES JENKINS

TRADING AND PROFIT AND LOSS ACCOUNT FOR THE YEAR ENDED 30 JUNE 20-9

	£	£	£
Sales			168,432
Less Sales returns			975
Net sales			167,457
Opening stock		9,427	
Purchases	105,240		
Less Purchases returns	1,237		
Net purchases		104,003	
		113,430	
Less Closing stock		11,517	
Cost of sales			101,913
Gross profit			65,544
Add income:			
Discount received			243
Reduction in provision for doubtful debts			54
			65,841
Less overheads:			
Discount allowed		127	
Wages and salaries		30,841	
Vehicle expenses		1,076	
Rent and rates		8,521	
Heating and lighting		1,840	
Telephone		355	
General expenses		1,752	
Bad debts written off		85	
Depreciation:			
vehicle		1,125	
shop fittings		600	
			46,322
Net profit			19,519

BALANCE SHEET AS AT 30 JUNE 20-9

	£	£	£
Fixed Assets	*Cost*	*Prov for dep'n*	*Net book value*
Vehicle	8,000	4,625	3,375
Shop fittings	6,000	3,000	3,000
	14,000	7,625	6,375
Current Assets			
Stock		11,517	
Debtors	3,840		
Less Provision for doubtful debts	96		
		3,744	
Prepayments		275	
Bank		21,419	
Cash		155	
		37,110	
Less Current Liabilities			
Creditors	5,294		
Value Added Tax	1,492		
Accruals	55		
		6,841	
Working Capital or Net Current Assets			30,269
NET ASSETS			36,644
FINANCED BY			
Capital			
Opening capital			36,175
Add Net profit			19,519
			55,694
Less Drawings			19,050
			36,644

CHAPTER 26 Accounting concepts and stock valuation

26.2

(a) Consistency concept: he should continue to use reducing balance method (it won't make any difference to the bank manager anyway).

(b) Prudence concept: stock valuation should be at lower of cost and net realisable value, ie £10,000 in this case.

(c) Business entity concept: car is an asset of John's firm, not a personal asset (in any case personal assets, for sole traders and partnerships, might well be used to repay debts of firm).

(d) Prudence concept: the bad debt should be written off as a bad debt in profit and loss account (so reducing net profit), and the balance sheet figure for debtors should be £27,500 (which is closer to the amount he can expect to receive from debtors).

(e) Accruals concept: expenses and revenues must be matched, therefore it must go through the old year's accounts.

(f) Going concern concept: presumes that business will continue to trade in the foreseeable future: alternative is 'gone concern' and assets may have very different values.

26.3

Proposal	Concept	Action
1	*Consistency*	*Continue to depreciate at 20%*
2	Business entity	The whole amount of £36,000 is drawings
3	Realisation or accruals (matching)	Do not include the sales in this year's accounts as this will anticipate profits

26.5

(a) £220 + £750 + £290 + £35,500 = £36,760

Note: replacement cost is not applicable here

(b) Prudence

(c) Net realisable value is the selling price of the goods, less any expenses incurred in getting the stock into a saleable condition

CHAPTER 27 Limited company accounts

27.4

CHAPELPORTH LIMITED
PROFIT AND LOSS APPROPRIATION ACCOUNT
FOR THE YEAR ENDED 30 JUNE 20-8

	£	£
Net profit for the year before taxation		135,000
Less corporation tax		48,000
Profit for year after taxation		87,000
Less interim dividends paid		
ordinary shares	21,000	
preference shares	8,000	
final dividends proposed		
ordinary shares	29,000	
preference shares	8,000	
		66,000
Retained profit for year		21,000

27.6

JOBSEEKERS LIMITED
PROFIT AND LOSS ACCOUNT (APPROPRIATION SECTION)
FOR THE YEAR ENDED 31 DECEMBER 20-6

	£	£
Net profit for year before taxation		68,200
Less corporation tax		14,850
Profit for year after taxation		53,350
Less interim ordinary dividends paid	10,000	
final ordinary dividend proposed	40,000	
		50,000
Retained profit for year		3,350
Retained profit at 1 January 20-6		7,350
Retained profit at 31 December 20-6		10,700

BALANCE SHEET AS AT 31 DECEMBER 20-6

Fixed Assets	Cost	Prov for dep'n	Net book value
	£	£	£
Intangible			
Goodwill	20,000	6,000	14,000
Tangible			
Premises	175,000	10,500	164,500
Office equipment	25,000	5,000	20,000
	220,000	21,500	198,500
Current Assets			
Stock		750	
Debtors		42,500	
		43,250	
Less Current Liabilities			
Creditors	7,250		
Bank overdraft	13,950		
Proposed dividends	40,000		
Corporation tax	14,850		
		76,050	
Working Capital or Net Current Assets			(32,800)
			165,700
Less Long-term Liabilities			
Bank loan			55,000
NET ASSETS			110,700
FINANCED BY			
Issued Share Capital			
100,000 ordinary shares of £1 each			100,000
Revenue Reserve			
Profit and loss account			10,700
SHAREHOLDERS' FUNDS			110,700

27.7 (a)

Ordinary shares

Advantage
- Voting rights
- Potential capital growth
- High dividends in good years

Disadvantage
- Risk of losing money invested
- Low (or no) dividend in poor years

7% preference shares

Advantage
- Fixed rate of dividend which will not go down if interest rates fall
- Less risky than ordinary shares

Disadvantage
- Generally, no voting rights
- Fixed dividends, so no growth in dividends
- Fewer capital growth prospects than ordinary shares

6% debentures

Advantage
- Fixed rate of interest which will not go down if interest rates fall
- Loans rather than shares
- Less risky than shares

Disadvantage
- No capital growth prospects
- Fixed rate of interest, whatever may happen to interest rates

(b)

- Jill is probably better off investing in ordinary shares
- The risk is that she could lose the amount invested but, if the company does well, she could make large capital gains
- Her income – in the form of dividends – will vary from year-to-year, depending on how successful the company has been

(c)

- Jack is probably better off investing in debentures
- These are the safest form of investment for him and will give him an income of £600 per year
- If he wishes to take a slightly higher risk he could invest some or all of the money in preference shares; if all, then his income will be £700 per year
- With preference shares there could also be some capital growth
- Debentures offer the safest investment: in the event of the company going into liquidation, debentures will be repaid before the preference and ordinary shareholders

27.9

	Net profit before appropriations	Retained profits	Shareholders' funds	Current assets	Current liabilities
(a)	*decrease* *£12,000*	*decrease* *£12,000*	*decrease* *£12,000*	*no change*	*increase* *£12,000*
(b)	increase £50,000	increase £50,000	increase £50,000	no change	no change
(c)	no change	decrease £25,000	no change	no change	no change
(d)	no change	decrease £43,000	decrease £43,000	no change	increase £43,000

27.11 (a) Authorised share capital – sets the maximum number of shares that can be issued to shareholders

Issued share capital – shows how many shares have actually been issued to the shareholders

(b) **GRIFT LTD: BALANCE SHEET AS AT 28 FEBRUARY 2002**

	£	£	£
Fixed Assets			
Premises			270,000
Machinery			150,000
Vehicles			170,000
			590,000
Current Assets			
Stock		17,000	
Debtors		8,500	
Bank		1,500	
		27,000	
Less Current Liabilities			
Trade creditors	6,000		
Proposed dividend	18,000	24,000	3,000
			593,000
Ordinary share capital			500,000
Retained earnings			93,000
			593,000

(c) Factors include (the question asks for one factor):

- to gain limited liability
- to have access to more capital, including the possibility of raising finance from debentures
- there may be taxation benefits

however,

- loss of control of business, as all ordinary shareholders will have voting rights
- more documentation required for a company than for a sole trader

Tutorial note: the factor selected needs to be developed further in order to obtain more marks.

27.13 (a) **FORALL LTD**

PROFIT AND LOSS APPROPRIATION ACCOUNT FOR THE YEAR ENDED 31 MARCH 2001

		£	£
Net profit before taxation			321,000
Less corporation tax			80,000
Profit for year after taxation			241,000
Transfer to general reserve			25,000
			216,000
Less ordinary dividends:	paid	35,000	
	proposed	50,000	
			85,000
Retained profit for year			131,000
Add balance of retained profits at beginning of year			72,350
Balance of retained profits at end of year			203,350

(b) Profit and loss account balance, £203,350 (£131,000 + £72,350)

(c) Share premium account, £115,000 (£40,000 + £75,000)

(d) **Capital reserves**

- created as a result of a non-trading profit
- cannot be used to fund dividend payments
- may be unrealised profits
- examples: revaluation reserve, share premium account

Revenue reserves

- retained profits from profit and loss account
- available to fund dividend payments
- come from realised profits
- examples: profit and loss account balance, general reserve, reserve for replacement of machinery

28.1
(a) manufacturing account
(b) manufacturing account
(c) manufacturing account
(d) profit and loss account
(e) profit and loss account
(f) manufacturing account
(g) profit and loss account

28.2

BARBARA FRANCIS
MANUFACTURING AND PROFIT AND LOSS ACCOUNT
for the year ended 31 December 20-8

	£	£
Opening stock of raw materials		31,860
Add Purchases of raw materials		237,660
		269,520
Less Closing stock of raw materials		44,790
COST OF RAW MATERIALS USED		224,730
Direct labour		234,630
PRIME COST		459,360
Add Production (factory) overheads:		
Rent and rates	24,690	
Power	7,650	
Heat and light	2,370	
Sundry expenses and maintenance	8,190	
Depreciation of plant and machinery	7,450	
		50,350
PRODUCTION (OR MANUFACTURING) COST OF GOODS COMPLETED		509,710
Sales		796,950
Opening stock of finished goods	42,640	
Production (or manufacturing) cost of goods completed	509,710	
	552,350	
Less Closing stock of finished goods	96,510	
COST OF SALES		455,840
Gross profit		341,110
Less Non-production overheads:		
Rent and rates	8,230	
Salaries	138,700	
Advertising	22,170	
Office expenses	7,860	
		176,960
Net profit		164,150

Memorandum

A manufacturing account has been prepared in order to show the main elements of cost which make up the manufacturing cost. In your business, the main elements of cost are:

- *direct materials* – the raw materials used to make the product
- *direct labour* – the wages of the workforce engaged in manufacturing the product
- *production overheads* – the other costs of manufacture; here rent and rates, power, heat and light, etc

The first two of these make up *prime cost*, the basic cost of manufacturing the product. Prime cost plus production overheads gives the production cost. The figure for production cost is carried down to the profit and loss account where it is used to calculate *cost of sales*. The profit and loss account then goes on to show *gross profit* and, after deduction of non-production overheads, *net profit*.

28.3 (a)

NORIV PLC
MANUFACTURING ACCOUNT – PRIME COST FOR THE YEAR ENDED 31 MAY 2003

	£	£
Opening stock of raw materials		21,450
Add Purchases of raw materials	234,090	
Add Carriage inward	750	
	234,840	
Less Returns outward	980	
	233,860	
Less Closing stock of raw materials	22,170	
		211,690
COST OF RAW MATERIALS USED		233,140
Direct labour*		266,000
Manufacturing royalties		6,560
PRIME COST		505,700

* 260,000 + (8,000 x three-quarters)

(b) Partly finished goods in course of manufacture, at a stage between raw materials and finished products.

28.5 (a) £11,200 – £12,100* = £900 increase in provision for unrealised profit

* £60,500 x 25/125

(b) **BALANCE SHEET EXTRACT AS AT 31 DECEMBER 20-8**

Current Assets	£	£
Stock of finished goods	60,500	
Less Provision for unrealised profit	12,100	
		48,400

(c) Provision for unrealised profit is made to reduce the closing stock value of finished goods to cost price. This enables the balance sheet valuation to comply with SSAP 9 and the concept of prudence.

CHAPTER 29 Ratio analysis

29.1

	Amero plc	*Britz plc*
• gross profit margin	11.85%	37.46%
• gross profit mark-up	13.44%	59.90%
• net profit margin	2.87%	14.55%
• return on capital employed	18.18%	13.70%

29.2

	Cawston plc	*Dunley plc*
• working capital ratio	1.51:1	1.04:1
• liquid capital ratio	0.82:1	0.65:1
• debtors' collection period	37 days	3 days
• creditors' payment period	57 days	46 days
• stock turnover	41 days	18 days

Cawston plc is the chemical manufacturer, while Dunley plc runs department stores.

All of the ratios for Cawston are close to the benchmarks for a manufacturing business: eg working capital and liquid capital ratios, although a little low, are near the 'accepted' figures of 2:1 and 1:1, respectively. Debtors, creditors and stock turnover show quite a high level of stock being held; debtors' turnover indicates that most sales are on credit; creditors' turnover is rather high.

For Dunley plc, the ratios indicate a business that sells most of its goods on cash terms: low working capital and liquid capital ratios, with minimal debtors' turnover. The stock turnover is speedy, whilst creditors are paid after 46 days (approximately one-and-a-half months).

29.5 (a) *Working capital*

Current assets – Current liabilities

Working capital, or net current assets, is needed by all businesses in order to finance day-to-day trading activities. Sufficient working capital enables a business to hold adequate stocks, allow a measure of credit to debtors, and to pay creditors on time.

Liquid capital

(Current assets – Stock) – Current liabilities

Liquid capital is calculated in the same way as working capital, except that stock is omitted. This is because stock is the most illiquid current asset. Liquid capital provides a direct comparison between the short-term assets of debtors/cash/bank and short-term liabilities.

(b)

- Working capital ratio = Current assets : Current liabilities
- Acid test ratio = $\frac{\text{(Current assets – Stock)}}{\text{Current liabilities}}$
- Debtors' collection period = $\frac{\text{Debtors}}{\text{Credit sales}}$ x 365 days
- Creditors' collection period = $\frac{\text{Trade creditors}}{\text{Credit purchases}}$ x 365 days

(c)

- Working capital ratio £13,450* : £7,865** = 1.71:1

  * (10,250 – 2,450) + 450 + 5,200

  ** 6,000 + 1,865

- Acid test ratio = $\frac{\text{£13,450 – £5,200 (stock)}}{\text{£7,865}}$ = 1.05:1
- Debtors' collection period = $\frac{\text{£7,800*}}{\text{£96,000}}$ x 365 days = 29.66 days

  * 10,250 – 2,450 (bad debt written off)

- Creditors' collection period = $\frac{\text{£6,000}}{\text{£56,000}}$ x 365 days = 39.11 days

(d) *Writing off the debt for £2,450*

- Writing off the debt as bad has reduced debtors to £7,800, and current assets from £15,900 to £13,450.
- The effect of this is that the working capital ratio has been reduced from 2.02:1 to 1.71:1.
- The effect on the acid test ratio has been a reduction from 1.36:1 to 1.05:1.
- By writing off the bad debt, liquidity ratios have reduced quite significantly.

Reducing the value of stock over the year

- Stock has reduced from £8,400 to £5,200.
- Had the higher level of stock been maintained, the working capital ratio at the year's end would have been £16,650*:£7,865 = 2.12:1.
  * (10,250 – 2,450) + 450 + 8,400
- The acid test ratio would be unchanged – because stock is excluded.
- A change in the level of stock affects the working capital ratio but has no effect on the acid test ratio.

CHAPTER 30 Costs and contribution

30.1 (a) See text, pages 513 - 518

(b)
- raw materials: variable
- factory rent: fixed
- telephone bill: semi-variable
- direct labour: variable
- indirect labour: fixed
- commission to sales staff: variable

Analysing costs by nature identifies them as being fixed, or semi-variable, or variable. This helps with decision making – the business might be able to alter the balance between fixed and variable costs in order to increase profits.For example, a furniture manufacturing business will have to make decisions on whether to use direct labour (variable cost) or machinery (fixed cost) for many of the production processes. The decision will be based very much on the expected level of sales, ie for lower sales it is likely to make greater use of direct labour, while for higher sales a more machine-intensive method of production might be used.

30.2 **Graph A**

- shows a *fixed cost,* which remains constant over a range of output levels
- as output increases, the *cost per unit* falls

Graph B

- shows a *variable cost,* which alters directly with changes in output levels
- as output increases then the cost increases, ie the cost per unit remains the same

Graph C

- shows a *semi-variable cost*
- here, a part of the cost acts as a variable cost, and a part acts as a fixed cost

Graph D

- shows a *stepped fixed cost*
- here, as the business expands, the fixed cost of rent increases as another factory needs to be rented

30.3

		fixed	semi-variable	variable
(a)	rates of business premises	✓		
(b)	royalty paid to designer for each unit of output			✓
(c)	car hire with fixed rental and charge per mile		✓	
(d)	employees paid on piecework basis			✓
(e)	straight-line depreciation	✓		
(f)	direct materials			✓
(g)	telephone bill with fixed rental and charge per call unit		✓	
(h)	office salaries	✓		

30.6 (a)
(i) fixed costs do not vary with the level of output
(ii) variable costs vary directly with the level of output
(iii) semi-variable costs are part fixed and part variable

(b) *Formula*

(selling price less variable cost) per unit = contribution per unit

Contribution per unit

$$\text{Variable cost} = \frac{£360{,}000}{40{,}000} = £9 \text{ per unit}$$

$$\text{Semi-variable cost} = \frac{£280{,}000 - £80{,}000}{40{,}000} = £5 \text{ per unit}$$

Therefore, contribution is £32 – (£9 + £5) = £18 per unit

(c)

		£
	sales £32 x 46,000 units	1,472,000
less	variable costs £9 x 46,000 units	(414,000)
less	semi-variable costs £5 x 46,000 units	(230,000)
equals	total contribution	828,000
less	fixed costs	(80,000)
less	fixed costs	(340,000)
equals	profit for the year	408,000

30.9 (a) Variable costs vary directly with the level of output, eg direct labour

Fixed costs do not vary with the level of output, eg rent

(b)

Total cost of 650 pumps:		£
Materials:	£20 x 400 pumps	8,000
	£18 x 250 pumps	4,500
Labour:	£15 x 650 pumps	9,750
	£3 x 50 pumps	150
Other variable costs:	£9,750* ÷ 5	1,950
Fixed costs:		2,400
Total costs:		26,750

* 'other variable costs' are one-fifth of the labour cost (excluding any bonus) of £9,750

CHAPTER 31 Break-even analysis

31.2 Graphical method

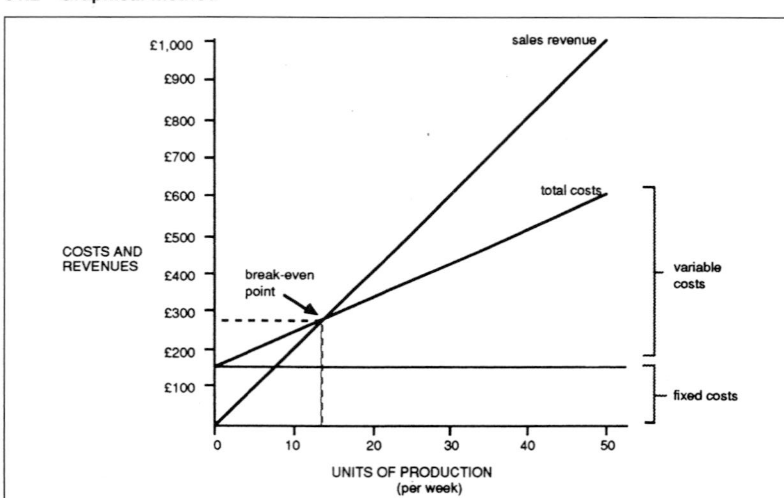

Calculation method

The contribution per unit is:

		£
	selling price per unit	20
less	variable costs* per unit	9
equals	contribution per unit	11

* materials £4 + direct labour £5

The break-even calculation is:

$$\frac{\text{fixed costs (£)}}{\text{contribution per unit (£)}} = \frac{\text{£}154^{**}}{\text{£}11} = 14 \text{ units (teddy bears) per week}$$

** factory rent and rates £100 + fuel and power £20 + other costs £20

31.3 (a) **table method**

units of output	fixed costs £	variable costs £	total cost £	sales revenue £	profit/(loss)* £
100	12,000	2,000	14,000	3,500	(10,500)
200	12,000	4,000	16,000	7,000	(9,000)
300	12,000	6,000	18,000	10,500	(7,500)
400	12,000	8,000	20,000	14,000	(6,000)
500	12,000	10,000	22,000	17,500	(4,500)
600	12,000	12,000	24,000	21,000	(3,000)
700	12,000	14,000	26,000	24,500	(1,500)
800	12,000	16,000	28,000	28,000	nil
900	12,000	18,000	30,000	31,500	1,500
1,000	12,000	20,000	32,000	35,000	3,000
1,100	12,000	22,000	34,000	38,500	4,500
1,200	12,000	24,000	36,000	42,000	6,000

* brackets indicate a loss

(b) **graph method**

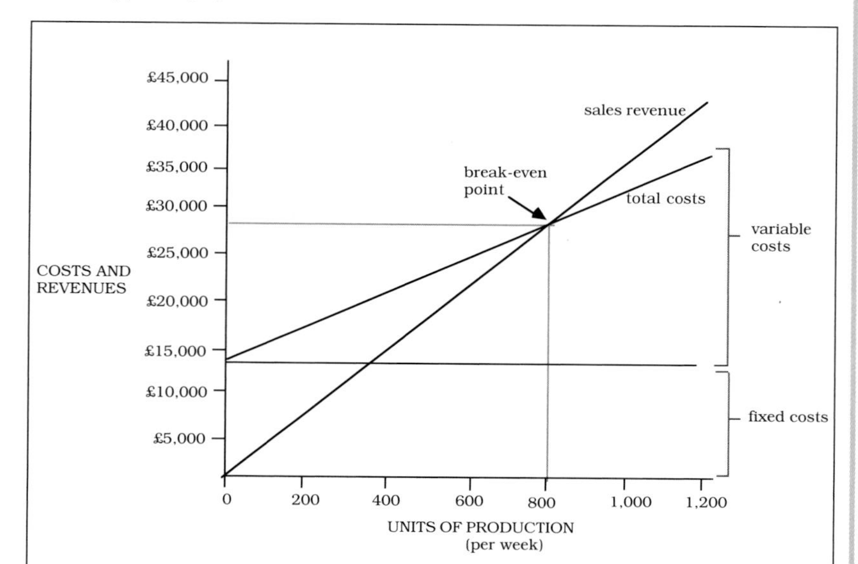

(c) **calculation method**

Fixed costs of £12,000 ÷ contribution of £15 per bat = 800 bats to break-even.

(d) **profit/(loss)**

- 200 bats

	£
Sales (£35 per bat)	7,000
Less variable costs (£20 per bat)	4,000
Contribution	3,000
Less fixed costs	12,000
Loss for month	(9,000)

- 1,200 bats

	£
Sales (£35 per bat)	42,000
Less variable costs (£20 per bat)	24,000
Contribution	18,000
Less fixed costs	12,000
Profit for month	6,000

(e) **margin of safety**

$$\frac{\text{current output} - \text{break-even output}}{\text{current output}} \times \frac{100}{1} = \frac{1{,}000 - 8{,}000}{1{,}000}$$

= 20 per cent, or 200 units

31.6 (a) (i) *Formula*: contribution per unit = selling price per unit – variable costs per unit

Definition: the amount that each unit contributes, firstly, to cover total fixed costs and, when they have been covered, secondly, contributes to profit

Calculation: £50 – £35* = £15 contribution per unit

* variable costs £12 + £16 + £7

(ii) *Formula*: break-even point (units) = $\frac{\text{fixed costs (£)}}{\text{contribution per unit (£)}}$

break-even point (sales) = $\frac{\text{fixed costs (£)}}{\text{contribution per unit (£)}}$ x selling price per unit (£)

Definition: the point at which neither a profit nor a loss is made

Calculation: $\frac{£450{,}000}{£15}$ = 30,000 units to break-even

30,000 units x £50 = £1,500,000 sales to break-even

(b)

Line or term	A, B, C or D
Fixed costs	B
Total sales revenue	D
Break-even point	C
Margin of safety	A

(c) From the graph (see page 544), at sales of 35,000 units:

		£
	revenue	1,750,000
less	costs	1,675,000
equals	profit	75,000

Check: margin of safety is 5,000 units (35,000 – 30,000) x £15 contribution per unit = £75,000 profit

(d)

- At a reduced selling price of £47, the contribution is reduced to £47 – £35 = £12 per unit
- Break-even point is higher at £450,000 ÷ £12 per unit = 37,500 units (and sales revenue of 37,500 x £47 = £1,762,500)
- As 37,500 units is the maximum capacity of Suddley Limited, no profit can be achieved
- The margin of safety is zero
- The reduction in selling price is not recommended

31.7 The limitations of break-even analysis are that:

- the assumption is made that all output is sold
- the presumption is that there is only one product
- costs and revenues are expressed in straight lines
- fixed costs do not remain fixed at all levels of output
- it is not possible to extrapolate the break-even graph or calculation
- the profit or loss is probably only true for figures close to current output levels
- external factors are not considered
- it concentrates too much on break-even point

See text, pages 533 - 534, for a fuller explanation of these points.

CHAPTER 32 Budgeting and budgetary control

32.1

production budget

	Month 1 (tables)	Month 2 (tables)	Month 3 (tables)	Month 4 (tables)
Sales	1,200	1,080	1,134	1,191
Opening stock	100	216	227	239
Closing stock	216	227	239	240
Production	1,316	1,091	1,146	1,192

32.5 (a)

Strudwick Stationers Ltd

Cash Budget for four months ending 31 August 2002

Details	May	June	July	Aug
	£000	£000	£000	£000
Receipts				
Cash sales	35.2	36.8	33.6	35.2
Credit sales	9.2	8.8	9.2	8.4
	44.4	45.6	42.8	43.6
Payments				
Purchases	32.2	30.8	32.2	29.4
Wages	9.0	9.0	9.0	9.5
Fixed costs	3.0	3.0	3.0	3.0
Variable costs	4.4	4.6	4.2	4.4
	48.6	47.4	48.4	46.3
Net cash flow	(4.2)	(1.8)	(5.6)	(2.7)
Add opening balance	12.1	7.9	6.1	0.5
Closing balance	7.9	6.1	0.5	(2.2)

(b)

- planning ahead – overdraft required in August (need to approach bank)
- monitoring and control of cash resources
- co-ordination of plans and resources – the pay rise might have been better offered in September
- communicating the budget to the directors and staff
- motivating staff to ensure that budget is met

32.6 (a) (i)

Cash Budget for Peversal Papers Ltd
for the three months ending 31 May 2002

	March	April	May
	£000	£000	£000
Sales – cash	4.851	5.390	5.929
– credit	83.600	94.050	104.500
	88.451	99.440	110.429
Production* costs (at £12 each)	55.200	61.200	64.800
Admin/distribution	28.000	34.000	38.000
	83.200	95.200	102.800
Net cash inflow/outflow	5.251	4.240	7.629
Opening balance	6.000	11.251	15.491
Closing balance	11.251	15.491	23.120

* see production budget, below

(ii)

Production Budget for Peversal Papers Ltd
for the three months ending 31 May 2002

	March	April	May
	units	units	units
Sales	4,500	5,000	5,500
Opening stock	900	1,000	1,100
Closing stock	1,000	1,100	1,000
Production	4,600	5,100	5,400

(b)

- Planning ahead
  - future receipts (from sales) and payments (for production costs and administration)
  - production of reams of paper, and stock position to meet next month's sales
- Monitoring and control
  - of cash resources
  - of production
- Co-ordination of resources to ensure that cash is available to pay for planned production
- Decision-making about production costs and administration expenses
- Communicating the budgets to managers and staff
- Motivating staff to ensure that the budgets are met
- Evaluation of systems and staff

32.8 (a)

Wilkinson Limited
Cash budget for the six months ending 30 June 20-8

	Jan	Feb	Mar	Apr	May	Jun
	£	£	£	£	£	£
Receipts						
Debtors	57,500	65,000	70,000	72,500	85,000	65,000
Total receipts for month	57,500	65,000	70,000	72,500	85,000	65,000
Payments						
Creditors	26,500	45,000	50,000	34,500	35,500	40,500
Wages and salaries	17,500	18,000	18,250	18,500	16,500	20,000
Other expenses	14,500	19,500	18,000	17,500	19,500	21,000
Total payments for month	58,500	82,500	86,250	70,500	71,500	81,500
Net cash flow	(1,000)	(17,500)	(16,250)	2,000	13,500	(16,500)
Add bank balance (overdraft) at beginning of month	2,250	1,250	(16,250)	(32,500)	(30,500)	(17,000)
Bank balance (overdraft) at end of month	1,250	(16,250)	(32,500)	(30,500)	(17,000)	(33,500)

(b)

WILKINSON LIMITED
FORECAST TRADING AND PROFIT AND LOSS ACCOUNT
FOR THE SIX MONTHS ENDING 30 JUNE 20-8

	£	£
Sales		465,000
Opening stock	15,500	
Purchases	232,000	
	247,500	
Less Closing stock	17,350	
Cost of sales		230,150
Gross profit		234,850
Less overheads:		
Wages and salaries	108,750	
Depreciation of fixed assets	6,000	
Other expenses	110,000	
		224,750
Net profit		10,100

CHAPTER 33 Decision-making and social accounting

33.1 (a)

- profit is a calculated figure which shows the surplus of income over expenditure for the year; it takes note of adjustments for accruals and prepayments and non-cash items such as depreciation and provision for doubtful debts
- cash is the actual amount of money held in the bank or as cash

(b)

	Profit	Cash
	£	£
Option 1		
new machinery	–	(450,000)
loan	–	600,000
interest on loan	(60,000)	(60,000)
redundancy	(160,000)	(160,000)
retraining	(30,000)	(30,000)
depreciation	(45,000)	–
net effect	(295,000)	(100,000)
Option 2		
new machinery	–	(250,000)
loan	–	300,000
interest on loan	(30,000)	(30,000)
retraining	(80,000)	(80,000)
depreciation	(25,000)	–
net effect	(135,000)	(60,000)

Note that depreciation is a non-cash expense which affects profit only

(c)

- For this first year, option 2 has the smaller effect on both profit and cash.
- If redundancy costs of £160,000 could be avoided in option 1 the effect on profit would be (£135,000), which is the same as option 2, and the effect on cash would be £60,000, compared with option 2 (£60,000).
- In subsequent years option 1 will have the larger effect on both profit and cash, with interest, retraining (year 2 only) and depreciation (affecting profit only); there will also be cost savings from employing fewer staff (affecting both profit and cash equally)
- There are social factors to consider:

  – redundancy (effect on workforce and local economy)

  – recycling (customers may be lost if non-recyclable paper is used)
- Making the assumption that sales will be the same under both options, then option 2 is to be preferred in the short-term. However, in the longer term, option 1 may be preferable, despite its higher costs, because it has the benefits of recycling.

33.2 (a) *Benefits of introducing checkout scanners*

- accuracy of till receipts and the total of each bill
- reduction in opportunity for fraud by employees
- faster turn-round time of customers at checkouts
- automatic updating of stock records and re-ordering
- better management information for marketing and financial decision-making

(b) (i) *Weekly cost of the scanners*

Cost of scanners £40,000

$$\text{per year} = \frac{£40{,}000}{2 \text{ years}} = £20{,}000$$

	£
yearly cost	20,000
training per year	1,840
total	21,840

£21,840 ÷ 52 weeks = £420 per week

(ii) *Number of weekly shifts to be cut in order to cover the weekly cost of the scanners*

cost per shift = £5 x 4 hours
= £20

$$\frac{£420}{£20} = 21 \text{ shifts per week}$$

(iii) *Number of employees to be made redundant if the scanners are introduced*

Each employee works 28 hours a week or 7 shifts a week

$$\frac{21 \text{ shifts}}{7 \text{ shifts}} = 3 \text{ employees must be made redundant to cover cost}$$

(c) (i) *Effects of the new system on current employees*

- it may lower job security and staff morale
- the need to retrain
- fear of 'big brother' computer monitoring speed and efficiency of staff
- fear of further redundancies as system becomes established

(ii) *Effects of the new system on the local community*

- anxiety of having to deal with new system
- expectation that investment in a new system may result in higher prices
- loss of jobs leading to element of local unemployment, particularly among part-timers such as students and returners to work

Index